The Stone-Campbell Movement

The Stone-Campbell Movement

An International Religious Tradition

Edited by

Michael W. Casey
and Douglas A. Foster

The University of Tennessee Press

Knoxville

Copyright © 2002 by The University of Tennessee Press / Knoxville.
All Rights Reserved. Manufactured in the United States of America.
First Edition.

The book was printed on acid-free paper.

Library of Congress Cataloging-in-Publication Data

The Stone-Campbell movement : an international religious
tradition / edited by Michael W. Casey and Douglas A. Foster.
    p.   cm.
Includes bibliographical references and index.
ISBN 1-57233-179-8 (cl.: alk. paper)
1. Restoration movement (Christianity)—History—19th century.
2. United States—Church history—19th century.
I. Casey, Michael W. II. Foster, Douglas A. (Douglas Allen), 1952–
BX7316 .S76 2002
286.6'09—dc21   2001004261

To our teachers

Contents

Introduction

The Renaissance of Stone-Campbell Studies:
An Assessment and New Directions   1
Michael W. Casey and Douglas A. Foster

Part I
Historiographical Issues
Intellectual History and Social History

The Sectional Origins of the Churches of Christ   69
David Edwin Harrell Jr.
The Apocalyptic Origins of Churches of Christ and the
Triumph of Modernism   85
Richard T. Hughes

Part II
An American Movement

1. ORIGINS

The Christian Movement and the Demand for
a Theology of the People   121
Nathan O. Hatch
The Agrarian Myth and the Disciples of Christ in the
Nineteenth Century   147
David Edwin Harrell Jr.

2. THE SIGNIFICANCE OF ALEXANDER CAMPBELL IN ANTEBELLUM AMERICA

A Rational Voice Crying in an Emotional Wilderness   163
John L. Morrison
Campbell's Post-Protestantism and Civil Religion   177
Mont Whitson
Early Cincinnati's "Unprecedented Spectacle"   189
Earl Irvin West
Republican Religion and Republican Institutions:
Alexander Campbell and the Anti-Catholic Movement   204
L. Edward Hicks

3. THE INFLUENCE OF A TRADITION ON THE PRESIDENCY

The Religious Thought and Practice of James A. Garfield   219
 William C. Ringenberg
Lyndon B. Johnson: The Religion of a Politician   234
 Monroe Billington
The Moral Inheritance of a President: Reagan and the Dixon Disciples of Christ   248
 Stephen Vaughn

4. AMERICAN MULTICULTURALISM: ETHNOCENTRISM, GENDER, AND RACE

"Living in a Land of Prophets": James T. Barclay and an Early Disciples of Christ Mission to Jews in the Holy Land   271
 Paul M. Blowers
Mainline Women Ministers: Women Missionary and Temperance Organizers Become "Disciples of Christ" Ministers, 1888–1908   292
 Glenn Michael Zuber
The Interracial Impact of Marshall Keeble, Black Evangelist, 1878–1968   317
 Paul D. Phillips

5. AMERICAN PRIMITIVISM

Hoosier Brethren and the Origins of the Restoration Movement   331
 David B. Eller
Two Restoration Traditions: Mormons and Churches of Christ in the Nineteenth Century   348
 Richard T. Hughes

Part III
A British Movement

The Churches of Christ in Britain: A Study in Nineteenth-Century Sectarianism   367
 Louis Billington
West End Chapel, Back Street Bethel: Labor and Capital in the Wigan Churches of Christ, 1845–1945   398
 Peter Ackers

Part IV
Social Ethics and Pacifism

David Lipscomb and the "Preferential Option for the Poor" among Postbellum Churches of Christ *Anthony L. Dunnavant*	435
Disciples of Christ Pacifism in Nineteenth-Century Tennessee *David Edwin Harrell Jr.*	455
From Pacifism to Patriotism: The Emergence of Civil Religion in the Churches of Christ during World War I *Michael W. Casey*	466
Who Speaks for the Christians? The Great War and Conscientious Objection Movement in the Churches of Christ: A View from the Wigan Coalfield *Peter Ackers*	481

Part V
Traditions Related to the Stone-Campbell Movement

A Different Kind of Loyalist: The Sandemanians of New England during the Revolutionary War *Jean F. Hankins*	499
Unity and Separation: Contrasting Elements in the Thought and Practice of Robert and James Alexander Haldane *Deryck W. Lovegrove*	520
"To Hear a Free Gospel": The Christian Connexion in Canada *Philip G. A. Griffin-Allwood*	544
The Boston Church of Christ *Russ Paden*	563

Contributors	575
Acknowledgments	577
Index	579

Introduction

The Renaissance of Stone-Campbell Studies: An Assessment and New Directions

Michael W. Casey and Douglas A. Foster

In the late twentieth and early twenty-first centuries studies of the religious tradition started by Barton W. Stone and Alexander Campbell have flourished. The three major religious groups of the movement, the Churches of Christ, the Christian Churches/ Churches of Christ, and the Christian Church (Disciples of Christ), all have first-rate historians producing monographs and significant essays about the tradition. Yet no major survey of Stone-Campbell studies has appeared since 1983.[1] An examination of this contemporary work is needed to put it into perspective and chart possibilities for new lines of research. We believe that the current trend is only a beginning and that the future is bright for Stone-Campbell studies.

Another major need is to make the wider scholarly world aware of this notable maturing of the tradition's historiography. Just as the renaissance of Stone-Campbell studies began, American historian R. Laurence Moore suggested that the Disciples of Christ and the Churches of Christ "may well be the most seriously overlooked and underestimated groups in the standard surveys of American religious history."[2] The Stone-Campbell tradition is one of the most significant native-born American religious movements: an "American Original," as Paul Conkin puts it.[3] Its rich history deserves to be known and studied by the wider scholarly community for insights that will enrich perspectives of the American story and the narratives of other countries where the tradition has had an impact. As a small effort toward this, we have gathered in this volume some significant essays on the Stone-Campbell tradition published in sometimes overlooked sources. The importance of each essay is heightened by bringing them together in this collection.

This introduction focuses on key historiographic issues raised by the renaissance of Stone-Campbell studies in general and by the essays collected here. We have not included everything published on the movement in the past two decades, but we have focused on what we believe to be the most significant materials and issues that need further investigation.

INTELLECTUAL HISTORY VS. SOCIAL HISTORY: WHICH USABLE PAST WILL WE USE?

Today Churches of Christ are facing a period of considerable disorientation and change. Many members are questioning their recent theological heritage and reacting against it. In such a time, it may be that some will discover again the countercultural, apocalyptic vision of Barton Stone.

Leonard Allen, "The Stone That the Builders Rejected," 1992

[T]he Restoration Movement/Churches of Christ is a development of post-Enlightenment Reformed theology. While much of its methodology is indebted to the Enlightenment, its fundamental theological commitments are Reformed.

Michael Weed, "Tradition at Risk," 1991

In 1988 two historians (Richard Hughes and Leonard Allen—best known for their historical work on primitivism) and one ethicist (Michael Weed) from the Churches of Christ collaborated in a remarkable little book titled *The Worldly Church: A Call for Biblical Renewal.*[4] Here for the first time within the tradition was a cry for a new "sectarianism," a call for a countercultural view of Christianity and the tradition. Sectarianism, variously defined, lies at the heart of much of the historiography of the Stone-Campbell movement in recent years. Allen and Hughes in particular have called for an intellectual history of the tradition to counter the method of social history used by American historian David Edwin Harrell Jr.

Harrell, Breeden Eminent Scholar in the Humanities at Auburn University and well known for his scholarship on Pentecostalism, in his 1960s work on the tradition completely revolutionized the historiography of the movement. Using Troeltsch's sect-to-church model he argued that contrary to most histories of the movement, the Stone-Campbell tradition did not escape the influence of antebellum American culture but in fact divided over sectional (Civil War), social (rural-urban), and economic issues. The northern, mainly urban, wealthy Disciples of Christ and the southern, rural, poor Churches of Christ went separate ways.[5] He concluded that the "twentieth-century Churches of Christ are the spirited offspring of the religious rednecks of the postbellum South."[6] Harrell belongs to the "anti-institutional" subdivision of the Churches of Christ. This group opposes congregational support of parachurch organizations—orphan homes, radio and television ministries—arguing that they are unauthorized by the Bible and supplant the work of the local congregation. Harrell embraced the radical sectarian theology of his splinter group and subtly asserted in his social history that both the liberal Disciples of Christ and the emerging sociologically denominational "mainstream" Churches of Christ of this century were wrong. He created a usable past for the sociologically sectarian Churches of Christ, and his method of social history allowed him to critique the majority views of the tradition while reaffirming his theological sectarianism.

Believing that ideas are more important than social and cultural circumstances, Hughes, professor of church history at Pepperdine University, and Allen, until recently a professor of theology at Abilene Christian University, have tried to counter Harrell's thesis by downplaying the role of the Civil War, arguing that the division predates it. Hughes asserts that the Disciples of Christ are the "embodiment" of an optimistic, postmillennial *denominational* vision of Alexander Campbell (1788–1866), while the Churches of Christ, in contrast, were at the end of the nineteenth century an "embodiment" of a pessimistic apocalyptic *sectarian* ideal most fully expressed by Barton Stone (1772–1844).[7] The Civil War merely exacerbated the tensions between these two worldviews. The social forces of southern sectionalism and economic deprivation "reinforced the theological tradition of Stone."[8]

What lies at the heart of the usable past for Hughes and Allen? In many ways their efforts parallel the new historiography of evangelicalism—the work of George Marsden, Mark Noll, Nathan Hatch, Grant Wacker, and others. These evangelical historians are engaging in "a form of what Germans call *Vergangenheitsbewtigung*—coming to terms with and overcoming the past by recognizing oneself as a product of the past and by mastering the history of one's own past."[9] These evangelical historians are trying to come to terms with and overcome "a fundamentalist movement that, thinly scarfed in tradition, went forth to battle the elements of modernity; that explicitly denied that it was shaped by a cultural context; that in varying degrees has embarrassed them, both by its anti-intellectualism and by its unfair share of leaders who, on the track of their souls, were creeps."[10] Hughes and Allen are on a similar quest. The hard-nosed debating, the rationalistic primitivism confident that the Churches of Christ had restored the church of the New Testament, the arrogant confidence that the tradition was above any cultural influence, and the often obsessive "defenders of the faith" have embarrassed the authors. Hughes and Allen, clearly a part of the more progressive Churches of Christ being assimilated into American evangelicalism, want to overcome these aspects of their heritage through the tales they tell about the past.

The "basic function of history," according to Leonard Sweet, is "to teach us who we are,"[11] and Hughes and Allen, like the new evangelical historians, are "restoring the didactic to the academic through a new version of history as moral discourse." In their intellectual history there are the heroes to be emulated (praised) and the villains to be overcome (blamed). Their work is an epideictic or ceremonial rhetoric by which they intend to educate a generation of people in the tradition who are ignorant of their history. Sweet says this historiography "poses questions to the past that not only resonate in the present but are relevant to the present." This history does not give "lessons" to "be fished out of history like some large-mouth bass," but it "does locate the fish within a school and the school within the sea." This praising of heroes and blaming of villains cannot help the movement "escape the sickness of our time." However, this history as moral discourse "believes that the process of historical consciousness and self-revelation uncovers the identifiable diseases, the recognition of which causes the symptoms to go away." To change the metaphor, one can begin to transcend the trappings of culture for a more pristine or biblical Christianity by scraping away the barnacles built up over time by human culture.

Hughes and Allen both have advocated the "apocalyptic" tradition of Barton Stone, David Lipscomb (1831–1917), and R. H. Boll (1875–1956) as worthy of praise. Unfortunately, neither author provides a precise definition of *apocalyptic* in their work. One can discern, however, a general theological point of view or "school within the sea" clearly as the Reformed tradition with Anabaptist and Lutheran components. Hughes articulates a minority position in antebellum America into which he places Barton Stone: "Often Calvinists convinced of the radical sinfulness of humankind" were skeptical "regarding human potential and progress . . . Instead these Americans often proclaimed their allegiance to a 'kingdom of God.'"[12] Stone had a Calvinist assessment of human nature as depraved. Stone's followers "generally joined to their Calvinist appraisal of human nature an experience of poverty and deprivation."[13] Later Hughes asserts: "we must first understand the strategic role of Calvinism in shaping the Stone-Campbell worldview," for "one simply cannot understand Barton Stone apart from his Calvinist yearning for the kingdom of God. For Stone, 'the kingdoms of this world' had not 'become the kingdoms of our Lord, and of his Christ.' Far from it. In truth, it was precisely the enormous gap between the kingdoms of this world and the Kingdom of God—a gap that seemed so apparent to Stone for a number of reasons—that fueled his apocalypticism."[14]

The model this historiography advocates is a particular strand within Reformed thought. Hughes recognizes that the appeal to the sovereignty of God cuts two ways in American history. One version "can and does sustain a powerful drive to reform all of society and to impose its vision on all of society."[15] The other version of "Reformed Christians," which includes the Separatist Puritans,

Separatist Baptists, and Barton Stone's Christians, "despaired when society failed to conform to the sovereign will of God." According to Hughes, "When that happened, they often focused their energies not on the construction of the kingdom of God for a future age but on a restoration of the ancient order in their own time and place. Such efforts sometimes prompted separation from the larger society and often generated a strong, countercultural resistance to the world and its values."[16] The Reformed tradition in its separatist countercultural version offers for Hughes and others a more biblical Christianity for the Stone-Campbell tradition and will allow the movement, especially Churches of Christ, to withstand the pernicious influences of secular society. Further, this tradition (along with Anabaptist and Lutheran aspects), the historians believe, will allow the movement to put behind the embarrassing and corrupting combative debating style and even overcome it with the Reformed view of the grace and sovereignty of God. While human actors seem center stage in the telling of the story, the search for God clearly lies at the heart of this historiography.[17]

Fundamental in Hughes's history is the idea of a sustained tradition of apocalypticism from Barton Stone, through David Lipscomb to R. H. Boll. He sees Lipscomb, Boll, and other figures as the full flowering of Stone's ideas. Lipscomb championed and brought to full flower Anabaptist conceptions of pacifism and separation from the world.[18] Boll, an immigrant from Germany, articulated Lutheran conceptions of grace.[19] Under the rubric of apocalypticism one will find the themes of separation from the world, premillennialism, pacifism, rejection of secular politics, rejection of wealth, and a focus on the sovereignty of God over human agency. Using a loose sect-to-denomination model, Hughes then argues that those who abandoned the sectarianism of the Stone tradition were essentially abandoning their heritage. The scattered evidence Hughes presents may not be enough to support his entire scenario, though this does not destroy the heuristic value of the usable past he lays out.

To critique adequately Hughes's work more spadework will have to be done in each of these themes. The genius of the new historiography is the stimulation for more work on the tradition. One topic to explore is Stone's view of noninvolvement in politics and premillennial eschatology. In 1826 Stone believed that Christians could be involved in public service to the government. He commended an early "Christian" preacher for his long service "as a legislator."[20] Newell Williams, a Christian Church (Disciples of Christ) historian at Christian Theological Seminary, sees Stone's change to a position of noninvolvement in government by Christians as a result of his "disapproval of the political party system that had emerged since the 1820s" and his "disappointment with America's failure to abolish slavery."[21] Hughes views Stone's premillennialism as part of his rejection of human agency in favor of the sovereignty of God. While Millerite premillennialists generally were indifferent and postmillennialism encouraged social reform, antebellum millennialism was not totally polarized over human agency.[22] Some antebellum premillennialists saw human agency as well as God's actions at work bringing about the end of the world.[23] For example, Stone asserted in an address:

> It is high time to awake out of sleep, and no longer indulge in dreams of better days, while we are inactive to hasten them on . . . Some of you say it [Christian union] will be effected in the millennium. No it must be effected before, that the world may be brought to believe and be saved. When Christ shall come the second time, it will be to judge, not to save the world . . . But you ask "what shall we do? I daily pray for the union of Christians, and am waiting for God to effect it." Do you wait for God to work a miracle to convince you of a plain duty? Do you wait for him to force his people to do right? In vain did you pray, in vain you wait, while you remain idle and inactive in the great work.[24]

Newell Williams argues that the "key to understanding Stone's millennialism was his view that 'the return and salvation of the Jews' and 'the fullness of the Gentiles brought in,' both of which he believed would precede the return of Christ, depended on the union of Christians."[25] Hughes may be overgeneralizing the relationship between human agency and premillennialism in Stone.

Furthermore, Hughes's model focuses solely on the division between the Disciples and the Churches of Christ, while the tradition actually has three major divisions. What role did the Stone and Campbell traditions as he describes them play in the second great division between the Disciples of Christ and the independent Christian Churches in the twentieth century? While Hughes sees the Stone churches located primarily in the Cumberland plateau, they also had a large presence in Ohio, Indiana, Illinois, and Missouri. In fact, Stone left Kentucky and settled in Illinois, ultimately dying in Hannibal, Missouri. Around half of the tradition's churches in these midwestern states were originally Stoneite. What happened to the Stoneite worldview north of the Ohio River? Did Stone's views simply fade away from these churches or was there another trajectory of ideas?

Some echoes of Stone's views have a "Disciples" trajectory suggesting that the division between the Disciples and Churches of Christ cannot be seen as simply a division between Stoneite and Campbellite worldviews. Stone did not insist on the necessity of immersion for all Christians, even for membership in the movement.[26] Open membership erupted as a contentious issue among Disciples in northern midwestern states from 1890 to 1930.[27] Disciples' scholar Joseph Belcastro traced open membership back to Stone and his movement.[28] Stone also took the moral influence theory of atonement opposing Campbell's idea of penal substitution, yet Stone's view of atonement ended up dominant among the Disciples in the *Christian-Evangelist* and was never present in the *Gospel Advocate* and the Churches of Christ.[29]

Harrell has reentered the fray with his recent work *The Churches of Christ in the Twentieth Century: Homer Hailey's Personal Journey of Faith* (Tuscaloosa: University of Alabama Press, 2000). While Harrell draws from Hughes's interpretation of the twentieth-century Churches of Christ and admits to some affinity between his work and Hughes's modified sect-to-denomination story, Harrell differs from Hughes on two key issues. First, Harrell believes that the noninstitutional controversy rather than the fight over premillennialism was the critical battle for Churches of Christ in the twentieth century. Second, while Hughes believes that the embarrassing debating style moved from the mainstream to the noninstitutionals, Harrell contends that the debating style with its common sense Baconian hermeneutic was found in the "arsenal of disputants on all sides of every argument."[30] Rather than a continuous intellectual trajectory of "apocalypticism," Harrell sees a continuous sociological stream of cultural alienation best exemplified by the noninstitutional Churches of Christ instead of the premillennial Churches of Christ. In contrast to Hughes, Harrell tells a tale of noninstitutionals who are faithful to the New Testament and progressives in the mainstream Churches of Christ, who are the "most overtly culturally captive group in the churches of Christ" as they look to evangelical theology and modern scholarship for new ideas.[31]

One of the most remarkable works on the tradition is an intellectual history written by Roman Catholic historian Richard Tristano.[32] It is one of the most compact and generally accurate overviews of the key intellectual streams flowing into the movement. Unfortunately, Tristano did his work before much of the new historiography emerged. Tristano also overlooked many rich journal articles on the movement, relying mostly on monographs and older standard histories. Still Tristano has provided penetrating insights into the tradition that probably only a sympathetic outsider could muster. He raises the possibility of dialogue between Catholics and the Stone-Campbell movement, particularly with "conservatives," that is, the Churches of Christ.[33] He saw two "very Catholic ideas" in Alexander Campbell: "reservations about denominationalism and baptism for the remission of sins."[34] Campbell distinguished between "real and formal" forgiveness of sins in baptism that he thought was a third way "between what he saw as the extremism of both Protestantism and Catholicism." While not identical to Catholic views, Tristano sees this as a "real basis for discussion." Furthermore, Tristano also sees the group's ecclesiology as a point of commonality. Both traditions share "a more highly developed notion of the unity of the church. Neither would consider 'their Church' to be a denomination." While he recognizes that each body offers differing solutions to denominationalism, "[t]he two models share some similarities and many differences, but a comparative approach could be useful."

Tristano also points to tensions within the tradition. He makes a strong case that a radical dualism permeated the Stone-Campbell movement, especially among "conservatives."[35] Both the Catholic and Stone-Campbell traditions perceived a threat in modern secular Enlightenment philosophy. The conservatives in the movement through emphasis on primitivism "have institutionalized a deep suspicion toward the secular." They have "maintained the nineteenth century separation between the natural and the supernatural worlds." This "world rejecting tendency" Tristano sees as a "dominant trait of Southern religious culture." It is possible that the Reformed model proposed by the new history of the tradition unconsciously maintains this perspective. Can a usable past for the movement be found that transcends this radical dualism? Tristano shows that it may be very difficult for Churches of Christ to construct a public theology or a positive role for the church in society.

Tristano also argues that the movement has rejected the "Relativism" and the "Eclecticism" of the Enlightenment and its idea of tolerance by restoring the idea of the "absolute authority" of the Bible.[36] At the same time, it has accepted "the rationalism and individualism of Lockean epistemology." The tradition has a dialectic "between Enlightenment individualism, relativism and rationalism; and a search for absolute authority." In other words, "the Restoration Movement is a synthesis, an attempt to unite absolute truth with individual opinion." Even though the tradition has failed to accomplish this synthesis, the genius of the movement was addressing important religious needs of American society. Tristano concludes his study: "The need which the Restoration Movement perceived was how to balance the human liberty which Americans cherish, with the message of the Gospel, which after all is not about the diversity but the unity of humanity. How can we balance the human need for pluralism and authority, individual conscience and community, toleration and religious certitude? These are questions for our own age."[37] And they certainly are questions that Stone-Campbell scholars should address in the future.

Three histories written in the 1990s are also worthy of note. Mark Toulouse, a Christian Church (Disciples of Christ) historian at Brite Divinity School in Ft. Worth, Texas, rejects the sect-to-denomination model used by both Hughes and Harrell. He believes that the early Stone-Campbell movement was not sectarian; instead, "the rich theological heritage" of the beginnings of the tradition were "dedicated . . . to the wholeness of the church."[38] Written for a Disciple audience, and believing that church history should "connect with theological, biblical, ethical, and practical ministry concerns,"[39] Toulouse traces various critical theological issues pertinent to the Disciples denomination rather than to institutional or social issues of Stone-Campbell history. Toulouse creatively reinterprets sacramental practice (baptism) to reflect current Disciples practice, rejects past choices of early restorationism and traditional mission practice, and celebrates what he sees as the centrality of ecumenism in the movement. Through his history Toulouse hopes to help Disciples reshape their tradition or be "a part of the traditioning of the denomination itself."[40] While Toulouse affirms the diversity of the Disciples, he admits sometimes Disciples find it difficult to "speak the language of faith" and settle for the "lowest common denominator faith" that plagues mainline Protestantism. He hopes that his analysis will start a dialogue in the Disciples concerning their Christian identity. Toulouse mines the best Disciples historical scholarship, yet he ignores most of the historical work done by scholars in the Churches of Christ and the independent Christian Churches. While he brilliantly analyzes the problem of the postdenominational age, this scholarship could enrich the dialogue that Toulouse seeks for the Disciples as they (and all of American Christianity) struggle with this contemporary enigma.

Henry Webb and James North have each written very different histories of the Stone-Campbell movement from the perspective of the Christian Churches/Churches of Christ (often know as the independent Christian Churches).[41] Their explorations of the division between the Disciples and the independents are their major original contribution. While both articulate a preference for the "middle-way" of the independents in contrast to the choices of the liberal Disciples and the sectarian conservative Churches of Christ, their histories significantly diverge from each other, reflecting differences in the independent churches themselves. North's work is primarily an intellectual history that reflects fundamentalist influence within the independents: North values unity but only on the basis of biblical authority. Teaching at Cincinnati Bible Seminary, which requires its faculty to affirm that the Bible is "infallible and inerrant in its entirety," North says, "we have no desire to initiate dialogue on Christian unity with denominations of liberal persuasion."[42] North clearly blames the division between the Disciples and the independent churches on liberalism. While North's history ignores efforts by moderates in the mid-twentieth century to bridge the growing gap between the rapidly polarizing groups, he has himself (along with Henry Webb) participated in internal unity efforts between the three Stone-Campbell bodies since 1998.

Webb, who taught at Milligan College, the only liberal arts school associated with the independents, takes a different view. Webb's history traces social as well as intellectual trends in the movement's history, more successfully for the nineteenth century than for the twentieth. Webb sees both hard-line liberals and fundamentalists at fault in the division between the Disciples and independents. He gives significant coverage to the moderates' unsuccessful efforts to preserve unity and details the takeover of the independents' main journal, *Christian Standard,* by fundamentalists. Webb's story of the failure becomes more significant as recent work by Newell Williams reveals that most Disciples laity are socially and theologically conservative.[43] In theory there was a social base for moderates to succeed in preserving unity. Webb's effort could now be considerably strengthened by setting the division between Disciples and independents into the larger developments of the American fundamentalist/evangelical movements as traced by evangelical historians.[44]

ALTERNATIVES TO THE SECT-TO-DENOMINATION MODEL

Both Harrell and Hughes, despite their different historiographical assumptions, use the sect-to denomination model for their histories. These constructs are ideal types that are difficult to find in history. Further, the transition from one type to another is extremely difficult to trace. Since these constructs are ideals, it becomes exceedingly difficult to detail how the change took place. Each historian has his weakness. Harrell focuses exclusively on social issues and mostly ignores the theology of the movement. Hughes, on the other hand, follows intellectual trajectories that are seemingly immune to all but the most obvious social factors. While giving invaluable clues, neither Hughes nor Harrell adequately address the question of how the intellectual beliefs of the movement interact with American culture. Alternatives to the sect-to-denomination model should try to take seriously how ideas interact with the culture in which they reside. While each of the following constructs has its own strengths and weaknesses, we think they are potentially useful in providing alternative understandings to the work of Harrell and Hughes.

From Boundlessness to Consolidation

John Higham suggests a model of transition from "boundlessness to consolidation" in mid-nineteenth-century American society.[45] After 1815 American society had little sense of limits and tended to be highly anti-institutional. This spirit of boundlessness was fueled by the democratization of politics and, as Hatch has shown, religion.[46] Clearly the Stone movement (as well as the larger "Christian" movement) fits Higham's description of the period of boundlessness. Richard McNemar (1770–1839) said of the early Stone movement: "it is difficult to paint the zeal for liberty and just indignation against the old aristocratic spirit, which glowed through every member of this new confederacy."[47] The Stoneites believed that freedom from the tyranny of clergy, creeds, synods, and anything associated with religious institutions would speed the natural ideals of the New Testament church. Even the early Campbell movement, though less "boundless" than Stone's, fits the pattern. In the iconoclastic *Christian Baptist*, Campbell attacked all human institutions, especially the hireling clergy who were the promoters of corrupt institutions. Higham points to the aggressiveness and popular restlessness of the period as "boundless" behavior. "The crusading mentality," he says, "evident in tract and missionary societies, in cold-water armies, in frenzied denunciations of the 'Monster Bank,' was a fighting mentality." Although Higham does not mention them, the crusading spirit and strife evident in the religious debates of the American frontier, mastered by Campbell and his imitators, may be seen as "boundlessness" behavior. Walter Posey in *Religious Strife on the Southern Frontier* said American denominations "sharpened their dissimilarities, assumed attitudes of extreme antagonism toward each other, and shunned cooperation among themselves in order to reach a scattered folk." Much of the religious fighting mentality can be attributed to Campbell. Posey claims Campbell's "harsh attacks on other churches, his pamphleteering crusades, his ceaseless debating, his contending and championing caused other groups to resent his new movement and to combine their resistance against him as the leader of a new sect." Campbell's "frequent appearance in public debates allowed Campbell to publicize his own opinion and to disparage the views of his opponents." Peter Cartwright claimed "that Campbellite preachers involved the Methodists in 'vain and hurtful debates,' in order 'to confuse the minds of the people, and draw them off from seeking God.'"[48]

By the 1850s, America "witnessed a subsidence of the radical hopes and reactionary fears of the early nineteenth century and the formation of a more stable, more disciplined, less adventurous culture." Control, order, and uniformity were now valued by Americans. The Campbell movement saw a shift to consolidation in the same period. In the 1830s Campbell began to press for greater cooperation among churches to accomplish evangelism. Although Campbell was not an enthusiastic supporter, the churches in his movement united with many of the Stone churches in 1832, necessitating greater coordination among the increasingly disparate movement. In the 1840s Campbell began to move beyond cooperation and press for greater organization: "There is now heard from the East and from the West, from the North and from the South, one general, if not universal, call for a more efficient organization of our churches."[49] Partially in response to Campbell's call there was a gradual development of state organizations in the 1840s. Finally this trend toward consolidation led to the establishment of the American Christian Missionary Society in 1849. This effort for order and uniformity continued in the north during the Civil War. Higham writes: "The conduct of the War required of course a major shift in priorities. It engendered respect for institutions, for discipline, for the principles of loyalty and authority."[50] The Missionary Society, with the southern churchmen gone, passed resolutions unofficially in 1861 and officially in 1863 endorsing the cause of the North. This set the stage for a new spirit of boundlessness in a segment of the movement as the Churches of Christ rejected the missionary society and all other human institutions. Jonathan Butler, who applied Higham's ideas to the emergence of Seventh-Day Adventism from Millerism, said that for Adventists the "institutional consolidation" was spiritually unsatisfactory. Therefore, "a new generation rebels against the closed, claustrophobic system by invoking the open, spontaneous spirit of boundlessness."[51]

It may be possible to view the development of various divisions within the movement as efforts to resist consolidation and to try to retain the sense of boundlessness. Of course there is heightened irony in the history of these efforts to conserve boundlessness, as most humans cannot tolerate much chaos. Those who attempted to reject consolidation inevitably consolidated their own positions and quickly lost the creativity they so desperately wanted to conserve. Still the attempts are important to consider.

Simplicity

David Shi offers an intriguing intellectual history of the idea of the "simple life" in America. He says simplicity "has always represented a shifting cluster of ideas, sentiments, and activities. These have included a hostility toward luxury and a suspicion of riches, a reverence for nature and a preference for rural over urban ways of life and work, a desire for personal self-reliance through frugality and diligence, a nostalgia for the past and a skepticism toward the claims of modernity, conscientious rather than conspicuous consumption, and an aesthetic taste for the plain and functional."[52] This array of ideas is unified by "the conscious desire to purge life of some of its complexities and superfluities in order to pursue 'higher' values—faith, family, civic duty, artistic creativity and social service."[53] The distrust of wealth, the preference for rural life, the stress on self-reliance, skepticism toward modernity, and the emphasis on the plain and functional are all prominent in Stone-Campbell history. The higher values the tradition pursued were the ideals of the golden age of the New Testament—pure church belief, practice, and structure and the resulting unity of the church. For Barton Stone simplicity consisted of holiness in one's life or separation from the world and a rejection of the "Babylon" of denominationalism. Campbell stressed simplicity in worship and in church structure. One could argue that the appeal to simplicity and the rejection of human complexity was at the heart of Campbell's program. In the second generation of the movement, a distrust of wealth and a skepticism about modernity emerged mostly among the conservatives. While neither Stone nor Campbell exactly fit Shi's schema of American simplicity, parallels between the movement and the American streams of the simple life are worth pursuing. How much of republican simplicity did Campbell accept? Did progressive simplicity influence the second and third generations of the Stone-Campbell movement? Were there parallels in the twentieth century between the simplicity of the Great Depression and the tradition? Lastly Shi describes the simplicity that emerged after the 1960s because of rising anxiety over affluence. Are the critiques of "worldliness" that emerged in the 1980s and earlier in mainstream circles in the 1960s within the Stone-Campbell movement especially in Churches of Christ and in evangelicalism generally, a part of this larger cultural phenomenon?

Primitivism

One of the ironies of Hughes's work is that the concept of primitivism he has encouraged and developed in conferences, essays, and books remains inadequately explored, Hughes himself adopting vague apocalypticism as his main heuristic label. The ideal of primitivism in its varied forms in the Stone-Campbell tradition needs further study. While primitivist rhetoric can be found in all three churches within the tradition, clearly each had a different understanding of primitivism.[54] In fact, it may be possible to understand the overall story of the movement as three different paths of restitution. While Hughes and Allen make a good case in one book about the primitivist soil of antebellum America,[55] did the "resoding" of America after the Civil War produce new versions of primitivism?

A significant omission in recent historiography of the movement is the story of its first "union." David B. Eller traces the fascinating union that took place by 1827 between renegade German Brethren congregations and Campbell's primitivist movement in Indiana. This was five years before the more well-known 1832 "union" between Stone and Campbell churches in Kentucky.[56] These Brethren churches brought a strong pacifist ethic, and some retained the practice of foot washing. Are there other Brethren ideas that might have influenced later Stone-Campbell developments? The impact of Brethren primitivism on the movement needs more exploration. A serious scholarly and critical examination of the tradition's ideal of restoring the primitive pattern of the church is still awaiting its historian.

Revitalization Movements

The Stone-Campbell tradition can also be viewed as an example of what anthropologist Anthony F. C. Wallace calls a "revitalization movement."[57] These movements arise in a time when society is in the midst of cultural upheaval. The internal map or "mazeway" that society provides for its people's stability in life has disintegrated. Without this, people feel deep dissatisfaction with their present situation and try to construct a new system where the old ways are placed into a new *Gestalt*. In one type of revitalization movement that Wallace calls "Revivalistic," people try to revive customs, values, or traditions thought to be lost. Only after a period of cultural distortion where people are alienated, disoriented and confused can revitalization happen.

Wallace explains that six major tasks must be performed by religious revitalization movements: mazeway reformulation, communication, organization, adaptation, cultural transformation, and routinization. *Reformulation* occurs with a restructuring of ideas already known to have gained some currency in society, though combined in a new and fresh way. Usually an individual or "prophet" has a dramatic change or moment of insight that shows the way for the new idea. In the wake of the Revolutionary War, Cane Ridge and the rise of the Christian movement fit the description. While less dramatic, Alexander Campbell and his movement, rising around the time of the War of 1812, clearly saw their program as a "restructuring" of Christianity to bring about Christian union. Wallace sees *communication* as primarily "preaching" or oral communication, but clearly other media can be employed. The leader or "prophet" feels compelled to share the new message with others, making converts to the cause and resulting in the need for *organization.* The role of leadership shifts to administration because the movement needs more political than religious guidance. Campbell clearly adopted this role far more successfully than Stone, who maintained a more "religious" focus on the ideals of the tradition. The new movement will encounter opposition and be forced to *adapt,* a process including doctrinal modification. Wallace says: "In most instances the original doctrine is continuously modified by the prophet, who responds to various criticisms and affirmations by adding to, emphasizing, playing down, and eliminating selected elements of the original visions." Both Stone and Campbell responded to the intense opposition the movement engendered. Campbell argued with his critics in formal oral debates and through his journals, *The Christian Baptist* and *Millennial Harbinger,* constantly adapting the tradition's original vision. At this point *cultural transformation* takes place. Reduction of alienation and stress in individuals occurs, and many enthusiastically start on "some organized program of group action." Finally, *routinization* occurs when the group action "becomes established as normal" and shifts to "preservation of doctrine and performance of ritual."

William G. McLoughlin took Wallace's concept and applied it to American history, tracing what he saw as five awakenings.[58] The first two, the Puritan and the First Great Awakenings, occurred before the emergence of the Stone-Campbell movement. The Second Great Awakening parallels and in some sense encompasses the Stone and Campbell movements. Little, if any, work has been done, however, on the connection and interaction of the other awakenings with later Stone-Campbell history.[59] McLoughlin argues that the Third Great Awakening, from 1890 to 1920, included the emergence of industrial society and new secular intellectual trends. Liberal Protestantism rose to accommodate Christianity to liberal thought in Darwinism and Biblical Criticism. The Social Gospel and other liberal movements emerged to spread humanitarian reform. The rise of liberal Disciples may be seen as a revitalization movement of the Disciples that parallels McLoughlin's pattern. While David Lipscomb (and the Churches of Christ) rejected liberal Protestant thought, his search for the primordial, peaceable kingdom could also be viewed as a revitalization effort.

The last awakening described by McLoughlin is rooted in the failure of liberalism and is probably the least coherent of his schema. However, the subsequent rise of postmodernism and postliberal theology puts his ideas into sharper focus. His hopes for a new consensus based in socialist options seem highly unlikely. Conservative options, both theological and political, have retained far more potency than he imagined. Disciples Renewal, the Boston/International Churches of Christ,[60] the effort to adopt and spread Evangelical/Charismatic worship styles among both independent Christian churches and a cappella Churches of Christ, and even the rise of political conservatism with George Benson (1998–1991) in Churches of Christ[61] and Billy James Hargis (1925–) in the independent Christian Churches[62] are all candidates for analysis with the revitalization model.

Religious Outsiders

R. Laurence Moore argues that religious outsiders or those who perceive themselves outside of the mainstream of American culture are the ones who have created American religious pluralism. The outsiders are actually at the center of the story of American religious life: "American religious experience began as dissent, and invented oppositions remained the major source of liveliness in American religion both in the nineteenth and twentieth centuries."[63] Robert Hooper, a professor of history at David Lipscomb University in his history of the Churches of Christ in the twentieth century, generally uses Moore's model to explain the changes in that body.[64] He identifies Churches of Christ as American outsiders in the early twentieth century and sees the transition away from pacifism symbolizing their shift to tentative insiders. Finally, in the 1950s, under the guidance of leaders who saw Churches of Christ as a national movement, the group reached insider status. Hooper also regards shifts in political stance as a marker of the change from outsider to insider. Much of Hooper's material, however, falls outside of Moore's paradigm as he narrates the internal issues and conflicts of the churches. The divisive issues from the 1930s through the 1960s are not clearly related to the outsider-insider thesis. Hooper's book is still important, as he lays out in broad outline how the Moore thesis could be applied to Churches of Christ. Nothing like this has been done for the Stone-Campbell tradition in the nineteenth century or for the Christian Churches/Churches of Christ and the Disciples of Christ in the twentieth.

Moore's approach suggests that the history of the tradition could be viewed as an overarching debate concerning who the insiders and outsiders in the movement were. The aim of this kind of narrative would be "to explore the sorts of social meaning, real or imagined they [the contestants] created."[65] An outsider label does not automatically assume a victim status, as they also may have victimized others to protect their social position and selfish interests. Some outsiders can be seen as agents of change, while others use the rhetoric of deviance to conserve, especially when used as "a well developed form of self-identification."[66] Moore points out that an outsider label over time "can provide a group with well-recognized social status within the structure of existing social arrangements." An exploration of "conservative" outsider rhetoric may reveal situations where the outsiders "had a substantial investment in many of the same cultural and social values that maintained the status of insiders." One example might be the racism of southern Churches of Christ in the pre–civil rights movement era. These and other concepts of Moore could be used to explore the outsider/insider roles in the Stone-Campbell movement. The use of Moore's categories would not automatically assume who the insiders and outsiders are before the history is investigated.

Dayton's "Methodist Paradigm"

Church historian Donald W. Dayton proposes a "Methodist paradigm" to explain the origins of evangelicalism in nineteenth-century revivalism, social reforms, and the Holiness and Pentecostal movements. Dayton contests the historiography of the new evangelical historians, which is overwhelmingly Reformed and from which Richard Hughes derives much of his perspective. Dayton labels this evangelical historiography the Presbyterian paradigm that stresses the origins of evangelicalism in the modernist-fundamentalist controversy and in "Old Princeton" theology.[67]

Dayton believes that the new evangelical historians have overlooked the dominance of Methodism in the nineteenth century as evangelical culture emerged. He views the Methodist, Holiness, and Pentecostal movements as correctives to the "Reformation tradition's . . . overemphasis on 'justification' as the organizing principle of Christian life and theology." Classic Reformation theology would view the Arminian emphases as "'semi-heretical' in their perfectionist tendencies, in a sometimes perceived Pelagianism, in their ethical 'activism' that sometimes appears to be a form of 'works righteousness,' and so on." Dayton further says that the Arminian movements shifted away from "orthodox" understandings of forensic justification, penal subsitutionary atonement, predestination, inerrancy, and total dependence on God with no room for human ability, moving instead toward sanctification, moral government, and moral influence theories of atonement, free will and human ability, and "less commitment to 'inerrantist' views of Scripture."[68] Many of these same themes can be clearly found in Barton Stone and some of his followers. Dayton further says his paradigm means that Holiness churches are not so much conservatives but more accurately a radicalization of the original Methodist revolt against Anglicanism. Similarly, Churches of Christ, especially with their strong early pacifist tendencies, might be seen as a radicalization of the original efforts of the Stone-Campbell movement. Dayton also says that his approach "puts greater weight on the factors of 'class' that were very prominent in the formation of the Holiness movement and Pentecostalism."[69] His paradigm applied to the Stone-Campbell tradition may also be a way to take more serious the class factors articulated by Harrell and downplayed by Hughes. Dayton sees an embourgeoisement of the new religious movements independent of modernity or the "liberalization" with which the Reformed historians are concerned. He says his paradigm has a different set of concerns: "the predominance of the revivalist/pietist protest *against* 'orthodoxy,' issues of dispensationalism and eschatological protest against the dominant society, factors of class and social location, dynamics characteristic of 'sectarianism' with its ambivalence toward traditional forms of religious life and traditional society, and other factors relatively independent of issues of 'modernity' and reaction to the Enlightenment."[70] Dayton's paradigm, while not a perfect fit, may prove to be a helpful heuristic model to transcend the differences between Hughes and Harrell and to correct some of the omissions of Hughes's approach.

Douglas Foster, a church historian at Abilene Christian University, begins this type of analysis in his application of Dayton's paradigm to one key historical controversy within the Churches of Christ: the fight over premillennialism. Foster overviews the rise of the premillennial party within the Churches of Christ as the mainstream became strongly amillennial. He then traces the affinities between David Lipscomb and R. H. Boll, a student of Lipscomb and the key leader in the development of dispensational views in Churches of Christ. After narrating the initial controversy in 1916, Foster traces the progress of the differences through the 1920s and 1930s. After a series of debates in the 1930s, Foy E. Wallace Jr. (1896–1979) took the lead in attacking missionaries, colleges, and leading preachers he suspected of being sympathizers with Boll. By 1940 the premillennial churches and leaders were isolated from the mainstream Churches of Christ. Foster argues that the controversy can be understood using Dayton's paradigm. The premillennialists were reformers or radicals trying to revitalize

Churches of Christ. They believed that the group had neglected prophetic literature and that dispensationalism was a needed corrective. However, traditional dispensationalism saw the primitive church as an accident of history, so most in Churches of Christ saw dispensationalism as a threat to their central tenet of restoring the New Testament Church. The effort to reform Churches of Christ failed because the premillennialists were forced to argue their case on the grounds of the traditional Churches of Christ. Dispensationalism became a set of propositions to be defended rather than "a vital belief motivating [Christians] to a life of joyous expectancy and zeal for spreading the gospel."[71] The premillennialist efforts to reform and revitalize the Churches of Christ fit Dayton's paradigm for evangelicalism.

Hughes's and Harrell's work have been pathbreaking and paradigm-shifting works in Stone-Campbell historiography. Any of these six alternatives to the sect-to-denomination model could provide new ways to extend and critique their efforts. Yet much of the needed work can proceed in a more localized, "postmodern" fashion. New paradigms can emerge from the exploration of specific issues of theology, society, and culture or from thick descriptions of minute more localized perspectives rather than from the top-down grand narratives or theories being imposed on the history. It is to these types of specific concerns that we now turn in the rest of this survey.

THEOLOGICAL ISSUES

Millennialism

Hughes's stress on the apocalyptic tradition in the Churches of Christ raises the issue of millennialism in the movement. Using a rhetorical approach, Disciples scholar Wayne Hensley argues that by using "various facets of secular postmillennialism," the Stone-Campbell movement "became a prime example of the nature and power of the rhetoric of postmillennialism."[72] After setting the movement into its historical context, Hensley says there were three main phases to the tradition's postmillennial rhetoric. First, to bring in the millennium Christians had to "evangelize the world." Second, world evangelization could not be accomplished until the church reestablished its primitive unity. Third, the basis for unity was the restoration of the ancient gospel and order found in the New Testament. Restoration was the foundation of the postmillennial rhetoric.[73] Drawing on the rural American culture that rejected urban influences, the movement's postmillennialism tapped into American beliefs of individual freedom, human equality, and the God-ordained destiny of America. The role of the chosen people was also co-opted by the tradition. The American Anglo-Saxon Protestants were the chosen people, as in other American postmillennial ideas, but the members of the movement "were the first-fruits" of this chosen people.

Every action by movement participants "was fraught with universal and eternal implications," giving them high motivation and commitment to the tradition. Hensley's article gives a good overview of how persuasive the movement was in early nineteenth-century American culture.

Nevertheless, millennial views were not uniform among leaders or followers. Hughes's work gives new stress to premillennial views, while Hensley's work tends to downplay them. Campbell held to a postmillennial view and its attendant optimistic worldview. At times he equated the destiny of America and Christianity.[74] Walter Scott (1796–1861) held both postmillennial and premillennial views at different points in his career.[75] Falling under the influence of leading American and British premillennialists, Scott expected the one-thousand-year reign of Christ to start in 1833 or 1834, but he spiritualized the millennium and returned to postmillennial views when nothing happened in the predicted years.[76] Barton Stone seems to have held premillennial views for his whole career. From 1829 to his death he clearly espoused those views, though before the start of his journal the *Christian Messenger* his views are more difficult to determine. Richard McNemar, one of the signers of the *Last Will and Testament of the Springfield Presbytery*, as early as 1801 held premillennial views that contributed to his and Stone's walking out of the jurisdiction of the Synod of Kentucky and forming the Springfield Presbytery.[77]

The diversity present in the first generation continued during the second. In the Campbell circle Robert Milligan (1814–1875) took a postmillennial view while Moses Lard (1818–1880) held premillennial stances. John Thomas (1805–1871), who was associated with Campbell and Scott but not Stone, developed premillennial views.[78] While some evidence suggests that in the north liberal Disciples held postmillennial views, other northern leaders took premillennial views. Arthur Crihfield (?–1852) was premillennial, as was Daniel Sommer (1850–1940) many years later. Paul Blowers, a church historian at Emmanuel School of Religion, traces the evolution of millennial thinking in James T. Barclay (1807–1874), the Stone-Campbell Movement's first missionary, sent to Jerusalem by the American Christian Missionary Society.[79] Barclay started out with postmillennial beliefs, but as he endured hardships in the Holy Land he gradually shifted to a premillennial view. He eventually came to believe that a political restoration of Israel would precede Christ's return. Barclay was clearly associated with Campbell, not Stone, during his career. In some cases it is conceivable that the premillennial trajectory that Hughes traces may have more Campbellite origins than Stoneite. For example, James A. Harding (1848–1922) was baptized by Moses Lard, a close friend to the Harding family. Harding admired Lard's ability to "take a passage of Scripture . . . analyze each part, and arrive at its full meaning as no other man" he "heard preach."[80] Harding graduated from Bethany College.[81] Much about the millennial views of other prominent persons remains unexplored. What, for example, were the millennial views of Benjamin Franklin (1812–1878)? What views dominated in the *Christian Standard, American Christian Review,* and the *Christian Evangelist*? How and why were the premillennial views persuasive to those who held them? How did the persons taking disparate views handle their disagreement over the millennium?

As mentioned in Hughes's own work, a large gap exists between the end of the Civil War and the start of the twentieth century. Except for scattered references to Lipscomb, Hughes provides little information on the millennial views found in the *Gospel Advocate*. In fact, some evidence supporting his apocalyptic trajectory from Stone through Lipscomb to R. H. Boll can be found. For example, Hughes mistakenly asserts there is "no evidence" that David Lipscomb's mentor, Tolbert Fanning (1810–1874), held premillennial views.[82] Fanning in 1866 said "that the subjects of Christ's kingdom will really subjugate, overcome and put down, by the Gospel of Peace, all Satan's subjects that can be saved; and afterwards the Lord will reign with his people a thousand years."[83] Conversely Hughes's theory may be found to oversimplify. What are the millennial views in the *Firm Foundation* and *Christian Leader,* other leading journals of the Churches of Christ after the Civil War? Were these millennial views central or peripheral to the group's theology? For example, while Hughes cites E. G. Sewell (1830–1924)—who co-edited the *Gospel Advocate* with David Lipcomb—as premillennial,[84] he ignores Sewell's assertion of an amillennial view and denial of premillennialism: "[T]he second coming of Christ will not be to take up his abode on the earth for the accomplishment of certain ends, but will bring all things pertaining to this earth to a close." The work of Christ on earth "will all be accomplished by the gospel, the words of Christ, through his church, his kingdom." Would Christ "come personally to dwell on the earth to restore all things?" Sewell said that "will have to be answered in the negative."[85]

In the independent Christian Churches, both premillennial and amillennial views are found.[86] How they evolved needs exploration. In Churches of Christ, premillennial and postmillennial views were present in the nineteenth century, but at some later time amillennial views appeared and became dominant. No one has carefully examined how or why this occurred. A debate over premillennialism that predates the fight over dispensationalism and R. H. Boll happened among Churches of Christ in Texas, but only cursory attention has been paid to this important event.[87] Possibly amillennial views emerged in this context. In the Disciples, evidence seems to indicate a long postmillennial tradition continuing into the twentieth century; however it is not clear how postmillennialism evolved and eventually collapsed in the Disciples.[88] Considerable work on the different trajectories of millennialism still needs to be done.[89]

Ethics: Pacifism

One prominent characteristic of the Stone-Campbell movement is a tradition of left-wing Protestant pacifism. Michael Casey, professor of communication at Pepperdine University, has found radical pacifists rooted in the American agrarian culture and the sectarian theology of the tradition. Peter Ackers, a labor historian at Loughborough University in England, has found a parallel pacifism in the British Churches of Christ grounded in the urban Midlands and labor union activism. Both manifest primitivist ideologies. A decline in pacifism and a hardening or radicalizing of a primitivist remnant occurred in both Britain and America in the face of war. The entire American movement experienced this during the Civil War[90] and again in Churches of Christ during World War I.[91] The movement in Britain divided along these lines in World War I.[92] Disciples of Christ in the U.S. had a resurgence of pacifism after World War I during the Great Depression, but it subsided with World War II.[93] Pacifism was also significant in the Stone-Campbell movement in Canada and probably in Australia.[94] One of New Zealand's foremost pacifists, Henry Ritchie Urquhart, was a member of the Churches of Christ.[95] It would be useful to trace and compare the pacifism of the movement across cultures and nations to see what, if any, is the theological core or, in anthropologist Clifford Geertz's terms, if this pacifism is a "system of symbols which acts to establish powerful pervasive and long-lasting moods and motivations" in the tradition.[96]

Ethics: Church and the Poor

One of the most interesting essays about the Churches of Christ was done by Anthony Dunnavant (1954–2001), formerly professor of church history and Dean at Lexington Theological Seminary. In it he explored the similarity of David Lipscomb's views of the poor with liberation theology. Dunnavant found seven themes of commonality: (1) a concern for the poor grounded "in concrete historical and personal experience"; (2) espousal of action for the benefit of the poor based on Matthew 25 "and in the kenosis of Christ"; (3) "an assumption that the poor are the fundamental historical basis of the Church"; (4) a focus on evangelizing the poor; (5) "an assumption that the poor are especially equipped to receive the gospel"; (6) that service to the poor is a measure of how faithful one is following Christ; and (7) a belief that the "institutional Church" should "distance" itself "from the corrupting influences of material wealth."[97] Dunnavant hoped the "resonance" he saw between Lipscomb and liberation theology will bring about both reexamination and "reappropriation" of these ideas "by North American Christians who value the heritage of David Lipscomb."[98] True to his Disciples ecumenical heritage, Dunnavant also hoped that the parallels between liberation theology and other conservative Christian groups would develop "ecumenical possibilities" that are "beyond the boundaries of familiar definitions of liberals, liberationists, Catholics, and conservative or evangelical Protestants." His goal was to develop a "family memory" across traditions.[99] His work is one of the finest examples of how a Stone-Campbell theme of unity is being usefully reclaimed in Stone-Campbell historiography.

Ecumenism

The profound irony of a Christian unity movement that is itself wracked by internal division continues to demand examination. Douglas Foster in his 1986 Vanderbilt dissertation studied conflicting ideas of Christian unity held by four principal leaders in the movement at the end of the nineteenth century: J. H. Garrison (1842–1931), Isaac Errett (1820–1888), David Lipscomb, and T. B. Larimore (1843–1929). He concluded that while all continued to use the rhetoric of unity characteristic of the movement's origins, very different understandings of the idea were actually at the heart of the division that was then taking place.[100] In his 1994 book *Will the Cycle Be Unbroken: Churches of Christ Face the Twenty-first Century,* Foster further suggests that conflicting ecclesiologies were heavily involved in a continuing propensity to divide in that segment of the movement.[101]

Disciples restructure was to a great extent driven by a perceived need to develop a formal denominational structure through which to act officially for the churches in ecumenical efforts. The 1991 publication of Anthony Dunnavant's Vanderbilt dissertation by Peter Lang publishers chronicles that process in detail.[102] A fascinating critique of restructure from one of its own architects, Ronald E. Osborn, appeared in *Mid-Stream* journal in 1989 and raises questions concerning concepts of Christian unity in Disciples circles that need further development.[103] Douglas Foster examined the variety and development of Disciples ideas of unity between 1880 and 1980 as part of the Lilly Endowment funded study examining Disciples in American culture.[104]

Several Disciples scholars have continued to be active in ecumenical studies. Perhaps the most significant recent publication is an anthology of ecumenical texts edited by Michael Kinnamon, former Dean of Lexington Theological Seminary now at Eden Theological Seminary, and United Church of Christ minister Brian Cope.[105] Other significant materials relating more specifically to Stone-Campbell ideas of unity appear with some frequency in *Mid-Stream* journal published by the Disciples' Council on Christian Unity.[106]

Remarkable shifts have taken place in the ecumenical movement away from a tendency to emphasize models of merger to focus on other understandings of unity such as covenant partnership and *koinonia*. These shifts may be partially responsible for what seems to be an increasing interest among members of

Churches of Christ and Christian Churches/Churches of Christ in appropriate participation in the ecumenical movement. A recent book jointly written by Barry Callen of the Church of God (Anderson, Indiana) and James North reports on a series of "unity" meetings between the two groups and lays out a model for "ecumenical" activities among conservative bodies.[107]

Other surprising ecumenical developments have occurred in recent years that need historical assessment. Despite abortive attempts at discussions of unity in the past, since 1984 meetings between the Churches of Christ and the Christian Churches/Churches of Christ known as "Restoration Forums" have produced a number of sometimes substantial studies on matters of doctrine and polity as they relate to unity.[108] These meetings need to be compared with the less successful Murch-Witty discussions of the 1930s and 1940s.[109]

In 1998 a new internal unity effort labeled the Stone-Campbell Dialogue began between members of all three major streams of the Movement. Papers and documents from these meetings have been made available on web sites hosted by the Disciples Council on Christian Unity and the international newspaper of Churches of Christ, *Christian Chronicle.*[110]

Recently there have been conversations between Churches of Christ and Southern Baptists sponsored by the Southern Baptist Home Mission Board. A comparison of these meetings with Disciples-Northern Baptist unity talks of the past would be fascinating.[111]

Work in this area has potential for particularly fruitful studies as the Stone-Campbell Movement and its constituent churches attempt to clarify issues of unity and ecclesiology that have been inadequately examined, understood, and articulated.

Pneumatology

Studies in the Holy Spirit have not been numerous in the movement. Newell Williams's 1979 Vanderbilt dissertation that treated the pneumatology of Barton W. Stone, one Doctor of Ministry thesis, and two Abilene Christian University master's theses are among the few academic treatments.[112] Thomas Olbricht, professor emeritus of religion at Pepperdine University, and Pat Brooks, a minister in the Churches of Christ, investigated how Alexander Campbell's Lockean philosophy shaped his views of the Holy Spirit.[113] Brooks also explored the controversy that emerged between Robert Richardson (1806–1876), biographer of Alexander Campbell, and Tolbert Fanning when Richardson tried to break from Campbell's Lockean views of the Holy Spirit.[114] Richard Hughes's article in the volume *Reaching Beyond* has some implications for pneumatology but more for ecclesiology.[115] Leonard Allen and Danny Swick have examined the role of the Holy Spirit and Spirituality in general in the early Stone-Campbell Movement and in twentieth-century Churches of Christ. The authors move toward constructing a full-blown trinitarian theology for the movement.[116]

Significant work needs to be done in this area. Campbell's view stands in stark contrast to the predominant view of Protestant revivalists and has put the movement on the fringe of Protestantism on this issue for much of its history. The Richardson controversy may indicate that differences over pneumatology played a role in the divisions of the movement. Many reformers of the tradition, from the obscure W. S. Russell (1832–1863) in the nineteenth century to Don Finto (1930–), who played a key role in the development of contemporary Christian music in the twentieth, have turned to revivalist, Holiness, and Pentecostal notions of the Holy Spirit to initiate change in the tradition.[117] Many in the tradition have left the movement and its rationalistic pneumatology for Pentecostal versions. Sidney Rigdon (1793–1876) and Parley Pratt (1807–1857) became Mormons partly because they were attracted to the idea that the Apostleship and the full range of gifts of the Spirit would be restored.[118] Maria Woodworth-Etter (1844–1924), who became a leading Holiness evangelist had left the movement in 1854.[119] In more recent times, Pat Boone (1934–) left Churches of Christ and openly embraced charismatic views.[120] Even a fledgling charismatic movement began with the Churches of Christ.[121] Two converts to Mormonism from the Stone-Campbell Movement articulated this attraction. Elizabeth Ann Whitney said, "My husband and myself were Campbellites. We had been baptized for the remission of sins, and believed in the laying on hands and the gifts of the Holy Spirit. But there was no one with authority to confer the Holy Ghost upon us." John Murdock noted, "finding their principal leader, Alex Campbell, with many others, denying the gift and power of the Holy Ghost, I began to think of looking for a new home."[122] These complex and intertwined relationships between revivalism, Holiness, Pentecostal, and Mormon views of the Holy Spirit and the Stone-Campbell movement need to be traced. Why have so many reformers turned to these views? Why have many in the movement been attracted to alternative pneumatologies? What has been the relationship between the Holiness, Pentecostal, and charismatic movements and the Stone-Campbell tradition? To what extent are twentieth-century pneumatologies in the three churches of the movement a reaction to these so-called three waves of the Spirit?

This quick survey of historical/theological matters is also significant for the absence or underdevelopment of major areas of systematic theology. Disciples scholar William R. Barr surveyed the Christological diversity of the Disciples of Christ that included Barton Stone's semi-Arianism, Campbell's orthodoxy, Scott's focus on what Christology meant for the praxis of the church, Robert

Milligan's focus on Christ's humanity, Edward Scribner Ames's idealist liberalism that Christ embodied the highest and best of human aspirations, and Frederick Kershner's eschatological Jesus, who raises humans to new levels of ethics.[123] John Mark Hicks, professor of theology at David Lipscomb University, has analyzed the varying views of atonement in the first-generation leaders. Campbell held a traditional penal substitution theory. Stone advocated a moral influence theory while Walter Scott supported a governmental theory.[124] Hicks's work is unique in its sustained analysis of a theological theme. Explorations of the tradition's understandings of God, anthropology, and ecclesiology are needed, along with further development of the history of the tradition's central theological concerns.[125]

PRACTICAL THEOLOGY

Communication Studies

Scholarship in religious communication has mushroomed in recent years. The Religious Communication Association sponsors a refereed journal and an annual conference. Despite the active scholarship of many from the Stone-Campbell tradition in RCA, no scholarly articles on the history of communication practices in the movement have appeared in the *Journal of Communication and Religion*.[126] Leonard I. Sweet, in his excellent book *Communication and Change in American Religious History,* amazingly has no citation of any study of Stone-Campbell communication activities. Despite this lacuna, the Stone-Campbell movement excelled in three areas of communication: the use of print media through religious journals, the spoken word through preaching, and argumentation through both oral and published debates.

W. T. Moore (1832–1926) is credited with originating the popular and accurate saying that the Disciples of Christ do "not have bishops, they have editors."[127] Elias Smith (1769–1846) of the New England "Christian" movement, a group that arose from the same American ethos as the Stone-Campbell tradition, began one of the earliest religious periodicals in America.[128] The rise of religious journalism was part of the explosion of printed material that Sweet calls "the institutionalization of print culture."[129] This new "communications environment" became what William Gillmore calls the "modernization of knowledge." Campbell certainly fits Sweet's description: "From here on, one could live in the backwoods but still be part of the cultural mainstream; isolation was not mutually exclusive with association." The torrent of print and the multiplicity of Stone-Campbell journals, however, goes unexplored by Sweet.[130] In his 1966 Vanderbilt dissertation, James Brooks Major explored the role of periodicals in the movement and found at least one hundred periodicals produced between 1820 and 1860.[131] However, Major focuses on how the journal editors functioned as power brokers rather than on how periodicals fit into the print culture of nineteenth-century America. How Stone-Campbell journalism fits this print culture is deserving of study.[132] Also, work is needed to trace the decline of the importance of "editor-bishops" and the overall decline of periodicals in the tradition in the age of the electronic culture.

Though some older studies of preaching and preachers in the movement have been published,[133] they represent the tip of the iceberg when one considers the numerous theses and dissertations on the preaching of the movement.[134] In one of those significant recent studies, Carisse Berryhill argued that Campbell's preaching depends largely on the theory of British rhetorician George Campbell.[135] Similar studies of other preachers are needed. What knowledge did other prominent preachers in the movement have of rhetorical theory? What training in rhetoric and homiletics did preachers in the tradition have? While in recent times Disciples Leander Keck and Fred Craddock have achieved national prominence in homiletics, surprisingly little is known about the history of how preachers have been trained in rhetoric. Michael Casey showed that Alexander Campbell shifted from classical to Enlightenment rhetoric in his preaching. Also, Casey has studied the influence of rhetorical theory and homiletic training specifically on the Churches of Christ and traces the evolution of preaching forms over the history of the movement.[136] Similar studies for the independent Christian Churches and the Disciples of Christ are needed. Joseph Jeter Jr., a Disciple homiletician, provides a starting point in an article that surveys early Disciples preaching, changes in preaching in the late nineteenth century, and the recent context where Disciples preaching has declined.[137] Newell Williams argues that there were two eras of Disciples evangelism. In the nineteenth century Disciples preachers "proclaimed the good news of what God has done for sinners." In the twentieth, preachers focused on "the good news of what people can gain if they will allow God to help them live lives of self-sacrifice."[138] In another article, Williams traces four stages of development in Disciples ministry: the practice of Barton Stone and the Christians, the views of Alexander Campbell, the emergence of the professional minister in the 1860s, and the current Disciples practice that emerged in the 1930s.[139] The content of sermons is largely unknown, so content analyses of sermons in different historical and contemporary settings are also needed.[140] In-depth studies of preachers, both prominent and obscure, along with exploration of particular periods of the movement, especially from 1865 to 1900, are needed to fill gaps in Casey's work. One potentially rich source for such work is the growing collection of sermons by twentieth-century ministers in Churches of Christ held by the Center for Restoration Studies of Abilene Christian University.

Debating quickly became a prominent characteristic of the Stone-Campbell movement.[141] The tradition mastered this prominent characteristic of the southern frontier[142] and of American culture.[143] R. Laurence Moore pointed to the debate between Robert Owen and Alexander Campbell as typical of the entertainment that religious controversy provided in antebellum America: the two men "who ought to have been bitter ideological foes, seemed to enjoy their performance as a team. They applauded each others jokes in public and dined together with apparent satisfaction in private." During the time of the debate "the two had the best and only show in town."[144] Alexander Campbell's proclivity and ability to debate has been widely chronicled by theses, dissertations, and in-house denominational publications.[145] Earl West's essay is an excellent overview of the "Unprecedented Spectacle" of the Campbell-Owen debate.[146] James Holm investigated Campbell's training in rhetoric under George Jardine at Glasgow University and how it served him in his debate with Owen.[147] Carroll Ellis provides the historical context of the debate with Catholic archbishop John Purcell.[148] Mark Weedman also examined the Purcell debate. Campbell and Purcell thought "historical precedent was authoritative" and "both believed that God acts providentially in history."[149] Campbell had a primitivist view of history giving authority only to the Bible, while Purcell had a "documentary view of history," where the documents of the church contain the genuine revelation of God "which guard against development and change."[150] Theological differences lay at the heart of the differences in this debate between two of the leading religious figures of the nineteenth century, which is worthy of a monograph in itself.[151]

Despite the wealth of studies about Campbell's debates, little has been done to understand them in the context of religious debate in America, which is itself a neglected area of study. Entertainment is the prominent paradigm, but other than a couple of short essays, little has emerged to explain this prominent genre of communication.[152] How do the debates of the tradition fit into the larger context of American religious controversy? How and why did religious debating in and out of the Stone-Campbell movement decline in the twentieth century?

Worship, Spirituality, and Aesthetics

As with most traditions, the movement has not escaped controversy over worship practices. James White in his important history of Protestant worship locates the Stone-Campbell movement in the frontier worship tradition.[153] While the pragmatic bent of the frontier tradition has played a key role in Stone-Campbell worship style, Dale Jorgenson, originally from the Churches of Christ and now a Disciple, argues that the Reformed tradition, Puritanism (English and American), and British/Scottish empiricist rationalism also shaped the worship and aesthetics of the Stone-Campbell movement.[154] The Reformed emphasis on the word rather than the image, simplicity in aesthetics, and opposition to instrumental music is echoed in the tradition.[155] The movement clearly inherited the Puritan rejection of a prepared liturgy, icons and ceremony, and an emphasis on congregational autonomy.[156] The elimination of the poetic and symbolic, "wit and eloquence," which Campbell learned from John Locke, along with the other factors, did not, according to Jorgenson, "provide a hopeful background for a faith expressed through the arts."[157] Jorgenson brilliantly traces the impact of these strands of thought on the movement showing the instrumental focus on art, the simplicity of church architecture, and the simplicity of "structure and style but with a high regard for theological soundness in the poetry" of the movement's hymnody.[158] Overall, the tradition's aesthetic created "a disinterest in metaphor, a bondage to literalism which at times became plodding, and a failure to enter into the alternative world represented by literature, visual arts, and non-vocal music."[159]

Other more narrowly focused studies have looked at the hymnody of the tradition. George Brandon traced the history of the hymnbooks of the Disciples of Christ from Alexander Campbell to the middle of the twentieth century. He found that Disciples hymnbooks had evolved to include "examples of almost all the types of hymnody found in mid-twentieth century middle-of-the road Protestant collections, from gospel songs to the formal hymns and tunes from the liturgical traditions."[160] Harold Holland, retired Pepperdine University librarian, performs a similar service for the hymnbooks in the Churches of Christ, concluding that the most used books "include mixtures (in varying proportions) of traditional Protestant (and a few Catholic) hymns, folk songs and spirituals, gospel songs which resulted from the interdenominational evangelistic campaigns and the Sunday School movement of the Nineteenth-Century, and modern songs in a wide range of musical and literary styles."[161] Holland also argues that two forms or preferences in music style developed in the Churches of Christ. The older rural tradition, encouraged by the gospel song business, favors gospel songs and often uses the shaped-note system. The newer "urban" tradition, encouraged by the group's colleges, has promoted "a somewhat traditional hymnody."[162] Forrest McCann, retired Abilene Christian University English professor, develops the story of the urban tradition by narrating the development of *Great Songs of the Church*, the hymnal that came to dominate the Churches of Christ.[163] McCann traces the story of the hymnal from its origins with E. L Jorgenson (1886–1968) of Louisville, Kentucky, to its continued revision and publication by Abilene Christian University. Jim Mankin, deceased Bible professor at Abilene Christian University, has narrated the efforts of prominent songwriter L. O. Sanderson (1901–1992) to improve the singing of the Churches of Christ. While Sanderson "sometimes catered" to the gospel song taste, some of his hymns are liked by the "urban" tradition.[164] Peter Morgan, director of the Disciples of Christ Historical Society, traced the early hymnals of the movement with their varying rationales and the resultant conflicts they engendered.[165]

These important studies need to be updated and supplemented as the worship styles of the tradition continue to evolve. While the rural and urban styles are still clearly present in all parts of the Stone-Campbell movement, a new worship style with origins in the Charismatic movement is becoming increasingly popular. The community church "suburban" style of worship needs to be analyzed.[166] As this suburban style of music and worship becomes more prevalent, a more comprehensive history investigating the trajectories of worship and aesthetics is badly needed.[167] Also comparative studies with the patterns of transformation in other traditions would be helpful.

Recently, Disciples scholars have explored spirituality in the tradition. William O. Paulsell looks at Disciples spirituality through prayer tracing the views of Campbell, Stone, and Robert Richardson, then ideas about prayer in leading Disciples periodicals: *The Christian-Evangelist*, *The Christian*, and *The Disciple*. Richardson and Stone differed from Campbell, who limited God to speaking to humans through Scripture. Richardson emphasized communion with God, while Stone saw prayer as a basis for holiness. Frederick Kershner was one of the first Disciples to take seriously the mystical dimension of religion. In a tradition that emphasized rationality, Paulsell found a surprising richness to prayer and spirituality.[168]

While scholars have made rich inquiries into the fields of communication studies and worship, other areas of practical theology need exploration. Religious education of adults and children, missions, pastoral care, and social ministries, among others, need historical treatment across the tradition, as well as comparative study with secular and religious trends.[169]

BIOGRAPHICAL STUDIES

Alexander Campbell

More attention has been devoted to Alexander Campbell by scholars both inside and outside the tradition than to any other figure in the movement. At least fourteen articles have been published on some aspect of Campbell's life and thought in nonmovement outlets.[170] Besides the articles considered under previous headings, several others are significant. John Morrison, independent Christian Church scholar, shows how Campbell's rational approach to Christianity functioned in the context of emotional frontier religion.[171] Campbell formed a "distinctive form of rationalism" that attacked religious emotionalism on the one hand and skeptical rationalism on the other. Believing that knowledge was power, Campbell trusted in the free marketplace of ideas and the triumph of his rational primitivism if both sides of issues were heard. Morrison traces Campbell's use of writing, public debate, and preaching to spread his theology on the frontier of the mid-nineteenth century.

Edward Hicks, Faulkner University (Alabama) history professor, shows that while Campbell was one of the leading anti-Catholic speakers in the western United States, "he was not the typical nativist nor did he reflect the more radical aspects of anti-Catholicism in America."[172] Campbell focused on the threat of Catholicism to republican institutions, especially democratic government, free education, and religious liberty.[173] Hicks places Campbell's anti-Catholicism into proper context. Hicks's study and Weedman's examination of Campbell's debate with Purcell mentioned earlier show that Campbell's anti-Catholicism cannot be reduced to the typical Nativism of antebellum America.

In another interesting study Richard Hughes compares the restitution motifs of Alexander Campbell and the early Anabaptists.[174] While Campbell and the Anabaptists began with similar presuppositions about the nature of Scripture and the effort of restoration, ultimately their primitivist agendas differed greatly. Campbell saw restoration "as a means to unity and produced a predominately outward and academic reform." Anabaptist primitivism was "limited in practice primarily to a revival of the spiritual, moral, dedicative aspects of the primitive church." They focused on external practices "only as they sustained a relationship to the spiritual concerns of the *corpus Christi*."[175] The two movements commenced in different contexts. The persecution of the Anabaptists and their reaction to medieval Catholicism encouraged their spiritual focus. The division and discord of Scotch-Irish Presbyterianism and American frontier religion galvanized Campbell to work for Christian unity and focus on the external factors of the apostolic church. Hughes argues that both movements "yielded to the prohibitive and determining influences of culture" and so were "partially thwarted" in restoring primitive Christianity. He concluded that "this comparison should reveal that restitution—or any biblicist motif—is not immune to cultural influences in any generation. To that extent the church of Christ will always be the church of the world."[176]

In recent works by movement historians, Campbell continues to receive prominent attention. Newell Williams makes the controversial claim that Campbell identified the gospel, not acceptance of the Bible, as an infallible revelation from God as the foundation for Christian union. The gospel is the "facts" proclaimed by the apostles, and for Campbell "the *meaning* of the facts about Jesus Christ reported by the apostles is that "God is love." Campbell advocated restoration of the ancient order because he "believed that 'apostolic' practices such as weekly observance of the Lord's Supper and believer's immersion for the remission of sins were more effective in communicating the message that God is love than 'modern' practices." Campbell's identification of the gospel as the foundation for Christian union was based on his conviction that the gospel, received in faith, has "the spiritual power to reconcile people to God and to one another."[177] Williams goes on to argue that Campbell believed the gospel could overcome social and cultural diversity. In the face of decline and internal division among Disciples, Williams proposes a usable past in Campbell that may help heal the divisions of the Disciples. In so doing he emphasizes Campbell's spiritual side while downplaying the scholastic dimensions of his thought.[178]

On the other hand, Hughes, in *Reviving the Ancient Faith,* sees Campbell as the father of the sectarian spirit and "a hard, combative style that prized verbal assault on the positions of opponents and enemies."[179] Campbell becomes a foil to blame as Hughes emphasizes Campbell's scholastic side. Unlike Williams, Hughes does not explore other positive dimensions of Campbell for a usable past. Instead he seems to want to jettison much of the Campbell legacy. He sees the later more ecumenical Campbell symbolic of the trajectory followed by the Disciples of Christ.

Leroy Garrett, another historian from the Churches of Christ, maintains that the "genius" of Campbell and the movement was not "restoration" but reformation. As a reformation movement the focus was on catholicity or unity. Garrett, a maverick within Churches of Christ, rejected sectarian exclusivism and called for a rediscovery of the tradition's plea for unity before it became more fashionable within the group. He also denies the claim that Campbell can be interpreted as a sectarian.[180] Garrett's own ecumenical agenda clearly shapes his interpretation of Campbell.[181]

The various searches for a usable past driven by the perspectives of each historian color how each views Campbell. Was Campbell a sectarian who later became ecumenical? Was he a reformer focused mainly on ecumenism, uninterested in restoration? Was his ecumenism based on his conviction of the spiritual power of the gospel of God's love to reconcile persons to God and to one another? Or was he more of a rational primitivist? These questions raised by recent historiography deserve exploration.

Despite the high interest in Campbell that has produced several excellent specialized studies by historians of all kinds,[182] no up-to-date biography of Campbell exists. Almost all the Campbell studies rely heavily on the first biography done by his close friend Robert Richardson.[183] Though not available to researchers at this writing, the manuscript of an original and thorough biography of Campbell by Disciples scholar Eva Jean Wrather has been deposited in the Disciples of Christ Historical Society. However, historical developments in the tradition, questions raised by the new historiography, and newly available archival materials open the door for a good critical biography and more focused specialized studies of Campbell.

Barton W. Stone

Scholarly interest in Stone and Cane Ridge has increased significantly since the reprint edition of his paper *The Christian Messenger* by Star Bible Publications in 1978.[184] Newell Williams has been the primary recent interpreter of Stone, culminating in 2000 with the first biography[185] of Stone in half a century. It is useful to compare Williams's work with that of Richard Hughes and Leonard Allen.[186] Like them, Williams sees Stone as a Calvinist who retained a Calvinist piety different from the revivalist leaders of the northern revival—Dwight, Beecher and Finney. Williams was the first scholar to publish the idea that Stone retained a Calvinist piety. Anthony Dunnavant correctly noted that Williams was one of the first to call into question the liberal Disciples idea that Stone was "an ecumenical founder" of the movement "whose commitment was not so closely tied to an insistence on" restoring the primitive church.[187] This ecumenical image found in William West's biography of Stone, Anthony Dunnavant argues, originated in the need by the liberals to find a "usable past in their Disciples of Christ tradition" that would justify their active involvement in the ecumenical movement.[188] Still, Disciples historians[189] and Leroy Garrett argue that Christian unity was the primary focus for Stone.[190] Nathan Hatch, on the other hand, does not see unity as Stone's banner; instead, freedom or liberty was the cry of the Stone movement. Hatch asserts that Stone and the other Christians declared their independence from "theology," Calvinist or otherwise, and from all institutional structures. This appeal to chaos resulted in more religious division than unity.[191] One is tempted to shout, "Will the real Barton Stone please stand up!" Paul Blowers is certainly correct in his assessment that Stone was a "complex mix" who "amalgamated seemingly contradictory elements from their religious culture: supernaturalism and rationalism, experimental religion and biblical literalism, [and] Calvinism and Arminianism."[192] With his complex mix, Stone will be fertile ground for new biographies and usable pasts.

Other Biographical Treatments

Three additional books deserve mention in this section. Though a volume of collected essays rather than a coherent biography, *Walter Scott: A Nineteenth-Century Evangelical*, edited by Mark G. Toulouse, sets Scott, the great evangelist of the movement, into a helpful social, cultural and theological context. The book is essential for understanding the shaping of Scott's career as one of the founding leaders of the tradition. In a revised version of her Georgetown University dissertation, Loretta Long, assistant professor of history at Abilene Christian University, has provided an excellent study of the life of Selina Campbell, Alexander Campell's second wife. Long depicts Campbell as a woman who conformed to nineteenth-century conventions concerning the role of women in society, yet was extremely active during and after her illustrious husband's life in the religious, educational and economic causes he espoused. Finally, though again not a biography proper, many of the essays in *The Quest for Christian Unity, Peace, and Purity in Thomas Campbell's Declaration and Address,* edited by Thomas Olbricht and Hans Rollmann, give never-before available insight into the early thought and career of Thomas Campbell.[193] These volumes are examples of what ought to be done with other key figures both in the early movement as well as in more recent years in the various streams.

RELATED TRADITIONS

Several religious traditions have ties with the Stone-Campbell movement. The Sandemanians, Haldanes,[194] and the Christian Connexion[195] all influenced key Stone-Campbell leaders with their ideas of restoring the primitive church of the New Testament. However, each of these traditions maintained its own independent heritage. The Stone-Campbell movement has also spawned new groups like the Christadelphians in the nineteenth century and the International Churches of Christ in the twentieth. The nexus of primitivism between these groups could be profitably explored.

In an important article, Jean Hankins explores how the New England followers of the Sandemanian sect fared during the Revolutionary War.[196] The Sandemanians were outside of the American religious mainstream and held tenaciously to their loyalty to King George in the face of great persecution. Unlike activist loyalists, the Sandemanians were passive: they did not fight or spy for England, give any food or information, or publish any pro-British propaganda. They believed in the separation of church and state; but they thought that the scriptural command to be subject to the higher powers meant that they had to be loyal to the political authority. Their primitivism and their belief that the American Revolution was unjust compelled them to remain loyal to Britain. Hankins concludes: "Sounding like activists, but acting like pacifists, New England's Sandemanians emerge as a different kind of loyalist."[197]

Deryck Lovegrove, religious historian at St. Andrews University, traces the evolution and resulting tensions in the theology and practices of Robert (1764–1842) and James Alexander Haldane (1768–1851).[198] The Haldane movement started with no intention of creating a new religious group. The Haldanes created a society with the goal of spreading the gospel and strengthening ministers of all denominations by discouraging "all bitter party spirit, wherever they discover[ed] it among Christians."[199] Gradually the Haldanes's theology shifted from Calvinist toward a concept of "apostolic order." They developed a "marked preference for a literal and commonsense treatment of the biblical text."[200] Slowly they began to insist on particular forms for worship and organizational structure and their original interest in unity came into tension with their interest in apostolic practice.

Frederick Norwood traces the career of James O'Kelly (1735?–1826), one of the founders of the Christian Connexion.[201] Writing from a Methodist perspective, Norwood sees O'Kelly expressing a democratic spirit present in American Methodism since his time. His democratic temper and cry for liberty fueled the group's separation from the Methodist Episcopal Church. O'Kelly equated "the Christian doctrine of freedom from sin with the political doctrine of democracy."[202] O'Kelly opposed the Methodist episcopal structure and the authority of Francis Asbury over the church. While viewing O'Kelly as a "divisive spirit," Norwood treats O'Kelly's views fairly and sympathetically.

Philip Griffin-Allwood, a Baptist minister in Nova Scotia, has written an interesting regional study of the Christian Connexion in Canada.[203] While at first two equal-sized conferences of the tradition developed simultaneously, in time the conference in the Maritime provinces increased in size, while the one in Ontario declined. In tracing the differences between the two conferences, Griffin-Allwood contends that the Ontario conference developed from and maintained its ties with the American Christian Connexion and was, therefore, simply an extension of the U.S. group. In contrast, the Maritime conference became an indigenous "transcongregational structure" for the Allinite revival, which sprang from the Nova Scotia Great Awakening (1776–1784). The Maritime churches accepted the premise of Canadian Protestantism that Canada was "God's last best country." While the distinctive Connexion doctrine was lost, the churches prospered by participating "in the Canadian religious version of 'His Dominion.'"[204] Griffin-Norwood's article suggests that the Christian Connexion had limited ability to transcend non-U.S. contexts without losing its distinctive core.

Charles Lippy, in an important study of the Christadelphians, sketches their history, theology, organizational structures, individual behavior, and social ethics.[205] Lippy explores John Thomas, his connection with the movement, and the controversy with Alexander Campbell that precipitated Thomas's departure.[206] Much of the Christadelphian restorationist and millennial thought has roots in the Stone-Campbell movement. Lippy argues that "in their firm commitment to what they believe are the teachings and practices of the apostolic church, Christadelphians constitute an important wing of the Restorationist movement in American religion."[207]

Russ Paden, from the Churches of Christ, traces the roots, growth, beliefs, and practices of the Boston or the International Churches of Christ in the only published scholarly account of the group.[208] Paden traces the historic ties of the Boston Movement to the Churches of Christ through the development of the campus ministry at the Crossroads Church of Christ in Gainesville, Florida, under Chuck Lucas. Believing that they were revitalizing "Christ's church," Kip McKean (1954–) took a small traditional congregation in a Boston suburb, the Lexington Church of Christ, and launched the Boston Church of Christ using the methods developed by Lucas in Florida. The congregation grew from 30 to 5,000 members and soon was planting churches all over the world. Paden says that in 1993 there were 42,855 members overseas and 27,055 in the United States. With their emphasis on evangelism, discipleship, exclusivist theology, and rigid hierarchical structure, the International Churches of Christ have experienced rapid though uneven growth. Paden also explores the controversies surrounding the practices of the movement. Paden's study is invaluable but more needs to be done on the early history of the Boston church when it was a satellite of Lucas's efforts known as the Crossroad's movement. Paden leaves the false impression that McKean and the Boston church were a new movement, when in reality it is a continuation of what started in Florida. Having completely severed ties with the Churches of Christ, this child of the Stone-Campbell tradition merits more study as it charts its own restorationist course.

THE STONE-CAMPBELL TRADITION AS AN AMERICAN MOVEMENT

The strength of Harrell's work as social history is that the Stone-Campbell movement can readily be seen as American. American culture and values are at center stage in the life of the tradition. While there is an "inner" dynamic being traced by intellectual and cultural historians, the movement has not and will not escape the American soil in which it was planted. Harrell's work raises the question of the tradition's impact on American society. Hatch has shown that the tradition captured the spirit of the American Revolution and helped democratize American religion.[209] In a seminal article, Harrell traces the agrarian myth of the Stone-Campbell movement, showing how it drew heavily from the central myth of nineteenth-century America that the West was to be "the garden of the world."[210] In this myth rural life was superior to the urban, the yeoman farmer was the hero, and millennial hopes were pinned on the agrarian. Harrell also traces the tensions that emerged as the agrarian myth waned. As American society urbanized, some in the heritage came to believe the evangelization of the city and reforming its evils were necessary for the millennium to take place. Others simply retrenched, feeling that the only way to maintain purity was separation from the threat of evil. In some places Disciples were prominent in the populist protests of farmers.[211] A large populist presence was common in places where the tradition was numerically strong.[212] Did members of the tradition participate in other agrarian-based protests?[213] How the myth plays itself out in the rest of the history of the tradition needs further work.

The American Presidents

The Stone-Campbell tradition also produced three American Presidents, all of whom went from agrarian backgrounds to the presidency: James A. Garfield (1831–1881), Lyndon B. Johnson (1908–1973), and Ronald Reagan (1911–). William C. Ringenberg, professor of history at Taylor University, gives an excellent overview of Garfield's religious evolution from a theologically narrow to a broadly open Protestant perspective that was respectful of other religions and secular ideologies. Ringenberg concludes that both liberal Protestants and Evangelicals would claim Garfield.[214] However, the relationship between Garfield's progressive Disciples theology and the optimistic "self-made man" philosophy of the gilded age has never been adequately plumbed. Garfield clearly took the agrarian myth and adapted it to the Lincolnian Log Cabin myth.[215] Monroe Billington argues that Lyndon Johnson's presidency cannot be viewed as coming "exclusively from selfish political motives," rather his religious heritage played a vital role in his positive accomplishments. Billington clearly shows that Johnson's religious beliefs lay behind many of his social programs and that Johnson was a person of piety and religious ecumenism.[216] While Billington does attempt to trace the explicit Disciples beliefs that were critical to Johnson's religion, clearly more exploration of the relationship between Johnson's Disciples background and his political orientation needs to be done. Stephen Vaughn's article shows the clear links between Ronald Reagan's values and his Disciples heritage. Reagan's mother and his minister at Dixon, Illinois, played decisive roles in the formation of the moral outlook Reagan exhibited in his presidency.[217] All three essays clearly mark the Stone-Campbell movement as quintessentially American and show how it has influenced American society through the power of the presidency.

Right-Wing American Political Movements

The story of these three presidents does not exhaust the stamp of the Stone-Campbell movement on American politics. Several from the tradition have played important roles, especially in conservative political movements. Edward Hicks makes a good case that George Benson, longtime president of Harding College, played a pivotal role in the emergence of present-day conservatism in America.[218] From the moment he testified in Congress about impending tax legislation during the New Deal era until his death in 1991, Benson was a national figure in political conservatism. William Buckley has named Benson a key architect of the emergence of the political right in the Reagan era.[219] Recent studies on creationism and the religious right by Ronald Numbers and William Martin reveal the participation of members of the Churches of Christ in those conservative movements.[220] James D. Bales (1915–1995), professor of Bible at Harding University, was involved with the British Evolution Protest Movement in the late 1940s. In the 1960s Doug Dean (1928–1992), professor of biology at Pepperdine University and a board member of the Creation Research Society, along with Rita Rhodes Ward (1910–), a high school biology teacher, fought against pro-evolution biology texts in Texas. Bales and Jack Wood Sears, professor of biology at Harding, debated Carl Sagan, then assistant professor of astronomy at Harvard, and Ernan McMullen, chair of the philosophy department at Notre Dame, on evolution in June 1966.[221] Bales, Dean, Ward, and others kept creationism and anti-evolution highly visible within the Churches of Christ.[222] In an effort pivotal to the rise of the current religious right, Alice Moore, wife of a minister in the Churches of Christ, led fights against sex education curriculum and particular textbooks in the K–12 language arts program in Kanawha County, West Virginia.[223] Almost as significant is Lottie Beth Hobbs, a devotional writer for the Churches of Christ, who established in the mid-1970s a traditionalist organization and a lobby group against the Equal Rights Amendment. In 1977 she also organized the National Pro-Family Rally in Houston to counter the pro-ERA National Women's Conference that had received $5 million from Congress. Hobbs later was appointed by President Reagan to the Family Policy Advisory Board.[224] A critical biography of independent Christian Church preacher Billy James Hargis, a key anticommunist speaker, has yet to be written.[225] Historians of the Ku Klux Klan have noted the high involvement of the early-twentieth-century Disciples.[226] One exploratory essay raises the question of the relationship between support for the Klan and opposition to "cooperation" with the United Christian Missionary Society.[227] The relationship between conservative political movements and each "branch" of the Stone-Campbell tradition remains to be explored. The agrarian myth theme again might be a key to understanding this phenomenon.

Multiculturalism

Another useful aspect of Harrell's material is that it raises the issue of multiculturalism in the Stone-Campbell tradition. While intellectual history plows deeper into the furrows of the dominant ideas of the tradition and mainstream American culture, it does not reveal the entire story. Social history gives voice not just to the ideas of the articulate elite, but to the inarticulate as well. Harrell shows that Native Americans, women, and African Americans all had significant roles in the tradition. Harrell did his work before the current emphasis on multiculturalism, so the areas he covered clearly need reinvestigating and expansion along those lines. Paul Phillips's important article on Marshall Keeble (1878–1968), one of the most influential African American preachers in the Churches of Christ, is an important first step.[228] The African American tradition in the Stone-

Campbell movement has a long and mostly unexplored history. Disciple scholar Hap Lyda's work is a good beginning. He traces the development of black Disciples in Kentucky and Tennessee from the earliest days of the Stone and Campbell movements through the Reconstruction period. Finding an estimated eight thousand black adherents at the end of Reconstruction, these members became the foundation of the African American tradition in the entire movement.[229] The tradition produced Fred Gray (1930–), civil rights lawyer for Martin Luther King and Rosa Parks,[230] and Franklin Florence, an admirer of Malcolm X and leader of a significant social protest against Eastman Kodak in 1966–67.[231] Both men studied under Keeble and remained lifelong friends despite the different paths of social protest they took.

Equally historic persons and events are waiting to be recovered in women's and Native Americans' history in the movement. For example, Selina Moore Holman (1850–1915), a member of the Churches of Christ, became president of the Tennessee chapter of the Women's Christian Temperance Union (WCTU).[232] She wrote extensively in the *Gospel Advocate* challenging David Lipscomb over the role of women in the church. The first female licensed as a physician in Canada, Jennie Trout (1841–1921), was an active member of the Stone-Campbell tradition.[233] Glenn Zuber traces the beginning of women ministers in the Disciples of Christ as a case study of how women's ministry evolved in mainline Protestantism.[234] Because of the development of the WCTU[235] and the Christian Women's Board of Missions (CWBM), the denominational women's missionary board, some women developed skills in organizing and in public speaking which eventually nurtured women preachers. The new developments "resulted in short term extensions of the traditional 'woman's sphere' to include the pulpit for numerous Disciples women, but failed to permanently alter that sphere." The WCTU and CWBM speakers gave women a more public role, dispelled the idea that women "were not physically capable of speaking in public," and gave many "the impression that they were preachers even though they were not." Yet these organizations illustrate the limitations for women. While men could, through opportunity, support, and education, develop their ministry skills, the few women who became ministers did so "only after proving themselves spectacular speakers." The women preachers never addressed the issue of their authority. Instead they asserted that the gospel itself converted rather than the preacher, and that they were needed simply to mitigate the urgent needs for ministers. Zuber also found that the women ministers often were either wives or widows of male ministers who were pressed into duty in emergencies or who played subordinate roles to their husbands. These women worked within traditional female roles rather than transcending them.

Disciple scholar Debra Hull, in her groundbreaking book, also traced many of these women and others who were preachers, reformers, educators, writers, and editors. Hull argued they shaped the entire tradition.[236] Her book is an excellent model and start in the recovery of the woman's voice in the movement. More recently Fran Craddock, Martha Faw, and Nancy Heimer have traced the influence of women specifically within the Christian Church (Disciples of Christ).[237]

Little scholarly work has been done on persons of Spanish-speaking origins in the movement. Among the few studies are Daisy L. Machado's paper presented at the 1996 Forrest H. Kirkpatrick Seminar for Stone-Campbell Historians, published in the summer 1997 issue of *Discipliana*, that surveyed social, theological, and historical matters connected with being Hispanic/Latino in a largely Anglo church.[238] While Machado found Hispanics in Texas to be on the margins of the Disciples of Christ, Mark Massa examined the highly successful Puerto Rican Disciples congregations of New York City that have developed their own indigenous worship styles largely independent of the Anglo Disciples.[239] Another successful effort among Hispanics is the growth of the Disciples in Puerto Rico.[240] Samuel Gonzalez, a minister in Churches of Christ, surveyed the history of the Iglesias de Cristo in Mexico and the United States in a paper delivered in two parts at the 1997 Restoration Lectures at Abilene Christian University.[241]

Marcos Ramos, a Southern Baptist and leading authority on religion in Cuba, reports that Manuel Muñiz evangelist at the Jovellanos Church of Christ and "a few other workers and members of local congregations joined the Revolution," while others migrated to southern Florida.[242] The Churches of Christ in Cuba started in 1937 with the efforts of J. R. Jimenez, and in 1939 E. R. Estevez joined him.[243] The mission efforts continued through 1961, but after 1962 the number of mission efforts were reduced. There are now several hundred members of Churches of Christ in Cuba and probably more of Cuban descent in Florida.[244]

In addition, a large initially indigenous restoration movement was begun in Spain under the leadership of Protestant journalist Juan Antonio Monroy that was "discovered" by leaders of U.S. Churches of Christ in the 1960s. Through his periodicals *Restauración* and *Alternativa 2000* Monroy has chronicled the development of Spanish Churches of Christ as well as Churches of Christ throughout Latin America. No scholarly work has been done, however, to trace the development of this vital body, as has been done, for example, for British Churches of Christ. This limited scholarship points to the obvious diversity that exists among Spanish-speaking persons within and without the United States. Future scholarship will need to wrestle with this diversity.

THE STONE-CAMPBELL TRADITION AS A BRITISH MOVEMENT

While the American context is primary for this volume, the Stone-Campbell movement has a significant presence in other countries. While the British Churches of Christ (the name used for the entire movement) have often been viewed as a "branch" of the movement founded by Alexander Campbell,[245] Labor historian Peter Ackers argues that the British churches had their own independent tradition "as a heterogeneous gathering of former Glasite, Scotch Baptist and Independent congregations and individual nonconformists."[246] The tradition can be viewed as a British movement paralleling in many ways the American one, but certainly different in its history and focus.

David Thompson, a Cambridge professor of church history specializing in English nonconformity, has told the denominational history from the modern ecumenical perspective, seeing the eventual union of the Association of Churches of Christ with the United Reformed Church as the culmination of the movement's plea for unity.[247] An excellent insider's history, it tells the story from the perspective of the Annual Meeting, the cooperative organization for the congregations, focusing on the hierarchy and official doctrine. Two key articles focus on areas neglected by Thompson: the appeal to primitivism and the working-class religiosity. Louis Billington, a leading historian of British and American sectarian religion, traces the development of the British Churches of Christ in the nineteenth century.[248] Billington traces membership size and regional distribution, social composition (mostly persons from humbler occupations and small tradesmen), organization of local churches, development of the national organization, and the separatist social and political views of the movement. Billington sees the movement, along with other traditions that emphasized the restoration of primitive Christianity, as indicative of "a widespread dissatisfaction not only with the Established churches, but with the older predominately middle-class Nonconformist and Methodist denominations" in the nineteenth century.[249] The gradual rise in affluence and cultural standing of the Churches of Christ occurred in part because the movement afforded the opportunity to develop "public speaking, administration and organizational" skills otherwise not available. Sectarian religion in the nineteenth century played an important role for the British working class.

Ackers picks up on this theme and explores the links between the Churches of Christ and the English labor movement.[250] He first does a "snapshot" of the origins of the Wigan Churches of Christ, showing a typical primitivist rhetoric.[251] Wigan and the surrounding area in Lancashire developed into one of England's leading coal-mining areas while at the same the Churches of Christ in Wigan developed into a power center for tradition. While stressing solidarity with the poor, the Churches of Christ did not adopt radical social attitudes, though they did produce local labor leaders. Next he explores the "Back Street Bethel from the 1870s to the 1920s," where mostly miners attended. Here the religious doctrine remained static, and pacifism, self-help for the needy, and the training and development of labor leaders were stressed as a cohesive community was created for coal-mining families. In the third section he explores the West End Chapel, where denominational consciousness was cultivated. The manufacturing dynasty of Timothy Coop (1817–1887) developed a national denominational identity for Churches of Christ and moved the chapel toward "mainstream denominational Nonconformity." Those seeking greater respectability sought out the West End Chapel, and this overall mix "dissolved the special conditions under which the coalfield chapels had produced labour leaders."

Ackers shows how many of the denominational trends (educated ministry, higher criticism of the Bible, and open communion) that Thompson painted as progress from an "intellectual theological" point of view can be seen as "a process of disempowering ordinary brethren." Instead of being accessible to all, the word of God was now the province of an educated clergy. The challenge to biblical literalism undermined the priesthood of all believers and mutual teaching. Open communion threatened to undo the church's strong stand against the world. Instead of unity by laying waste to all denominations, open communion invited accommodation to them. A denominational consciousness undermined "the role of the chapel as a school for labour movement activists."[252] Ackers, whose family has roots in the British Churches of Christ and coal-mining union activity, is a practicing Methodist and a former Labour Party activist. His own exploration of his family's past combined with excellent academic objectivity is recovering the significant and diverse role of nonconformist religion in the working class in Britain. Extending Ackers's work, Michael Casey shows that the Old Paths Churches of Christ, the sectarian division from the Associated Churches of Christ that became official in 1947, continued the pacifist and labor activism of the tradition resisting the denominational trends. The Old Paths Churches continued to produce pacifist and Labour Party activists throughout the twentieth century.[253] Ackers's scholarship exhibits the significance of the Churches of Christ in British society and culture.

THE STONE-CAMPBELL TRADITION IN CANADA, AUSTRALIA, AND NEW ZEALAND

While no comprehensive denominational history of the Stone-Campbell tradition in Canada exists, some valuable historical studies have been conducted. The standard work is Disciple scholar Reuben Butchard's chronicling of the tradition at both the national and local level.[254] Claude Cox, from the Churches of Christ, has edited a recent collection of essays focusing on key personalities, churches, and historical periods in the Canadian province of Ontario.[255] Brian Boden, using the Weber and Troeltsch typologies, argues that the tradition started as a frontier sect that gradually accommodated to Canadian culture, then spawned other sectarian protests.[256] Boden traced British (Scotch Baptist) and American (Campbell) roots in Canada and concluded that the Canadian Stone-Campbell churches were neither British nor American but uniquely Canadian. The tradition developed differently from those in the United States and Britain. Boden's schema could be a useful model for a comprehensive history of the Canadian Stone-Campbell churches. Other essays in Cox's volume indicate that Christian Connexion[257] and English Baptist[258] influences were also at work in the creation of the Canadian tradition.

As in Britain and the United States, the Canadian movement eventually fragmented into three "broad" groups. The divisions, however, did not develop precisely as they had in either the U.S. or British experience. A comparative study of the cultural influences at work in all three countries would be invaluable. One possible factor in the difference might be the continuing British and American immigration (and their ideas) into Canada. Ackers has shown a strong British expatriate presence early in the twentieth century when "Canada had overtaken the USA both in the intensity of its immigration and in absolute numbers of English immigrants."[259] What role did continuing British and American immigrants have in creating the uniquely Canadian Stone-Campbell tradition?

Despite the fact that the Stone-Campbell tradition in Australia and New Zealand is twice the size of the British Churches of Christ, no critical history of the tradition exists, and only one noncritical scholarly article has been published.[260] Graeme Chapman has written two denominational histories of the Australian movement, one of them self-published.[261] David Roper has published a history of the movement from the perspective of the conservative a cappella Churches of Christ.[262] No denominational history exists for the tradition in New Zealand. The presence of pacifist and labor movements in Australia and New Zealand makes comparative studies with the British Churches of Christ a potentially ripe field for exploration.

THE CULTURAL SIGNIfiCANCE OF THE ENTIRE TRADITION

A major lacuna in the rich historical work on the Stone-Campbell movement is an overview and assessment of the general cultural impact of the tradition. The only attempt to begin the effort is Leslie Galbreath's and Heather Day's bibliography of works by persons in the tradition, and it is skewed toward academic, theological, and historical works.[263] A cultural history of the Stone-Campbell movement has not been attempted by historians. Who are the musicians, writers, poets, artists, scientists, actors, and political activists that have been influenced by the movement? A list of culturally significant people who have had ties with the tradition would include the following, but needs much expansion.

With the tradition's deep interest in worship and hymns, it comes as no surprise that many and highly varied musicians have come from the movement:

Mike Alsup, lead guitarist for Three Dog Night (1947–), Pat Boone (1934–), Debbie Boone (1956–), Glen Campbell (1936–),[264] Chris Christian (1951–), Amy Grant (1960–),[265] Roy Orbison[266] (1936–1988), Patti Page (1927–), Meat Loaf (1947–), and "Weird" Al Yankovich (1960–) are significant singers in popular music. Ray Walker (1934–), a member of the Jordanaires, has served as a backup singer to many leading popular singers. Grant, Christian, and other significant figures in the contemporary Christian music industry have ties with the Belmont Church of Christ, a congregation in Nashville that became charismatic in the 1970s.[267] Several country music stars have roots or are still active in the Churches of Christ: Al Brumley (1933–),[268] the Delmore Brothers (Alton, 1908–1964; Rabon, 1916–1952),[269] Holly Dunn (1957–),[270] Merle Haggard (1937–),[271] Sonny James (1929–), Eck Robertson (1887–1975),[272] Marty Roe (lead singer of Diamond Rio),[273] Randy Travis (1959–), Kitty Wells (1919–),[274] Don Williams (1939–),[275] and Dwight Yoakam (1956–). Reflecting this rural or country music style, Albert E. Brumley (1905–1977) of Missouri was a significant composer of Stamps-Baxter Gospel music.[276] Jim McBride, Jackie White, Monty Powell, Tim Lewis, Roger Murrah, and Chris Waters are successful songwriters on the current country music scene. Other significant composers of music need to be traced. Marion Cawood and Arlene Auger are internationally known opera singers.[277] Several less-known singers have successfully pursued careers in opera in Europe. Dale Clevenger, a member of the Chicago symphony, is recognized as one of the most accomplished French horn players in the world.

The movement has also produced two of the most significant figures in American musical life: Robert Page (1927–) from the Churches of Christ and Robert Shaw (1916–1999) from the Disciples. Page is the choral conductor for the Pittsburgh Symphony Orchestra, founder of the Robert Page Singers, conductor of the Mendelssohn Choir of Pittsburgh, and director of choral studies at Carnegie-Mellen University.[278] Shaw founded the Collegiate Choir, the Robert Shaw Chorale, and has conducted the San Diego Orchestra, the Cleveland Orchestra and Chorus, and the Atlanta Symphony Orchestra. Shaw is considered by many to have been the premier American choral musician. Shaw's father, Shirley R. Shaw, was a Disciple minister in California. Along with his wife, Nelle, and his children, the family was known as the "singing Shaws." In a church that cultivated music, Robert Shaw's talents blossomed. While Shaw's biographer traces some of the influence of his family, the musical culture of the Disciples is not explored.[279]

Vachel Lindsay (1879–1931) and Edwin Markham (1859–1940) quickly come to mind as significant poets from the Disciples of Christ.[280] Are there others? Union Civil War General Lewis Wallace (1827–1905), son of Disciple temperance activist Zerelda Wallace, wrote the novel *Ben-Hur*.[281] Harold Bell Wright

(1872–1944), author of *Shepherd of the Hills* and other novels, trained at Hiram College and preached for the Disciples from 1896 until he abandoned the ministry in 1908 to pursue his career as a novelist.[282] Victor Allen wrote *In the Hands of God* and *The Borders of the Kingdom*. More recently, David L. Lindsey, an active member of the Churches of Christ, has written a large number of best-selling mystery novels. However, no other significant novelists from the heritage readily come to mind. Robert Rauschenburg (1925–), an influential artist involved in abstract expressionism, is from the Churches of Christ. He has been a colleague of John Cage and Merce Cunningham.[283] Artists other than those who are local, regional, or connected with the colleges of the tradition seem to be rare. Francis McDormand (1958–), daughter of a Disciple minister, Dean Jones (1931–), and Ronald Reagan are among the only actors of note.

The tradition has produced many practicing scientists for government, industry, and education,[284] including Michael Faraday (1791–1867) from the Sandemanians and naturalist John Muir (1838–1914), who grew up in the Disciples of Christ.[285] The movement is also noted for the large number of colleges and universities founded. Furthermore, several members have served as presidents of state and private institutions of higher learning. Many leading educators across several disciplines are from the Stone-Campbell movement.[286] Frank Knight (1885–1972), a leading neoclassical economist who taught at the University of Chicago and influenced Nobel Prize winners James Buchanan and Milton Friedman grew up in the Disciples and attended Milligan College, where he began a lifetime friendship with his teacher Frederick Kershner. Donald Dewey has made a preliminary attempt to access the Disciples' influence on Knight's career.[287]

In addition to U.S. presidents, politically conservative American social leaders, prominent women, and African Americans active in the movement, other prominent political and social activists had ties with the tradition. David Lloyd George (1863–1945), prime minister of Britain, was raised in the British Churches of Christ.[288] Sir Garfield Todd (1908–), a missionary from the New Zealand Churches of Christ and early supporter of black sovereignty, was prime minister of southern Rhodesia (Zimbabwe) in the 1950s.[289] Arthur Horner (1894–1968), one of the founders of the British Communist Party and a leader in British labor unions, was raised in the British Churches of Christ and was even a minister early in his career.[290] His American equivalent was Kate Richards O'Hare (1876–1948), who, after being active in a Disciples congregation as a child in Kansas City, became a leader in American socialism. An eloquent writer and speaker, she became known as "Red Kate."[291] Carry Nation (1846–1911), leading American temperance activist, was raised and baptized in the Disciples. She married Disciples minister David Nation (1821–1903) and even preached herself before becoming a temperance reformer. Her religious beliefs were central to her reformist rhetoric.[292] Several important British labor union leaders came from the tradition. W. T. Miller (1880–1963) was president of the General Federation of Firemen, Examiners and Deputies' Associations of Great Britain.[293] Amos Mann (1855–1939) and J. T. Taylor (1863–1958) established the Humberstone Cooperative near Leicester. Robert Fleming (1869–1939) from Belfast also was a prominent co-operator. Joseph Parkinson (1854–1929) was president of the Wigan Miner's Association and a Labour Party leader.[294] Many other less-known British labor leaders from the Churches of Christ need to be traced. Henry Wise Wood (1860–1941), leader of the farmer's movement in Alberta, Canada, from 1909 to 1931 was active in the Disciples until his early adulthood.[295]

Why did the tradition produce such a large number of diverse activists? Did the rationalism of the movement cultivate a pragmatic spirit and an attitude that society and culture can be changed and transformed? If culture is interpreted anthropologically as the symbolic webs of significance that humans weave and in which they are suspended, then the cultural and symbolic webs of the Stone-Campbell heritage that created these various artists and activists need to be assessed.[296] Why did the tradition nurture these technical, scholarly, and activist qualities while generally discouraging artistic qualities (except for music)? The dearth of actors, artists, poets, and novelists may indicate that Richard Hughes's assessment of the Churches of Christ is accurate for the entire tradition: "While Churches of Christ have produced a host of scholars who excel in fields requiring technical and logical expertise, they have produced relatively few scholars or professionals who excel in fields requiring creativity and imagination—literature, art, and music, for example."[297] While Hughes is clearly wrong about music, he is probably right in saying that the tradition's rationalist bent discouraged the development of imagination, thus truncating aesthetic quality. In addition, the large number of social activists indicates that the movement prizes pragmatic action over thoughtful reflection. Some may see this as the "positive" side of the movement's rationalism.

The Stone-Campbell heritage clearly has international cultural significance that merits further study by historians inside and out of the tradition. We hope that the search for usable pasts within the tradition continues. While the scholars surveyed may not agree with some of our assessments, and we have undoubtedly failed to identify every area of possible study, our hope nonetheless is that many will take up the challenge of continuing to investigate the significance of the meaning of the Stone-Campbell movement. We take pleasure in the fact that the conversation, debate, and dialogue over the importance of the Stone-Campbell heritage is being extended. It is our hope that in a small way the renaissance of Stone-Campbell studies is furthered by this survey and the reprinting of the following essays.

NOTES

1. Richard T. Hughes, "Twenty-five Years of Restoration Scholarship: The Churches of Christ—Part I," *Restoration Quarterly* 25 (1982): 233–56; "Part II," 26 (1983): 39–62.

2. Moore, "Insiders and Outsiders in American Historical Narrative and History," *American Historical Review* 87 (Apr. 1982): 420.

3. Paul K. Conkin, *American Originals: Homemade Varieties of Christianity* (Chapel Hill: Univ. of North Carolina Press, 1997), 1–56.

4. Richard Hughes, Leonard Allen, and Michael Weed, *The Worldly Church: A Call for Biblical Renewal* (Abilene: Abilene Christian Univ. Press, 1988). Weed teaches at the Austin Graduate School of Theology, Austin, Texas. For Hughes and Allen's work on primitivism, see Richard T. Hughes and C. Leonard Allen, *Illusions of Innocence: Protestant Primitivism in America, 1630–1875* (Chicago and London: Univ. of Chicago Press, 1988); Hughes, ed., *The American Quest for the Primitive Church* (Urbana: Univ. of Illinois Press, 1988); and Hughes, ed. *The Primitive Church in the Modern World* (Urbana: Univ. of Illinois Press, 1995). For Allen quote above see Leonard Allen, "'The Stone that the Builders Rejected': Barton W. Stone in the Memory of the Churches of Christ," in *Cane Ridge in Context: Perspectives on Barton W. Stone and the Revival*, ed. Anthony Dunnavant (Nashville: Disciples of Christ Historical Society, 1992), 56. For Weed quote above see Michael Weed, "Tradition at Risk," *Christian Studies* 11 (Spring 1991), 56.

5. David Edwin Harrell Jr., "The Sectional Origins of the Churches of Christ," in the present volume, 69–84.

6. Ibid., 79.

7. Hughes, *Reviving the Ancient Faith: The Story of the Churches of Christ in America* (Grand Rapids: Eerdmans, 1996), 17. See also Richard T. Hughes and R. L. Roberts, *The Churches of Christ*, Denominations in America Series, no. 10 (Westport, CT: Greenwood Press, 2001). This shorter version of Hughes's history includes "A Biographical Dictionary of Leaders in Churches of Christ" by Roberts.

8. Ibid., 133.

9. Leonard I. Sweet, "Wise as Serpents, Innocent as Doves: The New Evangelical Historiography," *Journal of the American Academy of Religion* 56 (Fall 1988): 402.

10. Ibid.

11. Ibid., 403. The quotations in this paragraph are all from this page in Sweet's essay.

12. Richard T. Hughes, "The Apocalyptic Origins of Churches of Christ and the Triumph of Modernism," in the present volume, 87.

13. Hughes, *Reviving*, 107.

14. Ibid., 257.

15. Richard T. Hughes, "The Meaning of the Restoration Vision," in *The Primitive Church in the Modern World*, ed. Richard T. Hughes (Urbana and Chicago: Univ. of Illinois Press, 1995), xvi.

16. Ibid., xvii.

17. See Sweet, "Wise," 404, where he makes the same point about the new evangelical historians.

18. Hughes, *Reviving,* 122. For more on how Anabaptist ideas inform Hughes, see his "Reclaiming a Heritage," *Restoration Quarterly* 37 (1995): 129–38.

19. Ibid., 169–71. On Hughes's own "Lutheran" views, see Richard T. Hughes, "The Subversion of Reforming Movements," in *Founding Vocation and Future Vision: The Self-Understanding of the Disciples of Christ and Churches of Christ,* ed. Anthony Dunnavant, Richard T. Hughes, and Paul M. Blowers (St. Louis: Chalice Press, 1999), 41–58.

20. Barton W. Stone, *History of the Christian Church in the West,* (Lexington: College of the Bible, 1956), 38.

21. D. Newell Williams, *Barton Stone: A Spiritual Biography* (St. Louis: Chalice Press, 2000), 231.

22. Ronald G. Walters, *American Reformers, 1815–1860,* rev. ed. (New York: Hill and Wang, 1997), 24–26.

23. Paul Blowers, "'Living in a Land of Prophets': James T. Barclay and an Early Disciples of Christ Mission to Jews in the Holy Land," in the present volume, 290. Also see Sacvan Bercovitch, "The Typology of America's Mission," *American Quarterly* 30 (1978): 137–41.

24. Barton W. Stone, "To the Church Scattered throughout America," in *Pioneer Sermons and Addresses,* 3d ed., ed. F. L. Rowe, 161–62 (Cincinnati: F. L. Rowe, 1925).

25. Williams, *Stone,* 224.

26. Michael D. Greene, "Barton W. Stone and Baptism for the Remission of Sins," in *Baptism and the Remission of Sins: An Historical Perspective,* ed. David W. Fletcher, 241–95 (Joplin, Mo.: College Press, 1990).

27. James B. North, "The Open Membership Controversy and the Christian Churches," in *Baptism and the Remission of Sins,* 333–66.

28. Joseph Belcastro, *The Relationship of Baptism to Church Membership* (St. Louis: Bethany Press, 1963), 22, 25, 27–29, 74, 80–82, 87.

29. John Mark Hicks, "Atonement Theology in the Late Nineteenth Century: The Pattern of Discussion within the Stone-Campbell Movement," *Discipliana* 56 (Winter 1996): 119–21.

30. David Edwin Harrell Jr., *The Churches of Christ in the Twentieth Century: Homer Hailey's Personal Journey of Faith* (Tuscaloosa: Univ. of Alabama Press, 2000), 174.

31. Ibid., 208, 366.

32. Tristano, *The Origins of the Restoration Movement: An Intellectual History* (Atlanta: Glenmary Research Center, 1988).

33. While Tristano's focus is on the Churches of Christ, he overlooks the official dialogue between the Christian Church (Disciples of Christ) and the Roman Catholic Church that began in the United States in 1962. These annual meetings became international in scope after the formation of the Disciples of Christ–Roman Catholic International Dialogue Commission in 1977. In its first series of meetings, the International

48   The Renaissance of Stone-Campbell Studies

Commission focused on the themes of "Catholicity and Apostolicity." This was followed by studies on "The Church as Koinonia in Christ" and "The Individual and the Church." The meetings do not aim at producing official statements of belief but in identifying areas of common affirmation and insights beneficial to both churches.

34. Tristano, *Origins*, 10–11. The quotations in the rest of the paragraph are from these pages.

35. Ibid., 13. The quotations following are from the same page.

36. Ibid., 153.

37. Ibid., 154.

38. Mark Toulouse, *Joined in Discipleship: The Maturing of an American Religious Movement* (St. Louis: Chalice Press, 1992), 6; see also revised and expanded edition *Joined in Discipleship: The Shaping of Contemporary Disciples Identity* (St. Louis: Chalice Press, 1997).

39. Mark Toulouse, "Church History as a Dialogue Partner in the Quest for Christian Identity," *Union Seminary Quarterly Review* 42, no. 3 (1988): 34.

40. Mark Toulouse, "The Problem and Promise of Writing Denominational History," *Discipliana* 57 (Winter 1997): 124.

41. Henry E. Webb, *In Search of Christian Unity: A History of the Restoration Movement* (Cincinnati: Standard Publishing Co., 1990), and James North, *Union in Truth: An Interpretive History of the Restoration Movement* (Cincinnati: Standard Publishing Co., 1994).

42. North, *Union*, 366.

43. D. Newell Williams, "Disciples and the Liberal/Conservative Divide," *Disciples Theological Digest* 7, no. 2 (1992): 5–25.

44. Joel Carpenter, *Revive Us Again: The Reawakening of American Fundamentalism* (New York: Oxford Univ. Press, 1997); George M. Marsden, *Fundamentalism and American Culture: The Shaping of Twentieth-Century Evangelicalism, 1870–1925* (New York: Oxford Univ. Press, 1980); Marsden, *Reforming Fundamentalism: Fuller Seminary and the New Evangelicalism* (Grand Rapids: Eerdmans, 1987); Mark A. Noll, *Between Faith and Criticism: Evangelicals, Scholarship, and the Bible in America* (San Francisco: Harper and Row, 1986). Kevin R. Kragenbrink has made some effort toward this in "Dividing the Disciples: Social, Cultural, and Intellectual Sources of Division in the Disciples of Christ, 1919–1945" (Ph.D. diss., Auburn Univ., 1996). Another place to start is C. J. Dull, "Intellectual Factions and Groupings in the Independent Christian Churches," *Seminary Review* 31 (1985): 91–118.

45. John Higham, *From Boundlessness to Consolidation: The Transformation of American Culture, 1848–1860* (Ann Arbor, Mich.: William L. Clements Library, 1969).

46. Nathan Hatch, *The Democratization of American Christianity* (New Haven: Yale Univ. Press, 1989).

47. Richard McNemar, *The Kentucky Revival* (New York: Edward O. Jenkins, 1846), 59. Original edition published in 1807. For more of the Christians' ideology, see Richard T. Hughes and C. Leonard Allen, "From Freedom to Constraint: The Transformation of the 'Christians in the West,'" *Illusions of Innocence*, 102–32. Hughes and Allen focus on the

consolidation of the ideas/theology of the Christians rather than the institutional consolidation of the movement Higham's theory outlines.

48. Walter Brownlow Posey, *Religious Strife on the Southern Frontier* (Baton Rouge: Louisiana State Univ. Press, 1965), xiii, 50–51, 53, 62.

49. Alexander Campbell, "Church Organization—No. 1," *Millennial Harbinger* (Feb. 1849): 90.

50. Higham, *Boundlessness*, 25.

51. Jonathan Butler, "From Millerism to Seventh-Day Adventism: 'Boundlessness to Consolidation,'" *Church History* 55 (Mar. 1986): 64.

52. David E. Shi, *The Simple Life: Plain Living and High Thinking in American Culture* (New York: Oxford Univ. Press, 1985), 3.

53. David E. Shi, *In Search of the Simple Life: American Voices, Past and Present* (Layton, Utah: Peregine Smith Books, 1986), 4.

54. For two older studies on restoration from the Disciples of Christ perspective, see Alfred T. DeGroot, *The Restoration Principle* (St. Louis: Bethany Press, 1960), and Ralph G. Wilburn, "A Critique of the Restoration Principle: Its Place in Contemporary Life and Thought," in *The Reformation of Tradition,* ed. Ronald E. Osborn (St. Louis: Bethany Press, 1963), 215–53. More recently Richard Hughes has edited two books of conference papers on the topic of primitivism, *The American Quest for the Primitive Church* (Urbana, Ill.: Univ. of Illinois Press, 1988), and *The Primitive Church in the Modern World* (Urbana, Ill.: Univ. of Illinois Press, 1995).

55. Hughes and Allen, *Illusions.* See the review by W. Clark Gilpin, "Recent Studies in American Protestant Primitivism," *Religious Studies Review* 19 (July 1993): 231–35.

56. David B. Eller, "Hoosier Brethren and the Origins of the Restoration Movement," in the present volume, 331–47.

57. Anthony F. C. Wallace, "Revitalization Movements," *American Anthropologist* 58 (1956): 264–81.

58. McLoughlin, *Revivals, Awakenings, and Reform: An Essay on Religion and Social Change in America, 1607–1977* (Chicago and London: Univ. of Chicago Press, 1978).

59. While McLoughlin ignores the revival of 1857–58, it would be useful for someone to explore the impact of that revival on the Stone-Campbell movement. On that revival, see Kathryn Teresa Long, *The Revival of 1857–58: Interpreting an American Religious Awakening* (New York: Oxford Univ. Press, 1998).

60. Martin Edward Wooten, "The Boston Movement as a 'Revitalization Movement'" (D.Min. thesis, Harding Graduate School of Religion, 1990).

61. On Benson see L. Edward Hicks, *"Sometimes in the Wrong, but Never in Doubt": George S. Benson and the Education of the New Religious Right* (Knoxville: Univ. of Tennessee Press, 1994), and John C. Stevens, *Before Any Were Willing: The Story of George S. Benson* (Searcy, Ark.: Harding Univ. Press, 1991).

62. Dale Leathers, "Billy James Hargis," in *Twentieth Century American Orators: Critical Studies and Sources,* ed. Bernard K. Duffy and Halford R. Ryan (Westport, Conn.: Greenwood

Press, 1987), 187–94; Donald K. Orban, "Billy James Hargis: Auctioneer of Political Evangelism," *Central States Speech Journal* 22 (1969): 83–96, and William Martin, *With God on Our Side: The Rise of the Religious Right in America* (New York: Broadway Books, 1996), 37–39.

63. R. Laurence Moore, *Religious Outsiders and the Making of Americans* (New York and Oxford: Oxford Univ. Press, 1986), 46.

64. Robert Hooper, *A Distinct People: A History of the Churches of Christ in the Twentieth Century* (West Monroe, La.: Howard Publishing Co., 1993).

65. Moore, "Insiders," 410.

66. Ibid., 404. The quotations for the rest of the paragraph are from this page.

67. Donald W. Dayton, "'The Search for the Historical Evangelicalism': George Marsden's History of Fuller Seminary as a Case Study," *Christian Scholar's Review* 23 (Sept. 1993): 12–33. In his published article Dayton uses *Pentecostal paradigm*, but he has changed it to *Methodist paradigm*.

68. Ibid., 15.

69. Ibid., 18.

70. Donald Dayton, "Rejoinder to Historiography Discussion," *Christian Scholar's Review* 23 (Sept. 1993): 69.

71. Douglas A. Foster, "Sectarian Strife in the Midst of the Fundamentalist-Modernist Crisis: The Premillennial Controversy in the Churches of Christ, 1910–1940," presented at the Methodism and the Fragmentation of American Protestantism, 1865–1920, Conference, September 29, 1995, Asbury Seminary, Asbury, KY.

72. Carl Wayne Hensley, "Rhetorical Vision and the Persuasion of a Historical Movement: The Disciples of Christ in Nineteenth-Century American Culture," *Quarterly Journal of Speech* 61 (Oct. 1975): 264.

73. Ibid., 254–55, 257.

74. Mont Whitson, "Campbell's Post-Protestantism and Civil Religion," in the present volume, 184–86, and Richard T. Hughes, "From Primitive Church to Civil Religion: The Millennial Odyssey of Alexander Campbell," *American Academy of Religion Journal* 44 (1976): 87–103.

75. Dan Danner, "History of Interpretation of Revelation 20:1–10 in the Restoration Movement," *Restoration Quarterly* 7 (1963): 230–32, and William A. Gerrard III, *A Biographical Study of Walter Scott: American Frontier Evangelist* (Joplin, Mo.: College Press, 1992), 180–87.

76. Blowers, "'Living in a Land of Prophets,'" in the present volume, 275–76.

77. Ronald P. Byars, "Cane Ridge from a Presbyterian View," in *Cane Ridge in Context*, 97.

78. Charles Lippy, *Christadelphians in North America* (Lewiston: Edwin Mellen Press, 1989), 13–20.

79. Blowers, "'Living in a Land of Prophets,'" in the present volume 273–84. Also see Jack Lewis, "James Turner Barclay: Explorer of Nineteenth-Century Jerusalem," *Biblical Archaeologist* 51 (Sept. 1981): 163–70.

80. As cited by F. W. Smith, "Lard's Quarterly," *Gospel Advocate* (Sept. 5, 1929): 855.

81. Kenneth Van Deusen, *Moses Lard: That Prince of Preachers* (Joplin, Mo.: College Press, 1987): 171–72.

82. Hughes, *Reviving,* 118.

83. Fanning, "The Coming of the Lord," *Gospel Advocate* (Sept. 18, 1866): 602.

84. Hughes, *Reviving,* 125. Hughes also ignores the rest of Sewell's statement in the cited passage: "[I know] so little about the millennium that I do not feel inclined to attempt to answer this [inquiry about the millennium]. It is an untaught question, and therefore no man's salvation depends upon an answer to it, and would aid no man in his soul's salvation to know about it." See *Gospel Advocate* (July 11, 1895): 437.

85. E. G. Sewell, "Restoration," *Gospel Advocate* (Mar. 11, 1885): 486.

86. For the premillennial views, see Doris Thompson, "History of an Ozark Utopia," *Arkansas Historical Quarterly* (Winter 1955): 1–15.

87. R. L. Roberts, "Premillennialism: A Historical and Restoration Perspective," in *Premillennialism, True or False?* ed. Wendell Winkler (Ft. Worth: Winkler Publications, 1978), 164–65.

88. Carl Wayne Hensley, "The Rhetorical Vision of the Disciples of Christ: A Rhetoric of American Millennialism" (Ph.D. diss., Univ. of Minnesota, 1972), 222–36, blames theological liberalism for the collapse of postmillennialism. Anthony L. Dunnavant, "Disciples Leaders' Changing Posture Regarding the United States and 'Denominationalism,' 1880–1980," in *A Case Study of Mainstream Protestantism: The Disciples' Relation to American Culture,* ed. D. Newell Williams (Grand Rapids: Eerdmans, 1991), 171–93, does not address the millennial question directly but points to possible lines of inquiry by noting the shift away from positive assessments of the United States by Disciples leaders in the Great Depression.

89. A start toward this can be found in Hensley, "Rhetorical Vision," 182–270.

90. David Edwin Harrell Jr., "Disciples of Christ Pacifism in Nineteenth-Century Tennessee," in the present volume, 455–65.

91. Michael W. Casey, "From Pacifism to Patriotism: The Emergence of Civil Religion in the Churches of Christ during World War I," in the present volume, 466–80.

92. Peter Ackers, "Who Speaks for the Christians? The Great War Conscientious Objection Movement in the Churches of Christ: A View from the Wigan Coalfield," in the present volume, 481–95.

93. Dunnavant, "Disciples Leaders' Changing Posture," 180–83.

94. See Thomas P. Socknat, *Witness against War: Pacifism in Canada, 1900–1945* (Toronto: Univ. of Toronto Press, 1987), 346–47, and Bobbie Oliver, *Peacemongers: Conscientious Objection to Military Service in Australia, 1911–1945* (South Freemantle, Australia: Freemantle Arts Centre Press, 1997), 35, 142.

95. H. Roth, *Pacifism in New Zealand: A Bibliography* (Auckland: Univ. of Auckland, 1966). David Grant, *Out in the Cold: Pacifists and Conscientious Objectors in New Zealand during World War II* (Auckland: Reed Methuen, 1986), 33. Three persons in New Zealand

from the tradition, including Urquhart, went to prison in World War I. See "C.O.'s in New Zealand," *Apostolic Messenger*, May 1918, 61–62. A photocopy of this rare British source is in the possession of Michael Casey.

96. Clifford Geertz, *The Interpretation of Cultures* (New York: Basic Books, 1973), 90.

97. Anthony L. Dunnavant, "David Lipscomb and the 'Preferential Option for the Poor' among Postbellum Churches of Christ," in the present volume, 444. All the quotations in this paragraph and the list are from these pages.

98. Ibid., 448.

99. Anthony Dunnavant, introduction to *Poverty and Ecclesiology: Nineteenth-Century Evangelicals in the Light of Liberation Theology*, ed. Anthony Dunnavant (Collegeville, Minn.: Liturgical Press, 1992), 8.

100. Douglas A. Foster, "The Struggle for Unity During the Period of Division of the Restoration Movement, 1875–1900" (Ph.D. diss., Vanderbilt Univ., 1986).

101. Douglas A. Foster, *Will the Cycle Be Unbroken? Churches of Christ Face the Twenty-first Century* (Abilene, Tex.: Abilene Christian Univ. Press, 1994).

102. Anthony L. Dunnavant, *Restructure: Four Historical Ideals in the Campbell-Stone Movement and the Development of the Polity of the Christian Church (Disciples of Christ)* (New York: Peter Lang, 1991).

103. Ronald E. Osborn, "The Irony of the Twentieth-Century Christian Church (Disciples of Christ): Making It to the Mainline Just at the Time of Its Disestablishment," *Mid-Stream* 28 (July 1989): 293–312.

104. Douglas A. Foster, "The Disciples' Struggle for Unity Compared with the Struggle among Presbyterians, 1880–1980," in *A Case Study of Mainstream Protestantism: The Disciples' Relation to American Culture*, ed. D. Newell Williams, 236–59 (Grand Rapids: Eerdmans, 1991).

105. Michael Kinnamon and Brian Cope, *The Ecumenical Movement: An Anthology of Key Texts and Voices* (Grand Rapids: Eerdmans, 1997).

106. See, for example, Thomas F. Best, "Disciples Identity, Ecumenical Partnership, and the Wider Ecumenical Future," *Mid-Stream* 32 (Oct. 1993): 9–27, and Anthony L. Dunnavant, "History and Ecclesiology in Recent Disciples Literature," *Mid-Stream* 32 (Oct. 1993): 51–64.

107. Barry Callen and James North, *Coming Together in Christ: Pioneering a New Testament Way to Christian Unity* (Joplin, Mo.: College Press Publishing Co., 1989).

108. See, for example, *Restoration Forum VI: Akron, Ohio, November 1, 2, 3rd, 1988* (Joplin, Mo.: College Press Publishing Co., 1989).

109. For one assessment of the Murch-Witty meetings, see Richard Cobb, "The Failure of the Murch-Witty Unity Movement in the Stone-Campbell Tradition, 1937–1947: Was the Church in the Way?" (master's thesis, Abilene Christian Univ., 1996).

110. The documents can be found at www.disciples.org/ccu/documents/ccudoc.htm#stone

111. Little has been published from the Churches of Christ—Southern Baptist Conversation except for a paper on baptism from the 1994 meeting. Douglas A. Foster, "Churches

of Christ and Baptism: An Historical and Theological Overview," *Restoration Quarterly* 43 (Second Quarter 2001): 79–94. On the Disciples and Baptists, see Eric C. Holmstrom, "The Northern Baptist-Disciple Quest for Union: A Lesson for Today?" *American Baptist Quarterly* 4 (1985): 397–407.

112. David Newell Williams, "The Theology of the Great Revival in the West: As Seen through the Life and Thought of Barton Warren Stone" (Ph.D. diss., Vanderbilt Univ., 1979); Stephen Pressley Berry, " An Inquiry into the Role of the Holy Spirit in the Development and Nurture of Faith: As Understood by Robert Richardson in Contrast to Other Leaders in the Stone-Campbell Movement Previous to 1906" (D.Min. thesis, San Francisco Theological Seminary, 1984); Jimmy Odell Strait, "The Indwelling of the Holy Spirit and Its Relation to God's Providential Activity in Representative Restoration Thinkers" (master's thesis, Abilene Christian Univ., 1968); Patrick Leon Brooks, "Lockean Epistemology and the Indwelling Spirit in the Restoration Movement" (master's thesis, Abilene Christian Univ., 1977).

113. Thomas Olbricht, "Alexander Campbell's Views of the Holy Spirit," *Restoration Quarterly* 6 (1962): 1–11, and Patrick L. Brooks, "Alexander Campbell, the Holy Spirit, and the New Birth," *Restoration Quarterly* 31 (1989): 149–64.

114. Patrick L. Brooks, "Robert Richardson: Nineteenth-Century Advocate of Spirituality," *Restoration Quarterly* 21 (1978): 135–49. The controversy is explored from Fanning's perspective in James R. Wilburn, *Hazard of the Die: Tolbert Fanning and the Restoration Movement* (Austin: Sweet Publishing Co., 1969), 198–201.

115. Richard T. Hughes, "Christian Primitivism as Perfectionism: From Anabaptists to Pentecostals," in *Reaching Beyond: Chapters in the History of Perfectionism,* ed. Stanley M. Burgess (Peabody, Mass.: Hendrickson Publishers, 1986), 215–55.

116. C. Leonard Allen and Danny Gray Swick, *Participating in God's Life: Two Crossroads for Churches of Christ* (Orange: Calif.: New Leaf Books, 2001).

117. For Russell, see Leroy Garrett, *The Stone-Campbell Movement: The Story of the American Restoration Movement* (Joplin, Mo.: College Press, 1994), 256, and for Finto, see Vinson Synan, "The Unexpected Renewal," *Charisma and Christian Life* (Sept. 1988): 85–89.

118. Hughes and Allen, *Illusions,* 137–40, and Hughes, "Two Restoration Traditions: Mormons and Churches of Christ in the Nineteenth Century," in the present volume, 357–58.

119. Maria Woodworth-Etter, *Signs and Wonders: God Wrought in the Ministry for Fifty Years* (1916; reprint, Tulsa: Harrison House, n.d), 19. Also see Wayne E. Warner, *The Woman Evangelist: The Life and Times of Charismatic Evangelist Maria B. Woodworth-Etter* (Metuchen, N.J.: Scarecrow Press, 1986).

120. Pat Boone, *A New Song* (Carol Steam, Ill.: Creation House, 1970).

121. Ken Waters, "Charismatics: The View from Within," *Mission* 9 (May 1976): 221–24, and *The Acts of the Holy Spirit in the Church of Christ Today* (Los Angeles: Full Gospel Business Men's Fellowship International, 1971).

122. As cited by Hughes, "Two Restoration Traditions," 358.

123. William R. Barr, "Christology in Disciples Tradition: An Assessment and a Proposal," in *Classic Themes of Disciples Theology: Rethinking the Traditional Affirmations of the Christian Church (Disciples of Christ)*, ed. Kenneth Lawrence (Fort Worth: Texas Christian Univ. Press, 1986), 9–27.

124. John Mark Hicks, "What Did Christ Accomplish on the Cross? Atonement in Campbell, Stone, and Scott," *Lexington Theological Quarterly* 30 (Fall 1995): 145–70; Hicks has extended this work into the late nineteenth century for the entire movement and into the twentieth century for the Churches of Christ. Hicks, "Atonement Theology," 116–27; Hicks, "K. C. Moser and Churches of Christ: A Historical Perspective," *Restoration Quarterly* 37 (1995): 139–57; and Hicks, "K. C. Moser and Churches of Christ: A Theological Perspective," *Restoration Quarterly* 37 (1995), 193–211.

125. Anthony L. Dunnavant, "Alexander Campbell on the Structure of the Church," *Disciples Theological Digest* 4 (1989): 21–39; W. Clark Gilpin, "The Doctrine of the Church in the Thought of Alexander Campbell and John W. Nevin," *Mid-Stream* 19 (Oct. 1980): 417–27; David Fletcher, ed., *Baptism and the Remission of Sins: An Historical Perspective* (Joplin, Mo.: College Press, 1990); Clark M. Williamson, "Disciples Baptismal Theology," *Mid-Stream* 25 (Apr. 1986): 200–223; Keith Watkins, "Naïve Sacramentalism: Barton W. Stone's Sacramental Theology," *Encounter* 49 (Winter 1980): 37–51; Richard L. Harrison, "Early Disciples Sacramental Theology: Catholic, Reformed, and Free," in *Classic Themes of Disciples Theology: Rethinking the Traditional Affirmations of the Christian Church (Disciples of Christ)*, ed. Kenneth Lawrence, 49–100 (Fort Worth: Texas Christian Univ. Press, 1986); Richard L. Harrison, "Sacraments in the Life Thought and Practice of the Disciples of Christ," *Mid-Stream* 27 (Apr. 1988): 94–108.

126. However, a few empirical studies about the communication practices of the tradition have appeared. See Garry Bailey, "New Church Member Perceptions of Socialization Strategies in High and Low Context Cultures," *Journal of Communication and Religion* (Sept. 1996): 29–36, and James R. Hallmark, "The Relationship between Ritualistic Religious Commitment and Communication," *Journal of Communication and Religion* 16 (Mar. 1993): 55–69.

127. W. T. Moore, *Comprehensive History of the Disciples of Christ* (New York: Fleming H. Revell Co., 1909), 12.

128. Nathan Hatch, "Elias Smith and the Rise of Religious Journalism in the Early Republic," in *Printing and Society in Early America*, ed. William L. Joyce (Worcester, Mass.: American Antiquarian Society, 1983), 250–77.

129. We follow Leonard I. Sweet, "Communication and Change in American Religious History: A Historiographic Probe," in *Communication and Change in American Religious History*, ed. Leonard I. Sweet (Grand Rapids: Eerdmans, 1993), 27–28.

130. For one assessment of Campbell, see Gary Holloway, "Alexander Campbell as a Publisher," *Restoration Quarterly* 37 (1995): 28–35.

131. James Brooks Major, "The Role of Periodicals in the Development of the Disciples of Christ, 1850–1910" (Ph.D. diss., Vanderbilt Univ., 1966), 6. See Hughes's review of Major, "Twenty-five Years, Part Two," 52–53.

132. A place to start is with Don Meredith's compilation of Stone-Campbell serials, found in library holdings of the colleges of the Churches of Christ. See Don Meredith, *Union List of Restoration Periodicals in Participating Christian College Libraries* (Memphis: Harding Univ. Graduate School of Religion, 1996). Also important is Thomas E. Friskney, "Periodicals in the Restoration Movement," *Seminary Review* 6 (Winter 1960): 33–46, which includes a chronological listing of restoration serials. Also see Sam E. Stone, "Journalism in the Early Restoration Movement," *Seminary Review* 20 (Summer 1974): 93–104, and Claude Spencer, *Periodicals of the Disciples of Christ and Related Groups* (Canton, Mo.: Disciples of Christ Historical Society, 1943).

133. Carroll Ellis, "The Preaching of Alexander Campbell," *Southern Speech Journal* 14 (1948): 99–107; William S. Banowsky and Wayne C. Eubanks, "The Preaching of H. Leo Boles," *Southern Speech Journal* 28 (1963): 318–29; Elbert G. Barnhart and Wayne C. Eubanks, "N. B. Hardeman, Southern Evangelist," *Southern Speech Journal* 19 (Dec. 1953): 98–107.

134. These studies are best accessed through two sources: Dwayne D. VanRheenen, Michael Casey, C. Wayne Hensley, Ronald Bever, and Paul Prill, "Rhetorical History and Criticism of the American Restoration Tradition: State of the Art" (paper presented at the Conference on the Religious Communication in the Campbell-Stone Movement, Abilene Christian Univ., Abilene, Tex., July 1985), and Dwayne D. VanRheenen, "Bibliography of Research on Religious Communication in the American Restoration Tradition through 1982: A Preliminary Report" (paper presented at the Speech Communication Association meeting, Louisville, Ky., Nov. 1982).

135. Carisse Mickey Berryhill, "Alexander Campbell's Natural Rhetoric of Evangelism," *Restoration Quarterly* 30 (1988): 111–24.

136. Michael W. Casey, "From British Ciceronianism to American Baconianism: Alexander Campbell as a Case Study of a Shift in Rhetorical Theory," *Southern Communication Journal* 66 (Winter 2001): 151–66, and Michael W. Casey, *Saddlebags, City Streets and Cyberspace: A History of Preaching in the Churches of Christ* (Abilene: Abilene Christian Univ. Press, 1995).

137. Joseph Jeter Jr., "Preaching among Disciples of Christ," *Disciples Theological Digest* 7, no. 1 (1992): 5–19.

138. D. Newell Williams, "The History of Disciples Evangelism: 'If I or an Angel Should Preach Another Gospel . . .'" *Mid-Stream* 26 (July 1987): 339–50. Also see W. Clark Gilpin, "Witness to the Deeds of God: Ministry in the Disciples Tradition," *Mid-Stream* 26 (July 1987): 265–72.

139. D. Newell Williams, "Historical Development of Ministry among Disciples," *Mid-Stream* 24 (July 1985): 293–315.

140. Joseph E. Faulkner, "What Are They Saying? A Content Analysis of Sermons Preached in the Christian Church (Disciples of Christ) during 1988," in *A Case Study of Mainstream Protestantism: The Disciples' Relation to American Culture*, ed. D. Newell Williams, 416–39 (Grand Rapids: Eerdmans, 1991), is an example. Although hampered

by methodological problems, see Bill Love, *The Core Gospel: On Restoring the Crux of the Matter* (Abilene: Abilene Christian Univ. Press, 1992).

141. Thomas Thrasher, a teacher in Decatur, Georgia, and a member of the Churches of Christ, has compiled a large bibliography of debates (mostly from the Stone-Campbell movement) and made it available on the World Wide Web at www.ptc.dcs.edu/teacher-pages/tthrasher/thomas.html.

142. Walter S. Posey, *Religious Strife on the Southern Frontier* (Baton Rouge: Louisiana State Univ., 1965), 43–75.

143. R. Laurence Moore, "The Market for Religious Controversy," *Selling God: American Religion in the Marketplace of Culture* (New York: Oxford Univ. Press, 1994), 118–45, and E. Brooks Holifield, "Theology as Entertainment: Oral Debate in American Religion," *Church History* 67 (Sept. 1998): 499–519.

144. Moore, "Market," 120.

145. See VanRheenen, "Bibliography," n. 134. For an important early in-house publication, see Bill Humble, *Campbell and Controversy: The Story of Alexander Campbell's Great Debates with Skepticism, Catholicism, and Presbyterianism* (Rosemead, Calif.: Old Paths Book Club, 1952; reprint, Joplin, Mo.: College Press, 1986). Also see Andrew Paris, "The Immediate Influences and Results of the Campbell Debates upon the Restoration Movement of the Nineteenth Century," *Seminary Review* 28 (Mar. 1982): 15–39.

146. Earl Irvin West, "Early Cincinnati's 'Unprecedented Spectacle,'" in the present volume, 189–203.

147. James N. Holm Jr., "Alexander Campbell: A Study in the Value of Effective Rhetorical Training," *Forensic* (Oct. 1976): 10–13, 31.

148. Carroll B. Ellis, "The Backgrounds of the Campbell-Purcell Debate of 1837," *Southern Speech Journal* 11 (1945): 32–41. Also see Eva Jean Wrather, "A Nineteenth-Century Disciples-Catholic Dialogue: The Campbell-Purcell Debate of 1837," *Mid-Stream* 25 (Oct. 1986): 368–74.

149. Mark Weedman, "History as Authority in Alexander Campbell's 1837 Debate with Bishop Purcell," *Fides et Historia* 28 (Summer 1996): 33.

150. Ibid., 23.

151. Don Haymes of the American Theological Library Association is working on this badly needed work.

152. Besides Moore and Posey, see Don Haymes, "Debates, Interdenominational," in *Encyclopedia of Religion in the South,* ed. Samuel S. Hill (Macon: Mercer Univ. Press, 1984), 195–96.

153. James F. White, *Protestant Worship: Traditions in Transition* (Louisville: Westminster/John Knox, 1989), 171–75.

154. Dale A. Jorgenson, *Theological and Aesthetic Roots in the Stone-Campbell Movement* (Kirksville, Mo.: Thomas Jefferson Univ. Press, 1989). Also see Johnny Miles, "The Origins of Alexander Campbell's Eclectic Theology of Worship," *Discipliana* 55 (Summer 1995): 35–45, where he develops similar ideas. Miles focuses more on the immediate Scottish

independent influence and overlooks the Puritan and Reformed traditions, but this influence obviously was mediated through the independents.

155. Jorgenson, *Theological and Aesthetic Roots*, 34–48.

156. Ibid., 51–55.

157. Ibid., 67.

158. Ibid., 195.

159. Ibid., 220.

160. George Brandon, "The Hymnody of the Disciples of Christ in the U.S.A.," *Hymn* 15 (Jan. 1964): 15–22.

161. Harold Holland, "The Hymnody of the Churches of Christ," *Hymn* 30 (1979): 263–68. The quotation is from 266.

162. Ibid., 267.

163. Forrest McCann, "A History of *Great Songs of the Church*," *Restoration Quarterly* 38 (1996): 219–28. Also see Forrest McCann, *Hymns and History: An Annotated Survey of Sources* (Abilene: Abilene Christian Univ. Press, 1997).

164. Jim Mankin, "L. O. Sanderson, Church of Christ Hymn Writer," *Hymn* 46 (Jan. 1995): 27–31.

165. Peter Morgan, "Disciple Hymnbooks: A Continuing Quest for Harmony," *Discipliana* 55 (Summer 1995): 46–63. Also see Daniel B. Merrick, "Sing to the Lord: Hymnology among the Disciples," *Mid-Stream* 36 (July/Oct. 1997): 309–18.

166. See also Forrest McCann, "'Time Is Filled with Swift Transition': Changes in Worship Music in Churches of Christ," *Restoration Quarterly* 39 (1997): 195–202. Unfortunately, this worthwhile article is not documented. The suburban category is our label to describe the newest trend in religious music style. For a longer historical and theological study of the topic see Dan Dozier, *Come Let Us Adore Him: Dealing with the Struggle Over Style of Worship in Christian Churches and Churches of Christ* (Joplin, Mo.: College Press Pub. Co., 1994).

167. Three older studies by Disciples scholars trace the evolution of Disciples worship practices from the frontier context to the 1960s. See Walter W. Sikes, "Worship among Disciples of Christ, 1809–1865," *Mid-Stream* 7 (Summer 1968): 5–32; Harry B. Adams, "Worship among Disciples of Christ, 1865–1920," *Mid-Stream* 7 (Summer 1968): 33–49, and W. B. Blakemore," Worship among Disciples of Christ, 1920–1966," *Mid-Stream* 7 (Summer 1968): 50–65. Fred Craddock, "Worship among Disciples: Literature and Practice," *Disciples Theological Digest* 3 (1988): 5–22, and Keith Watkins, "The Disciples Heritage in Worship," *Mid-Stream* 26 (July 1987): 291–98, continue the thread through the 1980s. Similar studies are needed for the Churches of Christ and independent Christian Churches.

168. William O. Paulsell, *Disciples at Prayer: The Spirituality of the Christian Church (Disciples of Christ)* (St. Louis: Chalice Press, 1995). Also see Ronald E. Osborn, "Hidden Heritage: Spirituality in the Disciples Tradition," *Mid-Stream* 36 (July/Oct. 1997): 239–71.

169. Some of this for the Disciples can be found in L. Dale Richesin and Larry D. Bouchard, eds., *Interpreting Disciples: Practical Theology in the Disciples of Christ* (Fort Worth:

Texas Christian Univ. Press, 1987), and L. Shelton Woods, "Early American Missionaries in Ilocos," *Philippine Studies* 45 (1997): 303–28. For Churches of Christ, see David Edwin Harrell, "The Disciples of Christ-Church of Christ Tradition," in *Caring and Curing: Health and Medicine in the Western Religious Traditions*, ed. Ronald L. Numbers and Darrel W. Amundsen (New York: Macmillan, 1986), 376–98; Thomas H. Olbricht, "The Churches of Christ," *Encounters with Eternity* (New York: Philosophical Library, 1986), 109–28; Wayne E. Wylie, "Health Counseling Competencies Needed by the Minister," *Journal of Religion and Health* 23 (Fall 1984): 237–49, and Randall J. Givens, "The Counseling Ministry of the Churches of Christ," *Journal of Psychology and Theology* 4 (Fall 1976): 300–303.

170. Besides the ones mentioned below and elsewhere in this essay, see Mary K. Dains, "Alexander Campbell and the Missouri Disciples of Christ," *Missouri Historical Review* 77 (Oct. 1982): 13–46; Terry Meithe, "The Social Ethics of Alexander Campbell," *Journal of the Evangelical Theological Society* 31 (Sept. 1988): 305–19; John Morrison, "The Centrality of the Bible in Alexander Campbell's Thought and Life," *West Virginia History* 35 (Apr. 1974): 185–204; Morrison, "Alexander Campbell Moral Educator of the Middle Frontier," *West Virginia History* 36 (Apr. 1975): 187–201; Morrison, "Alexander Campbell: Freedom Fighter of the Middle Frontier," *West Virginia History* 37 (July 1976): 291–308.

171. John Morrison, "A Rational Voice Crying in an Emotional Wilderness," in the present volume, 163–76.

172. L. Edward Hicks, "Republican Religion and Republican Institutions: Alexander Campbell and the Anti-Catholic Movement," in the present volume, 205.

173. Ibid., 208–12.

174. Hughes, "A Comparison of the Restitution Motifs of the Campbells (1809–1830) and the Anabaptists," *Mennonite Quarterly Review* 45 (Oct. 1971): 312–30.

175. Ibid., 329.

176. Ibid., 330.

177. Williams, "Future Prospects of the Christian Church (Disciples of Christ)," in *A Case Study of Mainstream Protestantism*, 563–64.

178. Also see Williams's review of Henry Webb's *In Search of Christian Unity: A History of the Restoration Movement* in *Restoration Quarterly* 34 (1992): 60.

179. Hughes, *Reviving*, 24.

180. Garrett, *Stone-Campbell*, 6–17.

181. Leroy Garrett, "Christian Unity: What I Hope For," *Theology Today* 40 (Jan. 1984): 444–47.

182. Some of the more significant specialized monographs on Campbell include Robert Frederick West, *Alexander Campbell and Natural Religion* (New Haven: Yale Univ. Press, 1948); Harold Lunger, *The Political Ethics of Alexander Campbell* (St. Louis: Bethany Press, 1954); Cecil K. Thomas, *Alexander Campbell and His New Version* (St. Louis: Bethany Press, 1958); D. Ray Lindley, *Apostle of Freedom* (St. Louis: Bethany Press, 1957); Granville T. Walker, *Preaching in the Thought of Alexander Campbell* (St. Louis: Bethany Press, 1954); Perry E. Gresham, ed., *The Sage of Bethany: A Pioneer in Broadcloth* (St. Louis: Bethany Press,

1960); Alger Fitch, *Alexander Campbell: Preacher of Reform and Reformer of Preaching* (Austin: Sweet Publishing Co., 1970; reprint, Joplin, Mo.: College Press, 1988).

183. Robert Richardson, *Memoirs of Alexander Campbell,* vols. 1 and 2 (Cincinnati: Standard Publishing Co., 1897).

184. Some of the better studies that include a focus on Stone are Paul Conkin, *Cane Ridge: America's Pentecost* (Madison: Univ. of Wisconsin Press, 1990), and John B. Boles, *The Great Revival, 1787–1805: The Origins of the Southern Evangelical Mind* (Lexington: Univ. Press of Kentucky, 1972).

185. Information for Williams's biography of Stone at footnote 21.

186. Williams did his dissertation on Stone and has published a series of articles based on that study: "Theology"; "The Social and Ecclesiastical Impact of Barton W. Stone's Theology," in *Explorations in the Stone-Campbell Traditions: Essays in Honor of Herman A. Norton,* ed. Anthony Dunnavant and Richard L. Harrison Jr., 11–42 (Nashville: Disciples of Christ Historical Society, 1995); "Barton Stone's Calvinist Piety," *Encounter* 42 (autumn 1981): 409–17; and "Barton Stone's Revivalist Theology," in *Cane Ridge in Context,* 73–92.

187. Anthony Dunnavant, "From Precursor of the Movement to Icon of Christian Unity: Barton W. Stone in the Memory of the Christian Church (Disciples of Christ)," in *Cane Ridge in Context,* 13.

188. Ibid., 12. See William G. West, *Barton Warren Stone: Early American Advocate of Christian Unity* (Nashville: Disciples of Christ Historical Society, 1954).

189. Richard Harrison, "Is Barton Our Cornerstone?" in *Cane Ridge in Context,* 63–70.

190. Garrett, *Stone-Campbell,* 88–93.

191. Nathan O. Hatch, "The Christian Movement and the Demand for a Theology of the People," in the present volume, 129–32. Also see Hatch, *The Democratization of American Christianity* (New Haven: Yale Univ. Press, 1989), 70–71, 173.

192. Paul Blowers, "Nearly 'Stone Silence': Barton W. Stone in the Memory of the Independent Christian Churches and Churches of Christ," in *Cane Ridge in Context,* 33.

193. Mark G. Toulouse, ed., *Walter Scott: A Nineteenth-Century Evangelical* (St. Louis: Chalice Press, 1999). Loretta M. Long, *The Life of Selina Campbell: A Fellow Soldier in the Cause of Reformation* (Tuscaloosa: Univ. of Alabama Press, 2001). Thomas H. Olbricht and Hans Rollmann, *The Quest for Christian Unity, Peace, and Purity in Thomas Campbell's Declaration and Address: Text and Studies* (Lanham, Md.: Scarecrow Press, 2000).

194. For the historical background to the Sandemanian and Haldane movements, see Lynn McMillon, *Restoration Roots* (Dallas: Gospel Teachers Publications, 1983). This is the publication of McMillon's dissertation, "Quest for the Apostolic Church: A Study of Scottish Origins of American Restorationism" (Baylor Univ., 1972).

195. Thomas Olbricht, "Christian Connexion and Unitarian Relations, 1800–1844," *Restoration Quarterly* 9 (1966): 160–86; Milo True Morrill, *A History of the Christian Denomination in America* (Dayton: Christian Publishing Association, 1912); Durwood T. Stokes and William T. Scott, *A History of the Christian Church in the South* (Burlington, N.C.: Southern Conference UCC, United Church of Christ, 1975), and Charles Hambrick

Stowe, ed., *The Living Theological Heritage of the United Church of Christ*, vol. 3, *Colonial and National Beginnings* (Cleveland, Ohio: Pilgrim Press, 1995).

196. Jean F. Hankins, "A Different Kind of Loyalist: The Sandemanians of New England during the Revolutionary War," in present volume, 499–519. See also Hankins, "Connecticut's Sandemanians: Loyalism as a Religious Test," in *Loyalists and Community in North America*, ed. Robert M. Calhoon, Timothy M. Barnes, and George Rawlyk (Westport, Conn.: Greenwood Press, 1994), 31–44.

197. Hankins, "Loyalist," 249.

198. Deryck W. Lovegrove, "Unity and Separation: Contrasting Elements in the Thought and Practice of Robert and James Alexander Haldane," in the present volume, 520–43.

199. Ibid., 521.

200. Ibid., 530. On the Haldanes see also Camille K. Dean, "Evangelicals or Restorationists? The Careers of Robert and James Haldane in Cultural and Political Context (Ph.D. diss., Texas Christian Univ., 1999).

201. Frederick Norwood, "James O'Kelly—Methodist Maverick," *Methodist History* 4 (Apr. 1966): 14–28.

202. Ibid., 20.

203. Philip G. A. Griffin-Allwood, "To Hear a Free Gospel": The Christian Connexion in Canada," in the present volume, 544–62.

204. Ibid., 554.

205. Lippy, *Christadelphians*.

206. Also see Roderick Chesnut, "John Thomas and the Rebaptism Controversy (1835–1838)," in *Baptism and the Remission of Sins*, 203–39.

207. Lippy, *Christadelphians*, 25.

208. Russell Paden, "The Boston Church of Christ," in the present volume, 563–73.

209. Hatch, *Democratization*, 67–81.

210. David Edwin Harrell Jr., "The Agrarian Myth and the Disciples of Christ in the Nineteenth Century," in the present volume, 147–59.

211. Keith Lynn King, "Disciples of Christ and the Agrarian Protest in Texas, 1870–1906," *Restoration Quarterly* 35 (1993): 81–91. Also see King, "Religious Dimensions of the Agrarian Protest in Texas, 1870–1908" (Ph.D. diss., Univ. of Illinois, 1985).

212. Richard C. Goode, "The Godly Insurrection in Limestone County: Social Gospel, Populism, and Southern Culture in the Late Nineteenth Century," *Religion and American Culture* 3 (Summer 1993): 155–69.

213. Karel D. Bicha, "Prairie Radicals: A Common Pietism," *Journal of Church and State* 18 (1976): 79–94, argues that the "behavior-reforming tenets of sectarian or pietistic Protestantism . . . exerted considerable influence on prairie radicals." He identifies two men from the Stone-Campbell tradition who were prominent farmer populists: Henry Wise Wood and Milo Reno.

214. William C. Ringenberg, "The Religious Thought and Practice of James A. Garfield," in the present volume, 230. Also see Howard E. Short, "President Garfield's Religious Heritage and What He Did With It," *Hayes Historical Society* 4 no. 2 (1983): 5–20, where he shows how Garfield fit into the progressive camp of the Stone-Campbell movement.

215. Irvin G. Wylie, *The Self-Made Man in America: The Myth of Rags to Riches* (New York: Free Press, 1954), 8.

216. Monroe Billington, "Lyndon B. Johnson: The Religion of a Politician," in the present volume, 234–47.

217. Stephen Vaughn, "The Moral Inheritance of a President: Reagan and the Dixon Disciples of Christ," in the present volume, 248–68.

218. Hicks, *"Sometimes in the Wrong."*

219. William F. Buckley Jr., "My Secret Right-Wing Conspiracy," *New Yorker*, Oct. 21, 28, 1996, 120, 122–24, 126, 128–29.

220. Ronald L. Numbers, *The Creationists* (New York: Knopf, 1992), and Martin, *With God*.

221. James Stephen Wolfgang, "Science and Religion Issues in the American Restoration Movement" (Ph.D. diss., Univ. of Kentucky, 1997).

222. Numbers, *Creationists*, 152–53, 234, 239–40, 314–15. See Wolfgang, "Science," for an assessment of the anti-evolution efforts within the Stone-Campbell movement.

223. Martin, *With God*, 117–43.

224. Ibid., 165–66, 214.

225. See the sources on Hargis cited in note 62.

226. Kenneth T. Jackson, *The Ku Klux Klan in the City* (New York: Oxford Univ. Press, 1967), 241; David M. Chalmers, *Hooded Americanism: The History of the Ku Klux Klan* (Chicago: Quadrangle Books, 1965), 111, 293, and Charles C. Alexander, *The Ku Klux Klan in the Southwest* (Lexington: Univ. of Kentucky Press, 1965), 89–90.

227. Edwin L. Becker, "1923: Year of Peril for Indianapolis Disciples Pastors," *Encounter* 54 (Autumn 1993): 369–86.

228. Paul D. Phillips, "The Interracial Impact of Marshall Keeble Black Evangelist, 1878–1968," in the present volume, 317–28.

229. Hap C. S. Lyda, "Black Disciples Roots in Kentucky and Tennessee, 1804–1876," in *Explorations in the Stone-Campbell Traditions*, 43–53. For a brief history of black Churches of Christ see Douglas A. Foster, "An Angry Peace: Race and Religion," *ACU Today* (Spring 2000): 8–20, 39.

230. Fred Gray, *Bus Ride to Justice: Changing the System by the System: The Life and Works of Fred Gray* (Montgomery, Ala.: Black Belt Press, 1995).

231. William C. Martin, "Shepherds vs. Flocks, Ministers and Negro Militancy," *Atlantic* 220 (Dec. 1967): 53–59.

232. C. Leonard Allen, "Silena Moore Holman (1850–1915): Voice of the 'New Woman' among Churches of Christ," *Discipliana* 56 (Spring 1996): 3–11.

233. Darrell Buchanan, "'In His Name': The Life and Times of Jenny Kidd Trout," *Leaven* 3, no. 3 (1995): 45–47, and Peter E. Paul Dembski, "Jenny Kidd Trout and the Founding of the Women's Medical Colleges at Kingston and Toronto," *Ontario History* 77 (Sept. 1985): 187.

234. Glenn Michael Zuber, "Mainline Women Ministers: Women Missionary and Temperance Organizers Become 'Disciples of Christ' Ministers, 1888–1908," in the present volume, 292–316. The following quotations are from Zuber's article. See Kathy J. Pulley, "Gender Roles and Conservative Churches: 1870–1930," in Carroll D. Osburn, ed., *Essays on Women in Earliest Christianity*, vol. 2 (Joplin, Mo.: College Press Publishing Co., 1995), 443–83.

235. Also see Glenn Zuber, "The Gospel of Temperance: Early Disciple Women Preachers and the WCTU, 1887–1912," *Discipliana* 53 (Summer 1993): 47–60.

236. Debra Hull, *Christian Church Women: Shapers of a Movement* (St. Louis: Chalice Press, 1994).

237. Fran Craddock, Martha Faw, and Nancy Heimer, *In the Fullness of Time: A History of Women in the Christian Church (Disciples of Christ)* (St. Louis: Chalice Press, 1999).

238. Daisy L. Machado, "From Anglo-American Traditions to a Multicultural World," *Discipliana* 57 (Summer 1997): 47–60. Also see Machado, "Of Borders and Margins: Hispanic Disciples in Texas, 1888–1945" (Ph.D. diss., Univ. of Chicago, 1996).

239. Mark Massa, "Disciples in a Mission Land: The Christian Church in New York City," in *A Case Study of Mainstream Protestantism*, 469–90.

240. Joaquin Vargas, *Los Discipulos de Cristo en Puerto Rico: Albores, crecimiento y madurez de un peregrinar de fe, constancia y esperanze, 1899–1987* (n.p.: Iglesia Christana en Puerto Rico, 1988).

241. Samuel Gonzalez, "History of the Iglesias de Cristo" (paper presented at the Restoration Lectures, Abilene Christian Univ., Abilene, Tex., Feb. 1997). Tape in Abilene Christian Univ. Library, PTC 252 Ab5 1997 no. 130, 133.

242. Marcos A. Ramos, *Protestantism and Revolution in Cuba* (Miami: Research Institute for Cuban Studies, Univ. of Miami, 1989), 111. For Muñiz's first name and the possible identities of other preachers who joined the revolution, see J. R. Jimenez, "The Gospel in Cuba," in *The Harvest Field*, ed. Howard L. Schug, J. W. Treat, and Robert L. Johnston Jr. (Athens, Ga.: C.E.I. Publishing Co., 1958), 94–100.

243. B. B. Harding and Foy Short, "Cuba," in *The Harvest Field*, ed. Howard L. Schug and Don H. Morris (Abilene, Tex.: Abilene Christian College Press, 1942), 41. Jimenez and Estevez were in Cuba as late as 1958, but it is unknown whether they stayed after the revolution. See Jimenez, "Gospel," and Earl Irvin West, *The Search for the Ancient Order: A History of the Restoration Movement, 1919–1950* (Germantown, Tenn.: Religious Book Service, 1987), 394–98.

244. Ramos, *Protestantism*, 111.

245. Bill Lancaster, *Radical Cooperation and Socialism: Leicester Working-Class Politics, 1860–1906* (Leicester: Leicester Univ. Press, 1987), 71.

246. Peter Ackers, "The 'Protestant Ethic' and the English Labour Movement," *Labour History Review* 58 (Winter 1993): 68. Also see T. Witton Davies, "The McLeanist (Scotch)

and Campbellite Baptists of Wales," *Transactions of the Baptist Historical Society* 7 (1920–21): 147–81.

247. David M. Thompson, *Let Sects and Parties Fall: A Short History of the Association of Churches of Christ in Great Britain and Ireland* (Birmingham: Berean Press, 1980), 195–201. The term *Churches of Christ* refers to the entire Stone-Campbell movement in Britain.

248. Louis Billington, "The Churches of Christ in Britain: A Study of Nineteenth-Century Sectarianism," in the present volume, 367–97.

249. Ibid., 386.

250. Peter Ackers, "West End Chapel, Back Street Bethel: Labor and Capital in the Wigan Churches of Christ, 1845–1945," in the present volume, 398–432. Also see Peter Ackers, "The Churches of Christ as a Labour Sect," *Dictionary of Labour Biography*, ed. Joyce M. Bellamy and John Saville (London: Macmillan, 1993), 10:199–206.

251. The quotations in the rest of the paragraph are from Ackers, "West End Chapel," 420–21.

252. Ibid., 417.

253. Michael W. Casey, "The Old Paths Churches of Christ: An Overlooked Pacifist Tradition, Part I: The Great War and the Old Paths Division" *Journal of the United Reformed Church History Society* 6 (May 2000): 446–60, and "Part II: Labourist and Pacifist Ties from the 1920s to the Present," *Journal of the United Reformed Church History Society* 6 (Dec. 2000): 517–28.

254. Reuben Butchard, *History of the Disciples of Christ in Canada since 1830* (Toronto: Canadian Headquarters Publications Churches of Christ [Disciples], 1949).

255. Claude Cox, ed., *The Campbell-Stone Movement in Ontario* (Lewiston, N.Y.: Edwin Mellen Press, 1995).

256. Brian Boden, "The Disciples and Frontier Religion: The Scottish Baptist Roots of the Restoration Movement in Nineteenth-Century Ontario," in *The Campbell-Stone Movement in Ontario*, 1–42.

257. Elmer S. Stainton, "The Contribution of Two Christian Connexion Preachers to Disciples History in Canada: McIntyre and Ashley," in *The Campbell-Stone Movement in Ontario*, 89–100.

258. Geoffrey H. Ellis, "A Note on the Distinction between 'Scotch Baptist' and 'Scottish Baptist,'" in *The Campbell-Stone Movement in Ontario*, 413–19.

259. Peter Ackers, "Exodus: Labour Emigration from English Churches of Christ to Canada during 1906 and 1907," *Journal of the United Reformed Church History Society* 6 (Oct. 1997): 33–46.

260. William Tabbernee, "The Influence of American Disciples in Australia during the Nineteenth Century," *Lexington Theological Quarterly* 33 (Spring 1998): 1–22.

261. Graeme Chapman, *One Lord, One Faith, One Baptism: A History of the Churches of Christ in Australia* (Essendon North, Australia: Vital, 1979), and Chapman, *No Other Foundation: A Documentary History of the Churches of Christ in Australia* (published by the author, 1992).

262. David Roper, *Voices Crying in the Wilderness: A History of the Lord's Church with Special Emphasis on Australia* (Salisbury, Australia: Restoration Publications, 1979).

263. Leslie R. Galbreath and Heather R. Day, *The Disciples of Christ and American Culture: A Bibliography of Works by Disciples of Christ Members, 1866–1984* (Metuchen, N.J.: Scarecrow Press, 1990).

264. Glen Campbell, *Rhinestone Cowboy: An Autobiography* (New York: Vintage Books, 1994), 10.

265. Bob Millard, *Amy Grant: A Biography* (Garden City, N.Y.: Doubleday and Co., 1986), 18–22, 24–25, 30–37, 92–93, 129.

266. Alan Clayson, *Only the Lonely: Roy Orbison's Life and Legacy* (New York: St. Martin's Press, 1989), 16, and Ellis Amburn, *Dark Star: The Roy Orbison Story* (New York: Carol Publishing Group, 1990), 74.

267. Synan, "The Unexpected Renewal," 85–89. Also see Millard, *Grant*, 33–36, 65–66, 72–73, 90, 107–10, 162, 174–75 for Belmont, and 43–45, 47, 72, 80–81, 116 for persons from Belmont with ties to the Christian music industry.

268. Ivan M. Tribe, "Al Brumley," in *Definitive Country: The Ultimate Encyclopedia of Country Music and Its Performers*, ed. Barry McCloud et al. (New York: Bumper Books U.S.A., 1995), 108–9.

269. Charles K. Wolfe, "The Delmore Brothers," in McCloud et al., *Definitive Country*, 224–25.

270. Janet Bird, "Holly Dunn," in McCloud et al., *Definitive Country*, 256–57.

271. Merle Haggard, *Sing Me Back Home: My Story* (New York: Times Books, 1981), 109, 128, 159.

272. Charles K. Wolfe, "Eck Robertson," in McCloud et al., *Definitive Country*, 688–89.

273. Barry McCloud, "Diamond Rio," in McCloud et al., *Definitive Country*, 230.

274. Ivan M. Tribe, "Kitty Wells," in McCloud et al., *Definitive Country*, 854–55.

275. Barry McCloud, "Don Williams," in McCloud et al., *Definitive Country*, 873–75.

276. Barry McCloud, "Albert E. Brumley," in McCloud et al., *Definitive Country*, 109.

277. Jorgenson, *Theological and Aesthetic*, 309.

278. "Robert Page: A Chorus of Kudos Headed His Way," *Pittsburgh Post-Gazette*, Sept. 20, 1998, G-3; *Abilene Reporter News*, May 3, 1990.

279. Joseph. A. Mussulman, *Dear People . . . Robert Shaw* (Bloomington: Indiana Univ. Press, 1979).

280. Jorgenson, "Vachel Lindsey: The Troubadour from Springfield," in Jorgenson, *Theological and Aesthetic*, 279–303, and Perry E. Greshem, *The Broncho That Would Not Be Broken* (Nashville: Disciples of Christ Historical Society, 1986).

281. Hull, *Women*, 54, and Lee Scott Theisen, "'My God, Did I Set All This in Motion?' General Lew Wallace and *Ben-Hur*," *Journal of Popular Culture* 18 (Fall 1984): 33–41.

282. Charles T. Jones, "Brother Hal: The Preaching Career of Harold Bell Wright," *Missouri Historical Review* 78 (1984): 387–413.

283. Jorgenson, *Theological and Aesthetic*, 312–13.

284. See Galbreath and Day, *Bibliography*, 166–81, for their citations of works by scientists associated with the tradition.

285. Gregory N. Cantor, *Michael Faraday: Sandemanian and Scientist: A Study of Science and Religion in the Nineteenth Century* (New York: St. Martin's Press, 1991); Gregory Cantor,

David Gooding, and Frank A. J. L. James, *Michael Faraday* (Atlantic Highlands, N.J.: Humanities Press, 1996), and Dennis Williams, "The Range of Light: John Muir, Christianity, and Nature in the Post-Darwinian World" (Ph.D. diss., Texas Tech Univ., 1992.)

286. Galbreath and Day's *Bibliography,* while incomplete, is the place to start. They neglect the considerable number of scholars in the Churches of Christ.

287. Donald Dewey, "Frank Knight before Cornell: Some Light on the Dark Years," *Research in the History of Economic Thought and Methodology* 8 (1990): 1–38.

288. There are several biographies of George, almost all of them do not understand his Stone-Campbell heritage by confusing it with the Baptists. See, for example, Bentley Brinkerhoff Gilbert, *David Lloyd George: A Political Life* (Columbus: Ohio State Univ. Press, 1987), 1:22–23, 43, 63, where he sometimes calls the Disciples of Christ "Free Baptists."

289. Ruth Weiss, *Sir Garfield Todd and the Making of Zimbabwe* (London: British Academic Press, 1999), and Dickson A. Mungazi, *The Last British Liberals in Africa: Michael Blundell and Garfield Todd* (Westport: Praeger, 1999).

290. Michael W. Casey and Peter Ackers, "The Enigma of the Young Arthur Horner: From Churches of Christ Preacher to Communist Militant (1894–1920)," *Labour History Review* 66, no. 1 (Spring 2001): 3–23.

291. Neil K. Basen, "Kate Richards O'Hare: The 'First Lady' of American Socialism, 1901–1917," *Labour History* 21 (Spring 1980): 165–99; Sally M. Miller, *From Prairie to Prison: The Life of Social Activist Kate Richards O'Hare* (Columbia: Univ. of Missouri Press, 1993), 14, 47.

292. Fran Carver, "From Sanctuary to Saloon: Carry A. Nation and the Religious Ethos of the Mid-Western United States, 1850–1910" (Ph.D. diss., Princeton Theological Seminary, 1997), and Carver, "With Bible in One Hand and Battle-Axe in the Other: Carry A. Nation as Religious Performer and Self-Promoter," *Journal of Religion and American Culture* 9 (Winter 1999): 31–65. Also Fran Grace, *Carry A. Nation: Retelling the Life* (Bloomington: Indiana Univ. Press, 2001).

293. Peter Ackers, "Miller, William Thomas (1880–1863): Pit Deputies' Leader and Nonconformist," in *Dictionary of Labour Biography,* 9:215–19, and Peter Ackers, "Christian Brethren, Union Brother: A Study of the Relationship between Religious Nonconformity and Trade Union Leadership, in the Life of the Coal Mining Deputies' Official, W. T. Miller, 1880–1963" (Ph.D. diss., Wolverhampton Univ., 1993).

294. H. F. Bing, "Amos Mann," 1:230–31; H. F. Bing, "Robert Fleming," 1:122; Peter Ackers, "Joseph Parkinson," 10:165–68; and Peter Ackers, "John Taylor," 10: 195–98 in *Dictionary of Labour Biography.* On Humberstone see Lancaster, *Radicalism,* 142.

295. William Kirby Rolph, *Henry Wise Wood of Alberta* (Toronto: Univ. of Toronto Press, 1950), 9–10, 62–64.

296. Clifford Geertz, "Thick Description: Toward an Interpretative Theory of Culture," in Geertz, *Interpretation of Cultures,* 3–30.

297. Richard T. Hughes, "What Can the Church of Christ Tradition Contribute to Higher Education?" *Restoration Quarterly* 36 (1994): 338.

Part I

Historiographical Issues

Intellectual History and Social History

The Sectional Origins of the Churches of Christ

David Edwin Harrell Jr.

One of the new churches spawned by the religious ferment in early-nineteenth-century America was the Disciples of Christ. Biblical literalists with an activistic faith, the early Disciples preached a "restoration of the ancient gospel"; their central plea was "to speak where the Bible speaks and be silent where the Bible is silent." By the early 1830s the Disciples of Christ had emerged as an independent denomination and, under the capable and energetic leadership of Alexander Campbell, made impressive gains during the decades between 1830 and 1860. On the eve of the Civil War the church had a membership of well over 200,000. The rapid growth of the movement continued unabated after the war. By 1880 the number of Disciples exceeded half a million, and by the first decade of the twentieth century the church had well over a million members.[1]

The nineteenth-century growth of the Disciples was accompanied by the development of serious internal tensions. Although nominally the movement remained united until the religious census of 1906 that listed separately the Disciples of Christ and the Churches of Christ, this official report was little more than a belated acknowledgment of an accomplished fact. For over half a century before 1906 the group had been divided into factions debating such issues as the use of instrumental music in worship services and missionary societies, and the pastor system. No official pronouncement of schism had been made because there was no authoritative organization to issue one; but most church-related institutions, editors of church periodicals, preachers, and local churches had aligned themselves with one faction or the other by the beginning of the twentieth century.

Division within the Disciples had roots deep into the nineteenth century. From the beginning of its organization in the 1830s the group had contained both men of moderate, unexcitable character and a more colorful array of unsophisticated exhorters. The dual plea of the early leaders of the church for the "restoration of the ancient order of things" and "Christian unity" lent itself to conflicting emphases. While most of the early reformers insisted that both ends must be accomplished before the millennium could begin, it became increasingly apparent that the extremely sectarian element in the group considered the legalistic restoration principle more important, while the more denominationally oriented liberals believed that the principle of Christian unity was primary. As the initial fervor of the pioneer venture began to wane, as a sense of denominational responsibility began to grow among the more influential church leaders, and as a loose denominational organization began to emerge, it was inevitable that the discordant elements within the group should go their separate ways. The specific doctrinal issues that arose were only incidental. If Disciples had not disagreed over instrumental music and missionary societies, they would have divided over something else, as from the beginning the movement had attracted people of antipodal sociological and psychological backgrounds.

The two major groups that emerged are best identified by their institutional loyalties. The liberals in the church were known as "society men" or "*Standard* men" to identify them as backers of the American Christian Missionary Society and the leading liberal journal of the 1870s, the *Christian Standard*. On the other hand, the conservatives were called "antis" or "*Advocate* men," which marked them as opponents of the society and supporters of the most powerful of the southern conservative periodicals, the *Gospel Advocate*. More and more the name Churches of Christ came to be quasi-official among the southern conservatives and the name Christian Church among the more liberal northern members of the movement. While the name Disciples of Christ was more widely used in the North, it continued to be acceptable in both sections and remains the most useful term to describe the entire movement.[2]

The conservative wing of the divided movement, the Churches of Christ, has grown very rapidly in the half century since 1906. By 1961, according to the estimate in the most recent *Yearbook of American Churches,* the Churches of Christ had a membership of around 2.25 million.[3] Together with the more liberal segment of the movement, the Christian Church, it forms the largest and most significant native American religious movement.

One of the most distinctive characteristics of the Churches of Christ from their beginning has been the marked sectional distribution of the membership.[4] According to the 1906 religious census, 101,734 of the churches' 159,658 members lived in the eleven former states of the Confederacy. Another 30,206 lived in the four border states of Kentucky, West Virginia, Missouri, and Oklahoma. The only state north of the Ohio River to have a membership of more than 5,000 was Indiana.[5] These statistics are even more striking when compared with the membership distribution of the more liberal wing of the movement that listed in the 1906 census as the Disciples of Christ. Only, 138,703 of the total Disciples' membership of nearly a million lived in the eleven southern states.

Excluding Virginia and North Carolina, where the liberal Disciples won virtually all of the churches, the group had a total membership of only 99,233 in the remaining nine states.[6] In sum, while the Churches of Christ had little appeal to the members of the Campbell reform movement outside of the South, they were highly successful in capturing their share of the church within that section.[7]

The sectional bifurcation of the Disciples of Christ—using the name to refer to the whole movement—is one of the most vivid American examples of the bending of the Christian ethos to fit the presuppositions of the community. All of the complex antagonisms in nineteenth-century American society—North and South, East and West, urban and rural, affluent and dispossessed—left their marks on the theology and institutional development of the group. Schism was a result of differences far more complex than doctrinal disagreement—far more than the simple statement that "The 'Christian Churches'" . . . took their instruments and their missionary society and walked a new course."[8] While it remains useful to define the schism within the movement doctrinally, the more fundamental question is, Why did some Disciples remain conservative while others were relaxing their doctrinal standards? Or even more pertinent: Why did such a large number of southern Disciples oppose "innovations" while most northern Disciples believed the Scriptures authorized them? The obvious fact that the Churches of Christ are sectional (and, for that matter, so is the northern-oriented Disciples church) leads to the obvious question: What are the sectional origins of the group?

The most likely place to look for the sectional origins of a church in the nineteenth century is in the wake of the bitter struggle centering around slavery and culminating in the Civil War. Historians of the Disciples have seriously underestimated the impact of these sectional pressures on the movement.[9] It is true of course, that there were moderates in the church, as there were moderates in the nation. Foremost among them was the revered Alexander Campbell, who worked feverishly to keep the social issue of slavery from destroying the religious movement he had initiated. Campbell and many other moderate Disciples leaders held to their views even during the war years, but after 1845 they had become more and more on the defensive against attacks from extremists in both sections.[10] One beleaguered moderate editor wrote in 1856, "We have been scolded, bemeaned, threatened, and called a 'coward,' a 'dumb dog,' and a 'popularity seeker,' not because of what we *have* said, but because of what we have *not* said—because of our silence."[11]

Some of the earliest Disciples preachers were ardent antislavery advocates. In 1834, Nathaniel Field, an abolitionist preacher from Jeffersonville, Indiana, wrote that he had "resolved not to break the loaf with slaveholders or in any way to countenance them, as Christians."[12] By the late 1850s many Disciples congregations in the North supported an abolitionist platform, and in 1857

John Boggs, who edited a militantly abolitionist Disciples monthly in Cincinnati, wrote, "Every congregation built on the Bible . . . would . . . prohibit the reception as members those who practice . . . slavery."[13]

A series of crises in the 1850s widened the breach between the radical antislavery element and the rest of the church. Abolitionist desire for a safe educational institution led to the establishment of North Western Christian University in Indianapolis in 1850. Four years later, frustrated by the suppression of controversial material by the moderate editors of the church, an antislavery religious periodical, the *North Western Christian Magazine,* was established in Cincinnati. From these institutional centers Disciples radicals inveighed against the sinfulness of the federal government and the silence of the moderates in the church and reserved special damnation for the course of the American Christian Missionary Society. The society, which was the only national organization in the church and the outstanding symbol of church unity, was repeatedly condemned as "the pliant tool of the slave-holding aristocracy" because its leaders solicited funds among southern churches and because of the employment of a former slaveholder as a missionary to Jerusalem.[14]

A complete rupture between the radical abolitionists in the church and the American Christian Missionary Society came in 1859 when the society refused to support an outspoken antislavery preacher as a missionary in Kansas. Disciples extremists in the North were infuriated and in the following year organized a society of their own with an antislavery constitution. The new organization, named the Christian Missionary Society, was relatively weak, but it was far from insignificant. The bolting abolitionists had able leadership, a periodical outlet, at least one educational institution supporting their cause, and the sympathy of many of the churches of the North.[15]

The Civil War by no means ended division within the church. Although it did bring the radical antislavery bolters back into the mainstream of the northern church (or, more correctly, brought the northern church to them), it generated new tensions that would not be eased so quickly.[16] While some churchmen in both sections remained aloof from the struggle, for the most part, Disciples North and Disciples South preached and prayed as their sons fought and died. Within the organizational structure of the church the war deepened the already present sectional antagonisms into a pattern that could still be discerned clearly in the 1906 schism. The crucial event in this realignment of forces came in the convention of the American Christian Missionary Society in Cincinnati in 1863.

The 1863 convention met at a time when tensions within the church were strong. The moderates, led by the aging Alexander Campbell and powerful Cincinnati editor Benjamin Franklin, had succeeded in squashing an effort to pass resolutions of loyalty to the Union in the 1861 convention.[17] But the moderates never represented a majority of the opinion at that convention; prowar preachers had acquiesced, but their silence was sullen and begrudging. By the time of the 1863 convention, the compromising temper of the loyalists in the North had changed. They were determined to push through loyalty resolutions.[18] Northern preachers were particularly goaded by accusations of disloyalty leveled at the church and the missionary society by the secular press.[19] Even more pressing in the minds of some was the refusal of the abolitionist Christian Missionary Society to abandon its organizational schism unless such resolutions were passed.

The 1863 convention began with a rousing prowar speech by the corresponding secretary of the society and reached a climax with the passage by an overwhelming vote of resolutions repudiating the "reports [that] have gone abroad that we, as a religious body, and particularly as a Missionary Society are to a certain degree disloyal to the Government of the United States." The society further "unqualifiedly declared" its "allegiance to said Government" and tendered its "sympathies to our brave and noble soldiers, who are defending us from the attempts of armed traitors to overthrow the Government."[20] The results of the loyalist triumph in the 1863 convention were predictable. The radicals in the North were pleased, and the renegade Christian Missionary Society was dissolved. By and large the church in the North was reunited.

On the other hand, it was immediately obvious that the sectional pronouncement would cause serious resentment in the border areas and in the South. Southern church leaders had no opportunity to express themselves publicly on the war resolution until 1866, but a number of influential preachers from the border areas immediately attacked the American Christian Missionary Society. John W. McGarvey, influential preacher from Lexington, Kentucky, wrote, "I have judged the American Christian Missionary Society, and have decided for myself, that it should now cease to exist."[21] His articles ripped open the festering sores of sectional bitterness. Opposition to the society spread through Kentucky. Aylette Rains, an eastern Kentucky preacher, tersely scribbled in his diary: "Bro. McGarvey has taken the position that the A. C. Missionary Society is dead!"[22]

In short, by the close of the Civil War the Disciples of Christ movement was deeply involved in the nation's sectional strife. The only question in 1865 was whether or not the nebulous unity of the movement could be restored—in spite of the seething sectional bitterness in the church. Was a rapprochement possible?

Hope for a cordial reunion was dampened by the appearance early in 1866 of two sectionally oriented weekly church periodicals. By 1863 most northern church leaders, joined by border-state loyalists, had become openly critical of the neutral *American Christian Review,* and a number of them had begun to formulate plans for the establishment of a Unionist paper.[23] These plans led to the founding in April 1866 of the *Christian Standard,* edited by Isaac Errett, one of the most respected churchmen of the North. It had the financial backing of such outstanding northern laymen as Rep. James A. Garfield and the wealthy Thomas W. Phillips of New Castle, Pennsylvania.

Unquestionably, the *Standard* was founded out of sectional interest. Shortly after the close of the war, the editor of the paper told the powerful southern preacher David Lipscomb that the journal was begun so that the "loyal brethren" would have somewhere to "express themselves . . . on the duty of Christians to support the government in its war upon the rebellion, its duty to punish traitors, and to express themselves on the infamy of slavery."[24]

More significant evidence of the growing sectional division is found in the *Gospel Advocate*, a Nashville weekly that resumed publication in January 1866 after an interruption of four years. David Lipscomb and Tolbert Fanning, the editors of the paper, denounced the activities of the church in the North during the war: "Those brethren who believe that political resolutions are the Gospel can do so; and those who desire to contribute to such an object can do so; *we cannot do it.*"[25] It became increasingly obvious that the editors of the *Advocate* were making a thinly veiled appeal for backing to the supporters of the lost cause. Isaac Errett charged that the *Gospel Advocate* "commenced its new issue with an appeal to men of southern blood, and proposed cooperation among them only. It has constantly denounced the brethren of the North who shared in the military defense of the government."[26] For the next several decades the editors of the *Advocate* rarely missed an opportunity to remind the Disciples of the South that the editor of the *Standard* and other northern church leaders had been "strong Union men" during the war.[27]

The most revealing facet of the postwar sectional agitation within the church was the persistent practice of both northern and southern church leaders of linking their sectional prejudices with their theological convictions. The doctrinal positions that eventually became the outward distinguishing marks of the Christian Church and the Churches of Christ were clearly and consciously tied to the sectional pressures in the nation. Especially in the South it was not unusual for orthodoxy to include both theological conservatism and southern sectional values.

The strongly loyalist action of the American Christian Missionary Society during the war virtually assured that it would be the center of a sectionally oriented theological controversy when the struggle ended.[28] Although purely biblical arguments soon abounded on both sides of the missionary society controversy, the sectional coloration remained strong. Lanceford B. Wilkes, one of the leading Kentucky conservatives, wrote in 1870: "I am opposed to the Cincinnati society . . . The society's political raid is regretted, I have reason to think, by its best friends."[29] A large portion of the church in Texas refused to support the formation of a state missionary society in 1892 because it was "as specifically an ecclesiasticism as the Baptist association or the Methodist conference" and because those who promoted the project were "following northern ideas and northern men."[30]

Northern editors repeatedly charged church leaders of the South with trying to propagate theological conservatism by fanning sectional prejudice. One preacher reported that a minister from "Yankeedom" could not even get a hearing in Texas, and accusations that "a few" southern editors were trying to "run a Mason and Dixon line through the Bible and the Church of Christ" were frequent by the 1890s.[31] The complaints of northern churchmen were not without justification. A fiery southern preacher argued that "neither Tennessee nor Texas would have had any progressive foolishness" if it had not been for the invasion of carpetbag pastors" from the North.[32] Thomas R. Burnett, vitriolic Texas "anti," summed up the conservative sectional gospel in 1892: "We know the doctrine advocated by them [writers in the *Christian Standard*] comes from the *North*. It is neither scriptural nor *Southern,* and is not suited to Southern people. But it is the determination of the *Standard* and its *Northern* allies . . . to force the new things upon the churches of this section."[33] Burnett's reasoning was effective in the South of the 1890s.

The heritage of bitterness was not the only force that shaped much of the South into a cultural and religious unit in post–Civil War society. The South also displayed an economic homogeneity well into the twentieth century; and, in spite of rumblings of a New South, the hero image in southern society remained the simple and austere yeoman farmer. Meanwhile, in much of the North the "Second American Revolution" wrought dramatic changes, not only in the industrialization of the section but also in the minds of the people. The businessman became the new idol, and financial success was equated with diligence, ability, and godliness. Diverging economic patterns combined with postwar bitterness to widen the sectional rift.

The relation of characteristic economic patterns, North and South, to the origins of the Churches of Christ is easily demonstrated. The 1936 religious census, recording urban and rural membership, points out one significant feature. In the northern-dominated Disciples of Christ, nearly 750,000 of the group's 1,196,315 members were classified as urban. On the other hand, more than 175,000 of the Churches of Christ's 309,551 members were affiliated with rural churches.[34] In most of the southern states the membership of the Disciples of Christ was overwhelmingly urban; in the Churches of Christ, rural membership outnumbered urban in nine of the eleven former states of the Confederacy.[35]

Even more impressive are the census estimates of the value of church edifices in each state. For the Churches of Christ the total value of church edifices divided by the total number of congregations amounted to less than $3,000; the comparable figure for the Disciples of Christ was nearly $16,000.[36]

This superiority of the Disciples, as measured by the average value of church property per congregation, was substantial in every state. For example, in Georgia the average for the Disciples of Christ was around $12,000, and for the Churches of Christ, $4,500; in Kentucky the Disciples led $13,500 to $2,500; in Tennessee, $14,000 to $3,000; in Texas, $20,000 to $3,500; and in Indiana, $13,000 to $2,300.[37] The meaning of these figures is obvious. The conservative Churches of Christ preachers of the South were identified not only with a sectional audience but also with an economic class.

The economic pattern so obvious in the 1936 religious census is discernible also in the writings of nineteenth-century Disciples leaders. The churches in the North, especially in the urban centers, became markedly more genteel in the decades following the Civil War. The successful businessman became the financial, and often the spiritual, dictator of middle-class congregations. The church in the South continued to be dominated by an agricultural outlook, and its theology smacked strongly of anti-aristocratic prejudices. All of the doctrinal issues involved in the division of the movement—organized mission work, instrumental music, the pastor system—required congregations to make a decision that concerned not only their faith but also their finances.

By the 1870s there is good evidence of the growing class consciousness in the church. In the 1871 convention of the American Christian Missionary Society, Benjamin U. Watkins, an acrimonious old conservative, shocked the assembly with a speech in which he suggested that most of the young preachers in the church were looking for "stylish places to preach in, rich congregations to minister to, and positions . . . among those who [have] large and well-filled pockets." He insisted the poor ought to be the "special object" of Christianity. Lewis L. Pinkerton, a Kentucky liberal, led a counterattack. Pinkerton asserted that "the most beautiful souls it had been his privilege to know—those who best illustrated meekness and gentleness . . . [were] not among the poor but the rich." He doubted "if Christianity could take root and flourish in the wretched, filthy, vermin-besieged houses of the poor of Cincinnati, or elsewhere."[38]

More often than not the class conflict within the church pitted agricultural poverty against urban middle-class affluence. "The modern rendering of the great commission," wrote a disgruntled rural layman in 1894, "appears to be, Go into the large cities and preach the Gospel, or go where the people will pay a good salary and entertain the preacher in good style." He complained that the "city preachers" were "continually begging in the country to build houses of worship in the cities."[39]

There was ample evidence to demonstrate the domination of the northern church by urban congregations, business leaders, and middle-class religious norms. The most sought-after preacher was the man whose "motto is vim, vigor and victory."[40] A leading northern preacher suggested the "greatest need" in the church was the use of "*strictly business principles* in our religious enterprises."[41] In 1894 the Board of Church Extension began publication of a quarterly magazine entitled *Business in Christianity* that, according to its promoters, would aid ministers in avoiding "so much blundering."[42]

The emergence of the church in the North as a middle-class denomination was evinced also by the increasing activity of businessmen in church work. City ministers were urged to make use of the talents of the businessmen in their congregations since the wealthy were generally "good planners" and "hustlers."[43] By the 1890s most of the very wealthy men in the movement had been pushed into places of national prominence in various church organizations both because their "business sense" was "sorely needed" and because of their "ability to aid financially."[44]

During the same decades the economic thought of most southern church leaders was running in entirely different channels. Conservative preachers attacked the "delusive idea of the overshadowing importance of the city churches" and insisted that the "best classes of people" lived in the rural areas.[45] "Great cities," stated a conservative Missouri magazine, "are the great corrupters of the morals of mankind, like lewd women."[46] Moses E. Lard, noted pioneer preacher in Kentucky and Missouri, conveniently summed up the ideals of the southern church: "The preacher of that golden age was a farmer . . . He geared his horse with dexterity, plowed with as much skill as ever did Lycurgus, and could whistle 'old Father Grimes' with an unction which will never be equaled by Bro. Moore's organist in Cincinnati."[47]

Southern church leaders frequently attacked "aristocrats" and what they thought were efforts by northern churchmen to cater to the whims of the wealthy. In 1892 David Lipscomb was disturbed by plans to build a $30,000 church building in Atlanta and predicted that such "extravagance" would "weaken instead of strengthen them."[48] Fletcher D. Srygley, the wit of the *Gospel Advocate*, wrote in 1891: "The Northern Christian publishes an article from the Oregonian on 'Why People Don't Go To Church.' This reminds me that a friend of mine asked a highly respectable and strictly moral but irreligious man why he did not go to church, and the man said he stayed away from such places out of respect for his deceased old mother who was a deeply pious woman and who always taught him never to attend places of fashionable amusement on Sunday!"[49] An editorial in the conservative *Octographic Review* clearly stated the anti-aristocratic prejudices of southern preachers: "The perils of religion thus consist in wealth and ignorance . . . Wealth brings worldliness, negligence . . . Rich men in the Church! Millionaires sons of God . . . ! Did godliness ever grow out of that kind of soil?"[50]

These diverging economic views were everywhere a part of the pattern of the dividing church. Conservative editors repeatedly charged northern church periodicals with domination by aristocrats. An early biographer of Isaac Errett wrote: "In Cincinnati it was believed at the time, or at any rate it was so represented that the 'Standard's' quarters were most gorgeous; and the 'Review' had visions of Brussels carpets, luxurious chairs . . . in which the editor . . . reclined and smoked his fragrant Havana! . . . It would make the impression that the 'Review' was the paper of the *people*—the 'Standard' was that of a select aristocratic *class*."[51] By the late 1880s the *Christian Evangelist,* then the leading liberal journal in the church, was accused of making a "constant bid" for the support of the "rich, high-minded, and half-converted" and ignoring the poor.[52]

Southern preachers frequently linked their economic opinions with conservative theology in condemning such "liberal innovations" as instrumental music and missionary societies. The outspoken Texas conservative Thomas R. Burnett betrayed his bias against wealth and fashion in an 1895 attack on the Texas Missionary Society:

> Last week about a hundred preachers and fashionable women assembled at Gainesville, Texas, in a state convention, and wasted enough of the Lord's money and time to have held a hundred protracted meetings . . . They also spent enough money for extra fine toggery, to appear in style, to pay the expenses of a half dozen evangelists to preach the gospel in destitute places all summer. What was their business at Gainesville? Principally a fashionable blow-out, and in addition to this, an effort to push forward the furor for societies and fads in religion, and to supplant the Lord's plan of work and worship in the churches.[53]

David Lipscomb surmised that the "fundamental difference between the Disciples of Christ [that is, Churches of Christ] and the society folks" was that the conservatives wanted people "to come to Christ," while the liberals wanted to build "a strong and respectable denomination" based on "moneyed societies, fine houses, fashionable music, and eloquent speeches."[54]

One of the most perceptive nineteenth-century analyses of the sociological roots of the Disciples of Christ schism was made by a conservative editor Daniel Sommer. He wrote: "As time advanced such of those churches as assembled in large towns and cities gradually became proud, or at least, sufficiently worldly-minded to desire popularity, and in order to attain that unscriptural end they adopted certain popular arrangements such as the hired pastor, the church choir, instrumental music, man-made societies to advance the gospel, and human devices to raise money to support previously mentioned devices of similar origin. In so doing they divided the brotherhood of disciples."[55] While Sommer's charge that liberals were responsible for the schism is biased, and his judgments on what is "unscriptural" are open to question, his understanding of the relationship between economic and theological outlook is a rare piece of insight.

A recent historian of the Disciples of Christ, in evaluating one of the conservative periodicals of the post–Civil War period, wrote, "If one were hunting incidents to illustrate a thesis for a modern volume entitled 'The Social Sources of Denominationalism,' an excellent example could be presented in the reaction [to the founding of the *Christian Standard*] of the *American Christian Review*."[56] The *Review* does vividly show the relationship between religious faith and social force; but no more or less than every other Disciples periodical of the nineteenth century.[57] Conservative and liberal theological positions, northern and southern sectional feeling, urban and rural prejudices, and agricultural and middle-class economic views were all important ingredients in the nineteenth-century fracturing of the movement. Every Disciples periodical and every Disciples minister during these critical years represented not simply a theological position but a describable mixture of one or another of these clashing viewpoints. The twentieth-century Churches of Christ are the spirited offspring of the religious rednecks of the postbellum South.[58]

NOTES

1. The two standard studies of the church are Winfred E. Garrison and Alfred T. DeGroot, *The Disciples of Christ* (St. Louis, 1948) and Earl Irvin West, *The Search for the Ancient Order*, 2 vols. (Nashville, 1957). See also, for a sociological interpretation of the movement, Oliver Read Whitley, *Trumpet Call of Reformation* (St. Louis, 1959).

2. The terminology in the Disciples movement is confusing. Actually, in both North and South all three of the names—Disciples of Christ, Christian Church, and Churches of Christ—are still used by both conservatives and liberals. In this study, the name *Churches of Christ* is used exclusively to denote the anti–instrumental music conservatives. The term *Christian Church* is used to describe the northern liberals. The name *Disciples of Christ* is most useful to describe the entire nebulous movement, although occasionally it appears as the official title of the liberal church.

3. Benson Y. Landis, ed., *Yearbook of American Churches* (New York, 1964), 255.

4. Although it has been nearly three decades since a census of the groups has been taken, a recent expert stated a self-evident fact when he described the church as a "predominantly Southern group." Wilbur Zelinsky, "An Approach to the Religious Geography of the United States: Patterns of Church Membership in 1942," Association of American Geographers, *Annals* 51 (June 1961): 143. This judgment probably is becoming increasingly less true. The mobility of southern population in recent years, along with the evangelistic efforts of the church, has created a more diverse pattern of membership. See Zelinsky's entire article for a sophisticated approach to religious geography. He ably discusses the reliability of various religious censuses. For the Disciples movement the only available statistics are those reported in the four government censuses between 1906 and

1936. Although these studies are far from flawless, for the purposes of this study they are adequate.

5. U.S. Bureau of the Census, *Religious Bodies: 1906,* 2 vols. (Washington: GPO, 1910), 2:240, 243. The Churches of Christ listed a membership of 10,259 in Indiana, while the liberal Disciples of Christ reported 108,188. Even here the more conservative wing of the movement controlled a relatively small part of the state. See notes 35 and 37 below for a fuller discussion of Indiana and other states that fail to fit neatly into the sectional pattern.

6. See note 37 below for a discussion of the course of the church in Virginia and North Carolina. According to the 1906 census, the Churches of Christ had a membership of only 415 in the two states.

7. By the time the last official religious census was published in 1936, the sectional pattern in the divided movement had deepened. Of the 309,551 members listed by the Churches of Christ in 1936, more than 192,000 lived in the eleven former Confederate states and another 65,000 lived in Kentucky, West Virginia, Missouri, and Oklahoma. Excluding Virginia and North Carolina, the Churches of Christ outnumbered the Disciples of Christ in the South by more than 30,000. In terms of relative strength, the Churches of Christ gained on the Christian Church in nearly every southern state during the thirty years between 1906 and 1936. U.S. Bureau of Census, *Religious Bodies: 1936,* 3 vols. (Washington: GPO, 1941), vol. 2, pt. 2, 464–66, 535–37.

8. West, *Search for the Ancient Order,* 2:448. To state the truism that some people in the movement believed it was unscriptural to use instrumental music in worship services and to support missionary societies contributes little to an understanding of the origin of the Churches of Christ.

9. Robert Richardson, one of the earliest historians of the church, wrote in 1868, "Mr. Campbell's conservative course in regard to this disturbing question [slavery] . . . preserved the reforming churches from division." Robert Richardson, *Memoirs of Alexander Campbell,* 2 vols. (Philadelphia, 1868–70), 2:534. More than sixty years later, a modern church historian wrote in a similar vein on the effect of Alexander Campbell's moderate stand on the slavery issue: "It cost him much criticism from both sides, but it established general lines of an attitude which not only saved the Disciples from a division in 1845, but enabled them to go through the Civil War still undivided." Winfred E. Garrison, *Religion Follows the Frontier* (New York, 1931), 179–80. See, for similar interpretation, Robert E. Barnes, "An Analytical Study of the Northwestern Christian Magazine" (B.D. thesis, Butler Univ., 1951), 126–30; Eileen Gordon Vandegrift, "The Christian Missionary Society: A Study in the Influence of Slavery on the Disciples of Christ" (master's thesis, Butler Univ., 1945), 81; and Robert O. Fife, "Alexander Campbell and the Christian Church in the Slavery Controversy" (Ph.D. diss., Univ. of Indiana, 1960), 255–73. See, for the opposite point of view and a general discussion of the Disciples and the slavery controversy, David Edwin Harrell Jr., "A Social History of the Disciples of Christ to 1866" (Ph.D. diss., Vanderbilt Univ., 1962), 233–344.

10. See Campbell's series of articles entitled, "Our Position to American Slavery," *Millennial Harbinger*, 3d ser., vol. 2 (Jan.–Aug. 1854). The best study of Campbell's social thought is Harold L. Lunger's *The Political Ethics of Alexander Campbell* (St. Louis, 1954).

11. Benjamin Franklin, "Where Is the Safe Ground, *American Christian Review* 1 (Feb. 1856): 35.

12. "Letter from Nat. Field, Jeffersonville," *Evangelist* 3 (Oct. 1834): 234.

13. "Querist's Department," *North Western Christian Magazine* 4 (Sept. 1857): 90. Such expressions were not uncommon. See, for example, A[lexander] C[ampbell], "An Excursion in Ohio," *Millennial Harbinger*, 4th ser., vol. 6 (Nov. 1857): 652; B. F. Perky, "News," *Gospel Proclamation* 2 (May 1849): 549; John Rogers to Isaac Errett, Nov. 6, 1851, in Disciples Manuscript Collection, Christian Theological Seminary Library, Indianapolis.

14. James S. Lamar, *Memoirs of Isaac Errett*, 2 vols. (Cincinnati, 1893), 1:217.

15. Eileen Vandergrift's thesis on the Christian Missionary Society is a very able study. Of course, it is impossible to say whether or not the abolitionist schism would have been permanent, but there is every reason to believe that it would have been. It would be possible to exaggerate the size of the bolting group but not the reality of the rupture.

16. The sectional impact of the Civil War on the church has been ignored almost completely by the historians of the movement. Winfred Garrison writes, "Its [the Civil War's] ultimate effect was less divisive than might have been expected; in fact, not divisive at all." *Religion Follows the Frontier*, 221. Another recent scholar writes, "The churches . . . weathered the issues created by the war without any serious disruption." West, *Search for the Ancient Order*, 1:350. The nineteenth-century historian William T. Moore insisted that nothing "like a division" was ever seriously contemplated by brethren on either side of the conflict." "Reformation of the Nineteenth Century: The Turbulent Period," *Christian Evangelist* 41 (June 1, 1899): 680. This misjudgment has been passed down from one generation of Disciples of Christ historians to another. It has been based partly on a companion misjudgment on the prevalence of pacifism in the church. One historian reports that the church's leaders opposed the war "almost to a man." Glen W. Mell, "A Study of the Opinions of Some Leading Disciples Concerning Pacifism" (B.D. thesis, Butler Univ., 1936), 53–54. The more general literature on American religion reflects this distortion. John R. Bodo, in his *The Protestant Clergy and Public Issues, 1812–1845* (Princeton, 1934), 227, writes: "The Disciples of Christ . . . began as a pacifist set. All of their leaders, with the exception of Walter Scott, were avowed pacifists." This interpretation of the movement is simply not true. Some of the leading preachers in the group were pacifists, but they by no means represent the majority of the church.

17. Loyalty resolutions were "unofficially" passed at the 1861 convention. See American Christian Missionary Society, *Report of Proceedings of the Thirteenth Anniversary Meeting . . .* (Cincinnati, 1861), 19–20.

18. Unionists insisted from the beginning that they represented the large majority of the church. "A Reply to 'Vindication of Ourselves and the Pioneer,'" *Christian Pioneer* 1

(Dec. 1861): 322–34; Elijah Goodwin, "A. C. Missionary Society," *Weekly Christian Record* 1 (Nov. 4, 1862): 2.

19. "A Reply to 'Vindication of Ourselves and the Pioneer,'" 322–34.

20. American Christian Missionary Society, *Report of Proceedings of the Fifteenth Anniversary Meeting* . . . (Cincinnati, 1863), 24.

21. "Missionary Societies," *American Christian Quarterly Review* 2 ([Nov.?] 1863): 342.

22. Diary, Dec. 27, 1863, in Aylette Rains Papers, College of the Bible Library, Lexington.

23. D. Pat Henderson to Isaac Errett, Nov. 21, 1861; William Baxter to Errett, Dec. 16, 1863; John Rogers to Errett, Aug. 10, 1863; and R. Milligan to Errett, Oct. 29, 1863, all in Disciples Manuscript Collection.

24. "The Truth of History," *Gospel Advocate* 34 (July 14, 1892): 436. Lipscomb is hardly an unbiased authority on the founding of the *Christian Standard*, but there is little reason to doubt that this conversation is accurately reported. John W. McGarvey's description of the motivations behind the establishment of the journal may be fairer: "After the death of Mr. Campbell and the subsequent suspension of the Harbinger, there soon arose a strong feeling among the leading brethren in the northern States, in favor of a weekly paper of higher literary merit than the American Christian Review then conducted by Benjamin Franklin and exerting a powerful influence throughout the brotherhood, and one which would be more 'loyal' as the phrase went, to the Federal Government then engaged in the struggle of the civil war." J. W. McGarvey, *Autobiography* (Lexington, 1960), 73.

25. "A Reply to the Call of W. C. Rogers, Corresponding Secretary of the A.C.M. Society for All to Disseminate the Gospel," *Gospel Advocate* 8 (Mar. 27, 1866): 109.

26. "The Gospel Advocate," *Christian Standard* 2 (Feb. 16, 1867): 52.

27. See, for a discussion of this facet of the struggle, David Edwin Harrell Jr., "Disciples of Christ Pacifism in Nineteenth Century Tennessee," *Tennessee Historical Quarterly* 21 (Sept. 1962): 263–74.

28. It should be said that there was some theological opposition to the missionary society prior to the Civil War, and it would have unquestionably been a source of friction had it not become involved in the sectional struggle. But the course that the society controversy did follow was without a doubt influenced by the society's wartime activities.

29. "L. B. Wilkes Sets Himself Right on Missionary Societies," *American Christian Review* 10 (Sept. 3, 1867): 285.

30. "Our Budget," *Christian Evangelist* 29 (July 28, 1892): 472.

31. "No North or South in Christ," *Missionary Weekly* 12 (Feb. 26, 1891): 4; "From the Papers," *Gospel Advocate* 33 (Mar. 25, 1891): 177.

32. T. R. Burnett, "Burnett's Budget," *Gospel Advocate* 38 (Nov. 26, 1896): 755.

33. "Our Budget," *Christian Evangelist* 29 (July 21, 1892): 456. In the same article, the editor of the *Christian Evangelist* wrote a discerning analysis of the sectional background of the doctrinal conflict in the church: "And after all, with the great majority of the members of the church in the South, for it is in the South that the opposition to cooperative

mission work is strongest, the chief reason for suspecting and opposing missionary work has been all along and now is that its headquarters and chief supporters have been in the north and west" (472).

34. *Religious Bodies: 1936*, vol. 2, pt. 2, 464, 535. A recent estimate that "about 80% of the Churches of Christ are in rural areas" is certainly incorrect. *Encyclopedia Britannica* (1962), 5:675. The Churches of Christ have been a part of the baggage of thousands of southerners who made the exodus into urban centers all over the country since World War II.

35. The four states in the South where Disciples rural membership outnumbered urban membership were Virginia, North Carolina, South Carolina, and Georgia. Virginia and North Carolina are discussed below in note 37. In South Carolina the combined membership of both Disciples and Churches of Christ was less than 3,000. Urban membership was greater for both churches in Georgia. In Indiana, the strongest Churches of Christ state outside the South, the figures showed 9,058 rural members and 3,794 urban. In the same state the large Disciples of Christ membership was well over 50 percent urban.

36. This figure has no particular meaning in itself, but it serves as a useful yardstick.

37. It is precisely at this point that Virginia and North Carolina, which simply do not fit into a North-South or a rural-urban interpretation of the Disciples schism, fall into place. The average value of church property per congregation in Virginia was over $10,000, and in North Carolina it was over $8,000. The churches of these states belong in the same category with those of such states as Kentucky, Missouri, Indiana, and Illinois, where the movement contained large, prosperous rural memberships. This element refused to follow the radical leadership of the sectarian conservatives of the Deep South, although it shared many of the prejudices of the radicals. But while these churches remained in the main body of the Disciples, they never really accepted the leadership of the urban liberals. Although no historian has studied the problem, it seems obvious that this is the sociological setting for the twentieth-century Independent Co-operative schism in the Disciples of Christ. One final qualification needs to be made in accounting for the local success of the various pleas within the restoration movement. It would be foolish to discount completely the personal influence of many magnetic preachers and editors. But, when all is said and done, these men were influenced by their sociological environment, and their leadership was effective because they fit the pattern demanded by their society.

38. American Christian Missionary Society, *Report of the Proceedings of the Twenty-third Anniversary Meeting* . . . (Cincinnati, 1871), 8.

39. "'Pathfinder,'" *Christian Oracle* 9 (Oct. 11, 1894): 596. See also "Our Budget," *Christian Evangelist* 32 (Feb. 7, 1895): 84.

40. James Small, "A Visit in Iowa," *Christian Standard* 33 (Oct. 23, 1897): 1356.

41. [J. Z. Tyler], "Business in Religion," *Christian Examiner* 12 (June 13, 1879): 2.

42. G. L. Brokaw, "Iowa Notes and News," *Christian Evangelist* 21 (Jan. 25, 1894): 60.

43. F. M. Cummings, "Business Men in the Sunday-School," *Christian Standard* 26 (May 30, 1891): 448.

44. J. C. Waggoner, "Christian Business Men of Illinois," *Christian Standard* 25 (July 19, 1890): 474.

45. W. B. F. Treat, "Religion in the Cities," *American Christian Review* 19 (Nov. 12, 1878): 361. See also David Edwin Harrell Jr., "A Decade of Disciples of Christ Social Thought, 1875–1885" (master's thesis, Vanderbilt Univ., 1958), 45–87, and Harrell, "Social History of the Disciples of Christ," 164–68.

46. "Great Cities," *Christian Pioneer* 7 (Aug. 1, 1867): 442.

47. "Pioneer Preaching in the West," *Apostolic Times* 3 (Feb. 8, 1872): 348.

48. "Fine Houses for Worship," *Gospel Advocate* 34 (Jan. 28, 1892): 52. See also "Miscellany," *Gospel Advocate* 34 (Apr. 21, 1892): 249.

49. "From the Papers" *Gospel Advocate* 33 (June 3, 1891): 338.

50. "The Chief Perils of Religion," *Octographic Review* 30 (June 23, 1887): 4.

51. Lamar, *Memoirs of Errett*, 1:308.

52. "'The Great Robbery,'" *Octographic Review* 31 (July 12, 1888): 1. David Lipscomb believed that as a general rule the "working people" of the North had been "weaned from the church by the building and conducting of churches, suited in style, buildings, and worship for the rich." "A Visit to Chattanooga," *Gospel Advocate* 31 (Apr. 3, 1880): 214.

53. "Burnett's Budget," *Gospel Advocate* 38 (July 4, 1895): 419.

54. "The Churches across the Mountains," *Gospel Advocate* 39 (Jan. 7, 1897): 4.

55. "Signs of the Times," *Octographic Review* 40 (Oct. 25, 1897): 1.

56. Garrison and DeGroot, *Disciples of Christ*, 357.

57. The *Review* is certainly not unique. It is interesting that a liberal historian should see the sociological roots of the conservatives in the movement but fail to see that sectionalism and economics also played a part in the policy of northern church papers.

58. Of course, the Churches of Christ have not remained an economic and cultural unit since 1906. The sociological and economic elevation of a portion of the membership of the church, especially since World War II, has motivated a large part of the church to begin the transition to denominationalism. The result is that the movement is once again dividing along sociological lines. Conservative appeals in the movement in the 1960s have a distinctive lower class and anti-aristocratic flavor, while the centers of liberalism are in the areas where the church is most numerous and sophisticated.

The Apocalyptic Origins of Churches of Christ and the Triumph of Modernism

Richard T. Hughes

The origins of the American-born Churches of Christ are exceedingly complex. While most historians have argued that Churches of Christ separated from Alexander Campbell's Disciples of Christ late in the nineteenth century, this essay will suggest that the genesis of Churches of Christ was not a matter of separation from the Disciples at all. Rather, Churches of Christ grew from two early-nineteenth-century worldviews that coalesced and intertwined with one another in ways that often defy disentanglement. The first was the apocalyptic perspective of Barton W. Stone; the second was the radically sectarian mentality of the young and brash Alexander Campbell of the *Christian Baptist* period (1823–1830). As early as the 1830s, these two perspectives wed, brought together in part by the matchmaking power of poverty, marginality, and social estrangement.[1] Together, they clearly shaped a portion of the Stone-Campbell movement that, in due time, would come to be known as a denomination separate from the Disciples; namely, the Churches of Christ.

While the perspectives of Stone and the early Campbell intertwined in the lives and thoughts of many in the early nineteenth century, and while the one rarely existed without the other, it is nonetheless possible to identify particular leaders and to discern particular streams of tradition that carried either the Stoneite or the early Campbellite perspective in especially powerful ways. Thus, for example, Campbell's sectarian perspective, which many of his early followers interpreted to mean that Churches of Christ constituted the one true church outside of which there was no salvation, fed through several influential editor-preachers. Most notable among these were Tolbert Fanning and John R. Howard of Tennessee, Arthur Crihfield of Ohio and Kentucky, and Benjamin Franklin and Daniel Sommer of Indiana.[2] Since this tradition is relatively well known, I will not trace it here.

This essay will focus, instead, on the worldview embraced by Barton W. Stone and the sizable corps of preachers he inspired in the Cumberland region of Tennessee in the early nineteenth century and on the ways in which that worldview helped define a sizable segment of Churches of Christ. This worldview could best be described, quite simply, as *apocalyptic,* embracing a radical sense of estrangement and separation from the world and its values and a keen allegiance to a transcendent vision these people described as the "kingdom of God." That kingdom had manifested itself in the earliest days of primitive Christianity, perpetually stood in judgment on the kingdoms of this earth, and would finally triumph over all things. Because Stone and his people identified so strongly with that kingdom, they typically refused to fight in wars, to vote, or otherwise to participate in the political process.

The apocalyptic worldview, however, should not be confused with premillennialism. There were those, as we shall see, who followed the apocalyptic perspective into a full-blown premillennial outlook. This, however, was not always the case. Indeed, on the Stone side of the movement, there were some who embraced the apocalyptic worldview but stoutly resisted premillennial thinking. On the Campbell side of the movement, there were some who arrived at premillennial convictions out of sheer biblical literalism with no reference whatever to what we here describe as an "apocalyptic worldview."

The irony here is that, while many in the movement uncritically fused the Stoneite and early Campbellite perspectives, in significant ways these perspectives were simply incompatible. For if Stone's worldview was predominantly apocalyptic, Campbell's outlook—even during the sectarian days of the *Christian Baptist*—was fundamentally optimistic regarding this world, progressive, and postmillennial. Further, the intellectual split between Campbell and Stone in this regard reflected a major split in American intellectual life at that time, the split between the "party of memory" and the "party of hope."

In the twentieth century, in the interest of modernization, key leaders of Churches of Christ literally drove from the church both the memory and the reality of the separationist and apocalyptic vision inspired by Barton W. Stone. Discredited and forgotten, this tradition therefore has played no meaningful role in the historiography of Churches of Christ.

HISTORIOGRAPHY, CULTURAL SETTING, AND BACKGROUNDS

In 1906 the U.S. Bureau of the Census recognized for the first time a division in the ranks of the Stone-Campbell restoration tradition and listed two separate denominations: Churches of Christ and Disciples of Christ. Until 1964 most historians rooted this division in a late-nineteenth-century dispute over missionary societies and instrumental music in worship, with the emerging Churches of Christ coalescing around the negative position on both these issues. In this view, the Disciples represented the mainstream of this tradition throughout the nineteenth century and even into the twentieth. On the other hand, Churches of

Christ departed from that mainstream, as well as from the parent denomination, the Disciples, over these issues and, therefore, possessed little theological identity apart from their resistance to these "innovations."[3]

However, in 1964 David Edwin Harrell took sharp exception to this interpretation and rooted the division in social forces related to the Civil War. Noting that Churches of Christ in the early twentieth century resided overwhelmingly in the upper South and that Disciples in the same period centered in the Midwest, Harrell concluded that the genesis of Churches of Christ as a denomination separate from the Disciples must have been sectional. Thus, poverty versus affluence and rural versus urban biases, along with deep sectional feelings, were all tensions that divided the movement and helped produce Churches of Christ as a separate and distinct denomination. Thus, he concluded, "the twentieth-century Churches of Christ are the spirited offspring of the religious rednecks of the postbellum South."[4]

There is considerable truth both in the traditional reading and in Harrell's revisionist interpretation. At the same time, neither of these interpretations recognizes the pivotal role played by the separationist and apocalyptic tradition of Barton W. Stone in shaping Churches of Christ, much less the cultural split that undergirded the differences between the Campbellite and the Stoneite perspectives.

How might one describe that "cultural split"? On the one hand, the dominant outlook of antebellum America was a postmillennial perspective that celebrated unbounded human potential and unrestrained progress into the modern world. Those who held this viewpoint composed the "party of hope," perhaps best epitomized by Ralph Waldo Emerson. Further, many who held this position were primitivists who took their bearings from a mythic, primordial age—a point underscored by Major L. Wilson in a seminal essay published in 1961. As Wilson put it, "the politics of restoration was not . . . a conservative flight to the past," but instead a vision of primordial perfections that "made further progress possible."[5] Those who took this view were confident that, through their own efforts, they could recover the perfections of that primal age and project those perfections into the American future. They would therefore re-create, in their own time, the kingdom of God on earth.[6]

Those Americans who embraced the minority position, on the other hand, placed themselves in radical opposition to this perspective and generally affirmed a pessimistic and antimodern worldview that frequently turned out to be profoundly apocalyptic. Often Calvinists convinced of the radical sinfulness of humankind, these Americans formed the "party of memory," of which Emerson so loudly complained. Many of these members were also primitivists, but their skepticism regarding human potential and progress prevented them from easily projecting the perfections of the first age into an American future. Instead, these Americans often proclaimed their allegiance to a "kingdom of God" that they saw manifest in the primordium and that they anticipated would manifest itself again in the millennium, but only at God's initiative. They simply had no confidence that the kingdom of God could appear between those end times of God-directed, primal perfections. For these Americans, primitivism often took on distinctly antimodern dimensions.[7]

The division that finally produced Disciples of Christ on the one hand and Churches of Christ on the other, while rooted in a variety of factors, had its oldest and deepest roots in this ideological polarization. Indeed, the Disciples of Christ are the legitimate children of the postmillennial, modernizing progressivism of the mature Alexander Campbell—a man who represented the "party of hope" as fully as any man of his age. Churches of Christ, on the other hand, ultimately descend, at least in part, from the separatist, antimodern perspective of Barton W. Stone, who stood squarely in the "party of memory."[8]

Yet, it must be said that for all their mutual enmity, the party of hope and the party of memory shared significant common ground. The fact that nineteenth-century Americans often rooted progress in the perfections of the primal past helps us understand how the Campbell and Stone movements, embracing as they did such radically differing worldviews, could unite in 1832. Indeed, most in both groups were convinced that they shared common restorationist presuppositions. How different those presuppositions really were became evident as the nineteenth century wore on, slowly revealing the existence of two denominations, not one: the Disciples and the Churches of Christ.

Indeed, recognition of these two divergent traditions helps account for the North/South sectional alignment of Disciples and Churches of Christ. While Professor Harrell's "sectional origins" thesis helps account to a great degree for the sectional alignment of these traditions, that thesis still leaves much unexplained.[9] In the first place, if the identity of Churches of Christ was principally defined by southern sectional prejudices, why did these churches thrive only in a relatively small region of the South—in Tennessee, southern Kentucky, and northern Alabama, but hardly at all in the Deep South and the Southeast? Even more important, when the two major terms of the Stone-Campbell movement's agenda—unity and restoration—finally broke apart, why did the restoration ideal make its home chiefly among Churches of Christ in the upper South, while the unity theme made its home chiefly among Disciples in the Middle West?

On the other hand, taking seriously the differences between Stone and the mature Campbell helps clarify answers to these questions. From the earliest years of the nineteenth century, a major strand of the movement that would become Churches of Christ centered in the Cumberland Plateau of Tennessee, an area where the leadership of Barton W. Stone was pronounced. R. L. Roberts, in fact, has compiled a list of approximately two hundred preachers in the Cumberland area, all influenced either directly or indirectly by Barton W. Stone, who were actively establishing Churches of Christ long before the mid-1820s, when Campbell was first known in that region. From that time on, Campbell made occasional visits to middle Tennessee, but he preached mainly in cities and towns, leaving the sizable corps of Stoneite preachers to dominate the rural countryside.[10]

On the other hand, Campbell's visits to Kentucky—an early bastion of the Stone movement—were far more frequent than his visits to Tennessee, and his long-term influence centered, therefore, especially in Kentucky and points further north. It is hardly any wonder, then, that the strength of Disciples of Christ is especially pronounced to this day in the original Campbell heartland of Kentucky and the Middle West, while Churches of Christ find their greatest strength in the region bounded by the Cumberland Plateau on the east and Texas on the west.[11]

The story that follows is one of competing perspectives on the value of this world, human progress, and modernity. The story concludes, however, with profound irony, for while Campbell's early, sectarian view of both church and Scripture dominated Churches of Christ from the 1820s on, his optimistic assessment of this world and of human progress finally came to dominate them as well. This was a slow development, gathering momentum for over one hundred years. Finally, in the World War I era, Churches of Christ took a decisive turn away from the old Stoneite worldview, increasingly embracing Campbell's optimistic assessment of human progress. As a result, these churches became agents of modernization as fully as did Campbell's Disciples; the primitivism of Churches of Christ became, not a foe of modernization, but a pivotal support for that process; and the traditional Stoneite insistence on separation from the world finally became little more than sectarian exclusivism, calling only for separation from the surrounding denominations.

ALEXANDER CAMPBELL

Alexander Campbell exerted little or no influence on the sizable Stoneite communities of Kentucky, southern Ohio, and middle Tennessee—communities most often called Churches of Christ—until 1823, when he traveled to Kentucky to debate William L. McCalla. The Stoneites, whose insistence on Christian freedom had left them almost vacuous theologically, found compelling Campbell's clear and detailed exposition of the forms, structures, and practices of primitive Christianity.[12] From that time on, Campbell exercised a growing, and finally decisive, influence over Churches of Christ in that region. Indeed, in January 1832 the Stone and Campbell movements formally united in Lexington, Kentucky.[13]

For almost a decade prior to that union, Campbell had contributed to Churches of Christ a Common Sense view of the Bible drawn directly from Scottish Baconianism,[14] a clear and detailed description of those aspects of the primitive church that ought to be restored, and great confidence that human beings were fully capable of reading Scripture aright, implementing its divine patterns, and restoring in full the grandeur and beauty of the apostolic age.

Campbell's great confidence in human insight and human ability to bring about moral and spiritual reform stood at the intellectual heart of his movement and, more than anything else, distinguished his movement from that of Barton W. Stone. But Campbell also differed from Stone in his understanding of Christian primitivism. For this reason, Campbell's position can be designated "rational, progressive primitivism." Indeed, restoration for Campbell was not so much a response to the sovereign rule of God, understood in Calvinist terms, as it was a response to the authority of Scripture, understood in some respects as a technical, even scientific, manual for the recovery of primitive Christianity. Clearly, Enlightenment perspectives significantly shaped Campbell's restoration vision, which, when all was said and done, focused on progress toward the rule of God, aided by rational analysis and technical reconstruction of the first Christian age. Ultimately, a complete restoration of the apostolic institutions would transform human society and launch the millennial dawn.[15]

However, Campbell also was convinced that the millennium would be the fruit of rational and scientific progress and simply would not—and could not—begin until scientific progress had run its course, enlightening all humankind. He made this point abundantly clear in 1858 in response to claims that the revival of that year was the harbinger of the golden age. In rebutting this claim, Campbell argued for the following "incomparably paramount" consideration: "it was but yesterday that the mariner's compass was discovered, that printing was shown to be practicable, that steam power was laughed at as an absurdity, and the electric telegraph ridiculed as the hobby of a vagarian's brain . . . We have too much faith in progress . . . to subscribe to the doctrines of these theological gentlemen who hint the last days are at hand."[16]

But there was no exchange that more clearly illumined Campbell's postmillennial principles than his quarrel in 1833–34 with Samuel M. McCorkle. Profoundly pessimistic about human progress, McCorkle challenged Campbell's most fundamental presupposition regarding the possibility of recovering a golden age. "The present cannot be renovated," McCorkle complained. "No means on earth can bring or restore the administration back to primitive rectitude; it grows worse yearly in despite of all the efforts that can be made to heal."[17] Writing under the pseudonym "A Reformed Clergyman," Campbell was incredulous. Had not Bacon, Locke, and Newton inspired tremendous progress in politics and science? And what of the noble contributions of Luther, Calvin, and Zwingli? Beyond this, "the invention of gunpowder, the mariner's compass, the printing press, the discovery of America, the American Revolution—what have they wrought!!" Even Campbell's own movement might well launch "a restoration" that would "bless the world in ten thousand ways." A millennium would dawn, to be sure, and its driving force would be "knowledge, scientific, political, and religious."[18] To Campbell, the conclusion of the entire matter was clear: "This is, of all ages and of all generations, the most unpropitious for the assertion of the dogma that moral and intellectual means can benefit society in no very valuable nor permanent way. Almost every common newspaper presents insuperable difficulties to such a preposterous opinion."[19]

By 1844 McCorkle found refuge not in Campbell's *Millennial Harbinger* but in Barton W. Stone's *Christian Messenger*. Indeed, Stone opened to McCorkle the pages of the *Messenger* for a lengthy series of articles in which McCorkle launched a massive counterattack on Campbell's views. "*'Restoration of ancient order,'* is a pleasing *dream*—a brilliant phantom," McCorkle began in July, and he specifically called on Campbell to show how the "man of sin" might be destroyed by merely "moral means." By August, McCorkle took the gloves off and came out swinging. "Great names in the Christian church have vetoed the doctrine of a personal reign of Messiah and our credulous brethren following in the perilous *wake*! . . . Half inebriate with the *fumes* of Babylon, . . . [editors] are harping upon, "Christianity restored," when we are approaching *a time of trouble,* such as never was . . . Will they counteract by the "Ancient Order" the strong delusion that God has promised to send . . . ?"[20]

BARTON W. STONE

It is significant that McCorkle chose to publish these strictures in Stone's *Christian Messenger* and that Stone chose to print them. Perhaps even more significant is McCorkle's confession to Stone: "With the exception of yourself, I have the editorial corps [of the movement] against me." While Stone did not approve of all that McCorkle wrote,[21] he was profoundly sympathetic with McCorkle's pessimistic outlook on human potential and progress. Indeed, in spite of their rejection of Calvinist theories of conversion, Stone and his followers—most of whom came from Presbyterian or Baptist backgrounds—continued to nurture for many years a Calvinist assessment of human nature.[22] Stone typified most when he wrote, "That mankind are depraved, is a lamentable truth, abundantly attested by the word of God, and confirmed by universal experience and observation . . . All are in want of what they were made to enjoy, which is God; and have a propensity to satisfy that want with meaner things."[23]

Stone's followers generally joined to their Calvinist appraisal of human nature an experience of poverty and deprivation. John Rogers, one of the early Stone preachers in Kentucky, later recalled that the pioneers "were mostly men of small means" who "knew nothing of the luxuries and refinements of modern society." Isaac Jones recalled that all the preachers in middle Tennessee and south central Kentucky early on were "poor men, (some having no homes of their own) having but little education."[24] While Campbell preached in meetinghouses, Stone's early preaching is described as largely itinerant, being "done under an Elm and Oak" and "under a Beech Tree, covered with a summer grapevine." And if Campbell moved among the cultured and the sophisticated, the work of Stone and his colleagues was among rustic and unlettered frontier people whose religious practices were often both primitive and emotional.[25] Further, the Stoneites typically idealized poverty as a Christian virtue—a fact that stands in stark contrast to Alexander Campbell, who died the wealthiest man in West Virginia, having plowed an inheritance from his father-in-law into farming, land speculation, book publishing, and educational enterprises.

Finally, the Stoneites were every bit as utopian and restorationist as Alexander Campbell, but for them restoration had less to do with the forms and structures of the primitive church and more to do with lives of simple holiness.

These features, taken together, nurtured in Stone and his people a distinctly antimodern bias and helped sustain their apocalyptic outlook. That outlook, in turn, expressed itself in three specific ways: their insistence on a radical separation from the world; an eschatology that often manifested itself in premillennial terms; and their disdain for political involvement of any kind.

The theme of separation from the world abounds on almost every page of fourteen volumes of Stone's *Christian Messenger*, which ran from 1827 through 1844. Stone himself is a case in point. Aiming originally at a career in law, Stone abandoned that for a career in preaching. Then, when he and four other dissidents left the Presbyterian church in the aftermath of the Cane Ridge Revival, Stone voluntarily relinquished all salary and committed himself to a life of poverty in the interest of the kingdom of God. If Stone had a creed, he surely expressed it in 1841 when he admonished his readers "that you must not mind earthly things, nor set your affections on them—not to be conformed to the world . . . Here you have no abiding place, but are as strangers and pilgrims seeking a better country."[26]

All of this stands in remarkable contrast to the world Martha Wilson, a mountain girl from North Carolina, found at Campbell's Bethany College in 1858. Having accompanied her husband to Bethany, Martha wrote home to her Aunt Julia in Yadkinville that she and Virgil, her husband, had "had invitations to tea at Mr. Campbell's and most of the Professors. They are all very sociable and friendly but there are rather more grades and circles in society than I think ought to be in a Christian community." In another letter, she complained, "I do not like to visit here—the people visit too fashionably." Yet her husband was awed with the prospects facing Bethany graduates. He wrote, "Tell Uncle that a great many young men go out from college to teach, but owing to the reputation of Bethany for its instruction, they command enormous prices never less than $800. One young preacher has been offered $1500 in S. Virginia to preach for three churches."[27] Without a doubt, the issue of orientation toward the world was a clear line of demarcation that separated the basic worldviews of the Stone and Campbell movements.

The Stoneites' radical sense of separation from the world grew quite naturally from their apocalyptic orientation—an outlook that often gave expression to an explicitly premillennial eschatology. Indeed, millennial excitement was central to the Stone movement from its inception at the Cane Ridge Revival of 1801. John Dunlavy recalled after the revival that many thought "the day of the Lord, or Millennium, was at hand, and that that revival would never cease until that day should commence." Levi Purviance remembered that during the revivals "many were fully persuaded that the glorious Millennial Day had commenced, and that the world would soon become the Kingdom of our Lord Jesus Christ."[28]

Due to paucity of sources, however, it is difficult to trace the progress of Stone's millennial thought between the revivals and 1827, when he launched the *Christian Messenger*. However, by the early 1830s no one could doubt where he stood on the millennial question. One sample of his thinking—a reply to the Elder William Caldwell—will suffice: "The second coming of Christ is at the commencement of his millennial reign on earth—here on earth he will reign till the 1000 years be finished—nor will he cease to reign on earth till he has raised from death the wicked, and judged them according to their works."[29] While the Millerite excitement of the early 1840s exacerbated Stone's interest in this theme,[30] his convictions regarding the premillennial kingdom of Christ predated those events by many years.

It is precisely here, tucked away in the union of separationism and apocalypticism, that one finds the origin of a third theme central both to Stone and to a major stream in Churches of Christ for more than a century. This tradition held that civil government—including American democracy—was both demonic and illegitimate and that Christians should refuse all active participation in government and politics, including voting. In fact, the Stoneites generally thought, following Daniel's vision in the second chapter of Daniel, that the kingdom of Christ would, in the last days, fill the entire earth, destroy every human government—democracies along with monarchies—and rule the earth along with Christ for a thousand years. Once again, Stone is a case in point: "The lawful King, Jesus Christ, will shortly put them [human governments] all down, and reign with his Saints on earth a thousand years, without a rival . . . Then shall all man made laws and governments be burnt up forever. These are the seat of the beast . . . We must cease to support any other government on earth by our counsels, co-operation, and choice."[31] Based on this fundamental presupposition, the Stoneites time and again admonished one another to total noninvolvement in civil government other than paying taxes and obeying civil law—but only those laws that did not conflict with the kingdom of God.[32]

In this connection, it should be noted that the Stoneites' rejection of ecclesiastical societies (missionary, Bible, temperance, etc.) grew out of the same apocalyptic vision that governed their refusal to participate in civil government. God had ordained none of these societies, and his coming kingdom would destroy them, along with all human governments and institutions devised by men's wits. On this point, the Stoneites stood once again in marked contrast with the Campbell movement. Campbell also stood opposed to ecclesiastical societies during the early years of his career, but he based his opposition not on apocalypticism but on the biblical pattern. Further, Campbell abandoned his opposition in the 1840s and became president both of the American Christian Bible Society (1845) and the American Christian Missionary Society (1849).

Finally, since Daniel, chapter 2, was such an important text for the apocalyptic visions of Stone and his people, it is interesting to note that Campbell tamed that passage and placed its meaning squarely in the context of human history and progress. For Campbell, the little stone that would fill the entire earth was not the coming kingdom of God but rather the Protestant Reformation, and the image that the stone destroyed was not human government but the Roman Catholic church.[33]

The contrast between Campbell and Stone with reference to the restoration vision can now be sharpened. If Campbell's vision can be called "rational, progressive primitivism," it is equally proper to name Stone's vision "apocalyptic primitivism." This designation points to his apocalyptic worldview which undergirded and sustained his premillennial perspective and which, in turn, reflected his Calvinist sense of the sovereignty of God. This meant that Stone was not so much interested in the church as in the *kingdom,* that is, the rule of God over all human affairs. That rule, he felt, was manifest preeminently in the restored church but would be consummated only in the premillennial second coming of Jesus Christ. Between the times, Stone felt, the kingdom of God was a countercultural reality that stood in judgment on all rational, scientific, and technical progress and, indeed, on all human creations whatsoever.[34] More than anything else, this conviction formed the basis for Stone's antimodern bias. Further, this apocalyptic and countercultural perspective provided the mainspring not only for Stone but also for a sizable segment of Churches of Christ until well into the twentieth century, even when that mainspring joined itself to the biblicism of Alexander Campbell.

DAVID LIPSCOMB

The man who more than anyone else carried this tradition into the twentieth century was David Lipscomb. Clearly the most influential person among Churches of Christ from the close of the Civil War until his death in 1917, Lipscomb edited the immensely influential *Gospel Advocate,* based in Nashville, Tennessee, for most of those years.

There is no question that Lipscomb was, in many ways, a Campbellite, holding a profoundly rational view of Scripture and even turning Campbell's biblicism toward legalism. As editor of the *Advocate,* Lipscomb inevitably stood at the heart of the fights between Churches of Christ and Disciples of Christ over missionary societies, the propriety of instrumental music in worship, the role of women in the church, and basic attitudes toward Scripture. Further, it was Lipscomb who responded to S. N. D. North, director of the federal census of 1906, who thought he detected a major rupture in the Stone-Campbell movement. North was right, Lipscomb responded, and he urged him to list Churches of Christ completely separate from Disciples of Christ.[35]

Yet, if Lipscomb was a Campbellite who turned Campbell's own biblicism toward legalism, he also stood squarely and profoundly in the Stone tradition of separationism, apocalypticism, and apoliticism. It is difficult, if not impossible, to know all the sources for this emphasis in Lipscomb's thought. Given the pervasiveness of the Stone movement in middle Tennessee, Lipscomb could have been influenced by any one or combination of a number of Stoneite preachers. Undoubtedly, however, the critical link between Stone, a first-generation leader, and Lipscomb, a third-generation leader, was Tolbert Fanning, founding editor of several journals, including the *Gospel Advocate,* and the most powerful second-generation leader among mid-South Churches of Christ. He was also mentor to David Lipscomb. Fanning had been deeply influenced in his youth by three Stoneite preachers in northern Alabama: Ephraim D. Moore, James E. Matthews, and Ross Houston. From these men, especially Ephraim D. Moore, Fanning learned that "the Church of God is . . . destined, finally, . . . to triumph over all the powers of the earth."[36]

While apocalyptic in his thinking, however, Fanning was not premillennial. He did not expect the literal rule of Jesus on this earth, nor did he expect any sort of divine rule for a literal thousand years. Nonetheless, he did expect God's rule to be realized on this earth when the kingdom of God would finally triumph over the kingdoms of this world. Accordingly, Fanning—like Stone before him—advised his people not to vote and espoused a consistently pacifist position.[37]

However, Fanning's apocalyptic worldview was different from that of Stone in other ways, for Fanning had absorbed the rational and technical perspectives of Campbell in a way that Stone had not. The kingdom of God remained for Stone a transcendent reality, never fully actualized in the present world, always standing in judgment of human creations and institutions, and destined to be realized completely in this world only at the end of time. Fanning's extreme Common Sense rationalism, however, led him to particularize the transcendent in ways that had been foreign to Stone. In Fanning's view, the kingdom of God was, in fact, the Church of Christ of his own temporal experience in Tennessee and the mid-South, and he wrote numerous articles explaining and defending this church to outsiders.[38]

The countercultural dimensions of Stone, therefore, while still alive in Fanning at one level, gave way at another level to sectarian exclusivism. Indeed, while it may appear that the increasingly dominant influence of Alexander Campbell in the Cumberland region simply obscured the old Stoneite worldview, this is not the case. Instead, Tolbert Fanning and his comrades, beginning in the late 1830s and 1840s, reshaped the Stoneite vision to make it more compatible with the sectarian vision of the early Alexander Campbell. Separation from the world, therefore, increasingly came to mean for Fanning and many of his generation simply opposition to the surrounding denominations.[39] For the remainder of the nineteenth century, more and more members of the Churches of Christ conformed themselves to this sectarian understanding, lost their apocalyptic orientation, and reconciled themselves to participation in the American political system. In this way, Fanning helped subvert the antimodern impulse in Stone and opened the way for the full-blown acceptance of the modernity and modernization that would occur among Churches of Christ in the early twentieth century.

There were some, however, who kept alive the original Stoneite vision, and none were more important in this regard than David Lipscomb. In part because he had been mentored by Tolbert Fanning, Lipscomb stood squarely in the two worlds of Alexander Campbell and Barton Stone. He therefore embraced in his own person both the drive toward modernization and a distinctly antimodern impulse.

Nonetheless, his success in combining the Campbell and Stone perspectives into a single outlook is a major reason for his tremendous power and influence throughout the increasingly heterogeneous fellowship of Churches of Christ. Had Lipscomb focused exclusively on the rational and legal side of Alexander Campbell, he would have alienated those whose roots ran deeply into the separationist piety of Barton Stone. And had Lipscomb focused only on the apocalyptic, separationist heritage of Stone, he would have alienated the legalists whose roots reached into the rationalism and biblicism of Campbell. Lipscomb's genius lay in the way he coherently combined these two perspectives into one. Further, Lipscomb was the last major leader in the history of Churches of Christ to combine these two perspectives successfully. Following his death in 1917, the mainstream of Churches of Christ increasingly relegated the apocalyptic and antimodern perspectives of the Stone movement to the status of heresy and built their house instead on the world-affirming foundation laid by Alexander Campbell, buttressed by the rational, legal, and technical themes that grew from

Campbell's biblicism. Lipscomb stands, therefore, as a pinnacle in the history of Churches of Christ, looking backward to both Stone and Campbell and forward to a monolithic Church of Christ that would expel Stone's apocalyptic antimodernism from its agenda.

Nonetheless, in his lifetime Lipscomb was an articulate proponent of the Stoneite worldview. In the years immediately following the Civil War, Lipscomb published a series of articles on the Christian's relation to the world and especially to civil government and, in 1889 he gathered these articles into a small book that received wide circulation among Churches of Christ. He called the book *Civil Government,* and a year after its publication he judged that "nothing we ever wrote so nearly affects the vital interests of the church of Christ and the salvation of the world as this little book."[40]

Lipscomb began with the Stoneite conviction that the Christian belongs to a kingdom ruled by God, not to the kingdoms ruled by humankind.[41] From this basic premise flowed the same themes that had characterized Stone: separation from the world, apocalypticism, and apoliticism.

Separation from the world meant for Lipscomb, first of all, reliance on the sovereign power of God. It was here that he found human institutions so objectionable. Indeed, the very existence of human institutions and governments represented for Lipscomb a profound departure from God's primordial design. In *Civil Government* Lipscomb argued that, from the beginning, God intended to be sovereign over all the earth. His sovereignty, in fact, formed the very essence of the Garden of Eden before the Fall. But "the act [by Adam and Eve] of . . . disobedience culminated in the effort of man to organise a government of his own, so that he himself might permanently conduct the affairs of earth, free from . . . God's government." This rejection of God's sovereignty meant for Lipscomb that humanity had transferred its allegiance from God to Satan. This, for him, was the meaning of Satan's statement to Jesus that all the kingdoms of earth "were delivered to me." For Lipscomb, then, human government was nothing less than Satan's dominion in rebellion against God.[42] Ever since humanity's rejection of God's government, Lipscomb claimed, God's intent had been to restore his sovereignty over the earth. This was the point of the Jewish wars against the Canaanite tribes. "The work to which they were called was a war of extermination against all people maintaining a human government." Again, God attempted a restoration with the advent of Jesus Christ into the world. At one level, Jesus' mission succeeded because he conquered "death and hell and the grave." At another level, however, Jesus' mission failed because it ultimately failed to destroy sin and rebellion.[43]

Precisely here Lipscomb introduced the same apocalyptic themes that characterized both Barton Stone and Tolbert Fanning before him. The day would come, Lipscomb claimed, when God would reestablish his sovereignty over all the earth and destroy all human governments, the best along with the worst. Like Stone and Fanning, Lipscomb also rooted this vision in Daniel, chapter 2: "The end of all the conflicts and strifes of earth will be the complete and final destruction, the utter consuming of the last vestige of human governments and institutions, and the giving of the dominion, and power, and authority of the whole earth to the people of the saints of the Most High . . . All these kingdoms are to be broken in pieces, and consumed[,] . . . but the little stone cut out of the mountain without hands is to become a great mountain, and fill the whole earth." Further, these themes for Lipscomb were the very "key notes . . . of the Old and New Testaments." Without them, the Bible was "without point of meaning."[44]

At this point, Lipscomb differed significantly, however, from his mentor, Tolbert Fanning, who had particularized the transcendent and had virtually identified the eschatological kingdom of God with the Church of Christ. Lipscomb agreed that when God established the church, he also reestablished his kingdom, rule, and authority. However, the kingdom of God in its church form was by no means the same as the eschatological kingdom that would break in pieces all the kingdoms of the earth. Lipscomb made this point abundantly clear in a key article he wrote in 1903 on "The Kingdom of God": "The kingdom in its present stage is not called 'the everlasting kingdom,' but it will grow into it. It is the same kingdom in a lower stage of growth and development." In *Civil Government* he spoke of the church as the present manifestation of the coming kingdom of God. Like Stone before him, Lipscomb could not imagine final human perfection between the times of primordium and millennium.[45]

Clearly, Lipscomb's apocalypticism embodied a profound eschatological expectation that governed his worldview. But was Lipscomb also premillennial? This question is important since premillennialism became such a pivotal issue for Churches of Christ during the first half of the twentieth century, and since Lipscomb's position on that issue was so hotly disputed following his death.

If by premillennial one means that when Jesus returns he will reign on the throne of David in Jerusalem for a literal thousand years, then Lipscomb apparently did not fit the description. In the first place, Lipscomb displayed little or no interest in the role of Israel and the throne of David in the millennial age. In the second place, Lipscomb always spoke of the kingdom of God "fill[ing] the whole earth, and stand[ing] forever."[46] The millennium for Lipscomb, therefore, was not a thousand-year interlude but rather the eternal rule of God on this earth.

However, if one means by premillennial simply that Jesus' return to earth will precede and inaugurate this final golden age, then Lipscomb clearly advocated a premillennial position. One finds glimpses of this position in an assortment of articles Lipscomb wrote for the *Gospel Advocate* over a period of years. For example, in 1878 Lipscomb commented favorably on the First American Bible and Prophetic Conference, convened at the Holy Trinity Episcopal Church in New York City in October of that year.[47] The speeches of the conference, he noted, focused on "the idea of the re-appearance of the Savior before and preparatory to the advent of the millenium [sic]," and he commended those speeches as doing "honor to the word of God." While Lipscomb was not then certain whether Christ's "coming precedes or succeeds the conversion of the world to God," he urged his readers to acquire copies of the speeches by writing to the *New York Tribune,* cautioning only that no one make this topic "a hobby to disturb the peace of churches."[48] Later in the century, Lipscomb spoke explicitly of a "reign of Jesus on earth" and declared that "'the times of restoration of all things' must be when Jesus returns again to earth—the restoration of all things to their original relation to God."[49]

Further, there can be no doubt that the millennium Lipscomb envisioned was a literal kingdom on this earth. Thus, for example, he spoke clearly of "the glorious millennial morn" in connection with "the re-establishment [of] the kingdom of God on earth." Again, he wrote, "the one purpose of God was to re-establish his authority and rule on earth." Or again, "This earth in the material, moral and spiritual world must become a garden of God's own planting." Further, to those who asked regarding God's rule on earth, "How would the mails be carried? How could the affairs of Railroads, Manufactures, and the many large corporations . . . be managed?" Lipscomb simply replied, "We will cheerfully commit the adjustment and management" of these things to God.[50]

Many in Lipscomb's circle shared these basic positions, though with differences in emphasis. James A. Harding, cofounder with Lipscomb of the Nashville Bible School, first president of that institution, and coworker with Lipscomb on the *Gospel Advocate,* candidly and explicitly advocated a view much more in keeping with classic premillennialism: "When the saints are caught up to meet him, Christ comes with them to earth . . . Satan is then caught, chained and cast into the abyss . . . [where] he is confined for one thousand years . . . [while] Christ and his saints reign; but the rest of the dead live not until the thousand years have expired. This, the resurrection of the righteous, is the first resurrection." Others in Lipscomb's circle revealed time and again, often in an offhanded way, their premillennial assumptions. For example, when answering a question from a reader of the *Gospel Advocate,* E. G. Sewell simply assumed a millennium bounded by a "first resurrection" of the righteous and a "second resurrection" when "the thousand years of peace are finished." Phillip S. Fall—contemporary of Stone in Kentucky, close friend of Campbell, relative of Tolbert Fanning, and preacher for the Church of Christ in Nashville from 1858 to

1877—wrote to Mrs. Alexander Campbell: "In regard to the pre-millennial advent, the New Testament . . . impresses me with the hope that this earth . . . is to be the home of the righteous I can conceive of no higher ideal of heaven than that [we] will dwell together with him . . . in this renovated spot."[51]

Finally, Lipscomb and those in his circle strongly resisted elaborating on their premillennial perspectives and engaging in speculation regarding "what the millennium is or when it begins or ends."[52] They refused to speculate on the millennium because they did not wish to press beyond what they viewed as the bounds of Scripture. Further, they did not argue or debate the premillennial question simply because it was not an issue. Rather, it was a working assumption, one that characterized many in the Tennessee, Kentucky, and Alabama Churches of Christ from the days of Stone throughout the nineteenth century. In spite of all this, historians generally have failed to see that Lipscomb was premillennial at all.[53]

The third component in Lipscomb's antimodern outlook was his rigorous pacifism and his refusal to vote or otherwise participate in civil government.[54] "The mission of the kingdom of God is to break into pieces and consume all these kingdoms, take their place, fill the whole earth, and stand forever," Lipscomb declared. "How [then] could the individual citizens of the kingdom of God found, enter into, and become part and parcel of—upbuild, support, and defend, that which God's kingdom was especially commissioned to destroy?" In this, Lipscomb by no means stood alone, for many premillennialists of his era embraced the same antipolitical posture and for precisely the same reasons. The Presbyterian dispensationalist James Brookes, for example, suggested that "those who are dead to the world and alive to Christ should avoid the polling place, because 'dead men do not vote.'"[55]

On the other hand, in perpetuating the old Stoneite worldview, Lipscomb stood fundamentally at odds with the Disciples of Christ of the late nineteenth century who perpetuated the Campbellite assessment of the world, modernity, and human progress. If Lipscomb had thought that the kingdom of God would "break into pieces" all the kingdoms of this earth, the editor of the Disciples-oriented *Christian Oracle* argued for "a very intimate relation between the advancing influence of Christian nations and the advancement of the kingdom of God." J. C. Tully typified the Campbellite/Disciples faith in progress when he asked, "Will the earnest desire in the hearts of men for freedom from the shackles of the past ever fade away and die?" and then rejoiced: "Never, never, no never. The forces are going forward, not back . . . So rapidly has the spirit of the age come upon us, that it may be affirmed of a truth: We are not in the same world, although on the same planet, with those who lived in the last century. We live in the age of progress in civilization and in all things which, in human judgment, minister to its perfection."[56] These two opposing worldviews stood, in many ways, at the heart of the debates over missionary societies and instrumental music in the late nineteenth century and finally contributed to the emergence of two well-defined denominations: Churches of Christ and Disciples.

Indeed, when one understands Lipscomb's commitment to "the kingdom of God," one then can understand the genius of his restoration vision and why he took the positions he did on music, societies, and a host of other issues. If one imagines Lipscomb simply a legalist, committed only to restoring the forms and structures of the primitive church, then one has missed the heart of David Lipscomb. Lipscomb was a legalist, to be sure, but his legalism pointed beyond itself in two directions. First, it pointed to Eden before the Fall, when God's sovereign rule prevailed in sublime perfection. Second, it pointed to God's inevitable, final, and future rule over all the earth, when the perfections of Eden would be restored.[57] In between these times of perfection, the church was the finite manifestation of God's kingdom on earth. Moreover, because the restoration of the primordial and Edenic rule of God was absolutely certain, Christians must therefore live their lives and order their churches according to God's law in its every detail. In this sense, Lipscomb's efforts to restore biblical forms of worship and biblical patterns of church organization all pointed beyond themselves to the restoration of the kingdom of God in "the glorious millennial morn."

When this becomes clear, one also begins to see how Lipscomb could hold together in a single movement the modernizing heirs of Alexander Campbell and the antimodern heirs of Barton W. Stone. The heirs of Stone fully understood the apocalyptic context of Lipscomb's legalism and his ethics. For them, rejecting instrumental music in worship and refusing to vote were two sides of the same apocalyptic coin. On the other hand, those who rooted their legalism in the biblicism of Alexander Campbell could simply ignore Lipscomb's apocalyptic thrust as well as his position on civil government. If Lipscomb wanted to refuse to vote, that was an idiosyncrasy they could tolerate. For them, it was enough that Lipscomb railed against departures from the "ancient order" among the emerging Disciples of Christ.

During Lipscomb's lifetime, however, more and more of his people exchanged the antimodern, apocalyptic vision of Stone for the rational, progress-oriented outlook of Alexander Campbell. Symptomatic of this shift was Lipscomb's lament in 1880 that a majority of the readers of the *Gospel Advocate* did not share his antipolitical position.[58] Those who made this shift would form the vanguard of Churches of Christ in the twentieth century. On the other hand, many who continued to hold the apocalyptic, antimodern, and apolitical perspectives of Stone, Fanning, and Lipscomb would be cast from the mainstream as heretics.

POSTSCRIPT: THE R. H. BOLL AFFAIR

Beginning in 1915 and continuing for one-third of a century into the 1940s, the emerging mainstream of Churches of Christ launched a sustained and, at times, ferocious attack against premillennial eschatology. The chief object of this attack for all those years was a German immigrant named Robert H. Boll, who enrolled in 1895 in the Nashville Bible School in Nashville, Tennessee. There he studied under James A. Harding and David Lipscomb, from whom he learned the separationist and apocalyptic perspectives that had energized many in Churches of Christ throughout the nineteenth century. Stridently antimodern, Boll questioned whether "the boastful splendor of the twentieth century" and "the roar of its civilization" represented any serious progress at all. When the United States entered World War I in 1917, Boll counseled Christians to refuse to fight. He dismissed the notion that the war was "a struggle . . . to make the world safe for democracy," grounding his counsel in the Stone-Lipscomb vision that the Christian simply does not belong to the kingdoms of this world.[59]

There is no question that Boll had learned his apocalyptic lessons from his teachers at the old Nashville Bible School, especially David Lipscomb and James A. Harding. At the same time, however, he expanded those themes to include the dispensationalism of protofundamentalists like Dwight L. Moody, Arno Gaebelain, Isaac M. Haldeman, Philip Mauro, James M. Gray, Reuben Torrey, W. E. Blackstone, and Cyrus I. Scofield—an outlook foreign to the nineteenth-century apocalyptic tradition of Churches of Christ.[60]

The battle against Boll marked the beginning of a great war on premillennialism that preoccupied and sapped the energies of preachers and editors in the emerging mainstream of Churches of Christ well into the 1940s. The question is, Why? Why the concern to destroy the premillennial sentiment when the mainspring of the Stone side of Churches of Christ had been anchored to a profoundly apocalyptic worldview that often had borne premillennial fruit throughout the nineteenth century? To call this turn of events ironic is, if anything, an understatement.

One is tempted to suggest that Churches of Christ made war on R. H. Boll because Boll had adopted a dispensational position with which Churches of Christ were largely unfamiliar. To some degree, that is true. The explanation is inadequate, however, both because dispensationalism was by no means the principal target of attack and because Churches of Christ rejected not just dispensationalism but the entire apocalyptic frame of reference.

Two reasons for this dramatic turnabout seem clear. First, Boll's premillennial outlook completely undermined the fundamental identity of Churches of Christ that prevailed in the early twentieth century—namely, the common conviction that Churches of Christ were identical, in all essential respects, to the churches of the apostolic age. Some, like Tolbert Fanning, Arthur Crihfield, and John R. Howard, had held this viewpoint since the late 1830s and early 1840s, but it blossomed in the early twentieth century as never before. This development was due in part to the fact that, between roughly 1880 and 1906, Churches of Christ passed through a bitter division with Disciples of Christ, who retained, in most locales, both the buildings and the majority of wealthy and influential members, especially in urban settings. In effect, Churches of Christ were left to begin all over again. Angered and defensive, Churches of Christ increasingly embraced the conviction that they, and they alone, were the true church, descended from the days of the apostles.

Boll's premillennial outlook, however, stood altogether at odds with this position. Boll argued, in fact, that the church most assuredly was *not* the kingdom of God in its fullness of perfection, either in its Pentecost beginnings or in its modern manifestation. Instead, that kingdom would come only in the last days, when Christ would rule the earth with his saints. In the meantime, the church was a manifestation of that kingdom but was in no sense perfect or complete. J. C. McQuiddy, publisher of the *Gospel Advocate,* typified the mainstream response when he charged that Boll's doctrine "belittles the church of Christ." Similarly, N. B. Hardeman complained that premillennialism made "the church of Christ absolutely an accident."[61]

Moreover, Boll provided a concrete demonstration of his own rejection of the sectarian exclusivism of Churches of Christ when he routinely ran articles from early fundamentalists like Gaebelain, Mauro, Torrey, and Blackstone on the pages of his journal, *Word and Work*. While most in the emerging mainstream of Churches of Christ sympathized with the fundamentalists' fight against modernism, they nonetheless stood separate and apart from the formal fundamentalist movement for two reasons. First, they viewed the various denominations that fundamentalism represented as false churches. Second, they opposed the premillennial sentiments held by many in the fundamentalist camp as simply unbiblical. Typically, therefore, they viewed Boll's fraternization with fundamentalists as nothing short of scandalous.

Also prompting the loss of apocalypticism among Churches of Christ in the early twentieth century was a constellation of factors surrounding World War I. Popular pressure on all Americans to support the war was overwhelming, and Churches of Christ felt the pressure intensely. In the first place, support for the war was an obvious way for Churches of Christ to lift themselves from the position of social marginality that they occupied as a result of their rupture with the Disciples. In the second place, the U.S. government brought tremendous pressure on Churches of Christ to abandon their pacifist position in the interest of patriotism. The U.S. Attorney General for middle Tennessee, for example, threatened J. C. McQuiddy, publisher of the *Gospel Advocate,* with arrest if he continued to publish articles judged "seditious" and that discouraged "registration of young men under the Selective Service . . . Act." McQuiddy responded by halting all promotion of pacifism and all criticism of militarism on the pages of the *Advocate*. One observes among Churches of Christ from that date forward a gradual disintegration of the pacifist sentiment until, by the early 1960s, pacifism had almost entirely vanished from this fellowship.[62]

One witnesses the erosion during this period of not only pacifism but also the basic Stone-Lipscomb worldview that sustained the pacifist sentiment. Humpty Dumpty–like, the themes of apocalypticism, separation from the world, and reliance on the power of God rather than on human wit and ingenuity all took a great fall, and all the preachers and all the editors would never be able to piece them together again with any semblance of coherence. In fact, for the most part, no one tried.

Thus, for example, while Stone, Fanning, and Lipscomb had held that human institutions were impotent to renovate the world and that God, at his initiative alone, would bring the millennial dawn, M. C. Kurfees now suggested that the League of Nations might well do God's bidding. "Who knows," he wrote, "but . . . [that the League's] adoption may be a long step toward the glad time when the nations shall beat their swords into plowshares, and their spears into pruning hooks'; and when 'nation shall not lift up sword against nation, neither shall they learn war any more.'" Moreover, if Stone, Fanning, and Lipscomb had embraced a fundamentally pessimistic view of human potential and progress, it was precisely that pessimistic outlook that the editors of the *Gospel Advocate* now sought to undermine. "It is not Christlike, it is not manly, it is not noble," McQuiddy complained in 1919, "to sit down and whine that it is impossible to bring about such a condition [as the end of all war]. The same spirit would never have broken the Hindenburg line; the same spirit would never have conquered Germany and made her sue for peace . . . The same spirit will never overcome the world, the flesh, and the devil, and bring the crown that is sure to come to the faithful." Indeed, most *Advocate* editors no longer perceived tension between human civilization and the gospel. Instead, Western civilization was the fruit of the gospel. "Our civilization is its offspring," declared A. B. Lipscomb in 1914.[63]

If the "Boll issue" during World War I represented a rite of passage from Stoneite apocalypticism to Campbellite progressivism, Boll himself served as a surrogate target in the place of David Lipscomb. After all, Lipscomb was the "editor-bishop,"[64] a legend in his own time. No one dared attack David Lipscomb before his death or even for the twenty years following—no one, at least, who cared about his or her standing in the Churches of Christ. Further, almost no one was willing to recognize that Boll's teachers at the old Nashville Bible School— Lipscomb and James A. Harding—were chiefly responsible for Boll's apocalyptic worldview. Instead, Boll's opponents repeatedly charged that Boll derived his theology—lock, stock, and barrel—from Charles Taze Russell, founder of the Watch Tower Bible and Tract Society. This tactic clearly was an effort to discredit Boll, who denied any connection with Russell time and again.[65]

However, Lipscomb would not be able to escape attack forever. Indeed, by World War II, many who sought to accommodate themselves to modernity saw in Lipscomb and his theology a clear and obvious impediment to that transition. So long as his perspective was alive and well, Churches of Christ simply would be unable to join the modern world. Further, twenty years and more had elapsed since Lipscomb's death. The "modernists," therefore, imagined it was now safe to attack Lipscomb himself.

The man who more than anyone else engineered that attack was Foy E. Wallace, perhaps the most powerful person in Churches of Christ from the 1930s through the 1950s. A Texan, Wallace edited the *Gospel Advocate* from 1930 to 1934; he established his own paper, the *Gospel Guardian,* in 1935 for the express purpose of destroying premillennialism among Churches of Christ; and he founded yet another paper in 1938, the *Bible Banner,* where he launched stinging attacks on both premillennialism and pacifism.

Wallace's fundamental objection to premillennialism was the standard complaint that it undermined the restoration of true, apostolic Christianity and therefore also the identity and integrity of Churches of Christ. "The [Boll] theory," Wallace charged, "makes the church an accident, . . . the result of a prophetic default; a mere afterthought."[66]

Wallace himself had been a pacifist prior to World War II, but he underwent a conversion to militarism apparently due to Japan's attack on Pearl Harbor in December of 1941.[67] He immediately launched a withering attack on pacifists in Churches of Christ, labeling them as "men with a dwarfed conscience" and "freak specimen[s] of humanity."[68]

In 1942 Wallace opened the pages of the *Bible Banner* to an attack on David Lipscomb himself. W. E. Brightwell fired the first shot, noting that the pacifists in the church were only "those who have attended certain schools or have read a certain book [Lipscomb's *Civil Government*]." Brightwell simply could not fathom Lipscomb's claim that human government was the domain of Satan. "The purpose of civil government is good," he countered. "The devil does not have anything to do with it. The Lord does."[69]

Brightwell's comments reflect the extent to which World War I had indeed separated Churches of Christ from their nineteenth-century intellectual underpinnings. He, along with many others in Churches of Christ in this period, displayed a complete inability to fathom the Stone-Fanning-Lipscomb position that human institutions were flawed to the core. To the contrary, government was good, especially the government of the United States. Minor defects may have existed, but the notion that government was fundamentally flawed, due to human sin, was for these moderns pure myth.

Perhaps no one reflected this new perspective more completely than did O. C. Lambert, who imagined government bad only if it did bad deeds. "I have been living sometime and the United States government has never persecuted me for my religion," Lambert crowed. "If that is the way the devil resists the church it seems to me he is wonderful." Lambert was simply incredulous that Lipscomb would make "the devil . . . the head of the United States government." Indeed, Lambert rightly pointed out, "Lipscomb recognizes no difference in the kingdoms. The United States government is just as bad as the rest. The government that gives so much freedom to Christians is no better than one that persecutes them."[70] Lambert simply stood amazed.

Though Lambert himself had earlier accepted Lipscomb's positions, he now announced, "I lose faith in the Lipscomb Lion and Lamb story!" Further, he felt certain that "the Lipscomb book would be outlawed now if the FBI knew its contents," and he encouraged Churches of Christ to "call all of them [copies of *Civil Government*] in and burn them."[71]

By October 1943 Wallace himself joined the attack and focused on the foundational apocalyptic perspectives of Lipscomb's *Civil Government*. "In looking back over the years in which this book and others like it were circulated among the brethren, it is not hard to see how the theories of Premillennialism found soil to grow among churches of Christ." Moreover, he rightly observed that "premillennialism calls for the very things that are taught in 'Civil Government' by David Lipscomb. The two theories go together; they fit each other perfectly." For these reasons, Lipscomb's book was "about as rank with false doctrine as one book of its size could be," and Wallace expressed shame "that any recognized leader in churches of Christ, past or present, should espouse and promote such a doctrine" as that taught by David Lipscomb.[72]

By 1949, when Wallace discontinued the *Bible Banner*, premillennialism—along with the entire apocalyptic worldview—was a lost cause among Churches of Christ except for a group of congregations loyal to this position and centered in and around Louisville, Kentucky, and New Orleans. Further, Wallace and his followers had convinced most members of mainstream Churches of Christ that premillennialists were badly deceived and perhaps even somewhat evil. Indeed, as early as 1944 E. R. Harper rejoiced that "R. H. Boll has been fought by every paper, pulpit, preacher and most schools," and that he and his people had been rejected "as unsound and therefore have been 'marked and avoided' by the church in general." He added, "The papers no longer allow him space to write his views and the pulpits are closed to him, . . . and most schools will not allow him to enjoy their fellowship."[73]

By World War I, no one represented the old nineteenth-century "party of memory" more fully than did fundamentalists. Alienated from the modern world; suspicious of urbanization; resistant to the massive influx of immigrants foreign to the white, Anglo-Saxon, Protestant worldview; hostile to the intellectual developments of modernity, especially evolution, biblical criticism, and the scientific study of religion, fundamentalists yearned for an America of memory—or, perhaps, for a mythic America that never existed at all. The tension between these yearnings and the reality of modernity helped foster among many fundamentalists a premillennial eschatology that summoned the judgment of God on the kingdoms of this world. For the most part, however, the rest of America was marching triumphantly into the modern age, fighting a war to end all wars and making the world safe for democracy.

Given their nineteenth-century apocalyptic underpinnings, one would think that Churches of Christ would have stood shoulder to shoulder with fundamentalists, hurling judgment on proponents of modernity. It is true that Churches of Christ, due to their biblical primitivism, were deeply sympathetic with the biblicism of the fundamentalist movement. Yet, their exclusivism prevented them from formally joining the fundamentalists, and in their defense of human progress and their strident stand against apocalypticism, Churches of Christ unwittingly allied themselves with modernists with whom, ironically, they shared considerable common ground. Indeed, in opposing the apocalypticism of R. H. Boll, Churches of Christ joined hands with liberals like George Eckman, Shailer Mathews, Shirley Jackson Case, James Snowden, and George Preston Mains who were determined to drive premillennialism from America's churches.[74] In opposing Boll, Churches of Christ finally opposed the one person in their fellowship most in tune with the fundamentalist outlook and most at odds with the modernist worldview. Moreover, in opposing Boll, Churches of Christ separated themselves once and for all from the "party of memory" and aligned themselves decisively with the modernist "party of hope."

Even more, however, in opposing R. H. Boll and driving him from their fellowship, Churches of Christ brought to completion a shift in understanding of the restoration ideal that had been in process for at least a hundred years. Indeed, the anti-Boll and anti-apocalyptic crusade among Churches of Christ meant—at long last—that the *rational, progressive primitivism* of Alexander Campbell, fully in tune with the spirit of modernity, had emerged victorious over the antimodern, *apocalyptic primitivism* of Barton W. Stone. In fact, it was only when Churches of Christ finally and decisively cut themselves loose from their nineteenth-century apocalyptic underpinnings that they could become friends of the modern world and allies of progress. From that time on, the mainstream of Churches of Christ faced itself in a decidedly modernist direction though, ironically, still professing its allegiance to a primitivist worldview.

NOTES

1. Poverty was not the defining factor in the 1830s, but it was important. Later, in the South, the Civil War helped to enhance the sectarian outlook, as Prof. David Edwin Harrell has amply documented. See Harrell, "The Sectional Origins of Churches of Christ," *Journal of Southern History* 30 (Aug. 1964): 261–77.

2. While Alexander Campbell never claimed, even during the *Christian Baptist* period, that the movement he led comprised the one and only true church, much of his early rhetoric pointed in that direction. By the late 1830s, Crihfield and Howard, in particular, were defending the Church of Christ as the one true church. For Crihfield and Howard, see Richard T. Hughes and C. Leonard Allen, *Illusions of Innocence: Protestant Primitivism in America, 1630–1875* (Chicago: Univ. of Chicago Press, 1988), 128–31.

3. This historiographic perspective has been shaped chiefly by historians writing from within the Disciples of Christ side of this movement. See, e.g., W. E. Garrison and A. T. DeGroot, *The Disciples of Christ: A History* (St. Louis: Christian Board of Publication, 1948), 404–6; and William E. Tucker and Lester G. McAllister, *Journey in Faith: A History of the Christian Church (Disciples of Christ)* (St. Louis: Bethany Press, 1975), 251–54. Most major histories of American religion rely on precisely this interpretation. See, e.g., Sydney E. Ahlstrom, *A Religious History of the American People* (New Haven: Yale Univ. Press, 1972), 822–23; Edwin S. Gaustad, *A Religious History of America*, rev. ed. (San Francisco: Harper and Row, 1990), 258; and Winthrop S. Hudson, *Religion in America: An Historical Account of the Development of American Religious Life*, 4th ed. (New York: Macmillan, 1987), 260 n. 25. Interestingly, the only text to date whose chief interest is a synthetic history of Churches of Christ employs the same interpretive assumptions but for opposite purposes. Thus, Earl I. West argues that "by 1906 . . . the 'Christian Churches' or 'Disciples of Christ,' as they preferred to be called, took their instruments and their missionary societies and walked a new course." See *The Search for the Ancient Order*, 2 vols. (Indianapolis: Earl West Religious Book Service, 1950), 2:448.

4. Harrell, "Sectional Origins," 264, 277. See also David Edwin Harrell, *Quest for a Christian America: The Disciples of Christ and American Society to 1866* (Nashville: Disciples of Christ Historical Society, 1966); and David Edwin Harrell, *The Social Sources of Division in the Disciples of Christ, 1865–1900* (Atlanta: Publishing Systems, 1973). Bill J. Humble shared the view that the Civil War, with its attendant social factors, played a significant role in dividing the Disciples into two separate communions. See B. J. Humble, "The Influence of the Civil War," *Restoration Quarterly* 8 (fourth quarter 1965): 245.

5. Major L. Wilson, "Paradox Lost: Order and Progress in Evangelical Thought of Mid-Nineteenth-Century America," *Church History* 44 (Sept. 1975): 352–54. R. W. B. Lewis made the same point when he argued that "the more intense the belief in progress toward perfection, the more it stimulated a belief in a present primal perfection." See *The American Adam: Innocence, Tragedy, and Tradition in the Nineteenth Century* (Chicago: Univ. of Chicago Press, 1955), 5. Richard Hofstadter concurred in *The Progressive Historians:*

Turner, Beard, Parrington (New York: Vintage Books, 1970), 7, arguing that American progress often was progress backward to "the primitivist sense of the ideal human condition." There was by no means consensus in antebellum America on the specific content of the primordial age.

6. Clearly, many of the Transcendentalist communal experiments reflected this outlook. Thus, Bronson Alcott saw America as the site of "the second Eden," in which humankind might be restored to "rightful communion with God in the Paradise of Good." See Clara E. Sears, *Bronson Alcott's Fruitlands, with Transcendental Wild Oats by Louisa Alcott* (Boston: Houghton Mifflin, 1915). John Humphrey Noyes imagined that the millennial age in which he lived, patterned after the perfections of the primitive church, would sustain not only social relationships free from selfish pride but even the scientific breeding of the perfect human being. See Maren Lockwood Carden, *Oneida: Utopian Community to Modern Corporation* (Baltimore: Johns Hopkins Univ. Press, 1969; reprint, New York: Harper and Row, 1971), 12–13. Similarly, the humanitarian crusade aimed at nothing less than the complete elimination of evil from the social fabric of American life.

7. Why, in an age dominated by postmillennial dreams and anticipations, would this minority voice exist at all? In the first place, Calvinism—with its emphasis on the sovereignty of God and the fallenness of humankind—led some to view with profound suspicion the assumption that human beings might create, through their own efforts, the kingdom of God on earth. In the second place, many who embraced such skepticism were people estranged from the progress and optimism of the age by social and economic circumstances. Thus, many found in William Miller's prediction that Christ would return in 1843 meaningful compensation for economic losses occasioned by the depression of 1837.

8. Almost alone among historians, Martin Marty recognized that the division between Disciples and Churches of Christ was finally a division between modernism and primitivism. See *Modern American Religion*, vol. 1, *The Irony of It All, 1893–1919* (Chicago: Univ. of Chicago Press, 1986), 163–64. Marty's account does not recognize, however, that this ideological split was rooted in the differing worldviews of Alexander Campbell and Barton W. Stone.

9. Professor Harrell does speak of the "divided mind" of the movement. Thus, he writes: "two distinct emphases emerged. One group conceived of Christianity in the denominational framework of practical religion, social and political activism, and, often, a nationalistic postmillennialism. A second group emphasized the sectarian tradition of Biblical legalism, a fanatical disposition, and uncompromising separation from the world" (*Quest for a Christian America*, 66). However, Harrell does not recognize that, among the various roots of the sectarian side of the movement, the Stoneite tradition played a prominent role, nor does he emphasize the apocalyptic dimensions that often accompanied the sectarian phase of the movement, especially in the South.

10. R. L. Roberts, "Early Tennessee and Kentucky Preachers," unpublished paper.

11. For delineation of the sectional alignments of Disciples and Churches of Christ in 1906, see Harrell, "Sectional Origins," 263–64. By 1950 Disciples of Christ had their

greatest strength in the five states of the original Campbell heartland—Kentucky, Ohio, Indiana, Illinois, and Missouri—and in Texas, with slightly lesser strength in Iowa, Kansas, and Oklahoma to the west and in Virginia and North Carolina to the east. See Edwin S. Gaustad, *Historical Atlas of Religion in America* (New York: Harper and Row, 1962), 65. On the other hand, by 1960 Churches of Christ were especially concentrated in middle and western Tennessee, northern Alabama, Arkansas, Oklahoma, and Texas. See Edwin S. Gaustad, "Churches of Christ in America," in *The Religious Situation: 1969*, ed. Donald R. Cutler (Boston: Beacon Press, 1969), 1030–31. Both Disciples and Churches of Christ by the mid-twentieth century had significant strength in southern California, a phenomenon explained by westward migration patterns.

12. See Hughes and Allen, *Illusions of Innocence*, 115–16.

13. See Dean Mills, *Union on the King's Highway: The Campbell-Stone Heritage of Unity* (Joplin, Mo.: College Press, 1987).

14. See Samuel Morris Eames, *The Philosophy of Alexander Campbell* (Bethany, W.Va.: Bethany College, 1966), esp. 19–32, and Robert F. West, *Alexander Campbell and Natural Religion* (New Haven: Yale Univ. Press, 1948), 220–21, 225.

15. On Campbell's postmillennialism, see West, *Alexander Campbell and Natural Religion*, 163–217; and Carl Wayne Hensley, "The Rhetorical Vision of the Disciples of Christ: A Rhetoric of American Millennialism" (Ph.D. diss., Univ. of Minnesota, 1972).

16. Campbell, "The Millennium," *Millennial Harbinger*, 5th ser., no. 1 (June 1858): 335–36.

17. S. M. McCorkle, "Signs of the Times," *Millennial Harbinger* 4 (Oct. 1833): 483.

18. A Reformed Clergyman, "The Millennium—No. 3," *Millennial Harbinger* 5 (Oct. 1834): 549; "The Millennium—No. 7," *Millennial Harbinger* 6 (Mar. 1835): 105; and "The Millennium—No. 8," *Millennial Harbinger* 6 (Apr. 1835): 148.

19. A Reformed Clergyman, "The Millennium—No. 3," *Millennial Harbinger* 5 (Oct. 1834): 549–50.

20. S. M. McCorkle, "Conversion of the World, No. 4," *Christian Messenger* 14 (July 1844): 70–71; and "Conversion of the World—No. 4 [sic]," *Christian Messenger* 14 (Aug. 1844): 97–98.

21. S. M. McCorkle, "The Laymen [sic]," *Christian Messenger* 13 (Mar. 1844): 349.

22. See Newell D. Williams, "Barton W. Stone's Calvinist Piety," *Encounter* 42 (autumn 1981): 409–17; and Hughes and Allen, *Illusions of Innocence*, 112–16.

23. B. W. Stone, "A Compendious View of the Gospel," in *The Biography of Eld. Barton Warren Stone, Written by Himself* (Cincinnati, 1847), reprinted in Hoke S. Dickinson, ed., *The Cane Ridge Reader* (Paris, Ky.: Cane Ridge Preservation Project, 1972), 191–92.

24. John Rogers, "Funeral Discourse on Elder H. Dinsmore," *American Christian Review* 6 (Sept. 17, 1863): 181; and Isaac N. Jones, "The Reformation in Tennessee," included in J. W. Grant, "A Sketch of the Reformation in Tennessee," c. 1897, typescript, 35, manuscript housed in Center for Restoration Studies, Abilene Christian Univ., Abilene, Tex.

25. Grant, "A Sketch of the Reformation in Tennessee," 9–10; compare with Jones, "The Reformation in Tennessee," 31–32, and Joseph Thomas, *The Life of the Pilgrim Joseph Thomas* (Winchester, Va., 1817), 124, 160, 162–63, and passim.

26. Stone, *Biography*, 49–50, and "Christian Union. Lecture III," *Christian Messenger* 11 (May 1841): 316–17.

27. Martha Wilson to Aunt Julia, Bethany, Va., July 21, 1858, in Jones Family Papers, Southern Historical Collection, Wilson Library, Univ. of North Carolina, Chapel Hill; Martha Wilson to Aunt Julia, Bethany, Va., Sept. 11, 1858, and postscript, Martha Wilson to Aunt Julia, Bethany, Va., July 21, 1858.

28. John Dunlavy, *The Manifesto, or a Declaration of the Doctrine and Practice of the Church of Christ* (New York, 1847), 437; and Levi Purviance, *The Biography of Elder David Purviance* (Dayton, Ohio, 1848), 248–49. See also B. W. Stone and others, *Observations on Church Government, By the Presbytery of Springfield*, 1808, in Dickinson, *The Cane Ridge Reader*, 12.

29. B. W. Stone, "To Elder William Caldwell," *Christian Messenger* 8 (May 1834): 148; see also B. W. Stone, "The Millennium," *Christian Messenger* 7 (Oct. 1833): 314; and B. W. Stone, "Reply," *Christian Messenger* 7 (Dec. 1833): 365–66.

30. See B. W. Stone, "The Signs of the Last Days," *Christian Messenger* 12 (Aug. 1842): 301–6; B. W. Stone, "Signs of the Last Days—continued," *Christian Messenger* 12 (Oct. 1842): 363–67; and B. W. Stone, "The Coming of the Son of God," *Christian Messenger* 12 (Apr. 1842): 166–70.

31. B. W. Stone, "Reflections of Old Age," *Christian Messenger* 13 (Aug. 1843): 123–26. See also B. W. Stone, "Civil and Military Offices Sought and Held by Christians," *Christian Messenger* 12 (May 1842): 201–5; letter to T. P. Ware and letter from T. P. Ware, *Christian Messenger* 14 (Oct. 1844): 163–71; and "An Interview between an Old and Young Preacher," *Christian Messenger* 14 (Dec. 1844): 225–300.

32. See James M. Mathes, "Number III," *Christian Messenger* 10 (May 1836): 65–66; and Jn.T. Jones, Jno. Rigdon, M. Elder, and D. P. Henderson, Committee, "Report," *Christian Messenger* 9 (Nov. 1835): 250–51.

33. Alexander Campbell, "American Christian Missionary Society President's Address," *Millennial Harbinger*, 4th ser., no. 2 (Mar. 1852): 124.

34. Most contemporary historians have not come to grips with the profound difference between Stone and Campbell regarding the restoration ideal. This is not surprising, for they also have failed to take seriously the apocalyptic worldview of Stone. David Edwin Harrell's work is a case in point. Harrell argued that Stone and Campbell alike were committed to a "spirit of moderation" and to postmillennial visions of social progress. Harrell, *Quest for a Christian America*, 36, 41, 45. Indeed, "prior to 1830, both [men] . . . linked their religious reform efforts with the eventual spiritual and social regeneration of the world." Interestingly, the one passage from Stone that Harrell cited to support this claim finds Stone arguing just the reverse, vehemently criticizing the postmillennial vision and contending that

"God would overturn, and overturn, and overturn, till Messiah shall reign alone, and all submit to his government." Harrell, *Quest for a Christian America*, 41. The passage Harrell cites from Stone is from "Remarks on Liberty of Conscience," *Christian Messenger* 3 (Feb. 1829): 91. Harrell did recognize that "the sectarian emphasis of nonparticipation in civil government centered around the influence of Barton Stone in the early years of the church," but he never connected that emphasis either with Stone's apocalyptic, countercultural worldview or with the very same perspective one finds later in both Tolbert Fanning and David Lipscomb. Harrell, *Quest for a Christian America*, 54–55.

35. David Lipscomb, "The 'Church of Christ' and the 'Disciples of Christ,'" *Gospel Advocate* 49 (July 18, 1907): 457.

36. Fanning, see James R. Wilburn, *The Hazard of the Die: Tolbert Fanning and the Restoration Movement* (Austin, Tex.: Sweet Publishing, 1969; repr., Malibu, Calif.: Pepperdine Univ. Press, 1980). On Fanning's debt to Moore, Matthews, and Houston, see Wilburn, *Hazard*, 13–16; and Tolbert Fanning, "Obituary," *Gospel Advocate* 6 (Jan. 1860): 31. On Fanning's early apocalypticism, see Tolbert Fanning, "Ministers of Peace in the World's Conflicts," *Gospel Advocate* 7 (Nov. 1861): 347–48.

37. See Tolbert Fanning, "Reply to Brethren Lillard, Harding, and Ransome," *Gospel Advocate* 7 (Sept. 1861): 265–76; "The Church of Christ in Prophecy No. 2," *Religious Historian* 2 (Feb. 1873): 40–44; "Political Strife amongst Christians," *Christian Review* 1 (Aug. 1844): 184–85; "'The Kingdom of Heaven': A Spiritual Empire," *Christian Review* 3 (May 1846): 101; and "Peace," *Christian Review* 3 (Mar. 1846): 65.

38. Fanning, for example, ran an entire series of fourteen articles entitled simply "The Church of Christ" in the *Gospel Advocate* from October 1855 through December 1856.

39. Most notable among Fanning's colleagues in the 1840s who employed an apocalyptic worldview to undergird their sectarian exclusivism were Arthur Crihfield and John R. Howard. On both, see Hughes and Allen, *Illusions of Innocence*, 128–31.

40. Lipscomb, " Religion and Politics," *Gospel Advocate* 32 (March 26, 1890): 199.

41. Lipscomb, *Civil Government* (Nashville: Gospel Advocate Pub. Co., 1889), 13–14, 16–17, 88–89, 91, 92, 128, 145.

42. Lipscomb, *Civil Government*, 8–9, 48, 9–10.

43. Lipscomb, *Civil Government*, 14, 46–47; "The Kingdom of God," *Gospel Advocate* 45 (May 21, 1903): 328; and *Civil Government*, 51–53.

44. Lipscomb, *Civil Government*, 25, 27–28 (see also 83–84), 96.

45. Lipscomb, "The Kingdom of God," *Gospel Advocate* 45 (May 21, 1903): 328; *Civil Government*, 60.

46. Lipscomb, *Civil Government*, 28.

47. For this conference, see Timothy P. Weber, *Living in the Shadow of the Second Coming: American Premillennialism, 1875–1925* (New York: Oxford Univ. Press, 1979), 28.

48. David Lipscomb, "The Prophetic Conference," *Gospel Advocate* 20 (Nov. 21, 1878): 725.

49. David Lipscomb, "Queries," *Gospel Advocate* 37 (June 23, 1898): 397; and David Lipscomb, *Queries and Answers*, ed. J. W. Shepherd (Cincinnati: F. L. Rowe, 1918), 360.

50. David Lipscomb, *A Commentary on the New Testament Epistles: Ephesians, Philippians, and Colossians*, vol. 4, ed. J. W. Shepherd (Nashville: Gospel Advocate Co., 1939), 76; Lipscomb, *Civil Government*, iii, 28 (see also 12–13); and Lipscomb, *Civil Government*, 136.

51. James A. Harding, "The Kingdom of Christ versus the Kingdoms of Satan," *The Way* 5 (Oct. 15, 1903): 929-31; E. G. Sewell, "Queries," *Gospel Advocate* 37 (July 11, 1895): 437; and P. S. Fall, "Interesting Reminiscences" [letter to Mrs. Alexander Campbell], *Gospel Advocate* 21 (May 15, 1879): 310.

52. See David Lipscomb, "Queries," *Gospel Advocate* 40 (June 23, 1898): 397; and Sewell, "Queries," 437.

53. Three factors help account for this oversight. First, the tendency of Disciple historians to understand their movement principally in terms of Alexander Campbell's faith in progress has obscured not only the premillennial sentiments of Stone but also those of Lipscomb. Second, the fervent refusal, especially of Lipscomb and his circle, to speculate on the Second Coming has led some to assume that he simply had little or no interest in millennial themes. Thus, for example, David Edwin Harrell argued that Lipscomb was "persistently unwilling to discuss the subject," something Harrell attributes to the general decline of interest in premillennial themes dating from before the Civil War. Harrell, *Quest for a Christian America*, 44, esp. n. 68. Third, beginning with World War I, Churches of Christ launched a frontal attack on premillennialism that lasted fully one-third of a century. When that attack had run its course by the mid-1940s, most mainstream Churches of Christ had come to view premillennialism as a heresy. Historians working within the context of the church, therefore, might well have little inclination to discern the significance of such views among revered leaders such as Stone and Lipscomb. Thus, both of Lipscomb's biographers—Earl West and Robert Hooper—simply ignore the premillennial theme in Lipscomb. West identifies the "kingdom" with the "church" and simply fails to see the apocalyptic dimension in Lipscomb's thought. See West, *The Life and Times of David Lipscomb* (Henderson, Tenn.: Religious Book Service, 1954), 97–99. Hooper spiritualizes Lipscomb's notion of the kingdom, suggesting that a "perfect kingdom," in Lipscomb's view, "could not be attained in this world," but only "in the world to come." Hooper, *Crying in the Wilderness: A Biography of David Lipscomb* (Nashville: David Lipscomb College, 1979), 110–22, esp. 121.

54. Johnnie A. Collins has argued that Lipscomb's pacifism was principally a function of southern, post–Civil War sectionalism. Collins, "Pacifism in the Churches of Christ, 1866–1945" (Ph.D. diss., Middle Tennessee State Univ., 1984). That claim, however, is only partly true. In the first place, Lipscomb claimed that he arrived at these conclusions "early in life," long before the Civil War (*Civil Government*, iii). In the second place, to ascribe Lipscomb's position only to the war is to diminish the importance of a long intellectual tradition that began with Stone and of which Lipscomb was heir. On the other hand, it is clear that the Civil War drove Lipscomb to take the Stoneite tradition seriously in a way he had not before. Indeed, Lipscomb cast his vote in 1860 for John Bell, the presidential candidate of the Constitutional Union Party (*Gospel Advocate* 54 [August 22, 1912]: 954). But he never voted again after the war.

55. Lipscomb, *Civil Government*, 28 (see also 83–84 and iv); and James Brookes, "Gentile Dominion," *The Truth* 6 (1880): 536, cited in Weber, *Living in the Shadow of the Second Coming*, 92–93. Compare with J. J. Robinson, "Is Social Service Part of the Apostasy?" *Christian Workers Magazine* 14 (July 1914): 729–32, also cited in Weber, *Living in the Shadow of the Second Coming*, 92–93.

56. J. C. Tully, "The Divine Law of Expansion," *Christian Oracle* 16 (Jan. 18, 1899): 2; and J. C. Tully, "Responsibility of the Disciples of Christ to the Present Age," *Christian Quarterly Review* 4 (1885): 581–82. For a brief discussion of the doctrine of Anglo-American progress among Disciples at century's end, see Harrell, *The Social Sources of Division in the Disciples of Christ*, 23–25. Harrell also notes that some Disciples leaders joined a postmillennial faith in American progress to prophetic themes.

57. Lipscomb, *Civil Government*, 136–37, 53–56.

58. David Lipscomb, "Withdrawal," *Gospel Advocate* 22 (Sept. 16, 1880): 597.

59. Robert H. Boll, "What Shall the End Be?" *The Way* 2 (Apr. 1900): 60–61; and "The Christian's Duty as to War," *Word and Work* 11 (Dec. 1917): 493–94.

60. Evidence abounds for the influence of dispensationalists on Boll. See, e.g., R. H. Boll, "About Books," *Word and Work* 10 (Feb. 1916): 88; "Bible Study Course," *Word and Work* 10 (Jan. 1916): 28; and "Jesus Is Coming" *Word and Work* 10 (Dec. 1916): 551. On Boll's dispensationalism, see R. H. Boll, *The Kingdom of God* (Louisville: Word and Work, n.d.).

61. R. H. Boll, "Words in Season," *Word and Work* 10 (July 1916): 338–39, and "The Olivet Sermon," *Word and Work* 10 (Nov. 1916): 487–92; J. C. McQuiddy, "Do the Kingdom and the Church Mean the Same Thing?" *Gospel Advocate* 61 (Apr. 17, 1919): 367, and "Is the Church the Vestibule of the Kingdom?" *Gospel Advocate* 61 (Mar. 20, 1919): 271–72; N. B. Hardeman, *Hardeman's Tabernacle Sermons*, vol. 4 (Nashville: Gospel Advocate Co., 1938), 157.

62. F. W. Smith, "As a Matter of Simple Justice," *Gospel Advocate* 62 (Sept. 23, 1920): 931. Compare with J. C. McQuiddy, "Conscientious Objectors," *Gospel Advocate* 59 (July 26, 1917): 720–21.

63. M. C. K., "The League of Nations and the Peace of the World," *Gospel Advocate* 61 (Sept. 4, 1919): 866–67; J. C. M'Q., "The Peace League," *Gospel Advocate* 61 (Mar. 27, 1919): 297–98; and A. B. Lipscomb, "Is Orthodox Christianity Today a Waning Power?" *Gospel Advocate* 56 (Mar. 5, 1914): 282–83.

64. See Richard Hughes, "The Editor-Bishop: David Lipscomb and the *Gospel Advocate*," in *The Power of the Press: The Forrest F. Reed Lectures for 1986* (Nashville: Disciples of Christ Historical Society, 1986), 1–34.

65. See, e.g., Cecil Douthitt, "Russellism Alias Bollism," *Bible Banner* 1 (Sept. 1938): 13; and T. B. Wilkinson, "Heaven—the Kingdom—and Premillennialism," *Bible Banner* 6 (Nov. 1943): 11. But compare also R. H. Boll, "Studies in Prophecy: Some Distinctions between Russell's Teaching and Bible Doctrine," *Word and Work* 10 (July 1916): 312–15.

66. Foy Wallace, "What Is It All About—And What Difference Does It Make?" *Bible Banner* 1 (Nov. 1938): 7, and "The 'New Spiritual Contingent Called "The Church"'—or, the Prophecies and Promises of God," *Bible Banner* 1 (Aug. 1938): 3.

67. Foy Wallace, "The Government—Civil and Military," *Bible Banner* 4 (July 1942): 2; Glen E. Green, letter in "The Christian and the Government," *Bible Banner* 4 (July 1942): 7; and Cled Wallace, "What Pearl Harbor Did to Us," *Bible Banner* 6 (Nov. 1943): 1.

68. Foy Wallace, "The Christian and the Government," *Bible Banner* 4 (Mar. 1942): 8. Highly inflammatory, this article was unsigned. In July, however, W. E. Brightwell revealed that Foy Wallace had written the article using Brightwell's notes. W. E. Brightwell, "For the Vindication of the Cause," *Bible Banner* 4 (July 1942): 6.

69. Brightwell, "For the Vindication of the Cause," 5, 7.

70. O. C. Lambert, "The David Lipscomb Book," *Bible Banner* 7 (Sept. 1944): 9–10.

71. O. C. Lambert, "The Lipscomb Theory of Civil Government," *Bible Banner* 5 (Oct. 1943): 3, "The David Lipscomb Book," 15; "Canonizing Campbell and Lipscomb," *Bible Banner* 6 (May 1944): 10; and letter from Lambert in Foy Wallace, "The Lipscomb Theory of Civil Government," *Bible Banner* 6 (Oct. 1943): 3.

72. Foy Wallace, "The Lipscomb Theory of Civil Government," *Bible Banner* 6 (Oct. 1943): 6, "'The Glorious Millennial Morn,'" *Bible Banner* 6 (May 1944): 5, and "The Lipscomb Theory of Civil Government," *Bible Banner* 6 (Oct. 1943): 5.

73. E. R. Harper, "Is It the Truth—Or the Person?" *Bible Banner* 6 (Mar. 1944): 7.

74. George Eckman, *When Christ Comes Again* (New York: Abingdon, 1917); Shailer Mathews, *Will Christ Come Again?* (Chicago: American Institute of Sacred Literature, 1917), and *The Faith of Modernism* (New York: Macmillan, 1924); Shirley Jackson Case, *The Millennial Hope: A Phase of War-Time Thinking* (Chicago: Univ. of Chicago Press, 1918), and *The Revelation of St. John: A Historical Interpretation* (Chicago: Univ. of Chicago Press, 1919); James H. Snowden, *The Coming of the Lord: Will It Be Premillennial?* 2d ed. (New York: Macmillan, 1919), and *Is the World Growing Better?* (New York: Macmillan, 1919); and George P. Mains, *Premillennialism: Non-Scriptural, Non-Historic, Non-Scientific, Non-Philosophical* (New York: Abingdon, 1920). For a discussion of the modernist attack on premillennialism, see Weber, *Living in the Shadow of the Second Coming*, 117–21.

Part II

An American Movement

Section 1

Origins

The Christian Movement and the Demand for a Theology of the People

Nathan O. Hatch

In 1776 John Adams posed the question that would preoccupy his generation of American citizens and their children. "It is certain, in theory," he said, "that the only moral foundation of government is, the consent of the people. But to what extent shall we carry this principle?" The Revolution brought an accent of reality to a new self-evident truth, the sovereignty of the people, which Edmund Morgan has recently described as a "political fiction." For the Founding Fathers the fiction of popular sovereignty held some resemblance to the facts, but they fully expected the governed and the governors to "join in a benign conspiracy to suspend disbelief" in the new fiction, in other words, to believe it rhetorically rather than literally. The people were not so kind, however, and the shrill and unending debate that characterized American history from Adams to Andrew Jackson concerned how seriously this fiction should be taken.[1]

A number of scholars have recently explored the dimensions of this cultural ferment over the meaning of freedom. In the wake of their own and the French Revolution, Americans witnessed the rapid growth of voluntary organizations and popular newspapers, the formation of organized political parties amid heated and increasingly popular political debate, the armed protest of unprotected economic groups, sharp attacks upon elite professions and upon slavery, and new ideas of citizenship and representation, of old age and women's identity.[2] Eugene Genovese has even argued that a revolutionary ideology of liberty and equality transformed the character of slave resistance in North America and in the Caribbean.[3] Lamenting the awakening to political consciousness of the common man, Harrison Gray Otis gave to a Harvard audience in 1836 his view of what had happened since the Revolution: "Everywhere the disposition is found among those who live in the valleys, to ask those who live on the hills, 'How came we here and you there?' accompanied with intelligible demonstrations of a purpose in the former, to partake of the benefits of the mountain air."[4]

122 The Christian Movement and the Demand for a Theology of the People

What became of American religion in these years—roughly 1780 to 1820—when traditional values were being turned upside down by what Gordon S. Wood has called a "democratization of mind"?[5] Despite a wealth of recent scholarship on the role of religion in the coming of the American Revolution, surprisingly little work has been done on the changing nature of popular religion after the Revolution. This imbalance stems in part from the conventional division between the era of the republics founding and that of the middle period, but it also reflects the simple fact that a quickened interest in religion as a cultural force has emerged within a broader historiographical tendency to downplay the social impact of the Revolution. The result has been that while historians have noted many links between the Great Awakening and the Revolution, they have not followed through to ask how rapid social change in the young republic affected structures of religious belief and organization.[6] What happened when people began to call for a strenuous application of popular sovereignty to the church? What did Christian freedom come to mean for people ready to question any source of authority that did not begin with an act of individual choice?

To explore these questions, this essay will focus on the cultural roots of a movement that assumed the name "Christian" or "Disciples of Christ." Between 1790 and 1815 this loose network of religious radicals demanded, in light of the American and French revolutions, a new dispensation set free from the trammels of history, a new kind of institutional church premised on the self-evident principles of republicanism, and a new form of biblical authority calling for the inalienable right of common people to interpret the New Testament for themselves. The central figures in the reform movement—Elias Smith in New England, James O'Kelly in Virginia, Barton Stone in Kentucky, and Alexander Campbell in Pennsylvania—were a motley crew with few common characteristics, but they all moved independently to similar conclusions within a fifteen-year span. A Calvinist Baptist, a Methodist, and two Presbyterians all found traditional sources of authority anachronistic and found themselves groping toward similar definitions of egalitarian religion.[7] In a culture that increasingly balked at vested interests, symbols of hierarchy, and timeless authorities, a remarkable number of people would wake up one morning to find it self-evident that the priesthood of all believers meant just that—religion of, by, and for the people.

At the dawn of the nineteenth century, the Federalist citadel of Essex County, Massachusetts, witnessed a major assault on its well-bred and high-toned culture. Religious enthusiasm had taken hold among common people, and its rude challenge to authority dismayed even the tolerant Jeffersonian diarist William Bentley of Salem. As late as 1803, Bentley had confided smugly that Essex County remained virtually free of sects. During the next five years, he watched with dismay the lower orders of his community championing "religious convulsions," "domestic fanaticism," and "Meeting-Mania." In chronicling the parade of sects that won attention—Baptist, Freewill Baptist, Methodist, Universalist, and Christian—Bentley noted the first field meeting in the county since George Whitefield, preaching by blacks and illiterate sailors, and servants angering their employers by frequenting night lectures "as in Mother Hutchinson's time." What Bentley found most appalling was that "the rabble" not only noised abroad strange doctrine but actually went beyond what they were told, attempting "to explain, condemn and reveal" religious matters. The people, he groaned, were doing theology for themselves.[8]

Bentley saved his sharpest barbs for an itinerant preacher, the "notorious" Smith, who regularly barnstormed through Essex County, preaching in the open air, singing in the streets, and accosting people to question their spiritual state. If this was not enough to discomfit the respectable citizens of Salem, Smith kept the pot boiling by leaving behind bundles of his tracts and pamphlets.[9]

For all its parallels with the dissent of a Whitefield or an Isaac Backus, Smith's gospel for the people did have one different twist. It was laced with the language of politics and reflected the experience of a man whose radical pilgrimage began with a political conversion. Until 1800 Smith filled the pulpit of the respectable Baptist Church in Woburn, Massachusetts, and gave little attention to political questions of the day. During the election of 1800, however, he fell under the influence of the radical Jeffersonian publicist Benjamin Austin Jr., who wrote regularly for the *Boston Independent Chronicle*. Smith quickly imbibed Austin's heady wine, which made much of the right of common people to think and act for themselves. Resigning from his church—as a manifesto of his own liberty—and denouncing formal religion of every kind, Smith began to translate the sovereignty of the people to the sphere of religion.[10] "Let us be republicans indeed," he declared in 1809. "Many are *republicans* as to *government,* and yet are but half republicans, being in matters of religion still bound to a catechism, creed, covenant or a superstitious priest. Venture to be as independent in things of religion, as those which respect the government in which you live."[11] From Portsmouth, New Hampshire, Smith launched the first religious newspaper in the United States, a fortnightly *Herald of Gospel Liberty,* which he edited from 1808 to 1818. From that forum, and in scores of pamphlets and sermons, he and a band of fifty or so itinerants, who called themselves merely Christians, carried on a blistering attack upon Baptists, Congregationalists, Methodists, and Federalists of any religious persuasion. The *Herald of Gospel Liberty,* which by 1815 had fourteen hundred subscribers and more than fifty agents around the country, became a vehicle of communication for other individuals who were moving independently to the same conclusions as Smith.[12]

From Virginia came word of O'Kelly's Republican Methodists, founded in 1794 to undo the "ecclesiastical monarchy" in the Methodist church. A prime mover among early Virginia Methodists, O'Kelly could not abide the bishopric of Francis Asbury and withdrew with more than thirty ministers to form a connection that had as many as twenty thousand members when it merged with Smith's forces, under the name Christian, in 1809.[13] "Episcopacy makes a bad appearance in our republican world," O'Kelly argued in 1798. "Francis was born and nurtured in the land of Bishops and Kings and what is bred in the bone, is hard to get out of the flesh."[14] O'Kelly, who had taken up arms in the Revolution and served a brief stint as a British captive, argued that he was "too sensible of the sweets of liberty, to be content any longer under British chains . . . As a son of America, and a Christian," he challenged Asbury, "I shall oppose your political measures and contend for the Saviour's government. I contend for Bible government, Christian equality, and the Christian name."[15]

Stone was an equally interesting figure who had ventured upon much the same pilgrimage prior to the appearance of the *Herald of Gospel Liberty*. In 1802, in the wake of the Cane Ridge Revival in Kentucky, Stone decided he could no longer live under Presbyterian doctrine or church organization. A year later, he and five other ministers pushed this idea to its logical extreme and proclaimed that it was not just the Presbyterians who were wrong: all church structures were suspect. Signing "The Last Will and Testament of Springfield Presbytery," these men vowed to follow nothing but the Christian name and the New Testament.[16]

Scholars have generally viewed Stone's beliefs as the product of the rough-and-tumble context of the frontier and of the rampant emotionalism of the Great Revival.[17] Stone was a rawboned character, no doubt, but he also spent his formative years during the Revolution, and his theology of "gospel-liberty" reflected this early experience. "From my earliest recollection I drank deeply into the spirit of liberty," he confessed late in life, "and was so warmed by the soul-inspiring droughts, that I could not hear the name of British, or tories, without feeling a rush of blood through the whole system . . . I confess their magic influence to this advanced day of my life." It was not without deep connotation that Stone characterized his break with the Presbyterians as the "declaration of our independence."[18]

The final member of the quartet whose democratic theology this essay analyzes is the Scottish immigrant Alexander Campbell—the only college graduate among the four and the only one not to participate in the American Revolution.[19] Whatever Alexander Campbell may have brought to America of his Scottish and Presbyterian heritage, he found much of it convenient to discard for an explicitly American theology. Writing to his uncle back in Scotland in 1815, he described his seven years in the United States: "During this period of years my mind and circumstances have undergone many revolutions . . . I have . . . renounced much of the traditions and errors of my early education." He described the change elsewhere in these words: "My mind was, for a time, set loose from all its former moorings. It was not a simple change: but a new commencement . . . the whole landscape of Christianity presented itself to my mind in a new attitude and position."[20] By 1830 Alexander Campbell's quest for primitive Christianity led his movement, the Disciples of Christ, into union with Stone's Christians. By 1860 their denomination claimed about 200,000 adherents, the fifth largest Protestant body in the United States.[21] More important, for our purposes, his theology fell into an unmistakable pattern that was emerging in the early republic. Smith, O'Kelly, and Stone all knew what Campbell meant when he proclaimed that July 4, 1776, was "a day to be remembered as was the Jewish Passover . . . This revolution, taken in all its influences, will make men free indeed."[22]

In many ways the message of the Christians built upon the kind of radical piety that Americans had known since the Great Awakening of the 1740s. These new reformers hammered relentlessly at the simple themes of sin, grace, and conversion; they organized fellowships that resisted social distinctions and welcomed spontaneous experience; and they denounced any religion that smacked of being bookish, cold, and formal. What sets the Christians apart from earlier revivalists is the extent to which they wrestled self-consciously with the loss of traditional sources of authority and found in democratic political culture a cornerstone for new foundations. Taking seriously the mandate of liberty and equality, the Christians espoused reform in three areas. First, they called for a revolution within the church that would place laity and clergy on an equal footing and would exalt the conscience of the individual over the collective will of any congregation or church organization. Second, they rejected the traditions of learned theology altogether and called for a new view of history that welcomed inquiry and innovation. Finally, they called for a populist hermeneutic premised on the inalienable right of every person to understand the New Testament for themselves.

A zeal to dismantle mediating elites within the church, more than anything else, triggered the Christians' revolt against tradition. O'Kelly broke with Asbury when the Methodist bishop refused to put up with representative government in the church. Smith bade farewell to Backus and the Warren Association after influential colleagues criticized his plain dress and suggested that the respectable parishioners of Woburn, Massachusetts, deserved more decorum. Both Stone and Thomas Campbell—Alexander's father, who had preceded him to America—withdrew from the Presbyterians when their orthodox colleagues began to clamp down on their freedom of inquiry concerning Presbyterian standards. Before their respective separations, each of these men in his own way had offered stern opposition to received tradition; yet their dissent was contained within taken-for-granted cultural boundaries. Once they had severed organizational ties, however, mild questions reappeared as seething hostility, and suggestions for reform turned to ecclesiastical defiance.

The Christians excelled at popular communication. They ferreted out converts with an unremitting itinerancy and cranked out an avalanche of pamphlet and newspaper copy, which, in its form and content, conspired against social distinction.[23] Smith was aware of his innovative role when he began the first religious newspaper in the United States; he confessed on its opening page that the utility of such a paper had been suggested to him by the explosion of popular print all around. "In a short and cheap way," he asserted, "a general knowledge of our affairs is diffused through the whole." While his paper did include accounts of revivals of religion throughout the world, its overall strategy showed little resemblance to previous revival periodicals such as the *Christian History* of the Great Awakening, largely an intramural communication among the clergy. By promoting in common language the idea that *"right is equal among all,"* Smith knew that he would incur the judgment that he was "stirring up the people to revolt" and "turning the world upside down."[24] Just as he expected, the established clergy found his "vulgar stories and malicious sarcasm" totally beneath them, but they could hardly ignore the popularity of his "poisoned arrows of ridicule and reproach."[25]

The style of Smith's communication is well illustrated in one of his early pamphlets, *The Clergyman's Looking-Glass,* a stinging attack on men of the cloth that went through at least a dozen printings. Smith juxtaposed passages of the New Testament with satirical jibes at the contemporary clergy in mock-Scripture style. After quoting from I Peter the instructions that elders were to serve God's flock "not for filthy lucre . . . neither as being lords over God's heritage," Smith gave his Petrine rendition of the modern clergy:

> The reverend clergy who are with me I advise, who am also a clergyman, and a D.D. a member of that respectable body, who are numerous, and "who seek honor one of another;" and a partaker of the benefit of it; feed yourselves upon the church and parish, over which we have settled you for life, and who are obliged to support you, whether they like you or not; taking the command by constraint, for filthy lucre, not of a ready mind, as lords over men's souls, not as ensamples to them, and when commencement day shall appear, you shall receive some honorary title, which shall make you appear very respectable among the reverend clergy.[26]

In a similar vein, Alexander Campbell used his first newspaper, the *Christian Baptist,* to mock the pretensions of the clergy. In a burlesque "Third Epistle of Peter," a document reportedly discovered by a monk, he instructed preachers to live well, wear the best clothes, adorn themselves with high-sounding titles, drink costly wine, and fleece the people.[27] Evangelicals in the past had often questioned the spiritual state of individual clergymen; the Christians now took the liberty to slander the entire profession as money-grubbing tyrants.

This kind of billingsgate journalism employed two very powerful appeals. In the first place, it portrayed society as horizontally polarized: the people were arrayed against elites of all kind, military, legal, civic, and religious. In an early edition of the *Herald of Gospel Liberty,* Smith sketched a most revealing dialogue between the people and the privileged class. "The picture, is this: two companies standing in sight of each other, one large, the other small. The large containing every profession useful to society, the other small, wearing marks of distinction, appearing as though they did no labour, yet in rich attire, glittering with gold and silver, while their plump and ruddy countenances, prove them persons of leisure and riches." Seething with resentment, the people of Smith's dialogue happened to overhear what the privileged were saying to each other: "To mix and place ourselves on a level with the *common people,* would be beyond all measure degrading and vilifying. What! are they not born to serve us? and are we not men of a totally distinct blood and superior pedigree?" In response, the people insisted that they were going "to take the management of our affairs into our own hands . . . When the people declare themselves free, such privileged classes will be as useles[s] as candles at noonday."[28]

Abel M. Sargent, another radical figure associated with the Christians, used his paper, the *Halcyon Itinerary and True Millennium Messenger,* to present a virtual class analysis of society. Writing in 1807 to extol Thomas Jefferson as the forerunner of a new millennial age, Sargent demanded that life, liberty, and happiness be extended to "the oppressed who have been deprived of them." His images of society bristle with the ongoing conflict between the powerful and the oppressed: "How often do we see it the case in earthly courts, under the dominion of the beast, that the power and influence of money and false Agency overbalance equity and right; so that the poor have but a dull chance to obtain justice in carnal courts; and again, how often is the poor industrious and honest labourer, reduced to the absolute necessity of yielding up his rights and falling a prey to cruelty and injustice, merely for want of money enough to discharge the fees of those whose interest and livings (like the wolf and raven) depend on the ruin and destruction of others."[29]

For all its innovation, however, this bombast against the privileged also employed a second appeal. It appropriated the rhetoric of civil and religious liberty that the respectable clergy had made popular during the Revolution and marshaled it for an entirely new purpose, to topple its very architects. The Christians exploited to the hilt the potent themes of tyranny, slavery, and Antichrist; they delighted in regaling their audiences with the latest chapter in the saga of the beast and the whore of Babylon. Simply put, Antichrist now worked his evil machinations through elites of all kind, particularly the clergy. In a splendid example of the multivalency of language, rhetoric that had seemed benign when used by respectable clergymen during the Revolution came to have radical connotations when abstracted from a restricted context and transferred to people who had reason to lash out at vested interests.[30]

But what end did the Christians have in view when decrying ecclesiastical authority? What positive implications did they wring out of the notion of religious liberty? Smith came right to the point in an early issue of the *Herald of Gospel Liberty* when he contrasted the mere separation of church and state with "being wholly free to examine for ourselves, what is truth." He argued that every last Christian had the "unalienable right" to follow "the scripture wherever it leads him, even an equal right with the Bishops and Pastors of the churches ... even though his principles may, in many things, be contrary to what the Reverend D.D.'s call Orthodoxy."[31] Using the same language, Alexander Campbell pressed for "the inalienable right of all laymen to examine the sacred writings for themselves." Brimming with conspiratorial notions of how clergymen of every stripe had "hoodwinked" the people, this logic eventually led each of these Christian leaders to demand that the traditional distinction between clergy and laity be abolished and that any leadership in the local church function according to new rules: "liberty is no where safe in any hands excepting those of the people themselves."[32] With demands for this sort of liberation afoot, it is little wonder that Congregational and Presbyterian clergymen came to view the Christians as but another tentacle of the Bavarian Illuminati's conspiracy to overthrow authority in church and state.[33]

The Christian idea of religious liberty stands in marked contrast to the eighteenth-century notion that religious liberty meant the civil right to choose or not to choose affiliation with a church. The religious dissent that had come out of the Great Awakening, despite its popular sources, had never begun to suggest that power should be surrendered to the people in this fashion. The Baptists in Virginia set themselves off from the culture of gentlemen by striving for more order, more discipline, and more social control within the local congregation.[34] In New England, as well, Baptists and Separatists called for closed communion and a tighter discipline within the pure church. By the 1760s, they were educating their clergy, forming associations to regulate doctrine and local disputes, and, as their people began to drift away to other sects during the Revolution, actually imposing stiff creedal tests upon local churches. Backus did not long for some new order that leveled the clergy and exalted the laity; he reminisced, instead, about the pious fathers of early New England. He argued time and again that his Baptists agreed "with the most eminent fathers of New England, except in sprinkling infants upon the faith of their parents and calling it baptism."[35] The same point has been made about the Separatists of New England: "they were reformers, not rebels; . . . they wished to fulfill their history as Puritans, not repudiate it."[36]

In contrast, the Christians called for the abolition of organizational restraints of any kind. In the "Last Will and Testament of Springfield Presbytery," Stone and five colleagues dissolved their association, already a splinter group from the Presbyterian church. Only by renouncing all institutional forms could "the oppressed . . . go free, and taste the sweets of gospel liberty."[37] Alexander Campbell did not even want to hear the words *church government:* "We have no system of our own, or of others, to substitute in lieu of the reigning systems. We only aim at substituting the New Testament."[38] In a similar vein, Stone and his associates declared that the attempt "to impose any form of government upon the church . . . should be justly abandoned by every child of gospel liberty." They went on to say that any human form of government would be "like binding two or more dead bodies together" and coercing people "like parts of a machine."[39] The organization of Protestant churches, which in colonial culture had been seen as vibrant and alive—the very body of Christ—now smacked of being dead and mechanistic.

By their appeal to "Bible government," the Christians removed the issue of power and authority from any concrete application, They opposed all ecclesiastical names not found in the New Testament, advocated the right of the individual unilaterally to withdraw from church membership, and refused to adhere to creeds as tests of fellowship, to undergo theological examinations, or to offer a confession of faith upon joining a church. In short, no human organization could exist that did not spring from the uncoerced will of the individual. When pressed by Bishop Asbury to heed the scriptural injunction, "Obey them that have rule over you," O'Kelly responded: "Rule over, is no more than for the church to follow those guides who delivered unto them the Word of God." O'Kelly was suggesting that, by submitting to the New Testament, a Christian in 1800 never would have to doff his hat to any mere mortal.[40]

In a passing reference in *The American Revolution Considered as a Social Movement*, J. Franklin Jameson noted the growth in numbers and zeal of those religious bodies that were revolting against Calvinism—the Methodists, Universalists, Unitarians, and Freewill Baptists.[41] He might also have included the loose combination of mavericks that called themselves merely Christians. Except for O'Kelly, whose Methodist background made Calvinism a dead issue, the other primary figures in this movement—Smith, Stone, and Campbell—were all zealous Calvinists early in life and experienced a conversion to what they called gospel liberty.

On one level this revolt seems simple enough to understand. The heady concepts of liberty that had led to denunciations of institutional constraints also rendered meaningless such concepts as unconditional election and limited atonement. After great intellectual turmoil, each of these men came to the point of harmonizing theology with their social experience. As a Calvinist, Stone confessed that he was "embarrassed with many abstruse doctrines."

"Scores of objections would continually roll across my mind." What he called the "labyrinth of Calvinism" left his mind "distressed," "perplexed," and "bewildered." He found relief from this dissonance of values only as he came to attack Calvinism as falsehood.[42]

The revolt against Calvinism, however, becomes somewhat harder to understand when placed in its full context. The Christians were venting their hostility not against Calvinism in some narrow sense, as if they might find their niche as Methodists or Freewill Baptists, but against an entire system. "We are not personally acquainted with the writings of John Calvin," wrote Robert Marshall and John Thompson, two of Stone's colleagues, "nor are we certain how nearly we agree with his views of divine truth; neither do we care."[43]

This was no mere revolt against Calvinism but against theology itself. What was going on that gave Stone the audacity not only to reject the doctrine of the Trinity—Unitarians right and left were doing that—but also to maintain, "I have not spent, perhaps, an hour in ten years in thinking about the Trinity"? What made it credible for Smith, after seriously debating whether he would be a Calvinist or a Universalist, to remove the dilemma altogether by dropping them both? "I was now without a system," he confessed with obvious relief, "and felt ready to search the scriptures."[44] How could these men convince themselves, not to mention their followers, that the stage was set for a church without organization and a theology without theory?

Whatever else the Christians demanded, the rallying cry of their theological revolution was a new view of history. They called for a new dispensation of gospel liberty, radically discontinuous with the past. They advocated new theological ground rules that dismissed everything since the New Testament as irrelevant, if not destructive. What led Americans in the finest evangelical tradition of Jonathan Edwards, John Witherspoon, Backus, and Asbury to repudiate their heritage? Furthermore, what gave credence to the idea that they were standing on the brink of a new age?

One cannot understand the Christians apart from their deep conviction that they had witnessed in the American and French revolutions the most momentous historical events in two millennia—a *novus ordo seclorum*. The opening line of *the Herald of Gospel Liberty* proclaimed that "the age in which we live may certainly be distinguished from others in the history of Man," and Smith was quick to point out that it was the struggle for liberty and the rights of mankind that set it apart. According to Smith, the foundations of Christ's millennial kingdom were laid in the American and French revolutions. "The time will come," he said, "when there will not be a *crowned head* on earth. Every attempt which is made to keep up a Kingly government, and to pull down a Republican one, will . . . serve to destroy monarchy . . . Every small piece, or plan, of Monarchy which is a part of the image [of Antichrist] will be wholly dissolved, when *the people* are resolved to 'live free or die.'"[45]

The following year in Washington, Pennsylvania, Thomas Campbell published the first salvo of their movement and pointed to the same state of revolutionary and apocalyptic affairs: "Do ye not discern the signs of the times? Have not the two witnesses arisen from their state of political death, from under the long proscription of ages? . . . Who amongst us has not heard the report of these things—of these lightnings and thunderings, and voices, of this tremendous earthquake and great hail; of these awful convulsions and revolutions that have dashed and are dashing to pieces the nations like a potter's vessel?" In their view, such political convulsions spoke as the voice of providence "loudly and expressly calling us to repentance and reformation . . . Resume that precious, that dear bought liberty, wherewith Christ has made his people free; a liberty from subjection to any authority but his own, in matters of religion. Call no man father." Alexander Campbell argued that the War for Independence unveiled a new epoch that would deliver men from "the melancholy thraldom of relentless systems." America's "political regeneration" gave her the responsibility to lead a comparable "ecclesiastical renovation."[46] An expectancy and overt respect for novelty characterized the Christians, as Stone's two associates confessed: "We confidently thought that the Millennium was just at hand, and that a glorious church would soon be formed; we thought, also, that we had found the very plan for its formation and growth." Opponents of these men agreed, moreover, that a sense of apocalyptic urgency had fueled the movement from the start.[47]

If the age of democratic revolutions gave the Christians good reason to sever ties with the past, it also suggested egalitarian models for a new age. In describing the true gospel that would revolutionize the world, Alexander Campbell called it "the declaration of independence of the kingdom of Jesus." Smith and Stone chose the same term to describe their withdrawal from the Baptists and Presbyterians, respectively. Similarly, O'Kelly claimed that he broke with the Methodists because they left him no option but "unlimited submission" or separation.[48] The lengths to which they allowed political idioms to color their thinking are sometimes difficult to comprehend: for example, they referred to the early church as a republican society with a New Testament constitution. In 1807, however, one maverick Christian in Marietta, Ohio, outdid them all, claiming that "the great potentate of the world, in principle, is the most *genuine* REPUBLICAN that ever existed."[49]

From a modern viewpoint, it may seem odd that men so committed to the separation of church and state held up a given political structure as a model for the church. They endowed the republic with the same divine authority as did defenders of the Standing Order such as Timothy Dwight and Noah Webster, but for opposite reasons. The republic became a new city on a hill, not because it kept faith with Puritan tradition, but because it sounded the death knell for corporate and hierarchic conceptions of the social order. For these radical sectarians, the constitutional guarantees of separation of church and state laid the groundwork for a new age. In sum, a government so enlightened as to tell the churches to go their own way must have also had prophetic power to tell them which way to go.[50]

Millennialism, then, served different functions for the Christians from those that it had during the Great Awakening. Revivals of the 1740s drew upon millennial themes to challenge traditionalists in the name of a greater commitment to traditional values.[51] This sense of eschatological drama, furthermore, served to define an evangelical identity over against political culture. By contrast, the democratic ferment experienced by the Christians convinced them that, in thinking about the future, they should work to erase the memory of the past and should learn from political culture whatever they could about a gospel of equality.

The Christians expressed their revolt against history most clearly in the radical way they chose to read the Bible. Amid unraveling cultural norms, they clung tenaciously to one final, unassailable authority, the ipse dixit of the New Testament. The direct propositions of Scripture became the only ground of certainty. In a letter to the *Herald of Gospel Liberty* in 1809, seventeen Christian ministers spelled out this central plank of the Christian platform: "In consequence of your receiving Christ as only head, and ruler of his church, it necessarily follows, *that his law as contained in the New Testament,* should be received without any addition, abridgment, alterations, or embellishments, to the exclusion of all articles of religion, confessions of faith, creeds, &c. &c. &c. composed by men." "The New Testament has been as the law once was, *among the rubbish,"* proclaimed Smith. "Now we have found it, let us read it to the people from morning till evening."[52] These were fighting words, no doubt, to the genteel clergy, men accustomed to covenants being the linchpin of society and to thinking of America as the new Israel. But even more radical than dismissing the Old Testament as a priestly rag used to hoodwink the people was the approach that Christians used to interpret Scripture. "I have endeavored to read the Scriptures as though no one had read them before me," claimed Alexander Campbell, "and I am as much on my guard against reading them to-day, through the medium of my own views yesterday, or a week ago, as I am against being influenced by any foreign name, authority, or system whatever." Protestants had always argued for sola scriptura, but this kind of radical individualism set the Bible against the entire history of biblical interpretation. In this hermeneutic, no human authority, contemporary or historical had the right to advise the individual in his spiritual quest. In order to ward off any systematic theology, these men insisted that religious discussion be limited to Bible language, as Smith put it, "to prove every particular from plain declarations recorded in the Bible."[53]

This fresh hermeneutic had considerable appeal because it spoke to three pressing issues. First, it proclaimed a new ground of certainty for a generation perplexed that it could no longer hear the voice of God above the din of sectarian confusion. If people would only abandon the husks of theological abstraction, the truth would be plain for all to see. Second, this approach to Scripture dared the common man to open the Bible and think for himself. All theological abstractions—such as the trinity, foreordination, and original sin—were abandoned, and all that was necessary to establish a given point was to string together texts from the King James Bible. Any Christian using New Testament words could fend off the most brilliant theological argument by the simple retort that he was using God's word against human opinion. All the weight of church history could not begin to tip the scale against the Christian's simple declaration, say, that the New Testament did not contain the word *trinity*.

This approach had a third appeal—obvious success in befuddling the respectable clergy. Smith, O'Kelly, Stone, and Alexander Campbell were to a man brilliant theological debaters, but they refused to abide by the etiquette of the opposition. Their coarse language, earthy humor, biting sarcasm, and commonsense reasoning appealed to the uneducated but left the professional clergy without a ready defense. In a pamphlet written in 1817 to combat Smith's influence in Massachusetts, the Congregationalist Thomas Andros recognized the new tactics: "Ridicule, sneer, malignant sarcasm and reproach, are the armor in which he goes forth. On this ground, and not on sober argumentation, he knows the success of his cause depends . . . If he knows the doctrine of original sin is not true, let him sit down and write a manly and candid answer to President Edward's great work on that subject . . . Were he a dignified, candid, and intelligent controversialist, there would be enough to answer him, but who would wish to attack a windmill? Who can refute a sneer?" Andros also recognized that popularity rather than virtue was the clarion call of the movement: "They measure the progress of religion by the numbers, who flock to their standard; not by the prevalence of faith, and piety, justice and charity, and the public virtues in society in general."[54]

Other Congregationalists and Presbyterians, less sensitive to the new measures, continued to use the language of orthodoxy to lambaste the Christians as a new form of the threadbare heresies of Arius, Pelagius, and Socinius.[55] The Christians merely sidestepped these attacks by putting the disputed points before their followers and letting them choose between the language of Scripture and that of metaphysical subtlety. This democratic revolution in theology wrenched the queen of the sciences from the learned speculations of Harvard,

134   The Christian Movement and the Demand for a Theology of the People

Yale, and Princeton men and encouraged the blacksmith, cooper, and tiller of the soil not only to experience salvation but also to explain the process. Its genius was to allow common people to feel, for a fleeting moment at least, that they were beholden to no one and were masters of their own fate.

How does one explain the theology of the people that came to be championed between 1790 and 1815? What kind of cultural context gave rise to similar movements in New England, the South, and the Midwest? Many historians have imagined that these radical pietists simply continued a tradition of dissent that had rippled through American culture since the 1740s. Others have viewed the Christians as prophets of the American frontier, men who developed notions in keeping with the self-sufficient characters that pushed into the hill country of New England and made their way across the Appalachians. This was religion following the frontier par excellence. Still other scholars have linked the Christian movement to the general revolt against Calvinism that followed the American Revolution. Rigid notions of depravity and predestination simply could not stir a generation that had witnessed at home and abroad the electrifying effects of liberty and natural rights. All of these—the ongoing tradition of evangelical dissent, the surge westward after the Revolution, and the disdain for Calvinistic explanations of the world—figure importantly in any explanation of the Christian movement.[56]

Yet these points of reference fail to locate the most intimate link between the Christians and American culture at the turn of the eighteenth century: a pervasive collapse of certainty within popular culture. From the debate over the Constitution to the election of Jefferson, a new and explicitly democratic revolution united many who were suspicious of power and many who were powerless in a common effort to pull down the cultural hegemony of a gentlemanly few. In a complex cultural process that historians have just begun to unravel, people on a number of fronts began to speak, write, and organize against the authority of mediating elites, of social distinctions, and of any human tie that did not spring from volitional allegiance.[57]

This crisis of confidence in a hierarchical, ordered society led to demands for fundamental reform in politics, law, and religion. In each of these areas, radical Jeffersonians, seizing upon issues close to the hearts of the people, resurrected "the spirit of 1776" to protest the control of elites and the force of tradition. Rhetoric that had once unified people across the social spectrum now drove a powerful wedge between rich and poor, elite and commoner, privileged classes and the people. Federalists, members of the bar, and the professional clergy heard the wisdom of the ages ridiculed as mere connivances of the powerful to maintain the status quo.

The violence of politics from 1780 to 1800, more than anything else, gave sharp definition to egalitarian impulses in American society. From the Revolution onward, republican equality became a rallying cry for people seeking to challenge all sorts of political authority. Incidents in South Carolina, Massachusetts, and New York illustrate how thoroughly the "virtue" of subjection and deference was giving way to an itching, smarting, writhing awareness of inferiority. In 1784 the South Carolina legislature threatened William Thompson, a tavern keeper, with banishment from the state for insulting the eminent John Rutledge. Thompson responded with a newspaper article that blasted the claims of "self-exalted" characters like Rutledge who had "conceived me his inferior." Thompson refused to "comprehend the *inferiority*" and denied the right of a conspicuous few to speak for the people.[58] During the debate over the Constitution, Antifederalists turned repeatedly to such arguments. At the Massachusetts ratification convention, for example, the self-taught Worcester County farmer Amos Singletary denounced the Constitution as a plot to consolidate the influence of the great: "these lawyers and men of learning, and moneyed men . . . talk so finely, and gloss over matters so smoothly, to make us poor illiterate people swallow down the pill . . . They expect to be the managers of this Constitution, and get all the power and all the money into their own hands. And then they will swallow up us little fellows, like the great Leviathan."[59]

A decade later the urban democratic leader William Keteltas was able to shake Federalist control of New York City by a shrewd media campaign depicting politics as a clash between rich and poor. Keteltas made into a cause célèbre the case of two Irish-born ferrymen whom Federalist magistrates punished summarily for reportedly insulting one of their number. Keteltas dramatized the issue in the popular press and eventually came to attack the New York assembly for not impeaching the responsible magistrates. This led to his own arrest by the Federalist legislature on a charge of breach of privilege. When Keteltas appeared before the assembly, a crowd of several thousand gathered in protest. His release from a brief prison sentence prompted a grand celebration in which the people pulled Keteltas through the streets in a carriage decked with American and French flags, a cap of liberty, and a picture of a man being whipped with the inscription, "What you rascal, insult your superiors?" By championing the cause of the ferrymen—what Keteltas called "'the most flagrant abuse of [the peoples] rights' since Independence"—he effectively mobilized the common people of New York to challenge Federalist domination.[60]

Such repeated attacks on the capacity of a conspicuous few to speak for the whole of society struck at the root of traditional conceptions of society.[61] Extending the logic of Antifederalists, radical Jeffersonians came to ridicule the assumption that society was an organic hierarchy of ranks and degrees; they argued, rather, that it was a heterogeneous mixture of many different classes, orders, interest groups, and occupations. In such a society the elites could no longer claim to be adequate spokesmen for people in general. In this climate, it took little creativity for some to begin to reexamine the social function of the clergy and to question the right of any order of men to claim authority to interpret God's word. If opinions about politics and society were no longer the monopoly of the few, why could not anyone and everyone begin to think for themselves in matters of religion?

The 1790s also witnessed fundamental challenges to the legal profession and the common law. Richard E. Ellis has documented the strident attacks against the legal system that surfaced in the popular press and in serious political movements to reform the law in Kentucky, Pennsylvania, and Massachusetts.[62] Radical republicans such as Boston's Austin denounced the legal profession for needlessly confusing court cases in order to charge high fees, deliberately making the law inaccessible to laymen, bartering justice to those who could afford to pay, and monopolizing legislative and judicial posts.

Those who called for radical legal reform addressed three primary issues. First, they demanded a simplified and easily accessible legal process, "a system of laws of our own, dictated by the genuine principles of Republicanism, and made easy to be understood to every individual in the community."[63] Second, they attempted to replace the common law—authority by precedent—with fresh legal codes designed for the new republic. For many of these radicals, the common law conjured up images of complexity, mystery, intolerance, and bias in favor of the elite: "Shall we be directed by reason, equity, and a few simple and plain laws, promptly executed, or shall we be ruled by volumes of statutes and cases decided by the ignorance and intolerance of former times?"[64] Third, having jettisoned the "monkist priesthood" of lawyers and the "absurdity of the common law," those who sought root-and-branch reform exhibited great faith in the ability of ordinary citizens to ascertain and dispense justice before the law. "Any person of common abilities," said Austin, "can easily distinguish between right and wrong" and "more especially when the parties are admitted to give a plain story, without any puzzle from lawyers,"[65]

In retrospect, this faith in democratic, personalized, and simplified law appears hopelessly naive and utopian. Yet it reflects a moment of historical optimism, a time when many in politics, law, and religion, flushed with the promise of the American Revolution, found it reasonable to take literally the meaning of *novus ordo seclorum* and to declare a decisive expatriation from the past.[66]

That Smith came to jettison orthodox Calvinism through reading Austin's articles in the *Independent Chronicle* in 1799 and 1800 underscores the correlation between the Christian movement and reform efforts in politics and law.[67] In method, substance, and style, Smith championed the cause to which radical Jeffersonians were committed: an appeal to class as the fundamental problem of society, a refusal to recognize the cultural authority of elites, a disdain for the supposed lessons of history and tradition, a call for reform using the rhetoric of the Revolution, a commitment to turn the press into a sword of democracy, and an ardent faith in the future of the American republic. Smith's primary interest, of course, was the spread of evangelical religion; yet he could never divorce that message from the egalitarian principles that the frantic pace of the 1790s had made self-evident.

That other individuals came to advocate virtually identical reform is further evidence that questions were raging in popular culture that popular religion simply could not avoid. While other claims to truth also flourished in this atmosphere, the Christian movement stands out as an attempt to bring some harmony between denominational traditions and egalitarian values. In lashing out at the tyranny of the clergy, the foolishness of abstract theology, and the bondage of church discipline, the Christians fulfilled a mandate for reform that was widespread in popular culture. In exalting the idea that every man was his own interpreter, they brought a measure of certainty to people committed to the principle that all values, rights, and duties originate in the individual—the principle that Alexis de Tocqueville later called individualism.[68]

The legacy of the Christian movement is riddled with irony. Instead of taking America by storm, the Christian Connection under Smith and O'Kelly vanished into insignificance, while the Disciples in the West grew into a major denomination only by practicing the kind of organization they had once hoped to stamp out. Instead of calming sectarian strife and restoring Edenic harmony, the Christians engendered controversy at every step and had to put up with chronic factionalism within their own ranks.[69] Instead of offering a new foundation for certainty, the Christian approach to knowledge, which made no man the judge of another's conscience, had little holding power and sent many early advocates scrambling for surer footing.[70] Instead of erecting a primitive church free from theological tradition and authoritarian control, the Christians came to advocate their own sectarian theology and to defer to the influence and persuasion of a dominant few. These ironies suggest that the real significance of the Christian movement is not to be found in its institutional development or in the direct influence of Smith, O'Kelly, Stone, and Alexander Campbell. What the movement does illustrate graphically is a moment of wrenching change in American culture that had great import for popular religion. Many followed the path even if they did not know its trailblazers.

The Christian movement illustrates, in the first place, the intensity of religious ferment at work in a period of chaos and originality unmatched, perhaps, since the religious turbulence of seventeenth-century England.[71] As in England a century and a half before, common folk in America at the dawn of the nineteenth century came to scorn tradition, relish novelty and experimentation, grope for fresh sources of authority, and champion an array of millennial schemes, each in its own way dethroning hierarchy and static religious forms.[72]

The resulting popular culture pulsated with the claims of supremely heterodox religious groups, with people veering from one sect to another, with the unbridled wrangling of competitors in a "war of words."[73] Scholars have only begun to assess the fragmentation that beset American religion in the period generally referred to as the Second Great Awakening, which they have too often viewed as a conservative response to rapid social change. The Christian movement serves as a helpful corrective and invites fresh appraisals of the popular culture that nourished people like William Miller, John Humphrey Noyes, and Joseph Smith. Theirs was a religious environment that brought into question traditional authorities and exalted the right of the people to think for themselves. The result, quite simply, was a bewildering world of clashing opinion—to the sympathetic Smith, an "Age of inquiry," to the distraught David Rice, a "hot bed of every extravagance of opinion and practice." Another erstwhile pilgrim, the Presbyterian-turned-Christian-turned-Shaker Richard McNemar, took up verse to capture the spirit of his times:

> Ten thousand Reformers like so many moles
> Have plowed all the Bible and cut it [in] holes
> And each has his church at the end of his trace
> Built up as he thinks of the subjects of grace.[74]

The Christians also illustrate the exaltation of public opinion as a primary religious authority. They called for common folk to read the New Testament as if mortal man had never seen it before. People were expected to discover the self-evident message of the Bible without any mediation from creeds, theologians, or clergymen not of their own choosing. This explicit faith that biblical authority could emerge from below, from the will of the people, was the most enduring legacy of the Christian movement. By the 1840s one analyst of American Protestantism concluded, after surveying fifty-three American sects, that the principle "No creed but the Bible" was the distinctive feature of American religion. John W. Nevin surmised that this emphasis grew out of a popular demand for "private judgment" and was "tacitly if not openly conditioned always by the assumption that every man is authorized and bound to get at this authority in a direct way for himself, through the medium simply of his own single mind."[75] Many felt the exhilarating hope that democracy had opened an immediate access to biblical truth for all persons of goodwill. What was difficult for Americans to realize was that a commitment to private judgment could drive people apart even as it raised beyond measure their hopes for unity.

The Christian movement also demonstrates the process by which popular culture became Christianized in the early republic. One reason that evangelical churches and sects grew so rapidly during these years was that they proclaimed value systems that endowed common people with dignity and responsibility.

People gladly accepted a theology that addressed them without condescension, balked at vested interests, and reinforced ideas of volitional allegiance and self-reliance. While such egalitarian strains were deeply rooted in the Great Awakening and subsequent revivals, historians have failed to appreciate the ways in which the founding of the American republic wrought, in Devereux Jarratt's words, "a vast alteration" in American religion. A staunch evangelical minister in Virginia prior to the Revolution, Jarratt by the 1790s had come to fear the volatile mix of things evangelical and egalitarian. Bemoaning the "levelling" spirit in "our high republican times," Jarratt recoiled from a religion "under the supreme controul of tinkers and taylors, weavers, shoemakers, and country mechanics of all kinds."[76] The theology that emerged between 1790 and 1815 to empower just these kinds of people certainly helps to clarify a process by which an America that had been largely Presbyterian, Congregational, Anglican, and Calvinist Baptist became a cauldron of Methodists, Disciples, Freewill, Free-Communion, and Primitive Baptists, Universalists, Mormons, and Millerites—to name a few. This new religious culture, which sanctioned the right of the individual to go his own way, would have been unthinkable apart from the crisis of authority in popular culture that accompanied the birth of the American republic.

NOTES

1. Charles Francis Adams, ed., *The Works of John Adams, Second President of the United States,* 10 vols. (Boston, 1850–56), 9:375, Edmund S. Morgan, "The Great Political Fiction," *New York Review of Books* 25 (Mar. 9, 1978): 13–18.

2. James A. Henretta, *The Evolution of American Society, 1700–1815* (Lexington, Mass., 1973); Richard D. Brown, *Modernization: The Transformation of American Life, 1600–1865* (New York, 1976); Richard D. Brown, "The Emergence of Voluntary Associations in Massachusetts, 1760–1830," *Journal of Voluntary Action Research,* 2 (Apr. 1973): 64–73; Jackson Turner Main, "Government by the People: The American Revolution and the Democratization of the Legislatures," *William and Mary Quarterly* 23 (July 1966): 391–407; Bernard Bailyn, *The Ideological Origins of the American Revolution* (Cambridge, 1967); Richard E. Ellis, *The Jeffersonian Crisis: Courts and Politics in the Young Republic* (New York, 1971); David Brion Davis, *The Problem of Slavery in the Age of Revolution, 1770–1823* (Ithaca, 1975); David Hackett Fischer, *Growing Old in America* (New York, 1977); Robert A. Cross, *The Minutemen and Their World* (New York, 1976); and Mary Beth Norton, *The Revolutionary Experience of American Women, 1750–1800* (Boston, 1980).

3. Eugene D. Genovese, *From Rebellion to Revolution: Afro-American Slave Revolts in the Making of the Modern World* (Baton Rouge, 1979).

4. Harrison Gray Otis, who had delivered the English oration at Harvard when he graduated in 1783, was asked to give the primary address at Harvard's bicentennial celebration in 1836. His speech is the lament of an old man who had witnessed the "fiery furnace of

140 The Christian Movement and the Demand for a Theology of the People

democracy" destroy much of what he held dear. While he had hoped that the Revolution had been "completed by the establishment of independence," he lived to see a "new school" take charge that "would identify revolution with perpetual motion. They would put all ancient institutions, laws, customs, courts, colleges, and schools upon wheels, and keep them whirling for ever with the steam of their own eloquence." Josiah Quincy, *The History of Harvard University*, 2 vols. (Cambridge, 1840), 2:662–70.

5. Gordon S. Wood, "The Democratization of Mind in the American Revolution," *Leadership in the American Revolution* (Washington, 1974), 63–89; and Gordon S. Wood, "Social Radicalism and Equality in the American Revolution," *The B. K. Smith Lectures in History* (Houston, 1976), 5–14.

6. On the new scholarly interest in religion, see Henry F. May, "The Recovery of American Religious History," *American Historical Review* 70 (Oct. 1964): 79–92. The broader trend to dismiss the social repercussions of the Revolution is evident in Frederick B. Tolles, "The American Revolution Considered as a Social Movement: A Re-Evaluation," *American Historical Review* 60 (Oct. 1954): 1–12. Studies of the Second Great Awakening in New England and the Great Revival in the Southwest have generally not addressed the question of how cultural ferment might have altered religion; they have focused, rather, on how traditional religion championed the revival technique in order to impose social order upon a disordered and secularized society. See Perry Miller, "From Covenant to Revival," in *The Shaping of American Religion*, ed. J. W. Smith and A. L. Jamison (Princeton, 1961), 350; Lois W. Banner, "Religious Benevolence as Social Control: A Critique of an Interpretation," *Journal of American History* 60 (June 1973): 23–41; and John B. Boles, *The Great Revival, 1787–1805: The Origins of the Southern Evangelical Mind* (Lexington, Ky., 1972). More sensitive to the ongoing impact of the Revolution in religious affairs is Donald G. Mathews, "The Second Great Awakening as an Organizing Process, 1780–1830: An Hypothesis," *American Quarterly* 21 (Spring 1969): 23–43.

7. Luther P. Gerlach and Virginia H. Hine define a social "movement" as "a group of people who are organized for, ideologically motivated by, and committed to a purpose which implements some form of personal or social change; who are actively engaged in the recruitment of others; and whose influence is spreading in opposition to the established order within which it originated." Luther P. Gerlach and Virginia H. Hine, *People, Power, Change: Movements of Social Transformation* (Indianapolis, 1970), xvi. The Christians, like the movements of which Gerlach and Hine speak, were decentralized and segmented, their weblike structures without clear lines of authority and often dependent upon shared publications. Their unity stemmed from little more than common ideology and perceived opposition from religious and political elites.

8. William Bentley, *The Diary of William Bentley, D. D.*, 4 vols. (Salem, Mass., 1911), 3:65, 271, 503, 515.

9. In May 1805 William Bentley commented about Elias Smith that "the press has lately vomited out many nauseaus things from this writer." Bentley, *Diary*, 3:157, 291, 370.

10. Elias Smith, *The Life, Conversion, Preaching, Travels, and Sufferings of Elias Smith* (Portsmouth, N.H., 1816), 341–42.

11. Elias Smith, *The Lovingkindness of God Displayed in the Triumph of Republicanism in America: Being a Discourse Delivered at Taunton (Mass.) July Fourth, 1809; at the Celebration of American Independence* (n.p., 1809), 32. Smith's colleague Abner Jones also experienced what he called a "disintegration" of his Calvinist beliefs and was quick to note the theological implications of demands for social equality. "In giving the reader an account of my birth and parentage," Jones wrote in 1807, "I shall not (like the celebrated Franklin and others,) strive to prove that I arose from a family of eminence believing that all men are born equal, and that every man shall die for his own iniquity." Abner Jones, *Memoirs of the Life and Experience, Travels and Preaching of Abner Jones* (Exeter, N.H., 1807), 3.

12. For a brief sketch of Smith's life, see William C. McLoughlin, *New England Dissent, 1630–1883: The Baptists and the Separation of Church and State*, 2 vols. (Cambridge, 1971), 2:745–49. Otherwise, no one has undertaken a serious study of Smith, despite his prominence as a religious and political radical in New England from 1800 to 1820, his scores of publications addressed to a popular audience, his newspaper that ran for a decade, and his fascinating memoir. The number of his itinerant followers is taken from one of his Congregational assailants. Thomas Andros, *The Scriptures Liable to be Wrested to Men's Own Destruction, and an Instance of This Found, in the Writings of Elias Smith* (Taunton, Mass., 1817), 18. A list of agents for Smith's newspaper is found in *Herald of Gospel Liberty*, Aug. 18, 1809, 104. For the number of subscribers, see ibid., Sept. 29, 1815, 720. On Smith's movement, which became known as the Christian Connection, see Thomas H. Olbricht, "Christian Connection and Unitarian Relations," *Restoration Quarterly* 9 (Sept. 1966): 160–86.

13. The best treatment of James O'Kelly is Charles Franklin Kilgore, *The James O'Kelly Schism in the Methodist Episcopal Church* (Mexico City, 1963). See also Edward J. Drinkhouse, *History of Methodist Reform*, 2 vols. (Baltimore, 1899), vol. 1; and Milo T. Morrill, *A History of the Christian Denomination in America* (Dayton, 1912). O'Kelly's primary works are James O'Kelly, *The Author's Apology for Protesting against the Methodist Episcopal Government* (Richmond, 1798), and James O'Kelly, *A Vindication of the Author's Apology* (Raleigh, 1801).

14. O'Kelly, *Author's Apology*, 4, 21.

15. O'Kelly, *Vindication*, 60–61.

16. "The Last Will and Testament of Springfield Presbytery," in John Rogers, *The Biography of Elder B. Warren Stone* (New York, 1972), 51–53. For other primary accounts of this movement, see Barton W. Stone, *An Apology for Renouncing the Jurisdiction of the Synod of Kentucky* (Lexington, Ky., 1804); [Richard McNemar], *Observations on Church Government, by the Presbytery of Springfield* (Cincinnati, 1907); Robert Marshall and James Thompson, *A Brief Historical Account of Sundry Things in the Doctrines and State of the Christian, or, as It Is Commonly Called, the Newlight Church* (Cincinnati, 1811); Levi Purviance, *The Biography*

of *Elder David Purviance* (Dayton, 1848); and Robert H. Bishop, *An Outline of the History of the Church in the State of Kentucky, during a Period of Forty Years: Containing the Memoirs of Rev. David Rice* (Lexington, Ky., 1824).

17. There is a considerable body of uncritical denominational literature on Barton W. Stone by the Disciples of Christ. See William Garrett West, *Barton Warren Stone: Early American Advocate of Christian Unity* (Nashville, 1954). For emphasis on Stone's contribution to the revivalist heritage of the South, see Boles, *Great Revival*. For appreciation of Stone in his full cultural context, see Ralph Morrow, "The Great Revival, the West, and the Crisis of the Church," in *The Frontier Re-examined*, ed. John. P. McDermott (Urbana, 1967), 65–78.

18. Rogers, *Biography of Elder B. Warren Stone*, 3, 47.

19. For discussions of the origins of the Campbellites, see David Edwin Harrell Jr., *Quest for a Christian America: The Disciples of Christ and American Society to 1866* (Nashville, 1966); Robert Frederick West, *Alexander Campbell and Natural Religion* (New Haven, 1949); Lester C. McAllister, *Thomas Campbell: Man of the Book* (St. Louis, 1954); and Errett Gates, *The Early Relation and Separation of Baptists and Disciples* (Chicago, 1904). In addition, see the extensive memoirs of father and son: Alexander Campbell, *Memoirs of Elder Thomas Campbell* (Cincinnati, 1861), and Robert Richardson, *Memoirs of Alexander Campbell*, 2 vols. (Cincinnati, 1913).

20. Richardson, *Memoirs of Alexander Campbell*, 1:438, 465–66. Many scholars have assumed that Thomas and Alexander Campbell applied to an American context beliefs that they had learned under the influence of Scottish reformers such as Robert Haldane and James Alexander Haldane. See, for example, Sydney E. Ahlstrom, *A Religious History of the American People* (New Haven, 1972), 448–49. The early documents of the Campbellite movement, however, manifest a keen awareness that the issues to be faced were, in their intensity at least, peculiarly American and demanded new solutions. See, for example, Thomas Campbell, *The Declaration and Address of the Christian Association of Washington* (Washington, Pa., 1809).

21. Lester G. McAllister and William E. Tucker, *Journey in Faith: A History of the Christian Church (Disciples of Christ)* (St. Louis, 1975), 154–55.

22. Alexander Campbell, "An Oration in Honor of the Fourth of July, 1830," *Popular Lectures and Addresses* (Philadelphia, 1863), 374–75.

23. "Elias Smith was here last week, distributing his books & pamphlets, & preached a lecture last week without sparing any of the hirelings as he calls them." Bentley, *Diary*, 3:388.

24. *Herald of Gospel Liberty*, Sept. 1, 1808, 1.

25. Stephen Porter, a Presbyterian clergyman, attempted to ward off the influence of Smith and his lieutenants among his congregation. Stephen Porter, *A Discourse, in Two Parts, Addressed to the Presbyterian Congregation in Ballston* (Ballston Spa, N.Y., 1814), 42–44.

26. Elias Smith, *The Clergyman's Looking-Glass: Being a History of the Birth, Life, and Death of Anti-Christ* (Portsmouth, N.H., 1803), 11. For examples of Smith's sensitivity to elitist codes of all sorts, even while he was still a Baptist, see Smith, *Life*, 279–80.

27. *Christian Baptist*, July 4, 1823, 280.

28. *Herald of Gospel Liberty*, Dec. 8, 1808, 29–30.

29. Abel M. Sargent founded a radical sect in Marietta, Ohio, where he published six issues of *Halcyon Itinerary and True Millennium Messenger*. The quotation is found in *Halcyon Itinerary and True Millennium Messenger* (Dec. 1807), 147–48. For a letter from Sargent to Smith, see *Herald of Gospel Liberty*, Aug. 16, 1811, 310. On Sargent, see John W. Simpson, *A Century of Church Life* (Marietta, 1896), 31.

30. Christians assailed the clergy as "tyrannical oppressors," "the mystery of iniquity," "friends of monarchy religion," "old tories," "an *aristocratical body of uniform nobility*," and "hireling priests"; people who would submit to such tyrants they labeled priest-ridden, slavishly dependent, passively obedient. See Smith, *Life*, 384, 402–3; *Herald of Gospel Liberty*, Oct., 13, 1809, 117; O'Kelly, *Vindication*, 47. In 1815 Smith claimed that most people in New England from forty to seventy years old could remember the respectable clergy emphasizing apocalyptic themes such as *"Anti-Christ, mystery Babylon,* the *great whore* that sitteth on many waters, the *beast* with seven heads and ten horns, the *man of sin* &c."* Herald of Gospel Liberty*, May 20, 1815, 695. On the multivalency of language, see J. G. A. Pocock, *Politics, Language, and Time: Essays on Political Thought and History* (New York, 1971), 3–41; and Harry S. Stout, "Religion, Communications, and the Ideological Origins of the American Revolution," *William and Mary Quarterly* 34 (Oct. 1977): 538.

31. Smith, *Lovingkindness of God Displayed*, 26–27; Smith, *Life*, 352–53. See also *Herald of Gospel Liberty*, Apr. 14, 1809, 67.

32. *Christian Baptist*, Jan. 2, 1826, 209; Smith, *Life*, 402–3; *Herald of Gospel Liberty*, Sept. 15, 1808, 6. See also Richardson, *Memoirs of Alexander Campbell*, 1:382–83.

33. See David Rice, *An Epistle to the Citizens of Kentucky, Professing Christianity* (Lexington, Ky., 1805), 11–12.

34. Rhys Isaac, "Evangelical Revolt: The Nature of the Baptists' Challenge to the Traditional Order in Virginia, 1765 to 1775," *William and Mary Quarterly* 31 (July 1974): 345–68.

35. Isaac Backus, *A History of New England with Particular Reference to the Denomination of Christians Called Baptists*, 2 vols. (Newton, Mass., 1871), 2:487. For evidence of the Baptist quest for respectability in the generation after the Great Awakening, see C. C. Goen, *Revivalism and Separatism in New England, 1740–1800* (New Haven, Conn., 1962). For the reaction of Baptists to the dissent spawned by the Revolution, see McLoughlin, *New England Dissent*, 2:710.

36. James Patrick Walsh, "The Pure Church in Eighteenth Century Connecticut" (Ph.D. diss., Columbia Univ., 1964), 143.

37. Rogers, *Biography of Elder B. Warren Stone*, 51–53.

144   The Christian Movement and the Demand for a Theology of the People

38. *Christian Baptist,* Nov. 3, 1823, 25; Richardson, *Memoirs of Alexander Campbell,* 2:63–64.

39. [McNemar], *Observations on Church Government,* 4, 9, 15. This pamphlet, the best-developed statement of Christian ecclesiology, rejects "external rules" and insists that all human organization spring from the deliberate and uncoerced choice of the individual.

40. O'Kelly, *Vindication,* 49. For similar expressions of resistance to human mediation of divine authority by Alexander Campbell and Thomas Campbell, see *Christian Baptist,* Apr. 3, 1826, 229, and Campbell, *Declaration and Address of the Christian Association,* 3. For the recurrence of this line of thought a generation later, see Lewis Perry, *Radical Abolitionism: Anarchy and the Government of God in Antislavery Thought* (Ithaca, 1973).

41. J. Franklin Jameson, *The American Revolution Considered as a Social Movement* (Princeton, 1926), 157.

42. Rogers, *Biography of Elder B. Warren Stone,* 14, 31, 33.

43. Marshall and Thompson, *Brief Historical Account,* 3–4.

44. Elias Smith, Sermons, *Containing an Illustration of the Prophecies* (Exeter, N.H., 1808), vi.

45. *Herald of Gospel Liberty,* Sept. 1, 1808, 1; Elias Smith, *A Discourse Delivered at Jefferson Hall, Thanksgiving Day, November 25, 1802, and Delivered (by Request) the Wednesday Evening Following, at the Same Place: The Subject, Nebuchadnezzar's Dream* (Portsmouth, N.H., 1803), 30–32. The sociologist Guy E. Swanson has argued that the political forms under which a people live significantly color their theological perceptions, particularly in times of rapid change. See Guy E. Swanson, *Religion and Regime: A Sociological Account of the Reformation* (Ann Arbor, 1967), 231.

46. Campbell, *Declaration and Address of the Christian Association,* 14; Campbell, "Oration in Honor of the Fourth of July," 374; *Christian Baptist,* Feb. 6, 1826, 213.

47. Marshall and Thompson, *Brief Historical Account,* 255. Presbyterian David Rice complained in 1803 about Stone and his followers: "Another thing that prepared the minds of many for the reception of error, was their high expectation of the speedy approach of the Millennium." Rice, *Epistle to the Citizens of Kentucky,* 13.

48. Campbell, "Oration in Honor of the Fourth of July," 377; Smith, *Life,* 292; Rogers, *Biography of Elder B. Warren Stone,* 47; O'Kelly, *Author's Apology,* 52.

49. Abel Sargent, *Halcyon Itinerary and True Millennium Messenger* 5 (Dec. 1807): 146.

50. Smith devoted a sermon of more than 120 pages to the subject of how republican values should be applied to the church. See Elias Smith, *The Whole World Governed by a Jew, or the Government of the Second Adam, as King and Priest* (Exeter, N.H., 1805). On the Standing Order's conservative use of millennial themes, see Nathan O. Hatch. *The Sacred Cause of Liberty: Republican Thought and the Millennium in Revolutionary New England* (New Haven, 1977), 97–138. See also Richard M. Rollins, *The Long Journey of Noah Webster* (Philadelphia, 1980).

51. James West Davidson, *The Logic of Millennial Thought: Eighteenth-Century New England* (New Haven, 1977), 122–41.

52. *Herald of Gospel Liberty,* June 23, 1809, 87; Feb. 2, 1809, 47. The Christians repeatedly suggested that Americans accord the New Testament the same kind of exclusive authority that they did constitutions in civil affairs. See Smith, *World Governed by a Jew,* 114; and Campbell, *Declaration and Address of the Christian Association,* 16.

53. *Christian Baptist,* Apr. 3, 1826, 229; Smith, *Life,* 292.

54. Andros, *Scriptures Liable to be Wrested to Men's Own Destruction,* 6, 21.

55. Porter, *Discourse in Two Parts,* 14; Rice, *Epistle to the Citizens of Kentucky,* 9–12.

56. William C. McLoughlin views the later wave of dissent as but an extension of the revivalism of the Great Awakening. McLoughlin, *New England Dissent,* 2:697–750. William Warren Sweet described the Christians as "a new denomination which arose directly out of the soil of the west." William Warren Sweet, *Religion in the Development of American Culture, 1765–1840* (New York, 1952), 221; and Winifred Ernest Garrison, *Religion Follows the Frontier: A History of the Disciples of Christ* (New York, 1931). Sweet also links the Christians to the broader revolt against Calvinism.

57. For the importance of the idea of volitional allegiance in this period, see James H. Kettner, *The Development of American Citizenship, 1608–1870* (Chapel Hill, 1978), 173–209. See also Gordon S. Wood, *The Creation of the American Republic, 1776–1787* (Chapel Hill, 1969), 483–99; Alfred F. Young, *The Democratic Republicans of New York: The Origins, 1763–1797*(Chapel Hill, 1967); and Edmund S. Morgan, *The Challenge of the American Revolution* (New York, 1976), 211–18.

58. Wood, *Creation of the American Republic,* 482–83.

59. Jonathan Elliot, *The Debates, Resolutions, and Other Proceedings,* in *Convention on the Adoption of the Federal Constitution,* 4 vols. (Washington, D.C., 1827–30), 1:112.

60. Young, *Democratic Republicans of New York,* 468–95.

61. Wood, *Creation of the American Republic,* 483–99. One of the clearest calls that common people should resist the traditional distinction between gentlemen and commoners came from the pen of the uneducated Massachusetts farmer William Manning in 1798. Samuel Eliot Morrison, ed., "William Manning's *The Key of Libberty,*" *William and Mary Quarterly* 13 (Apr. 1956): 202–54.

62. Ellis, *Jeffersonian Crisis.*

63. Benjamin Austin Jr., "Observations on the Pernicious Practice of the Law" (1786), in *American Journal of Legal History* 13 (July 1969): 258.

64. "Decius," *Independent Chronicle,* Jan. 30, 1804, 1.

65. Ellis, *Jeffersonian Crisis,* 171, 177; Austin, "Observations on the Pernicious Practice of the Law," 264.

66. For the importance in Thomas Jefferson's thought of breaking the grip of custom and precedent, see Edmund S. Morgan, *The Meaning of Independence: John Adams, George Washington, Thomas Jefferson* (Charlottesville, 1976), 71–79, and Daniel J. Boorstin, *The Lost World of Thomas Jefferson* (Boston, 1948).

67. Smith, *Lovingkindness of God Displayed,* 32.

146   The Christian Movement and the Demand for a Theology of the People

68. Alexis de Tocqueville, *Democracy in America*, trans. Henry Reeve, 2 vols. (New York, 1959), 1:104–5.

69. For an excellent example of the potential for factionalism within a local Christian church, see Don Harrison Doyle, *The Social Order of a Frontier Community: Jacksonville, Illinois, 1825–70* (Urbana, 1978), 157–60.

70. Smith himself left the Christian Connection in 1818 to join the Universalists, and two of his colleagues, Joshua V. Himes and Joseph Marsh, became early advocates of William Miller. David L. Rowe, "A New Perspective on the Burned-Over District: The Millerites in Upstate New York," *Church History* 47 (Dec. 1978): 408–20. Of five men who signed the "Last Will and Testament of Springfield Presbytery," two returned to the Presbyterians, two became Shakers, and only Stone retained his identity as a Christian. Alexander Campbell, similarly, saw his best preacher, Sidney Rigdon, defect to the Mormons. Mario S. De Pillis, "The Quest for Religious Authority and the Rise of Mormonism," *Dialogue: A Journal of Mormon Thought* 1 (Spring 1966): 68–88.

71. Christopher Hill, *The World Turned Upside Down: Radical Ideas during the English Revolution* (New York, 1972).

72. J. F. C. Harrison, *The Second Coming: Popular Millenarianism, 1780–1850* (New Brunswick, 1979), 163–206.

73. The phrase is that of Joseph Smith, who reacted strongly to the sectarian competition he knew as a young man. Joseph Smith, *The Pearl of Great Price* (Salt Lake City, 1891), 56–70. In this period evangelicals were preoccupied with a sense of the transforming power of the printed word. See Joan Jacobs Brumberg, *Mission for Life: The Story of the Family of Adoniram Judson* (New York, 1980), 44–78.

74. Elias Smith, *The Age of Enquiry* (Exeter, N.H., 1807); David Rice, "A Second Epistle to the Citizens of Kentucky, Professing the Christian Religion," in *An Outline of the History of the Church in the State of Kentucky*, ed. Robert Bishop (Lexington, Ky., 1824), 354; Richard McNemar, "The Mole's Little Pathways," as quoted in De Pillis, "Quest for Religious Authority," 75.

75. John Williamson Nevin, "Antichrist and the Sect," in *The Mercersburg Theology*, ed. James Hastings Nichols (New York, 1966), 93–119.

76. Devereux Jarratt, *The Life of the Reverend Devereux Jarratt* (Baltimore, 1806), 14–15, 181.

The Agrarian Myth and the Disciples of Christ in the Nineteenth Century

David Edwin Harrell Jr.

The prospective glory of the United States is a subject which overwhelms the imagination. No citizens of ancient or modern times ever had such a country to contemplate as those of the United States.
　　Alexander Campbell, "Prospective Glory of the United States," 1846

More than nationalistic bravado was involved in this statement in an 1846 issue of Alexander Campbell's religious monthly, the *Millennial Harbinger*; it was the full-blown flower of a Christian version of what Henry Nash Smith has called "*the* myth of mid-nineteenth-century America."[1] The faith that the American West was destined to be the "garden of the world" had a powerful appeal to nineteenth-century Americans. "It had strong overtones of patriotism," according to Smith, "and it implied a far reaching social theory."[2] The myth also became deeply enmeshed in the theology of such western religious groups as the Disciples of Christ.

The Disciples, the largest American-born religious movement, began amid the social ferment of the early-nineteenth-century trans-Appalachian West. From its beginnings the sect proved to be adept at meeting the religious needs of the frontier; by 1860 it was the sixth largest religious body in the nation. The Disciples successfully followed the frontier to the Pacific, although the center of the church's strength remained in the Mississippi Valley. By 1900 there were more than a million Disciples. The denomination divided in the twentieth century, but by the mid-1960s around four million American Christians belonged to sects that trace their religious origins to the Disciples movement of the nineteenth century.[3]

The Disciples of Christ grew out of two early-nineteenth-century religious reforms. One of these streams, the "Christian" movement, was the result of a Presbyterian schism led by Barton Stone during the great revival in Kentucky. In 1832 Stone and his followers united with another stream: a reforming group led by Alexander Campbell. Campbell, who lived in western Virginia, had by this time attracted a sizable following in the old Northwest and in the states of the upper South.

The Disciples, emphasizing a return to primitive Christianity and the need for Christian union, early gained converts from almost every element of western society. Colorful, and sometimes illiterate, "Campbellite" exhorters scoured the backwoods with their plea for the "restoration of the ancient order"—a simple gospel which found ready acceptance among the simple folk of the frontier. The Disciples, however, were never entirely a lower-class sect. The early movement included men of education, social standing, and wealth. According to one of his biographers, Alexander Campbell died the richest man in West Virginia.[4] In his *Social Sources of Denominationalism,* H. Richard Niebuhr suggests that the Disciples, perhaps more than any other religious group, were "a true product of the West."[5] The church was a truly American product, and the Disciples' version of the myth of the garden is a significant variation of the great American legend.

At the heart of the myth of the garden was the conviction that rural life was superior to urban life. Although the "Western yeoman had to work as hard as a common laborer or a European peasant," and his economic status was little better than theirs, the lot of the western farmer was idealized persuasively all through the nineteenth century.[6]

Western religious leaders were prominent dispensers of this myth. "I know of no class of men better situated to enjoy life than the farmer," wrote a Disciples preacher in 1882. "He can eat the fruit of the land cultivated by his own hand, and look up to his God and be thankful."[7] From Alexander Campbell's observation in 1830 that "the country gentleman . . . has advantages over his equal in town"[8] to the pronouncement that "the farmer is king"[9] by a late-nineteenth-century Texas evangelist, the belief in rural preeminence pervaded the church. "If you can get the use of a blind mule and two acres of land," advised a Tennessee journal in 1879, "do not come to New York."[10] The myth persisted to the very end of the century, in spite of the "yawning gap between agrarian theory and the actual circumstances of the West after the Civil War."[11] In 1895, in the midst of the farm unrest of the period, a Tennessee Disciple wrote: "There is certainly a striking contrast in the life and surroundings of contented farmers and that class of wage-workers who never look elsewhere for a living than to public works and the operators of large factories."[12]

The foremost hero of the garden myth was the yeoman farmer.[13] An article in the Tennessee *Gospel Advocate* proclaimed that "of all the pursuits of life that of a farmer is the most respectable."[14] The yeoman farmer was healthier, had the benefit of more "social enjoyment," and was free of the "anxiety, envy, and unprincipled ambition" found in urban occupations.[15] Another writer avowed that while farming was a "laborious employment," it was "ease itself compared with that of the business-driven, care-worn merchant."[16] And, perhaps most important, the yeoman farmer possessed a "high sense of independence," a fact which made him the political backbone of the nation.[17]

The pervasive myth of the yeoman farmer even penetrated into the South, where it overwhelmed the rival plantation myth.[18] Postwar southern Disciples were as dedicated to the ideal of a nation of small independent farmers as were northern Disciples. Just so much as southern society failed to conform to the yeoman image, most Disciples judged it a failure. "The best community in the world is that in which every man owns his own land, small farms with industrious owners," wrote David Lipscomb, editor of the Nashville *Gospel Advocate*, in 1875.[19] Another southern writer grumbled that one of the chief "curses left by slavery" was the unwillingness of southerners to labor on small farms.[20]

There is ample evidence of the practical commitment of Disciples leaders to the agrarian myth. In 1841 Alexander Campbell established the most important college in the early history of the church. The school was located in Bethany, Virginia, near his home. He justified the isolated site of the school in terms that illustrate the hold of the agrarian myth: "From the rural location of Bethany College, more favorable to health, morals and study than a village or city location, much may be expected, and we doubt not realized, in the physical, intellectual, and moral improvements of the youth admitted into this institution."[21]

The most significant facet of Campbell's statement was his injection of the element of morality into the myth of the garden. The agricultural West was God's area. A southern preacher wrote in 1877: "It is an ancient saying that 'God made the country and man made the town.' From the Bible . . . we learn that the first occupation of the first human pair was *tilling the ground*."[22] A society of yeoman farmers was not only the desideratum of the "political economist" and the "patriot" but also of the "Christian."[23]

That a relationship existed between "moral improvement" and rural living was accepted widely as a truism by Disciples leaders.[24] Even as the church became more urban in the last quarter of the nineteenth century, many of the preachers believed that people in the cities "would be better off physically, financially, and spiritually in the country."[25] In 1872 one of the most influential Disciples preachers in Kentucky nostalgically summarized the Christian myth of the garden:

> The preacher of that golden age was a farmer . . . He geared his horses with dexterity, plowed with as much skill as ever did Lycurgus, and could whistle "old Father Grimes" with an unction which will never be equaled by Bro. Moore's organist in Cincinnati . . . But he was more. He was the neighborhood justice of the Peace; in winter, the country school master, and always, on big meeting occasions, the innkeeper of the church. He was useful, popular and tenderly loved. As a rule, he was kind hearted, deeply pious, and always hospitable even to a fault . . . From his lips they caught lessons of wisdom which guided them like beacons through life's cheerless nights, and comforted them in death. Their hearts grew stout as he philosophized

on life's ills; their resolutions petrified as he counseled them to be true to the Master, and as, in his artless but often eloquent style, he pointed them to the time when they should all meet in the Savior's presence, and neither go out nor part more, they wept as if their hearts would break.[26]

Never was the agrarian myth more strongly linked with moral values than when the city and farm were contrasted. In 1843, after a trip through the major cities of the East, Alexander Campbell wrote: "American cities, like all other cities, are not favorable to the prevaleace [sic] of religious influences . . . They [urbanites] are generally neither so intelligent in scriptures, nor so pious as the people of the country."[27] "Great cities," wrote a Missouri preacher in 1867, "are the great corrupters of the morals of mankind, like lewd women to whom they are compared by the sacred writers of both Testaments."[28]

To many Disciples the great crime was that these sores on the landscape continued to grow throughout the nineteenth century despite the presence of "millions of acres uncultivated" in the garden of the West.[29] The West as a haven for the poor, a refuge for surplus city population, and as a stabilizing deterrent of class conflict was a major component of the garden myth. The image of the West as a safety valve was as old as the country and persisted well into the twentieth century.[30]

In 1847 Alexander Campbell made a tour of the British Isles and was appalled by the condition of the workers in the industrial centers of England. But he was convinced that Americans would not have to face such an economic crisis for a long time since they were blessed with a "large and roomy country," a "vast patrimonial inheritance," which would be an adequate safety valve for "unborn millions of our race."[31] A few years later he wrote: "An agrarian spirit has gone abroad . . . Other new settlements must be formed."[32]

Other Disciples leaders echoed Campbell's confidence in the western safety valve. Jacob Creath Jr., a hardhanded pioneer preacher who followed the frontier from the Kentucky bluegrass to western Missouri, suggested that the solution to the nation's economic problems was simply for the government to set aside one of the territories for "poor men with families." Creath's uncomplicated program called for the distribution of one hundred acres to all "family men" who would "swear they are not worth more than three hundred dollars."[33] In 1877 a southern church periodical advised: "The obvious remedy for the excess of the supply of labor . . . is dispersion; migration to other regions, where there is work to do and room to work."[34]

The safety valve myth combined with a vital millennialism in Disciples thought to form a Christian variety of the garden myth.[35] Most of the early leaders of the church believed that a millennial religious, political, and economic age was rapidly approaching—an era when injustice would give way to Christian order. "Things are in process," wrote Alexander Campbell, "in progress to another age—a golden—a blissful period of human history." According to Campbell, "selfishness, violence, inordinate ambition . . . oppression and cruelty" would be overcome in the not very distant future.[36]

Most preachers for the Disciples of Christ shared with other American Protestants during the nineteenth century a deep faith in progress and were confident that Christianity was God's instrument for bringing it about.[37] They believed that the return to "primitive Christianity" initiated by the Disciples movement was the harbinger of the beginning of events leading to the millennium.[38] Some of the exuberance of the early millennialism dimmed in the years following the Civil War when it became obvious that the religious reforms of the Disciples would not immediately transform the world.[39] But around the turn of the century millennialism experienced an enthusiastic resurgence. In 1899 an editorial in a leading Disciples journal stated: "Year by year, we can discern in the rapidly occurring events of our time, the growing power of the kingdom of God and its steady advance towards supremacy. The nations and kingdoms that conform closest to God's law . . . are the leading nations in the world."[40]

In 1898, during the months of rampant nationalism leading to the Spanish-American War, a Disciples preacher wrote: "We fully believe that the time is at hand in the gracious and beneficent purposes of God when he will bring into judgment all nations which are oppressing the people, and when he will overturn . . . the nations that are hindering the Christianization and elevation of mankind."[41]

The most persistent elements of millennial anticipation among the Disciples were racism and nationalism. Alexander Campbell and other early church leaders were almost unanimously racists.[42] "To the Saxons in Europe, to the Anglo-Saxons in Britain, to the American Anglo-Saxons on the continent," wrote Campbell, "God has given the scepter of Judah, the harp of David, the strength of Judah's Lion, and the wealth of the world."[43] Campbell believed that the "great . . . masters of nature have been found . . . almost exclusively" among the Anglo-Saxons.[44] Because of their unique characteristics God had given to the Anglo-Saxons the gospel of Protestantism; it was their providential destiny to spread truth to the world and to introduce the millennium.[45]

This theme of Anglo-Saxon Protestant millennialism persisted throughout the century. In 1899 a prominent preacher wrote: "The Anglo-Saxon race is the great missionary race and the conservator of the great missionary religion . . . We must bring America to Christ and then, use it as the base of supplies for the conquest of the world."[46] The "White Man's Burden" implied not simply a cultural responsibility, but a religious one also.[47] "It is the Anglo-Saxon race," wrote another Disciples editor, "that is in the forefront of every reform. It is the head of Protestantism; . . . it is the missionary race of the world."[48]

152 The Agrarian Myth and the Disciples of Christ in the Nineteenth Century

America was a land prepared for the introduction of the Anglo-Saxon Protestant millennium.[49] In 1899 a Disciples editor wrote, "The ends of the ages are come upon us. Dewey and destiny are strangely linked together . . . Anglo-Saxon supremacy . . . seems about to be realized . . . History is hastening and we must hurry! 'The king's business requires haste!' . . . Americanism has become a new, factor in world-parcelling."[50] This millennialistic imperialism was the legitimate offspring of the confident expectation of the early days of the movement. Exactly forty years earlier, Walter Scott, one of the foremost preachers of the early movement, had heralded the United States as the "first of the Messianic nations."[51]

Scott elaborately outlined the steps leading to the American millennium. "Luther and Washington," he wrote, "gave us *new* religion and *new* society in this *new* world."[52] He asked: "Can the symbols and imagery of the prophets then ever be more fully realized? Can the 'new heavens and the new earth'. . . ever be more evidently verified than by the case in which we have a new world, a new people, a new government, and a new hero?"[53] Thus, the agrarian myth and millennial hope were drawn together. The key to the introduction of the millennium was that God had provided "a new world"—a new garden of Eden. Into this garden he led his chosen people to construct a chosen government, and to rediscover the chosen religion; it was the fabled garden of the West.

Alexander Campbell aired his faith in the religious destiny of the new world, this land of plenty provided for God's purposes: "The Mayflower ferried over the Atlantic the seeds gathered from the early harvest's, the choicest first fruits of European Protestantism . . . God sent them, to a new world, that they might institute, under the most favorable circumstances, new political and ecclesiastic institutions. Such, most assuredly, was their divine mission."[54]

In an 1854 address before a Disciples convention in Cincinnati, David S. Burnet, the leading Disciples preacher of the Midwest, voiced the garden myth: "Between the sources of the Ohio and the headwaters of the Platte, is the largest body of fertile land on our globe and here will be the densest masses of men, and the greatest number of schools and colleges and churches."[55] He also echoed the Disciples version of the myth: the western garden was a "divinely chosen theater of *new measures*"—a haven for the restoration of religious purity. He said: "Here the woman [the church] has found her wilderness-sanctuary and may act . . . without fear of blood-red dragons, beasts, and false prophets."[56] In 1898 an editorial in a major Disciples journal summed up the Disciples myth:

> And in this country Protestantism has developed its ripest fruit. Here the movement for Christian union, the consummation of Protestant Christianity, has taken root and flourished. In no other country in the world would this have been possible. Here in America, and here alone, was it possible for primitive Christianity to be restored. Here, and here alone, was it possible to plant the standard of the New Testament

alone, and win to its support a million adherents within the short space of seventy-five years. It was not chance that brought the Campbells to America.[57]

With the passage of time the myth of the garden became "a less and accurate description of a society transformed by commerce and industry."[58] In the last quarter of the nineteenth century agricultural America passed through a traumatic period of readjustment. Poverty-stricken and embattled farmers launched vigorous protest movements, but change came slowly, both in action and in mind. The idyllic agrarian myth persisted long after its basis in fact had vanished.

From 1875 to 1900 most leaders of the Disciples of Christ held tenaciously to their Christian version of the agrarian myth, but they became increasingly defensive in attitude. Millennial hope was linked less and less frequently with the garden myth. The most fervent millennialists in the movement by the end of the century were the supporters of the new industrial order. Many still believed that the American farmer was a specially prepared instrument of God, but it was perfectly obvious that he was neither gaining in influence nor improving his status in society.

Church leaders were deeply concerned over these threats to the agrarian myth. Rural preachers often reminisced about the good old "days of the spinning-wheels and looms. . . and hard work by the men instead of flocking to the towns to be ruined by dissipation."[59] They were genuinely frightened by the rise of cities. "The cities are moral and spiritual deserts," wrote an Ohio preacher. "They contain the *dangerous classes*."[60]

The threat of urbanization to the Disciples agricultural myth was multiple. Cities were where "Catholicism has her greatest power." They were also centers of immorality: "Here is where Satan has his seat, where the saloon does its demoralizing work, and where vice, poverty and wretchedness make men desperate." Most dangerous of all were those urban radicals who preached economic heterodoxy, the "anarchists, socialists and wild dreamers of every type."[61] In 1885 a St. Louis editor warned: "The laboring classes of the great cities are largely irreligious . . . These all have loose ideas of the rights of property, openly preach the right to take whatever is wanted, and to burn, blow up and destroy."[62]

The reaction of some church leaders to this late-nineteenth-century challenge to the agrarian tradition was a plea for increased missionary work in the cities. "Patriotism," wrote one preacher, "as well as the love of Christ calls upon the churches to arouse themselves, and to seriously undertake the evangelization of the cities."[63] Armed with Boards of City Evangelization, an evangelical faith, and the moral and social convictions of a nineteenth-century farmer, these conservative Disciples stormed the citadels of Satan. Their attachment to the agrarian myth did not serve them well in the battle to win the cities.

A second group within the church simply reinforced its earlier class prejudices. Rural preachers became increasingly suspicious of those within the movement who showed any interest in cities and their problems. The division between the Churches of Christ and the Disciples of Christ, which was officially recognized in 1906, had clear rural-urban undertones. The theological conservatism of southern and western Disciples was repeatedly linked with distrust of city churches and a lingering faith in the agrarian myth.[64]

As early as 1865, John R. Howard, a Disciples editor in Missouri, warned that one of the greatest dangers to the church was "the constantly growing taste for what is termed elegance and refinement . . . in our large cities and towns."[65] By the last quarter of the nineteenth century the older preachers were becoming more and more conscious of the changes that were taking place in the movement. They prided themselves in being "old fogies" and repeatedly warned that "city preachers" were ruining the church. In 1894 a rural Iowa preacher protested that "the modern rendering of the great commission appears to be, Go into the large cities and preach the Gospel, or go where the people will pay a good salary and entertain the preacher in good style."[66] Rural readers frequently protested that the church papers were "catering to wealthy subscribers."[67]

Instead of emphasizing city evangelization, many conservative Disciples believed that the church should ignore these centers of sin and concentrate on farmers. A Kentucky preacher wrote: "A great cry has been made in certain quarters over what is sometimes styled 'Our failure in the great cities' . . . And it seems to be pretty well settled in certain circles that unless we can establish ourselves in the cities, we will never amount to much as a Church." He dismissed "this delusive idea of the overshadowing importance of city churches" as a "worldly" doctrine and urged renewed efforts in the country.[68]

City churches came under persistent fire from devotees of the agrarian myth. When the Disciples church in Portland, Oregon, announced plans to build a $30,000 church building, a Tennessee editor cited this "extravagance" as a typical example of the worldly nature of city churches.[69] In 1875 a rural Alabama evangelist wrote: "Our own brethren . . . are beginning to catch the liberal spirit in preaching. There is now a prevailing desire in many places to grow up as the popular and fashionable church."[70] City preachers, according to their rural critics, were particularly corrupted by contact with "fashionable society." "The most difficult task that many city preachers have to perform," wrote a caustic Kentucky editor, "is keeping on good terms with the choir."[71]

This distrust was frequently linked with the specific doctrinal issues that divided the movement in 1906. The Churches of Christ objected to the introduction of instrumental music into worship, the existence of missionary societies and other church organizations, and the employment of "located pastors." All of these "issues" were, in the conservative mind, connected with the influence of cities. "The reason why city churches gape for flutes, horns, and organs," wrote a disgruntled conservative, "is because the opera . . . has educated them to it."[72]

And there was real perception in the conservative analysis. The diverging theological points of view within the church were deeply rooted in conflicting agrarian and urban emphases. With considerable insight, a conservative editor wrote in 1897: "As time advanced such of those churches as assembled in large towns and cities gradually became proud, or, at least, sufficiently worldly-minded to desire popularity, and in order to attain that unscriptural end they adopted certain popular arrangements such as the hired pastor, the church choir, instrumental music, man-made societies to advance the gospel, and human devices to raise money to support previously mentioned devices of similar origin. In so doing they divided the brotherhood of disciples."[73]

In sum, by the end of the nineteenth century the Disciples' agrarian myth was being subjected to serious pressures. A few sophisticated preachers recognized the fallacy of the myth and increasingly turned to new sets of symbols, which centered around the importance of the city and the potential of industrialism.[74] But to most of the church the old truths remained sacred. Leaders reacted to the challenge of urbanization in two ways. Some became frantically concerned about city evangelization. They believed that somehow they must cleanse these centers of evil before the millennium could begin. The devoted agrarians in the church, however, simply refused the challenge. They believed that "true religion" had little future in the cities. As a matter of fact, urban churches were generally polluted by their environment rather than being a purifying source within it. Doctrinal purity and morality could be maintained only by separation from the source of evil. Their answer was a renewed emphasis on traditional religious values and an unswerving dedication to the agrarian myth.

NOTES

1. Henry Nash Smith, *Virgin Land* (reprint, New York: Vintage Books, 1957), 153.

2. Ibid., 154. See 139–305. See also Charles L. Sanford, *The Quest for Paradise* (Urbana, Ill., 1961), and Arthur K. Moore, *The Frontier Mind* (Lexington, Ky., 1957).

3. The best general studies of the movement are Winfred E. Garrison and Alfred T. DeGroot, *The Disciples of Christ* (St. Louis, 1948), and Earl Irvin West, *The Search for the Ancient Order*, 2 vols. (Nashville, 1957). For current statistics, see Benson Y. Landis, ed., *Yearbook of American Churches* (New York, 1964), 255. Two articles that discuss the frontier origins of the Disciples are William C. Bower, "The Frontier Mind," *The Scroll* 40 (June 1943): 300–309, and Sterling W. Brown, "The Disciples and the New Frontier," *The Scroll* 32 (May 1936): 153–65.

4. Benjamin Lyon Smith, *Alexander Campbell* (St. Louis, 1930), 147.

5. H. Richard Niebuhr, *The Social Sources of Denominationalism*, 5th ed. (New York: Meridian Books, 1960), 178.

6. Smith, *Virgin Land*, 153.

7. J. L. Parsons, "Life in the Country," *Christian Foundation* 3 (Nov. 1882): 404.

8. "The Four Great Sources of Health," *Millennial Harbinger* 1 (June 1830): 280.

9. John T. Poe, "God Bless Them," *Gospel Advocate* 27 (Feb. 25, 1885): 116.

10. "Going to the City," *Gospel Advocate* 21 (Oct. 9, 1879): 649.

11. Smith, *Virgin Land*, 224.

12. "Moving to Town," *Gospel Advocate* 37 (May 23, 1895): 331.

13. See Smith, *Virgin Land*, 151–64.

14. "Office-Seeking and Farming," *Gospel Advocate* 17 (Apr. 22, 1875): 377.

15. "Farming a Safe Pursuit in Life," *Millennial Harbinger*, 3d ser., no. 2 (Apr. 1846): 200.

16. "The Farmer's Life," *Gospel Advocate* 20 (Mar. 28, 1878): 102.

17. David Lipscomb, "Destitution, Its Cause," *Gospel Advocate* 17 (Mar. 25, 1875): 300.

18. See Smith, *Virgin Land*, 163–77.

19. "Destitution, Its Cause," *Gospel Advocate* 17 (Aug. 12, 1875): 750.

20. "Extract from E. D. Hicks' Address," *Gospel Advocate* 21 (Mar. 6, 1879): 154.

21. "Bethany College," *Millennial Harbinger*, n.s., no. 5 (Aug. 1841): 378. Tolbert Fanning, the most influential early church leader in Tennessee, also established a school with an agrarian emphasis. See James E. Scobey, ed., *Franklin College and Its Influence* (reprint, Nashville, 1954), 19–25.

22. "The Labor Question—The Evil and the Remedy," *Christian Examiner* 10 (Oct. 26, 1877): 3.

23. "Small Farms," *Gospel Advocate* 20 (Nov. 14, 1878): 716.

24. See Scobey, *Franklin College*, 269–83; "Preaching to the Poor," *Apostolic Times* 5 (May 8, 1873), 5; "Fortunate Farmer's Boys," *Octographic Review* 40 (June 8, 1897): 7.

25. E. A. Elam, "Going to Town," *Gospel Advocate* 37 (Apr. 25, 1895): 262.

26. Moses E. Lard, "Pioneer Preaching in the West," *Apostolic Times* 3 (Feb. 8, 1872): 348.

27. "Notes of an Excursion to the Eastern Cities, No. II," *Millennial Harbinger*, n.s., no. 7 (Feb. 1843): 64. See also John R. Howard, "Cities," *Christian Age and Protestant Unionist* 6 (Jan. 4, 1850): 2.

28. "Great Cities," *Christian Pioneer* 7 (Aug. 1, 1867): 442.

29. "Editorial Jottings," *American Christian Review* 23 (June 15, 1882): 196.

30. See Smith, *Virgin Land*, 234–45.

31. "Letters from Europe—No. VII," *Millennial Harbinger*, 3d ser., no. 4 (Oct. 1847): 544. In 1844 R. French Ferguson, a Kentucky editor, wrote in the same vein: "What manner of people ought we of this happy, plentiful country, to be, . . . having enough to sustain our own existence and enough to feed the starving nations of Europe." "Distress," *Christian Journal* 11 (Feb. 10, 1844): 393.

32. "An Address," *Millennial Harbinger*, 3d ser., no. 7 (May 1850): 261.

33. "Suggestion," *Christian Evangelist* 9 (Jan. 1858): 30–31.

34. "The Labor Question—The Evil and the Remedy," *Christian Examiner* 10 (Oct. 26, 1877): 3.

35. For good analysis of the continuing impact of millennial hope on American Protestantism, see David E. Smith, "Millenarian Scholarship in America," *American Quarterly*, 17 (Fall 1965): 535–49, and Ira V. Brown, "Watchers for the Second Coming: The Millenarian Tradition in America," *Mississippi Valley Historical Review* 39 (Dec. 1952): 441–58. This article is not intended to deal with all the implications of millennialism on Disciples' thought but simply the persistent linking of the millennium and the garden myth.

36. Alexander Campbell, "Address on the Amelioration of the Social State," *Popular Lectures and Addresses* (Philadelphia, 1863), 69. Most pre–Civil War Disciples leaders were firm postmillennialists. They believed that a perfect Christian society would soon arrive—perhaps in their own lifetimes. The key to the arrival of the millennium was the progress of their religious reform. For a general discussion of this subject, see David Edwin Harrell Jr., *Quest for a Christian America: The Disciples of Christ and American Society to 1866* (Nashville: Disciples of Christ Historical Society, 1966), 39–53. See also Samuel Montgomery Whitson Jr., "Campbell's Concept of the Millennium" (master's thesis, Butler Univ., 1951). Arthur Moore notes briefly the relation between millennial anticipation and the garden myth, *The Frontier Mind*, 30 ff., 140–43.

37. See Campbell, "Conclusion of Volume II," *Millennial Harbinger* 2 (Dec. 1831): 568; Forrester, "Progressive Development," *Protestant Unionist* 1 (Aug. 6, 1845): 138. Ralph Gabriel describes briefly the relationship of these two ideas and the American democratic hope in *The Course of American Thought*, 2d ed. (New York, 1956): 34–39.

38. Early in his career Campbell believed that the millennium would begin before the year 2000. See Whitson, "Campbell's Concept of the Millennium," 171–72. Other early preachers in the church shared this view. See, for example, Amos S. Hayden, *A History of the Disciples on the Western Reserve* (Cincinnati, 1875), 183–90.

39. See "The Second Coming of the Lord," *Christian Standard* 1 (June 2, 1866): 68; "Queries," *Gospel Advocate* 40 (June 23, 1896): 397.

40. "The Divine Law of Expansion," *Christian Oracle* 16 (Jan. 18, 1899): 2.

41. "The King of Nations," *Christian Oracle* 15 (May 12, 1898): 290. The reemphasis on the millennium around the turn of the century was largely confined to the nationalistic middle-class segment of the church. For some of these the nature of the millennium had come to include industrial and urban symbols, but for others the old views remained unchanged.

42. See Harrell, *Quest for a Christian America*, 50–53.

43. "The Destiny of Our Country," *Millennial Harbinger*, 4th ser., no. 2 (Aug. 1852): 452.

44. "An Address," *Millennial Harbinger*, 3d ser., no. 7 (May 1850): 265.

45. Ibid., 241–72. See also Campbell, *Popular Lectures*, 17–46; Alexander Campbell, "Progress of the Anglo-Saxon Race," *Millennial Harbinger*, 4th ser., no. 1 (Dec. 1851): 683–85.

46. "This and That," *Christian Oracle* 16 (Apr. 27, 1899): 6.

47. "The White Man's Burden," *Christian Standard* 35 (Mar. 4, 1889): 274.

48. "The Divine Hand in History," *Christian Evangelist* 26 (Jan. 3, 1889): 2.

49. See Harrell, *Quest for a Christian America*, 48–49.

50. "The Conflict of the Ages," *Christian Oracle* 15 (Aug. 4, 1898): 482.

51. *The Messiahship or Great Demonstration* (Cincinnati, 1859), 313.

52. Ibid., 323.

53. Ibid., 298; see also 297–335.

54. Campbell, *Popular Lectures*, 169. Charles L. Sanford surmises that "the Edenic myth . . . has been the most powerful and comprehensive organizing force in American culture" (*Quest for Paradise*, vi; see 74–113). See also Arthur Moore's chapter entitled "Eden Recovered," in *The Frontier Mind*, 11–24, and Edward McNall Burns, *The American Idea of Mission* (New Brunswick, N.J., 1957), 213–34.

55. Report of the *Proceedings* of the Convention of Churches of Christ, at the Anniversaries of the American Christian Bible, Missionary, and Publication Societies . . . 1854 (Cincinnati, 1854), 15.

56. Ibid., 14.

57. "The Standard Bearers of Protestantism," *Christian Standard* 34 (Apr. 16, 1898): 483. The Disciples of the nineteenth century were quick to react against any force that seemed to menace the garden as a haven for religious purity. In 1855 Jacob Creath Jr. warned that the "great Valley of the Mississippi, which for fertility of soil and inexhaustible resources . . . surpasses Ancient Egypt, was being threatened by "that most Loyal Son of the Devil, the Pope of Rome"; "Correspondence," *Christian Evangelist* 6 (Jan. 1855), 37–38.

58. Smith, *Virgin Land*, 139.

59. Jacob Creath, "My Reply to Bro. J. C. Risk of Canton, Mo.," *American Christian Review* 19 (Jan. 8, 1878): 9.

60. B. A. Hinsdale, "The Poor and the Gospel," *Christian Standard* 1 (Nov. 10, 1866): 254.

61. "The Problems of the Cities," *Christian Evangelist* 22 (Apr. 28, 1882): 258.

62. "Why Does Crime Increase?" *Christian Evangelist* 22 (May 28, 1885): 339.

63. "The Problems of the Cities," *Christian Evangelist* 29 (Apr. 28, 1892): 258.

64. "Evil Days," *Apostolic Times* 6 (Aug. 17, 1881): 4.

65. "Dangers to Christianity and Christians," *Christian Pioneer* 5 (June 1865): 257.

66. "Pathfinder," *Christian Oracle* 9 (Oct. 11, 1894): 596.

67. "The Christian Evangelist and Labor Reform," *Christian Evangelist* 26 (May 9, 1889): 292.

68. W. B. F. Treat, "Religion in the Cities," *American Christian Review* 19 (Nov. 12, 1878): 361.

69. "Miscellany," *Gospel Advocate* 35 (Apr. 21, 1892): 248.
70. J. T. Poe, "Christian Liberality," *Gospel Advocate* 17 (May 13, 1875): 467.
71. "Editorial Notes," *Apostolic Guide* 18 (Nov. 27, 1885): 5.
72. "Editorial Items," *Octographic Review* 30 (Oct. 13, 1887): 4.
73. D. Sommer, "Signs of the Times," *Octographic Review* 40 (Oct. 5, 1897): 1.
74. See, for instance, R. J. Tydings, "The Grinding of the Mill," *Christian Evangelist* 32 (Mar. 14, 1891): 167.

Section 2

The Significance of Alexander Campbell in Antebellum America

A Rational Voice Crying in an Emotional Wilderness

John L. Morrison

Alexander Campbell immigrated with his mother, brothers, and sisters to the United States from Ireland and Scotland in 1809, two years after his father, Thomas, had come to eastern Pennsylvania to prepare the way. The Campbells were a hardy lot; their Seceder Presbyterian background had endowed them with a strong sense of rugged individualism that expressed itself in the New World. They joined the religious controversy on the middle frontier, their intellectual swords cutting a broad path in the thinking of men. In one sense, Thomas Campbell was the sword bearer; Alexander, the warrior.

According to Robert West, Alexander Campbell was a "rugged and unlettered American believer in democracy and liberty."[1] His deep interest in the democratic process was acknowledged by Henry Clay, who described Campbell as "a distinguished member, about twenty years ago, of the convention called in the State of Virginia to remodel its civil constitution, in which, besides other distinguished men, were ex-Presidents Madison and Monroe, and John Marshall, the late Chief-Justice of the United States."[2] In spite of Campbell's expressed opposition to Madison's oligarchical leanings, the former president ventured that Campbell was the "greatest man at the convention."[3] Even if Madison exaggerated, Campbell distinguished himself among his contemporaries. In agriculture, he became one of the most progressive, successful, and wealthy farmers in West Virginia. His sixty published volumes testify to his vigorous writing career and popularity. In the field of education, he wrote extensively, campaigned for the "common school," attended educational conventions, and founded Bethany College, of which he was president for twenty-five years. Public speaking took Campbell on domestic and overseas tours. His famous frontier debates earned envy and venom from his contemporaries. As the founder of one of the largest indigenous religious bodies in America, the Disciples of Christ, Campbell stamped his image upon the religious character of the nation. Campbell's leadership in American religious life was noted by Henry

Clay, who said: "Dr. Campbell is among the most eminent citizens of the United States, distinguished for his great learning and ability, for *his successful devotion to the education of youth,* for his piety and as the head and founder of one of the most important and respectable religious communities in the United States."[4]

Although some judged him "modest and unassuming," Campbell was something of a celebrity. He attracted throngs everywhere he went and carried on an almost endless monologue. Robert Richardson, Campbell's chief biographer, reported that "nobody wished to talk in his presence. His themes were much out of the range of ordinary conversation."[5]

Undergirding this distinguished life was Campbell's belief that "knowledge is power."[6] Whether in the Sunday sermon, the daily classroom, frontier debates, lecture tours, legislative campaigning for common schools, pleas for colleges with a moral culture, or copious written polemics, he stressed knowledge. He faced a knowledge-hungry middle frontier. Not always did it sense its hunger nor favorably respond to his diagnosis of "malnutrition." Nevertheless, he diagnosed and prescribed; not infrequently the patient listened and sometimes got well. For instance, Campbell's advocacy of the Bible-based liberal arts college was not fully understood by all his contemporaries. Many who commended his biblical emphasis saw something sinister in his liberal arts appreciation. Some advocates of liberal arts colleges with accompanying theological seminaries saw something provincial in Campbell's belief that every educated person needed a thorough Bible education. Right or wrong, Campbell wanted to combine both in a "New Literary and Moral Institution." He justified the liberal arts because they freed "the human mind from vulgar prejudices, ignorance, and error." More important, however, their generality of "character and application" opened to humans "an extensive acquaintance with literature, science and art." Most important, they furnished humanity "with the means of extending his acquaintance with nature, society, and the Bible, to an extent commensurate with the wants of his nature and the limits of his existence."[7]

Although Campbell sang the religiously critical tune of his time, he took exception to some of its skeptical harmony. At times his atonal character—as many others saw it—earned him the enmity of religious friends and the praise of agnostic enemies. West says: "It is not surprising that bitter and hasty critics of Campbell branded him as an infidel, a deist, as well as an Universalist or Unitarian. There is a certain meeting of minds and temper between Campbell and the opponents of revealed religion in their onslaught against traditional Christianity and ecclesiasticism."[8] The meeting of the "minds and temper" that put Campbell in such an awkward position between friends and enemies of Christianity partly revolved around his anticlericalism. Campbell could not have expected a prize for diplomacy after this echo of Jefferson: "The clergy have ever been the greatest tyrants in every state, and at the present they are, in every country of Europe, on the side of the oppressors of the people who tramp on the rights of men."[9] He rankled others because he believed that speculative theology and philosophy, the strong arms of the clergy, were erroneous grounds for church doctrine. He further thought John Locke right in claiming that most churches required more of humanity to become a Christian than Christ did! Beyond stepping on the toes of the clergy and kicking the shins of church doctrine, Campbell ridiculed a multitude of time-honored traditions and customs that he believed availed against reason and/or revelation. Although Campbell shared many views with those who opposed traditional Christianity, he did not fancy himself in the destructive role of the skeptic. To him skeptics were indiscriminate reasoners who failed to distinguish between true Christianity and its many corruptions; corruptions of it, Campbell argued, were "no argument against its divine origin."[10]

The divine ship had to be put on an even keel, not given up! In order to aright the ship, Campbell invited those he attacked to respond. A less confident man might have shrunk from such an approach; his contemporaries testify that this was not one of his weaknesses. His motto: "Hear both sides, and then judge."[11] Campbell confidently believed that those who understood his position regarding the New Testament Church would accept it. In religious matters, people must judge for themselves and allow others the same privilege. The free market of ideas would prevail. In 1846, after twenty-three years of publishing the *Christian Baptist* and *Millennial Harbinger,* Campbell claimed that "we have uniformly and without a single exception, given to our readers both sides of every question upon religion, morality or expediency, that has appeared upon our pages."[12]

Besides writing, public debate was another medium in which Campbell exchanged ideas. Moses Lard, editor of a quarterly bearing his name, called him "the champion of Christianity in America" because of his debate with Robert E. Owen.[13] Walter B. Posey, in his lectures at Louisiana State University, said Campbell "brilliantly defended Christianity against the champion of skepticism." Protestants and Catholics alike considered twice before accepting his forensic challenges, a certain Thomas Cleland declining such a confrontation because he feared "certain defeat; sharing the same fate of . . . all other writers of the brotherhood."[14]

Campbell's preaching likewise attracted the attention of his contemporaries. Robert West maintains that Campbell's "satire, irony, simplicity of speech, and the analogy of Kingcraft and Priestcraft were choice weapons which he used to arouse the frontier folk of the Jacksonian era of American democracy."[15] Campbell suspected his satirical vein and, according to Richardson, often read his manuscripts to Mrs. Selina Campbell to rid them of some of their harshness. Richardson reported that Campbell discontinued *The Christian Baptist* in 1830 and started publishing *The Millennial Harbinger* partially because he preferred a milder-toned chronicle. *The Christian Baptist* had been designed to awaken the Christian world to the evil of clerical despotism, ecclesiasticism and all their attendant evils. *The Millennial Harbinger* was slanted toward showing "the incompatibility of any sectarian establishment, now known on earth, with the genius of the glorious age to come."[16] Although highly opinionated, Campbell was not an inflexible dogmatist. He could and did bend with the times.

Campbell's contemporaries—friend and foe alike—unanimously acknowledged his public speaking ability. At the Virginia Constitutional Convention of 1829, Madison said of Campbell's preaching: "It was my pleasure to hear him very often as a preacher of the gospel, and I regarded him as the ablest and most original expounder of the scriptures I have ever heard."[17] When Campbell preached, he minimized enthusiasm and emphasized logic. He seldom appealed to pathos or tenderness but, as his contemporaries put it, "He was clear."[18] His biblical mastery and literary knowledge commanded the respect of all. Moses Lard judged Campbell "a *fine* scholar, but not a *profound* one."[19] The dry, factual style in which he both wrote and spoke prompted Lard to complain: "he never vivified them [facts], and made them sparkle with the bright light of genius as they left his hand."[20] Lard regretted that Campbell often "seemed to invest his efforts, whether written or spoken, with the appearance of the poetic and imaginative. But he has left us hardly a genuine trace of either upon record."[21] Lard supposed that if Campbell had written biographical history, he "would have shown . . . men's faces; but they would have been the expressionless faces of men as seen beneath the coffin lid."[22] In spite of this shortcoming—perhaps because of it—Campbell's journalism and public speaking appealed to the eyes and ears of a sizable audience enamored with his unpoetic efforts.

The factualness of Campbell's preaching portended a historical, not philosophical, emphasis. This is in part correct. He believed history, the most important of all disciplines, "first in order because it was first in importance."[23] Believing that "the knowledge of facts is the most useful of all knowledge" and that the Bible "is the only authentic history in the world of almost half its existence,"[24] Campbell made a good case for history's primacy. His sermons and lectures were often historically ordered and so freighted with historical allusions that they could hardly have been as "popular" as he intended them. Robert Owen's survival through Campbell's historical wanderings during his "long speech" in the "Great Debate" redounds to Owen's good humor and endurance.

The pulpit and pulpiteer received Campbell's special attention. Campbell's view of the clergy greatly affected his views on preaching. The pulpit did not belong to the clergy. According to Campbell, the claims of power of the clergy were no less unbiblical than their titled names, Reverend or Doctor. A person needed no special call to preach the gospel, thus no special title. The call to preach came through the gospel as contained in the Bible and was instrumentally effected by a local congregation (or a denomination) in conjunction with the individual's desires and qualifications. Ministers were fallible people who differed from others only in the extent of their Christian work, not in the kind of work done. As Campbell put it: "In short there is no need to have men among us professing to be *called and sent* of God.'"[25] Campbell believed in a literal priesthood of believers.

Although Campbell wished the full-time ministry to be well educated, he believed the seminarial approach ill-advised. He was convinced that something artificial happened to the speaking style of seminary students that other professionally inclined graduates escaped. He complained: "my young priest gradually assumes a sanctimonious air, a holy gloom overspreads his face, and a pious sedateness reigns from his eyebrows to his chin . . . With his Sunday coat, on a Sabbath morn, he puts on a mantle of deeper sanctity, and imperceptibly learns the *three* grand tones—the Sabbath tone, the pulpit tone, and the praying tone—these are the devout, the more devout and the most devout."[26] Campbell thrust home his rapier of disdain by concluding that "one hundred such students of divinity" were not worth much. He concluded that "One Benjamite with his sling and stone would put a thousand such to flight."[27]

A good Benjamite with his sling and stone was armed—above all else but not to the exclusion of everything else—with biblical knowledge. Campbell's first sermon delivered in 1810 was an exposition of Matt. 7:24–27, the parable of the man who either builds unwisely on the sand or wisely upon the rock. Campbell was said to have exercised those analytical powers that he would wield with such force throughout his lifetime. Given to little gesticulation and to simplicity of language, he evoked a positive response. According to Richardson, many thought him immediately a better preacher than his father.[28]

But he was not only the Bible's expounder; he was its advocate. On one occasion while visiting in Cincinnati, Campbell had addressed the Young Men's Mercantile Library Association. Dr. Herman Humphrey, former president of Amherst College, listened in the audience and later wrote in the *New York Observer* that "Dr. Campbell's first discourse was an exceedingly interesting eulogy, if I may so call it, upon the Bible, glancing rapidly at some of the internal proofs of its divine origin, dwelling as much as his time would allow upon its wonderful history, biography and prophecies."[29] Dr. Humphrey further described Campbell as the "most perfectly self-possessed, the most perfectly at ease in the pulpit of any preacher I ever listened to, except, perhaps, the celebrated Dr. John Mason of New York."[30]

Campbell's views on the nature and function of the Bible greatly affected the character of his theology, and, consequently, his preaching. Although the Bible contained the revelation of God, everything in the Bible was not revelation, but the entire Bible was inspired, that is, "divinely authenticated."[31] Not all that was inspired could be urged upon humanity as revelation; in fact, because of Campbell's dispensationalism, not all revelation, though inspired, was obligatory upon people. Campbell remonstrated with those covenanters who would put the yoke of Jewish law, obviously inspired and revealed, upon Christians.

Campbell avoided a literal or mechanical view of inspiration wherein the writer transcribed exact dictation given by the Holy Spirit, and he also avoided the plenary view of inspiration wherein the total content, but not style or words, was inspired. The Bible, therefore, blended elements both human and divine, but it was not humanity who determined the blending; it was the Holy Spirit.[32]

But the Holy Spirit's influence upon the individual was never intended to contradict the Bible. Since the Holy Spirit always worked with the Scripture, not beyond or in opposition to it, the study of the Bible became imperative for the Christian, especially the preacher. What might appear to be the leading of the Holy Spirit could not be ascertained short of an empirical base against which to judge the leading; that base was the Bible. Therefore, one's personal experience did not determine the meaning of the Scriptures; instead, the Scriptures' meaning determined the validity (meaning) of the experience.[33]

Since metaphysical regeneration, according to Campbell, was not infused in the heart upon conversion, it was the person's obligation to know the Scriptures both before and after conversion. Since the Holy Spirit indwelled the individual after conversion, it could assist her or him through its empowering influence to act correctly, if the person knew what correct behavior was; or, upon having had some apparent religious experience, the validity of the experience could be checked against biblical standards. In either case, the objective revelation was superior to the untutored subjective judgment. The preacher, therefore, had to study the Scriptures; he could not rely upon the Holy Spirit to directly reveal its truth to him in any mystical manner. The individual acquired biblical knowledge by the same means as any other kind of knowledge.[34]

The nature and source of Campbell's theory of knowledge, then, had some bearing upon his rationalistic views. He held that all knowledge had its origin in experience. Ideas in the mind came via the senses. Having accepted this essentially Lockean, empirical doctrine and having denied intuitive knowledge (be it Platonic, Plotinian, or Kantian), the idea of God, for instance, though supernatural in origin, had to come into the mind via the senses, Campbell insisted. In the Campbell-Owen debate, which made Campbell famous on the frontier, he asked Owen, the English industrialist, materialist, and Utopian reformer, to agree that anything known came through the five senses. Owen agreed. Although believing in a God, Owen asserted that Divinity had not given any revelation to humans. Whereupon Campbell questioned how one could have knowledge (or an idea) about God when God had never been seen, heard, tasted, felt, or smelled. Campbell posed the skeptic's dilemma in this manner: "The Christian idea of an Eternal First Cause uncaused, or of a God, is now in the world, and has been for ages immemorial. You say it *could not* enter into the world by *reason,* and [you say] it *did not enter by revelation.* Now, as you are philosophers and historians, and have all the means of knowing, *How did it come into the world?*"[35]

Garrison stated the problem this way: "Granted that we can have no natural knowledge or idea of God, it is nevertheless true that we actually do have such an idea. Our ideas of spiritual things are facts to be explained. They must have a cause since it cannot be the natural reason, must be divine revelation."[36] Campbell held that the world was the effect of God; but one really could not know this to be true apart from revelation. He concluded that "To require us, then, to know a designer, in order to the proving of a design, is to require us to *know* a matter which is *to be proved,* that we may prove the evidences by which we are to prove itself! To make a designer the proof of design, is absurdity itself. How can we know a designer? By looking into his cranium and seeing his thoughts?"[37] His answer was an emphatic "no." One had knowledge of God by "observing his outward manifestations of mind."[38] These manifestations, the things he had said and done, told humans of God because revelation confirmed that God existed.

In short, the preacher should transmit revealed knowledge: it was in the Bible, the depository of all spiritual ideas available to people. The responsibility of the preacher was logically and accurately to relate these ideas to the listener. The Holy Spirit did not directly operate on the listener's mind during preaching, but the preacher did!

Campbell looked upon his audience with deep respect in spite of the revivalistic emotionalism of the times. The Baptists and Methodists placed a low value on dignity and beauty in their revival efforts, and, as Miyakawa concluded, "emotionalism was not conducive to long systematic study."[39] Campbell feared emotionalism. He appeared to his contemporaries as a rationalist. Miyakawa characterized the whole Campbellite movement as a "western religious version of rationalism and liberalism" that attracted "the more prosperous and better educated Baptists."[40] In 1839, upon returning from a speaking tour in the South, Campbell criticized the emotionalism of the Baptists, using the Methodists for invidious comparison: "They have adopted the recruiting and converting tactics of the Methodists even to a superfluity of excitation. Their new converts are born in a tempest of passion and feeling, under the inflammatory process of long protracted meetings [Campbell was hardly an after-dinner speaker himself], and of deeply impassioned appeals to their feelings. They live only in the high temperature of excitement and languish under the dispensation of reason and truth."[41] Campbell stressed the distinction between the "religion of excitement" and the "excitement of religion." People who lived in the atmosphere of a "religion of excitement" were "mushroom Christians" who "grow to perfection in a night, and wither in a day . . . They are deluded by the idea that religion is the effect, and not the cause of feeling. Religion, with them, is the fruit of excitement, rather than the root and reason of it."[42] And on the relationship of feeling to religion, Campbell said: "Let not one hence infer that we are opposed to feeling. God forbid! A religion without feeling is a body without a spirit. A religion that does not reach the heart and rouse all our feelings into admiration, gratitude, love, and praise, is a mere phantom. But we make feelings the *effect*, not the *cause* of faith and of true religion. We begin not with feelings but with the understanding: we call the upon men first to believe, then to feel, and then to act. The gospel takes the whole man—the head, the heart, the hand."[43]

Campbell actually enjoyed the company of religious anti-emotionalists who were, in many doctrinal circumstances, his enemies. He said little about the Episcopalians, who, in their aloofness from emotionalism, quietly condemned revivalistic proceedings. The Presbyterians, according to Perry Miller, "never condemned the principle of the Revival *in toto*, but simply objected (however strenuously) to inflated eloquence, to a neglect of theology, to allowing emotions to run away with logic."[44] In December 1830, during a tour that took Campbell to Franklin, Tennessee, he complained about "the icebergs of Calvinism," although he commented favorably upon a Mr. Jennings of Nashville who spoke with a "fine Presbyterian voice, with a very evangelical tone."[45] The Unitarians, blessed with the passion of Orville Dewey and the warmth of William Ellery Channing, dismissed revivalism as artificial, delusionary, and thus un-American. In 1840 Campbell made essentially the same charges when he accused the users of the "mourning bench" and "anxious seat" of creating delusion with "dreams, anecdotes, fictions . . . and unmeaning vociferations." He concluded that "the machinery of modern revivals is not divine, but human. It is certainly delusive."[46] The evil of "fanaticism," similar to that of the Crusades, had prompted revivalists to put unchristian bait "on the evangelical hook."[47] The solution to the problem was succinct: "From all this scene of raging enthusiasm, be admonished, my friends, to open your Bibles and to hearken to the voice of God, which is the voice of reason."[48]

Always suspicious of the mystical, Campbell, in an address on "phrenology, Animal Magnetism, Clairvoyance, etc." delivered at Washington College, Pennsylvania, in 1852, concluded "that spirit speaks in a style of lofty argument, of moral dignity and Divine grandeur, worthy of a Christian's heaven; . . . [of] his lofty port and heavenward aspirations, and not in the grimace and silly buffoonery of those spirits that peep and mutter tales unworthy of man, and still more unworthy of woman. From such demons, such silly demons, whether of imagination, fraud or fiction, let every man and woman of self-respect, of good sense and of sound discretion, turn away with scorn and contempt."[49]

Human dignity and their high destiny were prominent in Campbell's thinking and preaching. He noted that "it is mind alone that works on mind. It is educated mind that educates mind. It is living men and living books that quicken, inspire, develop, energize and polish mind. It is not theory nor a dead letter that animates and actuates the faculties of man . . . It is the present living generation that gives character and spirit to the next. Hence the paramount importance of accomplished and energetic teachers [and preachers] in forming the taste, the manners and the character of the coming age."[50]

Paramount to humanity's dignity was a person's free will. The preacher was persuader, not an echoing mouthpiece. Campbell was convinced that necessity destroyed virtue. Robert Owen, as interpreted by Campbell, had argued that lack of social virtue in the world was due to necessity since humanity had not created themselves and was therefore not responsible. Campbell called Owen "short-sighted" for his position and asked: "Will not this principle of necessity inevitably exterminate all good, kind, and generous feelings?"[51] Owen himself, claimed Campbell, had some "good, kind and generous feelings" because he had proposed to change certain malevolent conditions in society and in some cases had actually done so. But if the absence of social virtue was occasioned by humanity's irresponsible actions brought about because of necessity, Campbell questioned how Owen could logically campaign for the reversal of necessity by people who were no better than necessarily irresponsible. Campbell concluded that Owen agreed with him that "we change our circumstances, and our circumstances change us."[52] And that freedom meant responsible human action, which Owen had amply demonstrated in his own philanthropic pursuits. Of course Owen did not so conclude.

According to Campbell, testimony was essential to belief, and when that testimony was sufficient, humanity's determination or volition might constrain belief.[53] God's testimony, and thus humanity's preaching, was compelling but not compulsory in its effect upon the mind, for one acted ultimately out of self-interest, that is, acted voluntarily and according to reason.[54] The mind could examine and reexamine any issue before willing to act, but Campbell, noting humanity's limitations and their lack of complete freedom, did not subscribe to the idea that limited freedom meant no freedom. Without freedom of will, however limited, people would have no responsibility to themselves or to others. Humankind was a dependent, not an independent, creature, since freedom to act was valueless unless people had a standard by which to gauge the responsibleness (value) of their actions.[55]

The sinner, a certain kind of listener, was active in regeneration since his or her mind was "a thinking, rational principle."[56] Thus when Calvinists claimed that any activity of the unregenerated mind was necessarily against God, Campbell shrugged off the matter as a "comfortable theory."[57] The empirical, nonintuitive thought of Campbell can be seen in his unqualified, negative reaction to "Calvinism's Five Points," or more accurately, the "Five Points" of the Synod of Dort, 1618–1619.[58] Campbell came close to being an Arminian in his position on the Five Points, although he insisted that both were "equidistant from the true Gospel."[59]

If this "true" gospel were to be rationally, not supernaturally, conveyed to the listener, then the language of communication was vitally important. Campbell gave no small amount of attention to this matter. In an address in 1849 on "The Anglo-Saxon Language, Its Origin, Character and Destiny," he glowingly described all the achievements of the Anglo-Saxon, paying particular attention to the language which was "that ethereal instrument, that spiritual symbol, by which one spirit operates upon another, in simultaneously producing views, feelings and emotions, corresponding with its own."[60] The Anglo-Saxon language, blessed more than any other because it had drawn upon all other languages, had within it a greater diversity of sentiment and emotion. It "directly, clearly, fully and impressively utter[ed] all the soul" desired. The language was the mind of a people. The Anglo-Saxon had the best mind because everyone envied it. Germany, France, Prussia, and Russia had intellectual accomplishments but did "homage to the Anglo-Saxon mind . . . [not only] by transferring their works into our language," even as we do theirs, but by "laying aside their own sciences, arts and inventions, and in adopting ours."[61] The language was better, therefore the mind was better.

All language began when God gave Adam the gift of speech, "not by inspiration, but by example";[62] he acquired language by imitation, according to Campbell. God, of necessity, gave Adam a religious vocabulary by which he received "knowledge of his origin, nature, relations, obligations and destiny."[63]

In the beginning language was almost wholly narrative because humanity wrote down or repeated what they saw and heard, which came to them either through direct experience or by revelation. Only later did language become abstract and theoretical. Since humanity's ideas originally depended upon sensations received from external sources, religious ideas would have had to come from an external moral source, God himself, and would have had to be accepted by faith—or as Campbell put it, by credulity. Labeled by Campbell as the "greatest moral power of man," credulity permitted people to receive "instruction upon the testimony of teachers," without which they were incapable of improvement. Even the ancient philosophers' syllogistic reasonings assumed, according to Campbell, that "their conclusions were wiser than their premises," but so to conclude involved possessing "previous information upon the subject which they did not derive from reason."[64] Without facts to be accepted, their reasonings were worthless.

Religious facts were in the Bible, and when uncovered, understood, and obeyed, would bring felicity and happiness as God had promised. The key that would unlock the Bible and would spill its unadulterated treasure upon humankind was proper biblical interpretation. If, said Campbell, "all students of the Bible [were] taught to apply the same rules of interpretation to its pages, there would be a greater uniformity in opinion and sentiment, than ever resulted from the simple adoption of any written creed."[65] These rules of interpretation had to be creedless, not those of "enthusiasts and fanatics of all ages [who] determine the meanings of words, from that knowledge of things which they imagine themselves to possess, rather than from the words of the author,— They decide by what they suppose he ought to mean, rather than by what he says."[66]

The Bible, therefore, was to be understood grammatically, not doctrinally; rationally, not intuitively. Although he noted that Calvinist and Arminian alike urged that "their respective doctrines . . . be tried by the scripture, and by the scripture alone," they argued in circles, said Campbell. They said in effect: "You are to try our doctrine by the Scripture only. But then you are to be very careful that you explain the Scripture solely by our doctrine." Undoubtedly "a wonderful plan of trial," Campbell mocked, which "begins with giving judgment, and ends with examining the proof, wherein the whole skill and ingenuity of the judges are to be exerted in wresting the evidence, so as to give it the appearance of supporting the sentence pronounced beforehand."[67] In this way Campbell disposed of those theologians who first decided their faith and then proceeded "to examine what the Scriptures say."[68] Although not without an a priori of "how" the Bible ought to be interpreted, he wished to avoid presuppositions that presumed the "what" of its content. The Bible was to be analyzed "by fixed and certain principles or rule of interpretation." Since the Christian institution was divine, the principles by which the Christian institution could be certainly and satisfactorily ascertained were of paramount interest. He warned that "unless the sacred *writings* could be certainly interpreted, the Christian religion could never be certainly understood."[69] And in all of this matter of interpretation Campbell contended that God would not intuitively reveal anything to people.

God, having addressed humans in human language, assumed that humanity could properly interpret and understand. The introduction of many dialects and the changing forms of languages made the art of interpretation more difficult. But a basic art of interpretation still remained, or else God in his subsequent speaking to humans was neither wise nor benevolent "in giving any verbal communications."[70] Thus the preacher, when he stood before his congregation, was obligated to demonstrate that he had good hermeneutical reasons for advocating the acceptance of any Scripture interpretation; there was to be no personality cult built around the preacher's whims and fancies.

In summary and conclusion, then, it appears that Campbell's rationalism left no room for the belief that spiritual understanding was the sacrosanct domain of the clergy; instead, it belonged to any Christian whose intellectual qualities were sufficiently developed so that she or he could spell out the gospel in understandable terms. Luther's "priesthood of believers" found fulfillment in Campbell, at least in his opinion.[71] The effective preacher disclosed to the audience his application of mental powers to the Bible's content. The Holy Spirit would not directly infuse the mind of the preacher or listener with spiritual ideas; spiritual ideas—any ideas, for that matter—would be just as good as their source (in this instance, the Bible) and their proper interpretation as given by the human mind. People were to be looked upon as rational and capable of being appealed to by reason and argument, whose dignity ought not to be subjected to disheveled evangelists, who, in the words of Peter Cartwright, were "borne to sea with full sail and no ballast." Those who listened to the clearly presented gospel should respond freely to its call. The revelation of God was clear enough; but however, the preaching of humans, churned by the rampaging waters of human speculation and drowned by emotionalism, was often alarmingly muddied. To correct this, the preacher ought to view the Bible as its own best interpreter, permitting God to speak to humanity in God's own words. The preacher was essentially a persuader who brought clearly to the mind of the listener—sinner and saint alike—a rational and logical appeal to biblical evidence that should bring an affirmative response to God's admonition. The preacher, in short, pleaded God's cause!

In the wilderness of American sectarian life, Campbell the prophet found the threads of primitivism that he rationally wove into a religious institution. In the temple of American sectarian life, Campbell the priest officiated over a vigorous housecleaning that turned many of the tables of religious emotionalism. After the performance of prophet and priest, things were different. His opposition labeled him "destructive"; his friends, "constructive," because he had broken the shackles of "sectarianism." Vigorous, ambitious, intelligent, and perceptive, Alexander Campbell skillfully guided an embryonic religious revolt into a reform, or, as he preferred to call it, a restoration of the "ancient order of things." Beyond his basic doctrinal position, his chief weapon of attack was a distinctive form of rationalism that set him apart from many of his less rational contemporaries and added a distinguished chapter to America's middle frontier life of the nineteenth century.

NOTES

1. Robert Frederick West, *Campbell and Natural Religion* (New Haven: Yale Univ. Press, 1948), 3.

2. Robert Richardson, *Memoirs of Alexander Campbell* (Cincinnati: Standard Publishing Co., 1897), 2:540.

3. *Alexander Campbell as a Preacher* (New York: Fleming H. Revell, 1908; reprint, Grand Rapids: Baker Book House, 1955), 58.

4. Richardson, *Memoirs of Alexander Campbell.*

5. Alexander Campbell, *Familiar Lectures on the Pentateuch,* ed. W. T. Moore (Cincinnati: Bosworth, Chase, and Hall, 1871), 44.

6. West, *Campbell and Natural Religion,* 29.

7. Alexander Campbell, ed., *Millennial Harbinger, 1830–1864* (Bethany, Va.: A. Campbell, 1849), 433.

8. West, *Campbell and Natural Religion,* 45.

9. Alexander Campbell, ed., *The Christian Baptist, 1823–30* (n.p., Gospel Advocate Co., 1955), 2:126.

10. Campbell, *Millennial Harbinger,* 1832, 311–13.

11. Ibid., 1851, 226.

12. Ibid., 1846, 4.

13. Moses E. Lard, ed., *Lard's Quarterly* (Lexington, Ky., 1866; reprint, Kansas City, Mo.: Old Paths Book Club, 1950), 3:269.

14. Walter Brownlow Posey, *Religious Strife on the Southern Frontier* (Baton Rouge: Louisiana State Univ. Press, 1965), 53–54.

15. West, *Campbell and Natural Religion,* 9.

16. Campbell, *Millennial Harbinger,* 1830, 1.

17. Richardson, *Memoirs of Alexander Campbell,* 313.

18. Lard, *Lard's Quarterly,* 3:258.

19. Ibid., 261.

20. Ibid., 259.

21. Ibid.

22. Ibid., 258.

23. Campbell, *Millennial Harbinger,* 1845, 320.

24. Ibid.

25. Campbell, *The Christian Baptist,* 1:49–56.

26. Ibid., 1:106.

27. Ibid., 2:6–10.

28. Richardson, *Memoirs of Alexander Campbell,* 1:313–14, 316.

29. Ibid., 582.

30. Ibid.

31. Alexander Campbell, *Campbell-Owen Debate* (Bethany, Va., 1829; reprint Nashville: McQuiddy Printing Co., 1946), 381.

32. Campbell, *Millennial Harbinger,* 1864, 79–81.

33. Richardson, *Memoirs of Alexander Campbell,* 226.

34. Campbell, *The Christian Baptist,* 5:227.

35. Campbell, *Campbell-Owen Debate,* 123.

36. Winfred E. Garrison, *The Sources of Alexander Campbell's Theology* (St. Louis: Christian Publishing Co., 1900), 191.
37. Campbell, *Millennial Harbinger*, 1831, 149.
38. Ibid.
39. T. Scott Miyakawa, *Protestants and Pioneers* (Chicago: Univ. of Chicago Press, 1964), 159–73.
40. Ibid., 104–5, 150, 157.
41. Campbell, *Millennial Harbinger*, 1839, 11.
42. Ibid., 33–34.
43. Ibid., 12.
44. Perry Miller, *The Life of the Mind in America* (New York: Harcourt, Brace & World, 1965), 17.
45. Campbell, *Millennial Harbinger*, 1831, 111–13.
46. Ibid., 1840, 167–70.
47. Ibid.
48. Campbell, *The Christian Baptist*, 1:149.
49. Alexander Campbell, *Popular Lectures and Addresses* (Philadelphia: James Challen & Son, 1863; reprint, Cincinnati: Standard Publishing Company, n.d.), 212.
50. Ibid., 488.
51. Campbell, *Campbell-Owen Debate*, 56.
52. Ibid., 57.
53. Ibid., 73.
54. Campbell, *Millennial Harbinger*, 1854, 425.
55. Ibid., 1854, 66–67.
56. Campbell, *The Christian Baptist*, 3:5.
57. Ibid.
58. Campbell, *Millennial Harbinger*, 1831, 109; *The Christian System*, 2d ed. (St. Louis: Christian Board of Publication, 1839), 4.
59. Campbell, *Millennial Harbinger*, 1858, 144–45; 241–44.
60. Campbell, *Popular Lectures and Addresses*, 18.
61. Ibid., 30.
62. Ibid., 21.
63. Ibid., 109–10.
64. Campbell, *Campbell-Owen Debate*, 91–92.
65. Campbell, *Christianity Restored* (Rosemead, Calif.: Old Paths Book Club, 1959), 15.
66. Ibid., 23.
67. Ibid., 67.
68. Ibid., 66.
69. Ibid.
70. Ibid., 17.
71. Campbell, *The Christian Baptist*, 1:132–36, 2:152–58.

Campbell's Post-Protestantism and Civil Religion

Mont Whitson

Alexander Campbell (1788–1866) was the founder and most influential leader of a religious restoration during the nineteenth century. Along with his father, Thomas Campbell, he forged the movement into the largest nativistic church in America.

Ahlstrom says Campbell was "an important figure in American church history, a curious compound of the rationalistic theologian on the one hand and the eccentric and legalistic sectary on the other."[1] Living on the American frontier, Campbell, filled with a sense of mission and the freedom of beginning something new, worked through his reformation impulse to come up with what he later referred to as a restoration of New Testament Christianity. Commenting on his efforts, Mead calls the movement "the most successful of the definitely Christian indigenous denominations in America."[2]

EUROPEAN BACKGROUND

Campbell was born in Ireland and later pursued his college studies at the University of Glasgow in Scotland. He and his family, having left the Church of England, belonged to the Antiburger Presbyterian Church. While Campbell was in Glasgow the university was in a state of excitement and tension following the French Revolution. Campbell became acquainted with the inductive sciences and the new questions being raised about revealed and natural religion. He read and carefully studied the works of Locke, Bacon, Hume, Newton, Rousseau, Voltaire, and other political and social philosophers. Campbell was especially enamored with the Scottish "common sense" philosophy, a conservative response to Hume's skepticism, and with Locke's views on the church, society, and the state. As a boy he was absorbed with Locke's *Letters on Toleration*. Debating Robert Owen in 1829, Campbell says it was this "essay" that "first burst the chains that held England and Europe fast bound under a religious and civil despotism."[3]

EARLY AMERICAN EXPERIENCE

At the age of twenty-one in 1809, Campbell, with his European early training and experience, arrived in the United States. He was soon united with his father in Washington, Pennsylvania, a small western town near Pittsburgh. Thomas had come to America two years earlier and was already deeply involved with the Seceder Presbyterian Church. By the time Alexander arrived, Thomas Campbell had already organized the "Christian Association of Washington," a left-wing religious organization protesting the narrow and sectarian practices of the Seceder Church. In response to the church, which had expelled him from their communion, Thomas Campbell had just published his fifty-six-page "Declaration and Address." One of the first readers was Alexander, who had just arrived on the scene. Garrison's assessment of this document follows:

> This address is, for the most part, a tract on Christian unity. Few more logical and more impassioned appeals for that cause have ever been written. Its first ten and its last five pages are devoted almost wholly to this theme . . . In Mr. Campbell's view, the Christian world was made up of many parties, all of which hold all essential Christian truth and practiced the ordinances of God. They were divided because they treated as of divine authority so many other things which, as a matter of fact, were only "human opinion," or "inventions of men," or "inferential truths" derived by fallible reason.[4]

After four years of looking for a spiritual home, the Campbells merged their "Association" and the Brush Run Church with the Redstone Baptist Association. For the next seventeen years (1813–30), they remained with the Baptists. In 1830 the restoration movement became a separate entity. From 1823 to 1830, Alexander Campbell published the hard-hitting and crusading *Christian Baptist;* however, now with a growing, active, newborn church, he began the publication of the *Millennial Harbinger.* During the thirty-six years of Campbell's editorship, the widely circulated publication was the definitive explanation of the movement. The growth of Campbell's church was phenomenal during the second quarter of the nineteenth century. For example, by 1850, after only twenty years, the Disciples of Christ, with 118,000 members, ranked sixth in size among the Protestant churches in the United States.[5] Ten years later the Disciples membership had risen to 192,000.[6] Their churches, centered in mid-America, were scattered across the total expanse of the nation, all the way from New York to California. In the early 1830s the membership rolls were greatly expanded when many churches under the leadership of Walter Scott and Barton Stone joined the Campbell crusade. These men, especially Stone, had participated in the Great Western Revival, which began about 1800 and reached its crest in 1803. Scott, with his "formula for salvation," became the most influential preacher of the movement. His formula, which included five steps to conversion (hearing, believing, repentance, confession, and baptism), was "no frenzy of emotion, but a blending of rationality and authority, an appeal to common sense and to the Scripture."[7]

By the first quarter of the twentieth century the Restoration movement, which its origin in a plea for Christian unity was divided into three distinct groups: the Disciples of Christ, Churches of Christ, and the Christian Church. Each of the three divisions actually represented different parts of Campbell's complex and developmental theology, ranging from left-wing to right-wing thought. The Disciples of Christ have carried with them Campbell's unity theme while the Churches of Christ and Christian Churches have continued to stress a rationalistic, legalistic, restorationist agenda. Total membership of the three branches ranges between five to six million, thus placing them in the top six among American churches.

CAMPBELL'S RELIGIOUS AND POLITICAL THOUGHT

The New Testament was the central theme of Campbell's theology. To him much of the confusion and decadence of religion had evolved because both Protestants and Catholics failed to make a clear distinction between the Old and New Testaments. Throughout his life, Campbell maintained a careful balance, including a cautious distinction as well as an underlying unity in God's progressive revelation between the three distinctive biblical dispensations: "The *Patriarchal* continued from Adam to Moses, the *Jewish* from Moses to the Messiah, and the *Christian* from the Messiah till now, and is never to be superseded by another."[8]

Each of the dispensations stressed different political, social, and religious norms. Religious *ethics* were revealed directly to man during the Patriarchal age. A *covenant theology* with a religio-political and moral constitution was the high point of the Jewish age. The Christian dispensation derived from the teaching and commands of Christ is a *government of principles* rather than legal precepts. The Decalogue was a highly specialized rule of life for Jews only, while the Christian dispensation is a universal principle of love and fellowship with "only general rules . . . to be filled up by our own reflection and reason."[9] Campbell's first complete presentation of his dispensational view was developed in 1816 before the Redstone Baptist Association in a celebrated and highly controversial "Sermon on the Law." "In it Campbell undertook to do for his own time what the Apostle Paul had done for the churches of the first century in his letters to the Galatians and to the Romans."[10]

Philanthropy increased with each of the dispensations. According to Campbell, Christian philanthropy transcends all selfishness, including family, tribal and national loyalty or patriotism. In the Christian age, national patriotism is always to be held checked and under judgment of Christ. Love, fellowship, and freedom broadened with each of the three dispensations: "In the Patriarchal Age it included family or tribe. For Jews the object was the welfare of the nation of one's fellow citizens. Christian love embraces the whole world and enjoins us to imitate the universal benevolence of our Creator."[11]

Campbell's dispensational theology was met with stiff opposition by most of the Protestant world. Following his "Sermon on the Law," many members of the Baptist Association viewed him as an erratic and dangerous preacher. Following the lecture, Campbell was "itenerated less," being restricted to three or four small communities in Ohio, Virginia, and Pennsylvania.

LEFT-WING RATIONALIST

Fundamentally, Campbell was a left-wing, rationalist New Testament primitivist, emphasizing in his writings and preaching the "ancient order" of first-century Christianity. "The apostolic days" (to Campbell), writes Schlesinger, "had somewhat the rule that the primeval state of nature had for Locke . . . a moment of historical purity which could serve ever after as the measure of the rights and duty of man."[12] The movement, Campbell believed, transcended history since the restored church would be freed from all corrupt baggage added during nearly two thousand years of Catholic and Protestant domination. Lunger says Campbell was not only a New Testament primitivist but also, in a very special way, an Acts-Epistles primitivist. This emphasis accounts "for his wide divergence from what are thought of as typical left-wing social and political views, and also for the ease with which he arrived at a denominational synthesis on many specific issues."[13]

To Campbell the church "is essentially, intentionally and constitutionally one." The only constitution for believers is the New Testament. Human opinions, primarily in the form of ordinances, divide rather than unite Christians. One of the mottoes of Campbell's early faith was, "Where the Scripture speaks, we speak; where the Scriptures are silent, we are silent."[14]

Local autonomy among the churches and the separation of the church and state within the nation were basic doctrinal positions of Campbell. Both of these views are close to Locke's thesis of church and state.[15] To Locke, the commonwealth was "a society of men constituted only for the procuring, the preserving, and the advancing of their own civil interests." Similar to Locke's social contract, the church to Campbell was a "spiritual contract" between individuals and Jesus Christ. Again, in the Lockean tradition, Campbell conceptualized the church as a "voluntary society of men, joining themselves together of their own accord."[16] An example of this voluntarism explains his position on baptism. Church membership is limited to adult members who, after a rational choice and confession, are baptized into the body of Christ. He was an ardent critic of infant baptism, which to him placed a person in the kingdom without his own will or consent.

MILLENNIUM

Basking in their Adamic innocence, nineteenth-century Americans began to assume their task of implementing the idealized society foreshadowed by the American Revolution.[17] The idea of progress and utopian bliss became a common ethic among many political and religious leaders during this period. Especially on the American frontier millennial hope for an ameliorated society motivated the pioneers to perform their tasks with high hopes and unlimited vigor. An irresistible force seems to propel them onward. They were no longer "free agents" in this pervasive, all-embracing thrust of history.[18] They had been chosen as eschatological agents in a unique historical, social, and political drama. As actors on the historical stage, they joyfully dramatized the saga for others to see and to emulate.

Soon after arriving in the exciting, revolutionary "new world," Campbell caught the millennial fervor. His millennial stirrings increased during what Bellah poetically refers to as the "rich and fruitful mid-19th century summer."[19] Campbell began a reworking of the "Garden of Eden" on the American frontier. "No other preacher," writes Tuvenson, "fused the religious and secular elements of the millennial utopia . . . one could say . . . for Campbell (that) Americanizing the world, in the right sense, is almost identical with millennializing it." Campbell, continues Tuvenson, "goes . . . further than most millennialists in implicitly transferring the focus of redemption from the individual to the 'world.' The purpose of God in his dealings with men is to bring about a peaceful and just democracy in which they may dwell."[20]

During his *Christian Baptist* days, while loosely associated with the Baptist Church, Campbell often interrelated the restoration of New Testament Christianity with the fulfillment of his millennial hopes. In the 1829 issue he referred to the progress from "Babylon to Jerusalem" and the heightening, "with every volume of this work," toward "the arriving of the Millennium."[21] In 1830, following the break with the Baptists, he began the publication of the *Millennial Harbinger*. By this, time he was using the expression "The Millennial Church." In the first paragraph of the new periodical, he set forth the underlying principles of his future course as a utopian reformer: "This work shall be devoted to the destruction of sectarianism, infidelity and antichristian doctrine and practice. It shall have for its object the development and introduction of the political and religious order of society called *The Millennium,* which will be the consummation of that ultimate amelioration of society proposed in the Christian Scriptures."[22] The arrival of the millennium would negate all the evils of society, including sectarianism in the church, selfishness in the society, and injustices, such as slavery, in the state. Along with promoting the millennium, he exposed and warned his readers against being taken in by the "wild eschatology" of Miller and other contemporary premillennialists.

Showing some of his concern for the American nation, Campbell envisioned Christianity finally subverting the "purely political" American government, but not before society became fully civilized. Some of the hindrances to human happiness, along with Judaism, Paganism, and Romanism are "selfishness, violence, inordinate ambition, revenge, duelling . . . tyranny, oppression and cruelty." Like the Anabaptist, Campbell, at least at this time of his theological ferment, blurred the differences between church and society once the amelioration had fully come. The "purified church" was to become "in effect a total society."[23] The present "legal model" was to be replaced with the "evangelical" or "gospel model." Unlike the present reality of the *Civitas*, in the future "ultimate reality is an ecclesia, or church. It affirms that God is known not in glory, but suffering."[24] The ends of government, Campbell argues, are justice, defense, freedom, and welfare, not the final stage of human happiness that will come with the millennial order: "The admirers of American liberty and American institutions have no cause to regret such an event, no cause to fear it. It will be but the removing of a tent to build a temple—the falling of a cottage after the family are removed into a castle. Not by might, nor by sword, but by the spirit of the Lord will the political institutions of our government be laid aside."[25]

During his American experience Campbell wavered between pessimism and optimism regarding the role of the republic in the Christianization of the world. Lunger, in *The Political Ethics of Alexander Campbell,* observes three distinct periods in Campbell's millennial hopes for America: (1) up to 1830, early enthusiasm for the republic; (2) 1830–46, some disillusionment and despair; and (3) 1847–67, returning enthusiasm and hopes.[26]

His more optimistic declarations of faith in the republic are discernible in a series of lectures delivered over a twenty-five year period:

1. "An Oration in Honor of the Fourth of July," 1830
2. "On Common Schools," 1841
3. "Address on War," 1848
4. "The Anglo-Saxon Language," 1849
5. "The Destiny of Our Country," 1852
6. "Address on Colleges," 1854

Specific references to these lectures will be made later in the discussion of Campbell's civil religion.

POST-PROTESTANTISM

There is a post-Protestant ring to many of Campbell's religious positions. Employing Bellah's five stages of religious evolution—primitive, archaic, historic, early modern, and modern—one must conclude that much of what Campbell taught belongs to the "modern" evolutionary stage. He stands somewhere this side of the Protestant tradition. Campbell's post-Protestant modernization of religion was to continue on into the twentieth century by many of his followers. For example, the Disciples of Christ, with their ecumenical spirit, have steadfastly remained fluid and open to change. They represent the most consistent post-Protestant stance of the Campbell movement. The Churches of Christ and Christian Churches fall more in the "early modern" stage, and at times they sound more "archaic" than "early modern."

Campbell was not horrified of or fearful of change. He stands in the best tradition of the "idea of progress" and newness in the Christian experience. Openness to change, writes Bellah, "requires a great social-psychological revolution." This revolution, if successful, produces "social and personality systems capable of combining continuity and change, identity and openness to even deep-going structural reorganization."[27]

Many of the religious leaders of his time looked upon Campbell as an antireligious, theological heretic because of his relentless attacks upon some of the basic traditional Christian symbols and doctrines. He was consistently anticlerical, anticreedal and antihierarchical. Creeds, clerics, and bureaucracies to Campbell robbed the church and its members of an openness and choice in their beliefs and practices. As he saw the movement pass from sect to denomination, Campbell remained relatively unchanged in his basic "unchurchly" tenets.

In some ways he was not unlike Mark Twain and Robert Owen in their agnostic criticism of religion. "Campbell," writes Tuveson, "could condemn most of mankind's religious history almost as vehemently as Owen." In comparing Twain and Campbell, Tuveson says, "for all Mark Twain's distrust of doctrinalism and revivals, Campbell's conception of history had much that might well appeal to the grown man Clemons."[28]

One of Campbell's earlier confrontations with Protestant churchmen occurred in 1824 when he strongly opposed the Moral Society supported by the clergy in West Middletown Pennsylvania. In the *Washington (Pennsylvania) Reporter* he called the society a "moral evil." The moral association was pushing for fines and imprisonment of Sunday lawbreakers (for example, Sabbath-breaking, profane swearing, drunkenness, card playing, ball playing, and gaming). These societies, argued Campbell, were "anti-evangelical, anti-constitutional and anti-rational." Following through on his constitutional argument Campbell reminded the citizens that observance or nonobservance of the Sabbath was a "right of conscience," therefore the Sabbath-breakers could be fined or proscribed by civil law for not following the religious convictions of church members.[29]

CIVIL RELIGION

Lecturing on "Common Schools" at Clarksburg, Virginia, in 1841, Campbell reported to his audience existence of a "common Christianity" in the United States: "It is also becoming more and more evident, that, notwithstanding all our sectarian differences, we yet have something called a common Christianity; that there are certain great fundamental matters—indeed, every thing elementary in what is properly called piety and morality—in which all good men of all denominations are agreed."[30]

Thirteen years later, in his "Address on Colleges," Campbell clarified his "common Christianity" by describing a kind of overarching civil religion existing alongside various denominations:

> Yes, fellow citizens, we have a by law established religion (in America). I do not affirm that we have a by law established Jewish, Christian or Pagan religion in the specific terms of a Jewish, a Christian or Pagan hierarchy. Still, we have a by law established religion, but in the right of conscience, in the administration of oaths, or appeals to God, on the part of all the organs of civil government from the President of the United States down to a common magistrate . . . In these we have a solemn recognition of the being and perfection of God, of a day of judgment, of future and eternal rewards and punishment.[31]

Campbell's "common Christianity" is an earlier expression of current constructions such as Mead's "the religion of the republic," Smylie's "the nation itself," Herberg's "the American way of life," and Bellah's "civil religion."[32] American "civil religion," according to Bellah, is "that tradition of religious symbolization through which Americans have interpreted their national experience."[33] The most basic symbols of civil religion have been born out of the American religious and civil experience. The human experience of tragedy, suffering, joy, and victory became the forging ground for the birth of these symbols. Symbolizing tells "us nothing at all about the universe except insofar" as it is a reflection of humans "struggling to make sense of the world."[34]

The symbols of American civil religion include God, freedom, providence, chosen people, exodus, promised land, and "Sacrificial Death and Rebirth."[35] These symbols, left empty and open, allow citizens to interpret them within their own religious and political tradition. The "notion of transcendence in a democratic polity," argues Bellah, "provides the highest symbolic expression and legitimation for the openness of a genuinely participational political process . . . it is essential that the transcendence . . . remain symbolically empty, for particularity of content would operate to prevent precisely the openness it is meant to guarantee."[36] There was an ebb and flow in Campbell's conceptualization of civil religion. At times he seems to envision himself as an almost solitary prophet proclaiming a spiritual kingdom separate and apart from the social and political environment in which he was a temporary hostage. At other times, more representative of his total experience, he speaks in glowing terms of the nation and its social, political, and religious institutions, seeing them as a collectivity of God's chosen people.

The notion of transcendence, along with the symbols of chosenness, freedom, exodus, and the promised land, are explicitly and implicitly evident in Campbell's major lectures. In his 1852 address, "The Destiny of our Country," he called attention to "our divinely favored and beloved country." To Anglo-Saxon Americans, "God has given the sceptre of Judah, the harp of David, the strength of Judah's Lion, and the wealth of the world . . . to Britain and America God has granted the possession of the new world; and because the sun never sets upon our religion, our language and our arts, he has vouchsafed to us, through . . . science and arts, the power that annihilates time and annuls the inconveniences of space."[37] America's mission was to free the enslaved and to raise up the fallen: "To Protestant America and Protestant England, young gentlemen, the world must look for its emancipation from the most heartless spiritual despotism that our disfranchised, enslaved and degraded human kind. This is our special mission into the world as a nation and a people; and for this purpose the Ruler of Nations has raised us up and made us the wonder and the admiration of the world."[38]

In his address "The Anglo-Saxon Language" three years earlier, Campbell struck the same chord heard in his "destiny of our country" lecture. Anglo-Saxon minds were more comprehensive, vigorous, and acute than any found in Europe. Engaging in some date setting, Campbell projected the end of the millennium within 150 years. By that time Anglo-Saxons will "direct and control the energies and the destiny of the world."[39] Along with its comprehensiveness, the Anglo-Saxon language was the language of Protestantism, the language of religion and the language of foreign missions. "No event in the future," Campbell affirmed, "next to the anticipated millennial triumph, appears more natural . . . more morally certain and desirable, than this Anglo-Saxon triumph in the great work of human civilization."[40]

As early as 1830, long before he felt the inseparable link between the destiny of Christianity and America, Campbell praised in a July Fourth address the government of "this most favored of all lands."[41] The worth and contributions of a "Washington, a Franklin and a Jefferson," he declared, "will long resound through the hills and valleys of this spacious country."[42] Calling to remembrance the events of the Fourth of July 1776 was to Americans as the Passover was to the Jews. Our ancestors, freeing themselves from Rome, conflicting sectarians and restrictions on the rights of conscience, "sought a city of refuge, a hiding place from the storm, in this discovered section of the patrimony of Japeth."[43]

As a churchman and citizen, Campbell hammered out his turning and twisting theology and political thought on the anvil of personal experience in a developing, vibrant democracy. During his own lifetime, the religious movement which he led moved from a sect to a denomination. During all these years he was faced with many complex problems and issues, but, in the midst of the storms, he never veered far from his post-Protestant views of Christianity. To the end, even with the growth in numbers and prestige, Campbell remained opposed to religious creeds, sectarian practices, and the bureaucratic structuring of the organic church.[44] To him, democracy and Christianity were historically and contemporarily interrelated in their mission and destiny.

NOTES

1. Sydney E. Ahlstrom, *A Religious History of the American People* (New Haven: Yale Univ. Press, 1972), 448.

2. Sidney E. Mead, *The Lively Experiment* (New York: Harper and Row, 1963), 111.

3. Alexander Campbell, *Campbell-Owen Debate* (Bethany, Va., 1829), 2:5.

4. W. E. Garrison and Alfred T. DeGroot, *The Disciples of Christ: A History* (St. Louis: Bethany Press, 1948), 150–53.

5. David E. Harrell Jr., *Quest for a Christian America* (Nashville: Disciples of Christ Historical Society, 1966), 3.

6. Garrison and DeGroot, *Disciples of Christ*, 329.

7. Ibid., 188.

8. *Christian Baptist* 6 (Nov. 1828): 96.

9. Alexander Campbell, *Campbell-Walker Debate* (Steubenville, Ohio: James Wilson, 1820), 47; also *Christian Baptist* 1 (March 1824): 148.

10. Garrison and DeGroot, *Disciples of Christ*, 165.

11. Harold L. Lunger, *The Political Ethics of Alexander Campbell* (St. Louis: Bethany Press, 1954), 35.

12. Arthur Schlesinger Jr., "The Age of Alexander Campbell," in *The Sage of Bethany*, ed. Perry Gresham (St. Louis: Bethany Press, 1960), 35.

13. Lunger, *The Political Ethics of Alexander Campbell*, 33.

14. Garrison and DeGroot, *Disciples of Christ*, 140–51.

15. Campbell was a careful sympathetic student of Locke. Nineteenth-century intellectual, political, and religious liberty were considered by Campbell to be major contributions of Locke's "Essay Concerning Human Understanding," "Two Treatises on

Government," and "Letters of Toleration." Campbell seems to be oblivious to the Lockean unchecked self-interest doctrine, which, taken to its logical conclusion, deludes or destroys the Christian emphasis on brotherhood and community. Like many of his contemporaries, Campbell followed the classical economic position of Smith, Ricardo, and Malthus. The capitalism of classical economics fused well with Lockean political philosophy. Locke's utilitarianism maximizes self-interest almost to the total absence of virtue and a community ethic.

16. John Locke, *Four Letters on Toleration*, 7th ed. (London: Alexander Murray, 1870), 5–10.

17. R. W. B. Lewis, *The American Adam* (Chicago: Univ. of Chicago Press, 1955), 13–27.

18. Hannah Arendt, *On Revolution* (New York: Viking Press, 1963), 43.

19. Robert N. Bellah, "Reflection on Reality in America," *Radical Religion* 1, nos. 3/4 (Summer/Fall 1974): 38–49.

20. Ernest L. Tuvenson, *Redeemer Nation* (Chicago: Univ. of Chicago Press, 1968).

21. *Christian Baptist* 7 (August 1829): 7.

22. *Millennial Harbinger* 1 (Jan. 1830): 2.

23. Robert N. Bellah, "Religion and Policy in America," *Andover Newton Quarterly* 15, no. 2 (Nov. 1974): 110.

24. Russell E. Richey and Donald Jones, *American Civil Religion* (New York: Harper Forum Books, 1974), 176.

25. Alexander Campbell, *Popular Lectures* (Philadelphia: James Challen and Son, 1863), 374.

26. Some of the disappointment no doubt resulted from his involvement with the 1829–30 Virginia Constitutional Convention. As a delegate to the convention, Campbell opposed what he called the "anti-republican principles" ratified by the people of Virginia by a vote of 26,055 to 15,563. Only two counties west of the Alleghenies voted for it. Brooke County, Campbell's place of residence, voted 371 to 0 against ratification.

27. Robert N. Bellah, *Beyond Belief* (New York: Harper and Row, 1970), 24, 66.

28. Tuvenson, *Redeemer Nation*, 81, 217.

29. Alexander Campbell, *On Moral Societies* (Battle Creek: International Religious Library Association, 1898), 7, 15.

30. Campbell, *Popular Lectures*, 259.

31. Ibid., 297.

32. Rosseau used the term *civil religion* in *The Social Contract* (chap. 8, book 4).

33. Bellah, "Religion and Policy in America," 107.

34. Bellah, *Beyond Belief*, 195.

35. Ibid., 186.

36. Robert N. Bellah, "American Civil Religion in the 1970s," in Richey and Jones, *American Civil Religion*, 258.

37. Campbell, *Popular Lectures*, 170.

38. Ibid., 174.

39. Ibid., 40.
40. Ibid., 45.
41. Ibid., 375.
42. Ibid., 375.
43. Ibid., 373.
44. W. E. Garrison, a Disciple and distinguished church historian, felt that the Campbell heritage made it comfortable for the Disciples of Christ to engage in ecumenical dialogue: "Disciples of Christ have contributed to the ecumenical movement some elements of value derived directly from one strain of their heritage. One of these is a certain simplicity of approach, because they have fewer vested interests to defend, whether institutional or theological, and are in the habit of believing with an almost childlike trust, that unity is not only desirable but actually possible even though the road to it may be long" (*Heritage and Destiny* [St. Louis: Bethany Press, 1961], 140).

Early Cincinnati's "Unprecedented Spectacle"

Earl Irvin West

When Isaac G. Burnet, Cincinnati's newly elected mayor, called a meeting of the city's leading citizens for Tuesday night, April 7, 1829, to make arrangements for a debate between Robert Owen and Alexander Campbell, this can be considered an official sanction for the extraordinary event that was being planned.[1] Robert Owen, social reformer, lecturer, and founder of the then defunct communitarian colony at New Harmony, Indiana, had issued a general challenge a year earlier from New Orleans to the Christian clergy to defend religion in debate. Alexander Campbell of Bethany, (West) Virginia, editor of the *Christian Baptist,* an aggressive periodical dedicated to nonsectarian religion, had accepted the invitation. After reading Owen's challenge and Campbell's reply, the mayor requested that notices be placed in all the city papers and that interested citizens meet again to continue plans for the event. Accordingly, a committee of ten was appointed to select a site for the debate with instructions to request the First Presbyterian Church for use of its facilities. The pugnacious and independent Joshua L. Wilson, minister of that church and leader of Old School Presbyterians in the western country, rejected this request. The committee then turned to the Methodist Church, "a capacious stone building with brick wings" located on Fifth Street, between Sycamore and Broadway and capable of seating a thousand people.[2]

The debate, which Frances Trollope called "a spectacle unprecedented, I believe, in any age or country," began on Monday, April 13, and ended on the following Tuesday, April 21, after fifteen sittings.[3] Timothy Flint, ex-Congregational minister and one of the moderators, was impressed that the audience "received with invincible forbearance, the most frank and sarcastic remarks of Mr. Owen, in ridicule of the most sacred articles of Christian belief." Afterward, a foreigner remarked to Flint "that he had seen no place, where he thought such a discussion could have been conducted in so much order and quietness."[4]

An over-capacity attendance of twelve hundred at each session attests to the importance the public attached to the discussion, although opinions varied greatly. Writing in advance of the event, Robert Dale Owen, son of Robert Owen, thought the debate would have "claim sufficient to attract the attention of every enlightened man." He regarded the subject to be discussed as "the most important . . . that can be brought before a public assembly." "Its influence extends," he said presciently, "to the cabin of the peasant as to the hall of kings."[5] Flint himself regarded it as a "combat, unparalleled in the annals of disputation."[6] On the other hand, the editor of the *Washington National Intelligencer* said, "Upon our word, we think that the good people of Cincinnati might be much more profitably employed than in encouraging this bootless wrangling."[7] Cincinnati's caustic visitor, the Englishwoman Frances Trollope, reflected later, "All this I think could only have happened in America. I am not quite sure that it was very desirable it should have happened anywhere."[8]

While the debate was not as epic-making as Campbell's friends thought, the united stand for Christianity on the final day did indicate an interest by the contemporary Westerner in religion beyond the sheer novelty of the performance. Reports had circulated in the eastern religious press that infidelity was widespread on the frontier, and Campbell's biographer states that the clergyman did not hope to convert Owen but went to fortify a "wavering and unsettled public," which he regarded as in danger of being carried off by infidelity.[9]

Another aspect of the attractiveness of the debate was the presence of the colorful personality of the internationally famous Robert Owen. Born in 1771 in Newton, Montgomeryshire, Wales, the son of a saddler and ironmonger, the precocious boy proved such a voracious reader that he dropped out of school at the age of nine and, some said, gave up all religious dogma by the age of ten. He borrowed freely from private libraries and argued religion sharply with three Methodist ladies who had loaned him books. At the age of ten he went to live briefly with his brother in London, and from there he went to Lincolnshire and later to Manchester. These were important years in Owen's development, for he continued his study of the beliefs of various sects and also attended both the Presbyterian and Anglican churches where he heard "conflicting doctrines." In abandoning all religious beliefs, Owen concluded that differences in religion were due to the influence of social institutions. It was not until 1817, however, that Owen would publicly attack religion.

The knowledge Owen gained at Manchester while working in the cotton industry, meanwhile, laid the foundation for his later wealth and renown. Before he was twenty he was managing one of the city's largest mills. In the 1790s his fortune grew steadily. His business ability led him in January 1800 to become manager of the New Lanark mills in Scotland with a salary of one thousand pounds and a ninth interest in the partnership that owned both factory and village. His marriage to the daughter of David Dale, the original owner, satisfied a social expectancy, but between husband and wife there was little rapport. Her devout Scotch Presbyterianism could never add substance to the dream world in which Owen increasingly resided. Driven on by the irresistible force of a magnificent illusion, Owen sought the limelight of European and American political institutions, while his wife walked silently in the lonely shadows he cast behind.

New Lanark was an isolated mill town of two thousand, of which more than five hundred were children who had been brought from poor homes in Glasgow and Edinburgh. The situation was one of child labor, immorality, crime, drunkenness, and laziness—all contributing to the squalor and diminishing productivity. The determined enthusiasm with which Owen proceeded to improve these conditions was motivated partly by the desire for increased efficiency of operation and partly for social reform. From Owen's viewpoint the inhabitants were trapped in a network of circumstances beyond their control; consequently, they were not responsible for either their vices or virtues. He would often repeat in monotonous staccatos: "Character is universally formed *for* and not *by* the individual." It is impossible to overstate Owen's fondness for this expression, by which he meant that if men were placed in the right environment, they would develop the proper moral ideas and order their lives in a productive way. Unlike the French Physiocrats, who conceived of the true role of government to be the adjustment of the social order to a basic natural order, Owen sought to control the forces of nature in the common interest.[10]

Owen worked sedulously to create a new social order around New Lanark. He instituted a compulsory education system, one of the first in the world. For the smaller children he began a kindergarten. Not only did he provide better housing for families, but he also started a health fund. His patriarchal instincts served him well, and in time, through his vigorous leadership, immorality diminished, crime was cut sharply, and the whole complexion of the village changed. New Lanark came to be regarded as one of the most efficient mills in Europe. Since England's Industrial Revolution had created in many areas the problems Owen saw upon his arrival at New Lanark, his social experiment invited closer inspection from philanthropists and businessmen everywhere.

This remarkable achievement, however, was not the fruit of wholehearted cooperation. Owen's partners, who were understandably concerned more with profits than with social reforms, complained incessantly of the high costs of operations. Jeremy Bentham had invested ten thousand pounds in Owen's mills and became one of the reformer's most vocal critics. "Owen," said Bentham, "begins in vapour and ends in smoke. He is a great braggadocio; his mind is an image of confusion, and he avoids coming to particulars. He is always the same, says the same things over and over again; he built some small houses, and people who had no houses of their own went to live in those houses, and he calls this success." Owen, on the other hand, continued his dreams of villages where "the meanest and most miserable beings now in society will . . . become the envy of the rich and indolent."[11]

The New Lanark reformer then pursued his expanding vista with absolute dedication. In 1813 he published his *A New View of Society,* in which he declared that character is formed in childhood entirely by environment. It is pointless to persecute people who commit crimes, he pointed out, for they are not responsible. The object of his new society would be to prevent crime by proper training in early life. In January 1815, in a bill sponsored by Sir Robert Peel, Owen tried to get a measure through the House of Commons that would have limited children's working hours. The bill failed and the Factory Act of 1819, a drastically altered version, displeased Owen. He, however, drove relentlessly forward.[12]

To sell churchmen and statesmen on his *New View* became a principal feature of his modus operandi. Owen visited John Quincy Adams in London in 1817 while the latter was serving as American minister to England. Adams wrote in his diary that the reformer was a "speculative, scheming, mischievous man." When Owen visited him in Washington in 1844, Adams wrote that he appeared "as crafty [and] crazy as ever."[13] When Owen visited Washington on his trip to New Harmony in 1824, the two discussed religion. Adams never relented in his opposition to Owen's social system after that, and he referred to Owen's state of mind as "rational insanity."[14] Nor were some other prominent Americans better impressed.

The turning point in Owen's career came during an address that he delivered at the City of London Tavern, August 21, 1817. When asked why his new views had not been adopted earlier, Owen replied it was because of the errors of religion, the crucial one being the preaching of the doctrine of human responsibility. In reality humans were creatures of their environment, but the churches taught that humans made their own character. They sought through doctrines of rewards and punishments to provide proper motivation, "whereas the only sound way of making men good was to give them a good material and moral environment . . . they would become good automatically." To Owen, all theologies "proceeded from the deluded imagination of ignorant men." He considered the priesthood as the chief of satanic institutions and concluded that "man is a geographical animal, and the religions of the world are so many geographical insanities."[15] As Owen expanded his views, he denied that the Bible was the revelation of "the mind and will of God," that there was any truth to the Calvinist doctrines of original sin and predestination, or that the soul was immortal. He stated flatly that matter was eternal, there was nothing but matter in the universe, and the bodies men now have may continue in other forms and animals.[16]

The religious press responded to Owen's attacks with a sustained cataract of malevolence. The *Christian Observer,* in October 1817, linked Owen with Voltaire, Condorcet, and Paine and denounced him for saying that religious teaching fostered false views of human nature and perpetuated "superstition, bigotry, hypocrisy, hatred, revenge, wars, and all their evil consequences."[17] But it was Owen's rejection of the doctrines of human depravity and original sin that touched a sore point, because the liberals thought the orthodox Calvinists were using these highly incendiary issues as a stalking horse to attack them. Nevertheless, Owen's "Declaration of Mental Independence" nearly united all religious forces against him.

Selecting July 4, 1826, the fiftieth anniversary of the Declaration of Independence, as the auspicious moment for his announcement, Owen stated his intention of freeing the world of three evils: private property, irrational systems of religion, and marriage.

> I now Declare, to you, and to the world, *that Man up to this hour, has been, in all parts of the earth, a slave to a* TRINITY *of the most monstrous evils that could be combined to inflict mental and physical evil upon his whole race.*
>
> I refer to Private, or Individual Property—ABSURD AND IRRATIONAL SYSTEMS OF RELIGION—AND MARRIAGE, FOUNDED ON INDIVIDUAL PROPERTY COMBINED WITH SOME ONE OF THESE IRRATIONAL SYSTEMS OF RELIGION.[18]

It was a basic presupposition during this period that the American nation was built on the foundation of good morals and that morality could be equated with religion.[19] A correspondent from South Carolina wrote to the *New Harmony Gazette* in October 1827 that "religion is in the estimation of most thinking men the only efficient sanction of moral obligation."[20] A cloud hung over the Indiana colony in the minds of most Americans. Because it lacked the cohesive element of morality, predictions of its imminent collapse increased.

The intellectual appeal Owen lacked was compensated for in personal qualities. Most Americans regarded him, as did Timothy Flint, as an "honest enthusiast, whose real intentions were the good of mankind."[21] His sparkling conversation, air of suavity, perfect self-command, and constant good humor brought him wide public esteem. He was always optimistic, for the millennium was always just ahead, and "he was running so fast towards it that he had no time to notice the pitfalls in the way."[22] He was almost totally free of anger and preferred to sum "pure and genuine religion" into one word: "*Charity.*"[23] While Mrs. S. H. Smith, that connoisseur of minutiae in Washington society, thought he was "ugly, awkward, and unprepossessing, in manner, appearance and voice, she thought him very interesting in conversation." After her visit with him, she was convinced that he was devoted to the all-absorbing idea of promoting the happiness of mankind. "He is extremely mild," she wrote, "and instead of being offended by opposition or difference of opinion he is pleased with free discussion and even bears being laughed at, with great good nature."[24] In short, Owen was one of the most fascinating and unique personalities ever to visit the country. His trip to America to inaugurate the New Harmony project was one continuous triumphal march during which time he addressed the nation's leaders.

The path that led Alexander Campbell to Cincinnati on that April day in 1829 was in sharp contrast to that of his challenger. Born near Ballymena in County Antrim, North Ireland, September 12, 1788, he was reared in the pious atmosphere of a Scotch Presbyterian home. His father, an Old Light Seceder Presbyterian, and his mother, a descendant of a French Huguenot family, guided their son toward an academic career that was heavily oriented toward theological studies. Under his parents' guidance he memorized large selections from the Bible and augmented his studies by attendance at a local academy. Although his father wanted him to enter the ministry of the Seceder Church, Alexander hesitated while he sought for solutions to the problems raised by variations in religious dogmas. While he searched for answers, his father joined the Scotch-Irish immigration to America in 1807, and Alexander waited with the family in Ireland for an appropriate time to follow.[25]

During the next three eventful years, Alexander shifted his theological position away from the Seceders toward Independency. He spent a year at the University of Glasgow, where he came under the influence of Greville Ewing, a well-known Scotch Independent. His contact with the teachings of James and Robert Haldane and those of John Glas and Robert Sandemann left a lasting impression on his religious thought. In Ireland, Campbell belonged to the Presbytery of Market Hill, and in Scotland, to that of Glasgow, keeping himself in good standing with the Seceder Church. Upon his departure from Scotland, however, he confessed that his confidence in the Confession of Faith was shaken. When he arrived in Washington, Pennsylvania, in the fall of 1809, he was "under the conviction that nothing that was not as old as the New Testament should be made an article of faith, a rule of practice, or a term of communion amongst christians."[26]

While completely dedicating himself to religious service for the next decade, Campbell at the same time established a reputation for being an independent thinker. At the close of a discourse on "The Sermon on the Mount," which he delivered to the Brush Run Church near his home at Bethany, near Wheeling, Virginia, in the summer of 1810, he stated his convictions of the independence of the Church of Christ from any denominational connections and "the excellency and authority of the scriptures." During that year he delivered 106 sermons on sixty-one "primary topics of the Christian religion" in the western part of Pennsylvania, Virginia, and eastern Ohio. Meanwhile, his fame as a preacher of unsurpassed talents and boldness of thought grew.[27]

When Campbell was immersed by Elder Matthias Luce in 1812, his relations with the Presbyterians were broken; at the same time, he was drawn into the Redstone Baptist Association. His famous "Sermon on the Law," which he delivered before the association in the summer of 1816, only accented how tenuous this connection really was. By the time of his debate with W. L. McCalla, a vitriolic Old School Presbyterian, in 1823, Campbell and his colleagues in the Baptist ministry glowered at each other over a chasm of distrust and suspicion.[28]

After a short fling with politics in 1829, the minister devoted his entire attention to what he called a religious reformation. His teachings, a syncretistic system that combined elements from many religious dogmas, began with a fundamentalist's view of the Bible as the inspired word of God; as a result, only doctrines and practices which he considered to be founded on the Bible could be accepted. He considered the "three great maxims . . . which have been three cardinal points in our theological compass" to be: "The testimony of God *believed* constitutes Christian *faith;* The testimony of God *understood* constitutes Christian *knowledge*; and the testimony of God *obeyed* constitutes Christian *practice*."[29] E. D. Mansfield heard Campbell several times in Cincinnati between 1826 and 1829 and summarized his doctrines to be: "The Bible alone is the only creed . . . regeneration is coincident with baptism." Campbell, he concluded, "was a man of learning, keen intellect, and an instructive speaker. He was interesting in discussion and conversation."[30]

Although Campbell was much admired, his unique system, his excessive self-confidence, and strong derogations invited vigorous opposition, particularly from the Baptists. John Waller complained that Campbell "seems to have imbibed the impression that he was a chosen vessel of the Almighty, appointed to set in order the crazy concerns of Christendom which had been in mournful confusion since the age of the apostles."[31] After admitting that Campbell was "a polemic ajax in the region where he began the propagation of his tenets," another Baptist minister recognized that Campbell was "incisive in sarcasm and caricature, shrewd in repartee, and possessed of an overwhelming confidence in his ability."[32] Campbell, in fact, could scarcely be ignored.

Americans on the western frontier, as a Louisville Unitarian minister said, "have a taste for oratory," which partly explains Campbell's popularity as a speaker. His lofty diction that tended often to become excessively sublime and verbose followed the general pattern of Henry Clay. Like the Kentucky orator, Campbell stood erect and made few gestures. As his deep-set eyes pierced the audience, his Scotch-Irish brogue poured forth a stream of eloquence. One listener said, "The great excellence of Campbell's delivery, consists in the feeling which it inspires, of his manly independence, entire conviction of the truth of what he says, and entire understanding of his whole subject. He is plain, forcible, and self-possessed; he is not hurried away by his words or by his thoughts, but has the command of both."[33] Alexander Campbell's popularity on the frontier, both as a unique religious leader and eloquent speaker, lured Cincinnati's citizens to this "unprecedented spectacle" as much as the singular career of the socialist reformer.

By the spring of 1827 it seemed evident that the courses of the two men would ultimately converge. Campbell had read in the *New Harmony Gazette* Owen's "Declaration of Mental Independence." Since he desired to get better acquainted with Owen before establishing his opinions too securely, he formed only two quick impressions: He agreed that circumstances *do* influence character, but he felt that Owen had glorified this principle excessively to the exclusion of other valuable considerations. "To make everything in human character depend upon the power of circumstances, is to me as great an error as to making nothing depend on it."[34] Furthermore, he agreed with most American religious leaders that it had never been demonstrated that a social system could be successful without religion. On this basis, Campbell rejected Owen's "Declaration of Mental Independence" as contrary to the events of human history. The principles on which New Harmony had been established, he thought, were "at war with reason, revelation, and a permanent cooperation."[35] In a series of articles in the *Christian Baptist* through the summer and fall of 1827 Campbell defended religion as a necessary base for any social system.

Campbell's hostility to the Owenite communitarian system intensified during the next year. A Dr. Underhill from an Owenite community at Kendal in Stark County, Ohio, popularized Owen's views in the state. When a reader of the *Christian Baptist* requested Campbell in February 1828 to debate this man, Campbell refused, but, answering in April, he said if Robert Owen "will engage to debate the whole system of his moral and religious philosophy with me, if he will pledge himself to prove any position affirmative of his atheistical sentiments as they lie scattered over the pages of the New Harmony Gazette . . . I will engage to take the negative and disprove all his affirmative positions, in a public debate to be holden any place equidistant from him and me."[36]

Owen was well aware that his New Harmony experiment had failed when he arrived in New Orleans from Liverpool in early January 1828. Nevertheless his dreams of another colony were rekindled when he learned of the population growth in Texas and of the land grants given to settlers by the Mexican government. Meanwhile, he saw it was necessary to popularize his views as extensively as possible. In the next three weeks he told New Orleans audiences that he had spent more than $500,000 and devoted forty years of his life to making his ideas a reality. He invited "all governments and enlightened people" to stop wars by following principles "which are in strict accord to our natures." Then, in late January an advertisement appeared in the papers addressed "To the Clergy of New Orleans":

Gentlemen—I have now finished a course of lectures in this city, the principles of which are in direct opposition to those which you have been taught it your duty to preach. It is of immense importance to the world that truth upon these momentous subjects should be now established upon a certain and sure foundation. You and I, and all our fellow-men, are deeply interested that there should be no further delay. With this view, without one hostile or unpleasant feeling on my part, I propose a friendly public discussion, the most open that the city of New Orleans will afford, or if you prefer it, a more private meeting, when half-a-dozen friends of each party will be present, in addition to half-a-dozen gentlemen whom you may associate with you in the discussion. The time and place to be of your appointment.

I propose to prove, as I have already attempted to do in my lectures, that all the religions of the world have been founded on the ignorance of mankind; that they are directly opposed to the never changing laws of our nature; that they have been and are the real sources of vice, disunion and misery of every description; that they are now the only real bar to the formation of a society of virtue, of intelligence, of charity in its most extended sense, and of sincerity and kindness among the whole human family; and that they can be no longer maintained except through the ignorance of the mass of the people, and the tyranny of the few over that mass.

Owen concluded the challenge with a postscript that if his proposition were declined, he would then regard these as unanswered truths.[37]

The reformer found it necessary in the next few weeks to repeat his challenge and to extend it to clergymen outside of New Orleans. As he departed from the city on a steamboat, he soliloquized that he had discussed religion with the highest dignitaries of the English and Irish churches, with leaders of dissenting churches and with a prominent Jew in London, so he had expected the New Orleans clergy to be willing to investigate the truth "for the good the knowledge of it would do mankind. They thought differently and did not accept my proposal."[38] What reasons the New Orleans clergy had for ignoring Owen are unknown, but his challenge continued to arouse public interest.

The question may be fairly asked why Owen was so set on a debate. He wrote later to the *London Times* that the object of the meeting was not to discuss the truth or falsehood of the Christian religion but to determine the errors in all religions and to select from each the kernel of truth so as "to form from them collectively a religion wholly true and consistent, that it may become universal, and be acted upon conscientiously by all."[39] The editor of the *Cincinnati Chronicle and Literary Gazette* explained Owen's challenge from the fact that his social system was falling into disrepute, and those who had once been enchanted by his theories were disgusted with their practical application. Since New Harmony was becoming "a *living* memorial of the egregious folly of his Utopian schemes," the editor thought Owen wanted the debate to sustain his reputation as a reformer "and gratify his ambition for notoriety."[40] Owen would hold other debates, but he was no debater: "He was far too intent on stating his own case, at inordinate length, to pay any attention to his opponents." Moreover, he regarded a public disputation as a means of providing a platform from which he could repeat his unvarying version of the truth![41]

Be that as it may, Owen's attention was soon drawn to Campbell's invitation of April 1828. Owen's acceptance was published in the *New Harmony Gazette* in mid-May; and in early July, on his return to England, Owen spent a night in Campbell's home in Bethany. Later in a letter to his son, Robert Dale, from Wheeling on July 13, Owen said that he and Campbell had agreed on Cincinnati as the place, and the time to be the second Monday in April 1829.[42]

In selecting Cincinnati as the site, both disputants acknowledged the importance of this growing Ohio River city, now so familiarly known as the "Queen City of the West." Next to New Orleans, Cincinnati was the chief city of the western country. In three years its population had jumped from 16,000 to almost 25,000. Four hundred ninety-six houses were erected there in 1828, and the newspapers boasted of the "extraordinary prosperity" of the city and that "peace, plenty and prosperity have pervaded all classes of our inhabitants."[43] Cincinnati had twelve newspapers and periodicals, thirty-four charitable organizations, twenty-three churches, twenty-eight religious societies, forty schools, two colleges, and a medical school. Its theater was considered the finest outside of New York and Philadelphia and presented some of the nation's greatest stars. Many of its citizens were descendants of prominent New England families, among whom was Timothy Flint, who described Cincinnati as "a picture of beauty, wealth, progress and fresh advance, as few landscapes in any country can surpass."[44]

The delay until the next spring for the discussion was ostensibly to allow Owen time to return to England and look after business. In reality, a plan for a new communitarian colony in Mexico was unfolding in the reformer's mind. In October 1828, Owen published in England a *Memorial of Robert Owen to the Mexican Republic, and to the Government of the State of Coahuila and Texas,* in which he requested from the Mexican government a grant of land in Texas to be colonized with Owenite communities. Despite the fact the Mexican minister in London informed Owen that his plan was fantastic, the reformer sailed for Mexico City in November, carrying letters from important men in England to the Mexican government. After spending only two short weeks in the capital, Owen departed, and "the entire [Mexican] project quietly vanished into the air."[45]

When Campbell left for Cincinnati on April 7, he was satisfied that he had made thorough preparation for the coming encounter. For months he had involved himself in the "skeptical system" as he tried to imagine what it would be like to be a doubter. More than ever he was convinced that not one good reason could be offered against the Christian faith, and that sectarianism was the greatest enemy of the Christian faith in the world. He was resolved that he would not try to defend what the creeds said, for "it is the religion of the Bible, and that alone, I am concerned to prove to be divine." He departed with the satisfaction that he had the prayers and good wishes "of myriads of Christians in all denominations."[46] Both men were in the Queen City by Friday anxiously awaiting Monday's opening session.

More than a thousand people, some from two and three hundred miles distant, came to the Methodist Church on Sycamore Street that bright spring morning. "All ages, sexes and conditions were there," said Flint. The chapel was equally divided with one side for the ladies and the other for the men with a separate door of entrance for each. The city's leading citizens were there. A seven-man board of moderators, headed by Judge Jacob Burnet, senator-elect from Ohio, sat on an elevated platform. Alexander Campbell brought with him his father, Thomas, and two younger brothers, while Owen was attended only by a young German friend. The contestants sat side by side waiting for the debate to begin.[47]

Owen, dressed in a fine suit of black broadcloth, with manuscript in hand, spoke slowly and deliberately in chaste English.[48] Mrs. Trollope noted that his voice was soft and gentle with nothing harsh in his expressions. As a matter of fact, "his whole manner, disarmed zeal, and produced a degree of tolerance that those who did not hear him would hardly believe possible."[49] After asserting that the whole history of Christianity was a fraud, Owen entrenched himself behind his famous "Twelve Laws," each of which merely described one or another aspect of the vast power of circumstances as determinants of all human development. For the remainder of the debate, Owen refused to do more than repeat them. This happened so often that Flint surmised that the reformer's sole purpose in the debate was to fly his reputation like "a kite, to take up his social system into the full view of the community, and by constant repetition to imprint a few of his leading axioms on the memory of the multitude."[50] At one point, Owen reiterated his contention that the particles of the body were eternal, without beginning and end, and that his body, when decomposed, would later reappear in "new forms of life and enjoyment." On hearing this statement, says Flint, a revulsion of horror swept over the audience, and he felt the "coals of eloquence burning in his bosom" so strongly that he himself wanted to answer.[51]

Campbell's perfect self-possession left no doubt that he was in thorough command. Now slightly over forty with the first sprinkling of white in his hair and possessing a finely arched forehead and a sparkling bright and cheerful countenance, the clergyman "wore an aspect, as one who had words both ready and inexhaustible." So sure was he of his ground that he left the impression "that he would not retreat an inch in the way of concession, to escape the crack and pudder of a dissolving world." Campbell tried, with withering satire, to shake the perfect composure of his antagonist. Undaunted, however, Owen retorted, making the audience roar with laughter, and the debate moved along in good humor.[52]

Campbell's thorough acquaintance with sixteenth- and seventeenth-century Christian Apologists provided him with the opportunity to fortify his audience's faith in the Christian religion. Late in the evening of the eighth day of debate, Campbell asked the audience to be seated. Then, in a moment of drama, he asked all who prize the Christian religion to please rise. "Instantly, as by one electric movement, almost every person in the assembly sprang erect." When he asked those who were "friendly to Mr. Owen's system" to rise, only three or four admitted to "this unenviable notoriety." For a moment there followed a pause, and then "a loud and instant clapping and stamping raised a suffocating dust to the roof of the church." The victory for Campbell seemed apparent to most of the audience for few were convinced that Owen's Twelve Laws had disproved the Christian religion. While the viewers were disappointed that the two men had not come to close grips on the question of the validity of Christianity, they departed in admiration of Campbell's superb powers. "Mr. Campbell left on the far greater portion of the audience," wrote Flint," an impression of him, of his talents and powers, and his victory over his antagonist, almost as favorable, as he could have desired."[53] In the long run the editor of the *Cincinnati Chronicle* was probably right when he observed that if Owen had anticipated that his challenge would have been accepted by one as capable as Alexander Campbell, he would not have issued it; and on the other hand, if Campbell had known all Owen had in mind, he might not have accepted it.[54]

While the debate was not cataclysmic, it came at a time when religion was reasserting its dominion over people's minds following the period of inactivity after the close of the Revolution. On the American frontier a spirit of inquiry was in the air and a vigorous individuality concomitant with the dawn of the Jacksonian era drove humans to seek for solutions to their doubts. The Calvinism that ruled so sedately in colonial America was now being put to rest and the frontier was seeking for new grounds of faith somewhere between atheism and dogmatic sectarianism. The crowds that came for miles to hear the debate were driven by numerous complex impulses, not the least of which was the search for new religious foundations in an age of dynamic transitions.

NOTES

1. *Cincinnati Daily Gazette,* Apr. 9, 1829. Debates on religious topics became commonplace in later years.

2. Ibid., Apr. 11, 1829.

3. Frances Trollope, *Domestic Manners of the Americans,* ed. Donald Smalley (New York, 1949), 147–53.

4. Timothy Flint, "Public challenged DISPUTE between ROBERT OWEN . . . and Rev. ALEXANDER CAMPBELL . . . the former denying the truth of all religions in general; and the latter affirming the truth of the Christian religion on logical principles," *Western Monthly Review* 2 (Apr. 1829): 646. Flint's article also appears in the *Washington National Intelligencer,* May 26, 1829.

5. *New Harmony Gazette,* Aug. 6, 1828, 326.

6. Flint, "Dispute between Owen and Campbell," 641.

7. *Washington National Intelligencer,* Apr. 21, 1829.

8. Trollope, *Domestic Manners,* 153.

9. Robert Richardson, *Memoirs of Alexander Campbell* (Cincinnati, 1872), 2:269. A Presbyterian paper published a jeremiad on the rapid growth of infidelity in Kentucky. See the *Pittsburgh Recorder* 2 (Nov. 6, 1823). A report of the American Home Missionary Society said of the West in 1841, "*Mormonism* is there to delude them. *Popery* is there to ensnare them. *Infidelity* is there to corrupt and debase them. And *Atheism* is there to take away their God as they go on to the grave, and to blot out every ray of hope that may beam on them from beyond." Quoted in Robert E. Reigel, *Young America, 1830–1840* (Norman, Okla., 1949), 257.

10. G. D. H. Cole, *Life of Robert Owen* (London, 1930), 3, 10, 39. Cole observed that Owen was "from first to last a deeply religious person, not least when he was denouncing all the creeds, and earning the reputation of an infidel and a materialist." See also Arthur Eugene Bestor Jr., *Backwoods Utopias: The Sectarian and Owenite Phases of Communitarian Socialism in America, 1663–1829* (Philadelphia, 1950), 62–63.

11. Arthur J. Booth, *Robert Owen: The Founder of Socialism in England* (London, 1869), 27, 28; quoted in Bestor, *Backwoods Utopias,* 73.

12. J. Bronowski and Bruce Mazlish, *The Western Intellectual Tradition, from Leonardo to Hegel* (New York, 1960), 456.

13. Charles Francis Adams, ed., *Memoirs of John Quincy Adams: Comprising Portions of His Diary from 1795 to 1848* (Philadelphia, 1877), 12:116, 117.

14. John Q. Adams to Rev. Bernard Whitman, Dec. 25, 1833. The Adams Family Papers, Massachusetts Historical Society. (The author used the microfilms of this collection in the Indiana Univ. library.)

15. Cole, *Life of Robert Owen,* 22, 93, 192; Booth, *Robert Owen,* 4; Marguerite Young, *Angel in the Forest: A Fairy Tale of Two Utopias* (New York, 1945), 268–69.

16. Timothy Flint, "A Tour," *Western Monthly Review* 2 (Sept. 1828): 198–201; *Christian Messenger* 2 (Jan. 1827): 44–46; *Indianapolis Journal,* Feb. 21, 1826.

17. Quoted in Bestor, *Backwoods Utopias,* 124.

18. Timothy Flint, "New Views of Society; or Essays on the Formation of Human Character, etc. Various Addresses Delivered by Mr. Owen, Dedicated to Those, Who Have No Private

Ends to Accomplish, and Who Are Honestly in Search of Truth, etc.," *Western Monthly Review* 1 (June 1827): 105–18; Young, *Angel in the Forest*, 233, quoted from the *Washington National Intelligencer*, Aug. 3, 1826.

19. Sidney Mead, *The Lively Experiment: The Shaping of American Christianity* (New York, 1963), 53; Perry Miller, *The Life of the Mind in America: From the Revolution to the Civil War* (New York, 1965), 67–69.

20. *New Harmony Gazette*, Nov. 28, 1827.

21. Flint, "New Views," 118.

22. Cole, *Life of Robert Owen*, 34.

23. *Washington National Intelligencer*, Aug. 12, 1826.

24. Margaret B. Smith, *The First Forty Years of Washington Society* . . . , ed. Gaillard Hunt (New York. 1906), 179, 222.

25. The standard biography of Alexander Campbell is Richardson's *Memoirs of Alexander Campbell*.

26. Alexander Campbell, "Address to the Public," *Christian Baptist* 2 (1824) in bound volume revised by D. S. Burnet (Cincinnati, 1835), 92.

27. Ibid.

28. Alexander Campbell, "Anecdotes, Incidents, and Facts," *Millennial Harbinger* 5 (June 1848): 344–49.

29. Alexander Campbell, "Andrew Broadus against Himself," *Millennial Harbinger* 3 (Apr. 1832): 151.

30. E. D. Mansfield, *Personal Memories: . . . with Sketches of Many Noted People, 1803–1843* (Cincinnati, 1879), 272.

31. John N. Waller, "Messrs. Campbell and Rice on Influence of the Holy Spirit," *Western Baptist Review* 1 (Sept. 1845): 23.

32. B. F. Riley, *A History of the Baptists in the Southern States East of the Mississippi* (Philadelphia, 1898), 174.

33. J. F. C., "Alexander Campbell at Louisville," *Western Messenger* 1 (June 1835): 57, 58.

34. Alexander Campbell, "Mr. Robert Owen and the Social System, No. I," *Christian Baptist* 4 (1827): 327.

35. Alexander Campbell, "Deism and the Social System, No. IV," *Christian Baptist* 5 (1827): 364.

36. Alexander Campbell, open letter to "Mr. A.," *Christian Baptist* 5 (1828): 433–34. Apparently Campbell did not yet know of Owen's challenge that had been issued in January 1828. Richardson, *Memoirs of Alexander Campbell*, 2:239–40.

37. *New Harmony Gazette*, Mar. 26, 1828, 169.

38. Ibid., Apr. 9, 1828, 186.

39. *Cincinnati Chronicle and Literary Gazette*, Feb. 14, 1829.

40. Ibid., Apr. 25, 1829.

41. Cole, *Life of Robert Owen*, 299.

42. *New Harmony Gazette,* Aug. 6, 1828, 326; Alexander Campbell, "A Debate on the Evidences of Christianity," *Christian Baptist* 6 (1828): 470.

43. *Chronicle and Literary Gazette,* Feb. 14, 1829.

44. Quoted in Russell A. Griffin, "Mrs. Trollope and the Queen City," *Mississippi Valley Historical Review* 37 (Sept. 1950): 294.

45. Bestor, *Backwoods Utopias,* 216–17.

46. Alexander Campbell, "Desultory Remarks," *Christian Baptist* 6 (1829): 552.

47. Flint, "Dispute between Owen and Campbell," 640–41.

48. Nathan J. Mitchell, *Reminiscences and Incidents in the Life and Travels of a Pioneer Preacher* (Cincinnati, 1877), 65.

49. For a general discussion of the debate see Trollope, *Domestic Manners,* 147–53; *The Evidences of Christianity: A Debate between Robert Owen, of New Lanark, Scotland and Alexander Campbell, President of Bethany College, Va., Containing an Examination of the "Social System"* (Nashville, 1912); for Owen's remarks, see Robert Owen, *Robert Owen's Opening Speech and His Reply to the Rev. Alex. Campbell in the Recent Public Discussion in Cincinnati to Prove That the Principles of all Religions are Erroneous, and Injurious to the Human Race* (Cincinnati, 1829). (This is a rare volume, but there is a copy in the Covington Collection of Miami Univ.'s Alumni Library.)

50. Flint, "Dispute between Owen and Campbell," 642.

51. Ibid., 643–44.

52. Ibid., 641, 644.

53. Ibid., 646–47.

54. *Chronicle and Literary Gazette,* Apr. 25, 1829.

Republican Religion and Republican Institutions

Alexander Campbell and the Anti-Catholic Movement

L. Edward Hicks

In *Democracy in America,* Alexis de Tocqueville explored the nature of equality and its profound effect upon American institutions. Having sifted the texture of political institutions, philosophical principles, artistic attitudes, and religious authority for egalitarian influences, he observed that while equality isolated humans from one another and nurtured self-gratification, religion inspired "diametrically contrary principles" in that it fostered mutual dependence, self-restraint, and moral obligations toward others.[1] This American zeal for equality appeared so intense that Tocqueville viewed the future of "Republican Religion" pessimistically,[2] and he doubted if American society could sustain indefinitely the tension he discovered between "complete religious independence and entire political freedom."[3] Surprisingly, though he labeled America "the most democratic country in the world," Tocqueville concluded that American egalitarians would resolve this tension by either moving "unconsciously towards Catholicism," even though the Roman Catholic Church possessed forms and attitudes not normally associated with republican institutions, or by embracing agnosticism and infidelity.[4]

To the contrary, this study proceeds under the assumption that the zeal for republicanism in Jacksonian America was much stronger than Tocqueville estimated.[5] In addition, republicanism offered a formidable challenge to Roman Catholicism, which Tocqueville did not anticipate. Neither Catholic dogma nor liturgy generated great animosity toward the Roman church in nineteenth-century America. Instead, the social attitudes and practices commonly assumed to be official Roman Catholic sentiment and perspective were seemingly in conflict with accepted republican notions and concomitant republican elements in civic affairs, education, and religion.[6] It is ironic, then, in the context of Tocqueville's assertions of possible Catholic popularity, that Jacksonian America, about which Tocqueville made many astute observations, witnessed the beginnings of nativism as an ardent and vocal movement in opposition to immigrants and to Roman Catholicism.

Several well-known figures in Jacksonian America contributed to the intellectual foundations of nativism.[7] They include Lyman Beecher, Samuel F. B. Morse, and Alexander Campbell. While Campbell never participated in formal nativist politics, the American party for example,[8] he was nonetheless a strident and influential anti-Catholic spokesman. His 1837 debate in Cincinnati, Ohio, with Catholic bishop John Purcell may have been the most important Protestant-Catholic discussion in the Jacksonian era.[9] In as much as Campbell attracted such widespread attention for his trenchant critique of the ancient Roman church,[10] and his acknowledged importance as a writer and lecturer in the development of American religious thought, this study explores Campbell's anti-Catholic opinions and makes comparative note of the degree to which his views reflected contemporary nativist tenets.

Jacksonian nativism arose out of the fear that Roman Catholic immigration to the United States in the post-Napoleonic period posed a serious threat to American social, economic, and political structures. As Catholic institutions and their authority structures grew in the 1830s to accommodate demands placed upon the church hierarchy by the flood of Catholic newcomers to North America, nativist fears became intense. In particular, nativism found patent evidence of alarming Catholic strength, amid rumors of Catholic conspiracies against liberties, in the aftermath of the first Provincial Council of Catholicity, which met in Baltimore in October 1829. Anti-Catholic newspapers and publications quickly announced a massive conspiracy afoot, controlled and directed from the Papacy, to flood America with Catholic immigrants and to establish Catholic tyranny. Otherwise divisive Protestants united in their attacks upon the alleged moral depravity promoted in convents, the danger to Protestant schoolchildren posed by parochial schools, and the subversive nature of the Catholic hierarchy.[11] Leaders in evangelical reform movements, such as Theodore Dwight Weld and Lyman Beecher, also led in the effort to "battle the Pope for the possession of the garden spot of the world."[12]

It was in the context of evangelical concern about Roman Catholic influence and power that Alexander Campbell became a leading anti-Catholic spokesman in the West. It is my opinion that, while Campbell spoke directly to almost all of the major anti-Catholic issues, he was not the typical nativist nor did he reflect the more radical aspects of anti-Catholicism in America. Instead, he argued almost exclusively against the despotic tendency of Catholicism and its apparent antagonism toward republican institutions of all kinds—particularly representative government, congregational religious polity, and free and equal opportunity for education.

By 1837 Alexander Campbell had emerged as the spiritual leader of the rapidly expanding Disciples of Christ movement. Campbell's Scotch-Irish grandfather, Archibald Campbell, was an Anglican convert from Roman Catholicism who had denied his son Thomas the same religious freedom that he had once exercised. Despite the family quarrel that ensued, Thomas left home to pursue a theological education and train as a Seceder Presbyterian minister. The family of Alexander's mother were French Huguenots who had fled Roman Catholic persecution after revocation of the Edict of Nantes in 1685. Thomas and his wife served the Ahorey Church, near Rich Hill, County Armagh, in Northern Ireland during a particularly troubled era. In the first decade of Alexander's life, tensions between Protestants and Roman Catholics in Ulster often broke out in armed conflict.[13] Alexander, seeking theological and political peace and independence at age twenty-one,[14] emigrated in 1809 from Northern Ireland to join his father and eventually established his home near Bethany, Virginia.

Alexander Campbell soon developed a reputation in Virginia as a noted biblical scholar and religious maverick. Strongly influenced by his association with theological independents both in his early years at Rich Hill and during his year at the University of Glasgow,[15] Campbell had suspended his training for the Presbyterian clergy before he joined his father's independent congregation, the Christian Association of Washington (Western Pennsylvania) in 1810. The Christian Association, of which Alexander Campbell became the chief spokesman, evolved into the Brush Run Church, which eventually entered into a controversial relationship with the Redstone Baptist Association in 1815.[16] After 1830 his already precarious association with the Baptists degenerated further and he broke with them also.

The theology of Campbell was strongly influenced by his training in the Scottish school of Common Sense Realism and the Baconian inductive method of biblical interpretation, which had gained much support in America.[17] He successfully combined these elements of formal theology with an energetic religious life on the American frontier, where the "rationalistic and optimistic philosophy of the Enlightenment was simply a sophisticated expression of the spirit that prevailed in the American West."[18] Individuality and self-confidence were the trademarks that distinguished the Disciples, and they generally were suspicious of many traditional sources of authority. Ecclesiastical and clerical authority were especially suspect, and most believed that religious truth could best be discovered by a rational investigation of Scripture.[19] Campbell's Disciples of Christ and other groups common to the "back-to-the-Bible" movement were biblical rationalists who conceived of their mission in terms of "restoring the gospel to its original first-century purity and of reordering the church according to the 'ancient order of things.'"[20] The natural result of this spiritual revolution would be the union of a divided Christendom and the reconciliation of Roman

Catholicism and Protestantism under the banner of "New Testament Christianity." The foundation upon which the "Restoration" rested was biblical literalism.[21] Biblical literalism was by far the most important aspect of Campbell's thought and even his anti-Catholic rhetoric stemmed from his understanding of the Bible.[22]

According to Campbell, the key to Christian unity lay in adopting the practices of the first-century church, which he understood to mean following only those "approved examples" and "precepts" recorded in the Book of Acts and the Epistles.[23] Instead of a literal interpretation of Scripture, the Catholics had relied on tradition and extra-biblical authority. Thus, restoring Christianity to its first-century purity would necessitate eradicating those elements of church structure and practice developed mainly by Roman Catholic dogma and tradition which Campbell deemed largely "perversions" of true Christianity.[24] Throughout this period Campbell's primary anti-Catholic theological arguments stemmed from the basic "Restoration" ideal that "nothing ought to be inculcated upon Christians as articles of faith; nor required of them as terms of communion, but what is expressly taught and enjoined upon them in the word of God."[25] In Campbell's opinion, strict biblical interpretation "freed the individual Christian and restricted the activities of the Church,"[26] and, as a result, much of Campbell's anti-Catholic rhetoric was directed against the expansion of Roman Catholic theology into Protestant America.

Another very important aspect of Campbell's biblical interpretation that strongly influenced his anti-Catholicism was an intense belief that America was God's chosen land and the agent for the Christian millennium. He did not share with William Miller the belief that Christ would return in 1843; instead, he advocated a postmillennial eschatology which stressed that Christian progress and the eventual perfection of Western civilization would precede the establishment of Christ's kingdom on earth. His monthly periodical, published from 1830 to 1870, was entitled *The Millennial Harbinger*. As did most other American Protestants, Campbell saw the founding of America as a divine mission where God had sent Protestant Christians "to a New World, that they might institute, under the most favorable circumstances, new political and ecclesiastic institutions."[27] Campbell saw these new institutions as a definite prerequisite to the beginning of the millennium. According to him, God had given "in awful charge, to Protestant England and Protestant America . . . the fortunes, not of Christendom only, but of all the world."[28]

In November 1833 Campbell declared his intention to become involved in the battle against Roman Catholicism. Until this time he had in great measure remained "a silent spectator of the varied, ingenious, persevering, and bold efforts of the Romanists to gain the political ascendancy in this country."[29] The prevention of Catholic political ascendancy then was Campbell's primary concern.

According to him, the progress toward the Christian millennium was directly challenged by this apparent attempt by the Catholics to gain political control. He proposed to present to the American people his argument for republican institutions and Protestant theology, because without them the fundamental principles of free government would be destroyed. For him the anti-Catholic question ultimately was reduced to "Whether it is possible for any earthly government to exist, under which men's political and religious rights and privileges can be kept perfectly separate and distinct."[30]

Campbell's primary anti-Catholic arguments can be broken into four major points, which he continually stressed both in his publications and his debate with Bishop Purcell. First, he denied any scriptural warrant for the claim that Roman Catholicism was the "universal Christian church." Second, he argued that its hierarchical organization embodied religious tyranny by claiming infallibility and thereby denying the "priesthood of all believers." Third, he believed the Roman church in America aimed at political tyranny by seeking union with the state and dominance over it; and fourth, he believed the Catholic Church undermined the true basis of culture by withholding the Bible as a textbook from the masses.[31]

Of primary importance to Campbell was the Catholic argument for infallibility, because it directly opposed the basic Protestant concept of the "priesthood of all believers." Campbell had wished that "the Roman Catholic faith, under the mild genius of our institutions, might become so modified as to be suited to the character of our republic"; however, this could only occur if the Catholics would "abandon the absurd pretensions of infallibility, which indeed, [they] must do, if ever [they] can become American."[32]

Infallibility was not only a challenge to political freedom but also a theological point of dispute. In the Purcell debate Campbell compared infallibility to "mental slavery." According to him, the Council of Trent (the nineteenth ecumenical council of the Roman Catholic Church, 1545–63) had declared the Catholic oral tradition as equal in authority to both the Old and New Testaments; had affirmed the Catholic Church as the only person or institution that was allowed to interpret the Scriptures, and had declared that each member was obliged to swear obedience first to the church.[33] According to Campbell, the acceptance of this doctrine tended to "enervate and anesthetize" the minds of believers. To Campbell, "free discussion, free thinking, free reading, and most of all freedom of action, expand and corroborate the human mind," while "Popery dethrones reason, inhibits inquisitiveness . . . and condemns to eternal perdition all beyond the precincts of her communion,"[34] and "ever must be a reign of terror to all who love liberty of thought and freedom of speech."[35] To a Protestant theologian in search of religious freedom, the Catholic concept of infallibility endangered both civil and religious liberty.

Particularly alarming to Campbell was the statement made in 1832 by Pope Gregory XVI that liberty of conscience and the press was the "most pestilential error."[36] Gregory also agreed with former Pope Clement XIII who advocated burning all books on the "Index," which included works by Locke, Milton, Bacon, Grotius, Galileo . . . Luther, Calvin, Melancthon—and, indeed, all the standard Protestant authors."[37] As far as Campbell was concerned, this "mental slavery" to the Catholic hierarchical establishment precipitated social slavery and threatened to "disqualify a person for the enjoyment of political liberty. For in all history, civil liberty follows in the wake of religious liberty." Campbell believed the proper maintenance of this relationship the primary challenge to American republican institutions, and regarded religious liberty as the "cause, and political liberty as an effect of that cause."[38]

Essential in political liberty, Campbell's second major argument was the Madisonian concept of separation of powers established by the Constitution. He argued that the theocracy of Catholicism was essentially "unbiblical" as well as antirepublican in nature. Campbell believed Catholicism was pure despotism instead of a theocracy because, "God himself was lawgiver—the priests kept and expounded the law—the judges and kings executed it. Where, then, were all these powers accumulated in one and the same dynasty?"[39] Consequently, Campbell believed that if the church of Rome is unsusceptible of reformation or is infallible, it is proved to be essentially anti-American and opposed to the genius of republican institutions.[40]

It is on this last point that Campbell was the most vocal. The danger of Catholic subversion of American republican political institutions appeared to him a very real danger primarily because these same institutions would allow Catholics free access to them.[41] While Campbell discounted the probability that the pope actually plotted to dominate the Mississippi Valley,[42] he did consider it a real possibility that at some time, through the natural freedom of our political institutions, the Catholic vote would become a significant force in American politics. Campbell lamented that the "Catholic vote of this country may be hawked to the highest bidder," and the "momentous interests of liberty of conscience and of a free Bible, may hang on the results of a Presidential election."[43] Campbell never considered the possibility that Catholics might make America their first loyalty and relegate the pope to second place in their political hierarchy. He was of the opinion that no good Catholic could swear allegiance to the Catholic Church and to the American government at the same time without perjury. In his "most deliberate judgement" it was impossible and improbable because history had proved the opposite.[44]

As far as Campbell was concerned, the only hope to prevent Catholic religious and political domination was free discussion and unbiased public education. The battle for control of education became, for Campbell, the ultimate struggle, and the Catholic attack on the public school system was a most significant threat, one that demanded most of his anti-Catholic energy. Much of the bitter anti-Catholic rhetoric erupted in America because of the Catholic demand that the church and not the state be allowed to determine the nature of the public education system and, more specifically, that the church be allowed to determine which version of the Bible was to be used as a common school textbook. Campbell quoted Catholic Archbishop John Hughes as the source of his understanding of Catholic intentions for American education. According to Hughes, American public education without specific Catholic instruction would be a curse and not a blessing. Attendance at public schools, where the Catholic religion was not taught, would result in Catholicism "wasting away." Therefore, Hughes urged Catholic parents to withdraw their children from public schools and create schools of their own to teach the principles of their religion. Finally he demanded that American governments, both state and local, should so regard their "conscientious scruples" on this subject as either "not to tax them at all, or if they do, have tax drawn from them, and appropriated to their own Catholic schools."[45]

On several occasions Campbell argued, either directly or indirectly, against all the demands of Archbishop Hughes. He believed the influence of a Catholic-dominated educational system would eventually lead to ecclesiastical despotism, political tyranny, the corruption of biblical Christianity, and the ruin of America as the vanguard of millennialism. Campbell was fearful that Catholic education would de-emphasize literary and scientific study and concentrate on a Catholic theology,[46] which he deemed antagonistic to scientific discovery and to the free discussion of literature, philosophy, and theology.

Campbell consistently advocated open discourse and rational decision making, which he considered basically anti-Catholic in nature. He pictured universal education as the "ark of safety" for a society on the verge of catastrophe. "The Roman hierarchy," said Campbell, "may, and in all probability will, dash the American ship upon a rock, and engulf us all in one common ruin." He argued for a public education system patronized, sustained, guarded, and controlled by the state, which would enlighten all, Catholic and Protestant,[47] and in which all would rationally come to learn the truth.[48]

Consistent with Campbell's philosophy of universal education was his belief in the literal interpretation of the Bible and the possibility that all humans could rationally avail themselves of its great revealed truths. Even Bishop Purcell conceded that the basis of Protestantism as it was transported to the New World had been the literal interpretation of the Bible.[49] To deny access to an authoritative Bible as a textbook in the common schools was, therefore, seen by Campbell and others as a potentially fatal danger to the American society, for its denial might eventually lead to agnosticism or atheism. The Bible read and universally taught in the public schools would be the "shield of the nation."[50] The nation could then continue toward its millennial destiny as the "last and best hope of the oppressed of all nations."[51] Campbell continually pleaded the need to "assail Romanism and infidelity with the Bible in every man's family, and with a good common school for every man's children in the land." He believed that a "well-educated, Bible-reading nation [had] nothing to fear from Popery, prelacy or infidelity; but without the Bible and common school no nation can be free, virtuous and happy."[52]

Alexander Campbell had actively participated in one of the more interesting debates in American religious history. He had felt a deep commitment to defend Protestant Christianity and American republican institutions against, what he perceived to be, a most serious challenge. Papal infallibility, the autocratic and hierarchical nature of the Catholic clergy, its unsupported claim to be the "universal church," and its overt challenge to free public education had each been debated by Campbell in his various public discourses and publications. The nature of his commitment might best be summarized in his address to the graduating class of Bethany College in 1847 when he told them: "You must take some side in the great controversies of the age. Survey the battleground before you. On the one side are ranged antiquated error, superstition, despotism and misanthropy; on the other truth, intelligence, liberty, religion and humanity."[53]

While Campbell's debate with Bishop Purcell in Cincinnati lasted only one week, the repercussions from it continued until the slavery issue seized control of the American conscience. The apparent challenge of the Catholic Church to American institutions would lay dormant until the force of increased immigration from southern and eastern Europe in the late nineteenth century sparked its periodic return to public consciousness. While there has been a certain degree of anti-Catholic sentiment expressed at various times since, it has been relatively mild compared to the anti-Catholic and nativist rhetoric of the Jacksonian era. To a large degree, the American Catholic Church in the nineteenth century had sought independence from Rome and an end to its status as a "missionary church." In 1908 its independence was granted when Rome finally recognized what America was becoming to "millions of Catholics who made pilgrimages to it and in it: their own land."[54] America had become their land not because the power of the Catholic Church had altered American republican institutions, but because the church had instead adapted itself rather quickly and quietly to traditional American Protestant political and religious values. In a relatively short period of time in the nineteenth century the Catholic Church in America became decidedly less Roman and more American in theology and practice and no longer presented a direct challenge to Protestantism and its millennial hope.

History has thus proved that, much to the surprise of both Campbell and Tocqueville, Catholicism has been enculturated in America society without the ruin of its Protestant millennial theology or its republican institutions. Tocqueville had failed to see that republicanism in the political sphere was a part of a larger cultural whole, of which the spirit of Protestantism was a vital part. In the final analysis, Campbell's argument with the Catholics constituted a cogent and articulate expression of this cultural whole.

NOTES

1. Alexis de Tocqueville, *Democracy in America*, ed. Richard D. Heffner (New York: New American Library, 1956), 151–52.

2. Republican religion refers to religious sentiments and practices that supported and confirmed "republican polity in government and rebellion against orthodox Christianity, dogmatic systems, a formal priesthood, and all church structures." William Gribben, "Republican Religion and the American Churches in the Early National Period," *Historian* 35 (1972): 63.

3. Tocqueville, *Democracy in America*, 152.

4. Ibid., 155.

5. Three important essays argue for the strength and persistence of eighteenth-century republican values into the nineteenth century: Robert E. Shalhope, "Toward a Republican Synthesis: The Emergence of an Understanding of Republicanism in American Historiography," *William and Mary Quarterly* 29 (Jan. 1972): 49–80; Dorothy Ross, "The Liberal Tradition Revisited and the Republican Tradition Addressed," in *New Directions in American Intellectual History*, ed. John Higham and Paul K. Conkin (Baltimore: Johns Hopkins Univ. Press, 1979), 116–31; and Linda K. Kerber, "The Republican Ideology of the Revolutionary Generation," *American Quarterly* 37 (Fall 1985): 474–95.

6. Three works that demonstrate how republicanism, as a form of civil religion, was at work in the political arena of Jacksonian America are Marvin Meyers, *The Jacksonian Persuasion: Politics and Belief* (Palo Alto: Stanford Univ. Press, 1957); J. Mills Thornton, *Politics and Power in a Slave Society: Alabama, 1800–1860* (Baton Rouge: Louisiana State Univ. Press, 1978); and Major L. Wilson, "Republicanism and the Idea of Party in Jacksonian America," *Journal of the Early Republic* 8 (Winter 1988): 419–42.

7. On nativism see the seminal work of Ray Allen Billington, *The Protestant Crusade, 1800–1860: A Study of the Origins of American Nativism* (Chicago: Quadrangle Books, 1964).

8. For a thorough analysis of nativism's contribution to the metamorphosis of American political parties before the Civil War, consult David Potter, *The Impending Crisis, 1848–1861* (New York: Harper & Row, 1976), 241–53.

9. Billington, *The Protestant Crusade*, 65.

10. According to David Edwin Harrell, Campbell was, at the conclusion of the debate, "probably the most widely known anti-Catholic spokesman in the West." *Quest for a Christian America* (Nashville: Disciples of Christ Historical Society, 1966), 217.

11. The 1829 Catholic Council issued from Baltimore a series of decrees that "definitely placed American Protestants on guard." The Council warned American Catholics against "corrupt translations of the Bible," urged them to build parochial schools to save their children from "perversion," and approved the baptism of non-Catholic children when there was a possibility they might be raised as Catholics (Billington, *Protestant Crusade*, 38). Also, what appeared to be an open attack by the Catholic Church against the separation of church and state occurred in the several "trusteeism" controversies between the Catholic hierarchy and its parishioners. These controversies came to light when control of Catholic Church property was openly disputed. The question was whether church property was owned by the Catholic diocese or by the local church itself. While most Protestant church property was owned by the trustees of the local congregation, the debate among the Catholics only ended when the pope himself issued an encyclical against "rebellious" trustees in 1824. "The impression which the whole struggle left in the average American mind was that Catholicism was a sworn enemy to democratic institutions and thus a dangerous influence in the United States" (Billington, *Protestant Crusade*, 39–40).

12. Billington, *Protestant Crusade*, 37.

13. Eva Jean Wrather, "Alexander Campbell's 'Beau Ideal': The Making of a Reformer," *Restoration Quarterly* 30 (1988): 75.

14. Much of Campbell's early enthusiasm for America may have stemmed from what he felt was the absence of established Roman Catholicism. "He had, indeed, long been convinced that life, property, character, as well as religious liberty, were all in greater jeopardy in papal than in Protestant states, and had been wont to regard the Protestant north of Ireland and the papal south of the same island as truthful and unambiguous exponents of the fruits and tendencies of the two respective religious systems." Robert Richardson, *Memoirs of Alexander Campbell* (Indianapolis: Religious Book Service, n.d.), 1:210.

15. Perhaps the most thorough analysis of the influence of Scottish independent theology on Campbell is Lynn A. McMillon's *Restoration Roots* (Dallas: Gospel Teachers Publications, 1983).

16. Although Campbell edited a religious periodical entitled *The Christian Baptist* until 1830, his association with both the Redstone and Mahoning Baptist Associations was conditional, and his independent theology was constantly under attack by leaders of both associations. Campbell had insisted upon not being bound by the Philadelphia Confession of Faith and "refused to unite with them if any other creed than the New Testament was presented to us." Alexander Campbell, *The Millennial Harbinger* (1830–70) (Joplin, Mo.: College Press, 1987), 1832, p. 3.

17. A comprehensive analysis of the philosophical influence of "Baconianism" is Theodore Dwight Bozeman's *Protestants in an Age of Science: The Baconian Ideal and Antebellum Religious Thought* (Chapel Hill: Univ. of North Carolina Press, 1977).

18. Harrell, *Quest for a Christian America*, 28–29.

19. Ibid.

20. The best exposition of Campbell's position on this return to apostolic practices in the church was his "Restoration of the Ancient Order of Things" (nos. 1–24), Alexander Campbell, ed., *Christian Baptist,* 1823–1830, reprint ed. (Nashville: Gospel Advocate Co., 1955), vols. 2–5.

21. Harrell, *Quest for a Christian America,* 27–28.

22. An important distinction of Campbell's movement was that it claimed to be a "restoration" and not another reformation. He believed that since the reformation had sprung from the Catholic Church it contained as much error as the original. In order to purify Christianity an attempt had to be made to return to Christianity before Catholic ascendancy. According to Campbell, "a successful assailant against the arrogant pretensions of the Romanists must begin at Jerusalem and neither at Rome nor Geneva." *Millennial Harbinger,* 1834, p. 266. Other examples of this idea are found in *Millennial Harbinger,* 1833, 288, 469–70, and 1843, p. 352.

23. Harrell, *Quest for a Christian America,* 29. Perhaps the clearest expression of Campbell's understanding of the authority of the New Testament examples and precepts for nineteenth-century Christians was given in his "Sermon on the Law," delivered to the Redstone Baptist Association in September 1816. Cited in C. A. Young, *Historical Documents Advocating Christian Union,* reprint ed. (Joplin, Mo.: College Press Publishing Co., 1985), 224.

24. In Campbell's debate with Bishop Purcell, the first proposition under discussion was Campbell's assertion that the Roman Catholic Institution was "not the 'mother and mistress of all churches,' but an apostasy from the only true, apostolic and catholic Church of Christ," which Campbell believed to be composed of those individuals who had "restored" in both faith and practice the form and spirit of "New Testament Christianity." Cited in Richardson, *Memoirs of Alexander Campbell,* 2:424.

25. Quoted in Young, *Historical Documents Advocating Christian Union,* 108. The most comprehensive statement of restorationist principles championed by Alexander Campbell are found in Thomas Campbell's 1809 organizational statement of the Christian Association of Washington. In his "Declaration and Address," Thomas Campbell appealed for simple evangelical Christianity in its original form, "expressly exhibited upon the sacred page; without attempting to inculcate anything of human authority, of private opinion, or inventions of men, as having any place in the constitution, faith, or worship of the Christian Church, or anything as a matter of Christian faith or duty, for which there can not be expressly produced a 'Thus saith the Lord, either in express terms, or by approved precedent" (75–76).

26. Harrell, *Quest for a Christian America,* 30.

27. Alexander Campbell, *Popular Lectures and Addresses,* 1861, reprint (Rosemead, Calif.: Old Paths Book Club, n.d.), 169.

28. Ibid., 179.

29. Campbell, *Millennial Harbinger,* 1833, p. 538. "I thought that the history of the Old World was enough for the New on this subject, and I did not imagine that the sons of

that tottering hierarchy would have the insolence, in the face of American light and liberty, to urge its claims, now nauseating to all the intelligence of Europe. But it seems it must be attended to" (1834, p. 234).

30. Ibid., 1833, p. 538.

31. D. Ray Lindley, *The Apostle of Freedom* (St. Louis: Bethany Press, 1957), 19–26.

32. Alexander Campbell and John B. Purcell, *A Debate on the Roman Catholic Religion* (Nashville: McQuiddy Printing Co., 1914), 203–4.

33. Ibid., 351.

34. Campbell, *Millennial Harbinger,* 1848, p. 672.

35. Campbell, *Popular Lectures,* 174: "The Popish religion is utterly incompatible with freedom in any nation. The slave of the altar is essentially the slave of the throne."

36. Ibid., 419.

37. Ibid., 415.

38. Ibid., 393.

39. Ibid., 381.

40. Ibid., 392.

41. "Our community is mixed, and the wisdom of our institutions is that, irrespective of sectarian opinions, men of moral worth are eligible to every office, and that our government knows no man according to his faith." Campbell, *Millennial Harbinger,* 1833, p. 470.

42. Ibid., 1835, p. 407.

43. Ibid., 1852, p. 667.

44. Campbell and Purcell, *Debate on the Roman Catholic Religion,* 409.

45. Campbell, *Millennial Harbinger,* 1853, p. 150.

46. "Indeed, Romanism is their body, soul, and spirit. They are sold to the Pope and absolutism. With them, the church and the state are one idea . . . Their influence is the only portentous cloud on our horizon." Campbell, *Popular Lectures,* 178.

47. Campbell, *Millennial Harbinger,* 1835, p. 66.

48. Campbell, *Popular Lectures,* 181.

49. Campbell and Purcell, *Debate on the Roman Catholic Religion,* 220. Also, according to Billington, leaders of the anti-Catholic movement were aware "that their best means of appealing to the middle class was through the Bible. If Catholicism could be demonstrated as an enemy of the gospel, it would become the religious duty of American Protestants to destroy American Popery." *Protestant Crusade,* 142.

50. Campbell, *Millennial Harbinger,* 1835, p. 66.

51. Campbell and Purcell, *Debate on the Roman Catholic Religion,* 442.

52. Campbell, *Popular Lectures,* 502.

53. Ibid., 503.

54. Martin E. Marty, *Pilgrims in Their Own Land: 500 Years of Religion in America* (Boston: Little, Brown and Co., 1984), 285.

Section 3

The Influence of a Tradition on the Presidency

The Religious Thought and Practice of James A. Garfield

William C. Ringenberg

The year 1981 marked the centennial of the presidency of the only preacher to live in the White House, James G. Garfield. Admittedly, Garfield pursued several careers in addition to the ministry. He was, however, a fully recognized minister of the Disciples of Christ; and during the 1850s he spoke regularly at a broad variety of denominational services, including camp meetings and revivals, where he was a great favorite. Later his eloquence served him well in political debate during his seventeen years in Congress and as president. After 1860, he preached very little if at all, but his interest in pursuing religious truth deepened. In fact, probably no chief executive—not even John Adams, Thomas Jefferson, Abraham Lincoln, or Woodrow Wilson—came to the presidency with a more intense intellectual interest in Christianity than did Garfield.[1]

During his childhood near Cleveland, Garfield's major religious influence came from his mother and the Disciples denomination. Eliza Ballou Garfield numbered New England Puritans, Baptists, and Universalists among her ancestors, the most famous being her uncle, Hosea Ballou (1771–1852), who for half a century led the Universalist Church in America. There is no record that Eliza or her husband, Abram, showed serious religious interest until the loss in 1830 of both a child and a major financial investment. Subsequently, they "resolved to live a different life provided they could find the right way." The Western Reserve at this time contained many persuasive Disciples preachers and laymen, and soon the receptive Garfields "obeyed the Saviour" by accepting baptism and membership in the local church. Four months later Garfield's father died when the lad was only eighteen months old, and this tragic event led Eliza Garfield to an even deeper religious faith than she had previously experienced. She became an enthusiastic Bible reader, and biblical phrases began to appear frequently in her speech and correspondence. She regularly read the Bible to her children in their log cabin home, and on Sundays she walked with them to the Disciples meetinghouse three miles away.[2]

The Disciples, or the Christians, originated about a generation earlier when Thomas Campbell, Barton Stone, and others led a movement to unify all Christians on the basis of a rejection of all "human" creeds, forms of worship, and church government, and a rejection of denominational names, while holding the Bible as the sole guide for faith and practice. The intention was expressed in the motto "When the scriptures speak, we speak; when the scriptures are silent, we are silent." The early Disciples believed that they had restored the simplicity and purity of the gospel as practiced by the first-century church. They believed that they were leading a "new reformation" that eventually would unite the various branches of a divided Christianity. Unfortunately, the result of the movement was not the creation of church unity, but development of yet another denomination. In fact, the Disciples were not as different from other Protestant groups as they thought. In their lack of regularly ordained preachers and in their nonresistance they were like the Quakers; in their nonresistance as well as in their suspicion of politics they resembled Mennonites; in their emphasis given to the separation of church and state and to adult baptism they followed the Baptists; and their early preachers used the circuit riding approach made famous by the Methodists.[3]

Garfield accepted the Disciples variety of Christian faith while growing to young manhood. He did not undergo a typical Disciples conversion experience, however, until March 1850 when, attending a series of Disciples revival meetings, he "determined to obey the Gospel," and was "buried with Christ in Baptism and arose to walk [in] newness of life." The entries in Garfield's diary reflect the intense change in the young man.[4] Before his conversion he made few references to religious subjects; after, such references became regular features of the diary. A week later he expressed "thanks be to God for His goodness . . . I'll praise my maker while I have breath by the help of God."[5]

Garfield experienced a sense of divine guidance when illness interrupted his career as a worker on the Ohio canal and provided the occasion for his intellectual development and spiritual conversion: "Two years ago today I was taken with the ague in Cleveland. When I consider the sequel of my history thus far, I can see the providence of God in a striking manner. Two years ago I . . . [was] ripe for ruin. On the canal . . . ready to drink in every species of vice—and with the ultimate design of going on to the ocean. See the facts. I was taken sick, unable to labor, went to school two terms, thus cultivating my moral and intellectual faculties, took a school in the winter, and greatest of all, obeyed the gospel . . . Thus by the providence of God I am what I am, and not a sailor. I thank Him."[6] The young Garfield continued to display the enthusiasm of an ideal convert. He faithfully attended the religious services of the local churches and also those in the nearby Disciples of Christ school, Western Reserve Eclectic Institute (to become Hiram College in 1850), where he was enrolled. He especially enjoyed being present at revival services, baptismal services, and prayer meetings. On the latter he wrote, "I love to attend them." The young man not only attended meetings but also meditated deeply on the purpose of God for his life. In June 1852 he prayed, "may God grant that I may so live that I shall be prepared for the events of His providence whatever they may be," and by the end of the year he expressed the confidence that he could "see the hand of God shaping circumstances and arranging providences to govern" his future. He read carefully in the best works of religion and literature. He expressed particular fascination with Thomas a Kempis's *Imitation of Christ*. Of the author he wrote, "Would that my own soul were as golden."[7]

Garfield exhibited not only the zeal but also the narrowness of a new convert. The Presbyterians and the Methodists, he noted, used "unscriptural names" for their organizations, and their ministers preached "historical" rather than "gospel" sermons. It is curious that despite his criticisms Garfield frequently attended the meetings of such groups. Shortly after his conversion Garfield visited a Presbyterian service where he "listened a few minutes and then slept soundly until the exercises were nearly closed. It pains my heart," he noted, "to see the ignorance and bigotry that is abroad in the land. I wish that men would let all human traditions alone and take the Bible alone for their guide." The Methodists were even worse since in addition to theological error they added the disorder of their assemblies. After attending such a meeting Garfield noted being "grieved and disgusted with this shamble proceedings. The most excessive shouting and roaring. My conclusion is that this religion is only adapted to the coarser order of mind, and has more of the animal than spiritual in it." A visit to a Dutch Reformed Church brought the following comment: "I endured an hour of . . . sermonizing on the . . . themes of original sin [and] Total Depravity that contain neither Gospel, logic, rhetoric nor truth."[8]

More surprising than Garfield's criticisms of other denominations was his early belief—expressed by many other Disciples as well—that the practice of the Christian faith and the practice of politics were inherently incompatible. The youthful future president stated that "it looks to me like serving two masters to participate in the affairs of a government which is point blank opposed to the Christian (as all human ones must necessarily be)."[9]

If young Garfield was unduly critical of Christians in other denominations and in politics, he was also very demanding of himself. In his diary in the early 1850s he frequently chided himself for lacking spiritual faithfulness. He criticized his unenthusiastic attitude while attending church: "I do not feel that burning interest in meeting today that I ought. There seems to be kind of indifference in my case that seems wholly inexcusable. Not that I have any disposition or desire to abandon the cause of Christianity, and return to the weak and beggarly elements of the world for they have no charms for me; but I am not enough devoted to the cause of Jesus of Nazareth. May the Lord fill my heart with love and keep me in the right way." Similarly he criticized the insufficiency of his Bible study: "I have not read enough today. I hope not to let another Lord's Day pass without doing more and learning more of the Holy Word." Gradually, however, through the late 1850s, Garfield became an increasingly tolerant person. His wide reading and intellectual curiosity enabled him to grow beyond the rigid narrowness which characterized the Disciples of his day.[10]

It is significant that Garfield chose not to complete his education at Bethany College, the new Disciples institute of higher education in Virginia. Although he continued throughout his life to identify with the denomination and had the highest respect for the college founder, Alexander Campbell, he thought it "best for the sake of liberalizing my mind" to spend some time in a different environment. He thus chose Williams College in Massachusetts, where he studied for two years under President Mark Hopkins. Garfield accepted his Williams College friends as "spiritually minded Christians" while retaining a disdain for their Calvinistic theology: "It is strange to me that any set of Christians can hold so tenaciously to any dogma so cold and comfortless as the Calvinistic faith and at the same time regard the Gospel as a scheme of benevolence and even-handed justice. Certainly, I could never rejoice in such a Gospel." If the Williams experience did not convert him to the New England theology, it did make him increasingly tolerant of it and other theological views. It also led him to reassess his earlier opposition to Christians participating in political and military activities; in 1859 he ran successfully for the Ohio state senate, and in 1861 he accepted the regimental command of the Forty-second Ohio Infantry in the Union army.[11]

After graduating from Williams College in 1856 and while serving as principal, or president, of the Eclectic Institute in Hiram, Garfield pursued a serious investigation of the relationship between science and Christianity. The immediate occasion was a nearly weeklong, day-and-night debate with William Denton of England on "the development theory." The debate, which took place a year before Charles Darwin published his *Origin of the Species,* was a major local event. Garfield supported the concept of the miracle of divine creation, and he held that Denton was trying to "invalidate the claims of the Bible and remove God from the immediate control of the universe." Garfield prepared intensely for the debate, and Denton acknowledged that he was the worthiest opponent he had ever met. As a result of the debate, Garfield gained much local recognition and popularity; and throughout the next year he lectured frequently on the subject of geology and religion. Garfield's primary mission in these lectures was to "pursue that miserable atheism to its hole." The intense preparation for his speeches gave him a broad understanding of the relationship between science and Christianity, and it changed some of his earlier views. For example, he now accepted the idea that the earth was millions of years old.[12]

Garfield was not only broadening his religious and intellectual views in the 1850s, but he was also doing most of his preaching during this period. Nearly three years after his conversion and while a twenty-one-year-old student at the Western Reserve Eclectic Institute, Garfield preached his first sermon—although he was not formally ordained, then or later. In fact, very few of the early Disciples preachers were ordained. A man simply became a Disciples minister if he felt the call to preach, possessed at least fair biblical knowledge and general speaking ability, and could gain the confidence of the church constituency. When Garfield attended Williams College (1854–56), he frequently accepted preaching assignments among the Disciples in Poestenkill, New York, and other towns near the college. After returning from Williams to teach at the Eclectic Institute, he became one of the most popular Disciples preachers in the Western Reserve. Until the Civil War interrupted his careers in the classroom and pulpit, he preached somewhere in the Reserve nearly every Sunday, most frequently in the Disciples churches at Hiram, Solon, Aurora, Chagrin Falls, Warren, and Newburgh. In addition to delivering the usual Sunday morning sermon he performed baptisms, presided at weddings and funerals, and spoke at "protracted," or revival, meetings. Periodically, Garfield noted in his diary the conversions that followed his sermons. His peak as a revivalist was reached in January–February 1858, when at Hiram he preached twenty-seven times in less than a month and won many converts.[13]

Garfield possessed the physical traits, the personality, and the oratorical skills desirable for a successful preacher. His physique gave the appearance of strength. A six-foot, two-hundred-pound frame supported a massive head, a thick neck, broad shoulders, a deep chest, and muscular arms and legs. His face was handsome, with light blue eyes conveying a kindly, genial look, and his whole bearing conveyed dignity. His voice was very strong, his words came easily, and he appeared untroubled by any self-consciousness. In a moment of crisis he could think quickly and speak effectively, as when in 1852 he quieted and put to shame the traveling militant atheist who visited Hiram, or when in New York City, following the assassination of Lincoln, he quieted a mob of thousands with his Old Testament prophetlike oratory.[14]

While Garfield in his preaching clearly identified with the Disciples, he was less sectarian in approach than were many of his brethren. His sermons would include references to the unique "Disciples Reformation" and other such denominational distinctions; but he went much beyond by emphasizing the role of reason in religion, science, and philosophy, as well as in personal ethics and morality. Always his sermons gave a central place to the exaltation of Christ.

Garfield avoided abstract theological reasoning about the person of Christ and instead emphasized the simple life and teachings of the Savior. Typical sermon topics included the following: "The Saviour's Second Coming," "The Evidences of Christianity," "The Parable of the Wedding," "Salvation as Illustrated by the Deluge," and "The Necessity of Obeying Whatever God Commands of Us."[15]

Garfield believed in thorough preparation for each sermon. Many of his evangelistic messages were written in advance of delivery, and these manuscripts are still preserved as a part of his voluminous papers. He thought that it was "not right to take the time of an audience unless one is prepared to say something which will instruct and arouse." In fact, he believed that "the people needed arousing more than instructing." In his effort to be a dynamic preacher he noted that he was getting somewhat "spurgeonic" (after Charles H. Spurgeon, the famous nineteenth-century English preacher known for his stirring sermons).[16]

Garfield's sermons drew criticism from some of the more conservative Disciples. One group wished him to be "more denominational." Others were concerned that his lectures at the Hiram College chapel were not limited to preaching Disciples theology or even theology in general, but included—in addition to Bible expositions—wide-sweeping lectures on geology, education, morality, history, and current events. One unusually harsh Disciples critic noted that "his religious meetings were always well attended and were even more popular with the sinners of the world than with the saints of the church. There was a lack of spirituality about him that grieved the latter, and it was noticed that the revivals never progressed under the spell of his preaching, but the sinners liked to hear his short, sparkling, logical discourses which did not unpleasantly trouble them with thoughts of righteousness, temperance, and judgment to come."[17]

Partly because of such criticisms, but probably much more because of the growing breadth of his interests and opportunities, Garfield decided in the early 1860s to reduce the extent of his preaching activities. While serving in the Civil War in early 1863, Garfield told a friend that, given the state of the Disciples organization and doctrine, he could not remain a preacher and only a preacher for the rest of his life. He saw the Disciples ministry as a field too narrow for the growth and development he felt he needed. In fact, he believed that "a person devoutly fulfilling a secular calling while an active member of a religious society would have a greater freedom and freshness to speak out the truths of philosophy, morality and religion than would a regular minister." Thus the Civil War, which changed so much in American history, helped to accelerate the vocational change in Garfield's life from religion and education to law and politics. During the middle and late 1850s, Garfield repeatedly expressed his mental struggle over his vocational future: "The law and the ministry encompass me on either hand." Perhaps the heart of Garfield's problem was that, while he was developing a preference for a legal career, his religious background and the attitudes of many of his friends led him to question the propriety of such a choice. "Were it not for the religion of Christ, I should long ago have placed my mark in that direction [the legal profession], and though I did not [continue to] regard the legal profession as incompatible to Christianity, still I think it would be much more difficult to cultivate and preserve . . . purity of heart and devotedness to the cause of Christ." When Garfield left for the state capital in 1859, his mother wept and one of his colleagues at Hiram College lamented that his "best friends in Christ all shake their heads when . . . [his] name is [mentioned] in connection with law and politics."[18]

Garfield's decision to become a politician was the major step in his unusually rapid rise as a political figure in the late 1850s and early and middle 1860s. Certainly no other American within so short a period was an academic leader, a state senator, a lawyer who argued his first case before the Supreme Court, a major general in a great war, and a member of Congress.[19]

If, after his election to Congress in 1862, Garfield ended his formal preaching career, he did not reduce his interest in observing preachers and offering commentary on their sermons. On Sundays he frequently noted in his diary the sermons he heard, together with a brief evaluation of them. Such judgments as "good," "passable," "fine," or "stupid" repeatedly appear. Garfield's close friend and successor as president of the Western Reserve Eclectic Institute, Burke Hinsdale, usually received very high marks. In addition to administering the college, Hinsdale was minister of the Hiram Disciples Church, where Garfield frequently attended Sunday services when he was home from Washington.[20]

Many ministers received much less kindly evaluations than did Hinsdale. While Garfield in many ways was a very generous person, he regularly expressed harsh criticism of what he conceived to be poor sermons. He was displeased with narrow-minded preachers who gave major emphasis to criticizing others. After one Sunday service he noted, "I am utterly wearied of this everlasting attack on other churches that has so long disgraced our people and is productive of no good." On another occasion he wrote: "Went to church and heard another scolding sermon. Did me no good but rather made me angry." In his later years he grew increasingly impatient with the conservative wing of the Disciples of Christ. It was probably a minister of such orientation who in 1872 Garfield heard preach "the dryest sermon of the most . . . legalistic order." He also disliked simplistic sermons such as one that included "an attempt to draw a mathematical line across the world, with Hell bound on one side and Heaven bound on the other." Garfield's response was that "the issues of life and death and the exact scope of moral works cannot be mapped out like counties on a blackboard." He was further irritated by ministers who offered religious zeal but little else as a qualification for preaching. After listening to such a preacher in 1873, he noted, "I was tortured by the feeblest little preacher it has been my misfortune to hear for many months. It is a fraud on the community, and a wrong to the young man. I presume he is the victim of . . . foolish zeal of Christian friends who think that the only conclusive evidence of piety is an attempt to preach. The sermon was not a landscape, not even so diversified as a prairie. It was a flat, foggy bog, in which preacher was too feeble even to flounder."[21]

Sometimes Garfield wondered whether it was worthwhile going to Sunday services. For example, on one occasion he "attended church and listened to a very stupid sermon from very a ordinary man . . . I could have spent the day more profitably in reading, writing, or resting." Yet he answered his own doubt with a statement affirming the worthwhileness of such attendance: "I do not always go because I prefer to for my own sake, but because I think a man should maintain the habit partly for his own sake and partly for the sake of others."[22]

If Garfield was quick to criticize poor sermons, he was equally ready to praise eloquent preaching. He traveled widely and was always alert for an opportunity to hear a prominent preacher. Garfield had early experiences with and favorable impressions of Thomas and Alexander Campbell. He noted that as a preacher the latter displayed the ability to use "striking comparisons and bold conceptions" while avoiding "high wrought language."[23]

Mark Hopkins served as another early model for Garfield. Garfield praised the president's teaching in words that evolved into the famous statement that the ideal college consisted of Mark Hopkins on one end of a log and a student on the other; and he viewed Hopkins's preaching with similar admiration. Hopkins impressed him with the idea that "every word comes up from his heart up through his understanding, and . . . he is a good man. He is certainly a great thinker though . . . not . . . a very original one."[24]

Henry Ward Beecher attracted Garfield's attention by both his pulpit skill and his legal difficulties. As he listened to Beecher preach, Garfield was impressed by his intelligence, his sympathetic heart, and his honest conviction; however, he reacted negatively to "something . . . in his voice which . . . [displayed a] shadow of consciousness that he is saying a smart thing." Garfield took a deep interest in the widely publicized and sensational Beecher-Tilton adultery trial. He attended a session of the six-month trial in 1874 and commented: "I believe in Beecher's innocence; but I think he is a great sentimental big-hearted booby in his relations to and his judgment of the people around him . . . It is manifest that he has fallen into the hands of a most unscrupulous set of rascals, and they have done their best to skin him for their own mercenary purposes, and then to ruin him for the purpose of covering their own tracks." Garfield was impressed with the masterly way in which Beecher defended himself and with the way in which Mrs. Beecher supported and clearly displayed confidence in her husband. [25]

When Garfield was in London in August 1867, he visited Charles H. Spurgeon's Metropolitan Tabernacle hoping "to discover what manner of man he was and what was the secret of his power." The result of this visit was an unusually long and laudatory description in his diary. Garfield was very much impressed with the congregational singing, but he gave primary attention to the sermon. "The foundation of [Spurgeon's preaching] power," Garfield believed, lay in the "unusual fullness" of his belief in the presence of God, the personal accountability of all men to God, and the Bible as the word of God, which upon microscopic examination reveals "ever opening beauties and blessings." Garfield was also impressed that Spurgeon gave painstaking study to the topics on which he preached and that he stayed very close to the doctrines and the literature of the Bible in his sermons. He found the sermon delivery to be clear, logical, perfectly comprehensible, and directly applicable to the hearers. In summary, Garfield explained: "Every good man ought to be thankful for the work Spurgeon is doing . . . He is helping to work out the problems of religious and civil freedom for England in a way that he knows not of." Garfield "could not but contrast" the more than seven thousand people who heard Spurgeon with the twenty who were in attendance at the service at Westminster Abbey, which Garfield had attended a few days earlier.[26]

In December 1875 Garfield joined one of the most distinguished delegations ever to visit a revival service in America. Dwight L. Moody's famous Philadelphia campaign coincided with the centennial exhibition in that city. During the Christmas recess approximately two hundred members of Congress joined President Ulysses S. Grant, a majority of his cabinet, the chief justice, and a majority of the associate justices of the Supreme Court on a visit to the centennial grounds. Garfield noted that "this was probably the largest number of U.S. officials that were ever on one railroad train together." During the long weekend visit, Garfield and other congressmen joined Grant and several cabinet members and Supreme Court justices in attending the Sunday evening session of the crusade. Garfield made this report: "I was very greatly impressed by the meeting. The singing of Sankey is very effective. Moody seems to me to be very far from a great thinker or great speaker, but there is a wonderful directness and earnestness in all he says. He drives straight toward his object without delay and reaches the hearts and wills of people to a wonderful degree. This phenomenon is remarkable in many ways but in none more than this: It shows by contrast the powerlessness of modern theological training, as compared with a direct address to hearts and consciences of men."[27]

Garfield audited other well-known religious leaders, including Brigham Young and James Freeman Clarke. When Garfield visited Salt Lake City in 1875 he had a forty-five-minute interview with Young. The next day was Sunday; and at the request of Garfield, the Mormon leader preached a long sermon on the historical basis of Mormonism to a tabernacle audience of eight thousand people. "He is a clear and powerful reasoner," Garfield observed, "and is manifestly an intellectual leader among his people." A year later in Washington, D.C., Garfield heard "a very interesting sermon" by Clarke, the Unitarian clergyman and transcendentalist, who preached on "The Letter Killeth but the Spirit Maketh Alive." Garfield observed: "I have not been so much instructed by a sermon in a long time. It was so free from cant and hypercriticism, and was full of instruction."[28]

A growing freedom of inquiry and breadth of perspective characterized Garfield's mature years. The former critic of government in general and its wars in particular could now declare that government was an ordinance of God and the Civil War was "an act of humanity, justice, and religion" because it was God's way of showing His disapproval of the sin of slavery. He was not reluctant to denounce traditional religious practices that he no longer accepted. After visiting the Flathead Indians on a government mission in 1872, for example, he argued that in an attempt to bring salvation to the Indians "most of our missionary effort has been made wrong end foremost." Instead of immediately attempting to convert the Indians we should, he thought, have begun with meeting their temporal needs: "There is a Gospel of clothing, of food, of shelter, of work that should precede the theology of the pulpit." He followed very closely the developing debate on the issue of evolution; and while it is clear that he was eager to examine the subject thoroughly, it is not clear how much of the new thought he accepted.[29]

Garfield examined with great intellectual curiosity the most unorthodox of views without making any outward change in his religious affiliation and without departing from the central core of Protestant teachings he had learned and accepted as a young man. For example, he examined the views of Robert G. Ingersoll with enthusiasm and even sincerely cultivated his friendship and then flatly rejected his major ideas. Of Ingersoll's atheistic views Garfield commented: "He is the victim of intellectual prejudice against the Christian religion to a degree that he is entirely unaware of . . . I doubt if [his] views will sustain . . . [him] when the shadows of life fall heavily, and deepen into the darkness of death." Also, after reading Ernest Renan's life of Jesus, which rejected Jesus' supernatural nature, Garfield noted: "It is pleasant to read the views of a strong man with whom you disagree. He is sure to give you some valuable thoughts."[30]

During his early years Garfield attended a number of spiritualistic séances, more out of curiosity than conviction. On one occasion he attended such a meeting in his mother's house and "had a long conversation with what proported [sic] to be the spirit of my father. He (or it) was pleased with the course I am pursuing . . . Told past events correctly, but I have no confidence in the prophecies." After attending a similar session in 1872, the interested but cautious Garfield noted: "Somewhere in that direction is a great series of truth yet to be developed but what and how, who knows?"[31]

Much of the expansion of mind that Garfield experienced was the result of the quality and breadth of the materials that he read. One of his leading biographers notes that his reading in his mature years "is a summary of most of the books which influenced the thought of his times." The authors of these books included Darwin, Huxley, Mill, Spencer, Comte, and Gibbon. On Garfield's reading habits while living in Washington, the librarian of Congress is quoted as saying that if a rare book was absent from the library he assumed that either Charles Sumner or Garfield must have it. He was always impressed with books, which explored new areas and analyzed new theories, yet he always read critically. For example, of John W. Draper's *History of the Conflict between Religion and Science*, Garfield wrote in 1877: "It is a powerfully written essay, very interesting; but Draper always impresses me with the suspicions that his generalizations are too broad to be altogether safe."[32]

Although Garfield grew beyond much of the narrowness of his early Disciples upbringing, he continued his identification with that denomination through all his years. In 1873 he wrote in his diary: "It is due to a man's life and soul that he stand by his past as long as he can reasonably approve it. And for this reason as well as others I am glad to stand by the old memories of the Disciples." The mature Garfield identified with the progressive Disciples in the period of struggle between those who saw the denomination as a group of Christian believers who should base every detail of faith and practice upon the New Testament model, and those who viewed the New Testament as the primary source of religious authority while not giving exact formulas for the details of church organization and practice. Garfield was a member of the progressive wing that founded *The Christian Standard* as a vehicle for their views. In Washington, Garfield was an active member of the local Disciples church, seldom missing a service when he was in town. Sometimes he spoke to the congregation, but this practice became less frequent as his congressional responsibilities increased. When he became president the attendance at the church doubled, and this disturbed him: "It gives me a sorry view of human nature to see a little church filled to double its usual attendance by the accident of one of its frequenters having been elected to high office." Garfield continued his earlier identification with Hiram College. To his previous roles of student, instructor, and president he now added that of trustee, a position he held from 1866 until his death. He had significant influence on the institution through his voluminous correspondence with President Hinsdale.[33]

The Disciples of Christ, like the Baptists, place much emphasis upon the importance of the separation of church and state, and some of Garfield's strongest public statements were made against groups which he thought violated that principle. "No political organization," he warned, "is wide enough or pure enough to control and direct sacred interests of religion, and . . . no ecclesiastical organization of the nineteenth century can wisely manage the political interest of a great nation." He especially argued against the efforts of some that used governmental funds to assist Roman Catholic schools. Similarly, the single specific reference to religion in Garfield's presidential inaugural address is a criticism of the degree to which the Mormon Church was controlling the legal process of Utah.[34]

While in most areas Garfield's perspectives widened as he grew older, this was not true of his attitude toward the propriety of a public role for women. In the 1850s when listening to a lady Methodist preacher who "screamed loud, frothed at the mouth, pounded, etc.," he "could not help thinking of the words of St. Paul, 'Let your women keep silent in church for it is a shame for a woman to speak in church.'" A few years later when he listened to a sermon by "the Reverend (!) Antonette L. Brown," the well-known reformer and widely publicized minister, he commented that "there is something about a woman's speaking in public that unsexes her in my mind, and howmuchsoever I might admire the talent, yet I could never think of the female speaker as the gentle sister, the tender wife, or the loving mother." Later in the 1870s and 1880s, Garfield explained—in letters of response to Elizabeth Cady Stanton and Susan B. Anthony—his lack of support for women suffrage. While he expressed sympathy "with all efforts that will elevate women and better her condition," he did not yet believe that suffrage would accomplish that result.[35]

In summary, the religious thought of the mature Garfield was such that probably both the contemporary liberal Protestants and the modern-day Evangelicals would like to claim him. The former notes the growing scope of his religious views and his intense intellectual interest in the new religious thought of the late nineteenth century. The Evangelicals note his continuing orthodoxy on the major issues and the fact that there is no clear record that he subscribed to the new thought. In the following diary passage, written in December 1875, Garfield came about as close as he did anywhere to questioning the uniqueness of the revelation of God in Christ:

> Are all religions, past and present, false except that of Christ? If so, what shall we think of the Goodness and Mercy of God in leaving mankind so many generations without the truth? It is asking a good deal to require us to believe that this alone is the final and perfect form of religious truth, when men of all past ages have so confidently believed they had it, and it is now universally acknowledged that none was final and true unless it be this. Is it not intolerable egotism in us to suppose that we are so exceptionally precious to God, that while He has never seen enough good in the race to make it worth saving until 1800 years ago, yet then its superiority of virtue and importance led him to make great exertions to save it? It may not be

unreasonable to suppose that each age has had as much light as it could use, and the future may open up religious truth on a plane higher than that we now know of. Who shall limit the methods of God?

Despite any seeming doubts Garfield affirmed a positive faith to the end of his days. In 1876, while discussing the development of his faith, he declared the following: "I recognize the fact that my general views of religion have broadened, but I hope that they have not weakened my faith in the central doctrines of Christ. I care less for denominational doctrines, but more for the spirit of Christ."[36]

If, during Garfield's life, his religious faith strengthened and his religious thought matured, it does not follow that his religious practice always remained exemplary. It is true that Garfield's enemies sometimes exaggerated the degree of his guilt in political scandal (the Credit Mobilier affair, for example) and that his friends sometimes misunderstood his motives in political controversy (such as the "salary grab" affair). Nevertheless, for a man known for his religious seriousness and an ability to exercise good judgment in affairs of state, Garfield at times displayed a surprising lack of ethical sensitivity (for example, the DeGolyer Pavement scandal and his relationships with a few women).[37]

Garfield came to the White House in March 1881, but his stay was to last for only a few months. Shot in July by a mentally unbalanced man who considered himself a theologian, he died in September. He was cut off at the moment when his large abilities were at last to be put to the supreme test as the nation's leader. Yet Garfield probably questioned this seeming waste of himself less than most. During his illness he retained a patient and thankful spirit and a constant hope in God. He wanted to live, but he was not afraid to die. One of his dearest biblical passages had long been Romans 8:38–39, which declares that nothing, including death—and by implication untimely death—can separate us from the love of God. Garfield died as he had lived, with faith in the ultimate goodness of his Creator.[38]

NOTES

1. The most comprehensive, recent biography of Garfield is Allan Peskin, *Garfield: A Biography* (Kent, Ohio: Kent State Univ. Press, 1978). Also see Margaret Leech and Harry J. Brown, *The Garfield Orbit* (New York: Harper and Row, 1978); Robert G. Caldwell, *James A. Garfield: Party Chieftain* (New York: Dodd, Mead, 1931); and Theodore Clarke Smith, *A Life and Letters of James Abram Garfield*, 2 vols. (New Haven: Yale Univ. Press, 1925).

2. W. W. Wasson, *James A. Garfield: His Religion and Education* (Nashville: Tennessee Book Co., 1952), 11–13.

3. Caldwell, *James A. Garfield*, 11; Wasson, *James A. Garfield*, 7–10.

4. Garfield's recently published diary (through 1877) is unusually complete and well edited. See Harry J. Brown and Frederick D. Williams, eds., *The Diary of James A. Garfield*, 3 vols. (East Lansing: Michigan State Univ. Press, 1967–73).

5. Brown and Williams, *The Diary of James A. Garfield*, 1:36 (Mar. 3–10, 1850); Wasson, *James A. Garfield*, 13–14.

6. Brown and Williams, *The Diary of James A. Garfield*, 1:60 (Oct. 1, 1850); see also 1:193–94 (May 22, 1853).

7. Ibid., 1:xviii; 1:138 (June 7, 1852); 1:167 (Dec. 31, 1852); 1:285 (Sept. 28, 1857). Wasson, *James A. Garfield*, 15–17, 21–22.

8. Brown and Williams, *The Diary of James A. Garfield*, 1:42–43 (May 19, 1850); 1:62–63 (Oct. 13, 1850); 1:98 (Oct. 12, 1851); 1:244 (Mar. 12, 1854); 1:263–64 (July 9, 1854).

9. Brown and Williams, *The Diary of James A. Garfield*, 1:57 (Sept. 6, 1850).

10. Brown and Williams, *The Diary of James A. Garfield*, 1:38 (June 13, 1852); 1:213 (July 31, 1853).

11. Wasson, *James A. Garfield*, 35–36, 39, 44–46; Edmund Fuller and David E. Green, *God in the White House: The Faith of American Presidents* (New York: Crown Publishers, 1968), 139–45.

12. Wasson, *James A. Garfield*, 65–73.

13. Wasson, *James A. Garfield*, 48–51, 104–5; Caldwell, *James A. Garfield*, 41.

14. Frederick D. Williams, ed., *The Wild Life of the Army: Civil War Letters of James A. Garfield* (East Lansing: Michigan State Univ. Press, 1964), viii; Caldwell, *James A. Garfield*, 40, 50; Brown and Williams, *The Diary of James A. Garfield*, 1:xx; Fuller and Green, *God in the White House*, 144.

15. Wasson, *James A. Garfield*, 51–56.

16. Caldwell, *James A. Garfield*, 357; Brown and Williams, *The Diary of James A. Garfield*, 1:289 (Oct. 4, 1857).

17. Caldwell, *James A. Garfield*, 41; Wasson, *James A. Garfield*, 68–70; Williams, *The Wild Life of the Army*, ix; Peskin, *Garfield*, 50.

18. Smith, *A Life and Letters*, 2:733; Williams, *The Wild Life of the Army*, 210; Wasson, *James A. Garfield*, 76–79; Brown and Williams, *The Diary of James A. Garfield*, 1:328 (Apr. 14, 1858).

19. Caldwell, *James A. Garfield*, 40.

20. For example of the list of sermons, see Brown and Williams, *The Diary of James A. Garfield*, 1:491, 2:443, 3:593.

21. Brown and Williams, *The Diary of James A. Garfield*, 2:5 (Jan. 7, 1872); 2:112 (Nov. 10, 1872); 2:198–99 (July 6, 1873); 3:208 (Jan. 2, 1876); 3:551 (Dec. 9, 1877).

22. Ibid., 2:107 (Oct. 27, 1872); 2:208 (Aug. 3, 1873).

23. Ibid., 1:205 (July 3, 1853).

24. Ibid., 1:267 (July 17, 1854).

25. Ibid., 1:363 (Nov. 4, 1866); 2:349 (July 25, 1874); 2:356 (Aug. 14, 1874); 3:53–54 (Apr. 4–5, 1875).

26. Ibid., 1:385–88 (Aug. 4, 1867).

27. Ibid., 3:201–3 (Dec. 17, 19, 1875).

28. Ibid., 3:94–96 (June 5, 6, 1875); 3:238 (Feb. 20, 1876).

29. Wasson, *James A. Garfield,* 82–83, 118, 133–34.

30. Wasson, *James A. Garfield,* 113–14, 121–22; Brown and Williams, *The Diary of James A. Garfield,* 3:166 (Oct. 17, 1875).

31. Brown and Williams, *The Diary of James A. Garfield,* 1:84–85 (June 4, 1851); 1:146 (July 18, 1852); 2:57 (May 25, 1872); 2:411–12 (Dec. 30, 1874).

32. Wasson, *James A. Garfield,* 114: James G. Blaine, *Memorial Address on the Life and Character of James A. Garfield* (Washington, D.C.: GPO, 1903), 127, 136; Mark Hopkins, "Memorial Discourse on President Garfield," *Teachings and Counsels: Twenty Baccalaureate Sermons* (New York: Charles Scribner's Sons, 1884), 380; Brown and Williams, *The Diary of James A. Garfield,* 3:479 (May 6, 1877).

33. Brown and Williams, *The Diary of James A. Garfield,* 2:213 (Aug. 17, 1873); Wasson, *James A. Garfield,* 89–97, 101–4, 107–11; Caldwell, *James A. Garfield,* 183–84; Mary L. Hinsdale, ed., *Garfield-Hinsdale Letters: Correspondence between James Abram Garfield and Burke Aaron Hinsdale* (Ann Arbor: Univ. Press of Michigan, 1949), 142–43.

34. Wasson, *James A. Garfield,* 136–41; James A. Garfield, "Inaugural Address," in *Messages and Papers of the Presidents,* James D. Richardson, comp. (Washington, D.C.: GPO, 1903), 8:11.

35. Brown and Williams, *The Diary of James A. Garfield,* 1:81–82 (May 18, 1851); 1:257 (July 2, 1854); 2:5–6 (Jan. 9, 1872); Leech and Brown, *The Garfield Orbit,* 300–301.

36. Brown and Williams, *The Diary of James A. Garfield,* 3:194 (Dec. 5, 1875); Wasson *James A. Garfield,* 121.

37. Leech and Brown, *The Garfield Orbit,* 238–49; Hopkins, "Memorial Discourse on President Garfield," 386; Blaine, *Memorial Address,* 154.

38. Leech and Brown, *The Garfield Orbit,* 40–43, 69–97, 177–81, 253; Peskin, *Garfield,* 160, 353–81.

Lyndon B. Johnson

The Religion of a Politician

Monroe Billington

Most biographers of Lyndon B. Johnson have been inclined to view that politician through sharply critical lenses.[1] These critics have contended that he was the most "political" of all of the nation's presidents; indeed, they have depicted him as being obsessed with politics. Collectively they have seen Johnson as a preeminently expedient politician without morals or scruples who practiced the art of the possible to such an extent that he neither embraced nor manifested any guiding principles. Some have painted a picture of a brutal man who ran roughshod over his opponents, while others have written of a wily man who deceitfully manipulated people for his own ends. They have seen him as a high-pressure politician, and extant cartoons caricaturing his arm-twisting tactics are legion. According to these writers, some of whom qualify as psychohistorians, Johnson hungered for power and success, yearned to be loved and appreciated, manifested a penchant for secrecy, possessed a massive ego, developed a paranoia about being surrounded by hostile forces, and sheltered an immense inner anger. The analysts have stressed Johnson's psychological shortcomings so much that they have sometimes failed to acknowledge his positive political accomplishments.

Much of the criticism of Johnson is justified, but the contention that his character was somehow flawed or that his programs stemmed exclusively from selfish political motives probably does him an injustice. This essay focusing on Johnson's religion is intended as a corrective to those interpretations that have overlooked an important dimension of both the private and public life of this national politician.

Lyndon B. Johnson was born and reared in a strongly religious environment in Blanco County, Texas. Two years before his birth, 34.7 percent of all Texans were affiliated with a church. Of these 1,226,906 church members, 913,917, or 74.5 percent, were Protestants. The four most populous denominations, which claimed 69.7 percent of the Protestants in the Lone Star State, were Baptists (32.7

percent), Methodists (25.9 percent), Disciples of Christ (6.0 percent), and Presbyterians (5.1 percent).[2] These statistics had not changed significantly when Johnson was born in 1908, and the central Texas counties where Johnson spent his youth were as overwhelmingly Protestant as the state as a whole.

In addition to growing up in this general religious milieu, Johnson was a member of a family that was religious. He was the descendant of a long line of Baptist preachers and leaders in Texas religious circles. His maternal great-grandfather, George Washington Baines Sr., was a scholarly pioneer Baptist minister, missionary, editor, and educator. For more than ten years Baines was a member of the Board of Trustees of Baylor College in Independence, Texas (now Baylor University in Waco), and he served as president of that school from 1861 to 1863. Also, he was an early editor of *The Texas Baptist,* the first Baptist newspaper in the state. One son of this illustrious ancestor was George Washington Baines Jr., a fourth-generation Baptist minister and a great-uncle of Lyndon Johnson. Another son, the grandfather of LBJ, was Joseph Wilson Baines, lawyer, editor, educator, lay preacher, and a leading member of the Baptist Church in Blanco, Texas. Grandfather Baines was "strict in doctrine, broad in charity, [and] large in enterprise" who took seriously his religious ideals, moral thought, and civic duty.[3] Rebekah Baines Johnson, the daughter of Joseph Wilson Baines and the mother of Lyndon Johnson, was greatly influenced by her "baptist upbringing, sermons, prayer meeting[s], and Sunday School."[4] This devoutly religious woman, deeply committed to the Christian gospel, had the primary responsibility for shaping her son's religious views. She read the Bible to him regularly, she presided over a home where daily prayers were "aloud, proud, and unapologetic," and she took her children to worship services and other meetings as often as the church doors opened. She stoutly believed in the scriptural promise: "Train up a child in the way he should go, and when he is old, he will not depart from it."[5] Having "learned his faith at his Mother's knee," Lyndon Johnson was "nurtured and strengthened in this faith throughout his life."[6]

In later years Johnson recalled that "my earliest impressions of spiritual and moral forces carry a Baptist identification," and "Baptists have a special place in my affections,"[7] most surely the result of his mother's commitment and the early training of her son. But Johnson did not choose to join the Baptist denomination. While attending a revival meeting at the Johnson City First Christian Church, Johnson experienced a religious conversion common to youths of similar Protestant backgrounds. He not only "dedicated his life to Christ" but also decided to join the Christian Church. In July 1923, when he was fourteen years old, Johnson was baptized (totally immersed) in a tributary of the Pedernales River a few miles from his home.[8] Johnson's ardently Baptist mother was not wholly happy about her son's choice to join the Christian

Church (whose denominational name was Disciples of Christ), but she accepted the decision in good grace, "believing that some religion—whatever the denomination—should be a part of his life."[9]

While Rebekah Johnson was inculcating in her son the tradition of Bible study, prayer, and church attendance, as well as sowing the seeds for his mature religious views, Sam Ealy Johnson Jr., who served five terms in the Texas legislature, was introducing his son to the fascinating world of politics. As a child, Lyndon listened for hours to his father's and his friends' political conversations. When he was a teenager, he accompanied his father on trips related to political matters (including campaign ventures). Traveling in the family Model-T Ford, father and son stumped the county fairs, picnic grounds, church ice-cream suppers, and main-street political rallies in the towns and rural communities of the 89th Representative District. Sam Johnson exhibited a brand of agrarian progressivism that was the primary characteristic of his career of public service. He was sympathetic to the needs of the poor and the unfortunate. He wrote a bill providing for the erection of a home for widows of Confederate veterans, and he supported legislation regulating corporations, including railroad, insurance, and telephone companies. He fought for good roads and a system of state highways, for bus transportation for school children, and for protection of small investors from the sale of worthless securities. In the vanguard of the Texas progressive movement, Sam Johnson fought the "interests" on behalf of the "common man." Lyndon Johnson was impressed by his father's activism and concern for people.[10]

In 1958 Johnson published an article detailing his political philosophy.[11] He made no specific references to his religious views; however, he indicated that his political philosophy was the sum of his life's experience, and for him that included religion. Alexis de Tocqueville has written that an intimate relationship exists between political and religious philosophy. The two were so closely intertwined within Johnson that to separate them would do an injustice to both.

Lyndon Johnson held fairly typical religious views common to members of the large Protestant denominations in the United States. He believed in a God who created the Universe and its moral government, who had infinite charity, justice, and mercy, and who was the source of every human strength. This God was manifested in a Trinitarian manner: Father, Son, and Holy Spirit.[12] For Johnson, belief in a divine providence was not "an escape or a tranquilizer." Rather it was a compelling challenge to him and others "to attain the ideals of liberty, justice, peace, and compassion."[13]

Johnson believed that the Bible was the divinely inspired word of God and that it was a strength and guide for the daily lives of all Christians.[14] Although he never identified himself as a biblical scholar, Johnson revealed an easy familiarity with the Bible when he quoted it in both public speeches[15] and private conversations.[16] The frequency of Johnson's quotations and references, and his almost ministerial tone of voice when he recited a Bible verse, all indicate Johnson's internalizing of the Holy Word.

Johnson engaged in prayer and believed in its efficacy.[17] Prayers were irregular after Johnson became a busy national politician, but when he suddenly became president, he and Mrs. Johnson, without spoken agreement, began regularly to pray before their private meals. When the burdens of high office increased, Johnson repeatedly turned to prayer for comfort and sustenance. The White House years deepened his spiritual life.[18]

Johnson believed in the brotherhood of all humankind, in racial and religious tolerance, and in the integrity and dignity of the individual.[19] He once said that "man is not just an atom, a random piece of matter living in a mechanical, purposeless universe." Rather each person has "as inner compass, a spark of divinity, which sets him apart from the rest of creation."[20] He believed that humanity was born to overcome evil with good and that the Christian's duty is to serve God, people, and his or her country.[21]

In regard to the role of religion in the life of the nation, Johnson believed that the United States had been founded upon religious convictions, that religious beliefs underlay Americans' traditional devotion to individual liberty, and that the nation must continue to maintain a strong spiritual and moral climate.[22] Equally important was "religion's role as part of the mortar unifying one of the world's most diverse populations into one of history's most unified nations." Furthermore, "our churches, along with our schools, have done far more than political beliefs and dogma to help us hold to stable values and to keep both the faith and determination that tomorrow can be better. That quality of faith is indispensable to a progressive nation." Finally, he said, "If we are to continue with a strong sense of useful purpose, I believe religion must be a more significant part of our lives in the future than ever it has been in the past."[23] Concerning national leaders, Johnson believed that if they were to be different from tyrants, "we must balance the powers in our hands with God in our hearts."[24] He once said, "The highest morality of national leadership is to create and maintain the strength essential to the preservation of our beliefs."[25] Again: "The private unity of public men and their God is an enduring source of strength for our country."[26]

Like his Baptist forebears, Johnson was a strong believer in the separation of church and state ("but this does not mean that men of Government should divorce themselves from religion"),[27] and like the many Methodists among whom he grew up, he had a strong sense of social justice and injustice.[28] He was a believer in religious ecumenism before that word gained popularity. The Disciples of Christ had a long tradition of religious tolerance and a commitment to Christian unity, and these characteristics of that denomination attracted Johnson from the beginning.[29] Another attraction was that the Disciples of

Christ believed in a rational—rather than an overly emotional—religion. Johnson's most oft-quoted scriptural verse—Come let us reason together—was in the Disciples tradition, and that injunction from the Book of Isaiah had been the text of the preacher's sermon on the night young Johnson experienced his religious conversion.[30]

Johnson retained his membership in the First Christian Church of Johnson City throughout his life. His wife, who had been reared a Methodist, became an Episcopalian after attending a girls' school of that denomination.[31] They were married in St. Mark's Episcopal Church in San Antonio. When they lived in Washington, they most often attended St. John's Episcopal Church on Lafayette Square, St. Mark's Episcopal Church on Capitol Hill, or the National City Christian Church on Thomas Circle. Johnson found much in Episcopalianism appealing, "although he sometimes regarded the long rituals with an amusement that did not verge on disrespect."[32] But Johnson did not limit his attendance to those houses of worship associated with his wife's or his own denomination. In view of his religious ecumenism, he had no ambivalence about any creed, and he was tolerant of others' beliefs. He was comfortable in any church, and he sometimes worshipped at two or three services a week. He attended church more regularly than any other president in the nation's history.[33] He often privately related to friends and associates the satisfaction and strength he derived from attending worship services.[34]

As time passed, Johnson was increasingly attracted to the Washington church of his own denomination. As Mrs. Johnson later said, "It was a warm harbor in troubled times."[35] He came to appreciate its senior minister, Dr. George R. Davis. While Johnson developed and maintained a friendship with the evangelist Billy Graham (who has been called Johnson's "unofficial chaplain" and "chief spiritual counselor"),[36] in fact his most intimate relationship was with Dr. Davis, who impressed Johnson with "his deep and practical sincerity," and with whom Johnson felt very "in-tune."[37]

Most of the ministers who became acquainted with Johnson were impressed with the president as a man of faith. Dr. Davis wrote, "He is a man of great strength, endurance and faith,"[38] and Billy Graham described him as "a deeply religious man" whose faith "greatly influenced" his political decisions.[39] As his Christian consciousness grew and his faith matured, Johnson identified himself as a man of faith on numerous occasions as he spoke of his faith in God, Jesus Christ, the nation, and humankind. He came to believe that religious faith was the key to individuals retaining their identities in an increasingly urbanized and thus dehumanized culture,[40] and he once said, "One source of spiritual strength is faith . . . faith in the reality of ideals, faith which enables man to transcend the vanities of life for the sake of ends beyond himself."[41]

But Johnson's faith was neither theological nor theoretical. He strove to implement his faith by his actions. Good works were a necessary complement to his religious faith. His strong desire to help others was closely related to this religious concept. He believed that his religion could best be applied through trying to serve in the political realm, that he could best express God's will for his life by serving humankind. Indeed, he was driven by the desire to serve and to do good.[42] He wanted to "translate Christianity into a work-day affair."[43] He adhered to the biblical command "love thy neighbor as thyself,"[44] and he admitted to having a "very urgent stake in answering that old Biblical question, 'who is my neighbor?'"[45] He wrote, "I am sure our religious values will help motivate us to lives of useful service rather than lives of wasteful and self-serving idleness."[46]

Johnson's religion undergirded his Great Society program, his civil rights legislation, and his stand on Vietnam. The Great Society, enacted with the passage of dozens of bills, was a broad-ranging social program addressing areas such as education, health care and health insurance, housing, poverty, jobs, Indian rights, drug control, help to youth and the aged, and rehabilitation services. However others viewed it, Johnson saw it in terms of the help it provided for individuals. Time and again as Johnson defended, explained, argued for, and praised this legislation, he couched his language in moral and religious terms.[47] Not by accident did he believe those in need who would profit from this legislation were his "neighbors." As he said, "This is not just a religious truth. I think it is a very urgent social fact."[48] Of his Great Society program Johnson wrote that "the fiber of tomorrow's society is woven with the thread of today's spiritual renewal," and "if we are going to have the kind of country and kind of society we want to have, we must be committed, we must care about what happens—not to ourselves but to our neighbors and our fellow man. This is the spirit of most of our religions—and it is a spirit essential to our success in building a greater society."[49] Also, he said, "Every one of these issues has its moral and spiritual dimensions."[50] Johnson's efforts to alter positively the American scene with his Great Society legislation was referred to as "the war of amazing Christlike compassionate service."[51]

In a sermon on the president's religion, one minister concluded that the Great Society program was specifically an outgrowth of Johnson's deeply embedded belief that humans should love (and thus care for) their neighbor.[52] Another minister preached a sermon entitled "The Great Society," in which he associated the Johnson program with a phrase in the Lord's Prayer that Jesus prayed: "Thy Kingdom Come."[53] Johnson's own minister, who knew the president better than any other churchman, has written that Johnson's "deepest [religious] feelings & caring had everything to do with his effort toward 'Great Society' goals."[54] In March 1981, the National City Christian Church dedicated to Johnson's memory a stained-glass window whose central theme emphasizes the social reforms of the

Johnson administration in the context of Christian service. Medallions in the window symbolize the acts of mercy listed in the book of Matthew, chapter 25, reminiscent of Johnson's efforts toward a Great Society.[55] Some supportive ministers and churches may have exaggerated the relationship of Johnson's Christian ideals and his political programs, but the evidence indicates that his religious principles were an important part of the foundation upon which the Great Society was built.

History will award President Johnson a prominent role in the legal advancement of civil rights for blacks. Passed during his administration and receiving the president's efforts to secure their passage, the Civil Rights Act of 1964, the Voting Rights Acts of 1965, and the Civil Rights Act of 1968 together constituted significant steps forward in the battle against racial discrimination. In addition, President Johnson identified himself with the nation's largest racial minority by issuing executive orders and making numerous public statements on its behalf. Detractors have argued that political expediency moved Johnson from anti–civil rights stands in the 1930s and 1940s to pro–civil rights stands in the late 1950s and 1960s. But these changing positions should be viewed in the perspective of Johnson's development as a public servant. Johnson's love for people, with him from his earliest years, compelled him to be concerned about minority groups—from the Mexican American children he taught as a young man in Cotulla, Texas, in the 1920s to the bitter black rioters in the 1960s. When he was a young legislator voting against civil rights bills, he had told blacks that he would help them when he had the power and when the timing was right. When those two conditions were met he carried out his promises. The story of Johnson's public stance on civil rights is one of evolution, of maturation, and of growth,[56] and by the time Johnson became president, he was privately speaking favorably about black civil rights with "burning conviction" and "passion."[57]

As with the Great Society program, to some extent Johnson's civil rights efforts were rooted in his religious beliefs.[58] He often referred to the moral implications of the civil rights proposals while they were being considered by the Congress,[59] and upon one occasion he reminded a group of religious leaders visiting the White House that civil rights was a "cause of human dignity, [a] cause of human rights [which] demands prophets in our time, men of compassion and truth, unafraid of the consequences of fulfilling their faith."[60] Upon passage of the omnibus bill in 1964, Johnson wrote: "Almighty God has blessed our nation with a new opportunity to redress the grievances of the past and to heal our regional and racial divisions," and he called upon all Americans "with charity and hope to join in the challenging task of building a society founded on mutual respect, justice, and good will among men."[61] He recognized that legislation was but one step in the unending effort to correct the injustice of racial discrimination and racial prejudice because "the battle must be fought also—and ultimately won—in the souls of men."[62] He said,

I am not a theologian. I am not a philosopher. I am just a public servant that is doing the very best I know how. But in more than 3 decades of public life, I have seen firsthand how basic spiritual beliefs and deeds can shatter barriers of politics and bigotry. I have seen those barriers crumble in the presence of faith and hope, and from this experience I have drawn new hope that the seemingly insurmountable moral issues that we face at home and abroad today can be resolved by men of strong faith and men of brave deeds.[63]

Why did President Johnson increase American military involvement in Vietnam, and why did he keep this nation in the conflict long after it was clear that by any reasonable standard its presence there was in vain? Many factors contributed to Johnson's decisions, each with its own degree of validity: he did not want South Vietnam to fall into the hands of the Communists; he feared such a fall would inevitably lead to the spread of Communism in Southeast Asia; he wanted to win the war; he did not want to preside over a losing war for this country; he did not want to injure national pride; he did not want to injure his personal pride; he listened too single-mindedly to his military advisors; U.S. withdrawal would not bring peace to that troubled land; withdrawal would imperil the security of the United States; we had pledged to support South Vietnam and could not dishonor our pledge or abandon our commitment; South Vietnam should not have any government forced upon it; he wanted to resist "men who hate and destroy" so that "all of our dreams for freedom . . . will [not] be swept away on the flood of conquest."[64]

But Johnson's adherence to Christian principles may also have contributed to his stubborn stand in Vietnam. While editor of the *College Star* at Southwest State Teachers College, young Johnson in an editorial on "Sincerity" wrote what he could have written in the middle of the Vietnam conflict: "If you believe in a thing, stand up for it. If you support a principle, give all you have to give. If you think a thing is wrong (or right?), do not waiver [sic] if you find that sentiment is against you."[65] Having been told repeatedly by his mother that the strong must care for the weak,[66] Johnson almost quoted his mother to justify the nation's involvement in Vietnam: "There is a great responsibility on the strong." He went on to say, "Now it's not true that we've got to police all of the world . . . but the good Lord has smiled kindly upon us and we have an obligation as fellow human beings to help protect our neighbors against a bunch of desperadoes."[67]

Johnson considered his nation's stand in Vietnam to be a "cause of honor and ultimate hope for man, the only course that will assure him the free and peaceful life that God intended for the human family."[68] As the war intensified, he wrote: "At times like these we need the strength to persist in doing what we think is right, and that inner strength can come only from a deep and abiding faith in God."[69] He believed that moral force was as important as military power in the endeavor to resolve the conflict.[70] Johnson viewed his stand on Vietnam in such moral terms that he came to consider criticism of his position as immoral. He *cared* about his stand on Vietnam; the issue became so highly moralized that it became a matter of principle.[71] He prayed for "God-given vision and determination to make the sacrifices demanded by our responsibilities [in Vietnam]."[72] He believed that "our struggle in Vietnam is just, because we believe that man is born to freedom and dignity and that peace is the House of all. Our ultimate purpose in denying aggression is to assure that man will find fulfillment as an instrument of God's will. With God's help, we will succeed."[73] Despite the cruelty of the Vietnam struggle, he wrote that "if we believe that man is too noble a creature to serve anyone but God, the fate of the human family leaves us no escape from our convictions or our duty."[74] Late in the conflict he wrote: "I am still certain in the light of my own faith that our commitment in Vietnam is vital—and that God will reward the justness and compassion of our cause with the blessing of peace."[75] Johnson could not admit mistakes in a situation like Vietnam, where the effort was defined solely by a goal and where failure, therefore, was a challenge to the rightness of belief, to some integrity of self, which must be even more fiercely defended when under attack.[76]

Can one trust Johnson's remarks and letters in which he expressed religious opinions? Can one be sure that Johnson's speech writers were accurately reflecting the president's religious views? All American presidents, including Johnson, have attempted to project favorable public images that have not always or necessarily coincided with their private thoughts. Johnson may have had his share of dissimulation, but this essay indicates that Johnson was not a latter-day Machiavellian who recognized that a leader or an aspirant to power should *seem* to be religious, sincere, faithful, and humane. Concepts of Christian duty, benevolence, morality, and principle were as inseparable from and as deeply rooted in his character as his legendary political skills and his inordinate pursuit of and use of power.[77] While many divergent and sometimes conflicting and subconscious forces effected Johnson, the evidence strongly supports the assertion that the religious background, training, experiences, and beliefs of Lyndon Johnson were important factors influencing that president's political philosophy and decisions.

NOTES

1. Lengthy works devoting major attention to Johnson and pointing up his less attractive characteristics include the following: Alfred Steinberg, *Sam Johnson's Boy: A Close-up of the President from Texas* (New York: Macmillan, 1968); Eric F. Goldman, *The Tragedy of Lyndon Johnson* (New York: Alfred A. Knopf, 1968); Rowland Evans and Robert Novak, *Lyndon B. Johnson: The Exercise of Power* (New York: New American Library, 1966); Louis Heren, *No Hail, No Farewell* (New York: Harper & Row, 1970); Merle Miller, *Lyndon: An Oral Biography* (New York: G. P. Putnam's Sons, 1980); Jack Bell, *The Johnson Treatment: How*

Lyndon B. Johnson Took Over the Presidency and Made It His Own (New York: Harper & Row, 1965); Philip Geyelin, *Lyndon B. Johnson and the World* (New York: Frederick A. Praeger, 1966); J. Michael Quill, *Lyndon Johnson and the Southern Military Tradition* (Washington: Univ. Press of America, 1977); Robert Sherrill, *The Accidental President* (New York: Grossman Publishers, 1967); J. Evetts Haley, *A Texan Looks at Lyndon: A Study in Illegitimate Power* (Canyon, Tex.: Palo Duro Press, 1964); Tom Wicker, *JFK and LBJ: The Influence of Personality upon Politics* (New York: William Morrow, 1968); Evelyn Lincoln, *Kennedy and Johnson* (New York: Holt, Rinehart and Winston, 1968); Robert A. Caro, *The Years of Lyndon Johnson: The Path to Power* (New York: Alfred A. Knopf, 1982); Ronnie Dugger, *The Politician: The Life and Times of Lyndon Johnson; The Drive for Power from the Frontier to Master of the Senate* (New York: W. W. Norton, 1982). For an excellent essay reviewing many of the above volumes as well as those more favorably disposed to Johnson, see Robert A. Divine, "The Johnson Literature," in *Exploring the Johnson Years*, Robert A. Divine ed. (Austin: Univ. of Texas Press, 1981), 3–23.

2. Bureau of the Census, E. Dana Durand (Dir.), Bulletin 103 (2d ed., revised and enlarged), *Religious Bodies: 1906* (Washington: GPO, 1910), 42, 54.

3. Doris Kearns, *Lyndon Johnson and the American Dream* (New York: Harper & Row, 1976), 20; Dave Cheavens, "George Washington Baines," *Baptist Standard* 77 (Jan. 20, 1965): 6–7; Dave Cheavens, "Baines, Baptist, Baylor: The "B" in Lyndon B. Johnson," *Baptist Program* (Jan. 1965), 13–14; Horace Busby to John Bird, May 18, 1964, Executive File (Ex) PP 13-3, White House Central Files (WHCF), Lyndon B. Johnson Library, Austin, Texas. (Hereafter cited as LBJ Library.)

4. Rebekah Baines Johnson, *A Family Album* (New York: McGraw-Hill, 1965), 28.

5. Remarks at the 12th Annual Presidential Prayer Breakfast, Feb. 5, 1964, *Public Papers of the Presidents of the United States: Lyndon B. Johnson; Containing the Public Messages, Speeches, and Statements of the President, 1963–64*, vol. 1 (Washington: GPO, 1965), 262. (Hereafter cited as *Public Papers of President Johnson*.)

6. Ivan Sinclair to William M. McNeill, Oct. 6, 1964, General File, Religious Matters (Gen RM) 2, WHCF, LBJ Library.

7. LBJ to James L. Monroe, June 22, 1965, Gen RM 3-3, ibid.; LBJ to J. W. Storer, May 15, 1964, ibid. See also Remarks to the Christian Citizenship Seminar of Southern Baptist Leaders, Mar. 26, 1968, *Public Papers of President Johnson, 1968–69* (1970), 1:441–42.

8. George E. Reedy to Robert W. Burns, Apr. 21, 1964, Ex PP 13-3, WHCF, LBJ Library; personal letter from George W. Davis, June 9, 1981.

9. Personal letter from Lady Bird Johnson, May 4, 1981.

10. William C. Pool, Emmie Craddock, and David E. Conrad, *Lyndon Johnson: The Formative Years* (San Marcos: Southwest Texas State College Press, 1965), 25–26, 28, 29, 42–43, 48, 57–59, 176; Johnson, *Family Album*, 24; Booth Mooney, *The Lyndon Johnson Story* (New York: Farrar, Straus, 1963), 9; Steinberg, *Sam Johnson's Boy*, 25. See also Lyndon B. Johnson, *The Vantage Point: Perspectives of the Presidency, 1963–1969* (New York: Holt, Rinehart and Winston, 1971), 71.

11. Lyndon B. Johnson, "My Political Philosophy," *Texas Quarterly* 1 (Winter 1958): 17–22.

12. Mooney, *Johnson Story*, 189; LBJ to John H. Ryder, Oct. 5, 1967, Gen RM 3-3; LBJ to George Jessee, Oct. 5, 1966, Gen RM 3-2; LBJ to Rt. Rev. Monsignor Frederick J. Stevenson, Apr. 28, 1966, Gen RM 3-1, WHCF, LBJ Library.

13. Remarks at the Presidential Prayer Breakfast, Feb. 1, 1968, *Public Papers of President Johnson, 1968–69*, 1:122.

14. Remarks at a Ceremony Marking 1966 as the "Year of the Bible." Jan. 19, 1966, ibid., 1966 (1967), 1:34; LBJ to Gerard N. McAllister, June 2, 1967, Gen RM 2; statement, LBJ to Spyros P. Skouras, July 28, 1966, Gen RM 1; LBJ to J. Edward Smith, July 20, 1964, Gen RM 1; statement, LBJ to William R. Raborn, Oct. 4, 1967, Gen RM 1; LBJ to Everett Smith, May 15, 1964, Gen RM 1; Douglass Cater to Grace L. Shipman, Jan. 11, 1965, Gen RM, WHCF, LBJ Library.

15. For a perceptive article on Johnson's and other presidents' references to the Bible and other religious subjects in their inaugural addresses, see James H. Smylie, "Providence and Presidents: Types of American Piety in Presidential Inaugurals," *Religion in Life* 35 (Spring 1966), 270–82. See also House Document No. 9, *Inaugural Address of Lyndon Baines Johnson 1965* (Washington: GPO, 1965).

16. Personal letter from Lady Bird Johnson, May 4, 1981.

17. George R. Davis Oral History Interview, p. 17, WHCF, LBJ Library; Remarks at the Presidential Prayer Breakfast, Feb. 1, 1968, *Public Papers of President Johnson, 1968–69*, 1:121; Remarks at the Presidential Prayer Breakfast, Feb. 4, 1965, ibid., 1965 (1966), 1:129–30; Busby to Bird, May 18, 1964, Ex PP 13-3; LBJ to George R. Davis, Mar. 29, 1965; Ex PP 13-3; LBJ to John C. Harper, Sept. 24, 1965, Ex PP 13-3; George E. Reedy to David E. Kucharsky, Sept. 1, 1964, Billy Graham Name File; Whitney Shoemaker to Robert D. S. Condit, Dec. 9, 1967, Gen RM 3-3; Whitney Shoemaker to Mrs. R. F. Jackson Jr., Feb. 26, 1968, Gen RM 2; Brooks Hays to Joe Persico, Mar. 4, 1965, Gen RM 2, WHCF, LBJ Library.

18. Remarks at the 12th Annual Presidential Prayer Breakfast, Feb. 5, 1964, *Public Papers of President Johnson, 1963–64*, 1:261; personal letter from Lady Bird Johnson, May 4, 1981; LBJ to His Eminence Patrick Cardinal O'Boyle, July 31, 1967, Gen RM 3-1; LBJ to C. Ray Akin, June 2, 1967, Gen RM 2; Davis Interview, 34, WHCF, LBJ Library. Billy Graham, who visited Johnson in the White House many times, recalled that the two men often prayed together, and on occasion Johnson voluntarily getting on his knees for the prayers. Personal telephone interview with Billy Graham, Oct. 10, 1983. This interview has been transcribed and deposited in the Oral History Collection, WHCF, LBJ Library.

19. LBJ to the Very Rev. Monsignor Thomas J. Leonard, July 15, 1967, Gen RM; Monsignor Frederick J. Stevenson, Aug. 26, 1966, Gen RM 3-1; LBJ to W. A. Walsh, Oct. 1, 1964, Gen RM 3-3; LBJ to Rabbi Morris Pickholz and Rabbi Harold Goldfarb, Dec. 20, 1963, Gen RM 3-2; Anthony J. Celebrezze to Owen B. Kiernan, Feb. 17, 1965, Gen RM 2, ibid.; Frank Cormier, *LBJ: The Way He Was* (Garden City, N.Y.: Doubleday, 1976), 165; William S. White, *The Professional: Lyndon B. Johnson* (Boston: Houghton Mifflin, 1964), 93, 104.

20. Remarks at the Presidential Prayer Breakfast, Feb. 1, 1968, *Public Papers of President Johnson, 1968–69,* 1:122.

21. LBJ to Gerard N. McAllister, June 2, 1967, Gen RM 2; LBJ to Dominic Le Blanc, May 28, 1968, Gen RM 3-1, WHCF, LBJ Library.

22. Ralph A. Dungan to Mrs. Thomas J. Hennessey, July 20, 1964, Gen RM 2; LBJ to the Rt. Rev. Monsignor Frederick J. Stevenson, July 1, 1966, Gen RM 3-1; LBJ to W. A. Welsh, Sept. 24, 1964, Ex PP 13-3; LBJ to Bishop Reuben H. Mueller, May 18, 1964, Gen RM 3; Ivan Sinclair to Mrs. R. G. Tyler, Sept. 22, 1964, Gen RM, ibid.

23. Quoted in memo, Horace Busby to John Bird, May 18, 1964, Ex PP 13-3, ibid.

24. Quoted in Mooney, *Johnson Story,* 188.

25. Ibid.

26. Ibid., 189.

27. Remarks in Austin at the Dedication of the Agudas Achim Synagogue, Dec. 30, 1963, *Public Papers of President Johnson, 1963–64,* 1:102.

28. Remarks in Baltimore at the Celebration of the Bicentennial of American Methodism, Apr. 22, 1966, ibid., 1966, 1:447.

29. Jack Valenti, *A Very Human President* (New York: W. W. Norton, 1975), 17; Davis Interview, 25–26, WHCF, LBJ Library.

30. Personal letter from George R. Davis, June 9, 1981; Davis Interview, 17, WHCF, LBJ Library.

31. Goldman, *Tragedy of Lyndon Johnson,* 346.

32. Personal letter from Lady Bird Johnson, May 4, 1981.

33. Cormier, *LBJ,* 256; Valenti, *Human President,* 17–18. Richard W. Pierard, "Billy Graham and the U.S. Presidency," *Journal of Church and State* 22 (Winter 1980): 122; White, *The Professional,* 92.

34. Busby to Bird, May 18, 1964, Ex PP 13-3, WHCF, LBJ Library.

35. Quoted in the *Washington Post,* Mar. 16, 1981.

36. Cormier, *LBJ,* 257; Pierard, "Billy Graham," 121–24. Graham believes that it is not appropriate for him to be designated as a special spiritual advisor to the president. Personal telephone interview with Billy Graham, Oct. 10, 1983.

37. Personal letter from Lady Bird Johnson, May 4, 1981; George R. Davis, "A Tribute to Lyndon Baines Johnson" (pamphlet), Jan. 25, 1973, National City Christian Church, Washington, D.C. (1974).

38. Quoted in *The National City Christian* 20, no. 25 (Feb. 25, 1963): 4.

39. Loyd Hackler to George Christian, Apr. 28, 1967, Billy Graham Name File, WHCF, LBJ Library; personal letter from Billy Graham, Oct. 14, 1981.

40. Memo, Busby to Bird, May 18, 1964, Ex PP 13-3, ibid.

41. Quoted in Mooney, *Johnson Story,* 189.

42. David, "Tribute to Johnson;" Davis Interview, 18–19, WHCF, LBJ Library.

43. LBJ to Malcolm Watson, June 22, 1964, Gen RM, ibid.

44. Remarks to Members of the Bishops' Council, African Methodist Episcopal Church, Sept. 27, 1966, *Public Papers of President Johnson, 1966,* vol. 2 (1967), 1071–72; Robert

Zinsmeister Jr., "The Religion of Lyndon B. Johnson," General File (Gen) PP 13-3, WHCF, LBJ Library.

45. Whitney Shoemaker to Murray A. Carson, Apr. 9, 1968, Gen RM, ibid.

46. Quoted in memo, Busby to Bird, May 18, 1964, Ex PP 13-3, ibid.

47. Special Message to the Congress on Education: "The Fifth Freedom," Feb. 5, 1968, *Public Papers of President Johnson, 1968–69*, 1:165–72; Special Message to the Congress: "Health in America," Mar. 4, 1968, ibid., 322–33; Text of the President's Prayer Read at Church Services Attended by the First Family, Jan. 19, 1969, ibid., vol. 2 (1970), 1367–68; Remarks to Leaders of Organizations Concerned with the Problems of Senior Citizens, Jan. 15, 1964, ibid., 1963–64, vol. 1, 132–34; Remarks upon Accepting the Big Brother of the Year Award, Mar. 25, 1964, ibid., 422; LBJ to Paul Moore, June 11, 1966, Gen RM 3-1; LBJ to Rabbi Abraham D. Hecht, July 1, 1966, Gen RM 3-2; LBJ to Brother Flavian Renaud, Sept. 21, 1966, Gen RM 3-1; LBJ to Donald J. Irwin, Nov. 3, 1966, Gen RM 3-1; LBJ to Mother Aloysius, Carmelite Sisters, Sept. 16, 1967, Gen RM 3-1; LBJ to the Most Rev. Ernest J. Primeau, Mar. 28, 1968, Gen RM 3-1; LBJ to C. D. Pettaway, Sept. 4, 1964, Gen RM, WHCF, LBJ Library.

48. Remarks to the Christian Citizenship Seminar of Southern Baptist Leaders, Mar. 26, 1968, *Public Papers of President Johnson, 1968–69*, vol. 1, 442.

49. LBJ to John Wesley Lord, Feb. 15, 1966, Gen RM 3-3; second quote from memo, Busby to Bird, May 18, 1964, Ex PP 13-3, WHCF, LBJ Library.

50. Remarks to Members of the Bishops' Council, African Methodist Episcopal Church, Sept. 27, 1966, *Public Papers of President Johnson, 1966*, vol. 2, 1073.

51. Frank C. Laubach to the President, Jan. 10, 1967, Gen RM, WHCF, LBJ Library.

52. Zinsmeister, "Religion of Johnson," Gen PP 13-3, ibid.

53. Copy attached to letter, James L. Sandlin to LBJ, Feb. 24, 1968; Whitney Shoemaker to Sandlin, Mar. 12, 1968, Gen RM, ibid.

54. Personal letter from George R. Davis, June 9, 1981.

55. "The Lyndon Baines Johnson Presidential Window," The National City Christian Church, Service of Dedication, Mar. 15, 1981 (pamphlet).

56. Details of this story are in Monroe Billington, "Lyndon B. Johnson and Blacks: The Early Years," *Journal of Negro History* 62 (Jan. 1977): 26–42.

57. Joseph A. Califano Jr., *Governing America: An Insider's Report from the White House and the Cabinet* (New York: Simon and Schuster, 1981).

58. Personal letter from Lady Bird Johnson, May 4, 1981; personal telephone interview with Billy Graham, Oct. 10, 1983; personal letter from Billy Graham, Oct. 14, 1981.

59. LBJ to J. W. Storer, May 15, 1964, Gen RM 3-3; LBJ to the Rt. Rev. Monsignor Joseph P. O'Brien, Apr. 28, 1964, Gen RM, WHCF, LBJ Library; Doris Kearns Goodwin, introduction, *The Johnson Presidential Press Conferences* (New York: Earl M. Coleman Enterprises, 1978), 1:272; Remarks to the Delegates to the White House Conference "To Fulfill These Rights," June 1, 1966, *Public Papers of President Johnson, 1966*, 1:571–75.

60. Remarks to Members of the Southern Baptist Christian Leadership Seminar, Mar. 25, 1964, ibid., 1963–64, 1:421.

61. LBJ to Rev. Canon Bayard Clark, July 10, 1964, Gen RM 3, WHCF, LBJ Library.

62. LBJ to Felix Gear, Apr. 28, 1964, Gen RM 3-3, ibid.

63. Remarks to Members of the Southern Baptist Christian Leadership Seminar, Mar. 25, 1964, *Public Papers of President Johnson, 1963–64,* 1:420.

64. J. Michael Quill, *Lyndon Johnson and the Southern Military Tradition* (Washington: Univ. Press of America, 1977), 1; Louis Heren, *No Hail, No Farewell* (New York: Harper & Row, 1970), 80–82; Goodwin, *Johnson Press Conferences,* 1:348–50; LBJ to Cotesworth P. Lewis, Nov. 18, 1967, Ex PP 13-3, WHCF, LBJ Library.

65. Quoted in Pool, *Lyndon Johnson,* 125.

66. Kearns, *Lyndon Johnson,* 255.

67. Ibid., 56.

68. LBJ to Rabbi Joseph S. Shubow, Mar. 28, 1968, Gen RM, WHCF, LBJ Library.

69. LBJ to Jose Joaquin Trejos Fernandez, Sept. 6, 1966, ibid.

70. LBJ to the Most Reverend Iakovos, July 13, 1966, Gen RM 3-1, ibid.

71. James David Barber, *The Presidential Character: Predicting Performance in the White House* (Englewood Cliffs, N.J.: Prentice-Hall, 1972), 42–43, 54–57, 94.

72. Remarks upon Signing Proclamation "National Day of Prayer, 1965," Oct. 7, 1965, *Public Papers of President Johnson, 1965,* vol. 2 (1966), 1053.

73. LBJ to C. Ray Akin, June 2, 1967, Gen RM 2, WHCF, LBJ Library.

74. LBJ to Gerard N. McAllister, June 2, 1967, ibid.

75. LBJ to M. H. Stryker, Nov. 15, 1967, Ex PP 13-3, ibid.

76. Kearns, *Lyndon Johnson,* 257.

77. Ibid., 56.

The Moral Inheritance of a President

Reagan and the Dixon Disciples of Christ

Stephen Vaughn

One thing I do know—all the hours in the old church in Dixon (which I didn't appreciate at the time) and all of Nelle's faith have come together in a kind of inheritance without which I'd be lost and helpless.

Ronald Reagan to Rev. and Mrs. Ben H. Cleaver

The values that Ronald Reagan took into the American presidency came from many sources, as do values that all people use to order their lives, but it does seem clear that they derived in important ways from two individuals. One was the minister of the First Christian Church in Dixon, Illinois, during the 1920s. The other was the future president's mother, whose influence upon him was strongly purposive.[1]

The Reagans had come to Dixon from Tampico, Illinois, in 1921. The Cleavers moved there the following year. An attraction between Ronald (family and friends called him Dutch) and the daughter of the Reverend Ben H. Cleaver developed soon after. Margaret (Mugs) Cleaver was witty, intelligent, delightful, and, according to her sister Helen, "Dutch fell head over heels in love with her— a genuine attraction" that never wavered until she returned his engagement ring in 1934. She was "all that mattered," Helen recalled. "For almost six years of my life I was sure she was going to be my wife," said Reagan.[2]

Because of Mugs, Dutch found himself in proximity to Ben Cleaver, and in many ways the minister became a second father. "Naturally, he was *often* in our home," Helen remembered, "and felt the influence of father's guidance during those formative years." "He was as close to being a 'minister's kid' as one can be without actually moving into the rectory," one of Reagan's biographers has written. Cleaver "advised him, helped him get into college, even taught him to drive." Many years later Reagan acknowledged his debt. "You were all so much a part of my life and had so much to do with charting my course," he wrote to Helen after her father's death in 1975.³

As for the importance of Reagan's mother, there hardly can be any doubt. She assumed the responsibility for his religious training, taking him first to Sunday school, and when he was older, to the adult services. "I was raised to believe that God has a plan for everyone and that seemingly random twists of fate are all part of his plan," Reagan reminisced. "From my mother, I learned the value of prayer, how to have dreams and believe I could make them come true."⁴

I

Ben Cleaver's life offers much insight to the way he influenced Ronald Reagan. He had dedicated himself to the Disciples of Christ ministry. In an era when many clerics aspired to large urban congregations, Cleaver felt an obligation to rural churches and spent most of his life in small communities in Missouri and Illinois. He came to the Dixon church in 1922 and remained almost nine years, longer than any predecessor. He resigned to take the church in Eureka, where he served from 1931 to 1935. He ended "settled pastoral service" in 1946 and removed to Cape Girardeau in southeast Missouri, where for the next twenty years he served churches temporarily without pastors or too weak economically to pay regular ministers.⁵

The Disciples denomination, in which Reagan grew up, traced its roots to the aftermath of the American Revolution and to leadership of Thomas and Alexander Campbell. Members based their beliefs on the New Testament.⁶ The movement originated in rural America and flourished on the frontier. When Cleaver began his ministry, almost all membership was in small communities in the South and Middle West—more than half the members lived in Kentucky, Illinois, Ohio, and Indiana. Membership was also strong in Missouri, Iowa, Kansas, Tennessee, and Texas.⁷ The Dixon Christian Church of Reagan's youth opened communion to "all believers in Christ" and sought to keep services simple and understandable. It tried to foster an "undenominational spirit" that encouraged fellowship with other Christian groups.⁸

Cleaver's background was not only rural but southern. He had been named after a Georgia senator, Ben Hill. The family had come from Kentucky and settled in northeastern Missouri in 1818 in an area that became Ralls County. North of the confluence of the Missouri and Mississippi Rivers, west of Illinois and south of Hannibal, the region was part of little Dixie. Of the people in Ralls County in 1840, one in four was a slave, and Cleaver's grandfather Thomas was among the slave owners.⁹

Ben's father achieved wealth and prominence, but his success hardly guaranteed family security.¹⁰ Life was harsh during Ben's youth and such circumstances shaped his view of the world. In a time when disease was largely untouched by medicine, life was fragile. Ben was born in 1881, the fifth of six children. Three died in infancy, of illnesses easily curable in later years. His mother died of tuberculosis in 1887. Nine years later an older sister Maggie, aged twenty-five, succumbed to measles. His father remarried; Roberta Dickey-Clapper was a childless widow, thirty-four, who thereafter bore four children. Ben felt deeply indebted to this woman "for her high standards of morality." She died at age fifty, broken from child rearing and farmwork.[11]

When Cleaver entered the ministry, the social views of most Disciples reflected the beliefs of American pioneers, Anglo Saxons who lived in the Midwest and South. These assumptions assuredly bore a relationship to Reagan's later convictions. Although Disciples differed over the extent of church participation in social reform, most shared views held by many other Americans at the turn of the century. These included a belief in Providence; faith in progress; a nationalistic spirit that equated the country's interest with God's will and occasionally explained America's mission "in prophetic, millennialistic terms"; and a conviction about Anglo-Saxon superiority. An agrarian, anti-urban outlook also was apparent in Disciples thought.[12]

Disciples disagreed over the meaning of wealth and poverty. Some warned about the dangers of affluence and revered farmers and laborers. Most shared a desire for wealth and believed that hard work combined with Christian honesty would bring worldly success. Many Disciples admired the wealthy and counted the businessmen who often became influential members of the church. Their beliefs "fit easily into the general scheme of laissez-faire capitalism."[13]

Possessed of this background and of a healthy intellectual independence, Cleaver appears to have accepted the Disciples' comparatively liberal understanding of human nature, sin, and redemption. Although believing humans sinful and in need of God's salvation, most Disciples did not accept the view that original sin had totally corrupted human nature. Free will and intelligence enabled a person "to accept the means of grace that have been provided."[14]

Cleaver preferred to distance himself from the city. He feared the effect of urban secularism on doctrine and thought the impersonalization of large churches undermined Christianity. The vitality of religion, he believed, depended on a strong relationship between the local pastor and his congregation.[15]

Although he preferred a small church in a rural setting, he was not provincial. As a young man he briefly attended the University of Chicago, although he apparently disagreed with the church's "liberal element" there. He was by no means a rigid or cold individual. He was "no hairsplitter in matters of theology" and was "very curious, very widely read," his daughter Margaret recalled. He was "not narrow in any of his views." He could read Hebrew as well as classical Greek; he appreciated good music and theater. He enjoyed sports and often hunted quail before breakfast. His home did not foster a "repressive atmosphere," Margaret remembered. "We were absolutely free to say anything that came into our heads." Indeed, during one summer weekend, Cleaver loaned Reagan his family car so he could visit Margaret, then working at a camp in Lake Geneva, Wisconsin.[16]

When Cleaver assumed the Dixon ministry at age forty-one, he had been a pastor for more than eighteen years and Dixon was his tenth congregation.[17] In Dixon, his congregation considered him an "able and popular minister," although at first he had problems. He was not a good speaker; some members thought him "too intellectual," and he worried that he could not inspire the young. He overcame this shortcoming to be remembered as a "splendid organizer, a hard working, conscientious pastor and a creditable preacher."[18] The congregation held him in regard because of his dedication. When the janitor became ill, Cleaver took over the duties. When the depression made it impossible for the church to meet its budget, he insisted the debt be retired first and he be the last paid.[19]

Reagan's early allegiance to the Christian Church was a testimony to the influence of Cleaver, to be sure, and also to his mother, Nelle. The president's adopted son, Michael, has recalled that Nelle "instilled a Christian attitude in the entire family." Rev. David Franklin Seyter, a minister from Pine Creek, baptized Ronald on August 22, 1922. His confession and baptism, required for membership, were among the first performed in the church's new building, dedicated only three days earlier. Whereas Ronald's brother Neil (also baptized in the Christian Church) later joined Dixon's Catholic Church and removed his name from the rolls, Ronald retained membership until he transferred to the Hollywood Beverly Christian Church in 1940.[20]

Nelle Wilson Reagan had been born near Morrison in northwestern Illinois in 1884. She met Jack Reagan in nearby Fulton and in 1904 the two were married in the town's Catholic Church. Jack was not nearly as serious about religion as his wife, and he attended Mass only irregularly. For Nelle, however, religion was indispensable part of her life, and on Easter Sunday, 1910, she became a member of the Tampico Church of Christ. The Reagans lived in Tampico several years and then made a series of moves to Chicago, Galesburg, and Monmouth before returning to Tampico, where Nelle renewed her church membership. When the family moved to Dixon she transferred it there in early 1921.[21]

Nelle became quite active in the Dixon church. She believed in tithing and "could even put it on an almost selfish basis," her son recalled, "by guaranteeing that the Lord would make your 90 per cent twice as big if you made sure He got His tenth." The Reagan family income, however, in the mid and late 1920s was meager and church records suggest that Nelle's donations were small.[22] She made her contribution in other ways. She was one of the congregation's most loyal members. For eighteen years she taught the True Blue Class in the Sunday school, made up of twenty-five adult women. She was song director for the choir. She belonged to the Women's Missionary Society and chaired the Committee on Missions. She had talent as a dramatic reader and gave readings not only to her class but to other church groups in Dixon. She was a leader in convincing the congregation to build a parsonage for the Cleavers.[23]

To friends Nelle was "a lovely woman who gave of herself in service to others," surely "a practicing Christian if ever there was one." She was small in stature, with blue eyes and a soft-spoken, prudent demeanor. Church members recalled her as cheerful and kind to everyone. Where Jack was a cynic, Nelle was an optimist who believed people were "basically good."[24]

Nelle Reagan's Christian charity extended to the community—she visited hospital patients and prisoners in the local jail. On at least one occasion after she followed her son to Hollywood, she wrote the White House asking Eleanor Roosevelt to intervene on behalf of an Illinois man who sought treatment at Warm Springs, Georgia. In California she made a point of calling on patients at an impoverished tuberculosis sanitarium, bringing celebrities and movies supplied by her son. "I'm no society lady," she explained. "I don't spend my time at social gatherings, my time is devoted to God's work."[25]

As a youth in Dixon, Dutch Reagan was similarly active in church, and it was here that he gained experience as a performer and speaker. He participated in Sunday school pageants written by his mother. At age fifteen he was one of two leaders in the Easter sunrise prayer service. He belonged to Christian Endeavor, a group of thirty young people (usually eight to ten attended) that met on Sunday evenings and occasionally led discussions on such topics as "What Would Happen If All Church Members Were Really Christians?" and "What Difference Does It Make What We Do on Sundays." At seventeen he served as toastmaster at the district Christian Endeavor meeting in the Congregational Church in Moline.[26]

The church of Reagan's youth joined religion with social and political issues. It offered perspective on the disadvantaged. It admired businessmen and enterprise and coupled Christianity and patriotism. Cleaver championed temperance and was skeptical about some types of popular entertainment. His church offered a formula for character and defined youth's place in society. Here lay a seedbed for attitudes of a future governor and president.

II

The "brotherhood of man" was part of the First Christian Church's creed, and Nelle Reagan took the idea to heart. In early 1928 she read to her Dixon Sunday school class an essay about black Christians that she entitled "Negro Disciples and Their Contribution." She was "absolutely color blind when it came to racial matters," Reagan recalled. "Judge everyone by how they act, not what they are," she told her sons.[27]

In this regard, Nelle was "way ahead of her time" during the late 1920s and early 1930s. Intolerance often appeared among the Disciples. At least a few members of the Dixon congregation belonged to the Ku Klux Klan, although Klan there "was more anti-Catholic than against blacks," according to one of Reagan's contemporaries who remembered parades and burning crosses. Few Disciples had given up the idea of black inferiority.[28] Moreover, Anglo-Saxon primacy was an ingredient in the Disciples' zeal to spread Christianity. Dixon church members heard frequently about the work of missionaries with "the warring tribes of the wild country of Africa," and about "the strange customs of a heathen people." Only a few blacks lived in Dixon during the 1920s and none attended the Christian Church.[29]

Cleaver's racial attitudes during this period were of restrained sympathy. He believed the New Testament—at least Paul and Timothy's epistle to Philemon—neither condemned nor sanctioned slavery. He knew that before the Civil War almost every church in Ralls County had blacks on the rolls "with a certain door for admittance, and seating space." Blacks later were dispatched to their own churches. Years afterward he was deeply embarrassed. "I bow my head in shame at recollection of no 'County Meeting', during my four or five years as Secretary, when either of our two Negro Congregations was ever mentioned," he wrote in 1965.[30] During retirement he and his daughter Helen were among the few whites in Cape Girardeau to join the National Association for the Advancement for Colored People.[31]

Another concern of the era was how to treat the poor, and in this regard Disciples disagreed. Almost all acknowledged that they should aid the needy, but whether it was better to rely on an individual, congregational, or government programs was a point of contention. Most Disciples emphasized individual responsibility. Those who admired wealth or were otherwise conservative equated poverty with sin. Many argued that the poor needed moral redemption more than material relief. Charity developed slowly among the Disciples and most of it went to helping orphans. Nelle and Margaret Cleaver took part in this activity. Mugs and her friend Dorothy Bovey in 1927 helped the church's Triangle Club prepare a package of dolls for a St. Louis orphanage. Nelle participated in a Benevolence Institute.[32]

Attitudes toward the poor surely were related to the way many Disciples thought about business and the necessity of making a living. The Dixon church esteemed local businessmen and encouraged their success. In this respect it was part of a larger pattern of boosterism. Because many members were merchants, the congregation invited such speakers as the "big-bodied, big-souled business man and preacher" from Rockford who talked to the Bible School on "How to Do the Most and Live the Happiest." The church opened its parlors to the local Kiwanis Club and offered instruction in business etiquette.[33]

How, one might ask, did Reagan, the youthful citizen of Dixon and devoted member of the Disciples, see the role of business in the better life? In 1928 Reagan was vice president of the Hi-Y Club, part of the Young Men's Christian Association, and headed the entertainment and program committee. If the club's speakers were any indication, he had a healthy respect for businessmen. A grocer talked about "Merchandising as a Profession," and a representative from General Motors explained how his corporation conducted its affairs.[34]

For Cleaver, though, in his role as minister, prosperity and worldly accomplishment were not enough. He believed materialism should not be placed above the church's mission and told his congregation as much in early 1926 when he said that "spiritual values escape the foot-rule and adding-machine. Of greater importance than full treasuries and receipted accounts are clean hearts . . . filled with faith" and "transformed lives." It was good that members rejoiced over their "record and standing of matters of business," but they should "covet a like high rank for our congregation as a believing, worshipping, and Christ-honoring body of disciples." We "must never allow ourselves to trust to our gifts of money and even of time and service" as a replacement for reverence. The object was to increase one's "conscience on stewardship" and "loyal adherence to church standards of conduct and doctrine," not to rely solely on "mercantile ways of raising money."[35]

Given the attitudes about businessmen and the impoverished, it should not be surprising that the Christian Church provided a foundation for Reagan's later anticommunism and hostility to the welfare state. The Disciples rejected Marxism as unchristian. Occasionally sympathetic to the complaints of organized labor, the church was suspicious of unions, equating them with radicalism. Most Disciples associated socialism with anarchy and denounced bolshevism "as tyrannical, immoral, and anti-Christian."[36]

Cleaver was pessimistic about communism. He traced his thinking on this matter to his father's experiences in antebellum Missouri when he once traveled thirty miles on horseback to hear Alexander Campbell speak in a crowded courtroom in New London. Ben observed that Campbell gained prominence not only for ideas about church doctrine but also for debating Robert Owen, "the British-Welsh Atheist Philanthropist." Owen had promoted a "Social System" that "opposed all religions" and had founded "a sort of communist colony at New Harmony, Indiana, where he had many followers." Reports of the debate between Owen and Campbell, which occurred in Cincinnati, attracted wide attention. Campbell's New London Talk made a deep impression on Cleaver's father, who remembered it "as one of the best he ever heard."[37]

As he was unimpressed with Owen's experimentation, Cleaver was also later unenthusiastic about the New Deal. During Roosevelt's first term, when Reagan considered himself "an ardent New Dealer," Cleaver told his young friend that Americans "could not spend our way into prosperity." Reagan had then been skeptical but later professed agreement with the minister's position.[38]

In addition to respecting free enterprise, the religion of Reagan's youth valued patriotism. Love of country and devotion to Christianity were not synonymous, but often the threads converged. Nelle's Women's Missionary Society united Christianity and patriotism, opening meetings with "America" followed by the Lord's Prayer. The programs at Reagan's Hi-Y Club also opened with "America" and a prayer, usually followed by an inspirational talk. In 1928 Ash Wednesday and Washington's birthday fell on the same date, and the program committee arranged for a minister to talk about Lent while a high school teacher discussed Washington's youth.[39]

Reverence for national heroes and leaders connected the gospel and secular issues. When leaders of the state's Disciples held their annual convention in Springfield in 1927, they ended with a memorial service at Abraham Lincoln's tomb and a pilgrimage to New Salem. Cleaver had used Lincoln's memory to support temperance, preached on "Maintaining Faith in Our Leaders" the week before Christmas 1927, and prayed for the country's dead heroes the following Memorial Day.[40]

Cleaver's church did not neglect the great questions of war and peace. Christian Endeavor considered "What Should Be the Christian's Attitude toward War?" Reagan's later opinions about pacifism perhaps began to emerge from such discussion. Although Cleaver admired the nonviolent philosophy of Mahatma Gandhi, he advised caution in admiration. He warned of "much 'slush' among Christians these days over the great and admirable characters outside the church." Gandhi may have been a good man, Cleaver noted, but he had rejected Christianity while at Oxford and later in South Africa.[41]

The religion of Reagan's youth likely endorsed the use of power. Reagan's baccalaureate service in May 1928, in which Cleaver participated, featured a sermon on "Life's Opening Doors" by the pastor of Dixon's First Baptist Church. "There are two kinds of religious experience," the Reverend Walter Marshall said. "They come from the same source but they seem to move in different directions . . . One Experience calls for Peace—the other for Power. One for Action, the other for Repose . . . Christ comes to you today and shows you life's opening doors. His is not a Gospel of peace alone but of progress and power."[42]

III

The Disciples believed brotherhood, charity, enterprise, and patriotism depended on character. To this end, the Dixon church counseled proper conduct for young adults.

Many Disciples associated poverty with alcohol, a sensitive topic in the Reagan household.[43] Reagan remembered his father as "a restless man, burning with ambition to succeed," one who "might have made a brilliant career out of selling" had he not "lived in a time—and with a weakness—that made him a frustrated man." Dutch understood what "occasional absences or the loud voices in the night meant" and poignantly recalled when, at age eleven, he discovered his father lying drunk on the front porch, "arms spread out as if he were crucified—as indeed he was—his hair soaked with melting snow, snoring as he breathed." He never told his mother about this episode. But Nelle knew better than her son the seriousness of Jack's drinking. She tried to explain to Dutch and Neil that alcoholism was an illness and they should never condemn their father "for something that was beyond his control."[44] Still, he was troubled enough to discuss the problem with friends. Later he told others that finding his father on the front porch "marked a turning point in his life."[45] During his senior year in high school he wrote of life as "a struggle . . . full of sorrow and pain. / A life that warps and breaks us, / And we try to run through it again."[46]

Christian Church members were aware of a "problem" in the Reagan household. Some of Nelle's acquaintances discreetly suggested she get a divorce, but she recoiled from this advice and spoke against divorce in her Sunday school class. Dutch had tried to keep his father's problem secret from Mugs, but she heard about the behavior and became so upset that it threatened the couple's romance.[47]

Margaret's father was strict about alcohol. Ben Cleaver may have had compassion for Nelle, but he was a vocal proponent of the eighteenth amendment. Indeed, if he was "overboard" on any issue, it was temperance; he had no sympathy for those who indulged or who would repeal Prohibition. And Cleaver was not alone in these views. Temperance had widespread support in Dixon. The local newspaper linked drinking to crime and local politicians enthusiastically endorsed temperance, associating it with good citizenship.[48]

How deeply Reagan believed contemporary admonitions about drinking is hard to say. As a college student, he wrote a short story that described a student drinking spree with amusement, but he also spoke of bottles of alcohol "shining in the lamp light like executioner's knives."[49] Once he left for Iowa to work in a radio station, he experimented with the forbidden. He "learned to drink," he said, "principally because it was against the law—and it was done out of a bottle that tasted like gasoline on the fraternity back porch or in a parked car." One particularly bad hangover, though, convinced him moderation was best. "I decided if that's what you get for drinking—a sense of helplessness—I didn't want any part of it." Still, for years his picture was mounted behind the bar at a hangout in Des Moines called Cy's Moonlight, where he and Neil drank near beer spiked with alcohol. At Cy's, "you could always get a drink, Prohibition or no Prohibition," Neil recalled.[50]

Dixon's elders also worried about modern entertainment. New music and dances combined with movies and radio had invaded town life by the later 1920s, assaulting its isolation. During his youth Reagan was an avid moviegoer (and radio listener). For thirty-five cents he entered Dixon's segregated theater, where he watched Tom Mix or Wallace Beery and saw a five-act vaudeville show accompanied by a nine-piece orchestra and a $15,000 pipe organ.[51]

Cleaver was not hostile to entertainment. He appreciated a good time and "thoroughly enjoyed a good movie," his daughter remembered. But he joined other ministers to close down Sunday films and encouraged Reagan's Christian Endeavor to discuss "What's Wrong and What's Right with the Movies." The congregation felt that Sunday night pictures attracted the wrong people. Cleaver believed there had "always been good and bad movies" and objected to "innuendo" and "ugliness."[52]

Nelle Reagan interestingly emphasized the potential of movies for good. In 1927 the Women's Missionary Society discussed a united Christian world made possible by modern communication and technology. Nelle and a few others explained how movies, newspapers, radio, steamships, and planes made nations interdependent. Here were instruments "to apply the spirit of Jesus to all . . . human relationships." They made possible the extension of one's "personal circle to world-wide fellowship," curing "war, crime and sin of every kind." The group agreed that in Christ there was no east or west, only the brotherhood of humankind, "drawing the world together with an increasing sense of common need and common purpose." Greatness of leadership involved having that "glorious vision" to view the world "as one great neighborhood, one great fellowship of love."[53]

Nelle's optimism about the movies most likely related to the way she thought about acting and public speaking. Both the Reagans and Cleavers looked on acting and oratory as more than entertainment; they were also a way of learning. Consider the manner in which the youthful Reagan graduated from high school. On a warm spring evening in early June 1928, Mugs, not yet eighteen and president of the northside high school class, rose to speak at her graduation ceremony. On the speaker's podium was her father, who delivered the invocation, and Reagan, a bespectacled youth of seventeen.

The message Margaret delivered seems in retrospect prescient. The modern world, she began, was a "social world. Every person, to be the fullest success, must be able to mingle with people." In a society filled with clubs and civic organizations the person who had the most contacts stood the best chance to succeed. The high school should set up a course in public speaking and dramatics. If one wished to study history, the ideal would be "to visit the world's famous spots, and get the setting and facts at the same time." Because such travel was impossible for most people, "an excellent substitute" was "dramatization and pageant work." Education, she said, involved more than absorbing facts, most of which were quickly forgotten. Equally important was understanding how to tell facts to another person, "how to convey an idea clearly and forcefully, and, in general, how to conduct oneself before an audience." If facts from books perished, "ease and poise" were things one could never lose.[54]

Dancing was a more awkward entertainment in Dixon than acting or the movies. When Dutch and Mugs were in eighth grade and the Elks Club held its annual dance for children of members, "it took some effort to convince Mr. Cleaver that Margaret should be allowed to go." The Christian Church prescribed proper conduct on the ballroom floor. It was not uncommon for people of that generation to be suspended from church for dancing.[55]

How to raise children was understandably a concern for the Dixon church. In 1928 the Ladies' Aid Society (Nelle was a member) put out a *Hostess Reference Book*. Filled with recipes and advertising, it was interesting for the more than 150 rules governing etiquette of children as well as relations between the sexes and businessmen. It emphasized personality, but unlike many early-twentieth-century success manuals, it divorced neither personality from character nor image from substance. Success required more than becoming "an empty vessel to be filled and refilled according to the expectations of others and the needs of the moment." It assumed Christian faith. If growing up in Dixon involved "swimming and picnics," football and acting, this manual suggests it included restrictions that to later-day observers seem confining. Yet there was something poignant in this code, guidelines promulgated by mothers whose own opportunities had been limited, who were uncertain, perhaps fearful, of the world their children would live in, who aspired to have them succeed.[56]

The guidebook was nothing if not explicit. Reputation was paramount. Children were to be obedient, defer to elders, and be "clean and neat looking at all times." Respect for parents was "a reputation every child should cherish." Obedience was a virtue. "Never do anything when forbidden by your elders," the pamphlet told the child. "Never talk back to older people, especially to your mother and father," and "never argue with your elders," because "they know best."

People were judged by "appearance as much as by . . . manners." It thus urged attention to demeanor. "Talk in-a low, even voice," it suggested. Such behavior "denotes refinement . . . Conduct yourself in an easy but refined way" and "at all times be pleasant to all with whom you come in contact . . . Never know more about the subject discussed than the other fellow. A know-it-all is the most unwelcome person in the world and has few friends." And even if one did not have good clothes, "there can be no excuse of not being clean," because "soap and water [were] in the reach of all."[57]

Personality was a "priceless . . . asset" in "becoming real, popular and respected." It developed in many ways but among most important was table manners. "The study and training of table etiquette should be part of the very foundation upon which the young people receive their education and is just as necessary as Mathematics, Spelling and English," according to the women of the Dixon Christian Church. "Never keep your lips apart when chewing . . . Never eat chicken with your fingers." (The list of "nevers" numbered almost fifty.) And "never brush up the crumbs on the table or gather up the dishes," young people learned. "That is the maid's job."[58]

The booklet prescribed the ideal relation between sexes. Men should be chivalrous. "A gentleman's first call on a young lady should be to her home to meet her family," and the best time for formal calls was between 3 and 5 P.M. He should "not hold the lady's arm" when walking with her. And when a man and woman met by chance, it was the lady's place to speak first.[59]

Admittedly, it is difficult to gauge the influence of all the advice received by young people who grew up in Dixon during Reagan's time. All we can be certain of is that what he heard from Cleaver and from Nelle must have been difficult to cast off. It is possible to argue that indeed Reagan did amend, if not abandon, many of the principles that he first encountered in central Illinois. If read in isolation, Margaret Cleaver pointed out, the handbook circulated by the Ladies Aid left an impression that she, Dutch, and their friends were "more quaint than we really were." Helen questioned the depth of Reagan's commitment to Disciples' doctrine. He "sometimes attended church but was far from any great feeling for it," she said.[60] Others have maintained that Reagan did not possess a profound understanding of his religious heritage. Reagan himself admitted that he spent more time in the Dixon church looking at Mugs than "I listened to the sermons." Still, years later, when he had become president, he clearly believed "very firmly in a few simple principles." Even before he reached the White House, Reagan acknowledged the Cleavers and the Christian Church. "One thing I do know," he told the Cleavers after he became governor of California, "all the hours in the old church in Dixon (which I didn't appreciate at the time) and all of Nelle's faith have come together in a kind of inheritance without which I'd be lost and helpless."[61]

At many points the positions taken by Disciples of Christ of Reagan's youth coincided with the words, if not the beliefs, of the latter-day Reagan. These positions included faith in Providence and prayer, reticence to use government to protect civil rights for minorities, presumption that poverty is an individual problem best left to charity rather than the state, trust in the work ethic and admiration for those who achieve wealth, antipathy toward communism, association of America's mission with God's will, sensitivity to problems involving alcohol and drugs, and an uncomfortableness with literature and art that questioned the family or challenged notions of proper sexual behavior.

Reagan's experiences with the Disciples and the Cleavers proved important in other ways. They provided early training in public speaking and, as Mugs' graduation address suggested, offered a way of learning exposition in which acting played a central part. Reagan emerged from this environment with a tendency to view life in moralistic terms.[62]

Reagan could have done far worse than to have taken advice from Ben Cleaver and his mother. He retained his relationship with Cleaver after leaving Dixon. As noted, Cleaver became a pastor in Eureka (where Reagan and Mugs attended college) in 1931. Indeed, the future president corresponded with the minister until the latter's death. In later years the two men disagreed over such international issues as Vietnam, China, and the United Nations. Reagan also apparently turned a deaf ear to the minister's admonitions about wealth and Christianity. But these were differences among men who remained "cordial friends." The minister was a presence in helping Reagan draw his future. "He was a wonderful man," Reagan recalled shortly after leaving the White House, "a great influence."[63]

And then there was the influence of his mother. Nelle provided stability for a shaky family. She was a woman whose opportunities were limited but who tried to make the most of them. She fostered an interest in acting, believing the stage could be a force for noble purposes. Devoted to Christian brotherhood and charity, she derived her strength from faith. It was fitting that many years later, in 1981, as her son took the oath of his nation's highest office, his hand rested on Nelle's tattered Bible.[64]

NOTES

1. This article uses archival sources previously untapped by Ronald Reagan biographers. They include Ben Hill Cleaver's papers in the Disciples of Christ Archive, Nashville (cited as DCHSN); the Reagan-Cleaver family correspondence at Culver-Stockton College, Canton, Mo. (cited as CSCC); and the Records of the First Christian Church, Dixon, Ill. (cited as RFCCD). This article is also based on a thorough reading of the *Dixon Evening Telegraph* (cited as *DET*) between 1926 and 1928, as well as on interviews with Reagan; Cleaver's daughters, Helen and Margaret; Reagan's boyhood friend in Dixon, Dorothy (Bovey) Potterveld; and professors Thomas Israel and Fred Goodwin, Cleaver's friends in Cape Girardeau, Mo. For Reagan biographies that deal with Reagan and the First Christian Church, see Garry Wills, *Reagan's America: Innocents at Home* (Garden City, N.Y.: Doubleday & Co., 1987), 16–26, 33, 35, 56–57, 59, 102, 112; Lou Cannon, *Reagan* (New York: A Perigee Book, 1982), 24, 34; and Anne Edwards, *Early Reagan* (New York: William Morrow and Co., 1987), 33–36, 39, 56–60, 65, 66–67, 75, 92.

2. Helen Cleaver to author, Mar. 25, 1985; Ronald Reagan, *An American Life* (New York: Simon and Schuster, 1990), 40, see also 76–77.

3. Helen Cleaver to author, Mar. 25, 1985; Wills, *Reagan's America*, 18, see also 59, 102, 112. Dutch [Ronald Reagan] to Helen Cleaver, Feb. 26, 1975, Reagan/Cleaver Correspondence, CSCC. Also, Margaret Cleaver Gordon, interview with author, June 8, 1988, Bon Air, Va.; and Edwards, *Early Reagan*, 68, 75, 142–43.

4. Reagan, *An American Life*, 20, 22, see also 32, 56. Nelle also apparently later took responsibility for the religious training of Reagan's children Maureen and Michael. Michael Reagan, *On the Outside Looking In* (New York: Kensington Publishing Corp., 1988), 20, 50.

5. See [Ben Hill Cleaver], "A Brief Sketch of the Christian Churches of Ralls County, Missouri, and the Ministers Therefrom," 1966, p. 1, copy in Ben Hill Cleaver File, DCHSN. See also "History of First Christian Church (Disciples of Christ), Dixon, Illinois, from 1895 to September, 1966," from the daily diaries of Charles W. and Frank M. Johnson, compiled by Bess Johnson, Jan. 1958, 4–5, RFCCD. Cleaver was minister at the Eureka Christian Church from May 1931 to April 1935. Burrus Dickinson, interview with author, May 11, 1988, Eureka, Ill.

6. Thomas Campbell set forth the Disciples' basic beliefs in his *Declaration and Address* (1809), and his son, Alexander, promoted them during the next half century. Others associated with the Disciples' development included Barton Stone and Walter Scott. These four men were formerly Presbyterians (many early followers of the Campbells had also been Baptists). In addition, nationalistic forces—"a British background and an American environment"—helped fashion the Christianity of these men. The Disciples grew from a "new religious culture" that appeared during the late eighteenth and early nineteenth centuries and which "sanctioned the right of the individual to go his own way." It "would have been unthinkable apart from the crisis of authority in popular culture that accompanied the birth of the American republic." The Disciples of Christ wanted "to simplify the doctrines of Christian faith and promote a union of all Protestant denominations." They hoped to restore "primitive Christianity," wanted members to follow the New Testament, and believed every person capable of understanding its message. The Disciples gave followers the choice to decide for themselves any remaining "doubtful and inferential matters." They exalted the individual's conscience above the will of the church or congregation. *DET*, Mar. 16, 1928, 6. Winfred Ernest Garrison, *An American Religious Movement: A Brief History of the Disciples of Christ* (St. Louis: Bethany Press, 1945), 9, 10, 14. Nathan O. Hatch, "The Christian Movement and the Demand for a Theology of the People," *Journal of American History* 67 (Dec. 1980): 551, 567. See also Winfred Ernest Garrison, *Religion Follows the Frontier: A History of the Disciples of Christ* (New York: Harper & Brothers Publishers, 1931), 3–144.

7. In 1906 the Disciples of Christ had a nationwide membership of 1,142,359 and almost 90 percent of the members lived in localities of 25,000 or less. See David Edwin Harrell Jr., *The Social Sources of Division in the Disciples of Christ, 1865–1900*, vol. 2, *A Social*

History of the Disciples of Christ (Athens: Publishing Systems, 1973), 3, 5–6, 71. See also, Martin E. Marty, *Modern American Religion*, vol. 1, *The Irony of It All, 1893–1919* (Chicago: Univ. of Chicago Press, 1986), 164.

8. *DET,* Dec. 9, 1927, 5; Apr. 20, 1928, 9. On Cleaver's efforts to improve cooperation between Protestant churches, see [Ben Hill Cleaver], "Christ among the Candlesticks" (paper for the 1934 Illinois Ministers' Retreat Concerning the Present Welfare of Local Churches, 1934), 6, DCHSN. See also B. H. Cleaver to Brethren, Jan. 13, 1926, "Annual Reports for Year Ending Dec. 31, 1925," RFCCD; and *DET,* Jan. 13, 1928, 6; Apr. 5, 1928, 10; Mar. 16, 1928, 6. The local church in the Disciples of Christ was sometimes referred to as a "Christian Church" or "Church of Christ" and less frequently as a "Church of Disciples of Christ." In 1906, the Disciples movement separated and a more conservative branch became known as the "Churches of Christ" (plural).

9. Goldena Roland Howard, *Ralls County Missouri* (New London, Mo.: Printed by Walsworth, Marceline, Mo., 1980), 57.

10. For background on Ben Cleaver's father, John, who was a landowner, county judge, and bank president in Ralls County, Missouri, see "Some Memories of John Stephen Cleaver by his son Ben Hill Cleaver," assisted by his sisters Mrs. Kate Coil and Mrs. Bess Caldwell, Cape Girardeau, Mo., Aug. 18, 1967, 1–11, 17–20, DCHSN. See also Howard, *Ralls County Missouri*, 109, 112.

11. See Cleaver, "Some Memories of John Stephen Cleaver," 14, 15.

12. Many Disciples were also active in post–Civil War politics, and one, James Garfield, reached the White House. Harrell, *Social Sources,* 3, 25, 29–31. Ben Cleaver attended Christian University, a Disciples school in Canton, Missouri, which was later renamed Culver-Stockton College, and he graduated in 1902.

13. Harrell, *Social Sources,* 33, 34, 36 37, 39, 43, 46, 49.

14. Garrison, *An American Religious Movement,* 9. Salvation depended not on predestination but upon one's willingness to forsake life "according to the flesh" and to "submit to God's law," Cleaver told his followers in Missouri in a 1904 sermon entitled "Who Are Condemned?" See "Sermons: When and Where Delivered," Ben Hill Cleaver file, DCHSN.

15. Disciples disagreed over how to respond to the problems of expanding cities, and urban evangelism had become a major point of discussion among leaders. Many felt adaptation to urban America essential. See Harrell, *Social Sources,* 5–6, 71, 72, 75, 83; and Marty, *Irony,* 164. For Cleaver's views, see [Ben H. Cleaver], "Lectures on the Last Twenty-two Books of the New Testament," prepared and presented during the spring of 1908, Ben Hill Cleaver File, DCHSN, pp. 1, 14. On the importance of local pastors, see [Cleaver], "Christ among the Candlesticks," 1, 3, 5. The church was also threatened by poorly educated ministers, Cleaver believed, and he advocated better training. See "A Brief Sketch of the Christian Churches," [1966], 9. See also [Ben H. Cleaver], "Lectures" [Spring 1908], Cleaver Files, DCHSN, p. 45; "From B. H. Cleaver," *Christian-Evangelist* (Jan. 29, 1931): 162; and [Cleaver], "Christ among the Candlesticks," 2, 4, 7, 8.

16. On Lake Geneva, Ronald Reagan, interview with author, Oct. 16, 1989, Century City, Calif. Cleaver attended the University of Chicago between October 1911 and March 1912. Thomas Israel to author, May 17, 1988. Observations about Cleaver's ability to adapt to urban life made by Margaret Cleaver Gordon, interview with author, June 8, 1988. Margaret recalled that her father, while living in Cape Girardeau during the 1960s, used his knowledge of classical Greek to teach English to the wife of an immigrant. Others who knew Cleaver in Cape Girardeau testify to his intellectual curiosity. Thomas Israel to author, May 17, 1988; Thomas Israel with interview with author, May 10, 1988; and Fred Goodwin, conversation with author, May 7, 1988.

17. See "Record of Ministerial Service," Ben Hill Cleaver Papers, DCHSN; B. H. Cleaver to [Frederick D. Kershner], *Christian Evangelist* (July 26, 1928): 950; and Howard, *Ralls County Missouri*, 362.

18. For Cleaver's awareness of his deficiencies, see B. H. Cleaver to Dear Brethren, Jan. 13, 1926, "Annual Reports for Year Ending Dec. 31, 1925," RFCCD. *DET*, Mar. 16, 1928, 6. Dorothy (Bovey) Potterveld, interview with author, Feb. 7, 1987 (this observation was confirmed by Margaret Cleaver Gordon, interview with author, June 8, 1988). Diaries of Charles W. and Frank M. Johnson, compiled by Bess Johnson, Jan. 1958, 4, RFCCD.

19. See, "History of the First Christian Church," 5. See also Standard Church Register and Record: Meetings of Church Officers, [Apr. 2?, 1931], [p. 230?], RFCCD. Margaret Cleaver Gordon noted that although her father did not earn a large salary in Dixon (about $2,400 annually), her grandparents "were people of some means" and that the family did not feel acute money problems. Margaret Cleaver Gordon, interview with author, June 8, 1988.

20. Neil left the Dixon Christian Church in 1927. He had apparently been baptized in the Catholic Church as an infant, but his mother felt uncomfortable with that arrangement. Michael Reagan, *On the Outside Looking In*, 20, 270. See also Standard Church Register and Record, 82–83, RFCCD. It is unlikely, as Garry Wills suggests, that Ben Cleaver baptized Reagan. Cleaver did not assume the Dixon ministry until August 22, 1922. The previous pastor, Harvey Waggoner, died June 1, 1922. For Ronald Reagan's baptism, telephone interview with Ron Marlow (historian of the Dixon First Christian Church), Dec. 14, 1992. See also "History of First Christian Church," 2, 4, RFCCD; and Wills, *Reagan's America*, 21.

21. See Standard Church Register and Record, 82, RFCCD; and Gordon P. Gardiner, "Nelle Reagan: Mother of Ronald Reagan, President of the United States," in *Bread of Life* (monthly publication from the Ridgewood Pentecostal Church), May 1981, 3–4, copy in RFCCD. See also Ronald Reagan, *Where's the Rest of Me?* (New York: Duell, Sloan, and Pearce, 1965), 10–13. Observations about Jack Reagan's Catholicism based on Margaret Cleaver Gordon, interview with author, June 8, 1988; and Reagan, *An American Life*, 22, 31.

22. Reagan, *Where's*, 55. For example, Mrs. Reagan pledged five dollars on May 30, 1926, and two dollars on June 24, 1927. See "Ledger," 123, RFCCD. Fan magazines during

World War II maintained that Reagan insisted on giving one-tenth of his earnings to charity. "Ronnie has a kind of feeling about tithes," one publication said; see undated, unnamed clipping in Eureka College Archive, Eureka, Ill. (hereafter cited as ECAC).

23. For Nelle Reagan's church activities, see "Business Meetings of the Church," Jan. 13, 1926, 237, Standard Church Register and Record, 237, RFCCD; ibid., May 20, 1926, 238; "Meetings of Church Officers," Jan. 2, 1929, ibid. [204]; "Other Records of Interest," Jan. 16, 1929; Dec. 11, 1929; Jan. 14, 1930, ibid., 250–52. See also *DET*, Nov. 9, 1927, 12; Dec. 2, 1927, 3; Dec. 20, 1927, 12; Jan. 13, 1928, 6; Feb. 17, 1928, 5; Mar. 19, 1928, 2; Apr. 6, 1928, 5; Apr. 10, 1928, 10; Apr. 26, 1928, 2; and Sept. 1, 1937, 3. See also Gardiner, "Nelle Reagan," 5. On Nelle's dramatic readings, see Evelyn Carpenter's observations in Lorraine Rutkowski's "Lorrie's Lookout," 25, a publication of the Ronald Reagan fan club, circa 1950, copy in *Dixon Evening Telegraph* Archive (hereafter cited as DETA); and Reagan, *An American Life*, 35. For Nelle's contribution to the parsonage, see "Report of Building Fund Treasurer for the Year Ending Dec. 31, 1926," [Jan 7, 1927, 1], RFCCD; and "Report of Parsonage Building Fund Secretary, Jan. 11, 1928, "List of Parsonage Pledges and Payments," in *Annual Reports*, ibid.

24. Helen Cleaver to author, Mar. 25, 1985. Gordon interview with author, June 8, 1988. Nancy Reagan, *My Turn: The Memoirs of Nancy Reagan* (New York: Random House, 1989), 107. See also Reagan, *An American Life*, 20–22; Gardiner, "Nelle Reagan," 5, 13; Potterveld interview with author, Feb. 7, 1987; and *DET*, Nov. 9, 1927, 2.

25. When Dixon gave Reagan and his mother a homecoming in August 1950, the local paper devoted an article to Nelle's social work in California and maintained that she visited the tuberculosis patients at least twice a month. Ronald, according to the piece, had given the county patients 800 pounds of candy the previous Christmas. See clipping of Beverly Strouss, "Mrs. Reagan Says, 'Dixon More Beautiful Than Ever,'" [undated, most likely appearing in *DET* in Aug. 1950], copy in DETA. See also Mrs. J. E. Reagan to Mrs. [Eleanor] Roosevelt, Oct. 10, 1939, Box 2257, Eleanor Roosevelt Papers, Franklin D. Roosevelt Library, Hyde Park, N.Y.; Secretary to Mrs. Roosevelt to Mrs. Reagan, Nov. 16, 1939, ibid.; Reagan, *Where's*, 10; and Gardiner, "Nelle Reagan," 6, 13.

26. See program for "Easter Week Services," RFCCD. See also Reagan, *Where's*, 15. For Reagan's participation in Christian Endeavor, see *DET*, Sept. 23, 1927, 12; and ibid., Jan, 20, 1928, 5. For Reagan as toastmaster, see ibid., Apr. 16, 1928, 2. The church and Christian Endeavor provided experience in public speaking and leading meetings. Gordon interview with author, June 8, 1988.

27. See also *DET*, Feb. 3, 1928. 3; and Nancy Reagan, *My Turn*, 106–7. Quotations, Reagan, *An American Life*, 30, 52. In addition to Nelle Reagan, other members of the church's Women's Missionary Society opposed racial intolerance. In late 1927 they discussed "Breaking Barriers to Brotherhood." The "first barrier to be crossed [was] race-hatred," according to the program's leader. Americans "should receive and respect other races because as Christians we are all equal." Mrs. Alfred Tue quoted in *DET*, Nov. 4, 1927, 3; see also Sept. 9, 1927, 3.

28. As one church leader acknowledged, the Disciples "generally followed the prevailing cultural pattern" in their dealings with other races. In some areas during the 1920s this meant giving "strong support to the Klan." Some members of the Dixon Christian Church belonged to the KKK, which was "against whites as well as blacks who were living in sin." Gordon interview with author, June 8, 1988. Dorothy Bovey Potterveld to author, May 31, 1988. James A. Crain, *The Development of Social Ideas among the Disciples of Christ* (St. Louis: Bethany Press, 1969), 178; see also 179–87. Lester G. McAllister and William E. Tucker, *Journey in Faith: A History of the Christian Church (Disciples of Christ)* (St. Louis: Bethany Press, 1975), 357. See also Harrell, *Social Sources*, 161, 206, 207.

29. Or they heard about the "great, wonderful and backward land" called India. *DET,* Apr. 20, 1928, 3; Mar. 3, 1928, 3; Feb. 21, 1928, 2. Also Margaret Gordon Cleaver, telephone interview with author, July 13, 1988; and Marty, *Irony, 1893–1919,* 162. On number of blacks in Dixon, Gordon interview with author, June 8, 1988.

30. On the New Testament and slavery, see [Ben H. Cleaver], "Lectures. . .," [Spring 1908], [p. 41], Cleaver File, DCHSN. [Ben H. Cleaver], "A Brief Sketch of the Christian Churches," 5, Personal Papers File, Cleaver File, DCHSN.

31. On Cleaver and the NAACP, Israel interview with author, May 10, 1988; also confirmed in Gordon interview with author, June 8, 1988. Disciples' thought often reflected nativistic assumptions present in early twentieth-century American culture. Within this denomination, anti-Catholicism was the most pronounced, although anti-Semitism and anti-radicalism also appeared. Cleaver occasionally criticized Catholicism and Judaism, but was neither strongly nativistic nor sympathetic to such groups as the KKK. His early lectures indicate that he considered elements of Judaism unfriendly to Christianity yet thought it possible for Jews and Christians to unite. See [Ben H. Cleaver], "Lectures," [Spring 1908], 10, 11, 18, 23, 34, 35, 38, 54, 59, 60; [1934], 6; and Richard E. Lessner, "The Imagined Enemy: American Nativism and the Disciples of Christ, 1830–1925" (Ph.D. diss., Baylor Univ., 1981), v–vi, 347–79.

32. Cleaver, a member of the Dixon Ministerial Association, helped organize the Benevolence Institute to help the disadvantaged. See *DET,* Dec. 5, 1927, 2; see also Dec. 6, 1927, 10; Dec. 13, 1927, 9; Dec. 14, 1927, 3; Dec. 16, 1927, 3; Nov. 22, 1927, 4; Nov. 28, 1927, 2; Dec. 20, 1927, 12; Dec. 23, 1927, 10; Jan. 7, 1928, 2; and Harrell, *Social Sources,* 40–42, 50, 62, 69.

33. See *DET,* Nov. 15, 1927, 5; Feb. 6, 1928, 3. Business etiquette, members were told, was "as important an asset as the capital that finances the enterprise." The church offered a variation on the Golden Rule: "do to other salesmen as you would want them to do to yours." Quotations, *Hostess Reference Book* (Dixon, Ill.: Ladies' Aid Society, First Christian Church, [1928]), 9, 11, copy in RFCCD.

34. See *DET,* Jan. 26, 1928, 2; Feb. 16, 1928, 9; and Mar. 16, 1928, 7.

35. B. H. Cleaver to Brethren, Jan. 13, 1926, "Annual Reports for the Year Ending Dec. 31, 1925," RFCCD. Cleaver taught his family that there were "lots of things more important than money." Gordon interview with author, June 8, 1988.

36. Cleaver, though, urged frugality and fair wages for workers. See *DET,* Oct. 7, 1927, 3. Lessner, "The Imagined Enemy," 355, 347. See also Harrell, *Social Sources,* 105, 108, 125.

37. Quotations "Some Memories of John Stephen Cleaver," 4. Disciples talked about the implications of the Bolshevism. For a Disciple leader hopeful that Christianity would survive in Russia after 1917, see *DET,* Aug. 12, 1927, 1, 5.

38. Ronald Reagan to the Cleaver Family, Dec. 16, 1974, Reagan/Cleaver Correspondence, CSCC. Reagan was recalling Cleaver's sentiments, not his exact words. Burrus Dickinson called Cleaver "a middle-of-the-road type" who was not as liberal as A. W. Taylor, the Eureka pastor from 1902 and 1909. Taylor had been educated in sociology and was a proponent of the social gospel. Cleaver succeeded Fred Helfer, who had been pastor in Eureka between 1926 and 1930. Dickinson believed that Helfer had been too liberal for the Eureka congregation but that Cleaver was not as likely to "stir up things" over social causes. Burrus Dickinson, interview with author, May 11, 1988.

39. Margaret Cleaver was president of the Girls Hi-Y Club at this time. The club promoted loyalty and school spirit. See *DET,* Jan. 26, 1928, 2; Feb. 23, 1928, 2; Feb. 25, 1928, 2; Apr. 4, 1928, 3.

40. On Missionary Society, see *DET,* Nov. 9, 1927, 7; see also Dec. 15, 1927, 6; May 29, 1928, 8; and Marty, *Irony,* 299, 309. Men in the Dixon church were expected to remove hats when the American flag passed. See *Hostess Reference Book,* 5, copy in RFCCD.

41. Cleaver recognized that many Disciples sympathized with Gandhi's beliefs but reminded them the Indian leader was a Hindu, not a Christian. Margaret Cleaver Gordon emphasized her father's admiration for Gandhi. Ben Cleaver hated war, she said, but "perhaps thought it inevitable"; interview with author, June 8, 1988. Charles G. Elsam, see [Cleaver], "Christ among the Candlesticks," 4, DCHSN. On Christian Endeavor, see *DET,* Nov. 9, 1927, 12.

42. *DET,* May 28, 1928, 1, 5.

43. Most church members supported Prohibition. Many Disciples believed pauperism resulted from drunkenness and hence had little compassion for the poor. See Harrell, *Social Sources,* 41, 208–42.

44. Reagan, *Where's,* 7, 8, 9. See also Reagan, *An American Life,* 25, 33.

45. Nancy Reagan, *My Turn,* 105. Nancy Reagan's words, not her husband's.

46. Ronald Reagan, "Life," *Dixonian: 1928 (Cinema Number)* 15 (Dixon: Senior Class, Dixon High School, [1928]), 95.

47. Gordon interview with author, June 8, 1988. See also Reagan, *An American Life,* 41. On Nelle Reagan's opposition to divorce, see Gardiner, "Nelle Reagan," 5.

48. Gordon interview with author, June 8, 1988. On Dixon and temperance, see *DET,* Apr. 25, 1928, 7; see also Apr. 10, 1928, 10. Cleaver was a member of the Women's Christian Temperance Union and he aligned his church with the Illinois Anti-Saloon League. On Cleaver's membership in the WCTU, see *DET,* Jan. 24, 1928. On the Illinois Anti-Saloon League, see B. H. Cleaver to Brethren of the Congregation, Jan. 14, 1925, "Annual Reports for Year Ending Dec. 31, 1924, RFCCD. For Cleaver's work and sermons on behalf

of temperance, see *DET,* Dec. 14, 1927, 11; Jan. 13, 1928, 5; Jan. 24, 1928; Feb. 10, 1928, 5; Apr. 20, 1928, 9; and Sept. 24, 1928, 5. See also B. H. Cleaver to [Frederick D. Kershner], *Christian Evangelist* (July 26, 1928), 950. Teachings about alcohol (and drugs) were later reinforced by Reagan's California Christian Church. See, for example, C. K. [Cleveland Kleihauer], "The Peace Terms of Evil," *Christian Challenger* 6 (July 20, 1947): 1, copy in Hollywood-Beverly Christian Church Library, Hollywood, Calif. (hereafter cited as HBCCL); and "The High Cost of Experience," *Christian Challenger* 6 (Oct. 12, 1947): 1.

49. I am indebted to Reagan's biographer, Edmund Morris, for this quotation. See [Ronald Reagan], "Night of the Rose-Colored Bulbs, Or, Too Much Gin for Him," excerpt in Edmund Morris, "The Indifferent Figure in the Sand: A Review of Ronald Reagan's Collected Juvenilia" (unpublished manuscript).

50. Reagan, *Where's,* 56, 61. Reagan, *An American Life,* 53. Neil Reagan, "Private Dimensions and Public Images: The Early Political Campaigns of Ronald Reagan," 13, 14, an interview conducted by Stephen Stern, 1981, Governmental History Documentation Project: Ronald Reagan Era, Oral History Program, Powell Library, Univ. of California, Los Angeles. See also on Reagan's drinking habits, Michael Reagan, *On the Outside Looking In,* 183; and Nancy Reagan, *My Turn,* 119.

51. See *DET,* Dec. 24, 1927, 16; Reagan, *An American Life,* 30; and Reagan, *Where's,* 17–18. Jazz, often associated with black culture, was one type of entertainment that troubled the city fathers. See *DET,* Nov. 16, 1927, 1.

52. *DET,* Sept. 16, 1927, 5. Gordon interview with author, June 8, 1988. On church members' opposition to Sunday night movies, Potterveld to author, May 31, 1988. See also B. H. Cleaver to Brethren of the Congregation, Jan. 14, 1925, "Annual Reports for Year Ending Dec. 31, 1924," RFCCD.

53. The theme for this meeting was "The World—My Neighborhood." *DET,* Sept. 9, 1927, 3.

54. Quotations from Margaret Cleaver's graduation address, "A Chair for the New Home," reprinted in *DET,* June 4, 1928, 5.

55. Mrs. Potterveld recalled her grandmother had been suspended for dancing and poor church attendance. Potterveld to author, May 31, 1988. See also *Hostess Reference Book,* 5, copy in PFCCD.

56. T. J. Jackson Lears, "From Salvation to Self-Realization: Advertising and the Therapeutic Roots of the Consumer Culture, 1880–1930," in *The Culture of Consumption: Critical Essays in American History, 1880–1980,* ed. T. J. Jackson Lears et al. (New York: Pantheon Books, 1988), 8. Reagan, *Where's,* 18. For the contrast between the child-rearing practices recommended by the Dixon church of Reagan's youth and those suggested by the Hollywood-Beverly Christian Church of Reagan's young adulthood, see *Christian Challenger* 4 (May 20, 1945): 1; (June 17, 1945): 1, HBCCL.

57. *Hostess Reference Book,* 3, 5, copy in RFCCD.

58. Ibid., 3, 13.

59. Ibid., 4, 5.

60. Margaret Cleaver Gordon to author, May 25, 1988. Helen Cleaver to author, Mar. 25, 1985. Both Helen and Margaret observed that Reagan did not attend church regularly as president. "Even Nixon held services in the White House," Margaret noted. Gordon interview with author, June 8, 1988. Even before Reagan became president, observers commented on his "casual . . . churchgoing habits." See Majorie Hyer, "Reagans Likely to Attend Several Churches," *Washington Post,* Jan. 18, 1981, A18.

61. Reagan, *Where's,* 22. Also, Don Littlejohn, interview with author, Mar. 19, 1985, Eureka, Ill. Steven V. Roberts, "A Mighty Russian Pulpit for Reagan," *New York Times,* May 31, 1988, 7. "Dutch" [Ronald Reagan] to the Reverend and Mrs. Ben H. Cleaver, Jan. 4, 1973, Reagan-Cleaver Correspondence, CSCC.

62. "If he felt strongly that something was right," another writer who studied the Disciples observed, "he didn't let the facts stand in the way." Dickinson interview with author, May 11, 1988. See also Wills, *Reagan's America,* 52.

63. Gordon interview with author, June 8, 1988. Reagan interview with author, Oct. 16, 1989.

64. Michael Reagan said it was the first he had seen of Nelle's Bible. See Michael Reagan, *On the Outside Looking In,* 186.

Section 4

American Multiculturalism

Ethnocentrism, Gender, and Race

"Living in a Land of Prophets"

James T. Barclay and an Early Disciples of Christ Mission to Jews in the Holy Land

Paul M. Blowers

In the nineteenth century the West truly rediscovered Palestine. A land many Western observers had long considered fallen from its former glory was roused amid its Ottoman occupation to abide the hopes, dreams, and designs not only of aspiring Jewish nationalists but also of British and American diplomats, explorers, archaeologists, adventurers, Christian pilgrims, missionaries, and others in that great entourage which Naomi Shepherd has dubbed the "zealous intruders."[1] Protestant missionaries in the Levant, to the extent that they established an early and enduring physical presence in the Holy Land and a living link with evangelical churches in Europe, Britain, and America, played a memorable, if limited, role in this modern reopening of Palestine to the West.[2]

Indeed, while Western diplomacy in Palestine was still in its infancy, and geographical and archaeological studies of the land were still coming into their own, Protestant missionaries were developing a sophisticated campaign to rally Western support for resurrecting Hebrew missions at home *and* in the Holy Land, whence the gospel had first emanated.[3] Christian hope for the conversion, and possible repatriation, of the Jews as part of the timetable of the last days was certainly not historically new. Christian chiliasts had been advancing literal interpretations of select biblical prophecies and apocalypses concerning the destiny of the Jews since the second century. In the early nineteenth century a series of ambitious efforts at converting Jews, together with Christian gestures toward a Jewish reenfranchisement in Palestine, seized the imaginations of two generations of Christian missionaries in the Holy Land, many years before the involvements of premillennial fundamentalists with the Zionist movement.

Various reasons have been adduced for this dramatic resurgence in Christian interest in the conversion of the Jews and their resettlement in Palestine: an evangelical vision of global expansionism; enthusiasm for voluntary associations in the wake of the revivals in Britain and America in the eighteenth and early nineteenth centuries; a Protestant triumphalism that aspired to displace old particularisms (be they Jewish, Roman Catholic, or otherwise) with an enlightened and universally enduring faith; a pietistic sense of Christianity's debt to Judaism, coupled in some cases with a genuine desire to compensate for the historic sufferings of the Jews at the hands of Christians.[4] This last rationale was passionately espoused by the first two missionaries dispatched to Palestine by the American Board of Commissioners for Foreign Missions (ABCFM) in 1819, Levi Parsons and Pliny Fisk. Parsons begged his prospective supporters "not to imitate the example of the crusaders, those deluded champions of the cross," and to recognize Christianity's obligation to Judaism in the spirit of forgiveness.[5] Fisk justified the mission on the sheer historical and sacred significance of the land itself, the intriguing character of the Muslims, Jews, and other religious communities present there, in addition to the benefits for the Church in a mission to the Jews of the Holy Land.[6] Casting himself like Paul, "going to Jerusalem, bound in the Spirit, not knowing the things that shall befall me there" (Acts 20:22), Fisk looked to counteract those sects (Roman Catholicism, Syrian and Greek Christianity, etc.) that were already planted in Palestine but "deplorably ignorant" of Scripture and the true faith; a strategic base in Jerusalem would in turn be a springboard from which to introduce "pure Christianity" to Jews, Muslims, Catholics, and Eastern Orthodox alike.[7]

Yet Fisk touched on arguably the most significant motivation for American Protestant mission work in the Holy Land when he projected its hermeneutical benefits:

> It may also be hoped, that the prosecution of missionary labors in the Holy Land, will in some measure at least, assist in elucidating the meaning of Scripture; for though God had addressed men in language so plain and intelligible that none need to mistake in things material; yet the figures, the parables, the prophetic language of Scripture have beauty, and richness and strength, which are seen only by an acquaintance with the customs and scenery of that land, "where the book of books was handed down from heaven." Though no important advantage of this sort should be realized immediately, yet the time will probably come, when this anticipation shall be answered, in an eminent degree.[8]

Parsons showed none of Fisk's tentativeness about the possibilities of scriptural mysteries being unfolded through the missionary endeavor, having already assembled testimonies (Jer. 29:10–14; Ezek. 37:21–25) that clearly previewed the repatriation of the Jews and their conversion to Christianity in the inception of Christ's millennial kingdom.[9]

Indeed, millenarian ideals and speculations about the Jews' providential return to Palestine in the end times had motivated many of the pioneering

British and American missionaries in the Holy Land. But no well-defined and comprehensive Christian agenda for the Jewish mission was shared by all the churches. The London Society for the Propagation of Christianity among the Jews (or "London Jews' Society"), which, along with the (Anglican) Church Missionary Society, began the first dispatch of British missionaries to Palestine in 1820, originally asserted in an 1810 policy statement its desire to distinguish between the national reinstatement and the Christian conversion of the Jews. As late as 1823 its leaders were still disclaiming any intention of disseminating particular views on the nature of the millennium, all in the interest of avoiding prophetic enthusiasm.[10] Moreover, while many American Protestants on the home front were convinced of the validity of converting Jews, not all were sold on the millenarian fervor for their political restoration in Palestine. As Moshe Davis has observed, there was no clear-cut denominational alignment for or against the restoration proposal, the major Christian initiatives in this direction being undertaken by ambitious individuals who sometimes cooperated across confessional lines.[11]

A particularly striking case in support of this pattern is the work of James Turner Barclay. As the first appointee of the new and internally controversial American Christian Missionary Society (ACMS) of the Disciples of Christ, Barclay served in a mission to Jews in Jerusalem beginning in 1849. Barclay has surfaced from time to time in histories of nineteenth-century Protestant missions to Jews and of Western activities in the Holy Land, though no comprehensive study of him has yet appeared.[12] As interesting as his missionary work itself is Barclay's behind-the-scenes struggle to rationalize this mission within his own Disciple tradition. While the Jerusalem enterprise enjoyed strong initial enthusiasm and support at home, the faltering of the mission after Barclay's two tenures in Palestine tested the missionary will of the Disciples of Christ at a time when they, like other evangelical traditions in America, were grappling not only with organized missions per se but also with the shaping of a "millennial" vision of the Christian future, and with defining their own unique role within that future according to the new "scientific" analysis of the biblical prophecies.

Barclay, from Scottsville, Albemarle County, Virginia, was a former Presbyterian layman and a descendent of Robert Barclay, the eminent Quaker apologist and one-time governor of colonial New Jersey. A graduate of the Universities of Virginia and Pennsylvania, he practiced medicine and for a time owned and operated the Jefferson estate at Monticello.[13] A self-made biblical scholar and preacher, and a powerful Disciple proponent of foreign missions, he had offered his services for missionary work in 1849 before the ACMS had even been fully organized.[14] Barclay's passion for the Jewish mission in the Holy Land, like that of Fisk and Parsons, combined confidence in the Bible, carefully reasoned strategy, and sheer quixotic zeal. His mission prospectus set forth an already familiar logic, for which Romans 11 provided the pragmatic outline. The Jews should be premier recipients of the "ancient gospel" because of the Christian debt to the Hebrew tradition, and because their conversion, their engrafting again into the "true olive tree," would have the profoundest effects for the universal ingathering of the Gentiles.[15] The gospel had to go out again from Jerusalem to the nations, as it had in the primitive Christian mission in Acts: "Would not the establishment of a mission at the Holy City also have a strong tendency to attract the eyes of all men to that holy hill, as the place whence the Law of the Lord went forth in all its purity, eighteen hundred years ago (and whence, according to the views of some observant students of prophecy, it is ordained it shall soon go forth again in its pristine purity), and thus accomplish more for the restoration of primeval Christianity than the same amount of labor bestowed anywhere else?"[16]

Barclay, like his predecessors, pointed to the "signs of the times" as thoroughly auspicious for the conversion of the Jews. Thirty years earlier, Fisk and Parsons had proclaimed a whole assortment of signs favorable to the Jewish mission: reports of greater openness of European Jews to the gospel, the support of international leaders for such an enterprise, the formation of mission societies to the Jews, distributions to the Jews of Hebrew translations of the New Testament, and the like.[17] Barclay too saw the accounts of recent Jewish conversions to Christianity as a crucial sign that God had not fully rejected his covenant people, and that modern Gentile Christians should now imitate the Apostles by concentrating a strong missionary initiative on the Jews.[18] Other Disciple leaders, Alexander Campbell included, had remained hopeful but skeptical about such conversions from Judaism.[19]

For Barclay, pragmatic considerations and millenarian expectations were inseparable in rationalizing the Jerusalem mission. The Jews were the most likely candidates for this enterprise not only because of their biblical heritage but also because of their historical tenacity as a people who, unlike the South Sea Islanders or American Indians or other races prone to enslavement, had proven themselves "absolutely indestructible by all the combined powers of the earth"; in the long term, unconverted Gentiles would thus "be glad to take hold of the skirt of the despised Jews."[20] The substantial concentration of Jews already in Palestine and the new glimmers of hope among Jews for a national restoration there made it the sensible and strategic starting point for gaining a sympathetic hearing for the gospel. But most importantly, without Jewish conversion, Christian hopes for the consummation of history in the grand prophesied events connected with Zion would be dashed. It was incumbent on the Disciples, therefore, to seize the moment and, in effect, realize their own missionary eschatology for the Jews, especially since other Western Christian constituencies already present in Palestine (that is, the Anglo-Prussian bishopric and the Roman Catholic Church) had so grievously failed to restore authentic apostolic Christianity. Barclay also believed that Protestant denominations already involved in overseas missions were far too concerned about retaining their own sectarian identity simply to drop self-interest and follow the strategy patterned in the Acts of the Apostles.[21]

The strong initial home support for Barclay's Jerusalem enterprise was predictable. After all, the Disciples of Christ, like other evangelicals, were intrigued with the current movements and nationalist impulses of Jews worldwide, and with the way that contemporary political and demographic patterns might signal new opportunities for Christian missionary activity abroad.[22] Alexander Campbell, whose support for Barclay's mission was indispensable, consistently and publicly embraced the vision of a global mission of Christianity again radiating from the Holy City as in apostolic times.[23] Fully lacking, however, was a solid ideological or biblical-hermeneutical consensus among Disciple leaders on focusing the Jerusalem mission principally on Jews, on adopting a specific position toward their national restoration (instead of simply a religious "return" to Palestine), or on connecting the mission with a particular millenarian strategy.

Barton Stone, whose "Christian movement" in the old Southwest had merged with the Disciples in 1832, was a premillennialist but was less interested in the Jewish restoration in Palestine than in the prospect, as he understood Romans 11:12–26, of the Jews' return to faith and total redemption in the future finale.[24] Stone died before Barclay's mission ever began. On the other hand, Walter Scott, the premier Disciple preacher in the North, was captivated by the prospective resettlement of the Jews and their ultimate conversion at the start of the millennium. In his journal *The Evangelist* he featured a long essay on the Jewish restoration by Mordecai Noah, the pioneering American advocate of Jewish repatriation in Palestine who regularly entreated Protestant churches, in a spirit of forgiveness and tolerance, to rally political and ecclesiastical forces in the West behind the resettlement of Jews in their homeland.[25] Scott himself, in a series of essays in 1833, had already investigated the prophetic foundations of a Jewish restoration in the Holy Land and the various interpretative options.[26] He quoted heavily from the Jewish scholar David Levi, an eminent British Hebraist and polemicist whose "religious zionism," as Nahum Sokolow calls it, read the prophecies of restoration literally but left the timing to God alone.[27] Scott also indicated his dependence on George Stanley Faber, an Anglican evangelical and prophecy scholar who had calculated the commencement of the millennium right into Scott's own time.[28] Affirming the clarity of the prophecies of Jewish restoration and the ingathering of the Gentiles in the last days, Scott confessed his own initial sympathy with those premillennialists who expected Christ's thousand-year earthly reign to commence in 1833 or 1834.[29] He was neither an enthusiast nor a conscientious Christian exponent of Jewish repatriation, but a devotee of the Baconian hermeneutic who was convinced that the prophecies of the Bible, if scrutinized *inductively,* could divulge the scheme of the eschaton. Later, after nothing happened in 1833 or 1834, Scott admittedly adjusted his millenarianism, giving up not only on dating the millennium but also on making its arrival absolutely contingent on the literal return of the Jews to the Holy Land or even on their conversion. His logic: the Old Testament evidence for such eventualities was finally too mixed; and the more authoritative New Testament evidence, namely Romans 11, indicated not a literal return (the Jews Paul was addressing were not yet scattered!), nor a certain conversion (the ultimate faith of the Jews in Christ was itself the great contingency!).[30] Christians could only wait and hope for the Jews' final conversion and reinstatement in the true *spiritual* Israel, the church. Indeed, Scott ended up with a spiritualized millenarianism, but that shift in thinking did not hinder James Barclay from later considering Walter Scott's theoretical backing of his Jerusalem mission, conceived as it was within a comparatively literalistic millenarian scheme, still to be secure.[31]

Alexander Campbell's precise reasoning in support of the Barclay mission in the Holy Land is harder to interpret. Clearly Campbell supported the idea of evangelizing the Jews as a strategic component in his own postmillennial vision of a progressive illumination of the whole human race through the efforts of the reunited Church.[32] Jewish infidelity and Christian sectarianism were joint enemies to be vanquished. But Jews were not just another people subsumed in spiritual darkness; they had a unique place in salvation history, a critical role in its consummation, according to Romans 11. Campbell entertained, on biblical grounds, the prospect of the Jews' restoration in Palestine. As early as his debate with socialist Robert Owen in 1829 he was stating what would later be quoted by James Barclay as evidence of Campbell's unflagging support for repatriating the Jews in the Holy Land:

> It would appear that nothing is wanting to gather this people into their own land but the destruction of the Ottoman Empire. This the prophecies seem to indicate. They are ever prepared to return; for they will not hold any real estate in any country in the world . . . Their expectation is to return; and who can say that the evidence in favor of such an event is at all doubtful, or the event itself at all improbable? Blindness, says Paul, has happened to them in part, till the times of the Gentiles be fulfilled; then all Israel shall be saved [Rom. 11:25–26]; then the Jews shall be consolidated, and become the light of the whole world; and so all Israel shall yet be saved. Then shall the funeral song of infidelity be sung.[33]

Again in 1849, the year Barclay was commissioned, Campbell was writing of the Jews:

> God has not kept them these many years for nothing. He will use them again, and yet again bless all the nations of the earth by the seed of Abraham his friend. "If casting of them away has been the reconciling of Gentile world, what shall the resumption

of them be but life from the dead" [Rom. 11:15]. We hear a rattling in the valley of dry bones. The Jews are intent on rebuilding their city and their temple. We intend to notice the Jews, and especially the converted Jews of this our own day, and their efforts to convert their nation to the belief of him, as the true and long promised Messiah, whom their fathers repudiated and persecuted to death.[34]

Yet while Campbell consistently respected the attempts of his scholarly colleague Robert Milligan, and of Barclay himself, to outline the sequence of events (including Jewish repatriation and conversion) in the inauguration of the millennium, and was thoroughly optimistic about the "true Baconian system" applied to prophecy, he carefully shunned millenarian extravagances—be it date setting or asserting, as some were, that the Messiah would return to Jerusalem and directly intervene to convert the Jews.[35] Like Walter Scott, Campbell's concern that Jews, like Gentiles, arrive at faith in Christ, and his conviction that their only true hope lay in the Jerusalem *above*, overshadowed any abiding for their material restoration in the Holy Land. Still this did not stop James Barclay from invoking Campbell's authority in support of his grand vision of the "destiny of Israel."[36]

Barclay's first tenure in Jerusalem lasted from the winter of 1851 to the summer of 1854. Certainly it was as much a pilgrimage as a mission, and was fraught with disappointments from the outset. Upon first stepping foot in the Holy Land, Barclay had earnest hopes of "benefiting its present benighted inhabitants, and hoisting anew the standard of Primitive Christianity," in the image of the ancient apostolic mission.[37] He was not prepared to find, as he intimates of his first impression of Jerusalem, that there was "no worse missionary ground on all the earth than this same city."[38] He recoiled at the degraded state of the "lapsed churches of the East," the general void of the purity and simplicity of the faith in the very birthplace of the Christian mission; but especially disturbing was the bitter hatred of the Jews for all things Christian.[39] The Jewish population of Jerusalem in 1850 was about six thousand (of a total of fifteen thousand inhabitants), growing to around eight thousand during the 1850s.[40] Indications are that Jerusalem remained a bastion of Jewish orthodoxy amid steady immigration and the initial overtures of Christian missionaries to the Jews.[41] Barclay lamented the Jews' trepidation toward receiving the gospel, the rabbis' "sophistry," "the dogged obstinacy of some of these cabalistic devotees of the Talmud."[42] More discomfiting perhaps was the necessity of having to open his medical practice in order to get a hearing, all the while the London Jews' Society and other Christian organizations had or were building hospitals in the city that would doubtless be attracting prospective converts.[43]

In the months following, Barclay's frustrations mounted. He confessed the sad irony that Muslims had received him more warmly than Christians in the Holy City.[44] Abrasive confrontations ensued, quite often with Roman Catholics.

Encountering a frigid welcome at Bethlehem's Church of the Nativity, Barclay defended himself as a "Bible Catholic Christian" in the presence of the Latin patriarch of Jerusalem.[45] Elsewhere he found himself disputing locations of holy sites with "ignorant, superstitious and designing monks."[46] Barclay was put off as well by the overly accommodating, even "Judaizing" spirit of some Protestant missionaries who would go so far as to allow Jewish converts to continue circumcising their sons.[47] Barclay and his family endured protracted illness, forcing a temporary suspension of mission activities.[48] Then too there was the meager harvest of converts. Barclay actually baptized more from the Christian than the Jewish community, the only Jews initially being a mother and three grown children, and a man formerly converted to Roman Catholicism.[49] Like other missionaries, Barclay discovered that converts to Protestant Christianity were vulnerable to reprisals from their native coreligionists, thus necessitating some sort of asylum or patronage. Yet when he attempted to acquire land at Wady Farah, south of Jerusalem, as a retreat for converts, and acted through an agent of the British consulate, the sale met with local resistance and its failure set Barclay angrily at odds with the British consul in Jerusalem, James Finn.[50]

Barclay nonetheless put the best face on his labors, insisting on the timeliness of his efforts at Bible distribution as long as Jerusalem remained a magnet of pilgrim Jews and Gentiles.[51] His great consolations were his thriving medical mission (treating some two thousand cases of malaria during his first year alone) and his geographical and archaeological investigations, which included some extended collaborations with the preeminent American archaeologist in Palestine, Edward Robinson. Barclay's medical services earned him access to many restricted holy sites in Jerusalem, and his extensive researches led him to publish *The City of the Great King* in 1858, even today an important source for the topography of nineteenth-century Jerusalem, while including also Barclay's vision of the topography of "Millennial Jerusalem."[52]

As early as the summer of 1853 Barclay was nevertheless intimating the burdens of his mission to Alexander Campbell and ascribing its lack of numerical vitality to the inherent difficulties of restoring apostolic Christianity in a land so replete with competing religious communities and so conducive to compromised allegiances:

> Our success in re-planting primeval Christianity on the soil of its nativity, where it succeeded so triumphantly at first, has neither been commensurate with our desires nor expectations—only twenty-two having, as yet, embraced the truth. But still I trust that the objects of the mission are such as to engage your attention, and secure your approbation and prayers. Had mere numerical strength been my object, I could easily have gathered a church of several hundred members; but it has always been my determination to have a pure church or none, so far as it could be secured by the due administration of the apostolic rule for its formation.[53]

By the next summer, 1854, financial pressures prompted Barclay to leave his mission in the hands of a Jewish convert and return to Virginia, "the 'signs of the times' indicating the expediency of an earlier visit to the United States than I contemplated."[54] In his mind it was a mere furlough. Campbell initially suggested that Barclay be dispatched to Boston since it was the "Jerusalem" of the American home missionary effort.[55] Barclay's heart, however, remained in the Holy Land. Financial revitalization in the ACMS enabled him to do so in the summer of 1858, though not without controversy. Abolitionist supporters of the society, long opposed to Barclay's appointment since he had once owned slaves in Virginia, attacked his recommissioning and ultimately broke to form their own missionary society.[56] Skeptics of Barclay's quixotic tendencies stretched to give him the benefit of the doubt. Isaac Errett, an emerging Disciple leader and corresponding secretary of the ACMS, wrote later in 1858: "Whatever might have been suspected of romantic zeal, in his first visit to the Holy Land, no thought of the kind can attach to his return . . . The romance and poetry of the movement have had a fine chance to escape amid the stern realities of missionary life."[57] Once back in Jerusalem, however, Barclay's hardships were legion: a devastating drought in Palestine, rampant sociopolitical turmoil, continuing Jewish intransigence, proselytes of dubious loyalty, and more. With little evangelistic success to show, he mused in one of his brighter moments in 1860 that "although there is nothing particularly encouraging, there is nothing positively discouraging."[58]

This time around, however, the enduring woes ignited in Barclay a new burst of millenarian urgency. While supporters at home were hoping just to stir sympathy for the Jerusalem mission as a "child of faith, in its infancy,"[59] Barclay began a campaign to redeem his work by an ardent recommitment to the spiritual *and material* restoration of the Jews. Crossing denominational lines he inaugurated the "Abrahamic League for the Restoration of Israel" to solicit support for the Jews' "emancipation from their political durance abroad as well as their liberation from the grinding oppression of the rabbis in their own land."[60] He also boldly set out the eschatological framework of his own mission in a series of essays addressed to Alexander Campbell, dramatically entitled "The Welfare of the World Bound Up in the Destiny of Israel." Urging that the *novus ordo seclorum* ("new order of the ages") was imminent for America and the world, Barclay repudiated the prevalent view among many Protestants that Israel was forever God's outcast, and asserted that the reenfranchisement of the Jewish nation, its ascendancy to universal dominion, and the total conversion of Israel were fast approaching. Moreover, this ingathering of Israel was without doubt to be "an honor specially devolved upon America, and particularly that class of her citizens whose motto is, 'the Bible, the whole Bible, and nothing but the Bible.'"[61]

Still carefully trying to distance himself from those he deemed the true "literalists" and prophetic charlatans of the day, Barclay insisted that his was a scientific reading of the biblical evidence that divulged the hidden links between prophecy and the status of land and people in Palestine. "I am living in a land of prophets, where the language of prophecy is the language of all nature, and stands out, inscribed in bold relief, upon every object that meets the eye."[62] The desolation of the land, the absence of its former glory, the degradation of its inhabitants were now but a paradoxical signal of the Holy Land's imminent return to its pristine beauty in a transformation, or restoration, that would assume cosmic proportions: "Not only shall the Holy City be thus renovated, beautiful and blessed, but according to a covenant divinely ordered in all things and sure, every portion of the Holy Land, at least, (if not all the earth) shall be so far regenerated and delivered from the curse under which the whole creation groaneth and travaileth, that it shall yield its increase as it never has yet done since Adam and Eve first sinned. Even the brute creation shall become gentle as in the original Eden."[63]

Barclay cited numerous Old Testament prophecies of restoration, but he made Romans 11, a Pauline apocalypse disclosing the universal conversion of "all Israel," the keystone of his teleology.[64] He proposed two principal stages of the restoration: one partial, initiatory, effected by human intervention, and involving only the tribe of Judah; the other full and complete, by divine interposition, embracing the whole house of Israel.[65] Barclay furthermore mapped out the dramatic series of events that would unfold this scheme. First, the Jews, *yet unconverted*, would return to the Holy Land. The Jewish state in Palestine would thereupon be reestablished. A period of persisting recalcitrance and godlessness of the Jews ("or at least of their rulers") under the restored nation would ensue, followed by the time of judgment and repentance, and the conversion of responsive Jews. Converted Jews would join ranks to evangelize the world and help ingather the "fullness of the Gentiles" and lost Israelites, ushering in a millennial age in which the whole condition of nature and society would be ameliorated. At last the Redeemer would manifest himself at Zion; the ten lost tribes of Israelites would subsequently return to the Holy Land (if not yet fully converted, at least already convicted of their sin); and "all Israel" would be saved at Zion.[66] Strictly speaking, this was still a *postmillennial* scheme since it envisioned the millennium coming about through a gradual process of component events set in motion by human agency; but at the end of the millennial era, it would take nothing short of a bold apocalyptic intervention of Christ to bring the whole process to completion.[67] Most important at the moment for Barclay, this eschatological outline projected a victorious outcome for the mission of Jerusalem and explained his record to date of failing to convert Jews *en masse*. Timing was everything.

For now, as the conversion of the whole world hung on the "full inclusion" of the Jews (Rom. 11:12), and this inclusion or conversion of Israel hinged on an intermittent political restoration, all Gentile energies had to be focused on repatriating the Jews. Barclay pored over scriptural proof texts to verify the prophets' plain sanction of human instrumentality in the restoration, and to show how they all elucidated a single coherent plan for Christian intervention on behalf of Israel.[68] Yet the diversity, indeed the divergence, of the prophecies of restoration required imaginative correlation of the texts, not only with each other but with the current signs of the times. Barclay was confident that careful, inductive scrutiny of the literal meaning of these prophecies would demystify them and clarify any obscurities between their original purview and their contemporary fulfillment. Inevitably, however, even Barclay's assiduously "literal" interpretation tended toward occasional allegorisms. Thus, for example, in an exacting exegesis of Isaiah 18—which he stretched to include among the oracles of Israel's restoration—Barclay judged that the "land shadowing with wings, which is beyond the rivers of Ethiopia," the land "that sendeth ambassadors by sea," was none other than America, international peacemaker and asylum of the oppressed. The "gifts" offered to God, being that people "scattered and peeled . . . meted and trodden down . . . terrible from their beginning hitherto . . . whose land the rivers have spoiled" (Isa. 18:7) were the Jews, presented to God by America—not necessarily, that is, by the U.S. government per se but by a "large and efficient association" of Americans leading other international friends of Israel in the restoration enterprise.[69] "Expositors generally term this prophecy one of the most obscure in all the Living Oracles; but in my estimation," Barclay urged, "a greater degree of perspicuity would have been (heretofore at least) as useless as inconsistent with the character of such prophicies [sic]."[70]

Barclay's vision of the glorious horizons of Gentile participation in the restoration of Israel failed to capture the imagination of the Disciple of Christ sufficiently to sustain and prolong his work in Jerusalem. Financial constraints, the grim evangelistic picture, but most decisively the devastation of the ACMS by the Civil War, forced Barclay to leave his mission again in the summer of 1862. He temporarily undertook evangelistic work in London before returning to the United States in 1863. In 1865 he went back to Palestine with hopes of resurrecting the mission but returned to the United States for good later that year. He thereupon joined the faculty of Bethany College as a professor of natural sciences, and though his missionary and millenarian exploits would never figure prominently in future annals of Disciples history, Barclay actually came to enjoy a certain celebrity status among Disciples as their first pioneer in foreign missions.

Barclay's aborted mission in many respects typified the pattern of American Protestant evangelism in the Holy Land in this period. With missionary societies like the ACMS still fledglings, and the idea of such agencies (let alone of a Jewish mission) still new and scandalous to many, individual missionaries to the Jews were often left to fend for themselves, attempting to engineer the restoration of Israel without concerted denominational backing. The door was wide open to romantic and entrepreneurial ventures, as seen in various episodes of millenarian involvement in Palestine over the course of the nineteenth century.[71] Yet Barclay had always insisted, and still insisted in the years after his mission as he continued to espouse the imminent resurgence of Israel, that his eschatology was impeccably scientific, based on the harmony of scriptural and empirical evidences, and not to be linked with the rash miscalculations of Millerites, Mormons, and other deluded enthusiasts of the recent and distant past.[72] He was sure of having carefully negotiated a *via media* between the extremes of the "metaphorical-spiritualistic" and the "ultra literal" schools.[73]

Barclay's most serious miscalculation for the moment lay not in his hermeneutics so much as in presuming that Alexander Campbell and other key Disciple leaders would adopt a peculiar plan for the repatriation of the Jews as part and parcel of their missionary vision. Technically, as was noted above, Barclay had remained a postmillennialist like Campbell during the term of his mission work, promoting human initiative as a catalyst progressively to inaugurate the millennial age before Christ's second advent. Only after he returned home in disappointment and began serious study of apocalyptic texts like Daniel and Revelation did he roundly reject "a gradual introduction of a kind of Millennium of which so many are fondly dreaming" and, like other frustrated postmillennialists of the time, embrace a patently *premillennial* eschatology.[74] Nevertheless, in forcing the issue of the precise outworking and timing of millennial events, Barclay had overestimated the resolve of the Disciples of Christ to commit to any strict millenarian strategy for the Christian world mission. Disciple moderates like Isaac Errett had urged freedom of opinion in the interpretation of prophecies concerning the Jews and the end times and strongly warned against speculations that tended toward dogmatism and literalism. Politely mentioning Barclay as an "earnest, practical" expositor of prophecy who only intended to encourage faith, Errett nonetheless openly dissented from the quoted views of B. K. Smith, a devout admirer of Barclay's interpretations concerning the "destiny of Israel" and the Messiah's return at Jerusalem. As an officer of the ACMS committed to the Jerusalem mission, Errett could hardly have censured Barclay's eschatology directly and publicly; instead he did it indirectly and succinctly: "Our past reading and studies have led us to very different conclusions from those which bro. Smith has reached."[75]

From Barclay's perspective, on the other hand, the Disciples—whose scholars were among the strongest advocates of the Baconian "inductive method" applied in biblical interpretation—had lost some of their hermeneutical nerve.

Just when the science of biblical prophecy was reaching fruition and promising to unfurl the Christian future in ever clearer light, the Disciples among others were succumbing to the old patristic sin of spiritualizing the texts.[76] With no small hint of sarcasm Barclay told his readers, "But let whoever *may* fritter away the prophetic scriptures by such spiritualizing processes, surely the well-instructed 'Disciple of Christ,' who is endeavoring, by holding fast the form of sound words, rightly dividing the word of Truth, and walking in all the ordinances and commandments of the Lord blamelessly, to restore primitive apostolic Christianity to the world, will be the very last to practise upon a principle so subversive of the Truth as promulged [sic] by prophets and apostles!"[77] A year after Alexander Campbell's death in 1866, Barclay concluded that this "greatest and best of all men and reformers in post-apostolic times" had not taken prophecy seriously until it was too late. Henceforth the Disciples, zealous for the gospel but ignorant of prophecy, threatened to wrest the New dispensation from its crucial roots in the Old—a momentous criticism of an evangelical movement that had endorsed the authority of "the Bible" but thrown the bulk of its energies into recovering "*New Testament* Christianity."[78]

It is questionable whether Barclay's crusade on behalf of Israel had a legacy as such in the subsequent history of the Disciples of Christ. His word did not immediately spark any widespread millenarian revivals (though a strong premillennial movement later emerged among the offshoot Churches of Christ beginning in 1915); nor was it resumed in any fervent new commitment to Hebrew missions. In fact the most immediate effect of Barclay's labors was probably only to confirm some Disciple standard-bearers in their conscientious ambivalence toward the restoration of the Jews as a hermeneutical and eschatological issue. In 1867, even as Barclay was still publishing on prophecy and the future of Israel, Moses Lard, a stalwart Disciple conservative and premillennialist, announced that

> The return of the Jews to Judaea is with me far from being a postulate. It may be true; but if so, the evidence is not in my possession. In this surely no wish is felt to dogmatize. I am simply without faith, and hence can not give expression to it . . . That there are passages in the prophets which seem to teach Israel is to return to the ancient land I well know; but these passages may have been fulfilled in too many other events to justify us in confidently affirming that they point to a great Jewish return. Prophecy often has a double meaning. The same announcement may have two or even more fulfillments . . . In such cases it is difficult to say when its meaning is exhausted, and when it is to be no longer used. Those prophecies which are supposed to teach the universal return of the Jews may relate to other dispersions, partial or complete, and hence have been fulfilled in other returns long past. At least, to my mind, the mode of interpreting them is not sufficiently unerring to necessitate the conviction of a great general return of the Jews.[79]

If the "return" of the Jews figured among the millennial events at all, it surely would "not consist in restoring them, as Jews, to their former national prosperity, but in receiving them into the divine favor in virtue of their obedience to Christ."[80] Certainly the Messiah would not come again to Zion in a special epiphany on behalf of Israel, and when Paul spoke of "all Israel" being saved he could only have meant a "large number" of Jews coming to Christ along with their Gentile counterparts.[81] Empirically Lard found it hard to fathom a universal conversion of Jews when at the moment he saw so many of them "turning to *Rationalism,* not to Christ."[82]

At the turn of the century, the premier of conservative Disciple biblical scholars, J. W. McGarvey, still affirmed in the name of prophetic science that the repatriation at least of *converted* Jews would have to transpire in Palestine in the coming of the millennium. "If, at that time," he warned, "there still be left in the world any of the people now called Germans, French, British, and Americans, the question may no longer be, Why are the Jews yet with us? but Why are we yet with the Jews?"[83] The Disciples, however, were deaf to any bold new initiatives toward converting or repatriating the Jews. Progressives had already turned to other missionary and ecumenical horizons. Primitivists had spurned missionary agencies altogether. Deepening ideological schism in Disciple ranks, among other things over the biblical precedents for operating foreign missions, effectively thwarted prospects of any new direct involvements with Jews in Palestine. J. W. McGarvey (and the protofundamentalists of his time) now determined to support the Jews' own emerging Zionist movement as the likely providential means to their restoration and as an instrument of the consummation of history.[84] James Barclay and other pioneering Christian millenarians in the Holy Land could scarcely have imagined such a shift of perspective and strategy. Even this new outlook, however, gained no significant momentum among Disciples. Barclay's call to action on behalf of Israel remained unheeded.

NOTES

1. Naomi Shepherd, *The Zealous Intruders: The Western Rediscovery of Palestine* (San Francisco, 1987).

2. Ibid., 37–38, 229–57. See also Yehoshua Ben-Arieh, *Jerusalem in the Nineteenth Century: The Old City* (Jerusalem, 1984), 250–64.

3. A British consulate was not established in Palestine until 1839, and then other European governments followed suit. The American consulate commenced a turbulent and unstable tenure in Jerusalem in 1844, yet was not fully functional until 1857. See Shepherd, *The Zealous Intruders,* 107–31, 132–36; Vivian Lipman, "Britain and the Holy Land: 1830–1914," in *With Eyes Toward Zion,* ed. Moshe Davis and Yehoshua Ben-Arieh, vol. 3, *Western Societies and the Holy Land* (New York, 1991), 195–207.

4. Robert Healey, "Protestant American Missions to the Jews in the Nineteenth and Twentieth Centuries: From Conversion to Dialogue," *Miscellanea historiae ecclesiasticae* 7 (1985): 301–2; John Conway, "Protestant Missions to the Jews 1810–1980: Ecclesiastical Imperialism or Theological Aberration?" *Holocaust and Genocide Studies* 1 (1986): 128.

5. Levi Parsons, "The Dereliction and Restoration of the Jews" (sermon preached in Park Street Church, Boston, Oct. 31, 1819) (Boston, 1819), reprinted in *Holy Land Missions and Missionaries,* America and the Holy Land Series, ed. Moshe Davis (New York, 1977), 17–18. On the Parsons-Fisk mission in its millenarian context, see Neil Asher Silberman, *Digging for God and Country: Exploration, Archaeology, and Secret Struggle for the Holy Land, 1799–1917* (New York, 1982), 28–36.

6. Pliny Fisk, "The Holy Land: An Interesting Field of Missionary Enterprise" (sermon delivered in the Old South Church in Boston, Oct. 31, 1819) (Boston, 1819), reprinted in *Holy Land Missions and Missionaries,* 24–30.

7. Ibid., 28.

8. Ibid., 31.

9. Parsons, "The Dereliction and Restoration of the Jews," 10–14. On the broader context of early-nineteenth-century millenarian interest in the restoration of the Jews in the Holy Land, see Ernest R. Sandeen, *The Roots of Fundamentalism: British and American Millenarianism 1800–1930* (Chicago, 1970), 9–12, 20–22.

10. See Vivian Lipman, "America-Holy Land Material in British Archives, 1820–1930," in *With Eyes Toward Zion,* ed. Moshe Davis, vol. 2, *Themes and Sources in the Archives of the United States, Great Britain, Turkey and Israel* (New York, 1986), 26–29.

11. Moshe Davis, "The Holy Land Idea in American Spiritual History," in *With Eyes Toward Zion,* ed. Moshe Davis, vol. 1, *Scholars Colloquium on America-Holy Land Studies* (New York, 1977), 20.

12. See, for example, Robert T. Handy, ed., *The Holy Land in American Protestant Life, 1800–1948: A Documentary History* (New York, 1981), 83–89. Barclay unfortunately receives no mention in the important studies of Silberman, *Digging for God and Country,* and Shepherd, *The Zealous Intruders.*

13. For a brief biographical sketch of Barclay, see J. H. Garrison, ed., *The Reformation of the Nineteenth Century* (St. Louis, 1901), 134–39; also Norman Q. Grey, "Pioneering in Missions: Being a Biography of James Turner Barclay" (B.D. thesis, Butler Univ., 1944).

14. James T. Barclay to the Corresponding Secretary of the American Christian Bible Society (Oct. 5, 1849); Barclay to the Board of Managers of the ACMS (Oct. 30, 1849), compiled by D. S. Burnet, ed., *The Jerusalem Mission under the Direction of the American Christian Missionary Society* (Cincinnati, 1853; reprint, New York, 1977), 5–9.

15. Barclay, proposal for the Jewish mission, in Burnet, *Jerusalem Mission,* 12–14.

16. Ibid., 22.

17. See Parsons, "The Dereliction and Restoration of the Jews," 14–16; Fisk, "The Holy Land an Interesting Field," 32. On the broader millenarian interest in the "signs of the times" in early American Protestant missions, see Charles L. Chaney, *The Birth of Missions in America* (Pasadena, 1976), 274–78.

18. Barclay, proposal for the Jerusalem mission, in Burnet, *Jerusalem Mission,* 15–16.

19. See Alexander Campbell, "Converted Jews," *Millennial Harbinger* 5 (Dec. 1834): 616–19; cf. also W. K. Pendleton, "Book Notice on Henry Luria, or the Little Jewish Convert; or, Memoirs of Mrs. S. J. Cohen," *Millennial Harbinger,* 5th ser., vol. 3 (Dec. 1860): 715.

20. Barclay, proposal for the Jewish mission, in Burnet, *Jerusalem Mission,* 16–17.

21. Ibid., 16, 17–18, 23–24.

22. Early Disciple journals are full of excerpted periodical material from publications relating information about the current dispositions of the Jews, often with comments by the Disciple editors: see Alexander Campbell, "Notices of the Jews—Their Land and Destiny," 3 parts, *Millennial Harbinger,* 3d ser., vol. 6 (Feb. 1849): 85–88; (Mar. 1849): 146–49; (May 1849): 257–61; "The Israelite Indeed," *Millennial Harbinger,* 5th ser., vol. 2 (Jan. 1859): 42; "Number of Jews," *Millennial Harbinger,* 5th ser., vol. 4 (Dec. 1861): 687–89; "State of the Jewish Mind in the East," *Millennial Harbinger,* 5th ser., vol. 5 (Oct. 1862): 452–54; "The Present Condition and Aspirations of the Jews," *Millennial Harbinger,* 5th ser., vol. 6 (Mar. 1863): 132–34; Barton Stone, "Restoration of the Jews," *Christian Messenger* 14 (Dec. 1844): 272–74; features on the Jews entered in the *Christian Messenger* 4 (Apr. 1830): 127–28; (Oct. 1833): 319; Walter Scott, "Return of the Jews," *Evangelist,* n.s., 7 (Nov. 1839): 249–52; also "The Conversion of the Jews in Palestine," *Evangelist,* n.s., 8 (Apr. 1840): 84–87; "Prospects of the Jews," *Evangelist,* n.s., 8 (May 1840): 112.

23. See Alexander Campbell, "The Christian Missionary Society," no. 2, *Millennial Harbinger,* 3d ser., vol. 7 (Feb. 1850): 87; Letter to J. Barclay (Jan. 16, 1854), *Millennial Harbinger,* 4th ser., vol. 4 (Feb. 1854): 90–94; "Missionary Address," *Millennial Harbinger,* 5th ser., vol. 1 (Nov. 1858): 610–11; "An Address Delivered to the American Christian Missionary Society," *Millennial Harbinger,* 5th ser., vol. 3 (Nov. 1860): 607–8.

24. Barton Stone, "The Future Restoration of Israel," *Christian Messenger* 14 (July 1844): 84–87.

25. Mordecai Noah, "The Restoration of the Jews," reprinted in *Evangelist,* n.s., vol. 8 (Sept. 1840): 209–11; Noah, "Discourse on the Restoration of the Jews" (delivered at the Tabernacle, Oct. 28 and Dec. 2, 1844) (New York, 1845; reprint, 1977), 25, 28–33. Noah urged the Christian societies evangelizing Jews instead "to promote the restoration of the Jews in their unconverted state, relying on the fulfillment of the prophecies and the will of God for attaining the objects they have in view after that great advent shall have arrived." He broached Hebrew and even Christian prophecies (including Rom. 11:26; John 4:22) to the effect that the restoration of the Jews was a plain fact of Scripture. In turn, Protestants were to be good Protestants and heed Scripture at its word ("Discourse," 25, 29–33).

26. Walter Scott, "The Restoration of the Jews," 4 parts, *Evangelist* 1 (July 1832): 150–53; (Aug. 1832): 176–81; (Oct. 1832): 223–30; 2 (Jan. 1833): 13–15.

27. On Levi's religious Zionism, see Nahum Sokolow, *History of Zionism, 1600–1918* (1919; reprinted New York, 1969), 1:93–94; also R. H. Popkin, "The Age of Reason versus

the Age of Revelation. Two Critics of Tom Paine: David Levi and Elias Boudinot," in *Deism, Masonry, and the Enlightenment: Essays Honoring Alfred Owen Aldridge*, ed. J. Lemay (Newark, Del., 1987), 158–64.

28. Scott, "The Restoration of the Jews," no. 4, *Evangelist* 2 (Jan. 1833): 14; idem, "New Government and New Society," no. 7, *Evangelist*, n.s., vol. 9 (Dec. 1841): 169–70. See Sandeen, *The Roots of Fundamentalism*, 8–58, on George Stanley Faber and the upswing of prophetic studies among nineteenth-century millenarians. Walter Scott had apparently used Faber's work *Dissertation on the Prophecies, That Have Been Fulfilled, Are Now Fulfilling, or Will Hereafter be Fulfilled, Relative to the Great Period of 1260 Years* (London, 1804).

29. Scott, "The Restoration of the Jews," no. 1, *Evangelist* 1 (1832): 150–53; no. 3 (Oct. 1832): 223–30; no. 4, *Evangelist* 2 (Jan. 1833): 13–15. For him, the "gospel facts" were clear enough: the prophetic witness of Jewish restoration (Balaam in Num. 23–25; Moses in Deut. 4:28–30, 32) were not fulfilled after the Babylonian exile, but attested a future consummation in which the Jews would again return to the Holy Land; and Isaiah's prophecy of the ingathering of the Gentiles (Isa. 2:2–5) pointed to an orderly finale in which the converted Jews would join the Gentile Church under Christ's millennial reign. Scott anticipates 1833 as the date of the millennium's arrival in "The Restoration of the Jews," no. 4, *Evangelist* 2 (Jan. 1833): 13.

30. Scott, "New Government and New Society," no. 9, *Evangelist*, n.s., vol. 9 (Nov. 1841): 246; no. 10 (Dec. 1841): 265–66.

31. See Barclay, "The Welfare of the World Bound Up in the Destiny of Israel," no. 1, *Millennial Harbinger*, 5th ser., vol. 3 (Dec. 1860): 665.

32. On Campbell's millenarianism in context, see Richard T. Hughes, "From Primitive Church to Protestant Nation: The Millennial Odyssey of Alexander Campbell," in *Illusions of Innocence: Protestant Primitivism in America, 1630–1875*, ed. R. T. Hughes and C. L. Allen (Chicago, 1988), 170–87; see also Sandeen, *The Roots of Fundamentalism*, 45–46.

33. *A Debate on the Evidences of Christianity; A Debate between Robert Owen, of New Lanark Scotland, and Alexander Campbell, president of Bethany College, Virginia, Containing an Examination of the "Social System" and All the Systems of Skepticism of Ancient and Modern Times* (St. Louis, 1852), 328–29; for Barclay's quotation of Campbell, see "The Welfare of the World," no. 1, *Millennial Harbinger*, 5th ser., vol. 3 (Dec. 1860): 663.

34. Alexander Campbell, "Notices of the Jews—Their Land and Destiny," no. 1, *Millennial Harbinger*, 3d ser., vol. 6 (Feb. 1849): 85.

35. See already the work of Robert Milligan, "Prophecy," no. 11 (Conversion of the Jews), *Millennial Harbinger*, 4th ser., vol. 6 (Nov. 1856): 601–7. Milligan argued emphatically from Ezekiel and from Romans 11 for the repatriation of the Jews and the conversion of all fleshly Israel. Milligan even presumed to date the final conversion of the Jews for the year 1922. Campbell's approval of such efforts at a scientific eschatology thereupon appears in his "Articles on Prophecy," *Millennial Harbinger*, 5th ser., vol. 3 (Dec. 1860): 715–16; idem, "Prophecy," no. 1, *Millennial Harbinger*, 5th ser., vol. 3 (Mar. 1860): 126–27. For Campbell's criticism of exaggerated speculations, see "Millennium," *Millennial*

Harbinger, 4th ser., vol. 6 (Dec. 1856): 697–700; idem, "The Throne of David," *Millennial Harbinger*, 3d ser., vol. 6 (May 1849): 289.

36. Barclay, "The Welfare of the World," no. 1, *Millennial Harbinger*, 5th ser., vol. 3 (Dec. 1860): 663–65.

37. Barclay, Journal (Jan. 25, 1851), in Burnet, *Jerusalem Mission*, 112. Barclay's journal was also independently published as a *Narrative of the American Mission in Jerusalem*, 3 vols. (Cincinnati, n. d.).

38. Letter to the Secretary of the ACMS (Feb. 28, 1851), *Millennial Harbinger*, 4th ser., vol. 1 (June 1851): 344. Such first impressions of the wretchedness of Jerusalem were not uncommon with Western pilgrims and travelers to the Holy Land in this period, including the likes of Mark Twain and Herman Melville. See Shepherd, *The Zealous Intruders*, 174–75; Davis, "The Holy Land Idea," 13–14; Yehoshua Ben-Arieh, "Perceptions and Images of the Holy Land," in *The Land That Became Israel: Studies in Historical Geography*, ed. Ruth Kark (Jerusalem, 1990), 42.

39. Barclay, Letter to the Secretary of the ACMS (Feb. 28, 1851), *Millennial Harbinger* 4th ser., vol. 1 (June 1851): 344–45.

40. Yehoshua Ben-Arieh, "Patterns of Christian Activity and Dispersion in Nineteenth-Century Jerusalem," *Journal of Historical Geography* 2 (1976): 51; idem, *Jerusalem in the Nineteenth Century*, 274–75.

41. See Shepherd, *The Zealous Intruders*, 231.

42. See Barclay, Letter to Brother Crane (May 1, 1851), in Burnet, *Jerusalem Mission*, 168; Report to the ACMS Board (Oct. 13, 1851), in Burnet, *Jerusalem Mission*, 206–9.

43. Barclay, Letter to Brother Crane (May 1, 1851), in Burnet, *Jerusalem Mission*, 168–69. On the charitable activities of various Christian groups in Jerusalem in this period, see Ben-Arieh, "Patterns of Christian Activity," 49–69. On Protestant activities in particular, see idem, *Jerusalem in the Nineteenth Century*, 250–64.

44. Barclay, Letter to Brother Crane (May 1, 1851), in Burnet, *Jerusalem Mission*, 174–75.

45. Barclay, Letter to D. S. Burnet (Dec. 29, 1852), in Burnet, *Jerusalem Mission*, 279–83.

46. Barclay, Letter to Alexander Campbell (Aug. 27, 1853), *Millennial Harbinger*, 4th ser., vol. 4 (Jan. 1854): 8–9.

47. Ibid., 7.

48. Barclay, Letter to eastern Virginia supporters (Oct. 7, 1851), in Burnet, *Jerusalem Mission*, 198; Letter to Brother Crane (Oct. 13, 1851), in Burnet, *Jerusalem Mission*, 200–202.

49. Barclay, Letter to Brother Crane (May 1, 1851), in Burnet, *Jerusalem Mission*, 172; Letter to D. S. Burnet (Apr. 1, 1853), in Burnet, *Jerusalem Mission*, 317.

50. On the proposed asylum, see Barclay's reports in Burnet, *Jerusalem Mission*, 227–34, 263–64, 305–10, 314–16. See also Lipman, "America—Holy Land Material," 28–29.

51. Barclay, Report to the ACMS Board, in Burnet, *Jerusalem Mission*, 206.

52. James Turner Barclay, *The City of the Great King, or Jerusalem As It Was, As It Is, and As It Will Be* (Philadelphia, 1858). See also Jack Lewis, "James Turner Barclay: Explorer of

Nineteenth-Century Jerusalem," *Biblical Archaeologist* 51, no. 3 (Sept. 1988): 163–70; and Ben-Arieh, *Jerusalem in the Nineteenth Century.*

53. Barclay, Letter to Alexander Campbell (Aug. 27, 1853), *Millennial Harbinger,* 4th ser., vol. 4 (Jan. 1854): 6.

54. Barclay, Letter (addressee unnamed, Aug. 28, 1854), *Millennial Harbinger,* 4th ser., vol. 4 (Nov. 1854): 613.

55. Alexander Campbell, "The Missionary Cause," *Millennial Harbinger,* 4th ser., vol. 4 (Oct. 1854): 548.

56. On this schism, see Eileen Vandergrift, "The Christian Missionary Society: A Study in the Influence of Slavery on the Disciples of Christ" (master's thesis, Butler Univ., 1945), esp. 13–29.

57. Isaac Errett, ACMS Report, *Millennial Harbinger,* 5th ser., no. 1 (Dec. 1858): 676. Also in support, see Benjamin Franklin, "Dr. Barclay and the Jerusalem Mission," *American Christian Review* 1 (Nov. 1856): 347; idem, "A Letter from Jerusalem," *American Christian Review* 2 (Apr. 1857): 122–23.

58. Barclay, Letter to Isaac Errett (Jan. 15, 1860), *Millennial Harbinger,* 5th ser., vol. 3 (May 1860): 260.

59. ACMS report, Oct. 1859, *Millennial Harbinger,* 5th ser., vol. 2 (Dec. 1859): 696. The report continues: "As the eye of the Hebrew mother lingered about the spot where the infant Moses lay, amidst the perils of the Nile, so with the nurturing fondness of a true mother's heart, does the Church of Christ look to this tender child of hope, as the agent under God, in whom Israel shall yet find deliverance and the walls of Zion once more rise in the beauty of holiness."

60. Barclay, Letter to Isaac Errett (Jan. 15, 1860), *Millennial Harbinger,* 5th ser., vol. 3 (May 1860): 261–62, 264–65.

61. Barclay, "The Welfare of the World," no. 1, *Millennial Harbinger,* 5th ser., vol. 3 (Dec. 1860): 662–63. Barclay is quoting Alexander Campbell, *The Christian System,* 4th ed. (Bethany, Va., 1857), 104.

62. Barclay, "The Welfare of the World," no. 1, *Millennial Harbinger,* 5th ser., vol. 3 (Dec. 1860): 665.

63. Ibid., no. 2, *Millennial Harbinger,* 5th ser., vol. 4 (Jan. 1861): 8–9; ibid., no. 4 (Mar. 1861): 128.

64. Ibid., no. 2, *Millennial Harbinger,* 5th ser., vol. 4 (Jan. 1861): 10–14; ibid., no. 3 (Feb. 1861): 61–62, 65ff.

65. Ibid., no. 2, *Millennial Harbinger,* 5th ser., vol. 4 (Jan. 1861): 13–14.

66. Ibid., no. 3, *Millennial Harbinger,* 5th ser., vol. 4 (Feb. 1861): 65–69; no. 5, *Millennial Harbinger,* 5th ser., vol. 5 (May 1862): 241–43.

67. It is no great surprise to find postmillennial and premillennial viewpoints simultaneously in Barclay. Some historians point out in early American millenarian traditions a fluidity between broadly postmillennial and premillennial trends, between the vision of a gradual or progressive fulfillment of the millennium and the expectation of a decisive

divine intervention needed to alter the course of history. The crucial link between Puritan premillennialism and later Edwardsean postmillennialism, for example, was the insistence that the drama of the millennium would play itself out according to the "signs of the times" in American experience, and that, whatever the exact timing of Christ's second coming, the millennial fulfillment would be a process integrating divine and human agency alike (see Sacvan Bercovitch, "The Typology of America's Mission," *American Quarterly* 30 [1978]: 137–41). Only in the second half of the nineteenth century, especially after the Civil War, did the disparity between post- and premillennial eschatologies truly harden in American Protestantism (a change later to be observed in Barclay's own thinking).

68. Barclay, "The Welfare of the World," no. 4, *Millennial Harbinger*, 5th ser., vol. 4 (Mar. 1861): 122–28.

69. Ibid., no. 6, *Millennial Harbinger*, 5th ser., vol. 4 (June 1861): 301–6; cf. Mordecai Noah, "Discourse on the Restoration of the Jews," 46. By most accounts, Isaiah 18 is considered an oracle against Ethiopia that closes (vs. 7) on the hopeful note that someday the Ethiopians themselves will come to worship at Zion, bearing gifts for the Lord.

70. Ibid., 306. Great Britain also was to have an assisting role in the restoration of the Jews. In Barclay's interpretation of Isa. 60:9 ("Surely the isles wait for me and the ships of Tarshish first, to bring thy sons from afar, their silver and gold with them, unto the name of the Lord"), the "isles" are Britain, and the "ships of Tarshish" the British navy. A little more than a century earlier Jonathan Edwards had insisted that America herself, with her ships and her unique mission, not Britain, was the referent of this text. See his *Thoughts Concerning the Present Revival of Religion* (1742), as excerpted in *God's New Israel: Religious Interpretations of America's Destiny*, ed. Conrad Cherry (Englewood Cliffs, N.J., 1971), 55–56.

71. The stories of millenarian entrepreneurs in the Holy Land are extensive. Cf. Shepherd, *The Zealous Intruders*, 228–57; Ruth Kark, "Millenarism and Agricultural Settlement in the Holy Land in the Nineteenth Century," *Journal of Historical Geography* 9 (1983): 47–62; and David Klatzker, "American Christian Travelers to the Holy Land, 1821–1939," in *With Eyes Toward Zion*, vol. 3, *Western Societies and the Holy Land*, esp. 67–68.

72. See Barclay, "Prophecy," no. 2, *Millennial Harbinger* 38 (Feb. 1867): 70–72.

73. See ibid., no. 4, *Millennial Harbinger* 38 (Mar. 1867): 222.

74. See ibid., 217–22 (Barclay offers here a wholly revised outline of the millennial events, commencing with the descent of Jesus as a thief in the night). On the theory that despondent postmillennialists sometimes turned into devout premillennialists because of the crushing circumstances of the Civil War, social change, etc. (or in Barclay's case, frustrations on the mission field), see Donald Dayton, *Theological Roots of Pentecostalism* (Grand Rapids, 1987), 158–63.

75. See Isaac Errett, "The Study of Prophecy," *Millennial Harbinger*, 5th ser., vol. 4 (July 1861): 410–12.

76. See Barclay, "Prophecy," no. 1, *Millennial Harbinger* 38 (Jan. 1867): 30–35; no. 2, (Feb. 1867): 64–69; no. 6 (July 1867): 337–42.

77. Ibid., no. 6, *Millennial Harbinger* 38 (July 1867): 342.

78. Ibid., no. 1, *Millennial Harbinger* 38 (Jan. 1867): 34–35.

79. Moses Lard, "O. [E. E. Orvis] on the Editor's Theory of the Millennium," *Lard's Quarterly* 4 (July 1867): 306, 307–8; cf. idem, "The State of the World at the Coming of Christ," *Lard's Quarterly* 5 (Apr. 1868): 151–56. David Lipscomb, Lard's younger contemporary, also a premillennialist, confessed a similar pious ignorance about the destiny of the Jews: "We do not know when their condition will change, or whether it ever will in this world. Some passages seem to indicate that it will change and that they will bear a prominent and efficient part in the conversion of the world. But then we do not know but that these passages refer to spiritual Israel instead of fleshly Israel. Other passages seem to indicate they will not be converted. We do not know when the fulness of the Gentiles will come, or what it is or will be. We have but little faith in our own interpretation of prophecy, and cannot help our brother any on these subjects" ("The Condition of the Jews," *Gospel Advocate* [1874]: 202).

80. Moses Lard, *Commentary on Romans* (Lexington, Ky., 1876), 359; cf. 371: "The future salvation of Israel does not imply their restoration to their ancient homeland in Palestine. The former is a great necessity, the latter is none. When converted, the Jews can be just as happy, dispersed as they now are, as though they were all crowded back into Judea; and certainly they can be far more useful. The gospel is not designed to prepare men for an earthly Canaan, but for a heavenly."

81. Ibid., 371.

82. Lard, "The State of the World at the Coming of Christ," 153. Lard was at last willing to claim, even without express scriptural support, that "all expectations . . . that the condition of the world is to be greatly altered for the better by the Jews may be dismissed. It will never be realized. We are hence still left to the conclusion that at the second coming of Christ the world will be about as it is at present, no better, no worse" (156).

83. J. W. McGarvey, "Why Are the Jews Yet with Us?" *Christian Standard* 39 (May 1903): 660, 696.

84. Ibid., 696. On the larger shifts of eschatological thinking that induced protofundamentalists to invest their hopes in "political Zionism," see David Rausch, *Zionism within Early American Fundamentalism* (New York, 1979), esp. 53–146.

Mainline Women Ministers

Women Missionary and Temperance Organizers Become "Disciples of Christ" Ministers, 1888–1908

Glenn Michael Zuber

Tracing the formation and expansion of national women's societies at the end of the nineteenth century provides a particularly incisive look at the more general upheaval in American society that was gradually changing established notions of "woman's sphere." The strength and influence of these societies were among the reasons that a small number of women were able to become ordained Protestant ministers. In the last few decades of the nineteenth century, changes in gender relations mirrored the intellectual and social turmoil among Protestants caused by Darwinism, "higher criticism" of the Bible, and the burgeoning cities and their attendant problems. Increased urbanization, northern prosperity, and expanding transportation networks after the Civil War, furthermore, were particularly important for the history of middle- and upper-middle-class, native-born Euro-American women.[1]

The greater ease with which women gathered in large numbers after the Civil War on matters of common concern, in part, created the means by which national women's organizations formed a popular voice and worked with various degrees of success, and with differing agendas, toward the end of improving women's status and expanding the presence of women in society. Temperance, missionary, and suffrage organizations competed for the time and loyalty of Protestant women across the country and among the farming middle and upper-middle classes. The new conventions in women's roles, brought by outside social trends and internal reformers, created a conducive environment for most Protestant church bodies to debate the position of women, especially in the late 1880s and early 1890s, and a powerful enough impetus for several smaller church bodies to approve women's ordination, although few women actually became ministers.[2]

Of the larger "mainline" Protestant churches—those denominations historically more powerful and broadly representative than other bodies—the Congregationalists, Northern Baptist Convention, and Christian Churches (Disciples of Christ) counted a small number of women in their ordained ministries by 1900.[3] As a large Protestant church that also ordained women at the turn of the century, the Disciples present an excellent case study of a mainline church that struggled to maintain the distinction between the sexual spheres as women in various reform movements employed, ironically, the "separate spheres" ideology themselves to justify their public activism and their emergence within Disciple denominational life in positions, such as evangelists and preachers, previously reserved for men. In the end, several institutions and actors reconfigured the denomination's gender ideology and fostered the rise of women ministers: the Women's Christian Temperance Union (WCTU), a denominational women's missionary society (the Disciples' own Christian Woman's Board of Missions), and individual Disciple women reformers. The denomination and reformers in the women's missionary society compromised their respective versions of the ideology of the separate spheres, which resulted in temporary extensions of the traditional "woman's sphere" to include the pulpit for numerous Disciple women. However, these compromises failed to permanently alter that traditional sphere.

The ecclesial debate over the role of women in public, begun at the end of the Civil War, determined the social conventions in which women preached twenty and thirty years later. Women experienced new freedom to organize and exert collective influence as a result of the North's postwar prosperity, expanding transportation networks, and urbanization. Disciples debated the desirability and significance of this new freedom of women. In the 1870s, Disciple women possessed many new avenues and a new freedom to enter the public eye through organizing and speaking at Sunday school, temperance and missionary meetings, and conventions.[4] Northern Protestants were forced to debate a new question: why was public speaking by women now acceptable while preaching was still prohibited? In 1872 Isaac Errett, an influential Disciple and editor of the *Christian Standard,* argued that a woman was still prohibited from preaching because it presumed unwarranted authority; such an act would subvert the social order, her marriage, and the home. A woman's preaching would also cause social scandal. More fundamental, preaching and governing were masculine "faculties"; women's abilities and skills lay in giving the more emotional exhortations and prayers, both termed by Errett as "the language of the heart," in Disciple prayer meetings.[5] Fellow editor E. Goodwin of the *Christian* believed that women should be prohibited from exerting authority, but he did not believe that all types of preaching exerted the prohibited authority. Goodwin wrote in

1875 that women could speak for "the edification and comfort of saints, and for the conversion of sinners" as long as they did not speak "in a manner, or under circumstances that would indicate a desire to rule over the man, or a want of regard for her husband's authority." He defined improper speaking as "having reference to governmental matters in the church." Such speaking was the domain of the church elders.[6] Thus, while promoting a greater freedom for women to speak publicly, the northern editors still maintained the need to preserve intact the relative spheres of men and women. In contrast with northern Disciples and their editors, southern Disciples under the leadership of editor David Lipscomb and the *Gospel Advocate* continued to hold that any public presence of women, whether from a convention rostrum or church pulpit, was an unwarranted assumption of masculine authority.[7]

Between the 1870s and 1890s a consensus formed among most Disciples that allowed women to speak in public for the cause of the growing WCTU or to further support their own denominational women's missionary society, the Christian Woman's Board of Missions (CWBM), but not to preach on a biblical text and exert institutional authority. Yet the acceptance of women's public speaking developed unevenly even within the Disciples. Although women's lecturing and speaking in prayer meetings had been accepted for more than twenty years by the 1890s in some Christian Churches, many other Disciple women and men continued to oppose what they considered the unwomanly desire on the part of some women to speak in prayer meetings and participate in the CWBM. Conflicts over women speaking in prayer meetings continued into the 1890s and beyond. The debate over women's public speaking tapered off among southern Disciples when large numbers of their churches, calling themselves the Churches of Christ, broke away from the main body of Disciples during the 1890s and early 1900s.[8]

This differentiation of women's speaking from regular preaching explains why women were allowed to start speaking at conventions in 1874 for the cause of the CWBM, while most Disciples still condemned women's preaching. A mere two years after Errett had condemned women's public praying in church services and women's preaching, he himself offered a successful resolution of support for the new Christian Woman's Board of Missions at the 1874 General Christian Missionary Convention after four CWBM women delivered addresses from the platform.[9] Those Disciples who accepted women's lecturing did so apparently because such speaking appeared to fit into the category of exhortation rather than preaching—women who lectured presumed no institutional authority. Because the Disciple women who began speaking in public did not directly challenge their subordinate position in the church, Disciples who supported the popular mission and temperance crusades came to endorse CWBM and WCTU speakers in the late 1870s. For their own part, the Disciple women who led the CWBM spoke in public themselves while endorsing female modesty. In 1896 Mrs. Marie Jameson, a CWBM leader, recalled "those who looked askance at the new [CWBM] movement" did so based on the perception that CWBM women "propose[d] taking possession of the pulpit." Such opposition had been won over to the side of the CWBM because "it became manifest that we were trying to behave as becoming women professing godliness, and that we did not propose taking possession of the pulpit."[10]

The fact that the first Disciple women preachers mostly came from the WCTU and CWBM heavily influenced the history of these women's ministries; indeed, the organizations made that history possible.[11] Most of the first Disciple women preachers arose from the dedicated troupe of speakers and lecturers who extended the influence and effectiveness of the women's temperance and missionary organizations such as the WCTU and CWBM. A smaller number of women preachers first had been preachers' wives. The emergence of Disciple women preachers from the CWBM and WCTU was indicative of the women's solid middle-class, Euro-American backgrounds. A relatively high amount of leisure time, a product of the labors of their professional or middle-class husbands (including preaching husbands) or their own school teaching enabled many of these women to devote enormous amounts of time to the CWBM and WCTU—often without remuneration. Some graduated from teacher training institutions, others from four-year church colleges. The prominent position most women held before preaching, that of "organizer," was the title given to CWBM women who were elected or appointed to organize new auxiliaries and infuse declining ones with new energy. At times, organizing auxiliaries was also the duty of a CWBM or WCTU secretary or president at the county or state level when funds were short or their positions included that responsibility.[12]

The WCTU and CWBM were the primary voices for women to assume a greater position in local and denominational affairs. The organizer was foremost an effective lecturer and communicator of these goals. Lecturers gave addresses designed to attract large audiences and impart an enthusiasm for the temperance and foreign mission causes. One CWBM leader stated the purpose of an organizer was "not merely giving information regarding the work, but she must give instruction that awakens, arouses and sets on fire the many indifferent women of our land, consumes them even—consumes self, indifference, lethargy—and then recreates them—makes them new women in Christ."[13]

Lecturers often challenged the limits set on women's work in the church. Noting the effect the foreign mission cause had on American women, Ella M. Huffman observed that the CWBM's "influence and worth" could "not . . . be measured by the money value of bungalows and chapels, hospitals and college chairs, but by the advancing place of women in the widening circles of spiritual culture, not in India, Japan, and Jamaica alone—but in our own Christian

America, the result of its reflex influence."[14] In an effort to further its "reflex influence," women lecturers poignantly questioned if American Protestant women, considering all the contemporary cultural and ecclesial prohibitions hindering their work, truly enjoyed more freedom than the non-Western women they sought to reform and convert on the mission field.[15] Other women questioned how committed their fellow Protestants were about reforming America on Protestant principles if they as women, and therefore society's caretakers of morality, were limited in what leadership they could exert. One organizer reasoned that "though few women may desire to enter the pulpit, yet while they are prohibited every moral message they utter suffers depreciation." Furthermore, an obvious incongruity existed between saying churchwomen were valued work partners of men and Disciples not supporting women in the pulpit. According to one reformer, "This *prohibition* [against women's preaching] . . . is a *mark* of *woman's subjection* [to men]."[16]

Although the CWBM and WCTU did not deliberately seek to train women to become preachers, many aspects of women's "organizing" prepared them effectively to fill that role. The two most important tasks of an organizer was speaking and training women leaders; organizers performed these tasks relying on the time-proven methods and nomenclature used by Protestant ministers. Women frequently recognized that their work resembled that of regular evangelists or missionaries. When speaking of the organizer's responsibility, one CWBM lecturer wrote: "An Organizer should not be expected to raise money, but to act as a missionary to the needy places—to sow the seed. The most permanent work done by an Organizer (and the same is true of an Evangelist) is not always, if ever, the work that makes the largest showing when tabulated."[17] The work done by woman organizers was often equated to the work done by men evangelists in other ways as well. For example, organizers for the WCTU were called "WCTU Evangelists,"[18] just as women who organized Sunday schools were "Sunday school Evangelists." Perhaps even more ambiguously, a woman lecturer "solicited" her audience to "come forward" to join or form a WCTU or CWBM chapter. Although the person in the audience did not convert to Christianity, the whole process mimicked the common scene of revivalists urging the "unbelievers" in their midst to "come forward" to be saved.

The practical skills which had to be developed in order for the organizer to win the loyalty of indifferent or mildly skeptical audiences were similar to talents men developed for the pastorate. For example, the organizer had to have a strong, clear voice. Like a preacher, the organizer could not be soft-spoken or self-conscious when in front of people. Organizer Mary Lyons recommended, "A woman who expects to stand before the public should have a voice that can be heard by the entire audience. If, by nature, she has not a strong, clear voice, then by careful training [she must] obtain it."[19] Women who became organizers had to overcome not only opposition to their speaking in public but their own insecurities. The State Organizer of South Dakota, Mrs. Millie Vercoe, commented in 1902: "The terrible feeling of shyness was hard to fight against. I am learning what others have learned in the past—how to speak in public. These difficulties have been, and are to be[,] overcome."[20]

Although some churches did not allow organizers to speak to the whole congregation, others allowed them to speak from the pulpit during Sunday services. Such a development blurred distinctions between preaching and missionary speaking and represented an important step in the acceptance of women's preaching. Mary A. Lyons, one the most effective and aggressive CWBM organizers, reported in 1894 that as Ohio state organizer she visited one district at a time, organizing new auxiliaries and invigorating moribund ones. Along with District officers, Lyons thoroughly canvassed the district—she visited interested women, delivered addresses, held women's meetings, and "fill[ed] the pulpit on Sunday in most instances."[21]

Yet CWBM and WCTU lectures, even when delivered during Sunday services, were not usually confused with sermons. Women lecturers followed conventions that demonstrated to audiences they were not preaching. By the 1890s most Disciples confronted women speaking in public; the defining difference between the hundreds of women speaking, and the tens preaching, apparently was the degree of authority the women exerted over their audiences. Women presumed varying levels of authority according to the theme on which they chose to speak, whether or not they asked for non-Christians to convert under their speaking, and the number of weeks they spoke at a particular church. Even so, women did cross the line between speaking and preaching, at times intentionally, at other times unintentionally.

The first reason a CWBM or WCTU lecturer's speech was not usually considered "preaching" by many Disciples in the 1890s was because she spoke on the missionary or temperance cause, not exclusively on a Scripture. The addresses were perceived more as exhortations designed to convey information than expositions of a biblical text. The second reason CWBM and WCTU speaking was not preaching stemmed from the fact that women speakers did not exert authority by asking members of the audience who were not Christians to become Christians. One CWBM organizer unhappily noted that a woman could "stand behind the mechanical contrivance called a pulpit, and declare the unsearchable riches of Christ and plead with Christians to do their duty to sinners at home and abroad, but if she were then and there to call the sinners in her very presence to come to Christ, she would be transgressing what some regard [as] Paul's law of silence."[22] The third reason women speakers were not considered preachers was their limited time at speaking in any one particular church. By the early 1890s, it was common for women to speak during the Sunday service to promote the

CWBM and WCTU. They did not exert much authority, however, because their presence was transitional; they only spoke one week on the missionary cause during an allocated time in the Sunday service. They stepped down from the pulpit after their lecture and the next week the regular ministers preached. These three conventions—pertaining to how Scripture was used, whether listeners were asked to convert, and how many Sundays a woman spoke at one church—allowed women to speak from the pulpit without preaching, yet even then speakers could easily and unknowingly transgress them. In time, a few women developed a reputation for lecturing more on biblical texts or their audience's need for conversion than on the missionary or temperance causes.

These temporary CWBM and WCTU speaking engagements had three important effects on women's roles in the Disciples. First, through these speaking engagements women started to have a more public presence in the church. Not surprisingly, controversy over women's roles began between 1888 and 1893 in the largest Disciple papers, the *Gospel Advocate, Christian Standard,* and *Christian-Evangelist,* as more and more CWBM and WCTU women spoke from Disciple pulpits. Ruth Bordin argues that the controversy over women's roles in Protestant churches peaked around the year 1892, when the WCTU was reaching a peak in membership and power. Although Bordin does not mention the fact, Protestant women's missionary societies were also expanding at an unprecedented rate.[23] Second, women lecturers dispelled the widely held notion that women, as the "weaker sex," were not physically capable of speaking in public as were men. Evangelist A. P. Terrell, writing just before Disciple women became prominent lecturers, offered, "The voice of women is well adapted to talking baby-talk, soothing and comforting man in his hours of sorrow and trouble, and singing the Lord's songs; but for public speaking everyone knows it is a failure."[24] Third, many women lecturers proved themselves to be such powerful speakers that they gave the impression that they were preachers even though they were not. In fact, the history of Disciple women preachers was often one of lecturers giving speeches of such moving eloquence that they were encouraged, sometimes unexpectedly, either to remain at a church as their pastors or to become itinerant evangelists.

Positive responses to women's lecturing disproved the claim that social scandal would occur if women preached. From the 1870s to the 1890s, the expected resistance to women preachers was held up as important proof that both God and society were against women's preaching. One Disciple editorial sternly warned that "every woman therefore to-day that is . . . preaching publicly . . . is living, moving[,] acting and working in rebellion against God. Such women at once lose the respect of Bible loving people."[25] In actuality, CWBM, Sunday school, and WCTU organizers frequently found their lectures so popular that the response encouraged them to think about preaching.

Yet the arguments women used to cross over from lecturing into preaching also limited future opportunities for other women to become preachers. That most women first originated in the WCTU and CWBM suggests the importance of those organizations for women, but it also suggests the narrow opening available for women to become preachers. The obstacles that confronted potential women preachers remained so pervasive that only a few women, and mostly temperance and missionary lecturers, overcame the strong barriers that most others could not scale. For example, women lecturers became preachers only after proving themselves as spectacular speakers. While the men who were interested in becoming ministers received approval and opportunities for preaching from churches and other ministers, and for a small number of cases received some measure of formal theological education or training to develop their preaching abilities, women proved their persuasive pulpit skills before gaining a conditional approval from churches. Virtually the only acceptable forum for developing such speaking skills was found in the WCTU and CWBM.

The experiences of several women as organizers illuminate the reasons why some believed CWBM organizers were preaching, not just "lecturing," despite their lack of ordination, institutional authority, and official title. Francis "Birdie" Farrar (1874–1970) was twenty-two years old and single when she became organizer of the Virginia CWBM in 1896. At one place on her speaking tour, Farrar noted, "Many, I knew, had come from curiosity to hear what a woman had to say, for, in some parts of Virginia, the people think it very strange to hear a woman speak in public."[26] Often in the mountain churches she visited, people in the audience asked their neighbors, "Do she preach? Do she take a text?" The mountaineers wondered about the nature of Farrar's speaking. Was she preaching on a biblical text or merely exhorting the faithful?[27]

Farrar's experiences indicate that women's speaking could easily give the impression of preaching. Even as Farrar complied with unspoken rules about women's speaking, her audience still wondered if she was preaching; not only that, but she herself believed her speaking conformed to an understanding of preaching. To the common question asked by mountaineers, Farrar believed that, "Yes, she did take a text." She was "like hundreds of our other women going from coast to coast." Farrar understood her CWBM message as a special charge for women in her audience, for she told her audiences that "it was a woman who first carried tidings of the Risen Lord, and ever since Mary Magdalene gave that first joyous message[,] coming down through all the ages, women would continue to tell the old story until every knee should bow and every tongue confess Jesus as Lord to the glory of God the Father."[28] Thus, one can see the relative ease with which an organizer could theoretically preach in certain situations as long as she was not planning to stay long and did not ask audience members to convert.

When George T. Smith wrote in support of women's preaching in 1892 by citing the various kinds of public speaking and teaching Disciple women already performed with full approval, he revealed in the process how often women spoke from pulpits. Along with Sunday school teaching and missionary work, he listed women who "spoke" during the Sunday service in place of the regular preacher when he was absent and "occup[ied] the pulpit for a man when there is no preacher, and (even if she have no call to preach) the people have a call to hear her." Smith then asked of those who objected to women in ministry: "If any, how many of the above are permissible; why so, and how are they to be reconciled with Paul's declaration?"[29] A Wisconsin CWBM organizer in the mid-1890s, Isabelle Goodacre once recalled that "I was state organizer . . . and preached or spoke in all our Churches scattered over Wis." Goodacre apparently saw nothing wrong with herself preaching and found no difficulty preaching her sermons before churches as a CWBM lecturer. These ambiguous conventions allowed organizers to preach sermons but also stopped short of encouraging women to become long-term pastors. Organizers such as Farrar and Goodacre accepted the rules that restrained them from completing the transition from organizer to preacher. Only in the 1920s did the Disciple yearbook list Farrar with her husband as ministers of a church. Farrar first joined the CWBM to organize and strengthen CWBM auxiliaries, not to preach. Similarly, Goodacre only began regular preaching and received ordination when her husband's failing health in 1903 forced her to seek remunerative work.[30]

Occasionally, popular CWBM organizers more intentionally crossed the ambiguous line between women's speaking and regular preaching. By introducing revivalistic preaching in their lectures and presuming a certain authority, a few organizers not only informed audiences of the Disciple missionary cause but also performed missionary works themselves. Mrs. Clara H. Hazelrigg of Kansas (1859–1937) went further than mere speaking in her 1897 touring schedule when she asked members of her audience to convert under her preaching. Of Hazelrigg's 125 addresses that year, a contemporary noted that "she has frequently had confessions at the close of her addresses." Hazelrigg received ordination the same year and started holding revivals as a regular evangelist.[31]

The early experiences of CWBM organizers Farrar and Hazelrigg suggest that being mistaken as a regular preacher while organizing work was an important step in leading them to become preachers in their own right. The record of other early women preachers make this connection between initial positive reactions of audiences and becoming ministers clear; the initial authority to preach came from the positive reactions of audiences. Mrs. Clara C. Babcock (1850–1925), Whiteside County WCTU president, became a preacher in an Erie, Illinois, church because of a chance speaking engagement in 1888. The only record of Babcock's reasons for being in Erie that day is found in a 1915 *History of the Disciples in Illinois.* The author explained that after Babcock joined the Disciples from the Methodists,

> she went out into the service of the W.C.T.U. in Illinois. Being in Erie on a Sunday, she was induced to speak to the Christian congregation in the forenoon. The presence and approval of God were so manifest that she was led to continue in the service of that congregation. Later, after wise consel and mature deliberation, she was ordained to the Christian ministry in 1888.[32]

Although the specific reasons which "induced" Babcock to speak to the Erie Christian Church are vague, one can presume that Babcock was in Erie to speak for the WCTU. At the very least, the evidence indicates that Babcock happened to be in Erie, the church needed a sermon (or at least a speaker), and Babcock gave a sermon (or a WCTU lecture) impressive enough that the "presence and approval of God were . . . manifest" to her hearers. Finally, the one speech resulted in the church asking her to continue preaching from their pulpit.

While it is unclear whether Babcock preached or gave a WCTU lecture, it is doubtful she would have been asked to speak had she not been president of the Whiteside County WCTU. At the very least, her WCTU responsibilities developed her speaking abilities and earned her the respect of temperance supporters, of which Disciples (along with most U.S. Protestants) tended to be an enthusiastic part. Babcock had been organizing WCTU auxiliaries since at least July 1887, at which time she presided over the WCTU convention, where she was reelected president of the county WCTU. She reported holding forty-eight meetings in churches and schoolhouses and obtaining 148 new total-abstinence pledges.[33] Similarly, Illinois school teacher Sadie McCoy (1863–1948), almost by accident, became an evangelist while "lecturing" before a Sunday school in 1892. An unplanned revival followed one person's desire to convert at the conclusion of one of her addresses. McCoy would often tell future parishioners how "she was led from a school teacher to a temperance lecturer and Sunday school worker, never dreaming that she would become a 'Preacher of the Gospel.'" She became one of the more prolific evangelists and pastors during the next fifty years.[34]

Exceptional speaking ability was not the only reason congregations encouraged women to become preachers; low attendance and weak finances also led churches to ask women to preach for short periods of time. By the 1890s, organizers reported through the CWBM's *Missionary Tidings* that the problems of the scores of small churches across the South and Midwest had to be addressed if the CWBM was to continue to grow in numbers of auxiliaries and members. The CWBM had already established auxiliaries in the large urban churches, the easiest churches in which to organize auxiliaries—churches able to support a minister, capable of maintaining a stable membership, and located within the growing U.S. transportation network of railroads and well-traveled roads. The forward momentum of the CWBM had to be maintained by strengthening weak auxiliaries and establishing new ones in marginal churches with few resources to spare. Both the CWBM and the struggling church needed the potential resources of the other. WCTU and CWBM organizers possessed the practical experience of establishing new chapters and training volunteers to run the women's societies efficiently. Women organizers, in turn, acknowledged that the problems of struggling churches needed to be addressed and remedied before a healthy women's society was established. Mrs. Ella Beck reported: "It is very hard indeed to get a small band of women to see the need of missionary work when they have neither church home nor preacher. I find it very hard to start new work in a homeless or pastorless congregation." [35] Many organizers wanted to remedy the problems in struggling churches in order to indirectly strengthen CWBM auxiliaries or lay the groundwork for new auxiliaries. Organizer Mrs. Laura Gerould Craig commented, "The Organizer must give attention to the difficult problems of the Church as well as the Auxiliaries." [36] In 1902 and 1903, Mrs. Louise Kelly reported that as national organizer "much time has been spent in seeking to infuse new life and hope in discouraged churches and sowing the seed in virgin soil." During her term she visited thirty-two churches, gave thirty-six "public addresses," addresses to the men and women of the congregation, but had only visited sixteen auxiliaries.[37] Marginal churches served as fertile ground for training women pastors.

Struggling churches needed organizers to survive. Bertha C. Mason (1876–1959), a former CWBM missionary teacher in Mexico, served her second term as secretary and organizer (1902–8) of the Texas CWBM while preaching at several struggling churches. The character of these churches was revealed in a 1937 comment: "I have held many small pastorates in both Texas and Arkansas. Usually churches no one would have." Other women combined regular preaching with their duties as state superintendents of the CWBM's Young People's Department. For example, Daisy Schultz served as regional superintendent for the Inland Empire (north Idaho and east Washington) while performing pulpit supply as an ordained preacher.[38]

The ways prominent women preachers and supporters justified their position, or did not justify them, unintentionally limited opportunities for other women. A woman's authority to preach derived more from convincing other Disciples that all possible efforts should be employed to convert people than by claiming women and men possessed equal talents in ministry. Supporters of women's preaching often did not directly concern themselves with justifying a woman's right to preach or explain how the limits on women's preaching were in and of themselves undesirable. Rather, the few women who wrote defenses of their preaching concentrated on how more women in ministry would alleviate the pressing needs of the day. Virginia Hedges, Missouri CWBM organizer, told ministers, "The time is past when we are afraid of Sunday-school, missionary societies and Aid Societies . . . God speed the time when we are ready to use every agency for the furthering of Christ's kingdom." When so many people remained "unsaved" in the world, women were justified in preaching. Evangelist Clara Hazelrigg noted that "when defeat seems near, God's reinforcement saves the day." Women were the reinforcements that would *"help those men* to take the world for Christ."[39] Drawing on the assumption that women were naturally disinterested reformers and better moral examples than men, some women preachers asserted that the Prohibition cause would be victorious if more women were allowed to enter the ministry. Clara Hazelrigg claimed that when women preached, the day would come when the church could effectively "declare the saloon business to be outlawed by man and accursed of God, and that by his grace it must be swept off the earth." Conversely, if women could not preach, Virginia Hedges warned that though "few women may desire to enter the pulpit, yet while they are prohibited, every moral message they utter suffers depreciation."[40]

Well-known women Disciple preachers and lecturers revealed a telling aspect of their role among Disciples when they supported their ministry by citing the moral and political causes it furthered. While antebellum women itinerants preached in the face of family hostility, self-doubts, and public condemnation, Disciple women proved their acceptability by their popularity with audiences. Indeed, the latter often became preachers because of their popularity, not because of the dramatic religious experiences on which the former relied to defy accepted conventions. Of the few defenses made for women's preaching, most sidestepped the question of authority by claiming that since the gospel itself converted hearers, rather than the preacher, women could preach. Millie W. Mason, a former Australian lecturer, reported to *Christian Standard* readers that the famous revivalist who first convinced her to preach informed her that since "it was the 'gospel,' and not the preacher, that was the 'power of God unto salvation,' my ability to preach it (which has since then been demonstrated in Oklahoma) and my desire to serve God thereby was all the authority I needed."[41] The arguments of Disciple women preachers demonstrated that the society in which Disciple women preached was more open to their ministry than it had been in previous eras. They gained acceptance through promoting accepted women's causes, like temperance, not in defying the conventional roles of women.[42] This appeal succeeded for a time, but since the ideology underlying those conventions which restricted women from the pulpit remained largely untouched, regular preaching remained the domain of few women.

Despite their new status as popular preachers, women maintained their position in the Disciple ministry only with great difficulty. Disciple churches never granted women preachers the necessary institutional authority to consolidate and maintain their position in local congregations. To begin with, Disciples never held a high theology of the ordained ministry as in other Protestant communions. Disciples, unique among mainline Protestants, held that lay elders ruled the church while the position of the preacher remained ambiguous. At times, ministers acted in the capacity of elders, at other times, ministers served under the authority of the lay elders. Thus while women relied on their pulpit magnetism to establish their authority to preach, male preachers relied on their institutional, legal, and scriptural prerogatives as men, husbands, and church elders. These significant caveats to women's new public presence meant that Disciples perceived women's preaching as a new and temporary role for a few women—but not a radical, threatening, or often permanent one for many. Before 1912 the denominational yearbook did not list ministers with their churches. Therefore, one cannot be certain how many women held pastorates before 1912. Disciple yearbooks between 1907 and 1912 do contain a list of "Women Preachers," yet this list of preachers included women who did not preach regularly. These "women preachers" were primarily singing evangelists, CWBM leaders, preachers' wives, and evangelistic helpers. Although only fifteen women are known to have preached regularly during this period, instances of women preaching from pulpits were pervasive. The church periodicals of the period suggest that women's preaching, at least on a temporary basis, was a common occurrence, even if the woman was never ordained or chosen by a church to be its pastor.[43]

Many interpreted the Pauline injunctions to be primarily concerned with prohibiting women and wives from exerting governing authority over men and husbands. The most potent institutional roles of authority—ones even the most successful woman evangelist never performed—was that of elder and husband. The elders exerted authority in the congregations not because of their persuasive speaking ability but because of the fact that they were the appointed supreme rulers or "shepherds" of the church. Similarly, husbands exerted power, not persuasion, from their privileged legal and scriptural position. The fact a woman could preach by the 1890s did not indicate a new level of equality between the sexes, as much as that women preachers and their churches often managed to separate preaching and real institutional power. Women preached, and their audiences allowed them in good conscience, because they did not presume unwarranted authority. But without some authority in the particular church in which she preached, a woman maintained her position only by the support of others, but not her own official position, and by only holding temporary pastorates and revivals. Women preachers operated in a role not dissimilar to that of mothers in the Victorian family—women held a celebrated influence in swaying others but never the authority of the men in the family. Time proved that Isaac Errett had unnecessarily worried in 1872 that women's preaching subverted the "subordination of woman to man," which he found "so necessary to the perfection of social life, and incorporated alike into the systems of nature and of grace."[44]

The small number of women actually pastoring a church, the ambiguous authority and position of the women, and the decentralized polity of the denomination, partly explain the lack of significant conflict at the turn of the century over the issue among Disciples in comparison to other contemporary innovations, some of which foreshadowed the bitter Fundamentalist/Modernist controversy a decade later. It was not mere coincidence that northern Baptists, Congregationalists, and Disciples each had congregational governments and included ordained women among their ranks in 1900. Theoretically, women in each of these groups needed only the approval of sole congregations to be ordained. The hodgepodge of Disciple state and national missionary and benevolent societies at the turn of the century held no influence among the fissiparous Disciple congregations in internal matters such as selecting a minister. That being said, it is important to recognize that many Disciples knew about women preachers among their ranks if they read the popular church papers of the time. There are also many indications that women were supported in their new position.

The methods used to censure heterodox Disciple churches during this era were never applied to churches that had women preachers or to the women themselves.[45] Likewise, while many individual churches divided over the introduction of organs into church services in the 1880s and 1890s, there is no record of churches dividing over a woman becoming the preacher of a church or preaching temporarily in a church. In fact, there are many examples that show that women enjoyed a measure of support for their preaching efforts between 1888 and 1908. Respected Disciple revivalists and state missionary society officials ordained women organizers as preachers and evangelists. One woman served as state evangelist for the Illinois Christian Missionary Society (1892) and another as state evangelist for the California society (1904). Some women preached while simultaneously holding positions in the CWBM. Churches asked women evangelists to lead revivals and dedicate new church buildings. Regional missionary societies held their conventions, and local men preachers led revivals, in churches where women preached. Finally, the conservative *Christian Standard* and more moderate *Christian-Evangelist* both printed reports and photographs of women preachers and their work. *Christian Standard* editorials never assailed women preachers and their churches between 1888 and 1908, a significant fact considering the paper strongly criticized Disciple modernists in the 1890s and early 1900s for trying to reevaluate traditional Disciple practices and literal biblical interpretations. Only about fifteen women, though, managed to preach regularly and hold pastorates among the Disciples between 1888 and 1908.

By the 1890s, WCTU and CWBM lecturers and organizers credibly claimed that their preaching did not subvert the different spheres of men and women. The supporters of women's preaching managed to maintain a strict division of roles and power in the church and marriage. In an 1892–93 Disciple newspaper debate over whether women could hold the same church positions as men, T. W. Caskey wrote in support of the resolution and the new freedoms of women in society, but he also felt obligated to make some qualifications. "I will affirm the coequal rights of woman with man, religious and political, except the right to rule her husband, or be a bishop."[46]

Churches denied women preachers institutional authority in many ways. One minister explained the different roles that men and women performed in the church by saying, "[M]en *govern* the church, select its elders, deacons, employ preachers, dismiss them, collect all the moneys, appropriate it, withdraw from unruly members . . . Man governs the church, women sing, pray, exhort, teach, and even preach, but don't usurp authority over the man, but remain in subjection to the man." The fact that no record exists of a woman preacher being appointed an "elder," or being referred to as one between the 1880s and 1920s, indicates the pervasive rejection of women holding the highest lay position among the Christian Churches (Disciples). As late as 1952, only 1.1 percent of Christian Churches (Disciples) reported women elders in a national study. Five women served as lay elders in three churches—out of 277 churches reporting. In fact, Disciple women could conceivably preach in a church without being able to vote for a church officer—a startling contrast to other Protestant communions which usually allowed women to vote decades before they allowed them to preach.[47]

As with licensing of antebellum women itinerant preachers, ordination among Disciples did not abolish the distinction between the highest positions attainable by women and those attainable to men. Ordination could actually reinforce the traditional middle-class roles of women and men. Among Disciples, ordination served to recognize nonpreaching "women's work" as important and worthy of public notice. From the 1880s through at least the 1920s, most instances of women being ordained did not even involve the question of being a preacher. Preachers' wives, evangelists' wives, missionaries' wives, CWBM and National Benevolent Association organizers, and CWBM officers were ordained without a thought that they were authorized to preach in more than temporary situations—sometimes not even that.[48] Thus the role of full-time preaching elders in the Disciples resembled most closely the role of ordained ministers in other Protestant communions. Disciple women never acted as preaching elders but rather in roles more closely resembling evangelists.

The prohibition against women exerting institutional authority within the Disciple family reinforced the prohibition against women holding church authority. It was no accident that single women and wives of nonpreachers predominated among the ranks of Disciple women preachers. Because Protestants placed wives in subordination to husbands, women's preaching opportunities were limited and shaped in relation to those of their husbands. The success of women preaching while being subordinate to their husbands was decisive in their eventual acceptance as preachers. The hierarchical marriage relationship allowed women to preach only in unusual circumstances; a woman had more opportunity to become a preacher in her own right if she were single, widowed, or married to a man who did not preach. A single woman or widow was not obligated to decline opportunities for preaching and exerting authority in order to subordinate herself to her husband. The central concern to Disciples apparently was that a woman preacher not upstage her husband in his field. This convention manifested itself by women usually not preaching when their husbands could. A single woman usually gave up her independent ministry upon marriage to a fellow preacher. In a few instances, women could become preachers if their husbands were incapacitated by illness. Wives whose husbands were leading a revival or temporarily absent frequently preached from their husbands' pulpits. But she did not preach when he came back; such an occurrence implied the possession of equal authority. Both Millie W. Mason and Clara Babcock assured *Christian Standard* readers that women preachers would not "usurp" authority over their husbands. Both women accepted the Pauline injunctions which traditionally limited women's authority in the church. But they did not interpret the injunctions to prohibit preaching. They believed the injunctions merely described the obligations of wives and mothers, in Babcock's words, the "wifely relation." Mrs. Millie W. Mason explained that while Christianity gave women unprecedented opportunities to develop themselves, women were to fulfill first the "sacred duties which fall to the wife and mother." Mason claimed that she had done this; therefore, she enjoyed the benefits of advancement in the service of God that Christianity provided. She legitimately preached because she fulfilled her roles as wife and mother to the satisfaction of her husband and the congregations which called her to hold revivals.[49]

The first women preachers ministered within many paradoxes. On one hand, many justified their preaching and gained acceptance through their personal and ideological fidelity to traditional roles. Because they were good mothers and subordinate to their husbands, they could preach when the unusual circumstance arose. This indicated that traditional roles of Disciple women had changed from the years immediately following the Civil War. On the other hand, these same traditional roles still usually limited, or even prohibited, women's preaching. Conventional scriptural interpretation still excluded women from church eldership, usually prohibited them from regular preaching if their husbands preached, and only granted them enough acceptance to rescue declining churches so that those churches, paradoxically, could afford to hire men. The influence of women in the pulpit was only allowed to come from their ability to communicate and inspire, not from institutional position. Thus, while the first women ministers included among their rank some of the most impressive Disciple preachers of their era, these same women were often institutionally powerless. In this respect, the experience of mainline women ministers, at least Disciple ones, apparently differed little from that of women ministers in relatively more conservative churches that also ordained them—some Holiness and Pentecostal churches, for example.[50]

That a small number of Disciple women were able to create a long-standing, or even permanent, presence for themselves demonstrated that the "woman's sphere" among Disciples could be stretched—but only for one extraordinary woman at a time and in response to one unusual circumstance at a time. The all-pervasive prohibition against women's preaching fell between 1888 and 1908, but acceptance of women preachers remained elusive. Most Disciples held the contradictory positions of allowing women's preaching, but not women preachers. Women preachers did not help resolve the contradictions by moving into a traditionally masculine role while firmly upholding, in most cases, expected feminine roles. Not only did women preachers decline to rebel against the "woman's sphere," as antebellum women itinerants had, they embraced it.

Significantly, early Disciple women preachers found that forms of conventionality could be used to justify innovation—not unlike the WCTU's record of propelling women into the public arena to protect what was believed to be women's natural domain, the home. The record of a small number of CWBM and WCTU lecturers becoming preachers demonstrates the ability and influence of a modified cult of true womanhood to propel at least a few women into new positions of prominence in a mainline church. The transition of women lecturers into preachers also reveals the importance of women's organizations, such as the WCTU and women's missionary societies and their reformist program, on the active Protestant women of the period. The very possibility of this transition from organizer to preacher, no matter how incomplete, suggests the profound challenge the WCTU and CWBM were posing to Disciple women's views of themselves and their place in church and society.

The years 1888 to 1908 set a foundation for future growth in the number of Disciple women who preached and in the range of ministries in which they participated. After 1908, wives of preachers found more freedom to preach at churches located near their husbands. Husbands no longer had to be seriously ill or deceased to allow their wives the freedom to preach regularly. In fact, the wives and widows of preachers predominated among the expanding number of women preachers after 1914, a number that peaked in 1932. From 1914 to 1932 the number of women listed as preachers in the national yearbook increased from approximately ten to fifty. Although remaining a miniscule percentage of the total number of Disciple preachers, the significant increase demonstrates a greater openness to women's preaching and public leadership. The only mainline Protestant denomination that rivaled the Disciples in the number of ordained women ministers was the Congregationalists. In 1928 Congregationalists listed twenty-nine women pastors in that year's yearbook, while Disciples of Christ listed forty-three.[51]

A comparison between the contradictions and paradoxes within which early women preachers lived and ministered, and the public presence many women created for themselves despite those contradictions, reveals the profound accomplishments of early Disciple women preachers. Despite the optimism, though, of many Disciple women reformers in the WCTU and CWBM, that the accomplishments of their day heralded a new era for women, women remained visitors behind the pulpit. In 1893 CWBM Organizer Virginia Hedges wrote that she longed "to see the day when . . . both men and *women,* will fill the pulpits of the world." Yet this achievement, which she considered "the *legitimate results* of the *gospel,*" remained in a distant future for mainline Protestantism.[52]

NOTES

1. In its original development in the antebellum North, the cult of true womanhood had located men in the harsh public world of politics and capitalism while women—seen as humble, pious, submissive, and meek—became the industrialized North's protectors of the home, nurturers of children, and pillars of the church. The church's position in society, in turn, steadily weakened during the antebellum period and increasingly relied on the support of its female laity. See Barbara Welter, "The Cult of True Womanhood, 1820–1860," *American Quarterly* 18 (1966): 151–74, and her "The Feminization of American Religion: 1800–1860," in *Clio's Consciousness Raised: New Perspectives on the History of Women,* ed. Mary S. Hartman and Lois Banner, 137–57 (New York: Octagon Books, 1976).

2. See Ruth Bordin, *Woman and Temperance: The Quest for Power and Liberty, 1873–1900* (New Brunswick: Rutgers Univ. Press, 1981), 3–14, and Patricia R. Hill, *The World Their Household: The American Woman's Foreign Mission Movement and Cultural Transformation, 1870–1930* (Ann Arbor: Univ. Press of Michigan, 1985), 23–60. The "New Woman" of the late 1880s and 1890s who moved into public service roles to reform society "grew out of, rather than in direct opposition to, the cult of true womanhood." From Nancy F. Cott, ed.,

Roots of Bitterness: Documents of the Social History of American Women (Boston: Northeastern Univ. Press, 1986), 25–27.

3. Discussions of the meaning of the term *mainline Protestantism* can be found in William R. Hutchison, "Preface: From Protestant to Pluralist America" and "Protestantism as Establishment," in *Between the Times: The Travail of the Protestant Establishment in America, 1900–1960*, ed. William R. Hutchison (Cambridge: Cambridge Univ. Press, 1989), vii–xv, 3–18.

4. See Ruth Bordin, *Woman and Temperance: The Quest for Power and Liberty, 1873–1900* (Philadelphia: Temple, 1981), 162, and Anne M. Boylan, *Sunday School: The Formation of an American Institution, 1790 – 1880* (New Haven: Yale, 1988), 124–25. Bordin traces the early enthusiasm of the WCTU in promoting women's public speaking to the fact that the WCTU was fully controlled by women. Like the WCTU, the women's missionary societies of both the Disciples and the Methodist Protestant Church were fully independent women's organizations. See William T. Noll, "Laity Rights and Leadership: Winning Them for Women in the Methodist Protestant Church, 1860–1900," in *Women in New Worlds: Historical Perspectives on the Wesleyan Tradition*, ed. Hilah F. Thomas and Rosemary Skinner Keller, 219–31 (Nashville: Abingdon, 1982).

5. Although Errett felt compelled to discuss women's preaching in 1872, the discussion was theoretical rather than "one of much practical importance." He argued that "settle it which way you will, there will never be much of it. Nature is against it. The constitution of society forbids it. The duties of maternity put it largely out of the question. In the long run, nature will hold us level to our sphere." See Isaac Errett, "Shall Women Pray and Prophecy?" *Christian Standard* (Mar. 23, 1872): 92

6. E. Goodwin, "Woman Preaching," *Christian* (July 8, 1875): 2–3.

7. See David Lipscomb, "Woman's Work in the Church," *Gospel Advocate* (Mar. 14, 1888): 7; and "Home Life, Home Duties, Home Religion," *Gospel Advocate* (May 27, 1897): 325. Barbara Brown Zikmund provides a general overview of the Protestant debate over women's preaching in her "The Struggle for the Right to Preach," in *Women and Religion in America*, vol. 1, *The Nineteenth Century*, ed. Rosemary Radford Ruether and Rosemary Skinner Keller, 193–205 (San Francisco: Harper and Row, 1981).

8. Fred A. Bailey, "Disciple Images of Victorian Womanhood," *Discipliana* 40, no. 1 (Spring 1988): 7–12. The participation of women in public activities was only one issue that led the U.S. government to recognize the two Disciple churches in the 1906 religious census; the majority Disciples of Christ who accepted new church agencies and women's speaking and the minority, the mostly southern Churches of Christ, which condemned the innovative practices.

9. General Missionary Convention, *Report of Proceedings of General Missionary Convention* (n.p., [1874]), 43. Errett also wrote an influential "Help Those Women" editorial in the *Christian Standard* (July 11, 1874) that helped launch the newly proposed CWBM.

10. Mrs. Marie Jameson, *Missionary Tidings* (Dec. 1896): 201.

11. Hill argues that the influence and size of women's missionary societies has not been noted enough in histories of women's activism and the foreign missions crusade at the turn of the century. See her *World Their Household*, 195 n. 1.

12. Not all CWBM Organizers were Euro-American. See Bertha Mason Fuller, *The Life Story of Sarah Lue Bostick* (Little Rock, Ark.: by the author, 1949).

13. Anna M. Hale, "The Field Worker, Her Qualifications," *Missionary Tidings* (Dec. 1897): 183.

14. Ella M. Huffman, "The Higher Conquest," a CWBM speech reprinted in *Christian Oracle* (Nov. 9, 1893): 708.

15. Candace Lhamon Smith, "Whom We Serve," *Missionary Tidings* (Dec. 1896): 219.

16. Virginia Gilkeson Hedges, "'Dolly in the Pulpit,'" *Christian Standard* (Sept. 30, 1893): 778.

17. Lura V. Thompson, "Illinois," *Missionary Tidings* (Dec. 1896): 163. Starting in 1907, Organizers started to be called "state field missionaries" as well as the traditional title. At other times after 1909 they could be referred to as field missionaries or state missionaries. See Mrs. Jeanette H. Wells, "Indiana," and Mrs. George W. Oliver, "Virginia," *Missionary Tidings* (Nov. 1912): 253, 256.

18. The idea of a state WCTU organizer that promoted the temperance organization was borrowed from the Woman's Foreign Missionary Society (Methodist Episcopal). See Bordin, *Woman and Temperance*, 74, and Hill, *World Their Household*, 48.

19. Anna M. Hale "The Field Worker, Her Qualifications," and Mary A. Lyons, "The Field Worker, Her Preparation," *Missionary Tidings* (Dec. 1897): 183.

20. Mrs. Millie Vercoe, "South Dakota," *Missionary Tidings* (Nov. 1902): 252.

21. Mary A. Lyons, "Ohio," *Missionary Tidings* (Dec. 1894): 9. Mrs. Harlan, national CWBM speaker, reportedly spoke to one Sunday school and at three church services in a two-day stop in Denver in 1912. She was on a return swing from a western speaking tour. See Mrs. Sudie E. Flint, "Colorado," *Missionary Tidings* (Nov. 1912): 252.

22. Mrs. Persis L. Christian was a national CWBM organizer. See her "Woman's Interest," *Christian Standard* (Apr. 9, 1892): 324.

23. The debate was not limited to the Christian Churches (Disciples) but extended to American Protestant churches in general. Bordin claims that the debate over the role of women in American Protestantism and society in the early 1890s was in part because many women had grown accustomed to governing their own affairs in the WCTU. See Bordin, *Woman and Power*, 113. In the Disciples, CWBM women also governed their own missionary affairs.

24. A. P. Terrell, "Should Women Speak in Public?" *Apostolic Guide* (July 2, 1886), quoted in Mossie A. Wyker, *Church Women in the Scheme of Things* (St. Louis: Bethany, 1953), 50–52.

25. E.G.S., "The Elevation and Proper Position of Women under the Religion of Christ," *Gospel Advocate* (June 13, 1888): 8.

26. Birdie Farrar, "Virginia," *Missionary Tidings* (Dec. 1896): 164–65. Despite being new to the work she organized fifteen auxiliaries with 195 members and twenty mission bands with 293 participants in sixty-five days of travel and visiting churches.

27. Birdie Farrar Omer, *Mother, or the Aloe Plant* (Louisville, Ky.: Standard Printing, 1925), 69–70.

28. Omer, *Mother*, 69–70.

29. George T. Smith, "Does Woman Keep Silence in the Churches? To M. P. Hayden," *Christian Standard* (Aug. 12, 1893): 638.

30. Pension Fund of Disciples of Christ, "Minister's Application" (1931), and Commission on the Ministry, "Information Schedule" (1926), found in the Isabelle Goodacre File, Disciples of Christ Historical Society.

31. Mrs. C. U. Sims, "Kansas State C.W.B.M. Convention," *Missionary Tidings* (Dec 1897): 209. See Clara H. Hazelrigg, "Kansas Letter," *Christian-Evangelist* (June 7, 1900): 725. Before devoting her energies to the CWBM, Hazelrigg had been superintendent of Butler County, Kansas schools, a school teacher, and state-history textbook writer. In 1897 Hazelrigg spent 190 days speaking and traveling over nine thousand miles in the interest of the Kansas CWBM and organized forty-four new auxiliaries and Junior Christian Endeavor Societies with more than six hundred new members. Clara H. Hazelrigg, "Kansas," *Missionary Tidings* (Dec. 1897): 152.

32. Haynes, *Disciples in Illinois*, 464–66. Babcock's obituary notices also claimed she was ordained in 1888. See B. H. Cleaver, "Mrs. C. C. Babcock [obit.]," *Christian-Evangelist* (Dec. 31, 1925): 1703, and Ernest R. Babcock, "Babcock [obit.]," *Christian Standard* (July 25, 1925): 1045. However, according to a local paper Babcock was actually ordained in August 1889. Babcock probably began preaching at Erie Christian Church in 1888 but was not ordained until 1889. See "Saturday," *Sterling [Ill.] Gazette*, Fri., Aug. 9, 1889.

33. "Rock Falls," *Sterling [Ill.] Gazette*, July 20, 1888.

34. E. T. Sechler, *Sadie McCoy Crank (1863–1948), Pioneer Woman Preacher in the Christian Church (Disciples)* (Hermitage, Mo.: Index, 1950), 48; Ruth Black Aten, *She Kept Men Standing* (Chicago: Adams, 1967), 123. There are conflicting dates given within the E. T. Sechler biography concerning when Crank started to preach. In reconciling the information, it is most likely that Crank engaged in speaking similar to preaching but not in an official sense until her 1892 ordination. Sechler, *Sadie McCoy Crank*, 6. She continued for a time as State Sunday-school Evangelist holding revivals at Lomax, with thirty-seven additions, and Raymond, Illinois, with thirty-six additions. She then was appointed by the Illinois Christian Missionary Society as a state evangelist during the rest of 1892. She held five meetings that lasted more than twenty-five days. The meeting in Chicago resulted in a new church.

35. Mrs. Ella Beck, "New Mexico–West Texas," *Missionary Tidings* (Nov. 1913): 280. See also Mrs. Sarah K. Yancey, "Kentucky," *Missionary Tidings* (Nov. 1906): 286, "So many think because the church is small there should be no auxiliary."

36. Mrs. Laura Gerould Craig, "New York and New Jersey," *Missionary Tidings* (Nov. 1906): 287.

37. Louise Kelly, "Mrs. Kelly's Report," *Missionary Tidings* (Nov. 1903): 250. The *Kansas Messenger Yearbook* in 1908 and 1909 listed Kelly as preacher of the Hope and Madison, Kansas, churches. The 1912 National Disciple yearbook listed her as the Unadilla, Nebraska, church preacher. Kelly was heavily involved in training CWBM leaders starting at least in 1891, seventeen years before she was recorded as holding Kansas and Nebraska pastorates between 1908 and 1912. See Mrs. Helen E. Moses, "Organizer's Notes from Kansas," *Missionary Tidings* (Dec. 1891): 35.

38. Miss Bertha C. Mason, "Texas," *Missionary Tidings* (Nov. 1904): 251. See also "Texas," *Missionary Tidings* (Nov. 1904): 267. See also Bertha Mason Fuller Biography File at the Disciples of Christ Historical Society. Rachel Dangerfield, Colorado's CWBM superintendent of young people, was pastor at Severance, Colorado, and a successful evangelist. See "The Children, News Notes from the Young People's Department," *Missionary Tidings* (Sept. 1912): 149; "In the Eye of their Brethren," *Christian-Evangelist* (Mar. 14, 1912): 379; and J. E. Davis, "Ordination at Spokane University," *Christian-Evangelist* (Apr. 24, 1913): 578.

39. Mrs. Virginia Hedges, "Woman's Work in the Church," *Christian Standard* (May 20, 1893): 390; and Clara Hazelrigg, "Help Those Women," *Christian Standard* (Jan. 18, 1902): 82–83. See also Hedges, "'Dolly in the Pulpit,'" 778. Only rarely did women preachers confront hostility to their presence by relying solely on scriptural texts. See Mrs. Belle Reid Yates, "The Autobiography of a Pioneer," *Christian Standard* (Mar. 11, 1944): 167, and her "Let the Women Keep Silent," *Christian Standard* (Feb. 24, 1917): 622.

40. Virginia Hedges, "Woman's Work," *Christian Standard* (May 20, 1893): 390, and "'Dolly in the Pulpit,'" 778; Clara Hazelrigg, "Help Those Women," *Christian Standard* (Jan. 18, 1902): 82–83. For a more detailed discussion on the ways the temperance crusade influenced the rise of women as ministers in the Disciples see the author's "'The Gospel of Temperance': Early Disciple Women Preachers and the WCTU, 1887–1912," *Discipliana* 53, no. 2 (Summer 1993): 47–60.

41. Millie W. Mason, "A Woman's Voice for Women," *Christian Standard* (Nov. 14, 1908): 1956.

42. Catherine Anne Brekus, "'Let Your Women Keep Silence in the Churches': Female Preaching and Evangelical Religion in America, 1740–1845," vols. 1 and 2 (Ph.D. diss., Yale Univ., 1993), 193–200. Jualynne Dodson argues that antebellum African American Methodist women's preaching was tolerated more than accepted and that the hostility women endured came more from their attempt to gain ordination, rather than their actual preaching. See her "Nineteenth-Century A.M.E. Preaching Women," in *Women in New Worlds*, ed. Thomas and Keller, 276–81 (Nashville: Abingdon, 1982).

43. Some of the women who are known to have begun regularly preaching during this period are the following: WCTU Whiteside (Ill.) County president and organizer Clara C. Babcock in 1888, Missouri preacher's wife Jessie C. Monser in 1891, Illinois WCTU organizer and Sunday-school evangelist Sadie McCoy (later Crank) in 1892, Wisconsin CWBM organizer Isabelle Goodacre in the mid-1890s, former Good Templar temperance lecturer and Illinois resident Mrs. Alice Draper in 1896, Kansas CWBM organizer Clara Hazelrigg

in 1897, former Michigan Young People's CWBM organizer Pauline Barrows in 1897 (Idaho), Illinois resident Miss M. E. Very came from the Freewill Baptist ministry in 1902, Texas CWBM organizer and secretary Bertha C. Mason (c. 1905), and Kansas and National CWBM organizer Mrs. Louise Kelly (in 1908), Oregon Sunday-school worker and evangelist Clara G. Esson in 1906, Minnesotan Ada L. Forster (1907), and experienced itinerant lecturer and interdenominational evangelist Millie (Mrs. M. W.) Mason in 1907.

44. Isaac Errett, "Shall Women Pray and Prophesy?" *Christian Standard* (Mar. 23, 1872): 92.

45. Conservative and traditional Disciples censured heterodox churches and institutions in many ways: missionary societies returned donations from heterodox churches, delegates from heterodox churches to state conventions were not seated, well-publicized and strident attacks by the conservative *Christian Standard* were made over extended periods on Modernist proponents of the "New Theology," and colleges who employed theological liberals were accused of supporting heresy. In comparison, Nathaniel S. Haynes commented on the quiet rise of women preachers in the Disciples when he wrote, "The entrance of women into the public ministry of the churches of Christ in Illinois was as quiet as the rising sun. They served with efficiency in so many semi-public relations and places that this final step was easily taken." See "Women as Preachers and Pastoral Helpers," in his *History of the Disciples of Christ in Illinois, 1819–1914* (Cincinnati, Ohio: Standard Publishing, 1915), 650.

46. T. W. Caskey, "Woman and Preaching, the Caskey-Briney Discussion: T. W. Caskey's Tenth and Last Article," *Christian-Evangelist* (Mar. 23, 1893): 183, 184. The proposition debated: "According to New Testament teaching a woman may be an evangelist or pastor of a church, and do any work in the ministry, or fill any office in the church, that a man may do or fill."

47. David Nation, "The Woman Question," *Christian Standard* (Feb. 1, 1890): 74. Cf. E. Goodwin, "Woman Preaching," *Christian* (July 8, 1875): 2–3. For the report on women elders in 1952, see Howard Elmo Short, "The Service and Status of Women among the Disciples of Christ," in *Women in the Church: A Symposium on the Service and Status of Women among the Disciples of Christ* (Lexington, Ky.: College of the Bible, 1953), 30. Cf. Barbara Brown Zikmund, "Winning Ordination for Women in Mainstream Protestant Churches," *Women and Religion in America*, vol. 3, *1900–1968* (New York: Harper & Row, 1986), 340. The prohibition of women from institutional roles in local financial affairs meant that there was little or no possibility that women preachers could maintain a long-term pastoral presence at a particular church. Control over church money was an important symbol of institutional authority. The prohibition against women elders meant that women did not directly influence the monthly finances of a church. Because women could not control church donations they had less influence over the amount of their salary, what missionary and benevolence causes received funding, and issues related to the upkeep or expansion of the church building. Being unable to influence church finances meant that the female preacher retained less control over her ministry than did male preachers.

48. There is a temptation to overemphasize the importance of ordination—and under-emphasize the variety of ordained ministries and the reasons women were ordained—in the late-nineteenth and early-twentieth centuries among the Disciples of Christ. In fact, large numbers of Christian Churches did not even practice ordination into the 1880s. Women were ordained as early as 1883, but as missionary wives, not preachers. See Isaac Errett, "Ordination," *Christian Standard* (Sept. 15, 1883): 364. One of the most unusual reasons for ordaining women came in the 1890s. During this decade, railroads offered ordained clergy and mission board officials discount fares as part of public relations campaigns. The Indiana CWBM urged would-be organizers to be ordained by their local churches to take advantage of these discounts. Found in Lester G. McAllister and William E. Tucker, *Journey in Faith: A History of the Christian Churches (Disciples of Christ)* (St. Louis: Bethany, 1975), 263. See also J. E. Davis, "Ordination at Spokane University," *Christian-Evangelist* (Apr. 24, 1913): 578, and Minutes (Nov. 25, 1919) in "CWBM Executive Meeting Minutes" (Apr. 6, 1918–Oct. 1931).

49. Mrs. M. W. Mason, Australian evangelist, "A Woman's Voice for Women," *Christian Standard* (Nov. 14, 1908): 1956; and Clara C. Babcock, "Woman in the Pulpit" *Christian Standard* (June 4, 1892): 482. For information on one woman who began to preach because of the sickness of her husband, see Pension Fund of Disciples of Christ, "Minister's Application" (1931), and the Commission on the Ministry, "Information Schedule" (1926), found in the Isabelle Goodacre File, Disciples of Christ Historical Society. Similar circumstances propelled Jessie Coleman Monser (1868–1956) into the pulpit in 1891. Shortly after marrying Harold Monser, Jessie Coleman Monser preached from his pulpit because he became seriously ill with typhoid. See Mary Ellen Larue, "Women in the Ministry of the Church: A Disciple History" (B.D. thesis, College of the Bible, Lexington, Ky., 1960), 102. Mrs. Sadie McCoy Crank was one of the most prolific church workers of her era. Yet the Cranks were rarely referred to by the same title in church publications or local newspapers. While Mr. Crank would be termed "Rev. Crank," Mrs. Crank remained "Mrs. Crank." And while Mr. Crank was "Elder Crank," Mrs. Crank never exerted authority from this institutional role. See "Program," *Lawrence (Mo.) Chiefton*, Apr. 21, 1910, and Sechler, *Crank*, 20–21, 26.

50. Michael S. Hamilton gives an overview of the critical studies on the comparison between mainline and fundamentalist Protestantism in his "Women, Public Ministry, and American Fundamentalism, 1920–1950," *Religion and American Culture: A Journal of Interpretation* 3, no. 2 (Summer 1993): 172–96. He argues against an emerging consensus that understands mainline Protestantism as slowly opening up positions to women in the first half of the twentieth century, while conservative Protestants (i.e., Pentecostals and Fundamentalists) slowly closed off positions from women. How difficult it is to generalize about the experience of women ministers in conservative Protestant denominations can be seen in recent studies on the topic. Three separate patterns in the roles of women ministers in three Holiness/Pentecostal churches are found in Edith L. Blumhofer, *Restoring*

the Faith: The Assemblies of God, Pentecostalism, and American Culture (Urbana: Univ. Press of Illinois, 1993), 172–77; Rebecca Laird, *Ordained Women in the Church of the Nazarene* (Kansas City, Mo.: Nazarene Publishing, 1993), 139–52; and Mickey Crews, *The Church of God: A Social History* (Knoxville: Univ. of Tennessee Press, 1990), 92–98. Blumhofer notes that Assembly of God women evangelists were not allowed to vote in denominational meetings until 1920, and when women were granted ordination rights as pastors in 1935 the barriers remained high for all but the most dedicated. The most influential women preachers were itinerant evangelists who spoke in church settings controlled by men. While the Assemblies of God slowly granted women more privileges, the Church of the Nazarene, according to Laird, allowed women to be ordained from the beginning. But the proportion of women in ministry increased until reaching a plateau in the early 1930s and then declined after the Second World War. Crews, in contrast, argues that the second largest white Pentecostal denomination, the Church of God (Cleveland, Tenn.) initially allowed women to become preaching deacons but subsequently ruled against extending ordination to them in the first decade of the twentieth century. Soon after, the denomination further proscribed the role of preaching women and laywomen in general. It would appear that the Disciples followed a pattern similar to the Church of the Nazarene until the late 1960s, in that both gave limited acceptance to women in ministry, although the Nazarene church had a greater proportion of ministers who were women.

51. The *Congregational Year-Book 1928* (New York: National Council of Congregational Churches, 1928) listed the last record of solely Congregational Church statistics before a merger with another denomination created the Congregational Christian Churches. That yearbook listed twenty-nine women pastors (by evidence of having feminine names). Of these women, twenty were ordained and in full standing and four held licenses, while the remaining number were from other churches. A much larger number (ninety-nine) of Congregational women were listed as ordained and with full standing in the communion, but only some of these women were church pastors. Among Disciples, forty-three women were listed as church pastors in the annual yearbook. However, because the yearbook did not indicate if those who were listed were also ordained, there is no way to tell how many of these women were ordained. See the 1928 *Year Book of Disciples of Christ* (Indianapolis: United Christian Missionary Society, 1928).

52. Hedges, "'Dolly in the Pulpit,'" 778.

The Interracial Impact of Marshall Keeble, Black Evangelist, 1878–1968

Paul D. Phillips

In 1915, the year of Booker T. Washington's death, S. W. Womack, cofounder of the Jackson Street Church of Christ in Nashville, cried out for a "change in the moral and religious attitude of the two races toward each other." His plea published in a Nashville religious journal lamented the sad state of black-white relationships characterized by a mutual lack of trust. To Womack the burden of the responsibility for improving race relations lay at the door of white persons. He specifically called for "a more friendly attitude by the White people toward us." And in the words of Booker T. Washington he reminded whites "we are here and here to stay."[1]

Womack was one of many who believed that the solution to the race problem lay in Christian evangelism among blacks.[2] In the half century following Womack's appeal, Marshall Keeble, son-in-law to Womack, served valiantly as a dual apostle of evangelism among blacks and of goodwill among whites. His lifetime commitment to the evangelistic challenge met with phenomenal success. In an era that began before the turn of the century (Keeble began preaching at age eighteen and did not stop until his death in 1968), he reportedly baptized more than forty thousand individuals (many of whom were white) and established more than three hundred Church of Christ congregations. Moreover, his evangelistic ministry, which was centered in Tennessee and the South, extended across the United States from New York to California and included two tours to Nigeria.[3]

At the time of Keeble's death there was a journalistic outpouring of praise for this titan, not only because of his evangelistic success among blacks (whites flocked to his revivals sometimes in greater numbers than blacks) but also for his alleged achievement in breaking down racial barriers. The editor of the *Firm Foundation,* a Texas-based journal, wrote, "No man living, black or white, has done more to break down any racial barriers that might exist than has Marshall Keeble." He further praised this "apostle of goodwill," who had established the principle "that in Christ we are all brothers, regardless of nationality or color," and who "loved his brethren and . . . was a lovable brother."[4]

At Keeble's funeral, at the Madison Church of Christ, attended by a crowd of three thousand blacks and whites, one observer commented that he had not seen "a greater display of racial harmony and Christian love" than he saw expressed by the mourners who were "completely colorblind as they sang, prayed, and wept together." He noticed a "little colored boy about ten years old, who came by the casket of Brother Keeble, tears flowing down his cheeks, and behind him a white man with grey hair wept."[5] Chiefly because of him, another said, "racial tension . . . has been nil or non-existent in churches of Christ."[6]

But not everyone agreed with this idyllic view of racial harmony. R. C. Wells, writing two years after Keeble's death, charged that "the ideally desirable 'undivided church' while harmoniously scriptural is all but non-existent." Furthermore, he said, "Black Christians and White Christians in the past 'one hundred years' have never worked together as complete and total equals to any appreciable degree."[7] Angered by the closing of the Nashville Christian Institute, "Keeble's school," by the white-dominated board of directors just one year prior to Keeble's death, the editor of the *Christian Echo* charged that blacks in the Church of Christ had been robbed and cheated by their white counterparts in what he termed the "Grab of the Century."[8] In a similar vein, another said, "a great brotherhood had been stabbed in the back."[9]

White paternalism and racial inequality were the touchstones of the so-called interracial unity that R. C. Wells branded as nothing but a sham.[10] But to Marshall Keeble, who gave the strength of his life to the twofold task of elevating blacks by the proclamation of the gospel and of establishing a bond of interracial fellowship through white support of his ministry, the resulting unity was real. In his accommodation to white paternalism, Keeble never believed that he compromised his personal integrity or the integrity of blacks generally. His humility was genuinely Christian. He was so deeply committed to the Christian principles of turning the other cheek, self-denial, cross-bearing, and suffering for righteousness' sake that he was able to endure in silent uncomplaining resignation all the insults, indignities, threats, assaults, and racial slurs heaped on him. In speaking before the Jackson Street Church approximately a year before his death, he said, "You know in preaching the gospel of Christ over this country, I've suffered immense, I've weeped, I've cried."[11] But by the power of God he overcame all personal, demeaning attacks in order to accomplish his larger goals.

Standing in the tradition of Booker T. Washington, his boyhood idol whose principles of accommodation he readily accepted, Keeble said that he learned from Washington to hold a "high opinion of himself" and "respect for his race." Washington also taught him "how to get along with white people" and "how to get financial support from white people."[12] Beginning about 1920 and continuing until his death, Keeble did get financial support from whites. One of his earliest and most constant benefactors was A. M. Burton, founder of the Life and

Casualty Insurance Company and a fellow believer. Burton often provided Keeble with roundtrip railroad fare to a revival site, funds for tents and other expenses. Also, Burton urged other individuals and churches to contribute to Keeble's evangelistic support.[13] As Keeble's reputation grew, his sources of support came to include an increasing number of individuals and churches both white and black. White support paid costs of transportation, tents, boarding during revivals, support for himself and his family, and part or all of the cost for erecting permanent structures for the churches he established.[14] And the people to whom Keeble ministered the gospel shared their meager living with him. After closing a revival, he might walk the several miles to catch the train back to his home carrying a tow sack with "a gallon or two of sorghum molasses, two or three pounds of butter, perhaps a ham, some chickens, or if lucky a pig,"[15]

Keeble was able to arouse white interest in black souls by a constant reminder to whites of their centuries-old spiritual neglect of blacks. In expressing his gratitude for the "great missionary spirit among white churches" for trying to "reach all nations with the gospel," he reminded the white church that there was a mission work "right at your door among my race." For the white church to engage in the single effort of foreign missions while neglecting "your cooks, house girls, farm hands, chauffeurs, and nurses" is a mistake, "because if we can get the gospel to those who serve your homes and care for your little ones, you can put more trust in them, and save them from ignorance of the blessed gospel of Jesus Christ."[16]

A few months later Keeble thanked his white brethren "for turning their attention toward my race, trying to lift them with the gospel of Jesus Christ," but there remained literally "thousands" of unconverted blacks "living right around some of our largest white churches." These brethren must heed the charge of Jesus to "preach the gospel to every creature." In Marshall Keeble the white church had found its most effective evangelist to blacks.[17]

How did it happen that a son born to recently emancipated slaves in Rutherford County, Tennessee, who, as a boy growing up in Nashville received little formal education (he did not attend school beyond the seventh grade), became a great preacher? Keeble said that his grandfather, uncle, and father, all of whom preached, inspired him to want to preach. His grandfather, Marshall Keeble, began preaching while serving as a slave to Horace P. Keeble, prominent lawyer in Murfreesboro. He held revivals in schoolhouses, brush arbors, and under trees. His uncle, also named Marshall Keeble, preached "mighty near everywhere in Tennessee." His father, Robert Keeble, served as assistant minister for the Lea Avenue Christian Church, into which Keeble was baptized at age fourteen. Four years later Keeble began to preach, and in 1914 he launched his evangelistic ministry. Near the end of his long ministry, he paid tribute to the influence of preachers in his family, which "made me decide to preach."[18]

From the Jackson Street Church of Christ, Keeble's home church for nearly seventy years, he began his evangelism.[19] At the beginning of each year he would preach a revival meeting at his home church after which he would devote the remainder of the year to evangelism away from home. Early difficulties that he encountered in preparing and delivering sermons, for lack of an education, were in time corrected by the patient and diligent efforts on the part of Minnie Keeble, his wife, whose education at Fisk University equipped her to tutor her husband in correct speech and grammar.[20]

When Keeble became an effective evangelist attracting large interracial crowds and converting hundreds at two- to five-week revivals, he gave much of the credit to his wife. He also credited Booker T. Washington, who had much to do "with my entire work." With considerable pride he said, "I been able to do just about the same thing he done." Washington had disadvantages, too, but they "didn't bother or handicap him none." In the early years of his ministry, Keeble's white friends often compared him favorably with Washington, saying, "You're better than Booker T. Washington. You draw more people than he did."[21] Whether Keeble was preaching in tents as during the early years of his ministry or in church buildings or municipal auditoriums as in the later years, he often addressed capacity crowds.[22]

White interest in Keeble mounted with the growth of his reputation for making converts. In a five-week revival in Tampa, Florida, in 1927, his converts, which included four preachers of another faith, numbered ninety-nine.[23] His greatest number of conversions in any single year was in 1931, when more than a thousand blacks and whites responded to his gospel call for baptism.[24] In the fall of that year he baptized 115 in one day and a total of 286 at a tent meeting in Bradenton, Florida.[25] He had similar large harvestings of souls in Valdosta and Atlanta, Georgia, and in Muskogee, Oklahoma, in 1931.[26] Thirty-six years later, at age eighty-eight, Keeble's evangelistic powers seemed to have diminished but little. In a revival at his home church, ninety-nine responded to the gospel in what one writer termed the "crowning achievement" of his "later evangelistic career."[27]

White interest and white support of Keeble's evangelism stemmed not only from a desire to save black souls, but also from a practical aim to control behavior in the black community. According to Keeble, white brethren often told him that they "hoped all of the negroes in their section will obey the gospel, because when one accepts the gospel it seems to make a different man out of him in every respect."[28] In 1931, A. B. Lipscomb, minister and journalist, wrote, "We have never made a better investment for the Lord nor any which brought such quick and happy results." The preaching of Marshall Keeble "not only created a new religious and moral status for the negro element but it has brought to this community a new citizenry capable of thinking in terms of the Bible," he said.

And to Lipscomb this meant "that we now have better farm hands, better porters, better cooks, better housemaids than ever before."[29]

Undoubtedly, Lipscomb felt that blacks who had come under the influence of Keeble's preaching would not question the status quo in economic and social relations. "No question about racial differences or social equality has been raised," said Lipscomb, for there was "no occasion for it." Rather defensively Lipscomb added the absurd claim that the "duty of Christian brotherhood has been recognized and practiced to the fullest extent." To add weight to his allegation, he quoted Scripture on the equality and oneness in Christ.[30] On the issue of maintaining the status quo in race relations, the white church and the Ku Klux Klan stood together. (Many whites held membership in both organizations.)[31] Could Keeble be trusted to set the proper example of black subordination? In 1931, J. W. Brents, who later served as head of the Bible department at the Nashville Christian Institute, gave an affirmative response to the question when he said that the "greatest thing" about Keeble was that "he knows his place and at all times scrupulously keeps in it."[32]

Fearful that the basic touchstone of white supremacy was being violated at the Keeble meeting by so many whites apparently rubbing shoulders with blacks and committing interracial socializing, the Klan placed a ban on whites attending his meeting in a schoolhouse at Summit, Georgia, in February 1926. One evening during the meeting, about twenty-five Klansmen stomped into the revival, interrupted Keeble's preaching, and handed him a note. When he began reading it silently, the Klan leader demanded that he "read it out." Without hesitation Keeble obeyed the order. "The Ku Klux Klan stands for white supremacy. Be governed accordingly."[33] Recovering quickly from this startling threat, Keeble eased the tension by the submissive response, "I have always known the white man is superior. They brought us from Africa and have lifted us up." Turning to his black audience, he said, "Now you treat these white folks right and they'll treat you right. They are your friends and they'll take care of you."[34] (Years later, in recounting this incident, Keeble explained his response as an application of the biblical injunction to agree with your adversary quickly.)[35] Satisfied, the Klan left the meeting. Keeble later learned that the leader who handed him the note was a local doctor and a member of the Primitive Baptist Church. Keeble had baptized the doctor's cook, who recognized the Klansman. When Keeble returned to Summit the following year to hold another revival, the doctor met him on the street with a hearty welcome and offered the protective counsel, "If anybody bothers you, just let me know."[36]

Neither threats from the Klan nor assaults by lone ruffians silenced the apostle of Jackson Street. In 1939 at Ridgely, in West Tennessee, during a Keeble revival, a young white man approached Keeble ostensibly to answer his invitation to penitent sinners, but at the moment Keeble reached out his hand to receive the prodigal, he was struck a staggering blow to the head by brass knuckles. The assailant hit and ran, but Keeble recovered his balance and continued to call for sinners to repent. The incident brought Keeble community esteem when he refused to prosecute his attacker even though "leading citizens" urged him to prosecute. The people applauded his "Christlike" conduct.[37]

Most of the opposition Keeble faced was nonviolent but nonetheless real. The source of this opposition, he felt, lay in sectarian bias. Without doubt, this appraisal was accurate because Keeble waged an all-out war on all the other churches. His public enumeration of the alleged doctrinal errors of "the denominations" by name often resulted in a Keeble confrontation with the minister of the abused sect and his flock. But two factors—fairness and humor—worked in Keeble's favor in this confrontation. In fairness to any critic Keeble would allow him all the time he wanted to defend his beliefs. But because the open forum had its limitations, Keeble would not allow his opponent to make a rebuttal. For once his critic had sat down, Keeble would not allow him to speak again. And if he tried to interrupt Keeble's preaching, he was put down with the rebuke, "No, I didn't bother you while you were talking. Now you be quiet while I'm speaking."[38] Keeble found this evangelistic approach highly successful because he often converted the minister and his whole church.[39]

At a meeting in Los Angeles around 1930, according to Keeble's best recollection, he had been attacking the doctrines of different churches, which he had not hesitated to call by name, when a challenger rose to his feet and asked, "What about my church?" (To his audience at Abilene, Texas, where he was recounting the incident, he said, "Now there's a man made mad because I missed his church.") When Keeble learned that the man was a Latter Day Saint (Mormon), he knew that he had missed his church because he knew nothing about it. Stalling for time, Keeble asked the man to repeat the name of his church. "Did you say Latter Day Saint?" he asked. Upon getting an affirmative response, Keeble shot back, "You're too late—too late." Satisfied, the questioner sat down and the next night Keeble baptized him.[40]

Less bold critics and those who were simply seeking information often made use of the question box that had a spot in the format of the Keeble revival. Before beginning his sermon of the evening, Keeble would usually answer the questions. And he would also allow questions from the floor. When a scholar asked him for the Greek on a passage of Scripture, Keeble was caught in a dilemma. The scholar, a Lane College professor, probably knew that Keeble did not know the Greek on any Scripture. But his quick wit saved him from certain embarrassment. Keeble turned to his audience and asked for a show of hands of all those who knew Greek. When no hands went up, Keeble suggested to his learned critic that their discussion of Greek would be pointless because: "Nobody out there knows it."[41]

His good sense of humor prevailed in the face of the most offensive attacks. Once while supervising his white brethren in the process of erecting a tent for his revival in Hopkinsville, Kentucky, a racist approached Keeble with the taunt, "there's no need of your preaching to your people. Why you're not a nation. The gospel is not for you all—it's the nations—you're not a nation." Keeble deliberately answered the racial slur by quoting Mark's Gospel, "Go preach the gospel to every creature." The putdown intended for Keeble backfired when he said, "So if I happen not to be a nation, I'm creeping around here."[42] To the large interracial audience to which Keeble was telling the story, he charged, "I want to tell the colored people that are present here today if you are saved in heaven and you happen to recognize Mark when you get there, shake hands with him. Why? Mark says it's for every creature."[43]

His use of humor, whether for the purpose of silencing his enemies or just to "flavor my message" was masterful.[44] Humor enabled him to soften the harshness of his simplistic, literal use of the Scriptures' theology. His message was direct, "It's not Keeble, but the Bible is right."[45] And if one "rejects the Bible, he's hell-bound."[46] But he might hasten to add: "I don't mean no harm, just making it plain. So if you go to hell, I'd like to see you go there with your eyes wide open."[47]

Keeble taught a twelve-step gospel: five steps up one ladder took one from the world to the church; and, seven steps up the second ladder transported one from the church to heaven. In climbing the first ladder, the fifth step—baptism—was the one most emphasized by Keeble. He said that some of his brethren thought that he talked too much about water, but "might near the whole thing hinges on water." In creation, "God took some mud and dirt and made us."[48] To arm himself to fight Goliath, David stopped by a brook to get a stone because "God wanted him to use a stone that had been washed," said Keeble. "I'm trying to help y'all to see that . . . God put water in the plan."[49] Furthermore, "every piece of material in God's church had to be washed. If one didn't see anything in the water, He ain't never told you, you had to see something in the water. No, no. The people got to see you go in the water and be baptized for the remission of your sins cause the *Bible* says so."[50]

Climbing the second ladder from the church, which Keeble called "God's manufacturing plant," to heaven was a sanctifying process.[51] But adding the Christian virtues did not seem so important to Keeble as quitting the worldly practices of drinking whisky, wine and beer, smoking, snuff-dipping, card playing, theater going, dancing, shooting dice, and adultery. His attack on worldliness was a recurring theme. In emphasizing the importance of one's connection with God, he pointed out that the connection could be broken off by a "bottle of whisky." And "another woman between you and your wife will cut it off." To Keeble, cigarette smoking was intolerable. "And the ugliest looking thing you ever saw," he said, "is a cigarette-smoking Mama." He admonished, "Lay that filthy thing down. That bottle of whisky—lay it down, don't never buy another one. That's filthy. It will destroy both body and soul." Responding to the gospel, Keeble said, were all kinds of people: "not just hypocrites, liars, whoremongers, bootleggers, cigarette smokers, and snuff-dippers; all of them will come . . . and lay it all down and never dip another dip of snuff."[52]

To assist him in meeting the demands of a constantly widening ministry, Keeble trained other evangelists by apprenticeship. To accompany him on the revival circuit, he would take young men to lead the singing and to make short talks. After a time of training, these men would become independent evangelists or pastors of churches.[53] Keeble's great desire was to found a school to train ministers. In 1939 his dream became a reality in the establishment of the Nashville Christian Institute, a school to "supply the many millions of colored people of this land and other countries with gospel workers and evangelists."[54] From 1943 to 1958, Keeble served the institute as president and from 1958 to its closing in 1967, as president emeritus. By 1946 the institute had a student body of 350, nearly 20 percent of whom were preparing to preach. Keeble said that the institute offered brethren both black and white the opportunity to support the preparation of blacks for "better service in the kingdom of God."[55]

The meager support that the school received was never sufficient. In an apparent boast about the financial plight of the school, W. E. Brightwell, "News and Notes" editor of the *Gospel Advocate* said in 1948, "Marshall Keeble's school for the colored race . . . has never been pampered." In explanation, he added, "It has not been spoiled by doles which pauperize." It is "an orphan upon our doorstep . . . crudely pieced together out of second hand and salvaged materials." Perhaps white paternalists could find joy in knowing that "discarded equipment has been utilized with gratitude." Sadly, the school barely existed on a day-to-day basis. Brightwell said, "Where the next ton of coal will come from was a real concern."[56]

Despite the fact that the institute suffered from lack of strong financial support, it was a joy to Keeble who taught Bible at the school and who used boys ranging in ages from ten to fourteen in his apprenticeship program. At a revival held in Cookeville in 1953, Keeble took two of these boys with him each night. And they amazed the audience by their ability to quote long passages of Scripture from memory. Keeble reported that all who heard them "were convinced that Christian education is essential for carrying the gospel to the colored people of America." He added: "Everywhere these young men go with me, brethren are anxious to donate to our school."[57]

Keeble left an indelible Christian stamp on his students, who affectionately called him "Pop." He taught his students the love of God and love for all people. At the last graduation of the institute, June 1967, Keeble, in addressing the graduates, instructed them to "keep hatred out of their hearts and not to dislike anybody no matter what color he is." Emphatically he added, "Don't come up hating somebody. Don't let that get into your mind. You can handicap your work for the future."[58]

Seventeen years earlier, he had said, "The gospel of Christ will knock out of us all the prejudice and malice we have against any man." And to his white brothers he added the plea, "May the grace of God cause you to look upon no race as being inferior."[59] But Keeble never seemed to come to grips with the fact that the gospel had not knocked racial prejudice out of his white brothers who continued to draw the color line in their churches. While whites were flocking to Keeble's evangelistic meetings by the thousands, blacks never felt the freedom to respond in attending white meetings except by special invitation, and then only in roped-off sections and segregated balconies.[60]

He did not fail to tell his black audiences that they should not push for integration, that they should be patient. But he did not have a parallel message for whites. He never chastened whites for their segregated practices. He would chide blacks whom he said could think of nothing else but civil rights. Blacks and whites sitting across the aisle from each other at a Keeble revival might seem to be sharing the message and the humor of Keeble's preaching, but some observers said that blacks were biting the bullet. For they saw the shortcoming of the message, which urged patience for blacks and ignored the unchristian, discriminatory conduct of whites.[61]

Keeble's justification for not taking a stand and preaching against segregation was, "You don't win the Negro, just make him mad, and turn the white people against you."[62] But Keeble did not try to conceal his elation when segregation was declared illegal and the public schools were integrated. He stated in a public address, "We've been preaching it all the time, and now we're practicing it."[63] On occasion he had chastised his white brothers for branding blacks as inferior. He said, "God doesn't want you to call a man unclean because he's black. God created him. Don't you call him common or unclean."[64]

Marshall Keeble did not establish the racial harmony of which some whites boasted. But he did work toward reducing racial tensions in a day when race relations were frequently punctuated by violence. Although he did not accomplish everything, he did do something. He attempted to bring out the best in both whites and blacks. But blacks' willingness to suffer wrongs in silence at the hands of their white brothers ended with the passing of Marshall Keeble. Perhaps Keeble made his most lasting contribution in the churches that he founded. The editor of the *Gospel Advocate,* who was closely associated with his work for forty years, said, "Almost every Negro congregation [Church of Christ] in our state was either founded by Brother Keeble or reflects the imprint of his work through someone else."[65]

NOTES

Studies on Marshall Keeble include the following: Forrest N. Rhoads Sr., "A Study of the Sources of Marshall Keeble's Effectiveness as a Preacher" (Ph.D. diss., Southern Illinois Univ., 1970); J. E. Choate, *Roll Jordan Roll: A Biography of Marshall Keeble* (Nashville, 1968); B. C. Goodpasture, ed., *Biography and Sermons of Marshall Keeble* (Nashville, 1931); Arthur L. Smith Jr., "A Rhetorical Analysis of the Speaking of Marshall Keeble" (master's thesis, Pepperdine Univ., 1966); Marshall Keeble, *From Mule Back to Super Jet with the Gospel* (Nashville, 1962).

1. *Gospel Advocate* 57 (Dec. 30, 1915): 1326–27.

2. Ibid., 53 (Feb. 16, 1911): 206–7; 54 (Dec. 5, 1912): 1308–9; 57 (Dec. 2, 1915): 1226–27; 59 (Aug. 9, 1917), 762.

3. Ibid., 110 (May 2, 1968): 274; *Firm Foundation* 85 (May 14, 1968): 306; *Nashville Tennessean Sunday Magazine,* Mar. 29, 1964, 6–7, 15; Choate, *Roll Jordan Roll,* xiii.

4. *Firm Foundation* 85 (May 14,1968): 306.

5. *Gospel Advocate* 110 (May 23: 1968), 324.

6. Howard Winters, *Carolina Christian* 10 (June 1968): 9.

7. *Christian Echo* 68 (Feb. 1970): 2–3.

8. Ibid., 63 (Dec. 1968): 2.

9. Ibid., 3.

10. Ibid., 68 (Feb. 1970): 2–3.

11. Rhoads, "A Study of the Sources," 231.

12. Transcript of Rhoads interview with Keeble, June 7, 1967.

13. Choate, *Roll Jordan Roll,* 52; *Gospel Advocate* 66 (Jan. 3, 1924): 23.

14. *Gospel Advocate* 80 (Feb. 17, 1938): 163; 64 (Aug. 3, 1922), 742; 63 (Oct. 20, 1931): 1040; 83 (Feb. 27, 1941): 213; 82 (Oct. 10, 1940): 979; 57 (Dec. 16, 1915): 1227; 81 (Mar. 23, 1939): 282; 93 (Oct. 4, 1951): 638; 79 (Apr. 15, 1937): 352.

15. *Nashville Tennessean Sunday Magazine,* Mar. 29, 1964, 15; Rhoads, "A Study of the Sources," 103.

16. *Gospel Advocate* 63 (Jan. 1921): 78.

17. Ibid., (Sept. 15, 1921): 911.

18. Transcripts of Rhoads interview with Keeble, Apr. 29, 1967; Choate, *Roll Jordan Roll,* 17.

19. About the turn of the century, Keeble joined a group led by S. W. Womack out of the Lea Avenue and Gay Street Christian Churches to establish the Jackson Street Church of Christ; Rhoads, "A Study of the Sources," 59; Choate, *Roll Jordan Roll,* 7.

20. Rhoads, "A Study of the Sources," 72.

21. Transcript of Rhoads interview with Keeble, June 7, 1967.
22. *Nashville Tennessean Sunday Magazine,* Mar. 29, 1964, 6.
23. Choate, *Roll Jordan Roll,* 56.
24. Rhoads, "A Study of the Sources," 115.
25. Ibid.
26. Ibid., 113–15.
27. Ibid., 130.
28. *Gospel Advocate* 63 (Jan. 20, 1921): 78.
29. *Christian Leader* 45 (Aug. 25, 1931): 6.
30. Ibid.
31. Choate, *Roll Jordan Roll,* 54.
32. *Gospel Advocate* 83 (Oct. 15, 1931): 1289.
33. Rhoads, "A Study of the Sources," 106–8; Choate, *Roll Jordan Roll,* 53–54.
34. Ibid.
35. Ibid.
36. Ibid.
37. Rhoads, "A Study of the Sources," 120; Choate, *Roll Jordan Roll,* 78–79; Smith, "Rhetorical Analysis," 42.
38. Rhoads, "A Study of the Sources," 87–88.
39. Rhoads, "A Study of the Sources," 105; *Nashville Tennessean Sunday Magazine,* Mar. 29, 1964, 7, 15.
40. Marshall Keeble, "The Church among the Colored," *Abilene Christian College Lectures* (Austin, 1950), 151–52.
41. Ibid., 144; Choate, *Roll Jordan Roll,* 58–59.
42. Keeble, "Church among the Colored," 147–48.
43. Ibid.
44. *Gospel Advocate* 110 (July 18, 1968): 458–59.
45. *Christian Leader* 45 (Aug. 25, 1931): 6.
46. Rhoads, "A Study of the Sources," 269.
47. Ibid., 210.
48. Ibid., 224.
49. Ibid., 255.
50. Ibid., 269.
51. Ibid., 269; Goodpasture, *Biography and Sermons,* 61–62.
52. Rhoads, "A Study of the Sources," 210–50.
53. *Gospel Advocate* 75 (Sept. 21, 1933): 909.
54. Rhoads, "A Study of the Sources," 94–95; *Nashville Christian Institute Catalogue,* 1941–42, 11.
55. *Gospel Advocate* 86 (May 18, 1944): 341.
56. Ibid., 90 (Dec. 9, 1948): 1188–89.
57. Ibid., 95 (Sept. 24, 1953): 630.

58. Transcript of Rhoads's interview with Keeble, June 7, 1967. Laura Johnson Keeble, Marshall Keeble's widow (his first wife, Minnie Womack Keeble, died in 1932), was his devoted helpmeet for thirty-four years and his coworker in building the Nashville Christian Institute, where she shared with him the affection of the students. Her contribution to the school was so important that one writer called her "Keeble's eyes, ears, and hands" while he was away preaching and raising funds for the school. *Gospel Advocate* 98 (Feb. 9, 1956): 133.

59. Keeble, "Church among the Colored," 146, 156.

60. *Gospel Advocate* 80 (Nov. 3, 1938): 1040–41, (Sept. 22, 1938): 900.

61. Interview with R. N. Hogan, June 25, 1976; interview with David Jones, June 22, 1976.

62. Ibid., 107.

63. Marshall Keeble, "Turned Loose" (lecture delivered at Freed-Hardeman College, Feb. 1967, in Let the Bible Speak Cassette Study Series [West Monroe, La., 1974]).

64. Choate, *Roll Jordan Roll,* 107.

65. *Gospel Advocate* 110 (May 2, 1968): 278.

Section 5

American Primitivism

Hoosier Brethren and the Origins of the Restoration Movement

David B. Eller

Frontier Indiana was a patchwork of competing religious views and interests. The Great Kentucky Revival at Cane Ridge in 1801 had set the dominant spiritual mood for evangelical Protestants, and in the years following Cane Ridge the fires of revival had swept across the Ohio Valley. In the Hoosier State, as in the rest of the Midwest, the result was a tremendous increase in adherents to such sects as the Methodists and Baptists, who were ready and able to serve up religion warm, if not hot.

An important part of the story of the growth of evangelical Protestantism in the Ohio Valley was the rise of the Disciples movement, popularly known as the "Restoration" because of its emphasis on restoring simple or "primitive" New Testament Christianity as the norm for faith and practice. The Disciples are usually said to have been inspired by Alexander Campbell, a Presbyterian turned Baptist reformer, and Barton W. Stone, a veteran of Cane Ridge. Working independently before 1832 and cooperatively thereafter, these two pioneer ministers led a reform crusade that resulted in the formation of the Christian Church (Disciples of Christ) by about 1840. In Indiana, however, restoration activities previous to the mid-1830s were indigenous and largely independent of Stone and Campbell.[1]

Although historians of the Disciples of Christ have long recognized the significant contributions of the German Baptist Brethren, or Dunkers, to restoration reforms in southern Indiana, their accounts have usually been vague as to the congregations involved, their location, origin, and leadership. Brethren writers, who until recently were apparently unaware that several of their congregations merged into the restoration movement, have not clarified this picture. However, a comparison of Disciples source materials with those of the Brethren reveals an explicit relationship between the two groups.[2] And an understanding of the tradition and religious views of the German Baptist Brethren helps to place their involvement with the Disciples in its proper perspective.

The German Baptists of the early nineteenth century were a closed, noncreedal, pietist, and Anabaptist sect of European origin. Refugees of this group arrived in Pennsylvania as early as 1719. Like their Mennonite neighbors, with whom they were often confused, the Brethren grew and prospered in America. At least thirty congregation-communities were established before the Revolution, primarily in Pennsylvania, Maryland, and the Carolinas.[3]

The Brethren were distinguished from other religious groups by several important characteristics, perhaps the most significant of which was their form of baptism. The Brethren insisted on trine (that is, thrice repeated) immersion, with face forward, in flowing water. It was from this practice that the popular designation Dunker, or Dunkard, was derived. Most Baptist groups, by contrast, immersed once, face backward.[4] Another unique practice of the Brethren was their observance of love feast. This church ordinance was patterned after the last meal which Jesus ate with his disciples in the upper room in Jerusalem (John 13). It consisted of the washing of feet, a fellowship meal (the Lord's Supper), and communion with bread and wine. Love feast was held over a weekend, usually once or twice a year, and was one of the most important gatherings of the church.[5]

Several other characteristics made the Brethren a distinct people. They practiced nonresistance (defenseless pacifism) with regard to the state and civil authority. They developed an Annual Meeting, composed of representatives from each congregation, to decide matters of polity and doctrine. Like the Quakers and Mennonites, the Brethren also wore plain dress, which included bonnets and prayer coverings for the sisters and beards and broad-brimmed hats for the men. In addition, most Brethren in the early nineteenth century remained German in culture and preferred sectarian isolation to integration with the mainstream of American society.[6]

As was the case with many religious groups, Brethren were quick to move west with the frontier following the American Revolution. Dunker families had crossed the Allegheny Mountains into Kentucky shortly before 1790. Ohio had organized congregations by 1802, Indiana by 1809, and Illinois by 1815. Certain areas of southwest Ohio and north central Indiana became centers of Brethren activity in the mid and late nineteenth century.[7] As many as fifteen Dunker congregations across the Ohio Valley may have joined the restoration movement, and it is likely that most of these churches were located in southern Indiana.[8]

In contrast to most other pioneer Brethren congregations in Ohio or in other regions of the Hoosier State, Dunker congregations in southern Indiana had family roots in North Carolina, Kentucky, or both.[9] For example, Olive Branch, which may have had preaching services as early as 1803, had definite ties to North Carolina. The church was located in present-day Owen Township, Clark County, a short distance from the Ohio River. Jacob Stutzman, a Dunker minister from

Randolph County, North Carolina, settled in this area in 1802. Other families from Stutzman's former congregational area on the Uwharry River in North Carolina, including most of his large family, joined him in Indiana by 1806.[10]

Two of the earliest and largest Dunker churches in the Hoosier State were located to the west of Olive Branch in Orange and Lawrence Counties. Brethren who had moved to this area from Shelby County, Kentucky, organized the Lost River congregation in Orleans Township, Orange County, in 1819. These families included the Hostetlers, Leathermans, Sniders, and Hardmans. To the north of Lost River was the White River church, located in Indian Creek Township, Lawrence County, and organized about 1821. Important families identified with this congregation included the Kerns, Ribelins, and Sears. Both the Kern and Sears families were from Nicholas and Bourbon Counties, Kentucky, and prior to that from Rowan County, North Carolina. The Sears family had moved to the White River area by way of Harrison County, Indiana, where Brethren had previously formed the Bethel church in present-day Morgan Township. The Foutz and Hon families were also associated with the Bethel congregation. In addition to Olive Branch, Lost River, White River, and Bethel, there were also Brethren settlements of southern background in Jackson, Washington, Monroe, and possibly Dubois Counties before 1825.[11]

The merger of the Brethren from southern Indiana with the Disciples movement was a gradual process that took place in two stages. The first of these was the formation of an association of congregations independent of the Annual Meeting. The second was contact between leaders of the association and those of the emerging restoration movement.

Although all Brethren were supposedly unified by the Annual Meeting, close family ties, and traveling senior ministers called elders, the congregations in southern Indiana, because of their location and southern background, lacked adequate communication with other frontier Dunker congregations or the Annual Meeting. One restoration source suggests that about 1820 the Brethren in southern Indiana formed themselves into an "association" independent of the Annual Meeting because they were "unwilling to conform to all the rules observed by the brethren in Ohio, Pennsylvania and other states."[12] Brethren records indicate that at about this same time a group led by Adam Hostetler of Kentucky was removed from fellowship by the eastern church. It seems clear that the "Hostetler party" formed the basis of the independent association with congregations in Kentucky, Ohio, and Indiana. The number of members in this schismatic group has been estimated by some Brethren writers as high as fifteen hundred.[13]

Unfortunately, very little is known about Adam Hostetler. Originally from western Pennsylvania, he settled in Shelby County, Kentucky, in 1794 with his parents and other married brothers and sisters. At that time he and his father,

Christian Hostetler (Hochstetler), were already ministers in the Dunker faith, the father preaching in German and the son in English. In 1825, after an extensive itinerant ministry among Brethren settlements in Kentucky, Indiana, and Illinois, the younger Hostetler moved to the Olive Branch community in Clark County, Indiana. He died there in 1826.[14]

For reasons which are not known, Adam Hostetler and Peter Hon, a young minister, from Nicholas County, Kentucky, began to spread "strange doctrine" that was not in keeping with Brethren tradition. While existing Brethren records are vague, it is evident that Hostetler and Hon were expelled from the church sometime between 1816 and 1820. One source suggests that at least two church councils were held on the Hostetler-Hon controversy. The first met in 1820 in Muhlenberg County, Kentucky, and a second sometime later at Adam Hostetler's home in Shelby County, Kentucky. Brethren leaders from the eastern church attended both meetings. Hostetler and his followers faced several charges, including one that stated that they had become "too zealous in religious excitements," which more than likely suggests the sympathy of western Brethren for frontier revivalism.[15] Other issues included both Hostetler's and Hon's failure to conform to the standards of the Annual Meeting regarding plain dress, their acceptance of slave ownership among Brethren, and their use of an innovative and unacceptable procedure for feet washing during the love feast.[16]

Another Brethren source indicates that Hostetler and Hon were expelled from the church at a council held in Muhlenberg County, Kentucky, in 1816. The issues before this meeting were not given except that Hostetler and Hon were thought to have followed in the heretical footsteps of one John Ham. The identity of Ham is obscure. He was supposedly an eighteenth-century North Carolina Dunker leader who openly preached the final restoration of all souls from hell, or "universalism." The Annual Meeting of 1797 placed Ham and his sympathizers out of the church. Some of them later moved to the Green River country in Warren County, Kentucky. Universalist, or "restitution," ideas were widely held among the frontier Brethren in western Kentucky, Illinois, and Missouri.[17]

Universalism, however, was probably not a significant factor in the formation of the independent Brethren Association in Indiana. Of the churches in this group, only Olive Branch seems to have had connections with Universalists and may have embraced Universalist doctrine. The Stutzman family had close associations with Brethren universalism in North Carolina. Adam Bower, who had had contacts with the Stutzmans and other Brethren in North Carolina, moved near the Olive Branch community in 1805. He had "universalist preaching" in his Indiana home as early as 1812.[18]

In any event, by 1820 the Hostetler Brethren were in disagreement with Annual Meeting Brethren over a variety of issues concerning both doctrine and practice. It was not long, however, before the association itself was embroiled in a controversy over the form or mode of baptism. Peter Hon and Abraham Kern of the White River church began to advocate and employ a single action immersion rather than the customary dipping three times.[19] When this shift in practice began is not known. It may have dated from the very beginnings of the association, perhaps even earlier. The reasons for the change are also not clear. It is possible that both Hon and Kern were influenced in Kentucky by the more numerous Baptists.

Interestingly enough, the Brethren Annual Meeting of 1821, which assembled in Somerset County, Pennsylvania, addressed itself to the single immersion problem. The existing minutes do not record which congregation sent the following query, but it could well have originated out of the unrest in southern Indiana and Kentucky. Article 6 of the minutes questioned "Whether members (persons) might be received into the church who have been but once immersed (without rebaptizing them in the manner we believe it ought to be done according to the gospel)?"[20] The answer of the meeting is surprising, perhaps, in that it indicated flexibility on the part of the eastern leadership. After affirming that trine immersion was the true baptism, the Brethren decided that "if such persons would be content with their baptism and yet acknowledge the Brethren's order as right, we would leave it over to them and receive them with the laying on of hands and prayer."[21] This answer does not suggest that ministers were permitted to employ a single-action immersion. It may have been, however, a gesture of reconciliation to the western Brethren. Those baptized by Hon and Kern could remain in full fellowship with the brotherhood if the traditional practice was affirmed as correct. If the decision of the Annual Meeting was indeed such a gesture, it met with no known reply. So powerful was the move toward single immersion within the western association that by 1826 its advocates completely dominated the independent group.

It was at approximately this point in time, around 1827, that John Wright of Washington County, Indiana, leader of a small group of independent Baptist churches, suggested a merger between his group and the Dunkers.[22] This action marks the beginning of the second stage in the transition of the Brethren into the restoration movement. The necessary preparation for Wright's proposal, however, had taken place previously within the association under the leadership of Joseph Hostetler, a minister in the Lost Creek congregation and a nephew of Adam Hostetler. More was at issue than the mode of baptism. The very identity of the southern Indiana Brethren as a distinctive religious group was in question.

More is known about Joseph Hostetler than about any other minister in the association. Born in Kentucky, he moved to Indiana in 1818, when he was already a licensed preacher in the Brethren fraternity. After settling in Orange County he was ordained in 1821 by his uncle, Adam, during an annual gathering of the newly formed association. Young Joseph was known as the "boy preacher," and he apparently had considerable powers of persuasion. Between 1821 and 1825 he is believed to have visited several Brethren communities, baptizing more than one hundred converts. This period in his life was also marked by intense spiritual searching and personal study. One result was a growing dissatisfaction with Dunker sectarianism, a dissatisfaction that became intensified by his reading of Alexander Campbell's monthly periodical, the *Christian Baptist*.[23]

Published from 1823 to 1830, the *Christian Baptist* was an early voice of the Restoration movement and reflected its founder's criticism of narrow, sectarian, Baptist practices. Campbell and his supporters discarded denominational names, believing that "Christian" was sufficient title for the converted. They taught primitive, New Testament Christianity as the only rule of faith and practice, baptism by immersion for believers only and as necessary for the remission of sin, weekly observance of communion (the Lord's Supper), and local congregational autonomy. Campbell believed that higher levels of church government, such as the Brethren's Annual Meeting, were without biblical authority and should be purely advisory.[24]

A letter written by Joseph Hostetler to Campbell in December 1825 reflects not only the young preacher's searching but also the rapid growth of membership within the association:

> A sincere desire to know the truth as it is in Christ, is the sole cause of these lines . . . I belong to a church called "German, Baptists," sometimes "Dunkards," whose government is the New Testament only. They are not the same in principle or faith with those of the old connection in Pennsylvania, Virginia, Maryland, and Ohio; but an order that took rise from them in Kentucky, by one *Teacher* [Adam Hostetler], in Shelby about six years ago, amounting now to about two thousand, having about 24 teachers, and increasing fast. Our views of christianity you expressed in the *Christian Baptist* vol 2d, . . . and in the whole second volume I do not see anything to divide us in sentiment, though I do not approve of some things in your lst and 3d volumes.[25]

Hostetler went on to question Campbell on several points of doctrine. Why, for example, did not he, as an advocate of primitive Christianity, practice feet washing and the holy kiss of charity or observe communion at night, following the apostolic (and Brethren) practice? Reflecting the debate within the association, Hostetler also asked for Campbell's opinion on trine immersion baptism. "I yet think it [trine-immersion] is the proper action of baptism, and think that it should not be performed transversely, but forwards, in the most humble manner of obedience."[26]

Campbell lost little time in replying to the concerns expressed. Although Hostetler specifically requested a personal response, Campbell printed both the letter and his answer in the *Christian Baptist*. His basic point was that many Brethren practices, such as the holy kiss and feet washing, were social customs of the apostolic church and not rituals required for discipleship. He also expressed his preference for single immersion since baptism in the New Testament is spoken of as one act.[27]

Hostetler's biographer recorded the young Brethren's overall reaction to Campbell and the *Christian Baptist* in this way: "he read with eagerness though not with entire approbation; for being yet identified with a sect he felt that the blows descended too fast and too heavy. But still the light entered; the faith once delivered to the saints and long obscured by the traditions of men, became more and more apparent; objections to creeds and sects continued to be multiplied; until he found it impossible to refrain from a full and public avowal of his sentiments."[28] It seems evident that Hostetler was persuaded by Campbell's logic and soon adjusted his doctrinal perspective.

Accordingly, in the spring of 1826 Hostetler announced that he would preach on "primitive Christianity" at a specified day and time at Orleans, Orange County, Indiana. A crowd, perhaps generously estimated at one thousand and including several of his fellow Dunker ministers, gathered for the address. For an hour and a half the boy preacher spoke on the theme that "the disciples were called Christian first at Antioch." In doing so he squarely placed himself in sympathy with Campbell's emerging Restoration movement. So powerful was his preaching that the audience was moved against the use of denominational names. Some of the Brethren ministers, however, were not so easily convinced. Hostetler was informed that he would face stern charges at the next yearly meeting of the association. Not wanting to leave the decision of that body to chance, he undertook a personal visit to each member congregation explaining his position.[29]

Evidence suggests that the association meeting of 1826 took place in August at the Somerset Creek (East Union) meetinghouse, which was Peter Hon's home congregation in Nicholas County, Kentucky. The irony of the occasion must have been apparent to some. An independent Brethren association, formed after the expulsion of Adam Hostetler from the Annual Meeting church for holding non-Brethren views, now listened to his nephew explain why a Brethren identity should be altogether terminated. Young Joseph Hostetler so completely vindicated himself of all charges that he was asked to deliver the main address at the next annual gathering of the association. He reportedly thought to himself: "This day death passed upon this ecclesiastical body. About this time next year it will breathe its last; and my discourse shall be its funeral."[30]

It was apparently at the yearly association meeting of 1827 that John Wright and his brother, Peter, of the Blue River Baptists came to the Brethren with their plea of unity. Joseph Hostetler no doubt delivered his "funeral discourse." Adam Hostetler, who had been the strongest Brethren preacher of the previous generation and who might conceivably have been in a position to influence the

Brethren away from reforms inspired by Campbell, had died the previous September. The Dunkers and the Baptists agreed to form one fraternal organization and to call themselves "Christians." John Wright then proposed that the new coalition consider merger with the New Lights, and he was authorized to undertake correspondence with them for this purpose.[31]

Frontier New Light Christian churches are difficult to define precisely. One such group, based in Kentucky and led by Barton W. Stone, emerged out of the Great Kentucky Revival. Other unrelated and independent "old Christian" movements, primarily Methodist and Baptist in background, were active in New England, Virginia, and North Carolina before the turn of the century. The earliest New Light congregations in Indiana were of the "old Christian" connection rather than from the Stone group. It is likely that John Wright wrote to the "Eastern Conference of the Christian Church in Indiana," an organization formed in 1827 primarily of "old Christian" congregations. Beverley Vawter was the clerk of this conference.[32]

The traditional interpretation of John and Peter Wright's merger efforts has been that a unity conference of Baptists, Dunkers, and New Lights was arranged for July 1828. Representatives met on a farm just south of Edinburgh in Bartholomew County, Indiana. No detailed minutes or records of this meeting were kept, of course, for fear of setting up new denominational rules and creeds. Joseph Hostetler, John Wright, and Beverley Vawter, each representing their religious traditions, agreed to drop denominational names and creeds and to work cooperatively in a loose organization called the "Southern District."[33]

Two reports of the Edinburgh conference that appeared in Barton W. Stone's monthly publication, the *Christian Messenger,* describe the 1828 meeting in other terms which give an entirely different flavor to the proceedings. According to these reports, the meeting was merely the "second Conference of the Eastern District of the Christian Church." The presiding elder, Jesse Hughs, recorded the ministers present. Included were John Wright, Peter Wright, and Beverley Vawter. Neither the name of Joseph Hostetler nor that of any other clearly recognizable Brethren minister is on this list.[34] Another New Light minister, Joseph Hatchitt, described the Wright brothers at Edinburgh:

> The Wright Brothers, whose names you will see in the minutes have been formerly denominated "Depending Baptists," but lately have laid that name aside, and now call themselves the "church of Christ." I judge there are six to eight elders among them, and many churches. When we met in conference together, we could find nothing to separate us asunder. In fine, we saw as nearly eye to eye as any company of Elders who have assembled in modern times—and there was such a sweet spirit of love.[35]

The correspondence of Hughs and Hatchitt does not suggest that a formal merger of any kind took place. Indeed, Brethren participation in this meeting is doubtful. The number of elders listed as being in the "church of Christ" more nearly reflects John Wright's group of Baptists alone than it does a combined Dunker-Baptist organization. Still, it is evident that the Wrights were in full cooperation with the New Light body. They were asked to bear a letter of greeting to another New Light Christian conference in Harrison County, and John Wright was also chosen a member of a "presbytery" (committee) to ordain a candidate to the ministry.[36]

The mystery of who merged with whom remains. It is clear that after 1827 the Brethren Association ceased to function as a separate group and that its leaders became public advocates of the Restoration movement. Joseph Hostetler and Peter Hon traveled widely in 1829 and 1830 among Brethren communities in Indiana, Kentucky, and Ohio urging full participation in the movement.[37] It was John Wright, however, who played the crucial role of bringing the Brethren into restoration activities in Indiana. His personal relationship to the Brethren merits further attention.

The Wrights were a family of Quaker background from near the Uwharry Brethren area in Rowan and Randolph Counties, North Carolina. John Wright was born there but grew to adulthood in Powell's Valley, Virginia. After a short period in Wayne County, Kentucky, he moved to Clark County, Indiana, where he was baptized in 1808. In 1810 he relocated on the Blue River in Washington County. He was soon joined there by his father, Amos; uncle, Philbert Wright; younger brother, Peter; and other brothers as well. John, Amos, and Peter are credited with forming the Blue River Baptist Church in 1811. They all eventually became preachers. John Wright continued to reside in this general area until his death but spent his last eight years in an extensive itinerant ministry.[38]

The Blue River Baptist Church and others organized by the Wrights in a "Blue River Association" have been variously described as "free will" or "dependent" Baptists. Presumably this meant that like the Brethren, and in contrast to most American Baptist groups that developed out of the Calvinist tradition, the Wrights emphasized man's "free choice" in securing salvation. Also like the Brethren, their churches were non-creedal and organized on the principle of the Bible alone as sufficient guide for faith and practice. Accordingly, they did not identify with the more numerous "general" Baptists. Indeed, the closest and earliest association of the Wrights in Indiana was with the Brethren.[39]

Amos Wright had become a Dunker in North Carolina, probably when he married into a German Baptist family. His brother, Philbert, married into the Sears family, which was also Brethren. While restoration sources do not describe John Wright as a Dunker, there is at least one local tradition from Olive Branch that so remembers him:

> the Dunkards had a church early in this century [nineteenth] in what is known as Owen Township. It is known by the name of Olive Branch chapel. Revs. Messrs. John

Wright and Mr. Hughes, the former a Dunkard and the latter a New-Light, united and formed a union . . . Rev. John Wright, who came from North Carolina, had but few followers, and of course it was easy to go over to the new faith. The great hindrance to the coalition with the Dunkards was their mode of worship. But the union dispensed with trine baptism, or dipping three times, which according to their discipline was a necessary part of their religion. Feet-washing, too, was discarded by Rev. Mr. Hughes and between them both a satisfactory settlement of conflicting views was made.[40]

While no date is given in this account, it does confirm Brethren and New Light cooperation. Reverend Hughes may well have been the same Jesse Hughs who chaired the Edinburgh conference.[41]

This passage identifying John Wright with the Dunkers, however, raises more problems than can be resolved. Wright's merger proposal to the Hostetler Brethren supposedly came after they had agreed to adopt the single immersion mode of baptism. According to the above account, Wright himself practiced trine immersion. The passage also indicates that Hughes compromised on feet washing, a practice central to the Brethren but unknown in New Light circles. If Wright were indeed a Dunker, he, rather than Hughes, should have yielded on this point. And it is known that Wright, who regularly conducted services at Olive Branch in the 1840s, practiced feet washing in his later ministry.[42] Whatever Wright's religious background—Dunker, independent free will Baptist, or some combination of the two—his relationship to the southern Indiana Brethren was obviously close, and his influence among them was apparently quite strong.[43]

Several Brethren ministers became leading advocates of the restoration. Joseph Hostetler remained perhaps the most influential. He traveled widely in Indiana, Michigan, and Illinois; labored in and organized a number of new "churches of Christ"; defended Campbellism from Methodist attacks in a pamphlet entitled *Calumnies Refuted;* and while in Illinois debated publicly with pioneer Dunker Elder Isham Gibson.[44] John Ribble, David S. Lewis, and Christian Hostetler, a younger brother of Joseph Hostetler, also had Brethren backgrounds and worked in the Restoration movement. These men were from the Lost River church—today known as Old Liberty. Abraham Kern from White River—today called Old Union—his brother Conrad of Monroe County, and his first cousin Alexander Kern of Lawrence County became "Christian" preachers. Peter Hon and his brother Solomon, both of Kentucky, and George H. Hon of the Bethel and later Old Liberty congregations were still other ministers of Brethren background who were active in the restoration. Much like Joseph Hostetler, Peter Hon traveled and preached widely in Kentucky, Indiana, and Ohio, organizing new restoration congregations.[45] In fact, all the identifiable ministers in the independent Brethren association eventually joined the Campbell movement.

At about the same time that the western association Brethren were merging into the restoration, the Brethren of the Annual Meeting shut the door on single immersion. In 1827 the issue of the proper mode of baptism was raised, but the meeting reaffirmed its decision of 1821. The following year the matter was again introduced. This time the meeting counseled that candidates from other churches ought to be baptized again in the "true manner." Between 1832 and 1834 several new queries were introduced on the subject, but the language of the meeting became more and more uncompromising. Trine immersion became again the only form of baptism that the Brethren recognized.[46]

Although the Hostetler Brethren may be considered advocates of the Campbell restoration after 1827, the change from Dunker to Disciple was apparently gradual. Evidence suggests that Abraham Kern's congregation may not have fully embraced the movement until 1832; Olive Branch not until 1839.[47] Joseph Hostetler wrote that his father, a deacon in the Dunker faith from 1796, did not support the restoration until 1831. Other members may have retained a Brethren identity much longer.[48] It is also true that while the Brethren gave up some unique practices and customs, they retained others. Feet washing, for example, was practiced by John Wright, Peter Hon, and Joseph Hostetler until the close of their active ministry. Hostetler vigorously defended this service as a church ordinance in print as late as 1847.[49]

After 1827 the schism that began with the expulsion of Adam Hostetler and Peter Hon was complete. The noncreedal faith of the Brethren, their emphasis on New Testament primitivism, their similarity with Campbell on the necessity of adult (believer's) baptism—these factors made the Dunkers of Hostetler's association ripe for a redefinition of their religious identity along restoration lines. In 1820 it must have appeared to Adam Hostetler, Joseph Hostetler, Abraham Kern, and Peter Hon that the eastern Brethren were becoming more sectarian in terms of church government, distinctive dress, continued use of the German language, and integration into American culture and values—all in an age when unity and cooperation among frontier Christians were being stressed. The Brethren in southern Indiana and Kentucky clearly wanted to practice their faith without the restrictions of the eastern church and the Annual Meeting. They favored an independent frontier spirit, and their association was an attempt to capture that spirit. Once they abandoned trine immersion baptism, however, there was little that separated them from other frontier Baptist groups.

It is a paradox of the Disciples restoration that Campbell's crusade for undoing denominationalism eventually gave rise in fact to yet another denomination. The Hostetler Brethren, however, undoubtedly viewed their involvement as a return to primitive Christianity without the narrow strictures of Dunker tradition. The Hostetler-Wright merger in 1827 was the first of many in Indiana only indirectly influenced by Campbell that over time became identified as the Disciples of Christ.[50]

By 1839, when the Disciples held their first state convention in Indianapolis with Barton W. Stone as the featured speaker, the Dunker background congregations were in full cooperation. A partial census of participating congregations compiled at that time includes Lost River, White River, Olive Branch, and Bethel.[51] The southern Indiana Brethren had become Disciple Christians.

NOTES

1. The best study of the Indiana Restoration movement is Henry K. Shaw, *Hoosier Disciples: A Comprehensive History of the Christian Churches (Disciples of Christ) in Indiana* (St. Louis, 1966), esp. 19–111.

2. One of the first discussions of Brethren contributions to Disciples beginnings in Indiana was H. Clay Trusty, "Formation of the Christian Church in Indiana," *Indiana Magazine of History* 6 (Mar. 1910): 17–32. Commodore Wesley Cauble, *Disciples of Christ in Indiana: Achievements of a Century* (Indianapolis, 1930), 30–38; and Shaw, *Hoosier Disciples*, 48–51, 79–82, treated the role of the Brethren in somewhat more detail. The standard treatment of the Brethren in Indiana is Otho Winger, *History of the Church of the Brethren in Indiana* (Elgin, Ill., 1917). Winger does not mention any of the congregations herein discussed or the Brethren relationship to the Disciples movement. Roger Sappington, ed., *The Brethren in the New Nation: A Source Book on the Development of the Church of the Brethren, 1785–1865* (Elgin, Ill., 1976), 114–22, contains source materials on Brethren involvement with the Disciples, much of it focusing on Indiana.

3. An excellent volume of source materials on the Brethren in colonial America is Donald F. Durnbaugh, ed., *The Brethren in Colonial America: A Source Book on the Transplantation and Development of the Church of the Brethren in the Eighteenth Century* (Elgin, Ill., 1967). Pages 172–91 contain a statistical ordering of congregations made in 1770–72 by Morgan Edwards, a Baptist historian.

4. For a description of this form of baptism and a discussion of its importance for nineteenth-century Brethren, see Sappington, *Brethren in the New Nation*, 131–68.

5. The love feast is described in Sappington, *Brethren in the New Nation*, 168–77.

6. Floyd E. Mallott, *Studies in Brethren History* (Elgin, Ill., 1954), 149–63, 245–56, 267–74. A popular account of the Brethren in the 1840s is James H. Lehman, *The Old Brethren* (Elgin, Ill., 1976).

7. Sappington, *Brethren in the New Nation*, 15–102; Mallott, *Studies in Brethren History*, 112–48.

8. Madison Evans, *Biographical Sketches of the Pioneer Preachers of Indiana* (Philadelphia, 1862), 32. Not all of these fifteen congregations can be located or otherwise identified. Included in this figure may be Brethren congregations that joined the Restoration movement in Kentucky and Ohio. See David B. Eller, "Peter Hon of East Union," *Brethren Life and Thought* 18 (Spring 1972): 5–12.

9. Most Brethren pioneers in the Ohio Valley came from Pennsylvania, Maryland, or Virginia. See Winger, *History of the Brethren in Indiana*, 15–16; Mallott, *Studies in Brethren History*, 119–20; and Lester H. Binnie, "Migration of Early German Baptist Brethren within the United States," *Palatine Immigrant* 5 (Summer 1979): 6–7. Sappington, *Brethren in the New Nation*, 29–53, was one of the first to call attention to the importance of Brethren migration from the South into Kentucky and the Midwest. See also David B. Eller, "The Brethren in the Western Ohio Valley, 1790–1850: German Baptist Settlement and Frontier Accommodation" (Ph.D. diss., Miami Univ., 1976), 153–76, for a more detailed discussion of the southern background and origins of the Olive Branch, Lost River, and White River churches.

10. Traditional Brethren interpretation is that the Four Mile church, organized in 1809 in present-day Union County, is the oldest Dunker church in the state. Winger, *Brethren in Indiana*, 59–60. The evidence presented in the text, however, suggests that Olive Branch may have preceded it. The Olive Branch meetinghouse was built in 1821 and located a short distance northeast of Jacob Stutzman's land. *Christian Record* 4 (Apr. 1847): 293–94; 4 (June 1847): 365–67; Deed Book 26, 401–2, County Clerk's Office, Clark County Courthouse, Jeffersonville, Ind. The congregation is also described in *History of the Ohio Falls Cities and Their Counties with Illustrations and Biographical Sketches*, 2 vols. (Cleveland, 1882), 2:379. Stutzman's North Carolina ministry is briefly discussed in Roger E. Sappington, "Dunker Beginnings in North Carolina in the Eighteenth Century," *North Carolina Historical Review* 46 (July 1969), 224–28. Stutzman's family is described in John Scott Davenport, "A Multiple Census-Based Ordering of the Family of Jacob Stutzman (Sr.), Wife Barbara, the Dunker Minister Who Served the Uwharrie Congregation, N.C., 1764–1801" (typewritten manuscript dated Dec. 12, 1971), 1–5. A photocopy of this manuscript is in the possession of the author of this article. Davenport's research on the immigration of North Carolina Brethren into the Ohio Valley has been of invaluable assistance in preparing this study. Unfortunately, there is little in the Clark County records or in local tradition that sheds light on the religious activities of the Stutzman family in Indiana prior to 1820.

11. *History of Lawrence, Orange and Washington Counties, Indiana* (Chicago, 1884), 222, 544; William H. Roose, *Indiana's Birthplace: A History of Harrison County, Indiana*, rev. ed. (Chicago: Arville L. Funk, 1966), 28; *History of Jackson County, Indiana: From the Earliest Time to the Present . . .* (Chicago, 1886), 442–43; Sappington, *Brethren in the New Nation*, 44–46. The pioneer Brethren congregations nearest to this cluster were Four Mile (1809) and Nettle Creek (1820) to the northeast in Union and Wayne Counties and Raccoon Creek (1827) to the north in Putnam and Montgomery Counties. These congregations probably had little or no contact with those mentioned in the text.

12. Evans, *Biographical Sketches of the Pioneer Preachers*, 63. Joseph Franklin and J. A. Headington, *The Life and Times of Benjamin Franklin* (St. Louis, 1879), 163–64, suggests that the independent Brethren group broke away over the question of single immersion baptism. Such a conclusion is, however, unlikely. See note 22 below.

13. Abraham Harley Cassel, "Some Account of the Origin and History of the Far Western and Congregational Brethren also, of Eldr. [Elder] Rule and A.M. [Annual Meeting] Supremacy," June 7, 1886, Cassel Collection (Juniata College, Huntington, Pa.).

14. Harvey Hostetler, *Descendants of Jacob Hochstetler, the Immigrant of 1736* (Elgin, Ill., 1912; reprint, Berlin, Ohio, 1970), 869; John Henry Moore, *Some Brethren Pathfinders* (Elgin, Ill., 1929), 71, 74–76. It is assumed that Hostetler resided in Kentucky until his move to the Olive Branch community. He owned land in both Jackson and Washington Counties, Indiana, but is not listed in the 1820 Indiana census. Deed Book 25, p. 20, Clark County Courthouse; Deed Book C, p. 250, County Clerk's Office, Washington County Courthouse, Salem, Ind.; and Deed Book A, p. 1, County Clerk's Office, Jackson County Courthouse, Brownstown, Ind. Hostetler is buried in the Olive Branch cemetery.

15. Cassel, "Some Account of the Far Western Brethren."

16. Ibid. See also Moore, *Brethren Pathfinders*, 89–90; and Martin Grove Brumbaugh, *A History of the German Baptist Brethren in Europe and America* (Mount Morris, Ill., 1899), 535–36.

17. John Wolfe, "Pioneer History," *Brethren at Work* 7 (Feb. 22, 1882), 4. See also Moore, *Brethren Pathfinders*, 74–76; and Henry R. Holsinger, *Holsinger's History of the Dunkers and the Brethren Church* (Lathrop, Calif., 1901), 219–26, 762–64. Wolfe supposedly obtained his information from "minutes" of the 1816 council which had been attended by his pioneer minister father, George Wolfe (1780–1865). For more on John Ham see Roger E. Sappington, "Two Eighteenth Century Dunker Congregations in North Carolina," *North Carolina Historical Review* 47 (Apr. 1970), 192–99. See also John Scott Davenport, "The Quest for the Identity of John H., Banned Carolina Dunker Who Took Universalism West" (typewritten manuscript dated 1977), 19ff. A photocopy of this manuscript is in the possession of the author of this article. Davenport suggests that a more logical and definable candidate for the "John H." expelled by Annual Meeting is John Hendricks, not John Ham. Hendricks was a Dunker Universalist pioneer minister active in North Carolina, Kentucky, and Missouri.

18. Durnbaugh, *Brethren in Colonial America*, 330; *History of Ohio Falls Cities*, 2:416.

19. Franklin and Headington, *The Life and Times of Benjamin Franklin*, 163–64; and Evans, *Pioneer Preachers*, 32.

20. *Minutes of the Annual Meeting of the Church of the Brethren; Containing All Available Minutes from 1778 to 1909* (Elgin, Ill., 1909), 45. There is no direct mention in these minutes of Adam Hostetler's expulsion or of the formation of an independent association of Brethren in southern Indiana and Kentucky. The phrases in parentheses are most likely editorial clarifications by Henry Kurtz, a frequent clerk of the Annual Meeting who published the first edition of minutes in 1867.

21. Ibid.

22. An alternative sequence suggests that Wright proposed union with the Brethren several years earlier, about 1822, but clearly after the question of single-immersion baptism had been settled. The Brethren agreed, called themselves "Christians," and formed

a new organization with the Baptists. In this sequence the ministry of Joseph Hostetler, discussed below, would have taken place within the context of an already combined Dunker-Baptist association, which is unlikely. For varying interpretations of these events, see Evans, *Pioneer Preachers*, 32–33, 66–67; Trusty, "Formation of the Christian Church in Indiana," 19–20; Cauble, *Disciples of Christ in Indiana*, 34; and Eugene B. Scofield, "Indiana," in John T. Brown, *Churches of Christ: A Historical, Biographical, and Pictorial History of the Churches* (Louisville, 1904), 217–18. The reconstruction of events in Shaw, *Hoosier Disciples*, 49–51, 78, seems most accurate. It is clear that the Brethren merged with the Baptists before the Edinburgh unity meeting of 1828, discussed below.

23. A biographical sketch of Joseph Hostetler is given in Evans, *Pioneer Preachers*, 57–73. Evans's account must be considered primary data. Hostetler was living in Illinois when *Pioneer Preachers* was published in 1862, and he contributed a short address to his "dear brethren" at the conclusion of Evans's sketch. On page 6 of the book Evans states: "The materials for the work have been obtained, chiefly, "from the surviving pioneers— to whom the author acknowledges his obligations—and the facts, incidents, and in most instances the dates may be confidently relied upon."

24. Much valuable information on Campbell and his ideas may be found in Robert Richardson, ed., *Memoirs of Alexander Campbell*, 2 vols. (Philadelphia, 1869–70). The standard history of the Disciples is William E. Tucker and Lester G. McAllister, *Journey in Faith: A History of the Christian Church (Disciples of Christ)* (St. Louis, 1975). Also helpful is James D. Murch, *Christians Only: A History of the Restoration Movement* (Cincinnati, 1962). For a brief discussion of the influence of the *Christian Baptist* on the early Restoration movement, see Winfred E. Garrison and Alfred T. DeGroot, *The Disciples of Christ: A History* (St. Louis, 1948), 175–79.

25. J[oseph] H[ostetler], "To the Editor," *Christian Baptist* 3 (Mar. 6, 1826): 162–63.

26. Ibid.

27. A[lexander] C[ampbell], "Reply to the Above," *Christian Baptist* 3 (Mar. 6, 1826): 163–67.

28. Evans, *Pioneer Preachers*, 64.

29. Ibid., 65.

30. Ibid., 66; Margret Kern Garrard, *The Family of Conrad Kern* (n.p., 1968), 38.

31. Adam Hostetler's will was admitted to probate in Clark County, Indiana, in October 1826. Will Book B, p. 342, Probate Court, Clark County Courthouse. Wright's merger proposal is briefly discussed in Cauble, *Disciples of Christ in Indiana*, 34; and Trusty, "Formation of the Christian Church in Indiana," 19.

32. For more on the various New Light groups in the Ohio Valley see Shaw, *Hoosier Disciples*, 27–36, 60–71. Vawter was born in Virginia and baptized a New Light in Kentucky. He moved to Jefferson County, Indiana, in 1819 and was a popular preacher among various New Light and nominally Baptist churches. As with Joseph Hostetler, by 1827 Vawter had also come under the influence of Campbell and the *Christian Baptist*. Evans, *Pioneer Preachers*, 101–25. See also *Christian Messenger* 1 (Aug. 25, 1827): 240.

33. Cauble, *Disciples of Christ in Indiana,* 34, 37; Trusty, "Formation of the Christian Church in Indiana," 20, 22–23. Evans, *Pioneer Preachers,* 67, suggests that the unity conference of 1828 took place within the context of what would have been the last meeting of the Brethren Association. It seems clear, however, that the conference was not arranged by the Dunkers.

34. Jesse Hughs, "[Correspondence] for the Christian Messenger," *Christian Messenger* 2 (Sept. 1828): 259. Other ministers at the conference included Henry Logan, Jesse Frazier, James Doudle, James Daughterly, William Tracy, William P. Richie, Thomas Johnson, Josiah Ashley, and Joseph Hatchitt. The unordained ministers were Pliny Hatchitt, James McCoy, and Leonard Henry.

35. Joseph Hatchitt, "A Letter from Elder J. Hatchitt," *Christian Messenger* 2 (Sept. 1828): 260–61. Although Hatchitt refers to minutes, his and Hughs's correspondence contained personal reports not official minutes.

36. Ibid.; Hughs, "Correspondence," 260.

37. Evans, *Pioneer Preachers,* 33–34, 67.

38. Ibid. A biographical sketch of John Wright is given on pages 29–41.

39. Ibid., 30–31. It would be incorrect to assume that the Dunkers or the Blue River Baptists were much concerned about orthodox theological positions. As biblical literalists they were more interested in faithfully observing New Testament commandments. Calvinism is a body of doctrine based on the teachings of the Geneva Reformer John Calvin, which emphasized the omnipotence of God, humanity's sinful nature, and the salvation of God's chosen, or elect, by unearned grace alone. For a discussion of Brethren theology in the early and mid-nineteenth century see Sappington, *Brethren in the New Nation,* 123–98.

40. *History of Ohio Falls Cities,* 2:373.

41. Little is known about Jesse Hughs. He was apparently affiliated with the "old Christian" New Light movement of the eastern states rather than with Barton W. Stone. Although he was the presiding officer at the organization of the "Eastern District of the Christian Church" (Indiana) in 1827, Hughs is not considered by either Shaw or Cauble to have been a major figure in the Indiana restoration. The available Clark County marriage records do not indicate any ministerial activity for him beyond 1829; in Lawrence County he performed marriages from 1828 until at least 1835. Marriage Record C, 18, 22, Clark County Courthouse; Marriage Record A, 229, 391, 506, County Clerk's Office, Lawrence County Courthouse, Bedford, Ind. See also Shaw, *Hoosier Disciples,* 32, 35n.

42. The best source on Wright's later ministry is John Wright, "Record of the Life and Pilgrimage of John Wright, Sr., 1844–1850" (typewritten manuscript, Washington County Historical Society, Salem, Ind.). Wright kept this diary, which consists primarily of travel accounts, after the death of his second wife. There are numerous references to former Brethren congregations and personalities that he had known from the beginning of the Restoration movement, perhaps earlier.

43. Indicative of Wright's close relationship with the Dunkers was his friendship with Abraham Kern. Sometime before 1837 Kern assisted Wright in a merger of the "Southern District" with the Silver Creek Regular Baptist Association in Clark and Jefferson Counties. Evans, *Pioneer Preachers,* 34, 39.

44. Ibid., 68–71; Shaw, *Hoosier Disciples,* 50n; and Minnie S. Buckingham, ed., *Church of the Brethren in Southern Illinois* (Elgin, Ill., 1950), 220. There are no known copies of Hostetler's tract still extant.

45. Biographical data on many of these ministers are not readily available. For the Hostetlers see Hostetler, *Descendants of Jacob Hochstetler,* 846, 862. For the Kerns see Garrard, *Family of Conrad Kern,* 30–33, 37–39, 46–47. For the Hons see "Restoration Pioneers—The Honn Family," *Christian Standard* 53 (Apr. 13, 1918): 1; and Mamie Honn, "History of the Honn Family of Coles County, Illinois, 1676–1938" (typewritten manuscript dated Dec. 1938). A photocopy of this manuscript is in the possession of the author of this article. For a discussion of the life of Peter Hon, see Eller, "Peter Hon of East Union," 5–12. A brief sketch of Lewis, who also served in the Indiana legislature, may be found in *History of Lawrence, Orange and Washington Counties,* 340. Ribble, who died in 1828, was one of the earliest ministers in Washington County; he is buried in the Liberty (Lost River) cemetery.

46. *Minutes of the Annual Meeting,* 51–52, 55–57.

47. James M. Mathes, "Another Old Soldier Gone," *Christian Record,* 3d ser., no. 2 (Dec. 1858): 375; *Millennial Harbinger,* n.s., no. 3 (Dec. 1839): 471.

48. "Obituaries," *Christian Record* 4 (Feb. 1847): 256. In a letter to David B. Eller, Aug. 10, 1979, Jason Rainey Adamson states that his grandmother, Louise Sears Adamson, a member of the White River church, never changed from her Dunker faith.

49. Joseph Hostetler, "Feetwashing," *Christian Record* 4 (Jan. 1847): 205–8.

50. The Hostetler-Wright merger may well have been the first combination of different religious traditions in the Restoration movement. It took place five years prior to the 1832 agreement between Campbell and Stone to work cooperatively. Shaw, *Hoosier Disciples,* 49, suggests that, chronologically, the Brethren became churches of Christ (with Wright's group), then a New Light Conference (Christian), and finally, Disciples of Christ.

51. Francis W. Emmons, "Statistics of Indiana," *Millennial Harbinger,* n.s., no. 3 (Aug. 1839): 345, see also 551. Lost River had a membership of one hundred, with Joseph Hostetler, Christian Hostetler, and David S. Lewis as elders. White River had one hundred members, Abraham Kern and Alexander Kern, elders. Bethel's statistics, added somewhat later, credited that church with seventy members, Adam Sears, George H. Hon, and D[avid?] Fouts, "preaching Brethren." Olive Branch had ninety members in 1844. *Christian Record* 11 (Oct. 1844): 94.

Two Restoration Traditions

Mormons and Churches of Christ in the Nineteenth Century

Richard T. Hughes

In the spring of 1841, only eleven years after Joseph Smith and his colleagues had organized the Church of Jesus Christ of Latter-day Saints, four men met for debate at the Ridge Meetinghouse in the foothills of the Smoky Mountains just east of Nashville in Smith County, Tennessee. Those four were John D. Lee and Alfonso Young, representing the Mormons, and Abraham Sallee and Samuel Dewhitt, representing the Churches of Christ. The second proposition for debate defined the critical difference between these two traditions. That proposition read: *Are the gifts and offices of the ancient Apostolic Church of Christ, necessary in this age, in order to constitute a perfect church or body?*[1] The Mormon preachers affirmed; the Church of Christ preachers denied.

In spite of their very fundamental differences, one finds in this debate two upstart Christian movements that, in many ways, shared far more in common with each other than they shared with any of the older denominations. Indeed, Mormons and Churches of Christ alike rejected the surrounding denominations, which they viewed as "manmade churches" and based their authority instead on their respective understandings of the ancient church of the primitive era.

HISTORIOGRAPHIC PRESUPPOSITIONS

To come to terms with these two traditions in the nineteenth century, then, we first must assess the intellectual heart and soul of each, namely, their restorationist orientation. In this task, however, we will find little help from most historians who write of Mormons and/or Churches of Christ from the perspective of social history. While several social historians have produced some of the finest work in recent years dealing with these traditions, most of these same historians typically have not taken the restoration ideal seriously as a powerful and pervasive theme in its own right. Often, if they acknowledge this ideal at all, they implicitly—and sometimes explicitly—explain it chiefly as a function of various social factors without which, one presumes, the restoration sentiment would collapse and disappear.

Thus, Rhys Isaac, speaking of the profoundly restorationist Separate Baptists of Virginia, altogether missed the power of the restoration ideal and interpreted Separate Baptists simply "as a popular response to a mounting sense of social disorder." Likewise, Gordon Wood ascribed the popularity of several restorationist traditions in the new republic, including Baptists, "Christians," and Mormons, to "a social disintegration unequalled in American history."[2]

Again, Nathan O. Hatch explained the genius of both the "Christian" movement and the Latter-day Saints in terms of a populist, democratic revolt against their social betters. He viewed the "Christians" or Churches of Christ especially in terms of a "pervasive collapse of certainty within popular culture."[3] And Mormons he understood chiefly in terms of poverty and social estrangement. Thus, he wrote that "the *Book of Mormon* is a document of profound social protest, an impassioned manifesto by a hostile outsider against the smug complacency of those in power and the reality of social distinction based on wealth, class, and education . . . The single most striking theme in the *Book of Mormon* is that it is the rich, the proud, and the learned who find themselves in the hands of an angry God."[4]

David Edwin Harrell, who has written eloquently and perceptively of the restoration theme within the history of Churches of Christ, has nonetheless explained that theme and the peculiar directions it has taken within this fellowship, largely in terms of social forces. Thus, in attempting to explain the theological genius of Churches of Christ, he focused especially on the Civil War and argued that "social force, class prejudice, sectional bitterness, and theologies shot through with economic presuppositions were the base upon which doctrinal debates were built." He therefore judged that the sectarian theology of the largely southern Churches of Christ in the years following the Civil War often amounted to little more than "a thinly veiled appeal for backing to the supporters of the lost cause."[5]

Such judgments, I suspect, may often reveal more about the materialistic and scientific biases of those of us who inhabit the modern academy than they do about the spiritual struggles and insights of ordinary Americans some two hundred years ago. To the modern mind, steeped in the conviction that material reality is the only reality there is, and convinced that spiritual concerns are but reflections of more fundamental material issues, the nineteenth-century search for the kingdom of God almost inevitably becomes a search for social and economic standing.

I would be the last to deny the substantial merit of these historians' arguments, so long as one does not imagine that they take us to the center of these traditions. Likewise, I would be the last to suggest that social and economic factors play no role in shaping religious perspectives, for they clearly do. Further, it is obvious that the methods and presuppositions of social history are especially productive when one studies movements that clearly are driven by social rather than by intellectual or spiritual concerns. But it may well be that the presuppositions and methods of social and economic history are ill equipped to uncover in a meaningful way the driving power behind such religious movements as Mormons and Churches of Christ.[6]

Indeed, the historian who instinctively places social and economic issues front and center will almost inevitably miss the genius of restorationist movements in America, for most restorationist movements in antebellum America struggled with a profoundly spiritual crisis that simply cannot be explained by social, economic, and military pressures. That spiritual crisis typically revolved around the quest for the true church, for the kingdom of God, or for the sacred in the midst of a profane and fallen world. And that is a quest historians should take seriously in its own right.

One begins to grasp the immense dimensions of that spiritual crisis when one recalls how central had been the concern for the "true, apostolic church" among Puritans on both sides of the Atlantic.[7] Further, as Dan Vogel recently pointed out, this concern bedeviled a host of British and American Seekers from the seventeenth through the nineteenth centuries, including Lucy Smith, the mother of Joseph.[8] Moreover, this concern stood at the very center of American restorationist traditions like Mormons and Churches of Christ.

Religious pluralism in the United States, however, compounded the problem beyond measure for those who began with this concern. Joseph Smith tells us that he found himself "in darkness and confusion" over this very issue. Accordingly, the crisis that stood at the very heart and soul of the Mormon experience in the early nineteenth century was neither economic nor social, but spiritual, captured in the question Joseph put to the Lord in the spring of 1820: "which of all the sects was right—and which I should join."[9] John D. Lee echoed this same concern in his debate with the Church of Christ preachers at the Ridge Meetinghouse in 1841. "We now see six hundred and sixty sects," he lamented, "all professing to be the Church of Christ. Each sect contending for its own infallibility—and each contending that every other one is wrong." Then Lee asked that simple but penetrating question which lay at the heart of the spiritual crisis that ultimately defined both Mormons and Churches of Christ in the nineteenth century: "Why is this?"[10]

This question, however, seems both quaint and irrelevant to most Americans in the waning years of the twentieth century, when tolerance and pluralism have become an accepted way of life. Accordingly, historians with little sense of the spiritual urgency of that question, and schooled in the scientific methods and materialistic presuppositions of modern social history, often find lurking beneath such a question overtones of social and economic deprivation. Such presuppositons not only miss the spiritual core of many restorationist traditions; they also tend toward a variety of conclusions unsupported by the evidence. Thus, several recent studies have simply overturned, in many instances, the conventional wisdom that Mormon primitivism reflects social and economic deprivation. These studies have pointed out that the Kirtland Saints in the mid-1830s stood far closer to the economic mainstream of their neighbors than generally has been supposed.[11] After exploring the evidence in this regard, Grant Underwood finally concluded that "if Mormon millenarians wished to see the world destroyed, it was because it had deprived them of spiritual, not economic, opportunity."[12]

All of this suggests that intellectual history, not social history, may be the path that will lead us into the center and core of most of the restorationist movements of the antebellum United States.

THE SPIRITUAL CORE OF THE RESTORATION VISION

If we choose to follow that path, we quickly make several important and highly relevant discoveries. First, we learn that the restoration vision was in no way peculiar to antebellum America, much less to the process of democratization or to social marginality in the new republic. Instead, this vision in the modern world grew from the bias toward pure beginnings generated by the Christian Humanists in the Renaissance who despaired of the moral and intellectual corruption of their age. Through the influence of the universities, this theme quickly dominated the sixteenth-century Protestant Reformation, especially in Zurich. Reformed leaders like Heinrich Bullinger and Martin Bucer exerted powerful influences on the English to find the center and core of the Christian faith in the restoration theme. It is little wonder, then, that during the Marian exile, the commitment to primitive Christianity became a defining characteristic of the Puritan party.[13]

From there, the restoration vision took two routes in its journey to America. The first route, important for Mormons, took the Puritans across the Atlantic to the New World, where the restoration vision became fundamental to their task. In New England, then, one finds the intellectual tradition that finally shaped a young seeker by the name of Joseph Smith. Indeed, the ways in which both Puritans and Mormons virtually reenacted the sacred dramas from both Old and New Testaments were strikingly similar—and that was not coincidental.

The second route, important for Churches of Christ, was far more circuitous and involved an extensive layover in Scotland. John Knox carried the restoration vision from England to his native land, where it became central to Scottish and later to Scotch-Irish Presbyterianism. Thousands of those Presbyterians would later settle in the middle colonies, in the American South, and in northern Appalachia. Among them were the earliest leaders of Churches of Christ—Thomas and Alexander Campbell in northern Virginia and Barton W. Stone in Kentucky and Tennessee. Especially in the South, Baptists and Methodists also shared the vision of the primitive Christian faith. Little wonder, then, that Churches of Christ would find in that region an especially fertile soil for their appeal to "the ancient order of things."

Clearly, then, by the time of the American Revolution, restorationist thinking had become an important fixture in American intellectual life, from New England to Georgia. Further, it proliferated and thrived, especially between the Revolution and the Civil War. There are several social and cultural factors that prompted this proliferation and, indeed, it is precisely in this context that the work of the social historians is especially valuable.

First, there can be no doubt that the radically democratic and populist qualities of American life in the early nineteenth century rendered the restoration vision especially urgent. Here, the work of Nathan Hatch is especially helpful. Indeed, if Americans had abolished the tyrannies of princes and kings in the political realm, Christian primitivists now sought to do the same in the religious realm by declaring the jurisdiction of Christian history null and void.

Second, to Americans in the new republic, the American political system seemed radically new, altogether discontinuous with any political system that had ever gone before. The Great Seal of the United States captured this perception with the phrase *novus ordo seclorum* (a "new order of the ages"). But if the American political system was new, it was also ancient, even primeval, and descended as Thomas Paine insisted, from God himself, at the beginning of the world.[14] In short, this new democratic order stood outside human history, derived from the primordium, and now restored in the American millennial dawn. Such a powerful cultural myth would inevitably quicken and heighten the centuries-old restoration vision that a variety of English dissenters had brought to these shores.

But of all the social and cultural factors that facilitated the restoration vision, none was more important than the bewildering array of churches that competed on the American frontier. This was the problem that prompted Alexander Campbell to seek to unify American churches by pointing them to the apostolic faith. And this was the problem that prompted Joseph Smith to ask the Lord which of all the churches was the Lord's own. Indeed, this was the source of the spiritual crisis that demanded an answer. The solution came, both to Mormons and to Churches of Christ, in the venerable form of the restoration heritage, now quickened and heightened by democratic expectations and by the radical newness of the American experience.

Thus, Walter Scott, one of the early leaders of Churches of Christ, was simply mistaken when he ascribed the success of the early Mormons to principles he thought Mormons had learned from the Campbellites. Indeed, he charged, Sidney Rigdon "filched from us" the notion of immersion for the forgiveness of sins, and this accounted, Scott surmised, "for the success of the ministers of Mormonism."[15] This myth has been a powerful theme among Churches of Christ from the 1830s until the present day. Nothing, in fact, could have been further from the truth. Mormons succeeded for the same reason that Churches of Christ succeeded: each inherited a restoration vision that spoke in powerful and urgent ways in the cultural climate of antebellum America.

DIFFERENCES BETWEEN MORMONS AND CHURCHES OF CHRIST

Yet, for all their similarities, Mormons and Churches of Christ were radically different. The most striking difference obviously involved Mormonism's new Scripture, the Book of Mormon and its latter-day prophet, developments which Churches of Christ rejected. Indeed, those two developments have dominated anti-Mormon rhetoric on the part of Churches of Christ for more than a century and a half. Yet, to focus on the Book of Mormon and the prophet obscures both the fundamental similarity and the fundamental differences between these two traditions.

The fundamental similarity which must be recognized is the profoundly restorationist quality of both churches. Churches of Christ, however, find it difficult to discern in Mormonism any restorationist dimension whatsoever. A restorationist, according to most in Churches of Christ, is one whose restorationist efforts concentrate exclusively on the New Testament. Thus, one of several who took me to task for involving Latter-day Saints in a conference on "Christian Primitivism and Modernization,"[16] complained, "I am asking you to explain what rationale was used in including the Mormons in a conference such as this. Is it your view . . . that the Mormon church is seeking to restore primitive Christianity?" That, of course, is precisely my view; but to understand the crucial difference between Churches of Christ and Latter-day Saints in this regard, we must resort once again to intellectual history.

Our beginning point is the recognition that the restoration vision is, in a fundamental sense, a vacuous vision. It is finally nothing more than a method, a perspective, that looks backward to what one discerns as the first and therefore normative time. In this context, to say that one focuses on the Bible is hardly adequate, for there are many ways of reading and interpreting the Bible, each shaped and informed by one's intellectual presuppositions. This means that to understand Mormonism and Churches of Christ, we must first understand the intellectual traditions that shaped and molded these two movements. What we find, however, is not at all straightforward or simple to unravel, for both Mormonism and Churches of Christ drew on intellectual traditions that in many ways competed with one another and that pointed in very different directions.

Churches of Christ

In the case of Churches of Christ, the two competing traditions were apocalyptic revivalism and Enlightenment progressivism. The apocalyptic revivalistic perspective belonged to the earliest leader of Churches of Christ, Barton W. Stone, who performed the bulk of his ministry in Kentucky and Tennessee. Stone's thought bore the indelible imprint of Calvinism, on the one hand, and revivalism on the other. Indeed, by virtue of his teachers, Stone stood squarely in the heritage of the Great Awakening and then, in 1801, emerged as a pivotal leader of the Great Kentucky Revival at Cane Ridge.

Revivalism and Calvinism together bred in Stone an apocalyptic outlook that became the cornerstone of his life, often expressing itself in an explicitly premillennial eschatology and virtually defining his restoration vision.[17] Convinced that the kingdom of God would finally triumph over all human governments and institutions, Stone and his considerable band of followers remained fundamentally pessimistic about human progress.

Further, they exhibited far less interest in the formal structures of the church than in the rule of God over human affairs. They therefore conceived of primitive Christianity chiefly in terms of biblical ethics and refused both to serve in the military or vote, since all human governments, they imagined, stood squarely under the judgment of God. Time and again summoned one another to abandon themselves in the interest of the poor, to free their slaves, and to reject both fashion and wealth.

This apocalyptic/ethical emphasis, with its negative assessment of human progress and human culture, comprised the earliest understanding of primitive Christianity among Churches of Christ. Indeed, long before Churches of Christ in Kentucky and Tennessee had even heard of Alexander Campbell, Stone had gathered a corps of some two hundred preachers and a membership of perhaps twenty thousand.[18] It is little wonder, then, that his pessimistic, apocalyptic orientation prevailed among many Churches of Christ, especially in their Middle Tennessee heartland, until World War I when those churches embarked on the process of modernization and acculturation.[19]

In the meantime, however, the second intellectual tradition—that of the Enlightenment—increasingly came to dominate Churches of Christ, especially through the leadership of Alexander Campbell, whose restoration vision I choose to call *rational, progressive* primitivism. A Scotch-Irish immigrant who settled in

Bethany, Virginia (later West Virginia), Campbell arguably became the most influential first-generation leader among Churches of Christ over the long term.

Steeped in Lockean empiricism and the "Baconian" perspective of the Scottish "Common Sense" Realists, Campbell rejected the apocalyptic outlook of Stone and embraced instead a robust, postmillennial optimism about the world in which he lived. Indeed, Campbell imagined that through a rational and scientific reconstruction of primitive Christianity, he and the movement he led would unify a fragmented Christendom and, as a consequence, raise the curtain on the millennial dawn.

In keeping with his rational vision, Campbell concerned himself not so much with biblical ethics as with the forms and structures of the ancient church. He viewed the New Testament almost as a divinely inspired, scientific text that supplied precise directions for admission into the church, for church organization, for proper worship, and for a variety of other details pertaining to church life. Further, just as a scientific experiment carried out in the same way under the same conditions would yield the same results time and again, in the same way, Campbell imagined faithful attention to biblical directions would produce the same church today that it produced in the days of the apostles.

With such a scientific perspective, and in the political climate of antebellum America, it was inevitable that Campbell's followers would increasingly view the New Testament as a veritable constitution for the church. Indeed, this was the central metaphor that the Church of Christ preachers used against their Mormon opponents in the Tennessee debate of 1841. Accordingly, Samuel Dewhitt argued that the New Testament "is *perfect*, and . . . all which is necessary to constitute a perfect church or body is obedience to that law. The Apostles were lawgivers acting by divine authority. The elders were only executive officers whose business it was to see these laws enforced. If the laws, given by the Apostles, were sufficient to constitute churches in *their* day—we having the same laws, need nothing more."[20]

He continued: "When the framers of the Constitution of the United States of America had formed that instrument their work was accomplished, and that duty ceased and can never be resumed until the Constitution is abolished and it becomes necessary to make another. Now Jesus Christ and his Apostles made the laws for his government on earth, and the overseers of the Church now have nothing to do but to see those laws executed."[21] Here, in these statements, one finds the very heart and soul of the restorationist perspective, conformed to the contours of Enlightenment thought, that dominated Churches of Christ under the influence of Alexander Campbell.

It is important to recognize, however, that both Abraham Sallee and Samuel Dewhitt began their careers as Stoneite preachers, only later embracing the more rational and more progressive primitivism of Alexander Campbell. This point is instructive since Campbell's Enlightenment optimism eventually buried Stone's apocalyptic influence in virtually all quarters of the movement and, in so doing, paved the way for extensive modernization and acculturation among Churches of Christ in the twentieth century.[22]

Latter-day Saints

When one turns from Churches of Christ to the Latter-day Saints, one enters a radically different world, though no less restorationist. The restoration vision among Latter-day Saints drew from both apocalypticism and the Enlightenment, and in this they shared with Churches of Christ. But Romanticism quickly emerged as the defining intellectual influence on Latter-day Saints, and this was the difference that made *all* the difference.

Though he never spelled it out, Harold Bloom hinted at this point when he praised the imaginative genius of Joseph Smith, and he consistently placed Smith in the company of Ralph Waldo Emerson. Indeed, Bloom confessed, "I myself can think of not another American, except for Emerson and Whitman, who so moves and alters my own imagination."[23]

While American Romanticism shared with the Enlightenment a profound celebration of human potential, it stood starkly opposed to the scientific constrictions and materialistic biases of Enlightenment ideology. Indeed, romantics of practically every stripe—including both spiritualists and transcendentalists—sought to shed their earthy constraints, to enlarge the boundaries of the human spirit, and to touch in some meaningful way that spiritual realm that transcended the merely rational structures of the here and the now.

When we understand the genius of American Romanticism, we draw near to the genius of the restoration vision as articulated by Latter-day Saints. They cared little for the forms and structures of primitive Christianity, rationally perceived and reconstructed as ends in themselves. Instead, they hungered for communion with the divine, and they valued forms and structures only insofar as they facilitated that communion. They longed for the heavens to open and for God himself to descend once again to humankind, just as he had done in the days of Adam, Moses, David, John, and Paul. Moreover, they were convinced that no restoration could occur apart from immediate, divine authority that would come as contemporary and continuous revelation. Further, Romanticism served Mormons as the eclectic umbrella under which they drew from Judaism, Christianity, Masonry, and the American experience, fusing their selections into a grand perspective that pointed beyond itself and beyond all its singular components to the infinite that embraced them all.

Mormons, from their distinctly romantic perspective, occasionally lampooned and scorned the rationalist and materialist biases of their own age as grossly inferior to their own romantic vision. Perhaps no passage in all of early Mormon literature more effectively captured this contrast than the following from Parley P. Pratt:

> Witness the ancients conversing with the Great Jehovah, learning lessons from the angels, and receiving instructions by the Holy Ghost, . . . until at length the veil is taken off and they are permitted to gaze with wonder and admiration upon all things past and future; yea, even to soar aloft amid unnumbered worlds . . . Compare this intelligence with the low smatterings of education and worldly wisdom that seem to satisfy the narrow mind of man in our generation; yea, behold the narrow-minded, calculating, trading, overreaching penurious sycophant of the nineteenth century who dreams of nothing here but how to increase his goods, or take advantage of his neighbor, and whose only religious exercises or duties consist of going to meeting, paying the priest his hire, or praying to his God, without expecting to be heard or answered, supposing that God has been deaf and dumb for many centuries, or altogether stupid and indifferent like himself.[24]

Indeed, for Latter-day Saints, the fall of the church from its perfect original occurred not in the loss of material forms and structures which might now be rationally perceived and restored, but rather in the loss of divine revelation and the wonder-working power of the Holy Spirit. In the absence of immediate revelation, human beings had taken it upon themselves to interpret the Bible through human wisdom and human rationality, and to erect a myriad of denominations that were miserable substitutes for the true church of Christ, founded on the wonder-working power of God. Even Campbell, Mormons claimed, for all his restorationist rhetoric, had acted without immediate, divine authority, and therefore had founded yet another man-made sect.[25]

This was precisely the point that the Mormons made in their debate with Abraham Sallee and Samuel Dewhitt in 1842. Thus, when John D. Lee inquired into the reasons for religious pluralism in the United States, he quickly answered his own question. "We answer," he affirmed, "because they have lost the spirit which was possessed by the primitive Christians, and they lack the gifts which were originally and still are necessary to create a perfect church or body." Alfonso Young concurred. "The church was once perfect and united," he declared, "and why is it not so now? I answer, because the professed Christians of the present day deny spiritual influences. In short, because they neither possess nor seek the *gifts* which the apostles and primitive Christians possessed."[26]

In short, the debate at the Ridge Meetinghouse in Middle Tennessee in 1841 featured two religious movements that shared a common restoration heritage but had conformed that heritage to radically different intellectual moulds: the Enlightenment and Romanticism. Perhaps in no single exchange was the difference between these two molds more effectively illumined than in the exchange over the relation of faith to miracles. The Church of Christ preachers, following John Locke and Alexander Campbell, claimed that miracles functioned as empirical evidence that in turn produced faith. John D. Lee, however, turned this conception virtually upside down. "I will not only contend that miracles do not produce faith," he argued, "but that faith is necessary for the production of miracles." Later in the debate, he elaborated on this very point. "If Christians of the present day would exercise the same measure of faith and obedience as did the primitive Christians, they would receive the same blessings which were enjoyed by the first disciples of Christianity. *They* spake with tongues and wrought miracles. And so would Christians of the present day if they possessed the same faith and exercised the same degree of obedience and holiness.[27]

When one discerns the power of the romantic vision in antebellum America, one is hardly surprised to learn that disillusioned members of the Church of Christ in Mentor, Ohio, abandoned Alexander Campbell for Joseph Smith and thereby comprised the first corps of converts to the Latter-day Saints. At one level, those conversions are easily understood, for the converts simply moved from one restoration tradition to another. Yet, at another level, the conversions are puzzling. Why the disillusionment with Campbell and why the attraction to Joseph Smith? And even more puzzling, why would these converts begin with a church rooted in the Enlightenment, then abandon that church for one more in tune with the romantic mood of the time?

In effect, to ask that question is to answer it. Elizabeth Ann Whitney in many ways spoke for all the converts: "My husband, Newel K. Whitney, and myself were Campbellites. We had been baptized for the remission of our sins, and believed in the laying on of hands and the gifts of the spirit. But there was no one with authority to confer the Holy Ghost upon us." Or, as John Murdock, an 1830 convert from Churches of Christ to the Latter-day Saints, reported, "finding their principal leader, Alex Campbell, with many others, denying the gift and power of the Holy Ghost, I began to think of looking me a new home."[28] Indeed, Whitney and Murdock were essentially romantics whom Campbell initially attracted by virtue of his restoration vision. But the Enlightenment dimensions of Campbell's vision chilled them.

This romantic thirst for a direct encounter with the Spirit of God turned the restoration vision among Mormons in several directions the rationalistic Churches of Christ would find incomprehensible. First, it meant that Latter-day Saints viewed as normative the entire Bible, not the New Testament alone, for the entire Bible contained the records of a God who routinely broke into the orbit of human affairs to commune with humankind. For this reason, Latter-day Saints found no compelling reason to distinguish between Old and New Testaments as did Alexander Campbell. For his part, on the other hand, Campbell thought simply absurd the Book of Mormon idea that "the Nephites . . . were good christians, . . . preaching baptism and other christian usages hundreds of years before Jesus Christ was born!"[29]

Second, Latter-day Saints had little interest in mere obedience to biblical commands and replication of biblical data. Indeed, they never viewed the Bible as data at all. Instead, they viewed the Bible as story, as drama in which they themselves were participants along with Adam, Enoch, Moses, and Paul. As Philip Barlow recently observed, Joseph Smith "placed himself *inside* the Bible story" and put "endings . . . on stories that had their beginnings in the scriptural text." Or, as Jan Shipps has pointed out, Mormon restorationism involved far more than mere replication of events of the biblical long ago. It involved instead a "recapitulation" or a virtual living out of those events in the here and now.[30] To the rational mind of an Alexander Campbell, such an agenda seemed sheer nonsense. But to one who approached the restoration task from the perspective of Romanticism, as many did in antebellum America, such an agenda was enormously compelling.

Third, the romantic dimensions of the Mormon restoration led Latter-day Saints to place enormously more importance on the experience of God than on the Bible itself. Indeed, for Mormons, the Bible simply pointed beyond itself to divine power and authority that manifested itself not only in the first age but also in the here and now. This clearly accounts for the fact that Joseph Smith felt comfortable revising the Bible—an act that would have horrified Alexander Campbell. The act of revision itself abundantly proclaims the romantic dimensions of the Mormon faith. As Barlow points out, Smith never sought to determine "the intent of the ancient authors." Instead, he "used the Bible less as a scholar than as a poet," or as Barlow finally concludes, as "a prophet."[31]

Fourth, if the heart of Churches of Christ was their appeal to a fixed and permanent first-century norm that would never change, the principle of continuing revelation meant that the heart of Latter-day Saints was change and adaptation, guided by a latter-day prophet. This difference would have enormous implications for the way in which these two restoration traditions would adapt themselves to the modern age.

Finally, if Romanticism provided the intellectual underpinnings for the restoration vision of Latter-day Saints, and thereby dramatically separated Mormons from Churches of Christ, there is a sense in which the inner dynamics of Mormons and Churches of Christ in the early nineteenth century were fundamentally similar. For if early Churches of Christ split on their assessment of human progress, so did the Latter-day Saints. Indeed, like the followers of Barton W. Stone, Latter-day Saints were profoundly apocalyptic and even premillennial and, therefore, deeply suspicious of human potential apart from the divine initiative.[32] This theme dovetailed nicely with their peculiar brand of Romanticism, for the Saints looked not to human reason, but to the Spirit of God, to open the heavens and speak to humankind, to establish God's people in Zion, to defeat their enemies, and to renew the earth.

At the same time, however, Latter-day Saints shared profoundly in the spirit of optimism that characterized Alexander Campbell—but with a difference. If Campbell exuded optimism over human progress and the larger culture, the optimism of the Saints pertained not so much to the larger culture as to the Saints themselves. We find this optimistic strand especially in Mormon soteriology, perhaps classically expressed in Joseph's King Follett Discourse of 1844: "God himself was once as we are now, and is an exalted man, and sits enthroned in yonder heavens!" Lorenzo Snow later summarized the point, "As man now is, God once was; as God now is, man may become." Whatever one makes of this passage, it clearly expressed enormous confidence in human potential. Further, as the nineteenth century wound on, that confidence became more and more central to Mormon thought.[33]

There is no reason to ascribe the optimism expressed here to the Enlightenment, for it squares well with the exuberance over human potential that characterized many romantics. At the same time, however, Mormon optimism inevitably absorbed Enlightenment characteristics. Thus, an 1833 revelation proclaims: "The glory of God is intelligence" (D&C 93:36). By 1889, Orson F. Whitney combined that theme with the notion of eternal progression: "So says Joseph Smith. Intelligence is the glory of God. It is his superior intelligence that makes him God. The Gospel . . . is nothing more or less than a ladder of light, of intelligence, or principle, by which man, the child of god, may mount step by step to become eventually like his Father."[34] Little wonder, then, that Brigham Young could praise education "in every useful branch of learning," and urge his people "to excel the nations of the earth in religion, science, and philosophy."[35]

The fundamental question regarding Latter-day Saints, therefore, has to do with the relation between the pessimistic, *regressive* strands of Mormon thought, on the one hand, and the optimistic, *progressive* strands of Mormon thought on the other. In the case of Churches of Christ, Enlightenment optimism finally triumphed over apocalyptic pessimism and thereby paved the way for full-scale modernization. My sense is that precisely the same has been true with Latter-day Saints.

Finally, we conclude where we began, with a consideration of the scholars—in this case, Klaus Hansen. Hansen's work is relevant here in a backhanded kind of way, since his reading of Mormonism stands precisely opposite to my own. Indeed, Hansen found Mormonism essentially a reflection of Enlightenment optimism and order, standing in radical opposition to Romanticism. He drew this conclusion because he interpreted the restoration vision as an Enlightenment phenomenon, virtually antagonistic to the romantic mind, and because he imagined that few in antebellum America had much interest in such a peculiar, restorationist worldview. Joseph had asked, "Which of all the sects was right?"; however, "most American Protestants had been sufficiently influenced by the romantic mood so that the question simply never occurred to them. Conversion was an individual experience that could happen to a Baptist as well as a Methodist or a Presbyterian. All of them had a pathway to heaven; as long as they got there, it did not matter very much how. In the literal mind of Joseph, however, there had to be one church that was objectively true."[36]

It is manifestly the case that Joseph searched for a church that was objectively true. But objectivity for Joseph—and for Latter-day Saints in antebellum America—was not a matter of rational and scientific precision, as it was for Alexander Campbell and the Churches of Christ, and as it is for the modern mind today. It rather was a matter of the immediate power of God that carried for Latter-day Saints fully as much objective truth as the Bible carried for Alexander Campbell.

When all is said and done, that was the critical difference between Mormons and Churches of Christ in nineteenth-century America.

NOTES

1. Debate between Mormons and Church of Christ in *Crihfield's Christian Family Library and Journal of Biblical Science* 1 (July 18, 1842): 210. This journal published the proceedings of the debate in four issues: July 18, 25, Aug. 1, 15, 1842 (hereafter cited as Debate, by page). I am grateful to Mr. Verne R. Lee of Loomis, California, for a typescript of John D. Lee, Diary, May 28, 29, 1841. In the published debate, Lee's name appears as "John DeLee."

2. Rhys Isaac, *The Transformation of Virginia* (Chapel Hill: Univ. of North Carolina Press, 1982), 168; and Gordon Wood, "Evangelical America and Early Mormonism," *New York History* (Oct. 1980): 365.

3. Nathan O. Hatch, "The Christian Movement and the Demand for a Theology of the People," *Journal of American History* 67 (Dec. 1980): 561, 546. See also *The Democratization of American Christianity* (New Haven: Yale Univ. Press, 1989), 68–81.

4. Hatch, *Democratization*, 116–17.

5. David Edwin Harrell, *The Social Sources of Division in the Disciples of Christ* (Athens and Atlanta: Publishing Systems, 1973), ix; and "The Sectional Origins of the Churches of Christ," *Journal of Southern History* 30 (Aug. 1964): 270.

6. Furthermore, some restorationist movements were virtually driven by social and economic considerations. A case in point was Elias Smith's "Christian" movement in New England in the early nineteenth century, as Nathan Hatch accurately points out. Hatch,

however, is on far less solid ground when he finds central to Alexander Campbell and Barton Stone, also leaders of nineteenth-century "Christian" movements, the same social and economic motives he finds in Smith. Hatch, *Democratization,* 68–81.

7. Theodore Dwight Bozeman, *To Live Ancient Lives: The Primitivist Dimension in Puritanism* (Chapel Hill: Univ. of North Carolina Press, published for Institute of Early American History and Culture, 1988).

8. Dan Vogel, *Religious Seekers and the Advent of Mormonism* (Salt Lake City: Signature Books, 1988).

9. Joseph Smith Jr., "First Vision," in *History of the Church of Jesus Christ of Latter-day Saints,* 2d ed., 7 vols., ed. B. H. Roberts (Salt Lake City: Deseret Book Co., 1964), 1:4–6.

10. Debate, 238.

11. Mark R. Grandstaff and Milton V. Backman Jr., "The Social Origins of Kirtland Mormons," *Brigham Young University Studies* 30 (Spring 1990): 47–66; and Marvin S. Hill, C. Keith Rooker, and Larry T. Wimmer, "The Kirtland Economy Revisited: A Market Critique of Sectarian Economics," *Brigham Young University Studies* 17 (1977): 391–472.

12. Grant Underwood, *The Millenarian World of Early Mormonism* (Urbana: Univ. of Illinois Press, 1993).

13. This history is spelled out in more detail in Richard T. Hughes, "Christian Primitivism as Perfectionism: From Anabaptists to Pentecostals," in *Reaching Beyond: Chapters in the History of Perfectionism,* ed. Stanley Burgess (Peabody, Mass.: Hendrickson Publishers, 1986), 213–23. The Marian exiles were English Protestants who accepted self-imposed exile to the Continent to avoid persecution from Queen Mary, a zealous Catholic.

14. Philip S. Foner, ed., *The Complete Writings of Thomas Paine* (New York: Citadel Press, 1945), 1:273–75, 376.

15. Walter Scott, "The Mormon Bible," *Evangelist,* n.s., no. 7 (July 1, 1839): 160.

16. A conference on "Christian Primitivism and Modernization: Coming to Terms with Our Age," Pepperdine Univ., Malibu, Calif., June 6–9, 1991.

17. By *apocalyptic* I do not mean *premillennial.* The apocalyptic view is the conviction that one belongs not to the kingdoms of this world but to the kingdom of God that finally will triumph over all human institutions. Premillennialism, on the other hand, points to how God's kingdom will come, namely, through the premillennial second coming of Jesus Christ. As it turns out, Stone was both apocalyptic and premillennial in his outlook, but his apocalyptic perspective was the fundamental term in his thought.

18. R. L. Roberts, "Early Tennessee and Kentucky Preachers," photocopy of transcript in my possession.

19. Richard Hughes, "The Apocalyptic Origins of Churches of Christ and the Triumph of Modernism," *Religion and American Culture: A Journal of Interpretation* 2 (Summer 1992): 181–214.

20. Debate, 236–37.

21. Ibid., 237.

22. Anthony L. Dunnavant, ed., *Cane Ridge in Context: Perspectives on Barton W. Stone and the Revival* (Nashville: Disciples of Christ Historical Society, 1992).

23. Harold Bloom, *The American Religion: The Emergence of the Post-Christian Nation* (New York: Simon and Schuster, 1992), 102, 127.

24. Parley P. Pratt, *A Voice of Warning* (New York, 1837; reprint, Salt Lake City: Deseret Book Co., 1978), 88.

25. Parley P. Pratt, "Grapes from Thorns, and Figs from Thistles," reprinted from *Millennial Star* in *Writings of Parley Parker Pratt,* ed. Parker Pratt Robison (Salt Lake City: Parker Pratt Robison, 1952), 303.

26. Debate, 238, 236.

27. Debate, 217, 236.

28. Edward Wheelock Tullidge, *The Women of Mormonism* (New York: Tullidge and Crandall, 1877), 41–42; and John Murdock, "An Abridged Record of the life of John Murdock, Taken from His Journal by Himself," 4–10; typescript copy courtesy of Milton V. Backman, Brigham Young Univ.

29. Alexander Campbell, "Delusions," *Millennial Harbinger* 2 (Feb. 7, 1831): 87.

30. Philip L. Barlow, *Mormons and the Bible* (New York: Oxford Univ. Press, 1991), 21; and Jan Shipps, *Mormonism: The Story of a New Religious Tradition* (Urbana: Univ. of Illinois Press, 1985), 53–65.

31. Barlow, *Mormons and the Bible,* 73; see also 70.

32. See Grant Underwood, *The Millenarian World of Early Mormonism.*

33. O. Kendall White Jr., *Mormon Neo-Orthodoxy: A Crisis Theology* (Salt Lake City: Signature Books, 1987), esp. chap. 3.

34. Ibid., 83.

35. Ibid., 79.

36. Klaus J. Hansen, *Mormonism and the American Experience* (Chicago: Univ. of Chicago Press, 1981), 70–71.

Part III

A British Movement

The Churches of Christ in Britain

A Study in Nineteenth-Century Sectarianism

Louis Billington

The Brethren movement has been the subject of a number of recent historical and sociological studies, but there is a lack of adequate analyses of other nineteenth-century "restorationist" sects, their origins and the context in which they arose. By *restorationist* sects here is meant sects that, whatever their ultimate history, originally emphasized the recovery of "Apostolic" doctrines and usages, and the reestablishment of "primitive Christianity" as revealed in the New Testament.[1] Such sects generally rejected all forms of group identification except such terms as *Brethren, Christians,* or *Disciples.* Leaders of these restorationist movements saw themselves as part of a tradition that had produced many attempts at recovering "primitive Christianity," although each sect saw others as departing from the basis of Scripture in some major doctrine or practice.[2] The majority of these sects originated in secessions, direct or indirect, from either the Church of England or the Church of Scotland. Secessions from the established Church of Scotland would include the Glasites, or Sandemanians, the Scotch Baptists, the early Scottish Independents, and the Haldanites, while in England the Plymouth Brethren and other early nineteenth-century secessions from the Anglican establishment make up the majority of the restorationist movements.[3]

This discussion will focus on a sect that had contacts with both English and Scottish movements. Members of this sect called themselves Christians and later the Churches of Christ. They represent the British followers of Alexander Campbell, whose much more numerous American movement coalesced in the twentieth century into the Disciples of Christ and a more conservative breakaway group, the Churches of Christ. It is not proposed to provide more than an outline history of the British Churches of Christ (called here, for clarity, the Campbellites), but rather to concentrate on an analysis of their origins, size, social composition and values, and the major changes that occurred in those areas between 1842 and 1919, when the two groups into which the movement had divided were reunited.[4]

The first General Meeting of the Churches of Christ was held in Edinburgh in 1842, but that meeting reflected a history that went back to John Glas and his expulsion from the ministry of the Church of Scotland in 1730. Among the Glasites, or Sandemanians, as they were generally called outside Scotland, each congregation consisted only of believers and there was congregational autonomy. No separate, paid ministry was instituted, but each church had a number of elders and deacons who were collectively responsible for spiritual and material matters respectively. There was a weekly celebration of the Lord's Supper and some attempt was made to revive such New Testament usages as the fraternal kiss and foot washing.[5]

By the early nineteenth century there were at least three small groups of Sandemanians, each refusing fellowship with the others, but, although small, the Sandemanians had some influence among other Calvinistic sects. A recent historian of the American Disciples of Christ has emphasized that the Sandemanians reached startlingly similar conclusions to those emerging among the various "Christian" groups in the United States associated with Alexander Campbell, who was familiar with the Sandemanians in both Scotland and the United States.[6]

The introduction of believer's baptism by immersion into Scotland, about 1765, by Archibald McLean, Glasgow bookseller and printer, and a former Sandemanian, resulted in the formation of the group later called Scotch Baptists, to distinguish them from the English-style Baptist Church in Scotland. The Scotch Baptists were largely recruited from the Sandemanians, and they followed them in adhering to the "primitive" church plan of government. But mirroring the growing evangelical movement in Britain more than the Sandemanians, they vigorously condemned worldly pursuits and emphasized the work of evangelism. They made great efforts to win adherents and, by McLean's death in 1812, congregations had been organized in many areas in Britain and the United States. The movement also gained some members from the evangelical Haldane movement, when the Haldane brothers accepted the principle of believer's baptism by immersion and divided their own followers on that question.[7] Thus, by 1830, when the better-known secessions from the Church of England began, which produced the Plymouth Brethren and strengthened the ultra-Calvinistic Particular Baptists, there already existed a network of ultra-literalist, restorationist sects, and independent congregations.[8]

In the United States, the restorationist movement associated with Alexander Campbell shared the preoccupations of the British groups, but in America his followers did not organize as a separate movement until the early 1830s, preferring to cooperate with the Baptists. During his years with the Baptists, Campbell founded his first paper, the *Christian Baptist*. The fundamentals of his teaching on the "restoration," as well as the basis for his eventual separation from the

Baptists, appeared in its pages. He attacked the clergy, clerical education, creeds, and hierarchical patterns of church government and pleaded for a "restoration of the ancient order of things."[9]

Campbell's published works and the movement he led soon attracted the attention of British restorationist groups. The principal Scotch Baptist elder in London, William Jones, established contact with Campbell and received files of his *Christian Baptist* and the more recent *Millennial Harbinger*.[10] In 1835 Jones began to publish his own *Millennial Harbinger and Voluntary Church Advocate*, and the first eight issues were devoted to extracts from Campbell's writings. But in 1836 Jones closed his columns to Campbell because they disagreed on several points. Jones was a rigid Calvinist, a position Campbell rejected. Jones also saw Campbell as a threat to his own authority among Scotch Baptists, especially as some of Campbell's American followers declared apostate all sects founded before the Campbellite "reformation." But Jones's views did not prevent the growth of dissension among the Scotch Baptist Churches.[11] When Jones ceased publication of the *Millennial Harbinger,* James Wallis, a leader of the Scotch Baptist Church in Nottingham, founded the *Christian Messenger and Reformer,* which was sympathetic toward Campbell. Wallis carried with him a substantial part of the Nottingham congregation and gradually united dissident Scotch Baptists and scattered independent restorationist churches into a British Campbellite movement.[12] Some of these independent congregations had already established contact with Campbell, often through relatives who had emigrated to America, and joined Campbellite churches.[13]

The congregations that came to be associated with the British Campbellite movement thus had a variety of origins, but all saw themselves as a continuation of earlier restorationist sects: "How these churches came to exist may be accounted for by the fact that during the greater part of the eighteenth and the early part of the nineteenth century, the Spirit of God had been moving the minds of such men as Glas, Sandeman, Walker, McLean, the Haldanes and others."[14] The importance of the Scotch Baptist tradition for the developing Campbellite movement can be seen in the numerical strength of the latter's Scottish congregations and, indeed, in 1842 many members saw the recent divisions as nothing more than a further episode in the continuing search for "primitive" orthodoxy among the Scotch Baptists.[15]

After the first General Meeting in 1842, the Campbellites did not organize another General Meeting until 1847, after which they became annual events. During the years from 1842 until the mid-1850s, the movement was very loosely organized, and the principle of congregational autonomy made regional and national leadership slow to develop. Alexander Campbell's visit to Britain in 1847 helped to strengthen Wallis's position of leadership, but efforts toward interchurch co-operation produced further schisms, which did not subside until the mid-1850s. During the 1840s, in a period of severe economic and social dislocation, Campbellite congregations divided or disappeared fairly frequently, and members were much concerned with millenarianism, including the prophecies of the American William Miller, and the teaching of John Thomas, the founder of the Christadelphian sect.[16]

Premillennialism reached a peak among American Campbellites during the early 1840s, when William Miller predicted that the Second Coming would occur in 1844 and, despite Campbell's opposition to Miller's views, many of his followers joined the Millerite movement.[17] Millenarianism was already an important element in British evangelical Christianity, but the Campbellites with their American orientation, their ultra-biblical literalism, and their recent and unstable organization were particularly susceptible to the Millerite message. James Wallis followed Campbell in opposing Millerism, but Campbellite congregations in his own area of Nottingham and Derby were attracted to the new teaching, and a rival magazine, the *Gospel Banner,* challenged the authority of Wallis's organ when it attacked the Millerites.

Millenarianism created a wider interest in the Campbellite movement among members of other religious groups and converts were made, but Campbellite emphasis on prophecy also generated crippling schisms when rival Millerite congregations were organized around a dissident Campbellite core. With the decline of British Millerite congregations after 1847, some groups were reunited with Campbellite churches, while other Adventist churches that had no previous contact with Campbellites were also converted.[18]

Millenarian speculation among the Campbellites did not end, however, and in 1848 John Thomas found many "adventists" among these groups. After emigrating to America, Thomas had joined the Campbellite movement, but between 1837 and 1844 his differences with Campbell on such questions as baptism and prophecy became so pronounced that Thomas and his followers were declared to be schismatic. Thomas's monthly *Apostolic Times* already circulated among British Campbellites and, when he adopted Millerite views, his doctrines had even wider appeal. He arrived in Britain preaching that the Second Coming was imminent and, despite Wallis's opposition to him, the pro-Millerite *Gospel Banner* gave Thomas a hearing and there was the familiar sequence of schisms.[19] By 1850, the *Gospel Banner* claimed that the British Campbellite movement was in decline and that those congregations that had survived were deeply divided on questions of doctrine. Some churches were completely extinguished, and in 1873 David King, in reviewing the period 1848 to 1853, emphasized Thomas's part in dividing congregations, organizing separate groups, and preventing growth. But by 1853 many Campbellite congregations had begun to recover from the effects of Thomas's teaching, and some of his followers rejoined their old congregations.[20]

MEMBERSHIP

After 1847 there are available increasingly detailed statistics for the Campbellite churches. At first, officers of each church were urged to send to the General Meeting details of the number of members and how many had been gained and lost during the current year. Later a more standardized procedure developed, and churches were encouraged to make their returns under the following list of headings: "1, Present number of members; 2, Immersed during the year; 3, Received from sister congregations; 4, Received baptized believers; 5, Restored to fellowship; 6, Departed this life; 7, Expelled or fallen away; 8, Transferred to sister churches; 9, Removed to places where there are not churches; 10, Emigrated; 11, Number and title of officers; 12, Whether a Sunday school, and number of scholars."[21]

Apart from the obvious problem of the accuracy and regularity with which these returns were made by church officers, and the tendency for an individual to be recorded under a number of headings, a difficulty exists in using these statistics; a high percentage of churches failed to make any returns, and even churches known from other sources to have been large fail to appear in the statistics for years in succession. In 1842, eight churches supplied no data, and in 1850, during the dissension over John Thomas, twenty-three out of eighty-eight congregations failed to report, with fourteen out of the thirty Scottish churches providing no returns.[22] As late as 1892, approximately 20 percent of all churches failed to provide statistics, and it was often admitted by sect leaders that churches remained on the record which had long ceased to exist.[23] Bearing in mind these difficulties, however, the development of the sect can be traced in some detail and can conveniently be divided into three periods: 1842–55; 1856–75; 1876–1914.

1842–55

1842	42 churches	1,305 members
1848	80 churches	2,100 members
1850	88 churches	1,786 members (pro-Thomas *Gospel Banner*)
"	" "	1,816 members (anti-Thomas *Christian Messenger*)
1855	70 churches	1,823 members[24]

During this period there was a comparatively rapid growth of small churches but a lack of local leadership, dissensions over millenarian teaching, and disagreements over open or closed communion and the correct procedure for electing church officers resulted in a high failure rate. Some churches emerged by the grouping together of a number of tiny congregations, and the latter ceased to appear under their own headings in the returns. Some congregations moved from one village to another and reappeared as apparently new churches.[25] During a somewhat longer period than that under review—that is, from 1842 to 1872—eighty churches were removed from the records as being no longer in fellowship, and of these at least sixty ceased to exist, the majority disappearing before 1855. Of the remaining twenty or so congregations, a few preferred to adopt a full-time pastor and associated themselves with some section of the Baptists, while the remainder became the nucleus of Christadelphian or Adventist congregations.[26] Throughout this early period, the majority of the surviving congregations were small. The average for the sect as a whole was between twenty-five and thirty members per church, but a few congregations such as Nottingham and Edinburgh, with between 100 and 200 members, helped to produce an average figure for each congregation which was really atypical of the sect, churches of less than twenty-five members being not uncommon.[27]

1858–75

1858	83 churches	2,275 members
1862	90 churches	2,785 members
1866	108 churches	3,611 members
1872	110 churches	4,053 members
1875	126 churches	4,833 members[28]

After a slow recovery from the dissensions of the late 1840s there was a gradual upward turn in the late fifties that increased during the sixties with the greater use of full-time evangelists, who helped to develop major new churches in Birmingham, Manchester, and a few other centers. Many of the older churches, such as Nottingham, grew only slowly, and even successful new "causes" such as Birmingham grew most rapidly during their earliest years. By the end of this period second-generation members who had grown up in the sect were beginning to be significant.[29]

1876–1914

1876	126 churches	4,903 member
1886	133 churches	7,872 members
1891	150 churches	9,511 members
1914	200 churches	15,256 members[30]

This was a period of more rapid growth, with the employment of more full-time evangelists, the stimulus of a rival Campbellite group employing paid pastors, and the advantage of a significant group of second- and third-generation members. Few even of the larger congregations had owned their own chapels before 1870, but now, in an era of general Nonconformist church building, there was a widespread building program, with the construction or purchase of chapels that resembled many of the Primitive Methodist or Strict Baptist meetinghouses.[31] The Campbellites launched their own modest forward movement to increase the income of the sect and to extend the work of evangelism.[32] Like the Independent Methodists, the Campbellites made greater use of full-time workers while retaining the principle of an unpaid pastorate. The Quakers also made greater use of paid evangelists during these years and recruited some large, working-class congregations.[33] The Campbellites seem to have benefited from the reaction in some Nonconformist groups against the general drift of their denominations toward an apparently more secular culture, and Campbellite leaders agreed that the great majority of new converts came from members of other denominations and sects rather than from the unchurched.[34] The maintenance of strict standards of admission and behavior within the sect, as compared with the major Protestant denominations, meant that there was also a high rate of expulsion. For example, in 1890, 654 new members were admitted to the sect, but 629 were expelled or withdrew.[35] Many small churches formed during these years enjoyed a precarious existence and frequently failed to report to the General Meeting. By this late period, the regional distribution of the sect becomes clear: it was strongest in Lancashire and Cheshire (where the Independent Methodists were centered), and in the East Midlands, around Nottingham, Leicester, and Derby. There was a major congregation in Birmingham and a later and smaller one in Bristol, while the majority of the scattered congregations in the South and Southeast were to be found in the London area. After the early years, the sect never completely recovered in Scotland, although Glasgow, Edinburgh, and a few other places had comparatively large congregations. It was weak or nonexistent in Yorkshire, Lincolnshire, East Anglia, the Northeast and Southwest, all regions where the Primitive Methodists or the Bible Christians were strong. The Welsh Campbellites had a largely autonomous existence with about 250 members in a dozen Welsh-speaking congregations, and one or two of these had important local influence in mid-Wales.[36]

Throughout these three periods from 1842 to 1914, emigration created problems for some Campbellite churches. The percentage of members who emigrated each year varied, and the total number increased during the late fifties and sixties. Although emigration averaged only between 1/2 and 1 percent of the total membership in any one year, it often removed important local leaders who had provided pastoral supervision and funds, or it seriously weakened individual congregations, a few of which ceased to exist for this reason. Some members used the American contacts of the sect to emigrate to the United States, but probably as many went to Australia and New Zealand.[37]

SOCIAL COMPOSITION

The social composition of the Campbellites is difficult to assess with any accuracy, but sufficient evidence exists to establish the principal social groups in the sect and how these changed over time. During the 1840s and early 1850s, many congregations consisted largely of working men and their families, existing only by a narrow margin of subsistence. There were reports of churches weakened by local unemployment or industrial unrest.[38] Some congregations contained a high percentage of agricultural laborers unable to leave their employment to attend the General Meeting, especially when it coincided with a busy harvest period.[39] London congregations were described by their own leaders as "generally poor and occupying humble stations," and frequent conflict with slum missionaries and Mormon evangelists indicates the social milieu in which the Campbellites were making converts.[40] During the late 1850s David King reported that the depression was especially difficult for Campbellite congregations, the majority of which consisted of "that portion of the community who labour for their daily bread."[41]

From the beginning, the work of evangelism and leadership was exercised by a somewhat different social group than that which composed the members. Looking back in 1892, David King emphasized the lack of gentlemen and scholars in the sect, and the dominance in the leadership of a certain type of tradesman and small manufacturer.[42] An analysis of the men who led the most influential congregations, and financed and organized the sect's evangelism and literature, underlines King's view. James Wallis of Nottingham was a draper, as were George Tickle of Liverpool, Thomas Milner in Scotland, and Timothy Coop, a Lancashire leader and important financial contributor.[43] Coop was the only Campbellite leader to acquire more than modest wealth and an important place in the civic life of the local community. Others, like Wallis's associate Joshua Hines, were small textile and hosiery manufacturers, one a dye-works owner, some farmers, and some commercial travelers, often associated with the drapery trade, who acted as unpaid evangelists as they traveled. The support of these men guaranteed the existence of some larger congregations, the publication of literature, and intermittent maintenance of full-time evangelists. They also provided employment for rank-and-file members and for a few individuals who were themselves sect leaders.[44] In the smaller churches, where able leadership was always at a premium, skilled workmen and clerks assumed a more dominant role. We have evidence of churches led by printers, carpenters, shoemakers, engine drivers, colliers, excise officers, and bank clerks.[45] David King seems to have been the only Campbellite who was a full-time leader, evangelist, and editor over a period of many years, positions which helped to give him a commanding influence in the sect. By the sixties, King had attracted something of a reputation as a lecturer against secularism and, at that time, it is clear that the majority of the Campbellites consisted of the same type of skilled artisans who were attracted to the secular halls.[46] In the seventies, journalists who visited the larger Campbellite congregations in the major cities agreed in their impressions of these churches: "The better sort of working people and small tradesmen predominated, with a marked absence of the more well to do and better educated part of the middle class."[47] Although a small group of better-educated and more middle-class Campbellites had appeared by the 1890s and often represented a source of pressure for a liberalization of the sect, key spokesmen—like Bartley Ellis, a former postman—continued to be drawn from lower social groups.[48] The building program carried out from the mid-seventies suggests the greater permanence and affluence of the sect, but even the largest churches were modest buildings constructed in streets of small houses in the newer working-class suburbs.[49] As late as 1899 the *Newcastle Daily Chronicle* could report that it was difficult to obtain any information about the Campbellites, who were then holding their General Meeting in the city, as "those in touch with local church life . . . were unaware of the existence of the sect."[50]

LOCAL ORGANIZATION

The Campbellites claimed that in the New Testament the Christian gospel was essentially concerned with principles of church government and individual ethics rather than abstract, theological ideas, and this view has continued to be stressed by Campbellite apologists.[51] The Campbellites were not indifferent to doctrine, but, unlike the Scotch Baptists for example, theology in the sense of interpretation was given little emphasis. Instead, they stressed the desire to make church practice and worship conform to the New Testament model. The Lord's Supper was celebrated each Sunday, and the baptism of adult believers by immersion was made an essential condition of church membership. As was common with this type of restorationist sect, there was initially much uncertainty and controversy about what constituted New Testament teaching in matters of church government and practice; for example, foot washing, which had been used among the Sandemanians, was not adopted.[52] After much conflict, often associated with more general disagreements about millenarianism, Christadelphianism and practices associated with the Brethren, a generally accepted pattern of church government and organization emerged in the Campbellite sect.

The autonomy of each church was a central tenet of belief, but it was much modified in practice over time. The use of paid pastors was rejected, and the sect frequently attacked clericalism not only in the Anglican establishment but also among Methodists and Nonconformists. "The sacred Scriptures as the basis of belief and practice" led the Campbellites to elevate the office of elder, a member of the church who was appointed to supervise all matters of teaching and doctrine. Elders were also designated bishops, overseers, and pastors, and during the 1840s a wide variety of scriptural titles was given to elders as leaders of the churches. In addition, some churches selected their deacons who were responsible for financial and material matters from among the elders, while other congregations insisted that the office of deacon represented a separate order of church government from that of elder. The practice of electing elders and deacons as separate orders, with spiritual and material jurisdiction respectively, became generally accepted. Methods of selecting elders and deacons varied at first, as did their numbers in any congregation. Appointments to office were often for short periods of six or twelve months, and this necessitated frequent elections, which sometimes divided congregations and produced permanent schism.[53] In time, a number of principles were established for the election of church officers. Unanimity in elections had to be achieved and nomination for office came to be concentrated in the hands of the most respected members or the full-time evangelists, when these appeared. Often one individual dominated a church and his nominations were rarely opposed.[54] With many small congregations and a shortage of men able or willing to teach and supervise, many churches suffered from a lack of spiritual and financial guidance. During the early period some churches appointed too many elders and deacons, and throughout the sect there was some support for the view that all were entitled to exhort and teach, a practice adopted in some Brethren meetings. David King and other Campbellite leaders took the position that the majority was not equipped to speak regularly, and the *British Millennial Harbinger* stressed that liberty of speech, apart from education and discipline, produced more evil than good in a congregation: Christian learning and experience were necessary for profitable teaching.[55] In Birmingham, King occupied the position of evangelist and did not appoint elders for twenty years because no suitable candidates were available, and since he did not believe that *he* was scripturally qualified for the office, he declined to nominate others who might challenge his authority.[56] In practice, he retained de facto control to such a degree that his followers were known locally as Kingites, and his authority was bitterly resented.[57]

There was often a dogmatic insistence upon the minutiae of scriptural qualification for office, but, after a period of instability, a degree of general agreement was reached. This was helped by the secession of many dissident elements, and by the tendency of one individual or family to dominate a local church. Unpaid elders who taught week by week and deacons who supervised financial and allied matters became the key officials in each congregation, but many churches quickly found that it was difficult to obtain satisfactory and regular preaching when the great majority of their members were occupied with their secular callings and had little leisure time. Particular difficulty was met by small or recently established congregations and severe restrictions were imposed on the work of evangelism.[58] To meet these difficulties, the Campbellites gradually made use of evangelists who were recognized as fulfilling a scriptural office, separate from those of elder and deacon. These evangelists and their families were maintained from the earnings of the congregations they served, and they undertook preaching tours for weeks or months at a time. However, the bulk of preaching and pastoral work at a local level was undertaken by lay elders, some of whom, like Richard Lloyd of Criccieth, enjoyed a wide reputation.[59]

NATIONAL ORGANIZATION

Before about 1860 the Campbellites found it difficult to develop any formal structure of interchurch co-operation. Letters of introduction from one congregation to another were quickly introduced, but these tended to facilitate the schisms that characterized much of this period rather than to strengthen the churches. A division in one congregation often spread to another, because the second church had to decide which party in the divided church should be received into fellowship. Schisms could spread from church to church in this fashion, a process also seen among the Brethren and Christadelphians.[60] Unlike the Brethren, the Campbellites avoided frequent schisms after 1860, although important divisions still occurred. Suspicion of any agency of interchurch government, which had been reinforced during the early years, was gradually overcome. The annual General Meeting of the churches familiarized local leaders with one another and with common problems, but right down to 1914 it remains important to distinguish between the formal framework of interchurch co-operation and the de facto control of the sect by individual leaders. A declaration of the nature and limits of interchurch co-operation was drawn up in 1861, and this remained in effect throughout the remainder of the period. This document emphasized that co-operation was primarily for evangelism and involved no powers to settle matters of discipline within each autonomous church. Removal from the list of cooperating churches referred only to a church ceasing to assist in the work of evangelism, and every church was to judge for itself whether fellowship was lawful with any church that had withdrawn from the list. Arbitration and statements by the General Meeting declining further fellowship technically related only to matters of associated action for evangelism. In practice, because the General Meeting was dominated by a few men, especially those on the key committees and in control of the sect's journal, their authority was more effective than formal declarations would suggest.[61] After James Wallis died in 1867, David King dominated the sect until his death in 1894, although his authority and conservative interpretation of church polity and practice did not go unchallenged.[62]

Two problems underlined the division between the supporters of congregational autonomy and the advocates of some minimal apparatus of interchurch government and bureaucracy. The lesser problem arose when the sect began to acquire its own chapel premises. Some form of trust deed was needed, and members feared that such a document required specification of a creed or church title that was antiscriptural and an infringement of local church autonomy.[63] The second, more perplexing problem was the maintenance of full-time evangelists. Although they rejected paid pastors, the Campbellites, as we have seen, raised funds to maintain evangelists who visited the different churches and helped establish new congregations. Even before the first General Meeting, at least one evangelist had been maintained in this way, and at the Edinburgh meeting the churches agreed to cooperate to support evangelists and a committee was appointed to receive contributions.[64] During the first year £150 was raised, and £132 was spent on the support of one evangelist for the whole year and a second for some months.[65] Lack of funds remained a chronic problem, at least until the 1870s, but equally problematical was the lack of suitably qualified men for the work. Unlike the American Campbellite movement, the British sect failed to convert any professional ministers or clergymen until the late fifties, and even after that time such recruits were very few.[66] Between 1842 and 1845 the full-time evangelist was maintained largely at the expense of the Nottingham church, which employed him to assist the smaller congregations in the East Midlands.[67]

Alexander Campbell's visit to Britain in 1847 stimulated further demand for evangelists, but the sect looked toward the United States for suitably qualified teachers and, when these did not materialize, nothing further was done and no full-time workers were employed between 1848 and 1855, a period of bitter dissension.[68] The organizational structure that gradually emerged was similar to the cooperative association that had developed around the Nottingham church in the East Midlands. Local and regional associations came together to promote evangelism and to enable the larger churches to provide assistance for the smaller congregations. In this way there developed a pattern of preaching in a group of local churches by lay elders and the maintenance of an evangelist on a regional basis.[69] Such regional action stimulated the General Meeting to take part in the work of evangelism, but there were numerous areas of conflict. Many sect members preferred to subscribe funds for the support of a local evangelist under the control of a district committee, rather than contribute money to the General Meeting. Such an attitude was revealed in 1869, when the General Meeting wanted David King, who had built up successful churches in London, Manchester, and Birmingham, to move to Liverpool. King resigned as evangelist for the General Meeting and continued his work in Birmingham under the auspices of the Birmingham District Association, which he controlled. There was also much disagreement about the best method of utilizing evangelists, with some members preferring to see them located in one community for a lengthy period, building up a new church or sustaining a faltering one, while others saw the evangelist's role as making periodic visits to existing churches, rather in the manner in which Methodist ministers preached at least once a month in churches usually served by lay preachers.[70] The use of evangelists by the more active district committees, such as the Lancashire committee, in the late fifties resulted in their work being supported and taken over by the General Meeting, which developed its own Evangelist Committee.[71]

With the more general use of full-time evangelists, many Campbellites began to express fears of the growth of a professional ministry, and even the prospect of a training institute or theological college such as had developed among the American Campbellites. Although anxious to attract to the work of evangelism "men of education and culture," David King firmly opposed the idea of a denominational college: "Students devote some five years to the college courses, and generally come out largely unfit for the work before them. In scholarship they acquire considerable advantages, but in our larger towns, in the same time and less cost, superior results in the same direction could be realized."[72]

By 1872, the Evangelist Committee financed by the churches and by individuals and representing the district associations had become firmly established, and its yearly income of £707 was sufficient to maintain five evangelists throughout the year and four others for some months.[73] Although opposed to a separate theological college, King was prominent in the training of these men, by personal supervision and correspondence courses, and by 1882 a training committee had been organized that gradually consolidated and enlarged this work. As the income of the Evangelist Committee grew, some sect leaders remained convinced that larger resources would attract evangelists only interested in monetary reward, but the low average income of Campbellite evangelists when compared with that of Nonconformist ministers or skilled artisans made such a development unlikely. Local leaders feared a threat to church autonomy and their own authority. The majority of individual congregations remained dependent upon unpaid leadership, but these developments indicate the growing importance of paid evangelists in the expansion of the Campbellites even though the sect continued to emphasize the unscriptural nature of paid pastors.[74]

The sectarian ethos of the Campbellite churches was also emphasized by other controversies, such as the debate over the principle of open or closed communion, in which the closed communion party generally remained in control.[75] Attachment to unpaid pastors, congregational autonomy, and closed communion was reinforced by developments in the United States, particularly after Campbell's death in 1866. There was some truth in Campbell's claim that he had not changed his basic views on the restoration of "primitive Christianity" since the publication of the first volume of the *Christian Baptist,* but, from the 1840s, his emphasis did change. Among his followers this change was largely accepted during Campbell's lifetime, but with his death two distinct traditions among the American Campbellites began to appear. One group conceived of Christianity in the more denominational framework of practical religion, social and political activism, and an often nationalistic postmillennialism. The second group emphasized the sectarian tradition of restorationism, a rigid, biblical literalism and an uncompromising separation from the world. Even before Campbell's death, these two positions were clarified in debates over open and closed communion, the propriety of full-time pastors, theological education, and allied matters. By the beginning of this century, the first group had evolved into a major, new American denomination, the Disciples of Christ, and the second broke away and became known as the Churches of Christ.[76] After Campbell's death, the majority of British Campbellite leaders followed David King in supporting the more sectarian of the two American groups, although complete polarization did not take place among American Campbellites until the early twentieth century and many American leaders occupied an intermediate position.[77]

Through the *Ecclesiastical Observer,* King publicized his views attributing the supposed decline of the Disciples of Christ in the post–Civil War period to the introduction of paid pastors—"the one man system"—the introduction of organs into congregational worship, and the movements toward open communion. He corresponded with both moderate and conservative American leaders, including J. W. McGarvey, the spokesman for the anti-organ school, and T. D. Butler, originally from England, who confirmed King's belief that the American movement was backsliding: "Preaching is now a profession, as much as law or physic, and among us as a people as among other bodies of the religious world. We railed against 'the sects' vehemently for *this* which was *then* anything and everything that was bad; now we have radically changed, and we generally practice what we formerly universally condemned."[78] King reprinted other American attacks on the development of theological colleges, the ordination of "ministers," and the policies of the "progress" party in general. He found these "progressive" changes particularly difficult to accept in view of the American claim that they were the key to a massive expansion of the Disciples of Christ between 1880 and 1890, when it was claimed that the membership increased from 475,000 to 641,000, a trend that was to result in a denomination of 1,120,000 members by 1900.[79] The forward movement of the British Campbellites was in part an attempt to demonstrate that the British churches could make substantial gains without sacrificing fundamental principles and usages.

As early as the 1860s, David King faced challengers anxious to direct the British Campbellite churches into paths being followed in the United States. By far his most important critic was Timothy Coop, who had long been the treasurer of the Evangelism Committee and one of its principal benefactors. Coop was a wealthy man, active in the temperance movement, and anxious that his sect should exert a wider influence. He became alarmed at the exclusiveness of the British Campbellite churches and was convinced that little progress would be made in Britain under King's control. Clearly Coop wanted the British churches to follow the American Disciples of Christ and, ultimately, to transform themselves into a denomination that could claim equality with Baptists, Congregationalists, and Wesleyan Methodists. Coop frequently visited the United States and was instrumental in persuading the newly formed Foreign Christian Missionary Society of the Disciples of Christ to introduce American-style churches to Britain, meeting a substantial part of the cost himself. These churches with paid ministers, organ music, public collections, and pew rents were similar to contemporary major British Nonconformist churches.[80] H. S. Earle, an American missionary, was active in Southampton, where there was no Campbellite church from 1875, but from 1878 churches were established in towns where the British Campbellites already had congregations, with resultant bitterness on both sides. Coop's descriptions of the British Campbellite churches in the American press were especially distasteful to British leaders, who believed that their efforts were being ridiculed.[81] Coop's writings confirm the nature of his aspirations for his own churches as well as what he felt to be wrong with the Campbellite congregations:

> Our movement is yet in its infancy. It has few, if any of the elements of permanency to show the people. The Churches we have started are, with one exception, without suitable places for worship. And this fact alone stands greatly in the way of success before a class of people we ought to be able to reach. We must not consider it contrary to human nature if we do not find men willing to give up pleasant religious associations, social friendships and even, often, business advantages for what evidently seems to be a sort of experiment. . . . If the people whose ear we get were not religious at all, the difficulties I have hinted at would not be so prominent. But our movement is essentially an effort to lift people to a higher religious position. Almost everyone is already in some church or is in some way religious.[82]

By 1888 Coop had helped to organize and finance eleven churches that formed the Christian Association. These churchmen included the large West London tabernacle whose minister, W. T. Moore, directed the Disciples of Christ's efforts in Britain and edited the *Christian Commonwealth,* a magazine founded by Coop.[83]

Few British Campbellites followed Coop into this new movement, which did not go unchallenged by the older sect. Efforts by the Campbellites at evangelism and church building along more orthodox lines produced the modest successes already examined, while a bitter paper war with Coop and his American associates helped the British sect reaffirm their faith in the old ways.[84] Conservative American Campbellites continued to supply King with information about his opponents and their American activities, and the British Campbellites claimed fellowship "only with those men and churches in America . . . whose faith and practice are at one with the faith and order of the church as left by the Apostles."[85] Conflict reached a peak with the appearance of Moore's biography of Coop in 1889, which gave the Christian Association's version of events since the sixties, and King replied in the *Bible Advocate*.[86] With King's death in 1894, tension between the two groups declined. The tendency among the British Campbellites to make greater use of full-time evangelists, and a gradual liberalization of beliefs and practices, especially among the younger, second- and third-generation members who had been restrained by King, enabled them to move closer to the Christian Association, many of whose members had not been involved in the "betrayal" of the older sect by Coop and his immediate followers. In 1917 a union of both groups was accomplished, but not without schisms on both sides.[87]

SOCIAL RELATIONSHIPS AND SOCIAL AND POLITICAL VIEWS

The Campbellites believed that only baptized members of the church should contribute toward its financial maintenance, according to their ability, and at their public services no collections were taken. All seats were free and the sect made much of this point in its propaganda. Except for the weekly celebration of the Lord's Supper, the focal point of corporate worship, the Sunday services in the Campbellite churches resembled those in many small Baptist congregations, with unaccompanied hymn singing, prayer, and preaching having the central roles. Organs were not introduced into the churches until the present century and in 1917 were still opposed by some congregations.[88] By 1878 Campbellite services struck a sympathetic journalist in Liverpool as old-fashioned.[89] Members were generally recruited from dissident members of other sects and denominations, and the decision of an individual to join a Campbellite church was usually the result of a long period of Bible reading and discussion about the nature of "primitive Christianity" rather than a sudden conversion experience.[90] The sect opposed mass evangelistic crusades of the Moody and Sankey type as spurious and unscriptural, but in a number of areas the Campbellites gained members through an increase of pietism and Bible reading, the aftermath of revivals organized by other denominations.[91] Early recruits included Baptists, Methodists, Evangelical Unionists, and Brethren, and in the late nineteenth century the Salvation Army provided some members.[92]

An early minute book of one congregation mentions the exclusion of members for habitual neglect of divine worship, heretical opinions, immoral conduct and company, quarrelling with and disobeying parents and employers.[93] The sect emphasized separation from the world and the need for a strict division of church and state. The true sphere of the "primitive" church was spiritual and inward, not material and political, and the political duties of church members were to be exercised quite separately from the church as a spiritual community.[94] During the 1840s, some Campbellite leaders complained that the sect had been too much influenced by contemporary popular radicalism, and they attempted to combat its influence on church government. From then until the seventies it is difficult to find evidence of political and social activity outside the church by individual Campbellites.[95] During Alexander Campbell's visit to Britain in 1847, his followers vigorously opposed any discussion of American slavery, which Campbell was accused of condoning, and they emphasized that slavery as a social and political problem did not concern the church as an institution.[96]

David King fostered this sharp separation of religious and political activity by encouraging a strong sense of exclusiveness amongst Campbellites. He opposed the drift toward "worldliness," which he saw affecting many "so-called Christians." "Costly entertainments, dancing, novel reading, concerts, bagatelle, and other trifling games, luxury and extravagance and godless company," he complained, were all tolerated by "respectable families," which believed themselves to be Christians.[97] This type of criticism was common among conservative Methodists and Nonconformists at midcentury, but their denominations were in general moving toward the more accommodating attitude King described.[98] As the Campbellites moved away from the period of millenarian enthusiasm and schismatic divisions, their range of permitted recreations and activities widened. King shared with his secularist opponents a preoccupation with self-improvement and useful knowledge. He emphasized the importance of outdoor exercise and urged the benefits of reading history, biography, science, and works of travel. Sect members were encouraged to visit museums and to attend lectures on improving subjects, and King strongly approved of domestic musical evenings and family games. The good Christian should present "a happy and genial image" to the world, but he must always remember that he is *in* but not *of* worldly society. King reaffirmed the need to avoid the theater, the ballroom, the concert hall, the casino, the racecourse, and all forms of gambling.[99] The Campbellites in this respect resembled the Primitive Methodists, among whom a "neo-puritanism" concerning alcohol and gambling remained strong, although the Primitive Methodists had probably accommodated themselves more to other aspects of secular culture by 1900.[100] Like the Primitive Methodists, the Campbellites quickly endorsed total abstinence, although there remained, for some time, a reluctance to associate the churches in any formal way with such "unscriptural" agencies as temperance societies, and there was a fear that certain types of temperance agitation would involve the churches in political questions.[101] Individual leaders, such as Timothy Coop, were very active in the Prohibition movement and numerous obituaries in the Campbellite press suggest that by the late nineteenth century an overwhelming majority of members were total abstainers, although total abstinence was never made a condition of membership.[102] As individuals, Campbellites were also urged by their principal magazine to support other late-nineteenth-century "moral reform" movements, such as the anti-Contagious Diseases Acts agitation and the wider movement for personal purity.[103] Campbellite support for social reforms of this type suggests that the rigid sect ethos that dominated the group up to the seventies was declining despite David King's conservatism. Together with a wider interest in the social issues of the day, the sect developed more concern about the training of its children, and an earlier condemnation of Sunday schools as "unscriptural" by some members gave way to their general acceptance and establishment.[104]

While the churches became more closely associated with moral questions affecting the wider community, "party political" activity was left to the conscience of the individual. In the 1890s some Campbellites were still undecided whether Christians should vote, but limited evidence suggests that those who were qualified not only exercised the franchise but became active in local political affairs. Amos Mann, a Leicester Campbellite leader, became a leading advocate of producers' cooperatives, a Liberal town councilor, and then a Labour Party supporter. Fragmentary evidence suggests a probable predominance of Liberal voters amongst Campbellites in the late nineteenth century; Amos Mann's shift to the Labour Party was in no way unusual. At least one Campbellite evangelist became alarmed at the tendency of some members to try to thrust their political views upon the rest, but it is only possible to speculate about the tensions created by such an attitude within individual congregations, or about possible tensions between the small manufacturers, wholesalers, and shopkeepers who had played such an important role in the development of the sect, and more politically radical working-class members.[105]

THE CAMPBELLITES AND NINETEENTH-CENTURY SECTARIANISM

Twentieth-century apologists for the Campbellites, like apologists for some sections of the Brethren, stress the supposed ecumenical aspects of the Campbellite tradition with its emphasis upon the fundamentals of Christianity, worship, and practice. In the nineteenth century, little evidence of this "pioneering for Christian unity" can be found.[106] The Campbellites had their major contacts with other sects and denominations through the controversy and debate by which new members were recruited. There were early and prolonged exchanges with the Scotch Baptists, Adventists, Mormons, and Christadelphians, but the Campbellites also won members from the larger denominations and had particular success in persuading Baptist congregations with unpaid pastors to become Campbellites.[107] In the late nineteenth century, Christadelphians, Mormons, and Seventh-day Adventists seem to have been most persistent in proselytizing among the Campbellites, with the Christadelphians creating the most resentment among Campbellite leaders. Premillennial views remained widespread among the Campbellites and inclined members toward Adventist sects, while a literal reading of the Scriptures as the foundation of their "primitive order" made members particularly susceptible to the approaches of rival sects like the Christadelphians, whose method of conversion was by appeals to reason and history. Conflict with the Christadelphians was intensified by the interlocked origins of the two sects and by the location of their leaders in Birmingham. From the 1890s the methods of scriptural interpretation and persistent proselytizing employed by the Jehovah's Witnesses (or Russellism as the Campbellites called the new sect) produced frequent counterattacks from the Campbellites, as from the Christadelphians.[108]

In 1847 Alexander Campbell described the Brethren as more like his own followers than any other group he had encountered in Britain.[109] Campbellites and Brethren both sought the restoration of "primitive Christianity," in which there would be no separate order of paid ministers. Both groups celebrated the Lord's Supper each Sunday, and some Brethren shared a belief in the necessity of believers' baptism by immersion. Not all Brethren accepted this position, however, and disagreement with the Campbellites centered on the reception of non-immersed believers at the Lord's Supper, the nature of baptism, and the Brethren's dispensational theology. The Campbellites attributed the frequent schisms of the Brethren to the failure of the latter to adopt scriptural practices in all cases of church government.[110] Contacts were closest during the 1840s and 1850s, and it was in Scotland, where the Brethren had more middle- and lower-class members, that the two sects were most often confused. During the revival of 1859–60, one evangelist was claimed by both Brethren and Campbellites, and converts were attached to Brethren meetings or to Campbellite or Baptist churches. This confusion of sect boundaries continued into the 1860s, by which date the Brethren had come to dominate, and the Campbellites went into a relative decline in Scotland. Debate and controversy between the two sects continued, however, and David King thought that the Scottish Campbellite churches were too much influenced by Brethren teaching and practice.[111] At Peterhead, a strong center of Brethrenism, the Campbellites maintained two congregations, and elsewhere the two sects recruited from a common pool of potential members; as late as the 1880s, the Campbellites were able to build up a new church in another Brethren stronghold, Leominster in Herefordshire.[112]

The Campbellites had more friendly contacts with the loosely associated Free Gospel Churches, which in 1898 adopted their present name of Independent Methodists. The Independent Methodists rejected the use of paid ministers and emphasized congregational autonomy. Like the Campbellites, they experienced many years of fragmentation and frustration because of a lack of full-time evangelists, concern for congregational independence, and the disruptive impact of other proselytizing sects. They were concentrated in Lancashire, Cheshire, and adjacent areas of the West Riding, where the Campbellites had some support.[113]

Some Independent Methodists subscribed to the *Ecclesiastical Observer,* and each sect cited the other as evidence of the viability of an unpaid ministry.[114] In terms of their theological background and patterns of church government, the two sects represented different traditions, with the Campbellites looking back to a Calvinistic, Presbyterian, and Baptist background, while the Independent Methodists represented the ultimate in antiministerial dissent among the Methodists. Although the Campbellites and the Independent Methodists had different origins, the pattern of their social and political beliefs and development in the late nineteenth century was similar. Both possessed more stability and were capable of raising greater funds from the seventies onward. Both endorsed total abstinence and had leading members active in local politics and government, mostly as Liberals, although there is some evidence that the Independent Methodists possessed a rather larger proportion of small businessmen, accountants, journalists, teachers, and other middle-class members of the community.[115]

CONCLUSION

A study of the Campbellites indicates some characteristics of nineteenth-century lower-class religion and of the process of sect development that need to be examined in other religious groups. The number and range of sects that emphasized the restoration of "primitive Christianity" and that began to organize as separate sects during the 1830s and 1840s suggest a widespread dissatisfaction not only with the established churches, but also with the older and predominantly middle-class Nonconformist and Methodist denominations, although the pattern of recruitment to some sections of the Brethren, for example, should warn against seeing this dissatisfaction in exclusively economic or social terms. The existence and growth of the Campbellites also show the need to qualify descriptions of early Victorian popular religion, which dwell exclusively on revivalism, as conducted, for example, by the Primitive Methodists. Methodists and other revival-orientated sects may well have acted as a halfway house for those ultimately converted to sects where greater emphasis was placed upon a special eschatology or "restorationist" message, accepted by a "reasoned" study of the Scriptures rather than emotional conversion. Just as the revivalists themselves had their greatest successes where their audiences shared with them common assumptions about heaven, hell, and salvation, and were familiar with the basic language and format of the revivalists' message, so the Campbellites as well as the Brethren, the Millerites, the Mormons and a variety of other Adventist sects had most appeal among those dissatisfied with the nature of their own religious experience and the general state of the religious body with which they were currently associated. On the fringe of popular revivalism and conventional denominational life, there was considerable scope for sects that emphasized a legalistic set of doctrines and a more total alternative community—a sense of belonging to a favored and select body, often claiming a unique millennial role. The Campbellites and some other sects with which they were initially closely associated could also utilize popular anticlericalism both outside and within existing religious bodies by endorsing criticism of contemporary patterns of church government, clerical education, wealth, and power while emphasizing that such criticism did not apply to the "primitive Christianity" they offered.

The Campbellites' interpretation of "primitive Christianity," a general expectation of the Millennium, and a vigorous anticlericalism among early members combined to prevent the rapid growth of a paid ministry. Lack of funds, the instability of many congregations, and a lack of suitable candidates were additional practical reasons for the continued reliance on unpaid officials. After 1870, the improved economic position of many Campbellite members made a paid ministry more feasible, but the need to reconcile this with the sect's original interpretation of the Scriptures resulted in elaborate justification of the use of paid officials as evangelists, who in Campbellite doctrine remained distinct from a regular ministry. The early history of the Campbellites underlines certain features of Victorian society that made the organization of lower-class religious life difficult in general and the existence of individual congregations precarious. The practical difficulties that helped delay the appearance of a paid ministry also restricted and even destroyed the work of the congregations. Some instability can be attributed to prevailing economic conditions producing a decline in congregations for a variety of reasons; migration in search of employment, insufficient income to pay even modest church dues or to provide suitable clothes in which to attend meetings, and the counterattraction of industrial or political agitation. The experience of the Campbellites also suggests the problems of developing local leadership with adequate pastoral and organizational skills, and the disproportionate responsibility and power thrown into the hands of a minority of members who were sometimes better educated and generally more economically secure. In the early decades of Campbellite development, the lack of clear sect boundaries and the controversies through which the sect both grew and fragmented suggest a process that can probably be illustrated for other lower-class religious groups. Equally important for other sects as well as the Campbellites was the process by which control of the sect's literature and journals fell into the hands of a few men who wielded a power within the sect far greater than their official position would suggest. With this development was associated the growth of at least a rudimentary pattern of local, regional, and national organization, with informal methods of government within the sect being at least as important as their stated system of organization and operation.

Campbellite as well as other lower-class sect leaders often contrasted the comparative comfort and even affluence of their members in the late nineteenth century compared with their poverty during the decades before about 1850. This raises the question whether the standard of living of the groups of which the sects were predominantly composed had significantly improved, or whether the sects were recruiting from a slightly higher social class in the later period. Certainly, the history of the Campbellites suggests a local membership, after which about 1870 not only had more stability but also sufficient funds for the erection or purchase of churches, the publication of a wider and more varied range of sect literature, and the maintenance of an increasing number of paid evangelists. Local difficulties were still created by strikes or factory closures, but the predominant impression of the sect as a whole is not that it was a church for the poor, but that it was a church for respectable, teetotal, working, and lower-middle-class people who were increasingly involved in the wider political and social life of the community. This impression must be qualified by emphasizing that nothing is known about the 20 percent of members who were lost to the sect each year. Were they predominantly poor members who thus felt it difficult to maintain a place in the local congregation, or were some economically successful members who felt restricted by the otherworldly ethos stressed by David King up to his death? No simple equation between economic success and dissatisfaction with a strict sect ethos can usefully be drawn, but it is interesting that Bryan Wilson has stressed the comparative poverty of late Victorian Christadelphians and their rigid sectarianism, and there is much evidence that the latter sect had a strong appeal to many Campbellites, although it is impossible to say whether the attraction of the Christadelphians was greatest among those Campbellites who were most economically insecure.[116] There is also a need to know much more about other sects that were expanding in the late nineteenth century, such as the Seventh-day Adventists and the Jehovah's Witnesses, who appealed to some Campbellites anxious to remain within a close sect ethos and drawn toward the millenarian element neglected in their own tradition under King's leadership.

At a more general level, it is also important to stress that for the late, as for the early and middle years of the nineteenth century, popular lower-class religion took the form not only of more legalistic sects such as the Christadelphians and Jehovah's Witnesses, but also of emotional, revival orientated groups such as the Salvation Army and a variety of Holiness and, later, Pentecostal groups.

Proselytizing through discussion and debate, which the Campbellites favored and shared with other sects, assumed a common religious language among potential members. Nineteenth-century secularism also propagandized by discussion and debate and utilized a similar literalist view of the Bible and widespread working-class anticlericalism to advance its own militantly antisupernatural beliefs. There was the same concern with self-education among a predominantly respectable working-class membership in Campbellite and secularist groups. Among the Campbellites, talents for public speaking, administration, and organization could be developed by at least a minority of leading members within each congregation without any sense of the middle and upper class patronage and control associated with both the Nonconformist denominations and the large number of late Victorian mission halls designed to convert the poor. Whether such talents as were developed within the sect were ultimately utilized in a wider field depended on the inclinations and opportunities of individuals and the degree of otherworldliness maintained within the sect. By the end of the century, the Campbellites placed few obstacles in the way of their members taking part in a wider social and political arena, and they even cited the activities of such members as an indication of the sect's respectability and local standing, although tensions occurred as a result of the involvement of individual members with political parties or other movements not favored by the majority. A similar process and results can be shown among Independent Methodists and among Primitive Methodists in many areas.

It must be remembered, however, that as the Campbellite members moved away from a rigid sect ethos, the growth of other sects with a legalistic orientation, like the Jehovah's Witnesses, or with an emotional revivalistic emphasis, like the Holiness movements, demonstrated the continuing appeal of a rigid doctrine of separation from the world. But, by the end of the nineteenth century, all types of sectarian Protestantism touched only a small minority of the population, among whom the language of religious experience and discussion was growing increasingly unfamiliar.

NOTES

1. For recent studies of the Brethren, see B. R. Wilson, ed., *Patterns of Sectarianism* (London, 1967), 213–342; F. Roy Coad, *A History of the Brethren Movement* (London, 1968); and H. H. Rowdon, *The Origins of the Brethren* (London, 1967). The term *restorationist* was commonly used by the Campbellites, and it is here employed to indicate both a powerful ideological theme in a wide range of nineteenth-century religious groups and, in part, as an explanation of the nature and form of these groups. The term is not intended to indicate an additional type of sect, but an additional characteristic of some types of sects. The conventional typologies of sects developed by sociologists, and summarized and extended in Wilson's *Patterns of Sectarianism*, 22–45, seem too inflexible, as Wilson himself suggests in his more recent *Religious Sects* (London, 1970), 35. The latter work is of limited value for students of British religious groups in part because, as the bibliography indicates, there is insufficient data on nineteenth-century religious life.

2. See, for example, the histories of restorationist sects in the Campbellite magazines, the *Christian Advocate* (Edinburgh, 1858) and the *Ecclesiastical Observer* (Birmingham, 1882); and two popular handbooks used by the sect, J. F. Rowe, *History of Restoration*

Movements (Cincinnati, n.d.); and M. M. Davis, *The Restoration Movement of the Nineteenth Century* (Cincinnati, 1913).

3. An outline of the major restorationist movements of the late eighteenth and nineteenth centuries can be found in Coad, *A History of the Brethren Movement*, 80–81; Rowdon, *The Origins of the Brethren*, 1–26; H. Escott, *A History of Scottish Congregationalism* (Glasgow, 1960); and in a recent article by T. F. C. Stunt, "John Henry Newman and the Evangelicals," *Journal of Ecclesiastical History* 21, no. 1 (1970): 69–74. Some Anglican Seceders found their "primitive" church among the ultra-Calvinistic Baptist sects. For an introduction to one such group that had much in common with the restorationist sects considered here, see S. F. Paul, *Historical Sketch of the Gospel Standard Baptists* (London, 1945).

4. The "official" history is A. C. Watters, *History of the British Churches of Christ* (Indianapolis, 1948). This is a shortened version of Dr Watters's Ph.D. dissertation submitted at Edinburgh University in 1947. Book and dissertation are essentially uncritical, narrative descriptions of the sect's development. See also the brief sketch in William Robinson, *What the Churches of Christ Stand For* (Birmingham, 1926). The best history of the Disciples of Christ is David E. Harrell, *Quest for a Christian America: The Disciples of Christ and American Society to 1866* (Nashville, 1966).

5. J. T. Hornsby, "John Glas" (Ph.D. diss., Edinburgh Univ., 1936); *Christian Advocate* (Sept. 2, 1858); *London Christian Instructor* (Mar. 1819); Escott, *A History of Scottish Congregationalism*, 17–23.

6. Harrell, *Quest for a Christian America*, 6–7; W. E. Garrison, *Religion Follows the Frontier: A History of the Disciples of Christ* (New York, 1931), 201–2.

7. R. D. Mitchell, "Archibald McLean, 1857–1912: Baptist Pioneer in Scotland" (Ph.D. diss., Edinburgh Univ., 1952); George Yuille, ed., *History of the Baptists in Scotland* (Glasgow, 1926), 36–51; R. B. Hannen, "The 'Scotch Baptist' Churches: An Episode in Scottish Baptist History," *Chronicle* (Chester, Pa.) (Oct. 7, 1944); T. Witton Davies, "The McLeanist (Scotch) and Campbellite Baptists of Wales," *Transactions of the Baptist Historical Society* (London) 7 (1920–21): 147–81.

8. Coad, *A History of the Brethren Movement*, 81; Rowdon, *The Origins of the Brethren*, 23–26; *Millennial Harbinger and Voluntary Church Advocate* (1835): 10ff.

9. Harrell, *Quest for a Christian America*, 1–9; Garrison, *Religion Follows the Frontier*, 35–144.

10. William Jones, *Autobiography* (London, 1846), 36–138.

11. Ibid., 122–38; *Millennial Harbinger* (1835): 15–78; (June 1844): 281ff.

12. *Christian Messenger and Reformer* (Aug. 1838): 202–6; *British Harbinger* (July 1867): 221–27; Francis and John White, *History, Directory, and Gazetteer of Nottingham* (Sheffield, 1844): 150, 260.

13. *Christian Advocate* (Sept. 2, 1858); *Millennial Harbinger* (Bethany) (Aug. 1847); *Christian Messenger* (Apr. 1838): 72; (Feb. 1839): 428.

14. W. T. Moore, *The Life of Timothy Coop* (London, 1889): 137.

15. Numerous obituaries in the principal Campbellite periodicals indicate the Scotch Baptist background of many early members. Some early leaders like David King, Timothy Coop, and Joseph Rotherham had a Wesleyan background, although Rotherham came to the Campbellites via the Baptists; Louise King, ed., *Memoir of David King with Various Papers and Addresses* (Birmingham, 1897); Moore, *The Life of Timothy Coop;* Joseph B. Rotherham, *Reminiscences* (London, 1922). Alan Betteridge, "Asterby and Donington on Bain, Lincolnshire, Baptist Church," *Baptist Quarterly* (Jan. 24, 1971): 27, shows a rural Baptist pastor embracing Campbellism about 1839; the *Congregational Magazine* (London) (Mar. 1841): 180, reported that the Campbellites were proselytizing during the Kilsyth revival of 1839 in Scotland.

16. See my article, "The Millerite Adventists in Great Britain, 1840–50," *Journal of American Studies* 1 (Oct. 1967): 191–212.

17. Harrell, *Quest for a Christian America*, 39–48.

18. Billington, "Leicester Secular Society, 1852–1920." For the wider ramifications of mid-nineteenth-century millenarianism, see Ernest R. Sandeen, *Roots of Fundamentalism: British and American Millenarianism, 1800–1930* (Chicago, 1970).

19. Billington, "Leicester Secular Society, 1852–1920," 210–11; *Christian Messenger* (Aug. 1843): 204–6; *Gospel Banner* (London) (Aug.–Dec. 1848); *British Millennial Harbinger* (London) (Nov. 1850): 515–20.

20. *Gospel Banner* (July 1850): 192–96; *Ecclesiastical Observer* (Oct. 1873): 333–34; *Bible Advocate* (Sept. 1, 1892): 325–26; King, *Memoir of David King*, 1–61. Premillennialism continued to fascinate some Campbellites in spite of King's opposition; e.g., see obituary of James Collins in *Bible Advocate* (Nov. 30, 1917): 569–72 and James Anderson, *An Outline of My Life* (Birmingham, 1912).

21. *British Millennial Harbinger* (Sept. 1858): 457.

22. Ibid. (June 1850): 282–83 and *Christian Messenger* (Oct. 1842): 279–84.

23. *Bible Advocate* (Sept. 1892): 326. One Campbellite evangelist estimated that one-fifth of recorded members were "mere paper" (Jan. 16, 1914): 43.

24. The Churches of Christ yearbooks from the late nineteenth century contain summaries of early statistics except where possible original reports have been used. *Christian Messenger* (Oct. 1842): 279–84; *Bible Advocate* (Sept. 1, 15, 1892) reprints further details of the 1842 meeting; *British Millennial Harbinger* (Nov. 1848): 528–29; (June 1850): 282; (Sept. 1855): 453–54; *Gospel Banner* (July 1850): 192; *Ecclesiastical Observer* (Oct. 1873) gives further details of Campbellite statistics to that date.

25. This is based on an analysis of the statistics and comments in the Campbellite press during the 1840s and 1850s. The early life of James Anderson, the Campbellite evangelist, shows the frequency with which he and his family moved in search of employment: see Anderson, *An Outline of My Life*, 1–26. The instability of individual congregations with a working-class membership can be shown even for sects like the Primitive Methodists, which had a paid ministry, and more dramatically among the Independent Methodists, who, like the Campbellites, relied on an unpaid pastorate. See

Primitive Methodist Magazine (Bemersley) (Mar. 1838) and *Primitive Methodist Magazine* (London) (Aug. 1844) for typical reports of circuit losses due to members moving because of unemployment and strikes; and James Vickers, *History of Independent Methodism* (Bolton, 1920), 66.

26. *Ecclesiastical Observer* (Oct. 1873): 336–37; *Millennial Harbinger* (Bethany) (Mar. 1853): 173; Anderson, *An Outline of My Life*, 26–30; Bryan R. Wilson, *Sects and Society* (London, 1961): 238–39.

27. Analysis of statistics cited in note 24 above, and other issues of Campbellite periodicals. That congregations were often small is indicated by the example of Banbury, where the 1851 census recorded twenty-five Campbellites who met in a schoolroom; *Bishop Wilberforce's Visitation Returns for the Archdeaconry of Oxford in the year 1854*, trans. and ed. E. P. Baker (Oxford, 1954), 13.

28. *British Millennial Harbinger* (Sept. 1855): 453–54; (Sept. 1858): 457; (Sept. 1862): 317–18; (Sept. 1866): 321–22; *Ecclesiastical Observer* (Sept. 1872): 312–14; (Sept. 1875): 306–9.

29. Ibid. (Oct. 1873): 338–39. Obituaries of members in the age group of twenty-five to forty in the *Ecclesiastical Observer* during the 1870s show many second-generation members. See also below, under "Local Organization" and "National Organization."

30. *Bible Advocate* (Sept. 1892): 326 gives statistics for the period from 1876; see also issues for Aug. 14, 1914, 515.

31. This is based on reports and illustrations of chapel openings in *Bible Advocate* and *Ecclesiastical Observer*; in the latter see especially Jan.–Sept. 1873; also H. B. Kendall, *The Origin and History of the Primitive Methodist Church*, 2 vols. (London, 1909), and Ralph Frederick Chambers, *The Strict Baptist Chapels of England*, 4 vols. (London, 1952–63).

32. *Bible Advocate* (Sept. 1891): 232–41.

33. *Ecclesiastical Observer* (July 1882): 185; *Free Gospel Magazine* (London) (Nov. 1884): 402; Vickers, *History of Independent Methodism*, 291–307; Elizabeth Isichei, *Victorian Quakers* (London, 1970), 99–100.

34. This is based on numerous obituaries in the Campbellite press; also Moore, *The Life of Timothy Coop*, 364, and Anderson, *An Outline of My Life*, 1–13.

35. *Bible Advocate* (Sept. 1890): 232. The Independent Methodists had a similar turnover; report on five years' evangelistic work in *Free Gospel Magazine* (Oct. 1880): 361–63.

36. Annual returns give details for individual churches and later for regional groupings. *Ecclesiastical Observer* (Sept. 1, 1875): 306–9, e.g., gives the following details: Southern Division—648 members; Midland Division—1,153; Yorkshire—344; Lancashire and Cheshire—1,094; Northwest—161; Northeast—258; Scotland—862 (including Edinburgh—167 and Glasgow—197); Wales—c. 300.

37. Annual returns list members who emigrated, and the Campbellite press contains many letters from members overseas. Reference to the difficulties created by emigration appear as early as 1845; see *Christian Messenger* (June 1845): 92–93.

38. *Christian Messenger* (Oct. 1842): 325; *Millennial Harbinger* (Bethany) (Oct. 1846): 580–85, a report on the British churches by a visiting American leader, W. K. Pendleton; Anderson, *An Outline of My Life*, 1–21.

39. *British Millennial Harbinger* (June 1850): 286–87.

40. Letters from David King in *Millennial Harbinger* (Bethany) (Feb. 1855/Apr. 1856); see also *Gospel Banner* (May/June 1849).

41. *British Millennial Harbinger* (Sept. 1858): 459.

42. *Bible Advocate* (Sept. 15, 1892): 341–42.

43. For Wallis, see *British Harbinger* (July 1867): 221–27; White, *History, Directory, and Gazetteer of Nottingham*, 150, 260–62; *Nottingham Journal* (Festival Supplement) (May 3, 1951); for Tickle, *Bible Advocate* (Jan. 15, 1894): 34; for Milner, *British Millennial Harbinger* (Aug. 1866): 274–75; and for Coop, Moore, *The Life of Timothy Coop*.

44. Moore, *The Life of Timothy Coop*, 204, 441; White, *History, Directory, and Gazetteer of Nottingham*, 232; *Millennial Harbinger* (Bethany) (July 1848): 396; (Dec. 1857): 706–9; *Bible Advocate* (Sept. 15, 1892): 341–42; (Nov. 30, 1917): 569–72. For the employment of members and leaders by prominent members of the sect, see, e.g., obituary of James Alfred Dawson, *Bible Advocate* (Jan. 23, 1914): 50–51, and obituary of Amos Mann in *Christian Advocate* (Jan. 19, 1940): 46.

45. Obituaries in the Campbellite press yield information on this topic.

46. *Christianity v Secularism. Report of a Public Discussion between D. King . . . and C. Bradlaugh* (Birmingham, 1870); and King's polemical magazine *The Old Paths* (Birmingham), 1866–91, which was designed for distribution as a tract. Also see Rosamund Billington, "Leicester Secular Society, 1852–1920: A Study in Radicalism and Respectability" (Ph.D. diss., Leicester Univ., 1968).

47. *Liverpool Argus* (Aug. 3, 1878) quoted in *Ecclesiastical Observer* (Sept. 15, 1878): 242–45. A similar report from the *Nottingham Daily Express* (Feb. 26, 1878), was quoted in the issue for Mar. 15, 1878, 80–82. James Anderson, who had wide experience in the sect from 1860 onward, wrote in 1912: "Where the bulk of the people are made up of the better sort of the working class, the Gospel of Christ is more likely to take effect. Above or below that line you have harder work" (159).

48. T. J. Ainsworth, *Sydney Black* (London, 1911); Rotherham, *Reminiscences; Bible Advocate* (Aug. 18, 1899): 641; (May 26, 1911): 321–25; (June 2, 1916): 337–38.

49. *Bible Advocate* (Aug. 18, 1899): 641, and numerous other examples from the 1890s; also personal observations. For other reports of the location of Campbellite churches, see *Ecclesiastical Observer* (Mar. 15, 1878): 80–82; (Sept. 15, 1878): 242–45.

50. *Newcastle Daily Chronicle* (Aug. 7, 1899) quoted in *Bible Advocate* (Aug. 18, 1899): 641.

51. William Robinson, *The Shattered Cross: The Many Churches and the One Church* (Birmingham, 1945).

52. Coad, *A History of the Brethren Movement*, 118–36; Wilson, *Patterns of Sectarianism*, 214–15; Yuille, *History of the Baptists in Scotland*, 53–54; Rowdon, *The Origins of the Brethren*, 1–26, 227–30.

53. *Christian Messenger* (Nov. 1841): 318–20; (May 1842): 109–10; (Sept./Nov. 1844): 28–147; Watters, *History of the British Churches of Christ*, 118–19, 259–60; King, *Memoir of David King*, 240; Thomas Hughes Milner, *The Messiah's Ministry* (Edinburgh, 1858).

54. Anderson, *An Outline of My Life*, 14; *British Millennial Harbinger* (Jan. 1858): 50–51.

55. *British Millennial Harbinger* (Feb. 1853): 89.

56. King, *Memoir of David King*, 238–322; Watters, *History of the British Churches of Christ*, 193–94; *British Millennial Harbinger* (Apr. 1860): 102.

57. See *National Reformer* (London) (Nov. 17, 1867) for a secularist attack on the "Kingites." *A Birmingham Sect Maker: Teaching v Practice and Teaching, i.e. Absurdity Reviewed by Anti-Humbug* (Gatshead, 1873) was an attack on King by a dissident church in Newcastle.

58. *Ecclesiastical Observer* (Oct. 1, 1873): 325–41, article reviewing developments since 1842.

59. Ibid. *Christian Messenger* (Aug. 1843): 205; *Bible Advocate* (Mar. 16, 1917): 121–22.

60. *Christian Messenger* (May 1848): 236–37; (Sept. 1847): 428–30; *Ecclesiastical Observer* (Sept. 1, 1873): 319ff; Wilson, *Sects and Society*, 242–45; Wilson, *Patterns of Sectarianism*, 295ff.; and *A Birmingham Sect Maker*.

61. There is a statement of the purposes of interchurch co-operation in *The Churches of Christ Year Book and 78th Annual Report* (Birmingham, 1923): 2.

62. *A Birmingham Sect Maker; Bible Advocate* (Nov. 30, 1917): 569–72.

63. *Bible Advocate* (Jan. 27, 1899): 77; *Ecclesiastical Observer* (July 1875): 240ff.

64. *Ecclesiastical Observer* (Oct. 1873): 325–41, a good résumé of the work of evangelists from the 1830s to 1872; *Bible Advocate* (Jan. 19, 1917): 25–28, has a history of the Evangelist Committee; Moore, *The Life of Timothy Coop*, 139–44; *Christian Messenger* (Dec. 1841): 361–62; (Oct. 1842): 279–84.

65. *Christian Messenger* (Oct. 1843): 329; *Ecclesiastical Observer* (Oct. 1873): 326; Watters, *History of the British Churches of Christ*, 76–77.

66. *Bible Advocate* (Sept. 15, 1892): 341–46 gives King's views on the contrast between British and American churches with regard to converting clergymen; see also Rotherham, *Reminiscences*.

67. *Millennial Harbinger* (Bethany) (Oct. 1846): 585.

68. Ibid. (Feb. 1856): 118; *British Millennial Harbinger* (June 1850): 283; *Ecclesiastical Observer* (Oct. 1873): 333.

69. *Ecclesiastical Observer* (Oct. 1873): 333; *Millennial Harbinger* (Bethany) (Feb. 1856): 118; *British Millennial Harbinger* (June 1850): 283.

70. *British Millennial Harbinger* (Sept. 1858): 458–59; Rotherham, *Reminiscences*, 33–45; *A Birmingham Sect Maker*, 8–9; *Ecclesiastical Observer* (Sept. 1869): 309; (Sept. 1872): 314–15.

71. *Ecclesiastical Observer* (Oct. 1873): 325–41; (Sept. 1875): 300–301.

72. Ibid. (Mar. 1871): 105.

73. Ibid. (Sept. 1872): 314.

74. King, *Memoir of David King*, 12–13; *Bible Advocate* (Sept. 1891): 225–52; (Sept. 1890): 229–45; (Aug. 14, 1914): 519; *Ecclesiastical Observer* (Sept. 1875): 300–303 indicates that evangelists at that time received an average of about £45–50 per annum. For some indication of the range of incomes among Nonconformist ministers at a slightly later date, see *Congregational Year Book* (London, 1882), 45–47, 60–80.

75. *Ecclesiastical Observer* (Nov. 1871): 394; *Millennial Harbinger* (Bethany) (Oct. 1846): 580ff.; *British Harbinger* (Sept. 1866): 320; *Christian Advocate* (June 1859): 108–10; Moore, *The Life of Timothy Coop*, 220–48.

76. Harrell, *Quest for a Christian America*, 26–61; Garrison, *Religion Follows the Frontier*, 147, 224–45. For one of the few scholarly studies of an American conservative leader, see James R. Wilburn, *The Hazard of the Die: Tolbert Fanning and the Restoration Movement* (Austin, Tex., 1969).

77. Garrison, *Religion Follows the Frontier*, 276–77; *British Harbinger* (Sept. 1866): 320; (Sept. 1868): 318ff; *Ecclesiastical Observer* (July 1872): 240–41; (Jan. 1–Feb. 15, 1878).

78. *Ecclesiastical Observer* (July 1872): 241.

79. Ibid. (Aug. 1, 1883): 198–200; *British Advocate* (Feb. 1, 1893): 53–54; (Nov. 15, 1893): 427–29; also Anderson, *An Outline of My Life*, 185.

80. John T. Brown, ed., *The Churches of Christ: A Historical, Biographical, and Pictorial History* (Louisville, 1904), 130ff.; Moore, *The Life of Timothy Coop*, 326–60.

81. Moore, *The Life of Timothy Coop*, 364ff.; *Ecclesiastical Observer* (Dec. 15, 1878): 327–31, and succeeding issues.

82. Moore, *The Life of Timothy Coop*, 364.

83. Ibid., 406–18; Garrison, *Religion Follows the Frontier*, 266–67.

84. See *Ecclesiastical Observer* during 1879 and 1889.

85. *Bible Advocate* (Feb. 1, 1893): 53–54; (Nov. 15, 1893): 427–29.

86. Ibid. (Sept. 1, 15, 1892): 325–46.

87. Ibid. (Apr. 17, 1914): 241–42; Watters, *History of the British Churches of Christ*, 212–16; Anderson, *An Outline of My Life*, 185–86.

88. For use of organs see Watters, *History of the British Churches of Christ*, 202; Rotherham, *Reminiscences*, 33–34; *Ecclesiastical Observer* (Jan. 1873): 32–33.

89. *Ecclesiastical Observer* (Sept. 15, 1878): 242–45.

90. Moore, *The Life of Timothy Coop*, 364; Anderson, *An Outline of My Life*, 49; also many obituaries in the Campbellite press.

91. *Ecclesiastical Observer* (June–Sept. 1875); for Campbellite links with other revivals see *Congregational Magazine* (London) (Mar. 1841): 180; *Christian Advocate* (Nov. 1859): 219; (Dec. 1860): 199–215; Anderson, *An Outline of My Life*, 50. Alexander Campbell himself solicited confessions of faith during services he conducted in Britain, but he disliked "calling of persons to come forward in the midst of singing" and preferred more "simple, rational and practical methods." *Millennial Harbinger* (Bethany) (Sept. 1847): 527–31.

92. This is based on numerous obituaries and church reports in the Campbellite press.

93. Reprinted as an appendix to Watters, *History of the British Churches of Christ*, 259–61.

94. *Ecclesiastical Observer* (Dec. 1, 1877): 317–19; *Bible Advocate* (Mar. 1, 1894): 92–93; Anderson, *An Outline of My Life*, 179.

95. See Watters, *History of the British Churches of Christ*, 75–76, for the impact of popular radicalism in the 1840s. Campbellite sources reveal few comments upon political affairs until the 1870s, but see *Christian Messenger* (May 1845): 33–34.

96. See Campbell's journal of his British tour in *Millennial Harbinger* (Bethany), 1847 and 1848; Harrell, *Quest for a Christian America*, 126–33.

97. *Millennial Harbinger* (Feb. 1855): 114.

98. Robert Currie, *Methodism Divided: A Study in the Sociology of Ecumenicalism* (London, 1968), 112–40.

99. *Ecclesiastical Observer* (Dec. 1, 1877): 317–19.

100. See Currie, *Methodism Divided*, 112–40, for some rather exaggerated remarks on all branches of Methodism, including the Primitives. For an indication of the broadening attitude of Primitive Methodists, see Kendall, *The Origin and History*, 2:507ff.; and, for the continuing strength of the antiliquor and antigambling viewpoint, G. M. Morris, "Primitive Methodism in Nottinghamshire, 1815–1932" (Ph.D. diss., Nottingham Univ., 1967), esp. 324ff.

101. For Primitive Methodists and total abstinence, see Kendall, *The Origin and History*, 1:469–76; for the Campbellites, obituaries of early leaders; King, *Memoir of David King*, 1–62. For suspicion of formal links between Campbellite churches and temperance societies, see *Bible Advocate* (Sept. 1, 1891): 241; (Mar. 1, 1894): 92–93.

102. For Coop, Brian Harrison, "The British Prohibitionists, 1853–1872: A Biographical Analysis," *International Review of Social History* 15, pt. 3 (1970): 442. For wider temperance activity, see the Campbellite press and Anderson, *An Outline of My Life*, 179.

103. *Ecclesiastical Observer* (Sept. 1871): 292–99; (May 1872): 167–68.

104. Harrell, *Quest for a Christian America*, 76: Watters, *History of the British Churches of Christ*, 159–60. For later support, *Bible Advocate* (Sept. 1, 1891): 233ff.

105. "Should a Christian Vote?" *Bible Advocate* (Sept. 15, 1892): 353. For the career of Amos Mann, see Joyce Margaret Bellamy and J. Saville, *Dictionary of Labour Biography* (London, 1972), 1:230–31, which also contains a sketch of Robert Fleming, a Belfast Co-operator and Campbellite (122). Mann's father-in-law, James Leavesley, was a small leather manufacturer in Leicester, a town councilor, and member of the Board of Guardians. He was previously a Primitive Methodist: see *Bible Advocate* (Nov. 1, 1918): 354–57. Anderson, *An Outline of My Life*, 179, warned in 1912 of the dangers of political disagreement within the churches.

106. Robinson, *The Shattered Cross*, 77–92; Rowdon, *The Origins of the Brethren*, 267–93.

107. For contacts with Baptists see *Christian Messenger* (July 1839): 177; *Christian Advocate* (Dec. 1859): 236; Rotherham, *Reminiscences*, 27ff.; Betteridge, "Asterby and Donington," 27; see *Minutes of the Seventy-first Annual Association of the New Connexion of General Baptists* (Nottingham, 1840): 42ff, for the large number of part-time pastors.

108. Anderson's *An Outline of My Life* is largely devoted to the details of his, controversies with Brethren, Mormons, Christadelphians, Seventh-day Adventists, and Jehovah's Witnesses; see also Wilson, *Sects and Society*, 245 ff. Before the arrival of Jehovah's Witnesses in Britain, some Campbellites were interested in the idea that the unbelieving ceased to exist after death: see *Report of the Conditional Immortality Conference Held at the Cannon Street Hotel, London, May 15th*, 1876, London.

109. *Millennial Harbinger* (Bethany) (Aug. 1847): 475.

110. King, *Memoir of David King*, 239–40; Anderson, *An Outline of My Life*, 31–42; *British Millennial Harbinger* (Aug. 1859): 410–11; *Christian Advocate* (July 1860): 115–18.

111. Ibid. (June 1859): 119; Coad, *A History of the Brethren Movement*, 172–73; Yuille, *History of the Baptists in Scotland*, 79, 99.

112. For Peterhead, see Coad, *A History of the Brethren Movement*, 172, and *Bible Advocate* (Sept. 28, 1917): 467; and for Leominster, *Bible Advocate* (Sept. 1, 1890): 229ff and Rowdon, *The Origins of the Brethren*, 165–66. Analysis of the Brethren in Hereford from 1841 to 1876 shows that 80 percent of members came from the same social categories as Campbellite leaders—i.e., tradesmen, farmers, skilled artisans, and clerks—but only 14 percent were laborers and servants. Leadership and control were carried out by the 6 percent of members who were army officers, surgeons, doctors, dentists, solicitors, and gentlemen; see Rowdon, *The Origins of the Brethren*, 169–70.

113. *Free Gospel Magazine*, 1871–1910; Vickers, *History of Independent Methodism*.

114. *Ecclesiastical Observer* (15 July 1882): 185; *Free Gospel Magazine* (Nov. 1884): 402.

115. For Independent Methodist growth, social composition, and attitudes toward total abstinence, Vickers, *History of Independent Methodism*, and the *Free Gospel Magazine* have been used.

116. Wilson, *Sects and Society*, 242–55, 300–303.

West End Chapel, Back Street Bethel

Labor and Capital in the Wigan Churches of Christ, 1845-1945

Peter Ackers

There is a large and complex literature regarding the part played by working-class Nonconformity in the industrial revolution and the emergence of the English labor movement. For all its nuances, this writing can be separated into two main strands. The first, broadly Marxist, perspective sees working-class Nonconformity primarily as a form of capitalist control, inculcating bourgeois norms of hard work, thrift, respectability, and political moderation into the working class. However, even labor historians who subscribe to this view cannot help but be struck by the ubiquitous accounts of lay preachers at the forefront of Victorian labor movement campaigns, especially in the coalfields. Thus, the second view stresses the part played by working-class Nonconformists in leading their class toward political and industrial emancipation. To a considerable extent, the stance taken, particularly on Methodism, depends on whether writers draw their evidence from national, usually middle-class, denominational hierarchies or from local accounts of working-class religiosity.[1]

This article locates the history of one Protestant religious sect, the Churches of Christ, within this debate between control and emancipation and considers the complex interaction of the two in one industrial town between the middle of the nineteenth century and the Second World War. This group of self-styled "Christians" or "Christian Brethren" (often called by outsiders "Campbellites") later adopted the modern title "Churches of Christ." A definitive official history of the Churches of Christ has already been written, but this account shifts the center of attention away from national denominational developments downward to the provincial town and its local congregations, where the true arena of working-class religious activity lay. Drawing on a combination of primary and secondary documentary sources, and oral testimony from old members, the study examines the main characteristics of their "plea," as this evolved in the Wigan coalfield.[2] The approach adopted here is thematic rather than strictly chronological. In particular, the article explores two interrelated historical dynamics in order to explain the development of the Churches of Christ's religious beliefs, social character, and political impact. One is the spatial differentiation between the middle-class, town-center West End Chapel and the working-class, coalfield, Back Street Bethel. The other is the temporal sect-to-denomination evolution characteristic of such groups. Both these are sociological ideal types, and neither is followed neatly by the Wigan Churches. However, in tandem, they offer a more subtle historical understanding of the Churches than any analysis that restricts itself to their general religious features. The contrast between the democratic, proletarian Christianity of the Back Street Bethel in its sectarian phase and the paternalist, middle-class culture of the West End Chapel in its denominational phase illustrates a central contradiction within English Nonconformity and shows this recurring even within one of its primitive "reformation" movements.[3]

The first section explores the formation and early development of the Churches in Wigan up to the 1870s. It discusses their founding features under three categories—religious beliefs and practices, membership and social composition, chapel social life and attitudes toward the world—which provide a benchmark for tracking subsequent developments across space and time. The second section narrows its focus to the coalfield chapel of Platt Bridge and the working-class religious culture that emerged there. The third section returns to the Rodney Street town-center "mother church" to compare its historical evolution, under the leadership of a powerful manufacturing family, with that of the smaller, outlying mining chapels. Whereas the approach in sections 2 and 3 is deliberately static and sociological, section 4 addresses the issue of change in a more historical vein, using Platt Bridge to illustrate developments in the Back Street Bethels between the wars.

I

The first Churches of Christ congregation has been traced to Nottingham in 1836. At the first national meeting in 1842, the affiliated membership was still only 1,300, and it was not until the later decades of the century that the Churches' growth quickened, to reach a peak of 16,596 in 1930. By 1900, membership was concentrated geographically in a few industrial areas, notably Lancashire and the East Midlands.[4] If Wigan is compared to another major provincial stronghold, Leicester, a similar pattern of advance can be discerned. The Leicester church began in the homes of two shoemakers in 1859, and by 1879 there were two chapels.[5] In Wigan, the movement was launched by Timothy Coop, a young clothier's shop manager and former Wesleyan Methodist. The first convert was baptized by him on August 8, 1841, in the town's River Douglas.[6] By this time the

Wigan economy was already firmly founded on coal and cotton, with male employment concentrated in the former and female in the latter. Future decades saw the expansion of deep mining beyond the town and a process of urbanization that linked the outlying pit villages in a larger metropolitan area. Wigan miners were less well organized and endured worse pay and conditions than their equivalents in the coalfield settlements of County Durham, but they also enjoyed greater occupational choice and freedom from employer control. The religious character of the area was equally distinctive to Lancashire, with Nonconformity taking third place to a strong loyalist Anglicanism and a cohesive Irish Catholicism. The dissenting tradition in the town itself was weak and dominated by a rather genteel brand of Congregationalism. In this respect, the Churches of Christ, like another strong local group, the Independent Methodists, may be seen as a "new sectarian" working-class response to the neglect of the coalfield by mainstream, middle-class dissent.

Coop's "Church of New Testament order" was founded on the two cardinal principles: "That the Scriptures taught repentance and Baptism by immersion for the remission of sin, and that they were to gather themselves together on the first day of the week for the Breaking of Bread and prayer."[7] The main theological figure in the "restoration" movement, the Scottish American Alexander Campbell, visited the Wigan congregation in 1847. By 1850, Coop was reporting progress to their main national publication, *The British Millennial Harbinger*. The year 1853 saw the appointment of a local "evangelist" and announced a "thriving Sabbath School."[8] June 28, 1858, was a watershed for the 68-strong congregation and 130 scholars, who had been meeting in local halls. The foundation stone was laid for the "more commodious" town-center, Rodney Street "Christian Meeting House" (and Sunday school), with its upper room for celebrating the Lord's Supper.[9] The chapel trust deed demanded a "Copy of Matters Believed and Practised," which flew in the face of their hostility to nonbiblical creeds or denominational titles. This dilemma was resolved by asking the evangelist William McDougale to draft thirteen articles of faith, supported by scriptural "Proof Texts." In form, it was a series of quotations from the word of God, prefaced by the emphatic statement: "Each article has been separately examined by its proof-texts, in the view of their respective contexts in the Divine Word, in a gathering of the Church, called expressly for this purpose, and the whole unanimously and heartily adopted, as expressing their deliberate convictions—June 28th, 1860."[10]

The style and content of this biblical confession of faith echoes documents from much earlier Puritan separatist, and especially Baptist, congregations.[11] It provides a useful benchmark for comparing the Churches to other religious groups, and to the evolution of their own historical self over the next century. For analytical purposes, the contents can be divided into "beliefs" and "practices." Three key articles delineate the Churches' distinctive and central plea.

The first is straightforward biblical authority as a basis for Christian unity on simple New Testament principles. The second is the Baptist principle of believer's baptism; and the third is a weekly celebration of the Lord's Supper. The first article, and cornerstone, refers to "the Scriptures" of "the Old and New Covenants" as "the only accredited revelation from God to man, for his salvation [and] the sole sufficient rule of faith practice and order for the Church of Christ." The fifth article invokes biblical authority for "One Baptism" in water "for the remission of sins, and the gift of the Holy Ghost," obligatory by "the authority of the Lord upon every believer." The ninth article on "The Lord's Supper" insists that it is "the duty of members, on the first day of the week, to assemble to break the loaf, and drink of the cup, with thankfulness and reverent joy, remembering our Lord, who gave His body to be broken and His blood to be shed for us, and jointly participating in that body and blood, as 'spirit and life.'"

The "practices" declared embody a self-conscious attempt to re-create the ways of the early church, as laid down in the New Testament. The keynote is the rejection of a full-time priesthood, as a matter of egalitarian biblical principle, following the radical interpretation of a Protestant ideal, the priesthood of all believers.[12] The eleventh article on "The Ministry" represented a compromise between "the oversight and teaching of the Elders and Pastors of the church" and "the liberty of teaching, exhortation and admonition by all brethren thus gifted." Timothy Coop describes how they applied this New Testament blueprint to chapel government.[13] This fell short of straightforward democracy, with a strong element of "selection" for "the qualifications required" and a concern to achieve congregational consensus. The "oldest brother" was appointed to nominate three "pastors," who were subsequently approved unanimously. "When three brethren had been named, the church signified their entire approval of the choice of every member, rising, so that perfect consensus was obtained." Though unanimity was "not absolutely necessary," it was "very desirable." The predictable result was the appointment of three natural leaders, later prominent in the wider movement: John Corf, William McDougale (the evangelist), and Timothy Coop himself. They were, in turn, asked to select "two brethren qualified to sustain the office of deacon," again subject to the endorsement of the whole church. No doubt an open election would have achieved similar results, and perhaps a needlessly divisive contest was feared; but we must turn to the smaller, working-class-run chapels, with their labor-movement traditions, for a fuller expression of congregational democracy.

The final article on "Titles" underlines the Churches' Puritan ideal of simplicity and congregational equality, insisting "that the assumption of distinctive titles or honorary names, other than those found in the New Testament, by the brethren, however gifted, devout, or useful, is contrary to Christian humility and the equality of the brotherhood, and not to be tolerated." Thus all the brethren were expected to take their responsibilities seriously. Article 12, "Gospel without Price," refused to charge pew rents, because it was "a departure from the simplicity of the first churches 'in Christ,' and from the noble and generous love of the early believers, to ask for payment for sittings or occupation of a place used for the worship of Almighty God." And article 13 ruled against taking collections from outsiders, insisting that each congregation was "Self-Supporting," and that, "on no pretext whatever should any appeal be made to the world for money for the support of Christ's cause." Perhaps this practical emphasis on social equality between believers made the Churches more open to the working classes. Corf's opening speech promised, "No respect of persons—no inconvenience to the poor—no 'sit here in a place of honour' to the rich, or 'there at a footstool' to the poor." And Coop reported, "no boxes would be sent round."[14] This presupposed a strong voluntary obligation for members to attend regularly and maintain "their church." Discipline was strict, absence from the Lord's table was noted, and if it persisted for several weeks without "good cause" the member's name was excised from the church roll.[15]

The Wigan plea tells us little directly about the Churches' early social composition, though it does suggest that the poor might feel welcome there. Early accounts point to the lowly status of the new congregation, though often in rather lurid and exaggerated biblical language. They also suggest that most members had come from other churches after being "sorely perplexed" by the teaching there.[16] During the "particularly vicious" 1853 Wigan miners' strike,[17] Coop reported, "For the last two months our town has suffered much through the colliers and factory operatives turning out of employment to obtain an advance of wages . . . many of our members are depending on the working of the coal-pits and factories for their livelihood."[18] Shortly after the establishment of Rodney Street, attempts were made to spread the church into the poorer surrounding areas. On Sunday April 21, 1860, a second, makeshift meeting place opened at Wigan Lane. Members of the new congregation were "all in the humblest walks of life; men and women whose simple maintenance is earned by severe toil."[19] The brethren's lowly status is constantly restated: "From the first the audience was composed of men and women of the lowest class—men whose labor was expended in the bowels of the earth, with minds as dark as the coal mines in which they worked, and lives as begrimed with sin as were their persons with the filth consequent on their occupation. The majority of the women were the wives of these men."[20]

Article 10 of the plea, "The Fellowship," does suggest a broader social concern. "That it is also our duty, as it is the natural expression of the Divine Life in man, to contribute of our earthly goods for the use of those who are in need, 'according as the Lord has prospered us,'—laying it in store on 'the first day of the week,' according to Apostolic rule." However, at this early, intensely religious and conversionist stage, there is little evidence that the brethren had much time for those social issues preoccupying mainstream Victorian Nonconformity. Instead, they maintained a narrowly confessional focus of conversion, baptism, open-air preaching, Bible reading, tract distribution, and biblical debate devoted to winning souls. Nor were they obviously radical in their other social attitudes, except for their important stress on the equality of all male believers. Yet, in the decades following the opening of Rodney Street, the Churches took a sympathetic attitude to coal mining strikes and began to throw up labor leaders.[21] One possible factor was the nonprescriptive, or adiaphoristic, attitude of their plea on issues of the world that did not touch on their core scriptural faith.[22] This did not extend to matters of personal morality, over which there was strict congregational control. The newness of the Churches in the town and their mode of recruitment dictated that they were all first-generation adult converts to a highly distinctive group, with correspondingly strong levels of voluntary commitment. Moreover, they felt themselves outside the pale of the local religious establishments, receiving "little or no sympathy" from mainstream Nonconformity, "bitterly opposed" by Catholics, and "treated with contempt" by the established church.[23] Such early hostility may have been overdrawn for effect, yet as late as July 1907, the history of Hope Congregational chapel mentions a James Lowe, who had joined from Rodney Street five years before, after reaching "a broader view of the truth."[24]

II

During the last quarter of the century, the brethren founded a series of chapels in the growing coalfield villages surrounding Wigan. In 1868 a new chapel had opened in the mining village of Golbourne, on the town's southeastern outskirts.[25] This "meeting room for Christians, who decline to be called by any other name" closed during the 1870s.[26] More than a decade later, on the opening of Platt Bridge chapel, a few miles away, "the remaining brethren" were visited and "exhorted to come and aid the small church."[27] The first permanent coalfield chapel at Hindley village opened in 1874. Three further mining chapels were founded, at Albert Street, Newtown, in 1877; in the poor town-center area of Scholes in 1882; and at Victoria Road, Platt Bridge, in 1883; their development is explored in greater detail here. The 1883 General Annual Meeting welcomed these three to the "co-operation."[28] Platt Bridge, about four miles to the southeast of Wigan, was by the 1870s a growing mining village.[29] Here the coalfield was expanding and throwing up new settlements. With "several cotton mills and many collieries," it was neither an isolated pit village nor simply part of Wigan. The larger township of Hindley had a station on the Lancashire and Yorkshire railway, three miles from Wigan and seven from Bolton. "Formerly a single street, forming the road from Wigan to Bolton," it had grown greatly to an area of four square miles, with a population of 8,477 in 1861. Platt Bridge itself was a hamlet, situated about one and a half miles southwest from the town of Hindley, with a station on the Wigan and Tyldesley railway. Within the wider area, the Anglican Parish church of All Saints dated from 1766, and a new church dedicated to Saint Peter had been erected in 1864. In 1869, there were already some hallmarks of a working-class, self-help civilization, including "a successful co-operative store" connected to "a newsroom and library, and a commodious hall, used for public meetings, lectures etc." Just before the two Christian Brethren chapels in Hindley and Platt Bridge came on the scene, there were "various congregations of Nonconformists, several of which also have schools," including at least eight chapels.

The new coalfield chapels adhered closely to the original Rodney Street doctrinal position and Platt Bridge's early days reprise Coop's initiative.[30] The simple pattern of worship was first established by brethren assembling in a cottage, where the members "showed the Lord's death" in the morning and held open gospel meetings in the evening. The next step was to form a Sunday school from their own and other local children. "Some little time after, the Liberal Club-room was secured for the services on Lord's Days." At length came the construction of "a nice, substantial chapel," two cottages and a schoolroom, financed by Coop's heir, the manufacturer James Marsden. The chapel opened with fifty-one brethren, thirty of whom had joined during the past year, and a Sunday school of more than one hundred students. Apparently, there was "a deal of opposition, both honourable and otherwise," but this did not deflect the evangelical drive "both indoors and out-of-doors, and from house to house." A visiting Evangelist, Joseph Adams, conveys this optimistic mood of Christians overcoming adversity: "At Platt Bridge the truth has been rudely and slanderously assailed and the brethren maligned, yet all has turned out to the glory of God and the infant church rejoices in new brethren and sisters. Open air mission work goes on here." On a visit on July 22, 1883,

> [s]pecial services were held in the open air, and in the new chapel, and fresh ground opened up in the district within a radius of two miles. The young converts were formed into a class, instructed in Bible truth, and encouraged in devotional exercises. Several lectures were given, and relevant questions invited, which were put and answered. Four were baptised, the new baptistery being used for the first time, and one baptised believer received. Young and old were included among the new converts—notably one old man, once a slave of sin, now a servant of Christ. His daughter said—"O, what a change is in our house now that father is converted."[31]

The Sunday cycle of the Lord's Supper for members in the morning, Sunday school, then open evening gospel meetings took up the whole day, and brethren from outlying areas would bring sandwiches with them. There were experiments over the years, such as evening communion or extra Thursday night gospel services, but the basic pattern remained. More notable than the all-embracing Nonconformist Sabbath was the complete repudiation of the normal Christian calendar, including even Christmas and Easter. To begin with, the calendar was regarded as unbiblical, though it gradually seeped into Sunday school activities. The annual rhythm of chapel life was provided instead by more social occasions, like chapel and Sunday school anniversaries and New Year Watchnight events. Overall, chapel life bears a close similarity to the other accounts of working-class Nonconformity in the same period or phase of development.[32] Church government displays all the hallmarks of contemporary labor movement constitutional democracy and its fascination with procedural propriety and organizational minutiae.[33] The church meeting of the whole congregation was the sovereign body on issues of expenditure, discipline, and doctrine. There were regular quarterly church meetings plus additional special church meetings called to endorse important decisions. These included proposals to strike off members or to make a significant financial commitment. At the turn of the century, there were as many as a dozen meetings a year, attended, on average, by about a quarter of the 100-strong congregation. The brothers and sisters nominated and then elected six chapel officers, including a secretary and president. They required the support of three-quarters of those present and often failed to reach this. Monthly officers meetings conducted the day-to-day administration of chapel affairs and enjoyed a form of delegated authority, only calling a church meeting to make major decisions. Important items were dealt with by "resolutions," formally proposed, seconded, and amended. Organizational tasks, such as maintaining and letting the building, ordering hymn books, tracts, and other chapel equipment, loomed large. The main public activities consisted of sporadic missions, visits by evangelists, and chapel anniversaries. These entailed the arrangement of speakers, and the dissemination of bill posters, leaflets, and tracts. The 1923 mission required a bookstall, 5,000 handbills, an effective poster for the front of the chapel, 5,000 localized tracts, a Thursday evening gospel meeting, a prayer meeting, and open air meetings.[34] Advertisements would be placed at the local Miners' Hall, and there was door-to-door distribution of tracts, along with gospel meetings at the local Picture Palace led by visiting evangelists.

Voluntarism was a distinguishing feature of chapel life in two respects: the relationship of the local congregation to the wider Churches movement, and the responsibilities of the individual members to their chapel. The chapel could send delegates to the Churches' biennial Lancashire and Cheshire District Conference, to the annual Wigan and District Association meeting, as well as to the national Annual Meeting. The district periodically organized more concerted activities, and chapels could contribute names to and take preachers from an agreed "plan." They could also join other local chapels to support financially visiting evangelists for short local campaigns. In 1912 they joined Rodney Street in a "special mission"; and two years later they wrote to the evangelist James Smith requesting he "give the Church at Platt Bridge a month on the next plan."[35] They received regular publications from the national Churches' bookroom, plus communications and financial appeals from the evangelist, temperance, Sunday school and chapel-building committees. Yet affiliation to, and financial support for, all these activities remained a voluntary decision for the local congregation. Should they wish, they could withdraw at any time from "the co-operation" completely and operate in isolation. Even while affiliated, they could, and frequently did, forgo activities for doctrinal, financial, and other reasons. A 1911 district meeting on the "deepening of spiritual life" was not supported, and a resolution was passed in 1914 "that the letter from Lancashire and Cheshire appealing for finance be not entertained."[36] During the period of initial expansion, recruitment was of adults from "the world," as baptized believers. However, from the outset this included spouses, and the definition of *adult* was evidently flexible. One Platt Bridge youth, George Miller, was baptized at eleven years of age.[37] Furthermore, by the new century, the first-generation founders had been reinforced by their own large families and other Sunday school graduates. Nevertheless, in this period a high proportion of chapel members had been won from the outside world, and even for whose who had not, the responsibilities of membership still entailed a large measure of voluntarism. Discipline was monitored by the officers, who kept a constant check on nonattendance at the Lord's Supper, noted other transgressions, and sent out delegations of "visitors" to recalcitrant members. These visits mixed policing and pastoral elements, and they often provided intelligence of, and support to, members with problems. Ultimately, a church meeting would consider names to be struck off the register. On the odd occasion, this was for moral transgressions, as when "it was decided to withdraw from" Catherine Stopforth for "having committed fornication." A more normal reason was "negligence" or "absence from the Lord's table."[38]

In the first place, it was the social composition of the early coalfield chapel that established a vital link with the emerging labor movement. The Platt Bridge pioneers "were miners, almost to a man," men of "practically no education," yet "full of zeal for the Gospel." The nucleus of the new congregation was a handful of mining families who had moved from Albert Street, Newtown, "seeking employment at the new collieries which were opening in the area at the time."[39] Their migration was precipitated by the 1881 strike, "the biggest . . . in the Lancashire coalfield."[40]

> Early in the year 1881, when work was resumed after the long strike among miners in the Wigan district, a number of brethren were forced to remove with their families,

from Newtown to Platt Bridge, distant from Wigan about four miles, in another direction. Brethren and sisters together, they numbered about nine or ten, with no "speaking power" amongst them. But they loved the Saviour, and wished to make him known, and though removed from their former church association they did not forget the claims of their Lord.[41]

Platt Bridge grew around these large founding families and became known as the "Miller chapel." Albert Street, Newtown, their previous chapel, was a larger and more impressive building, with an upper room like Rodney Street, but it too had a large mining clientele. Around 1908 the nine chapel officers divided between four miners and five local tradesmen, while the rank and file were mostly miners.[42]

Even a small chapel had numerous subcommittees and other groups. Platt Bridge had its own Band of Hope Committee and a separate Sunday school, as well as periodic "nightclasses" and "young men's improvement classes." When the chapel wanted preachers for the 1922 plan, it looked no further than the male members of the church.[43] There were no women on the committee, but they did participate in church meetings. More predictably, women ran fundraising activities, like the "sewing circle" and "young women's class," which formed the chapel's financial backbone. They raised money toward the platform carpet and oilcloth, electric lights, decorating, the heating apparatus, or just made general donations. Apart from such work, they held sisters' teas with musical accompaniments. The appointment of three sister visitors in 1914 may reflect the high proportion of women nonattenders.[44] Overall, however, the most remarkable feature to a contemporary observer was "the preponderance of male members, which is something like two to one."[45] Male leadership was the norm for nineteenth-century religion, but a numerical dominance is more remarkable. The maleness of the chapels, and their sense of brotherhood, probably enhanced their contribution to the coalfield labor movement.

The original plea suggests an extreme religious seriousness and joyless austerity. Yet once the Churches entered the working-class coalfield, chapels became much more social institutions, with a wide range of more lighthearted activities to complement the core religious services. Platt Bridge chapel life involved frequent and lively get-togethers, most notably annual chapel and Sunday school anniversaries. New Year Watchnight services were preceded by tea and cakes. Social events were modest "tea parties" with sandwiches or Lancashire meat and potato pies, catering for between fifty and ninety people, for which members were charged admission. When James Miller immigrated to Canada in 1923, there was a "farewell tea" with "musical items and a presentation." Simon Miller's eightieth birthday occasioned the presentation of an inscribed walking stick and a social evening. A more common present was a copy of the New Testament.[46] Music played a central part in these chapel social events. These were genuine family affairs in which the men, women, and children mixed and all had a role. The chapel's twenty-fifth anniversary celebrations on July 1, 1908, took the form of a "tea and social evening," including an account of one brother's missionary trip to South Africa. "Brother Miller and family and a friend enlivened the occasion with song and recitation."[47] The chapel had a choir, and the combination of social events with church business or worship was common. Yet these small tight-knit communities were clearly frequently touched by the tragedy and suffering of the local coalfield. Thomas Miller's joyous report of Platt Bridge's annual Sunday school picnic carries a grim postscript. It

> [t]ook place at Lawton, St Mary's, in a field kindly lent by Mr Marsh (farmer), for the occasion, where the scholars, members and friends enjoyed themselves in various games and amusements, though the weather was somewhat threatening in the morning. About 240 persons travelled by the 10 o'clock train from Birkenshaw, and returned at 7.30. On leaving the school we sung in the street "Children of Jerusalem" and on the way from the field all stood in front of Mr Marsh's house and sung that beautiful hymn, "Hushed was the evening hymn," and gave the farmer three hearty cheers for his kindness shown towards us. Whilst writing the above we have received the sad news of our dear Bro. Jas Fairclough, who is a co-worker in the Sunday School, having met with a serious accident in the coal mine. He now lies in a very critical condition in the Infirmary. The teachers and members of the church are in deep sympathy, and our prayer is that our Heavenly Father may restore him to health.[48]

Three years later, Peter Speakman was "following his employment in the coal mine" when "a runaway tub caught him, the injuries being so serious that the doctor ordered his removal to the Wigan Infirmary, where he died in a few minutes after his admission."[49] At such time, their primitive religion does sound like "the sigh of the oppressed creature, the heart of the heartless world, and the soul of soulless conditions."[50] Witness Thomas Miller's bittersweet account of the turn-of-the-century New Year's Day Sunday school presentations and tea party:

> After tea, the Superintendent had the pleasant duty of distributing prizes to the scholars and the teachers who had made not less than 100 full marks. Afterwards we had the pleasure of hearing a few words from our esteemed Bro. James Smith, of Wigan who took for his subject the word "Watch," putting each letter to stand for a word, thus W stands for words, A for actions, T for thoughts, C for character, and H for hearts . . . After the address, a service of song was rendered splendidly . . . the sweet music of the scholars, as they went over the beautiful sentiments of their hymns, produced at times mingled feelings of sadness and happiness. Sadness caused by the absence of some who would have been among us had not the cold hand of death removed them. Sadness at the thought of what might happen if any of those now so young, should forget, or grow up to despise, the instruction of their

parents and friends, and also their Sunday teachers. But the bright side gives joy to our hearts. Jesus is the same yesterday, today, and forever. Our departed ones are not lost, only gone before, which is far better.[51]

There are three available indicators of the coalfield chapels' attitudes to industrial and political life. The first is the practical activity of chapel members. The second is the formal, minuted statements by the congregation or leading members on public affairs. The third involves those areas of social concern, such as poverty, where the chapel took action on its own part to support its members and the surrounding coalfield community. The Churches' clearest contribution to the labor movement was the provision of leaders and activists. Leicester produced two outstanding co-operators, Amos Mann (1855–1939) and J. T. Taylor (1863–1958), and there were others, such as Robert Fleming (1869–1939) from Belfast. The Wigan chapels nurtured a number of similar figures. From Platt Bridge there was W. T. Miller (1880–1963), full-time Lancashire secretary, national president, and national secretary of the colliery deputies trade union. His namesake and cousin, Thomas (the other W. T.) Miller was chapel secretary for many years, a justice of the peace, and a labor councilor on the local Abram District Council. In addition, there were the first W. T. Miller's brothers, James and George, both later colliery deputies' union branch secretaries. From Albert Street there was the miner and elder Swithin Meadows, a pastor and deacon and supporter of "all progressive causes, political or otherwise." From an earlier generation came Joseph Parkinson (1854–1929), a "well-known Wigan magistrate, miners' official and public representative." He was a miner's son who became president of the Wigan Miners' Association during the 1881 strike, MFGB agent by 1908, and a councilor and labor leader of Wigan council for four years. And there were others whose lives are less well documented.[52]

Temperance was the Churches' most accepted approach to public affairs, and a convenient panacea for social problems, capable of uniting the manufacturer and working man. Platt Bridge chapel supported temperance conferences and demonstrations and wrote to their member of parliament in support of the 1923 Liquor Traffic Prohibition Bill and against a related social evil, the "betting tax."[53] Otherwise, the most notable collective campaign of the coal mining chapels at Platt Bridge and Albert Street was that over-conscientious objection in the Great War, discussed elsewhere.[54] More generally, the labor sympathies of the chapel leadership were clear. In the 1920s, W. T. Miller drew up a resolution "protesting against the interventions of this country into Russia," and they gave two pounds out of church funds toward opening a fund for the Russian famine. In the 1930s, they wrote thanking Arthur Henderson "for his services to the League of Nations" and asking the minister of labor to restore "the cuts to the unemployed." For a primarily religious body, these minutes are significant glimpses of a deeper political sympathy.[55]

One distinctive feature of the original plea was the vision of the Churches as a self-supporting brotherhood that would not depend on the support of the outside world. The Poor Brethren Fund was the most enduring example of this self-help ethic. The chapel gave ten shillings to J. Hope in 1912 and two shillings a week to brother and sister Anderson in 1914 for as long as the fund lasted. The fund's rise and fall was a weathervane for the cycles of prosperity and poverty in the coalfield. The Andersons were again receiving payments two years later, as was a brother Naylor a decade on. At a 1916 meeting, ten shillings was paid to three brethren, but the fund became exhausted though there were "still brethren in need." Charity, even from their own number, went against the brethren's ethos, and when Jas Speakman was offered ten shillings for being "off work for several weeks through sickness," he refused it. Such unfortunate brethren were also granted concessions to chapel social events, such as chapel anniversaries. Social activities, like the 1912 anniversary and 1933 jubilee, offered a free tea to "any member in receipt of Poor Law Relief or receiving old age pension and not working."[56] The chapel also contributed more generally to the coalfield community. On December 13, 1931, a collection was made for the Bentley Miners Fund after many lives had been lost in a pit explosion and the proceeds were made up from chapel funds. During the general strike the chapel sent representatives to the meetings at the Miners' Hall in Platt Bridge. They reported back to a special elders' and deacons' meeting, which endorsed the centralization of distress relief, and organized Sunday evening collections for the local distress fund. The chapel offered the free use of the building to the local Relief Committee, and once the strike was over, the £4.10 residue from their own Miners' Relief Fund was transferred into the Poor Brethren Fund.[57]

The movement of the Churches into the coalfield put new flesh on the dry "restoration plea." It established a new milieu for the Churches, which became not only working class in social composition, but also independent of the leadership of Coop's growing manufacturing empire. While the basic restoration ideals found favor and persisted in the coalfield chapels, church government took a decidedly more democratic turn, training members to make their own religious and administrative decisions. The large coal mining contingent, the dense family networks, and even the maleness of the chapels all deepened their organic relationship to the coalfield labor movement. As time went on, this was expressed in statements and gestures of support, but, more importantly, the chapels gave of themselves, through individual leadership at all levels and through self-help within their membership and the surrounding community. Therefore, in the coalfield chapel independent labor became a social reality, as "pitmen preachers" learned the attributes of leadership and self-government. The "Protestant ethic" of individual calling and self-improvement marched hand in hand with labor movement commitment. The chapel trained the ambitious individual in the skills of reading, writing, speaking, and administration, so necessary to leadership positions, while tying this to a solidaristic ethos of brotherhood and social responsibility. Since for the chapel's mining clientele the labor movement offered one of the few avenues of opportunity, personal advancement and collective concern were natural bedfellows.

III

From one vantage point, the story of the Churches of Christ in Wigan is one of small, coalfield chapels. From another, it is the tale of the Coop industrial dynasty and the town center Rodney Street chapel. At its peak in 1932, Rodney Street had a membership of more than five hundred, compared to just more than one hundred each at Albert Street and Platt Bridge.[58] The chapel was centrally located and had large premises, with a spacious schoolroom and an impressive upper meeting room. As a national center for the Churches of Christ it provides a contrast to the egalitarian and working-class atmosphere of the smaller, coalfield chapels. When Timothy Coop (1817–1887) opened Rodney Street in 1858, he was at the threshold of a remarkable personal transition from weaver and shop manager to large-scale clothing manufacturer and "one of Wigan's foremost business men."[59] On March 4, 1872, his grand town-center factory opened, a secular partner to the town-center chapel. Coop had already moved to Southport in the spring of 1863 and,[60] disaffected with the Churches' narrowness, formed a rival "Christian Association" closer to the liberal U.S. Disciples.[61] The twin task of carrying his blend of business and religious leadership into the new century fell upon his new son-in-law and business partner.

James Marsden, J.P. (1841–1927), more than anyone else, shaped Rodney Street chapel during his "sixty years' leadership."[62] He was thereabouts when the chapel opened and remained there until his death in 1927. He was only thirteen when, in 1854, he began work for Coop, then a tailor and draper in Wigan. He lived on the premises with the other shop assistants, and under his new master's influence "gave his heart to the Lord."[63] On June 14, 1864, aged twenty-three, he married Coop's daughter, Lois. That year, he became Sunday school co-superintendent, a position he kept for forty years. On January 1, 1866, Coop took him into partnership and two years later, still only twenty-seven, Marsden became a church elder. Once again, business and religious status were marching in step. Like Coop before him, he displayed incredible energy, running a rapidly expanding enterprise whilst simultaneously conducting morning and evening services, Sunday school, and weeknight cottage meetings. As with Coop, Marsden's religious, business, and public interests ranged ever wider. He became a key figure in the national Churches: on its central body, the General Evangelical Committee, for twenty-five years; three times national conference president;

and chairman of the foreign missions committee for thirteen years. He also "exercised a wide influence" on the town's social and public life through his "religious, philanthropic, temperance and social work"[64] as a county and borough magistrate, vice president of the national Temperance Alliance, Liberal town councilor, vice president of Wigan Infirmary, governor of Wigan Mining and Technical College, and Trustee of the Wigan Savings Bank. Moreover, he made wider national and international contacts. Like Coop, "a lifelong Liberal and Free Trader," he became a friend of Lloyd George and a member of the Royal Geographical Society who "travelled in many lands, East and West, for pleasure and educational purposes."[65] His well-attended funeral was packed with local notables, and the town hall flag was flown at half-mast.

John Crook, a contemporary of Coop and Marsden, also belonged to the manufacturing family. He retired in 1900, but his son, R.K., and grandson, R.B., maintained the link between business and chapel leadership for more than a century. He pioneered overseas missions, initiated the first Churches' yearbook in 1886 as secretary of the General Evangelist Committee, and was the "organising genius of the last quarter of the century."[66] Coop & Co. Ltd. became a large and modern business that pioneered the manufacture of readymade suits. In Marsden's lifetime, the new factory was thrice expanded, growing to employ more than one thousand workers. The weight of the business family's influence on the development of the Churches of Christ in Wigan may be a distinctive local feature, for Billington claims that "Coop was the only Campbellite leader to acquire more than modest wealth and an important place in the civic life of a community."[67] In other provincial towns, such as Leicester, a humbler type of "tradesman and small manufacturer" dominated the Churches' leadership.

Rodney Street founded the Wigan restoration plea but was soon in the vanguard of new thinking. Coop became a strong advocate of employing U.S. evangelists, of open communion, and of a closer relationship with other Nonconformists. By the time of the Great War, his Christian Association had rejoined the Churches, and ideas that had appeared so audacious before were entering the mainstream of national thinking. Rodney Street remained very much abreast of the new ideas. "Due to Mr Marsden's zeal and foresight . . . the preaching at Rodney Street was for long years supplied by leading Divines, Professors, and Missionaries of the Churches of Christ, both from the homeland and overseas."[68] Rodney Street was always more hierarchical, socially and constitutionally, than the coalfield chapels. Part of Marsden's 1870s grand plan for the expanding Wigan Churches was for one central eldership to direct the whole Wigan area. Such a Presbyterian solution would have extended the business family's influence much more directly into the outlying coalfield chapels. According to Crook, "this sagacious view" was defeated by those who feared "a species of

Ecclesiasticism."[69] As a next best solution, a looser District Association of Churches was formed. By the 1920s, if not before, Rodney Street was not too dissimilar in organization from other local Congregational and Baptist chapels. Its large, relatively prosperous congregation supported a de facto minister who was usually a leading figure in the national Churches, a regular contributor to the weekly *Christian Advocate,* and a participant in the activities of the new Overdale Theological College.

Rodney Street always enjoyed a superior social composition to the other Wigan chapels. Miners probably became less numerous once the outlying chapels were established to cater for them. The large and powerful business family provided a quite different style of paternalist chapel leadership, reinforced by the presence of their employees among the congregation. However, most members were not in the large employer's pocket, and the majority of men were probably still in manual occupations. A comparison of the new trustees (an elite section of the membership) elected on March 13, 1956, with their predecessors suggests this.[70] In 1956, there were six male manual workers, and, with the exception of Robert Burton Crook, a company director and last representative of the mill-owning dynasty, the other ten men occupied a variety of generally modest white-collar occupations. Of the seven women, two were housewives, three were in white-collar occupations, and two had working-class jobs. With a third of this elite band of trustees still in manual occupations, and others in routine white-collar jobs, this was still far from a bourgeois chapel. If we examine the previous trustees, it becomes apparent that the postwar decline of the industrial dynasty and the local shopocracy had created more opportunities for ordinary members, particularly women. The old trustees were elected in the early twentieth century. All were men, seven held manual occupations, including a solitary collier, and there were eight local tradesmen. The manufacturing dynasty was particularly heavily represented: by James Marsden himself; his son; the clothing manager, Harry Marsden, killed in the Great War; and his other son and successor to the business, Sidney James Marsden, who lived until 1953.[71] Finally, Robert Kay Crook, the father of Robert Burton Crook, company secretary, was still alive as a company director of the new trustees. In addition, three trustees described their occupation as "gentleman," and a fourth as a "naturalist." The balance of seven were in white-collar occupations. Overall, then, in comparison to the coalfield chapels, Rodney Street was more middle class, though manual workers probably still formed a majority of the membership, with the manufacturing family dominating the leadership, especially in the early part of the twentieth century. In contrast to other large town-center Nonconformist chapels, such as Wigan's Hope Congregational, it remained fairly modest in social composition throughout its history.[72] Nonetheless, the combination of a powerful and cohesive manufacturing family leadership, a large trade and middle-class presence, and a sizable group of Coop & Co. employees in the congregation facilitated the emergence of a rather different religious culture.

Like the coal mining chapels, Rodney Street soon generated a lively and varied social life. Perhaps the main difference was the chapel's sense of better connections, both with the other religious, political, and business leaders of the town and with the Churches nationally. A characteristic public meeting, like that held to debate the Great War, was presided over by a couple of full-time evangelists, one of them the de facto minister, attended by a representative of the Coop dynasty, chaired by the mayor of Wigan, and supported by similar figures from the local community. Coop and Marsden were active citizens and politicians, and under the latter's "leadership" the chapel played a "prominent part in all the moral and social crusades."[73] There is no sharper reminder of this new progressive respectability than the rapid shift the Churches' national leadership, supported by Rodney Street, made from Boer War pacifism to Great War patriotism. By the Great War, Rodney Street had become a very different chapel from its coalfield counterparts. It retained a distinctive style of worship, but the overlap with respectable Nonconformity was growing and encouraged. In church government and attitudes toward social problems it increasingly converged with their agenda. As a West End town-center chapel, populated by the best-known figures of the local Churches, it became increasingly a magnet for the Churches' socially mobile membership. Educated, middle-class people expected a more sophisticated and liberal regime than the puritanical rigor of old, and this in turn attracted more of their kind. This was not a chapel deeply embedded in the surrounding coalfield, which might spark a generation of young men into trade union activism. Self-improving its membership remained, but the collective context to the individual advance was lost and the characteristic route was to white-collar and professional employment. In social terms, chapel became a vehicle for leaving the working class rather than for moving to positions of responsibility within its main political and industrial institutions.

IV

The variations, across geographical space and social structure, between Back Street Bethel and West End Chapel, were inevitably overlaid by change through time, broadly along sect-to-denomination lines.[74] There were three interrelated elements to the latter: the rise and fall of the Churches' membership; the changing social status of the Christian Brethren, largely as a consequence of their improving ethos, but also facilitated by external economic changes, such as the growth of white-collar employment; and modifications in the Churches' beliefs and practices. The changes in religious outlook were part of a national process that eventually touched every corner of the co-operation and divided congregations between the new revisionism and the "old paths." The reaction against the Churches becoming a denomination like any other had many expressions, from outright secession to a grudging acceptance of some new ideas and resistance to others. The aim here is not to adjudicate between the relative theological merits of the various positions, but to relate the changes in belief and practices to the type of people the Churches attracted and produced, and ultimately to their capacity to throw up labor movement leaders.

In 1858 the Churches had just one chapel in Wigan, Rodney Street, and none in the surrounding hinterland. Late starters, they reached their membership peak, both in Wigan and nationally, considerably later than most other Nonconformist groups, around 1930. By 1929, at the height of national and local membership, the Rodney Street "mother church" had nine daughters in the Wigan District. This section compares the raw national figures with those of Rodney Street, and the three south Wigan chapels which joined the co-operation together in 1883: Albert Street, Newtown; Scholes; and Platt Bridge.[75] The most striking general impression from both the national and the Wigan figures is the gradualness in both growth and decline. It took the national Churches twenty years to double their original membership in 1862; fifteen years to do it again in 1877; and twenty-three years a third time in 1900. Likewise, the growth of the four Wigan chapels over the forty years from 1886 to the late 1920s is steady but unspectacular. One indication is the complete absence of chapel rebuilding or extension, as in Methodism's main growth period.[76] The big leap in Wigan membership, injecting new coalfield blood and creating a new social base, appears to have occurred in the decade just before the official figures began in 1886. Most coalfield chapels date from these years, and when the three Wigan chapels joined the "co-operation" in 1883, they brought with them a new combined membership greater than Rodney Street. Thus the 1870s were the formative period for the Churches' coalfield presence. The seed had fallen on fertile ground, Marsden's chapel-building program harvested the new constituency, and the following decades saw its consolidation. Overall, the membership figures suggest that the Wigan Churches underwent three main growth periods: a founding phase in the 1840s, 1850s, and 1860s; a frontier phase, for the most part in the 1870s and 1880s, but in some cases extending into the twentieth century; and a consolidationist phase in the first two decades of the twentieth century. This latter stage began and ended at different times in the various chapels and neighborhoods. During it, the emphasis shifted from converting adults to nurturing the plentiful next generation of Churches' children, and any others who could be attracted in the neighborhood, through the Sunday school. If we turn to the pattern of decline, from the 1930s onward, gradualness is again evident, until the sudden exodus during and after the Second World War.

Whereas the Churches' growth begins much later than mainstream Nonconformity, and their decline starts later and proceeds more slowly, the wartime collapse is consistent with the wider experience. It reflected a speeding-up of economic, social, and cultural change that undermined the local communities, values, beliefs, and institutions—such as the Sunday schools and chapel outings—on which the regeneration of chapel life depended.[77]

However, the change considered here relates not only to numbers but also to the sort of people involved, how they regarded their commitment to the chapel, and how it formed their characters. Well before the Great War, a change in the Churches' social composition was becoming noticeable. The 1905 yearbook observed: "The last half century has made a change in the worldly status of the brethren. Fifty years since, even elders and leaders might usually be found in the lower ranks of life, among the humble handicraftsmen—now they may often be looked for among the locally influential."[78] The Churches began life primitive, equal and rigid, but as time wore on, patterns of social differentiation developed with implications for all three characteristics. Once members improved their social status, they became less tolerant of the primitive religious ideals and social restrictions. Moreover, they tended to leave the area of their local chapel and sometimes lose touch with the Churches as social status improved both within and between generations. There was no sudden transformation of the local Churches' membership. By and large the membership in 1939 was an older version of 1918, with their offspring and other Sunday school recruits failing to compensate for the intervening deaths and departures, and these children were far less likely to follow the manual occupations of their parents.[79]

Moreover, this century has seen the gradual dilution of the New Testament plea and the primitive practices associated with it, leading ultimately to the merger in 1980 of the bulk of the Churches' membership with the United Reformed Church (itself formed by the union of English Presbyterians and Congregationalists in 1972).[80] To the official leadership this was a logical principled progression as the ecumenical insights of the original plea bore full fruit at the expense of its more sectarian elements. To others, this was a betrayal of the original principles, leading to a loss of identity. These complicated divisions originated in the period after the Great War, when the pace of doctrinal revisionism quickened and proved increasingly unacceptable to some sections of the Churches. Once this process began to touch on more central issues, it threw up bitter doctrinal disputes, especially in the more primitive Back Street Bethels. These revolved around key elements of the original New Testament plea, like biblical literalism, closed communion, and the rejection of a professional ministry. Derived from these were primitive practices, such as the rejection of instrumental music and other trappings of nonbiblical ritual, or assumptions from Saint Paul about the role of women in religious worship. The founding Wigan brethren were "Bible Christians" in the most basic sense. Men of limited learning, largely self-taught, they regarded the English Bible as the direct word of God, equally accessible to all. By the start of this century, however, the Churches were producing educated, middle-class Bible scholars who went back to the original Greek and challenged misconceptions derived from a literal reading of the English edition. Their names began to appear in *The Christian Advocate* accompanied by "B.A." or "M.A." From an intellectual theological perspective this was progress. From a sociological point of view, it began a process of disempowering ordinary brethren by arrogating a special authority of biblical interpretation to an educated middle-class elite. In short, it recommenced the journey toward clerical authority, whereby the hard-wrought self-education of the working-class lay preachers began to count for less against the new middle-class learning. The dispute over biblical literalism often took on quite comical forms, centered on particular passages in the Bible. There were acrimonious interwar arguments over whether Jonah did literally survive in the belly of the whale.[81] However, the dispute had a deeper sociological import, for any challenge to biblical literalism touched on the notion of the priesthood of all believers and the ideal of mutual teaching. In short, it threatened to undermine the role of the chapel as a school for labor movement activists.

The argument over open versus closed communion is also too easily caricatured as a struggle between forward-looking ecumenicals and backward-looking sectarians. From a pragmatic modern religious perspective, it exposed a central contradiction in the Churches' original plea, between two biblically inspired calls: for adult believers' baptism and for a return to a universal Christian church that transcended sectarian divisions. Closed communion was an obstacle to ecumenical relations with other denominations, including the powerful American Disciples.[82] However, the Churches' founders had aimed not for an accommodation with the various fragments of Christianity, but to revolutionize that situation by creating a new unity on New Testament principles that superseded and laid waste existing denominational divisions and dogmas. Again, whatever the realistic prospects of success or the intellectual merits of this project, it had a sociological import. A chapel motivated by this sectarian fire and set against the established world was likely to leave a strong impression on its members. The communion question was a major reason for the "old paths" chapels, Albert Street, Scholes, and Hindley seceding in 1947. But even a chapel like Platt Bridge, which remained loyal to the "co-operation," became concerned. In 1920, it suggested an Annual Conference paper on "Who should be partakers at the Lord's Table." A year later, it demurred on the closely related question of "public collections at Rodney Street" during an evangelist's visit. The chapel was careful to check if someone wanting "fellowship" was an "immersed believer" before he was admitted to the congregation, and it protested against the Churches' national chairman for "engaging in propaganda for co-operation with the British and American Churches." Toward the end of the decade, the idea of "leaving the co-operation" was canvassed in some quarters but rejected.[83]

The use of instrumental music in the centerpiece of worship, the Lord's Supper, had been an important issue in the split between the U.S. Campbellites.[84] The argument originated from the attempt to replicate exactly the Last Supper and other early church practices described in the New Testament. Organs and pianos were seen as detracting from this Puritan authenticity, by adding a layer of human artifice. Hence it was a highly visible symbolic issue in the struggle over the new revisionism. Where chapels were still noninstrumental, this set them clearly apart from the atmosphere of mainstream Nonconformity. This doctrinal dispute tore small congregations apart. A letter from another Wigan chapel, Beech Hill, to Platt Bridge describes an exodus of thirty members to a chapel outside the "co-operation." It was considered newsworthy that "the organ played at last Sunday nights service for the first time," the Lord's Supper morning service being a distant Rubicon.[85] The dispute over instrumental music did not loom so large at Platt Bridge itself. Singing was already central to all chapel social and religious activities other than the Lord's Supper. Outside the inner sanctum, the chapel quite readily endorsed instrumental accompaniment. In 1930 they loaned the Sunday school money to buy a piano, and eventually this was introduced into the main members' service. In addition, they already held religious activities that could be regarded as going well beyond the New Testament plea. New Year's Eve Watchnight services began early in the century and were usually combined with a chapel social. Despite their earlier contempt for the unbiblical Christian calendar, carol singing was also practiced from quite early on. George Miller, the chapel impresario, was again on hand for Christmas 1934 to organize "Carol Singing."[86]

Even Rodney Street continued to pay lip service to the ideal of the priesthood of all believers.[87] In practice, however, a number of factors reinforced the view that some were more equal than others. Democratic congregational traditions were strongest in working-class chapels. Hence the strongest resistance came from these quarters when, in the train of biblical interpretation, the expedient of itinerant evangelists metamorphosed into *de facto*, full-time ministers with degrees and theological training. The idea of a theological training college had been first mooted in 1871 but rejected. Overdale College was established eventually in Birmingham in 1920, and Marsden of Rodney Street talent-spotted its first principal, William Robinson, who became the Churches' best-known twentieth-century theologian. The college immediately became the focus of controversy, reviving fears of a central creed with authoritative interpreters.[88] Again this challenged the Churches' tradition that all members could understand the Bible and preach its word. Platt Bridge seems to have taken a more relaxed attitude than some other small chapels. During 1922 it twice donated Sunday collections to the new college. Three years later it did "protest against the affiliation of the College to the Student Christian Movement," presumably because this implied some dilution of the Churches' distinctive plea.[89]

In addition to these deliberate changes in the national Churches' doctrine and practices, there was a more subtle interwar drift in chapel life associated with looser attitudes and outside cultural changes. On the surface, chapel life seemed much as always, but social change and theological liberalization also had implications for primitive patterns of church organization. They had least direct effect on the small, coalfield chapels, many of which retained their local autonomy and their democratic, lay principles beyond the Second World War. However, a decline in lay participation began to affect even these chapels. Over the quarter century from 1912 to 1939, Platt Bridge chapel membership remained fairly steady, hovering on either side of a hundred and only beginning a gradual decline in the late 1930s. However, the character of chapel life was changing, along with the wider society outside. A number of indicators—the frequency of church and officers' meetings, attendances at church meetings, and the exercise of discipline—suggest that the congregation was aging, increasingly reliant on endogamy, and becoming less voluntarist and participatory. In brief, those cultural factors that had molded a generation of labor movement activists were ebbing away. None of these changes was contested, and it seems likely that they simply reflected the practicalities of the situation. The chapel's two delegates to the 1934 Lancashire and Cheshire Conference were nominated by the officers' meetings and left to vote at their "discretion." But the earlier minute "that only Church Officers should occupy the position of servitor at the Lord's table," was rescinded in 1934 in favor of a looser construction that "whenever possible" one officer should be in attendance. Once more this suggests a loosening of commitment, even among the inner circle. The congregation was becoming correspondingly more passive. In the 1920s, while officers' meetings retained their frequency, there were, on average, about five church meetings a year. By the 1930s, even the frequency of officers' meetings had fallen to about five a year, and there was usually no more than one church meeting per annum. The demise of the earlier congregational participatory democracy is quite apparent.[90]

Another indicator is the chapel's approach to discipline, especially over nonattendance at the Lord's Supper. Members were regularly struck off the register until the late 1920s. Then, attention shifted from individual absentees to overall attendance. From 1930 no expulsions were recorded, and the approach to nonattendance changed from punitive to persuasive. In 1916, absentees received a leaflet followed by a visit. Eight years later the officers tried to extend visiting to "all members on the church book," presumably as a form of preventative medicine. By 1930, a letter "to members who are absenting themselves from the Lord's

Table" was considered sufficient. Three years later the tone was softer still: "That we invite our members out of fellowship free to our Jubilee Celebrations." A "reminder letter" was sent to members "who are not constant in attendance at the Lord's Table"—no more.[91] As this more relaxed attitude came to predominate, the chapel began to shed many vestiges of its distinctive voluntarist character, as a "peculiar people" different from other denominations. Interference in members' social and private life seems to have abated as well. In 1934, Gladys Gaskell's "position in the Wesleyan Girl Guides" was drawn to the committee's notice, but nothing seems to have been done about it. Veterans recall how strict the Churches had been about popular entertainment, like the cinema, and how their attitudes gradually moderated.[92] Naturally, there was a wider context. Between the wars, coal and cotton began to decline as local employers. As Nonconformity declined, the culture of biblical literacy dissipated. As the Churches took on the colors of their religious surroundings, their distinctive growth phase gradually merged into the wider experience of decline.[93]

V

This article has tried to divine what manner of religious community the Wigan Churches of Christ were, how they developed across space and time, and how they forged a link with the coalfield labor movement. The first section provided a snapshot of their origins, centered on their 1860 confession of faith, which aimed to restore a pristine New Testament Christianity: a literal approach to the Bible, a stress on adult believers' baptism, an obligatory weekly closed communion, the rejection of a separate ministry, and a primitive brotherhood of the humble. Many early members were coal miners, though there was no great evidence of the Churches adopting radical social attitudes, beyond extending a welcoming hand to the poor. Yet even in this intensely conversionist phase, the Churches had begun to nurture local labor figures.

The second section moved to the coalfield Back Street Bethel from the late 1870s to the 1920s. There was little change in religious doctrine, except for an even stronger emphasis on democratic church government. This cohesive community of mainly mining families re-created the Churches in the coalfield as an alternative social focus to the public house. They felt mining disasters firsthand, contributed labor leaders, formed self-help programs for their needy, and hosted a sizable antiwar movement. The chapel had labor sympathies, but its main contribution was to train and motivate local labor leaders. The reason for this was the participatory culture and improving ethic, found in those other branches of primitive, working-class Nonconformity, which produced pitmen, preachers, and labor movement leaders.[94]

The third section presented a very different scene, the West End Chapel. Here the manufacturing dynasty dominated the chapel, played a central part in national Churches' developments, and spearheaded the movement toward mainstream, denominational Nonconformity. As members rose in social status, the chapel became a social magnet for the socially aspiring and came to resemble less a "labour sect" than Joyce's model of religious-based employer paternalism.[95] The fourth section focused on change at the Back Street Bethel, especially between the wars. A mixture of denominational and wider social factors dissolved the special conditions under which the coalfield chapels had produced labor movement leaders. The rising status of the brethren and weakening links to the coalfield were accompanied by a new revisionism emanating from the national Churches and a more general loss of religious fervor. Membership participation declined, discipline became more lax, and the chapels began to lose their distinctive identity and this-worldly impetus. The primitive moment had passed.

How can we best understand the Wigan Churches' labor movement links? The conclusion drawn is that any novel aspects of the national Churches' beliefs came firmly second in importance to those features that formed a common ground with earlier radical primitives: the group's voluntarist character, "An egalitarian, democratic approach to church life . . . endemic in truly working class nonconformity,"[96] and puritanical values of self-improvement, self-discipline, and public service. These, rather than specific "doctrines," seem to hold the key. The twentieth-century *Christian Advocate* carried articles on "Social Christianity," and the Churches' Temperance and Social Committee ran appeals for miners in "distressed areas." But it was the activity of local chapel activists, rather than central initiatives from the hierarchy, that characterized the Churches' contribution to the labor movement. It "was not so much a contribution of ideology as a direct giving of persons of a new kind";[97] and it was the culture of the local chapel, rather than the ethos of the Churches as a whole, that, in the main, explained these phenomena. This influence waned as the Churches became more middle class, more hierarchical, and more theologically liberal. This still begs the question why other "new primitive" congregations, notably among the Christadelphians and the Plymouth Brethren, did not make such a contribution to the labor movement. These two shared with the Churches a puritanical "meetinghouse" ethos, a reverence for literalist biblical debate, and a liturgical emphasis on the sacrament. Perhaps, the most plausible answer is that the Churches were in the right place at the right time offering the right product to an industrial working-class constituency alienated from mainstream dissent and turning to labor. Maybe, a willingness to "open" sufficiently to the practical concerns of "the world" enabled their brand of working-class Puritanism to thrive in small ways among the tight-knit collier and shoemaking communities of late Victorian England.

This conclusion supports two methodological positions on the study of working-class religion.[98] The first is the need to track any religious movement across time and space, and to be specific about the where and when of religious experience. The Churches of Christ underwent their own sect-to-denomination evolution, and our understanding of their social composition and religious ideas depends fundamentally on where and when the snapshot is taken: whether we look at the early primitive Churches or their more sophisticated successor; the town-center "mother church" or their coalfield offspring. Yet, these changes ran no simple course. The smaller, poorer, outlying outposts changed more slowly and maintained the original primitive conditions much longer. In 1966, the Platt Bridge secretary could still report: "We have no Minister. We are dependent on local preachers"—and it so remains to this day.[99] The second observation is that the center of working-class religious experience is not to be found at the Churches' Annual Meeting, nor at its numerous national committees, nor in the pages of *The Christian Advocate*, nor even in the District structures or the hierarchy of the large, West End Chapels. It is by shifting our attention downward from the denomination to the local chapel, the Back Street Bethel, that we can understand more precisely the elements of working-class Protestant Nonconformity and its links to labor activism.

NOTES

Abbreviations

BMH = *British Millennial Harbinger*
BA = *Bible Advocate*
CA = *Christian Advocate*
PB = Platt Bridge Chapel Minutes.
For the location of these and other sources, see appendix 1.

    1. For the first view, see E. P. Thompson, *The Making of the English Working-Class* (London, 1980), on the earlier nineteenth century. P. Joyce, *Work, Society, and Politics: The Culture of the Factory in Later Victorian England* (London, 1980), gives this attitude a novel ethnic twist for industrial Lancashire, linked to employer paternalism. For the second view see R. Moore, *Pit-Men, Preachers, and Politics: The Effects of Methodism in a Durham Mining Community* (Cambridge, 1974), and R. F. Wearmouth, *Methodism and the Struggle of the Working-Classes, 1850–1900* (Leicester, 1954).

    2. For the Churches of Christ, see especially D. M. Thompson, *Let Sects and Parties Fall: A Short History of the Association of Churches of Christ in Great Britain and Ireland* (Birmingham, 1980), a good general history that includes a valuable bibliography. Two other studies are L. Billington, "The Churches of Christ in Britain: A Study in Nineteenth-Century

Sectarianism," *Journal of Religious History* 8 (1974/75): 21–48, and T. Witton Davies, "The McLeanist (Scotch) and Campbellite Baptists of Wales," *Transactions of the Baptist Historical Society* 7 (1920/21): 147–81. See also Peter Acker's larger study, "Christian Brethren, Union Brother: A Study of the Relationship between Religious Nonconformity and Trade Union Leadership, in the Life of the Coal Mining Deputies' Official, W. T. Miller, 1880–1963" (Ph.D. diss., Wolverhampton, 1993).

3. For Back Street Bethel and West End Chapel see H. McLeod, *Religion and the Working-Class in Nineteenth Century Britain* (London, 1984), 15. For sect-to-denomination see B. R. Wilson, *Sects and Society: A Sociological Study of Three Religious Groups in Britain* (London, 1961); and, *Patterns of Sectarianism: Organisation and Ideology in Social and Religious Movements* (London, 1967).

4. Thompson, *Sects and Parties*, membership appendix 2.

5. B. Lancaster, *Radicalism, Co-operation and Socialism: Leicester Working-Class Politics, 1860–1906* (Leicester, 1987), 71. For the Leicester Churches see G. J. Hammond, "The Ten Churches of Leicester: The Rise and Progress of the Restoration Movement in and around the Conference City," *CA* (20 July 1928): 451–54; Anon, *Churches of Christ, Nottingham and Leicester District Co-operation: A Record of Service, 1865–1915* (Heanor, 1915); B. Waterton and M. Waterton, *Churches of Christ in Leicestershire between the Wars* (Churches of Christ Historical Society Occasional Paper 2, 1986, 1–15).

6. *CA* (July 12, 1963). For a contemporary account of Coop's life see, W. T. Moore, *Timothy Coop: Or the Story of a Consecrated Business Career* (London, 1889). For a more detailed discussion of the Wigan background see Ackers "Christian Brethren, Union Brother," 40–91. This account follows A. D. Gilbert, *Religion and Society in Industrial Society: Church, Chapel and Social Change, 1740–1914* (London, 1976), 42–44, and Lancaster, *Radicalism*, 70–75, in seeing the Churches of Christ as part of a late Victorian "new primitive" or "new sectarian" working-class backlash against the increasingly middle-class character of mainstream Nonconformity. For some differences of interpretation with Lancaster, see Peter Ackers, "The 'Protestant Ethic' and the English Labour Movement: The Case of the Churches of Christ," *Labour History Review* 59 (1993): 67–72. K. Tiller, "Working-Class Attitudes and Organisation in Three Industrial Towns" (Ph.D. diss., Birmingham, 1975), and R. Gregory, *The Miners and British Politics, 1906–14* (Oxford, 1968), make interesting comparisons between Wigan, Lancashire, and other towns and coalfields respectively.

7. R. K. Crook and W. Robinson, *Centenary of the Churches of Christ, Rodney Street, Wigan, 1841–1941* (Wigan, 1941), 3.

8. *BMH* (1853): 45–46, 238.

9. Ibid. (July 1, Aug. 1, 1858).

10. *Rodney Street Chapel Trust Deeds (1860)*: "Matters Believed and Practiced by Christian Brethren Assembling in the Christian Meeting House, Rodney Street, Wigan."

11. See H. Foreman, *The Baptists of Bewdley: A History of Bewdley Baptist Church* (Bewdley, 1991). Other later Churches of Christ "confessions of faith" that the author has seen

bear a close resemblance to the Rodney Street plea. See the *1910 Trust Deeds of Humberstone Garden City Christian Meeting House, Leicester,* and the *1889 Trust Deeds of Loughborough Christian Meeting House.* Itinerant evangelists like McDougale probably encouraged such consistency, as did the Lancashire-based Chapel Building Fund; Thompson, *Sects and Parties,* 66–67.

12. Crook and Robinson, *Churches of Christ,* 12.
13. *BMH* (Jan. 1, 1858).
14. Ibid. (Aug. 1, 1858).
15. Crook and Robinson, *Churches of Christ,* 4.
16. Moore, *Timothy Coop,* 84.
17. R. Challinor, *The Lancashire and Cheshire Miners* (Newcastle, 1972), 46.
18. *BMH* (1853): 45.
19. Ibid. (May 1, 1860).
20. Ibid. (July 2, 1860).
21. See Thompson, *Sects and Parties,* 125, and Ackers, "'Protestant Ethic,'" 68–71.
22. J. Acheson, *Radical Puritans in England, 1550–1660* (London, 1990), 101.
23. Moore, *Timothy Coop,* 95.
24. J. B. Horsman, *A History of Hope Congregational Church, Wigan, 1812–1962* (Wigan, 1962).
25. *BMH* (Apr. 1, 1868).
26. *The 1869 Wigan Directory* (Blackburn: J. Worral, 1969; reprint, Swinton: N. Richardson, 1983), 1–37.
27. *CA* (1883): 85.
28. Ibid. (1883): 366.
29. See *Wigan Directory,* 18.
30. *CA* (1883): 347.
31. Ibid. (1883): 85, 527.
32. See R. W. Ambler, *Ranters, Revivalists, and Reformers: Primitive Methodism and Rural Society, South Lincolnshire, 1817–1875* (Hull, 1989), and Moore, *Pit-Men.*
33. PB, 1911–39.
34. Ibid., Apr. 29, 1923.
35. Ibid., June 16, 1912, and Apr. 12, 1914.
36. Ibid., Feb. 1, 1914.
37. *CA* (Oct. 1976): obituary.
38. PB, Jan. 14, 1914.
39. *CA* (July 26, 1963).
40. Challinor, *Lancashire and Cheshire Miners,* 164.
41. *CA* (1883): 347.
42. Annotated photograph, Albert Street and interview with Harry Ackers.
43. PB, July 16, 1922.
44. Ibid., Mar. 8, 1914.

45. *CA* (1883): 347.

46. PB, Mar. 11, 1923; July 1, 1934.

47. *BA* (July 24, 1908).

48. Ibid. (Aug. 18, 1899). Harry Ackers recalls a very similar Sunday school outing at Albert Street a decade or so later.

49. *BA* (Sept. 5, 1902).

50. T. B. Bottomore and M. Rubel, eds., *K. Marx: Selected Writing in Sociology and Social Philosophy* (Harmondsworth, 1976), 41.

51. *BA* (Jan. 12, 1900).

52. See Lancaster, *Radicalism*, 142, for Mann and Taylor. The former wrote an interesting autobiographical account of his co-operative endeavors: A. Mann, *Democracy in Industry: The Story of Twenty-one Years' Work of the Leicester Anchor Boot and Shoe Productive Society Limited* (Leicester, 1914). His obituary is in the *CA* (Jan. 19, 1940). See also Peter Ackers's entry for W. T. Miller in *The Dictionary of Labour Biography*, vol. 9 (Oxford, 1993), 215–19, and the entries for Mann and Fleming in vol. 1, 1972 (Parkinson and Taylor will appear in vol. 10). Parkinson's obituary is in *The Wigan Observer*, Feb. 2, 1929.

53. PB, Apr. 11, 1923, and June 27, 1926. Thompson comments, "Perhaps part of the appeal of the Temperance question was that it posited a solution to social and economic problems which did not involve any criticism of the economic structure of society," *Sects and Parties*, 125.

54. See Peter Ackers, "Who Speaks for the Christians? The Great War Conscientious Objection Movement in the Churches of Christ: A View from the Wigan Coalfield," *Journal of the United Reformed Church History Society* 5 (1993): 153–66.

55. PB, Aug. 29, 1920, Feb. 26, 1922, Feb. 4, 1934. By comparison, the *Minutes of the Humberstone Garden Christian Meeting House (1909–1945)*, led by the two radical co-operators, Mann and Taylor, which cover the same period, contain few political statements.

56. PB, May 14, 1921; Oct. 4, 1914; Apr. 2, 1916; Aug. 14, 1927; June 30, 1912; and May 1, 1933.

57. Ibid., Nov. 29, 1931; June 13, 20; Dec. 9, 1926.

58. *Churches of Christ Yearbook*, 1932. Due to the emphasis on the closed Sunday morning communion service, membership figures are probably fairly precise, especially for the earlier, more sectarian period. Sunday school figures were also published, but the more casual attendance of nonmembers at open evening gospel meetings and other church activities is harder to gauge.

59. *Portrait and Biographical Sketch of James Marsden, J.P., 1841–1927* (Wigan, 1927), 1.

60. Moore, *Timothy Coop*, 281.

61. Thompson, *Sects and Parties*, 82–5.

62. Crook and Robinson, *Churches of Christ*, 7.

63. R. K. Crook, "Mr. James Marsden: Biographical," *CA* (Mar. 11, 1927): 155–56.

64. *Portrait and Biographical Sketch*, 2.

65. Ibid.

66. Thompson, *Sects and Parties*, 63.

67. Billington, "Churches of Christ," 30. However, Leicester businessmen did dominate particular chapels, as when, in 1887, the boot and shoe manufacturer Benjamin Toone built the South Wigston Church; see Hammond, "The Ten Churches," 452.

68. Crook and Robinson, *Churches of Christ*, 8.

69. Crook, "James Marsden," 156.

70. *Rodney Street Chapel Deeds*.

71. *CA* (Jan. 30, 1953): obituary.

72. See Horsman, *Hope Congregational Church*, 131–34.

73. Crook and Robinson, *Churches of Christ*, 8. The experience of the Leicester "mother church" shows that the preeminence of the town-center chapel was not assured. Crafton Street, founded in 1865, had 266 members in 1907 (compared to Rodney Street's 256). However, due to changes in its urban setting, it had become by 1929 "a down-town church" with a membership of only 82 (compared to Rodney Street's 531). See Waterton and Waterton, "Churches of Christ," 8, and Hammond, "The Ten Churches," 452.

74. See the sociological analysis in Wilson's *Sects and Society* and *Patterns of Sectarianism*. At a national level, the British Churches of Christ followed a classic sect-to-denomination development, leading to merger with mainstream nonconformity in the form of the United Reformed Church. However, a substantial minority dissented from this movement at different periods in the twentieth century, particularly through the "old paths" movement, and at the grassroots the picture was far more complex. For instance, of the Wigan chapels discussed here only Rodney Street joined the United Reformed Church. If the predominant trend in the Churches of Christ was to "open-up," Wilson's earlier study shows how the Christadelphians, whose movement originated in the early Churches of Christ, followed an alternative "closed" path, as did sections of the Churches themselves. Individual congregations often negotiated their own balance between the two dynamics.

75. See appendix 2.

76. A. B. Barton, *Discovering Chapels and Meeting Houses* (Princes Risborough, 1990), 21; and Peter Ackers, "Churches of Christ in the Wigan Area," *Chapel Society Newsletter* 4 (1991): 44–45.

77. Gilbert, *Religion and Society*, 198–203.

78. Quoted in Thompson, *Sects and Parties*, 125.

79. Interviews with members of the Miller family.

80. See *United Reformed Church Act*, 1981.

81. Interview with Elsie Armstrong.

82. See the discussion in Thompson, *Sects and Parties*, 134–41.

83. PB, Apr. 4, 1920; Aug. 18, 1921; Apr. 16, 1924; June 6, Aug. 14, 1927. Clearly in some Nonconformist circles there were links between theological liberalism and labor political sympathies. Among the working-class members of the Churches of Christ, however, a measure of political radicalism and theological fundamentalism seem to have gone hand in hand. This was true of W. T. Miller, the Wigan subject of Acker's "Christian

Brother, Union Brethren," and J. T. Taylor, Leicester socialist and co-operator, who on October 14, 1928, moved, unsuccessfully, "That owing to the decision of the Annual Meeting again to have American preachers, who believed in open communion, come and preach in this country for the Churches, we sever our connection with the co-operation"; *Humberstone Church Minutes* (see above, note 11).

84. Thompson, *Sects and Parties*, 121.

85. PB, Sept. 8, 1939. Issues such as instrumental music also preoccupied the Humberstone brethren during the interwar years. *Humberstone Church Minutes*, Jan. 28, 1934.

86. PB, July 13, 1930; Dec. 26, 1911; Nov. 7, 1915; Oct. 14, 1934.

87. Crook and Robinson affirmed in 1941 that "this Church has ever stood for the priesthood of all believers," *Churches of Christ*, 12.

88. Thompson, *Sects and Parties*, 128–34.

89. PB, Apr. 30, Oct. 8, 1922; Apr. 7, June 21, 1925.

90. Ibid., Sept. 16, 1934.

91. Ibid., Feb. 6, 1916; Apr. 11, 1923; July 13, 1930; May 1, 1933; Mar. 4, 1934.

92. Ibid., Feb. 4, 1934. A point mentioned in several of the Wigan interviews.

93. A. D. Gilbert, *Religion and Society*, 206–7.

94. For this type of explanation, see Moore, *Pit-Men,* and R. Colls, "Primitive Methodism in the Northern Coalfield," in *Disciplines of Faith: Studies in Religion, Politics, and Patriarchy*, ed. J. Obelkevich, L. Roper, and R. Samuel (London, 1987), 323–34.

95. See E. J. Hobsbawm, "The Labour Sects," in *Primitive Rebels: Studies in the Nineteenth and Twentieth Centuries* (Manchester, 1971), 126–49, and Joyce, *Work, Society, and Politics*, 134–57.

96. Thompson, *Sects and Parties*, 53.

97. Colls, *Primitive Methodism*, 333.

98. See McLeod, *Religion and the Working-Class*, 44–56, and E. P. Thompson, "On History, Sociology, and Historical Relevance," *British Journal of Sociology* 27 (1976): 387–402.

99. G. Miller, undated letter, c. 1966, to Chapel Building Committee.

APPENDIX 1

SOURCES FOR THE WIGAN CHURCHES OF CHRIST

The main source for both published and unpublished material on the British Churches of Christ is their national archive located in the Selly Oak Colleges Central Library, Birmingham. This includes large quantities of national records as well as material from local chapels. Although this has been sorted into boxes, it remains uncataloged. Researchers wishing to use the archive need to contact the archivist, Mrs. E. M. Sewell, Room 105, First Floor, Central House, Selly Oak Colleges, Birmingham. The nearby Springdale College Library, 54 Weoley Park Road, Selly Oak, Birmingham, also has a substantial collection of published material. In addition, the author has drawn on local sources in Wigan and Leicestershire and on interviews with old members of the Churches.

Unpublished Primary Material

SELLY OAK ARCHIVE

Chapel Building Committee Correspondence.
Rodney Street Chapel Trust Deeds plus lists of trustees, March 13, 1956, and earlier, undated.
Platt Bridge chapel building plans, March 16, 1883.
Two letters from George Miller, Platt Bridge Secretary, Apr. 14, 1969, and c. 1966.
Annotated photograph, Albert Street, Church of Christ Elders, c. 1908–10.

IN AUTHOR'S POSSESSION

Platt Bridge Chapel minutes (1911–39).
"What the Church of Christ at Platt Bridge Stands For" (doctrinal notes, modern, undated).
Church of Christ, Victoria Road, Platt Bridge, Wigan Centenary Booklet (1883–1983).
Humberstone Garden City Christian Meeting House, Minutes (1909–45).
Humberstone Garden City Christian Meeting House, Trust Deeds, Dec. 31, 1910.
Loughborough Christian Meeting House, Trust Deeds, May 14, 1889.

Published Primary Material

SELLY OAK ARCHIVE

Specialist published material cited in the footnotes includes the *Churches of Christ Yearbook* from 1886, *The Christian Hymnary for Use of Churches of Christ*, Birmingham, 1938, and runs of the main periodicals: *British Millennial Harbinger, British Harbinger, Ecclesiastical Observer, Bible Advocate,* and *Christian Advocate.*
The Lancashire District box includes Portrait and Biographical Sketch of James Marsden, J.P., 1841–1927, Wigan.

IN AUTHOR'S POSSESSION

Personal interviews
  For Wigan, these include Elsie Armstrong, Apr. 15, 1989; Sydney Miller, Apr. 16, 1989; Ruth Miller, Sept. 8, 1989; Betty Miller, Sept. 8, 1989; Harry Ackers, Sept. 8, 1989.
  For Leicestershire, they include Peter Hill, Mar. 29, 1994; and Bernard and Grace Mee and Enid Shaw, Sept. 21, 1994.

APPENDIX 2
CHURCHES OF CHRIST MEMBERSHIP, 1842–1949

Table 1
1842–1885

Year	Great Britain	Year	Great Britain
1842	1,300[a]	1864[b]	3,400
1843	—	1865	3,868
1844	—	1866	3,616
1845	—	1867	3,971
1846	—	1868	4,023
1847	2,300	1869	4,040
1848	2,057	1870	3,988
1849	1,029	1871	3,776
1850	1,816	1872	4,053
1851	—	1873[b]	4,115
1852	2,081	1874	4,394
1853[b]	1,932	1875	4,936
1854	1,998	1876	4,903
1855	1,823	1877	5,764
1856	2,103	1878	6,166
1857	2,065	1879	6,003
1858	2,275	1880	5,844
1859	2,475	1881	6,451
1860	2,326	1882	6,632
1861	2,528	1883[b]	7,112
1862	2,782	1884	7,327
1863	3,148	1885	7,654[c]

[a] No accurate local figures.
[b] The Annual Meeting was held in Wigan.
[c] Accurate local figures begin following year.

Table 2

1886–1929

Est. Year	1878 (1) Rodney St.	1882 (2) Albert St.	1882 (3) Scholes	1882 (4) Platt Bridge	1916 (5) Mitchell St.	Great Britain
1886	211	76	94	57		7,872
1887	220	75	89	54		8,306
1888	266	101	111	76		8,608
1889	276	113	113	68		9,137
1890	307	114	107	59		8,985
1891[a]	305	59	101	54		9,511
1892	297	80	116	69		9,954
1893	293	90	113	56		9,944
1894	250	71	95	59		10,249
1895	234	72	98	75		10,559
1896	224	85	101	91		10,834
1897	220	90	101	85		10,932
1898	213	94	95	88		11,124
1899	—	—	—	—		11,117
1900	223	130	81	100		11,789
1901	229	133	79	101		12,224
1902	238	133	83	95		12,537
1903	253	136	78	80		12,841
1904[a]	261	150	78	90		13,063
1905	273	173	63	90		13,958
1906	—	—	—	—		14,265
1907	256	128	74	95		14,326
1908	258	108	64	85		14,500
1909	—	—	—	—		14,440

Table 2 *(continued)*

Est. Year	1878 (1) Rodney St.	1882 (2) Albert St.	1882 (3) Scholes	1882 (4) Platt Bridge	1916 (5) Mitchell St.	Great Britain
1910	281	158	68	78		14,822
1911	273	157	68	92		14,725
1912	311	150	68	91		14,778
1913	366	126	69	100		15,256
1914[a]	375	131	66	100		15,228
1915	382	146	68	106		15,182
1916	398	136	62	111	65	15,191
1917	445	114	67	117	61	15,101
1918	466	—	72	118	74	16,437
1919	480	120	80	—	77	16,243
1920	472	114	85	94	82	16,011
1921	496	138	78	101	82	16,068
1922	491	145	71	104	104	16,306
1923	487	157	72	99	109	16,465
1924	471	160	83	103	98	16,382
1925	449	135	81	100	101	16,349
1926	448	135	84	106	109	16,283
1927	445	140	77	102	112	16,447
1928	521	140	90	88	82	16,576
1929[a]	531	134	90	88	85	16,595

NOTE: [a] The Annual Meeting was held in Wigan.

TABLE 3

1930–1949

Est. Year	1878 (1) Rodney St.	1882 (2) Albert St.	1882 (3) Scholes	1882 (4) Platt Bridge	1916 (5) Mitchell St.	Great Britain
1930	564	117	87	80	79	16,596
1931	564	117	98	82	77	15,991
1932	565	117	104	90	77	16,126
1933	552	117	112	93	73	16,018
1934	410	114	112	90	72	15,527
1935	422	114	85	92	70	15,327
1936	525	121	93	90	74	15,838
1937	538	100	100	84	73	15,823
1938	551	84	100	82	58	15,482
1939	560	82	101	79	45	15,229
1940	556	85	101	74	45	14,948
1941	552	94	101	67	46	14,303
1942	295	74	106	48	44	13,511
1943	304	65	112	51	41	13,107
1944	315	71	110	55	41	12,764
1945	317	60	110	47	51	12,101
1946	316	60	110	50	48	11,660
1947	323	0[a]	0[a]	49	46	10,628
1948	323			51	31	10,359
1949	323			47	32	10,001

NOTES: [a]Left co-op.
SOURCES: *Churches of Christ Yearbook*; Thompson, *Sects and Parties*.

Part IV

Social Ethics and Pacifism

David Lipscomb and the "Preferential Option for the Poor" among Postbellum Churches of Christ

Anthony L. Dunnavant

In the quarter century since the Second General Conference of the Latin American Episcopal Council in Medellín, Colombia, the theme of a "preferential option for the poor" has become increasingly familiar in the theological discourse of Christians. However, part of the power of this idea is rooted in its claim to great antiquity within—and even beyond—the Christian tradition. The Catholic bishops at Medellín likened their discernment of God's presence in "the present-day transformation of Latin America" to that of "Israel of old," which "felt the saving presence of God" when God "delivered them from the oppression of Egypt by the passage through the sea and led them to the promised land."[1] In a similar fashion, when the Latin American Episcopal Council met in Puebla in 1979, its document on "A Preferential Option for the Poor" drew from both the ancient tradition of the people of God and the more immediate past. From the ancient past it invoked images of "the poor of Yahweh," the poor Christ, the Jesus who evangelizes the poor, the Mary of Magnificat, and the "evangelical poverty" of the gospels and the First Epistle to Timothy. But the immediate past of the "rise of grassroots communities" was also foundational to the document.[2] This kind of historical consciousness, one that is both deep-rooted and attentive to the contemporary scene, is characteristic of much Latin American Catholic theology, certainly of that associated with "liberation."[3]

As Robert McAfee Brown describes it, part of the challenge to North American Protestants that the Latin American statement of "a preferential option for the poor" presents is that this option is a "vocation that will appeal only to those few North American counterparts" of the grassroots church communities. Both the historical orientation of liberation theology and Brown's suggestion raise the possibility that within the stream of North American Christianity there might be traditions—or at least individuals—that have embodied or expressed "a preferential option for the poor." Furthermore, as North American Protestants seek ways to "embrace the notion," they might be helped by a recognition that the notion is neither entirely new nor entirely alien to the Christian tradition in their own cultural heritage. *This is not to suggest, of course, that the theological, social, historical, and cultural differences between North America and Latin America may be simply swept aside. Those differences are profound.* It is to suggest that those moments and movements that share a certain resonance of emphasis and insight might fruitfully be identified.[4]

It is in this spirit of striving to identify other discoveries of God's concern for the poor that we turn to the North America of the nineteenth century and the Campbell-Stone movement. This movement emerged on the western frontier of the United States in the early national period. In it are the roots of three major North American religious bodies, the Christian Church (Disciples of Christ), the undenominational fellowship of Christian Churches and Churches of Christ, and the Churches of Christ. It was in the closing years of the nineteenth and opening years of the twentieth centuries that the Campbell-Stone community divided. The division that produced the Churches of Christ as a distinctive body was rooted, at least in part, in a socioeconomic bifurcation in the movement. That Churches of Christ represented, during the generation after the Civil War, *much more* than the other branch of the movement a "religion of the disinherited" is suggested by both the actual wealth of congregations and the perspective of the group's leadership.[5] Clearly, Churches of Christ *saw themselves* as relatively materially poorer than their former religious compatriots. The time and place that the Churches of Christ arose gives credence to this self-image.[6] Within the Campbell-Stone movement, then, the focus will narrow to Churches of Christ between the Civil War and World War I. This was a period in which this group was—*relatively* and in self-perception—poor. Further, the focus will be on David Lipscomb, who was one of the principal leaders of this group, and on ways in which he approached articulating a "preferential option for the poor."

David Lipscomb is the figure most strongly associated with the emergence of the Churches of Christ as a distinct religious community within the larger Campbell-Stone movement. It was around his views as expressed in the *Gospel Advocate* during the two generations between the Civil War and World War I that the Churches of Christ "consolidated."[7] The fact that this religious body has been, and remains, overwhelmingly, a people of the southern United States is important to an understanding of Lipscomb. It was the southern strand of the Campbell-Stone movement that came closer to being identified with the "disinherited" than the other strands. Richard T. Hughes has recently suggested that Lipscomb was "not only . . . a man of God and a man of the book [the Bible], but also . . . a man of his region and a man of the people." This, then, is the first aspect of Lipscomb's views that resonates with the Latin American "commitment to solidarity with the poor, to being a church of the poor"—a simple identification with the poor, or the "common masses."[8]

David Lipscomb's views share other significant similarities with those arising from the orbit of Latin American Catholic liberation theology. Lipscomb's concern for the poor was not vague, abstract, or ahistorical. Like liberation theology, which is based on "concrete historical and political conditions," David Lipscomb's writings about the poor were based on his own personal experience of poverty in the concrete historical situation of the Civil War and Reconstruction-era southern United States. He understood this poverty as having both regional and economic (as opposed to *merely* individual and moral) dimensions.[9] Early in 1866 Lipscomb wrote: "We have in the South brethren impoverished, and suffering for the necessaries of life, whose misfortune it was to share the general desolation of the country in which they lived. We have brethren North of us who have grown rich by the very circumstances that impoverished our brethren South."[10] The "general desolation" of the Civil War was the large, historical background that fed Lipscomb's "insatiable desire to help the distressed people of the South."[11] But his experience with poverty was not confined to his efforts to help others who were impoverished. During the Civil War years, poverty had come very close. He reflected in late 1866, "It is but a year or two since we ourselves were in a condition of almost actual starvation. The writer of this has visited, within the last four years, our Senior Editor, who could not give him bread to eat; this was his condition for weeks . . . We have visited other families that were near to us, in which we felt that every mouth full of food we ate was taken from women and children who must suffer for the want of it."[12]

If Lipscomb's own experience of poverty, perceptions of its causes, and efforts on behalf of the poor "destitute" Christians of the South are seen as one "pole" of his concern, the other "pole" is clearly the example of Christ seen in Scripture. Again, there is a striking similarity with the familiar Christological basis of the Church's option for the poor in the Latin American liberation theology literature. On the one hand, there is the reference to the Jesus of the Gospels' claim that "God may be found in the poor" (Matt 25); on the other hand there is the imagery of *kenosis*.[13]

Lipscomb alluded to the first of these themes in the following passage:

> Christ is personified in his poor, helpless brethren. Matt. xxv:40. In them, Christ appeals for help to himself. Who realizes this? . . . Let us realize that every helpless, needy one of our brethren is the personification of Christ to us appealing for help. He is our Christ, to be kindly welcomed and generously treated. Shall we cast our Christ from our doors and let him become a beggar from others? Let us be careful, "Verily I say unto you inasmuch as you have done it unto one of the least of these my brethren, ye have done it unto me." "Inasmuch as ye did it not to one of the least of these ye did it not to me."[14]

He also invoked the image of Christ's self-emptying as the example that calls Christians to sacrificial giving on behalf of "the masses":

> Without timely aid, the masses, unable to raise crops the coming year, will be in as bad condition another winter as they have been during the past . . . It is folly in us to deceive ourselves on this subject . . . We must sacrifice our luxuries, our comforts, our wealth and pride, to relieve our brother's distresses, just as Christ sacrificed his honors, glories, joys and possessions in heaven, to help poor helpless, fallen man on earth. This was the fellowship of God to man. I will give of my honors and joys to you, and take of your weaknesses, sufferings, and sorrows to myself, is the language of Jesus to man, in his mission to earth. Our fellowship for one another must be of this character. I'll give of my plenty, and partake of your privations and self-denials, is the language of Christian fellowship.[15]

The language of *kenosis* and the apprehension of Christ (God incarnate) personified in the poor "brother" certainly suggests an orientation of the church "for the poor." But as liberation theologian John Sobrino says, "a church for the poor is not yet a Church *of* the poor." To use Sobrino's language for the question, is there in the writings of David Lipscomb a recognition that "the Church of the poor is a Church the social and historical basis of which is to be found among the poor"? Yes! Lipscomb repeatedly stated his assumption that "the great masses of professed Christians are now, [and] ever we trust will be from the poor, laboring classes."[16] Lipscomb traced the history of the poor people of God in sweeping terms, reminding his readers that God's

> prophets of olden time were poor, often clothed in sackcloth. His Son was born of an humble handmaid of the Lord, who was espoused to a carpenter. The reputed Father of our lord, Joseph, was a carpenter. The laboring, toiling classes were the associates chosen of God for his Son during his childhood and youth. The more prominent of his Apostles were from the laboring classes. Several followed the uncertain and precarious calling of fishermen. *They were the chosen vessels of the Lord in which his spirit dwelt, and through whom it guided and guides the nations of the earth to God and Heaven.* The poor of this world were the chosen vessels of mercy, the especially honored and blessed of God. They, as a class, constitute his elect. They are the chosen objects of his tender regard and true and faithful love. The great mass of his true and honored followers, in all ages of the world, have been, ever must be, from the poor.[17] (emphasis added)

The sentence underscored above moves us into another area of the "preferential option for the poor," which is echoed in Lipscomb's writings—the importance of the poor as evangel*ists* as well as evangel*ized*.

The bishops meeting at Puebla reflected that "the rise of grass-roots communities has helped the Church to discover the evangelizing potential of the poor. For the poor challenge the Church constantly, summoning it to conversion;

and many of the poor incarnate in their lives the evangelical values of solidarity, service, simplicity, and openness to accepting the gift of God."[18] Interestingly, one of the great controversies of David Lipscomb's life was related to his opposition to the missionary societies that arose within the Campbell-Stone movement in the middle of the nineteenth century.[19] He saw these societies as "concentrat[ing] the authority and power and means of all the Christians and all the churches in a few persons," who tended to be "chosen. . . for their capacity to raise money." Therefore, his opposition to the societies was based in part on the conviction that "Christ [would have] never established a religion among the poor, and committed its propagation especially to them as a class—[and] made them the objects of his most favored blessing, [if] that [religion] required the concentration and management of great sums of money in one mass in order to reach its highest prosperity."[20] Rather, Lipscomb believed that "the religion of Jesus Christ was adapted to the common people" and that "they are those best fitted to maintain and spread that religion." He thought that churches "manned by the working people, suited to the means and conditions of the working people," would be the "effective instruments under God of perpetuating and spreading the religion of Christ in its purity."[21] He made quite explicit his assumption that "it is altogether a mistake to think that the poor are to be preached to by the rich." Such a mistaken notion was alien to Lipscomb's belief that "the rich corrupt" the church.[22]

Lipscomb's belief that the rich corrupt the church was accompanied by an oft-repeated caution that the movement of which he was a part should not conform to the ways of the rich and thereby be drawn into this corruption. Again, this resembles the concern expressed at the Second General Conference of the Latin American Episcopal Council at Medellín that there was a perception "that the hierarchy, the clergy, the religious are rich and allied with the rich." This concern led to several suggestions, including that priests should know "how to assume the realities and the 'sense of the people' in their circumstances and mentality."[23] The priests were "exhorted" to "give testimony of poverty and detachment from material goods . . . particularly in rural areas and poor neighborhoods" and "encouraged," if they felt so called, "to share the lot of the poor, living with them and even working with their hands."[24]

Similarly, Lipscomb had a special desire that the preaching ministry be not conformed to "the tastes and habits of the rich." He therefore opposed, to some degree, education for the ministry and an itinerant, hired ministry. He maintained that both preachers and other Christians were well advised to support themselves through manual labor, at least partially.

On the issue of education, Lipscomb observed in 1866:

> There is just now a great anxiety manifested for an educated ministry. This is all right, if that education is properly conducted, we often-times think that the habits

acquired, and the tastes formed, in getting the education, are not such as are most desirable for enabling the preachers to do good service. Our schools, like our churches, are modeled and conducted to suit the tastes and habits of the rich. If a poor young man, by dint of his own energy or by the aid of friends, enters and passes through school, his associations and surroundings are those of the rich. He forms habits and tastes in consonance with these, loses sympathy with the habits and wants of the poor, and is deprived of his power for reaching those whom it is his especial duty to reach and benefit. The poor are those to whom the Christian minister should be prepared and trained to preach.[25]

Lipscomb's argument against an itinerant "hired" ministry sounds similar themes and adds others—including an encouragement to "live poor":

The whole plan of a Preacher's putting himself up to the highest bidder, shifting about from place to place, for the sake of a little higher salary is at once a degradation to Christianity, demoralizing to the man and the worst of policies for his support. It makes merchandise of the Christian religion, supplying the preaching of the Gospel to the rich because they are rich, leaving the poor destitute because they are poor, thus thwarting the plan of salvation, *for in it the Gospel is to be preached to the poor because they are poor*. This system keeps the Preacher ever in an unsettled and harassed state of mind, which disqualifies him for usefulness. Makes him in all his preaching over anxious to please, which destroys his independence and true self respect . . . When the brethren aid you, be thankful and preach the Gospel, when they neglect you, work, and toil and preach the Gospel. Don't grumble or complain. *Don't seek the rich and honorable to preach to, but preach to the poor, the neglected, the degraded, and if you live poor you will have the respect of the good and true, your own self-approval, and better than all, the approval of your Father in Heaven. You will be one of the world's true heroes and Heaven's crowned victors.*[26] (emphasis added)

Elsewhere David Lipscomb makes clear that his admonition to "work and toil" includes his assumption that labor with one's hands is to be preferred.[27]

Lipscomb believed that the preference for the poor in evangelism necessitates the church's maintaining an atmosphere that is not alienating to the poor: "Whatever is introduced into worship in the congregation, either in preaching, singing, praying or biblical reading, that . . . transcends the power of appreciation of the very large majority of the worshippers, and hearers . . . becomes, to use the figure of Paul, the veriest barbarism to that class of people to whom the Gospel was especially adapted and sent—the poor."[28]

Three other aspects of the "preferential option for the poor" that are associated with recent Latin American theology are at least implicit in the writings of David Lipscomb. The first of these is what has been called the "epistemological privilege of the poor," the second is service to the poor as the "privileged gauge of our following of Christ," and the third is the vocation of the church to be "herself bound to material poverty."[29]

"The epistemological privilege of the poor" is a phrase that has been used by Latin American liberation theologians to indicate "that the conditions of oppression endured by the poor make them more open to the liberating word of God than are those who stand in the way of liberation."[30] In other words, "the poor are accepted as constituting the primary recipients of the Good News and, therefore, as having an inherent capacity to understand it 'better' than anyone else."[31] Intimations of this view have already been seen in Lipscomb, who urged preachers to "not only preach to the poor in public, but in private also . . . Visit them at their houses, learn to appreciate their trials and difficulties, . . . and school [your]selves to a full sympathy with their condition. Don't be afraid of being troublesome to the poor. *No class of persons will be more benefitted by your conversation and association, or will more cheerfully be troubled with your presence* . . . [Christ] associated with and made himself one of the poor. His servants should act as he did" (emphasis added).[32] While this may fall short of being a full statement of an "epistemological privilege of the poor," it does seem to imply more openness on their part to the preacher and, indirectly, more openness to the gospel among the poor. Lipscomb thought of the capacity of the poor, or at least of the common people, as being that of "men and women of strong, native, discriminating minds and sterling, honest hearts, who have learned what of language they know chiefly from the simple style of the Bible, and that in every day use among the laboring classes of our community."[33] So convinced was Lipscomb that the poor were fully capable (*preferentially* capable) of understanding the gospel, that in theological education his "interest [was] in seeing schools adapted to the wants of the poor, at which the humble and unpretending can be educated, without separating them, in habits and sympathy, from the poor, and in which they will be taught the principles and practices of the Christian religion in the fullness of all their parts."[34] Although it lacks an explicitly sociopolitical liberation context, Lipscomb's language is in accordance with the general idea of a greater "epistemological" and "obediential" capacity of the poor (or at least of the common people) to understand and conform to the gospel. As he wrote, "the common or laboring people . . . are most easily reached, and . . . generally make the best members when converted . . . [They] have less to hinder their obeying the gospel, and less to hinder service after they obey."[35]

The Catholic bishops at Puebla stated: "When we draw near to the poor in order to accompany them and serve them, we are doing what Christ taught us to do when he became our brother, poor like us. Hence, *service to the poor is the privileged, though not the exclusive, gauge of our following of Christ*" (emphasis added).[36] David Lipscomb's view clearly concurred with the italicized portion of the statement above. On the same issue, Lipscomb's language in the following passage is especially impressive when one remembers how *central* baptism, by immersion, for the remission of sins, is in the conservative strands of the Campbell-Stone movement.

> The man that can spend money in extending his already broad acres, while his brother and his brother's children cry for bread—the woman that can spend money in purchasing a stylish bonnet, an expensive cloak, or a fine dress, merely to appear fashionable, while her sister and her sister's children are shivering with cold and scarce able to cover their nakedness, are no Christians—have not a promise of a single blessing from God; *and not withstanding they have been baptized for the remission of sins,* may be unremitted in their attendance upon the appointments of the Lord's house, and constant and regular in their family devotions—yet they are on the broad road that leads to death.[37] (emphasis added)

Alongside his powerful exhortation to material service to the poor stands Lipscomb's insistence, again, that preaching the gospel to the poor is what best embodies the spirit of the church:

> The crowning characteristic of the Christian religion in the esteem of its founder, is that the "poor have the gospel preached to them." The church that fails to exhibit that its first, most important work is to preach the gospel to the poor, has utterly failed to appreciate the true spirit of its mission, and the character of work it was established to perform . . . The thousands of the poor in the cities and in the country, must be sought out—preached to—must have congregations whose dress, style, manners and associations will draw them to them, rather than repel them from them, and these congregations, so conforming themselves to the true spirit of the Gospel, and adapting their habits to the necessities of the poor, will alone constitute the Church of Christ.[38]

Lipscomb's last line in the above even seems to suggest that "service to the poor," at least in his sense of preaching to the poor, *is* an *exclusive* "gauge of our following of Christ." This is confirmed by his statement that "the man who refuses to bestow his goods, to sacrifice his conveniences and luxuries in order to relieve the wants of his suffering brethren and sisters, and their helpless orphans, is no Christian man, and has no more chance of Heaven than the veriest infidel in the land."[39]

Third, the Medellín conference concluded that "a poor Church is herself bound to material poverty."[40] This theme was picked up by the bishops at Puebla who called for a "Church . . . more and more independent of the powers of this world." Such a church would "rely more on the being and power of God and his grace than on 'having more' and secular authority. In this way it will present an image of being authentically poor."[41] Lipscomb's challenges to congregations relative to the "habits" and styles of their members' dress and of their worship have already been noted. He also opposed concentrating the wealth of the church in two kinds of "structures"—buildings and societies. He despaired of congregations that committed to the course of erecting elaborate buildings, saying, "when I hear of a church setting out to build a fine house, I give that church up. Its usefulness as a church of Christ is at an end."[42] In similar fashion, he saw missionary societies as leading people away from God. His main objection to the societies was that they were, in his view, a "corrupting" modification of the divinely constituted order of the church.[43] However, Lipscomb was also opposed to what he saw as the societies' tendencies toward oligarchic control by "money-loving men."[44] His preference for a church "herself bound to material poverty," in some sense, is clear in his 1897 statement:

> I am fast reaching the conclusion that there is a radical and fundamental difference between the disciples of Christ and the [missionary] society folks. These desire to build up a strong and respectable denomination. To do it they rely on strong and moneyed societies, fine houses, fashionable music, and eloquent speeches, too often devoid of gospel truth. Disciples of Christ do not wish fine houses; they wish people to come to Christ, to be saved by the truth. They do not wish any denomination or party, do not rely upon the favor of the rich or fashionable.[45]

When division became clear and an identifiable religious community commonly called the Churches of Christ emerged as separate from the remainder of the Campbell-Stone movement, it largely followed Lipscomb's lead in repudiating extraparochial Church structures. However, Lipscomb's cautionary words were not simply calling for a fully congregational polity for the church. He also was concerned about the effects of wealth upon institutions that the church might in any way sponsor or support. He remarked relative to Bible colleges:

> The rich seldom profess Christianity, and when they do, ninety-nine times out of every hundred their influence is to corrupt the church, lower the standard of morality, and relax all discipline in a church . . . My memory now fails me of a single preacher that either was rich or set his heart upon being rich, that his usefulness as a preacher was not thereby destroyed. Hundreds are ruined as preachers by riches where one is by poverty. *If riches affect individuals so deleteriously in their religious character, is there not danger of too much wealth having an injurious effect upon a school?*[46] (emphasis added)

In sum, there are several themes that have arisen in the liberation theologies of Latin America in the recent past, and in the episcopal pronouncements that have reflected—to a degree—those theologies, that are similar to pronouncements by David Lipscomb, the principal founder of a significant North American religious community—the Churches of Christ. These themes include

(1) a concern for the poor that is rooted in concrete historical and personal experience; (2) an advocacy of activity on behalf of the poor that has its basis in the teachings of the Jesus of the Gospel (Matthew 25) and in the kenosis of Christ; (3) an assumption that the poor are the fundamental historical basis of the Church; (4) a recognition of the evangelizing power of the poor; (5) an assumption that the poor are especially equipped to receive the gospel; (6) a view that service to the poor is (at least) a "privileged gauge of our following of Christ"; and (7) a conviction that the institutional church (or institutions of the church) are challenged to distance itself (themselves) from the corrupting influence of material wealth.

Of course, these common themes may not be taken as evidence that David Lipscomb was a "liberation theologian." For one thing, such a statement would be simply anachronistic. But beyond the differences in historical and cultural context, there are substantive differences between Lipscomb's and the liberationists' understanding of the Church's option for the poor.

For example, Lipscomb stands in contrast to much Latin American liberation theology in his insistence that neither the poor—*nor any Christian*—should engage in political action in order to fundamentally change the social order. He bluntly opposed political revolution:

> The Christian is to pay his taxes, and perform all duties laid upon him by the government, that involve no active support of the government, and that involve no violation of the commands of God and the spirit of the religion of Christ, as a part of his duties to God—as his religious duty. God has so ordained that he must. The cheerful performance of these duties must not depend on the character of government, nor upon his approval or disapproval of the government.
>
> Christians are to be supporters and partisans of none. Quiet submission to the requirements in all things not contrary to the will of God and then a quiet submission but persistent refusal to do the thing commanded, is the part of the Christian. A Christian can engage in active rebellion against no government. Neither active support or participation, nor active opposition.[47]

From the foregoing, it may be concluded that a kind of "passive resistance" might be permissible. But no active participation in political struggles for liberation would be countenanced in such a view. Not only did Lipscomb oppose "active rebellion," but he also was severely critical of those who "despise their own condition, are discontented with their lot, and envy those who are possessed of more of the world's goods." This attitude he characterized as "positive sin" and "a violation of the plain letter of the law of God."[48]

Clearly, the language of liberation theologian Gustavo Gutiérrez with respect to political revolution is in sharp contrast with Lipscomb's. Gutiérrez writes, "Christ's liberation is not restricted to political liberation, but it occurs in historical happenings and liberative political actions . . . It involves immersion in the political process of revolution, so that from there we may proclaim and live Christ's gratuitous and liberative love."[49] Similarly, the discontent of the poor is not condemned, but rather lifted up in the liberation theology context as one of its fundamental premises—a premise resting on God's discontent with the oppression that creates and sustains poverty. Again, in the words of Gutiérrez: "One must keep in mind that the God of the Bible is a God who not only governs history, but who orientates it in the direction of establishment of justice and right . . . He is a God who takes sides with the poor and liberates them from slavery and oppression."[50]

The contrast between Lipscomb's identification with "the people" and that of Latin American liberationists may be better understood in connection with Lipscomb's concept of the church. It is in this context that Lipscomb's rejection of "active" participation in politics may be clarified.

In 1908 Lipscomb stated his long-standing convictions:

> For fifty years I have maintained that the church of God is God's institution through which his children can do and receive all good. I have no reason to turn from this. To turn to and rely on human governments and institutions is to forsake God and to distrust his power to save . . . The question, then, is: Will the Christian do more to promote and sustain the [moral] sentiment by standing aloof from the political strifes and maintaining high moral and religious sentiment or by entering the political strifes and besmirching his garments and his character by the strifes of political partisanship? [Church historian Johann August Wilhelm] Neander says: "The Christians stood aloof from the state, as a priestly and spiritual race, and Christianity seemed able to influence civil life only in that manner, which it must be confessed is the purest, by practically endeavoring to instill more and more of the holy feeling into the citizens of the state." This is God's way for Christians to influence legislation. I believe it is the best and only way . . . Political parties come and go, earthly kingdoms rise and fall; but God remains the same yesterday, today, and forever.[51]

This was Lipscomb's characteristic stance: for Christians, the *church,* as God's institution, is to be relied on; it is sufficient to work a spiritual revolution in the lives of people that will ultimately affect the social order. Any transformation of society by Christianity will be via the vehicle of the church. Therefore, a clear conception of the proper role of the church is necessary. This, of course, was one, if not *the* major focus of the Campbell-Stone movement in the nineteenth century.

Lipscomb was clear as to the church's tasks and their relative importance:

> The first and highest object in the establishment of the Church of God on earth is . . . the perfection of [members'] own character[s] in Christian purity and holiness . . . The secondary work of the Church . . . was the relieving of the physical ills that afflict

humanity—feeding the poor, nursing the sick, caring for the orphan, visiting those that are in prison, and exhibiting a tender sympathy for the bodily ills, sorrows, misfortunes and afflictions of our fellow-creatures . . . The third design was, "for the edifying or building up of the body of Christ" . . . When the first two objects have been gained . . . but little preaching will be needed to bring them into the Kingdom of God.[52]

In other words, the church should eschew political parties, strife, and active support for or rebellion against governments and attend to its own life of cultivating personal sanctity and of giving humane attention to the afflicted. The foregoing suggests an approach that is primarily focused on the internal life of the church and on suffering individuals.

While this church-based (ecclesiocentric) and individualistic orientation is strong in Lipscomb, and although this stands in sharp contrast to Latin American liberationists like Gutiérrez, the contrast should not be overdrawn. Lipscomb did see a role for Christians in the political world: "While Christians should not engage in political questions and strifes, *they have duties to fulfill with reference to all questions that arise in society*—that is, to stand on the side of right and justice, to study the moral questions that arise in the affairs of the world, and warn as to the principles of right and justice. These, in the end, must prevail; and he who teaches these benefits humanity"[53] (emphasis added). It was in connection with this duty that Lipscomb himself engaged in some discussion of "political questions."

In the wake of the election of 1896 and its controversy over the gold standard (the election with Bryan's famous "cross of gold" speech), Lipscomb wrote in surprisingly "social" terms about socioeconomic, political polarization and impending class-based violence:

> The recent political contest . . . was the occasion of aligning the laboring people against the capitalists in a political conflict as they had never been before. This question of the money standard may never come up again, *but the alignment and contest of these parties will remain.* Both parties to the conflict have been concentrating their forces for some years past. Capital has been increasing and concentrating in fewer hands, and the capitalists have been growing into a solid body. Labor has been learning to appreciate its importance, and the laborers have been learning their strength and concentrating their power. Neither party has been always just in the conflicts, nor is either likely to be always so in the future. Capital is selfish and overbearing. It has controlled legislation in its behalf and to the injury of the laborer. Jesus Christ taught the dignity and honor of labor. He who would be greatest of all, let him be servant of all. His sympathies were with the poor, the laborer, those humble in station, not with the rich or exalted. *In the end the dignity and honor of labor must prevail and its rights be vindicated.* Those possessed of riches may deal justly and cease to legislate for capital and help labor. That is Christian, and would be wise policy, and would prevent a

violent conflict. *If they pursue a selfish course, then a violent convulsion must be the end.*[54] (emphasis added)

According to Robert Hooper, the Civil War was the "catalyst for Lipscomb's thinking" about the relationships between rich and poor and between business and politics that set the trajectory of his thought for the remainder of the century. He arrived at the view that "business interests controlled the politics of the United States." He believed that the "panics" of 1873 and 1893 were caused by the "greed of big business and the power hunger of the trusts." He came to see the American laborer as "enmeshed in a kind of slavery."[55] With this perspective, it is not surprising that "Lipscomb was fully convinced that labor 'combinations' were good and necessary for protection against monopolists and capitalist[s]—'the great oppressors of humanity.'"[56] By the closing decade of the nineteenth century, he had reached the opinion that "money is more and more becoming concentrated in the hands of the wealthy" and "is more and more becoming a controlling element in all the affairs of society." He noted, for example, that "money can thwart justice," and he saw the emergence of "mob law" as the natural outcome of such corruption: "As things go now, money accumulates on the one hand, and is overbearing and disregardful of human rights. The unmonied masses combine on the other, and, by mob law, assert their power."[57]

In spite of this "social" analysis, Lipscomb did not conclude that the church should enter into political contests on the side of the poor or the laboring class. He saw the solution to such problems as going in the opposite direction—not that the church should enter into social struggles but rather that those "struggling" should be drawn into the church. Therefore, Lipscomb's was *not* a concept of "integral liberation" in which God and God's church are linked to the organized struggle of the oppressed. He did not see that as the vocation of the church.[58] However, given his doctrine of church, it is noteworthy that he would recognize "class conflict," acclaim the "rights of labor" as linked to Jesus' teaching, and associate money with injustice.

Another area where Lipscomb's view of the poor contrasts with that of the liberation-oriented Latin American Catholic theologians is in Lipscomb's willingness to make moral distinctions among the poor and assert: "There is a species of poverty that has never been honored of God—that is a crime in the sight of God—and that justly deserves to be stamped with disgrace and infamy by men. It is that poverty, want and penury that is brought about by idleness, debauchery and crime."[59] On the other hand, Lipscomb could make poverty into a kind of virtue. His understanding of poverty was not exclusively as a "spiritual poverty" (as in "the poor in spirit"). He was acquainted, as has been shown, with actual, historical, material poverty. But Lipscomb did promote what has recently been called "another kind of spiritualization: that of calling upon the poor to be satisfied with their state . . . of privilege in God's sight."[60] Of course, this observation must be softened by the reminder that such "spiritualization" did not relieve the church from service to the poor, nor did it imply that the principal basis of the church was other than the *materially* poor. But it is consistent with Lipscomb's general perspective of not seeing oppression as primarily a social, structural, and, *as such,* spiritual problem against which God acts in solidarity with the oppressed *in the world.*

After all, in Lipscomb's view this world was "the world from which God delivered us through Christ."[61] His theology was primarily a "theology of otherworldliness," even though it included a concern for the spiritual transformation of people in this world.[62] This "otherworldliness" is reflected in those areas where the contrast between Lipscomb's and Latin American Catholic liberations' views of the church and the poor are sharpest—in Lipscomb's aversion to political *action* by Christians (beyond allowable "study" and "warning"), his condemnation of the discontent of the poor, and his moralizing categorization of different "species" of poverty—the "disgraceful" versus the "spiritually" virtuous.

In spite of these very significant differences from much of contemporary liberation theology, and in spite of the radically different social, historical, and cultural contexts from which Lipscomb's and the liberationists' theologies arose, David Lipscomb sounded several themes that are in harmony with the recent call for a "preferential option for the poor." The resonance between Lipscomb's writings on this issue and the contemporary theological concern is sufficient to warrant a fresh examination of, and perhaps reappropriation of, these themes by North American Christians who value the heritage of David Lipscomb. This process might contribute to North American efforts to recognize a "preferential option for the poor" within their own cultural and religious heritage and through that recognition move closer to understanding that "option" as it is being advocated globally and ecumenically.[63]

NOTES

1. Second General Conference of Latin American Bishops, *The Church in the Present-Day Transformation of Latin America in the Light of the Council,* vol. 2, *Conclusions,* 2d ed. (Washington, D.C.: Division for Latin American-USCC, 1973), 33, 36.

2. John Eagleson and Philip Scharper, eds., *Puebla and Beyond: Documentation and Commentary,* John Drury, trans. (Maryknoll, N.Y.: Orbis Books, 1979), 264–66. As my quotation from these episcopal documents indicates, I am defining "Latin American Catholic liberation theology" loosely enough to include both the Medellín *Conclusions* and the Puebla document on "A Preferential Option for the Poor" within its orbit. The association

of the Medellín conference with liberation theology is, I think, quite defensible. The case for making the same association with the Puebla conference is weaker. However, I will draw mainly from Puebla's "Preferential Option" document, which has been interpreted by liberationists as in essential continuity with Medellín (see Gustavo Gutiérrez, *The Power of the Poor in History*, Robert R. Barr, trans. [Maryknoll, N.Y.: Orbis Books, 1983], 125–65). The "grassroots communities" mentioned here are the *comunidades eclesiales de base*. These are also called "base Christian communities," "basic ecclesial communities," "Grass-roots church communities," etc.

3. See, e.g., Gutiérrez, *Power of the Poor in History*, esp. 3–22.

4. Robert McAfee Brown, "The Significance of Puebla for the Protestant Churches in North America," in Eagleson and Scharper, *Puebla and Beyond*, 343. Elsewhere Brown himself has identified aspects of the "national song" of the United States that might be in harmony with the "key" of liberation theology. His examples reflect, for the most part, harmony on the central theme of socioeconomic and political liberation. I have chosen, in this work, to pursue similarities of focus that arise in the ecclesiastical and biblical (texts and themes) arenas more narrowly construed. (*Theology in a New Key: Responding to Liberation Themes* [Philadelphia: Westminster Press, 1978], 143–46).

5. David Edwin Harrell Jr., *A Social History of the Disciples of Christ*, vol. 1, *Quest for a Christian America: The Disciples of Christ and American Society to 1866* (Nashville: Disciples of Christ Historical Society, 1966), 79.

6. It has also been argued, in quite a different context, that "relative poverty may be more significant socially than absolute poverty" (Caroline Hodges Persell, *Understanding Society: An Introduction to Sociology* [New York: Harper & Row, 1984], 255). See also note 8 below; David Edwin Harrell Jr., *A Social History of the Disciples of Christ*, vol. 2, *The Social Sources of Division in the Disciples of Christ, 1865–1900* (Atlanta and Athens, Ga.: Publishing Systems Inc., 1973), 334–40.

7. Earl Irvin West, *The Life and Times of David Lipscomb* (Henderson, Tenn.: Religious Book Service, 1954), 7; on the importance of Lipscomb, see also Robert Eugene Hooper, *A Call to Remember* (Nashville: Gospel Advocate Co., 1977), 31.

8. Richard T. Hughes, "The Editor-Bishop: David Lipscomb and the *Gospel Advocate*," in *The Power of the Press: Studies of the Gospel Advocate, the Christian Standard and the Christian-Evangelist*, ed. Richard T. Hughes, Henry E. Webb, and Howard E. Short (Forrest F. Reed Lectures for 1986; Nashville: Disciples of Christ Historical Society, 1987), 23. I am indebted to Professor Hughes for alerting me to Lipscomb's general identification with the common people. The same theme is treated in some detail in the chapter "The Cry of the Poor" in Robert E. Hooper's *Crying in the Wilderness: A Biography of David Lipscomb* (Nashville: David Lipscomb College, 1979), 222–34. On the current geographic distribution of the Churches of Christ, see Wade Clark Roof and William McKinney, *American Religion: Its Changing Shape and Future* (New Brunswick and London: Rutgers Univ. Press, 1987), 136, 312. Part of Lipscomb's rhetoric about the poor and especially about the laborer must be seen in the context of that of the "greenbackers and freesilverites of the middle and late 1870s" and

of the Populists of the 1890s. As was the case for Lipscomb to some degree, in the writings of these groups, "the primacy of producers . . . was a constantly recurring idea" (Walter T. K. Nugent, *From Centennial to World War: American Society, 1876–1917*, The History of American Society Series, ed. Jack P. Green [Indianapolis: Bobbs-Merrill Co., 1977], 101). The regional identification of David Lipscomb is an important point relative to his perspective on poverty. Although there is considerable controversy surrounding the causes of poverty in the southern United States in the years between the Civil War and World War I, there is little doubt of the *fact* of poverty in that region in those years. Harold D. Woodman has provided a good review of the diverse economic-historical interpretations of the post–Civil War South in "Sequel to Slavery: The New History Views the Postbellum South," *Journal of Southern History* 63, no. 4 (Nov. 1977): 523–54. Woodman observes that "the masses of white population who never owned slaves were . . . undergoing a momentous process of social change for which they had little experience. Hill-country whites, who had been largely self-sufficient yeomen, were being transformed into commercial farmers. Like the former slaves [white yeomen] borrowed from local merchants to whom they gave crop liens, but they also secured their loans with mortgages on their lands. In the process, many lost their lands and came to occupy a status little different from that of the blacks" (552). In the years between the Civil War and World War I, there emerged "a special southern form of wage laborer" based on "share wages" and a resurrected form of the plantation modeled after the "large-scale, thoroughly capitalistic farm." The working class, "divided by racial antagonisms, failed to cooperate either in unions or in lasting political alliances." Furthermore, "disenfranchisement laws prevented political activity by virtually all the black and large sections of the poor white population. Planter capitalists, along with merchants and textile and other manufacturers enjoyed a kind of unfettered capitalism . . . The majority of the population—and hence the South as a whole—remained poor" (553). Even if one rejects Woodman's analysis, the fact of poverty in the post–Civil War South remains clear. The interpretation of Robert Higgs, for example, which sets out to correct "exaggerated" accounts of the "problems of Southern development," nonetheless concedes that "Southern income levels remained substantially below those elsewhere [in the United States] throughout the post–Civil War era." Furthermore, even during the period between 1880 and 1900, when the rate of growth in southern incomes kept pace with the nation as a whole, "the *absolute* difference between Southern and non-Southern income levels became wider." Despite a narrowing of this gap between 1900 and 1920, Higgs concludes his discussion recognizing a "relative poverty of the South in the post–Civil War era—and indeed right up to the present day" (*The Transformation of the American Economy, 1865–1914: An Essay in Interpretation*, The Wiley Series in American Economic History, ed. Ralph L. Andreano [New York: John Wiley & Sons, 1971], 108, 110, 114). With this perspective, it is perhaps not crucial to distinguish between "the poor" and "the common people." However, David Lipscomb does sometimes make a distinction between "poverty" and "a moderate competence." This is not consistent and Lipscomb uses phrases like "honest, industrious, independent poverty and toil" to represent a kind of ideal (D. L. [David Lipscomb], "Who Are to Blame?" *Gospel Advocate* 11 [May 6, 1869]: 422, 425).

9. Gustavo Gutiérrez, "Liberation Praxis and Christian Faith," *Frontiers of Theology in Latin America*, ed. Rosino Gibellini, trans. John Drury (Maryknoll, N.Y.: Orbis Books, 1979), 23; West, *David Lipscomb*, 112–15; Hooper, *Crying in the Wilderness*, 230.

10. D. L. [David Lipscomb], *Gospel Advocate* 8, no. 3 (Jan. 16, 1866): 46.

11. West, *David Lipscomb*, 114.

12. D. L. [David Lipscomb], "A Word to Our Southern Brethren," *Gospel Advocate* 8, no. 48 (Nov. 27, 1866): 758.

13. For an expression of these themes from the perspective of liberation theology, see Jon Sobrino, *The True Church and the Poor*, Matthew J. O'Connell, trans. (Maryknoll, N.Y.: Orbis Books, 1984), 137, 150, 152.

14. D. L. [David Lipscomb], "Aid to Christians in Need—How Shall It Be Administered?" *Gospel Advocate* 12, no. 11 (Mar. 17, 1870): 253.

15. D. L. [David Lipscomb], "The Destitute South," *Gospel Advocate* 9, no. 9 (Feb. 28, 1867): 171–72.

16. Sobrino, *The True Church*, 92, 135; D. L. [David Lipscomb], "New Publications," *Gospel Advocate* 8, no. 1 (Jan. 1, 1866): 11.

17. Lipscomb, "Who Are to Blame?" 422.

18. Eagleson and Scharper, *Puebla and Beyond*, 265–66.

19. West, *David Lipscomb*, 130–33.

20. David Lipscomb, "Societies and the Gospel Advocate," in *Queries and Answers by David Lipscomb*, 5th ed., J. W. Shepherd, ed. (Nashville: Gospel Advocate Co., 1963), 392; D. L. [David Lipscomb], "Mr. Brown's Article on Interest," *Gospel Advocate* 10, no. 36 (Sept. 3, 1868): 841. In contrast to what he viewed as the futility of "devising ways and schemes for raising money to hire men to preach," Lipscomb told the story of Madison Love: "While wise, learned men have been philosophising as to the impracticability of reaching men in the extreme South without a large amount of money, a poor shingle-maker from Tennessee . . . was guided by the hand of God to the extreme southern coast of our land, where, to an honest, simple-hearted people, he spoke the word of life . . . A human society would never have done this work. Your 'sensible plans' would have sought the chief cities and influential centres, and have squandered money and time in seeking the influential, while God guided his servant to his chosen—the poor . . . [Love] was not old when he died; he had baptized over five thousand persons with his own hands" (D. L. [David Lipscomb], "Response" [to Thomas Munnell], *Gospel Advocate* 9, no. 13 [Mar. 28, 1867]: 250).

21. D. L. [David Lipscomb], "A Visit to Chattanooga," *Gospel Advocate* 21, no. 14 (Apr. 3, 1889): 214.

22. D. L. [David Lipscomb], "The Churches across the Mountains," *Gospel Advocate* 39, no. 1 (Jan. 7, 1897): 4; Lipscomb, "Visit to Chattanooga," 214.

23. Second General Conference of Latin American Bishops, *Conclusions*, 188, 180.

24. Ibid., 193.

25. D. L. [David Lipscomb], "Educated Preachers," *Gospel Advocate* 8, no. 1 (Jan. 1, 1866): 175.

452   David Lipscomb and the "Preferential Option for the Poor"

26. Lipscomb, *Gospel Advocate* 8 (1866): 47.

27. D. L. [David Lipscomb], "What Callings Are Proper for Christians," *Gospel Advocate* 11, no. 6 (Feb. 11, 1869): 122. Lipscomb's view of Scripture convinced him of "a preference of the Holy Spirit for those [callings] which require physical, muscular toil." Even though he admitted that the more important point was that work must be honest and an influence for good, he nonetheless thought it "a sad omen for the religious and moral well-being of a church or community, to see a general disposition to avoid the callings demanding manual labor" (122). Lipscomb did not abandon this thesis. A generation later he wrote: "Manual labor is the labor taught in the Bible. Study, thought, and learning are desirable and helpful in directing manual labor; but the labor is the important thing for the healthy development and well-being of the man, morally, mentally, and physically . . . The laboring man and woman constitute the foundation (D. L. [David Lipscomb], "Manual Labor Good for Man," *Gospel Advocate* 66, no. 49 [Dec. 3, 1904]: 777).

28. Lipscomb, "New Publications," 11.

29. The first phrase is, according to Deane William Ferm, Hugh Assmann's (*Third World Liberation Theologies: An Introductory Survey* [Maryknoll, N.Y.: Orbis Books, 1986], 33); the second phrase is from the Puebla document "A Preferential Option for the Poor" (Eagleson and Scharper, *Puebla and Beyond,* 265); the third is from the Medellín conference (Second General Conference of Latin American Bishops, *Conclusions,* 190).

30. Ferm, *Third World Liberation Theologies,* 33.

31. Sobrino, *The True Church,* 140.

32. D. L. [David Lipscomb], *Gospel Advocate* 8, no. 9 (Feb. 27, 1866): 142.

33. Lipscomb, "New Publications," 11.

34. D. L. [David Lipscomb], "Our Educational Prospects and Difficulties," *Gospel Advocate* 8, no. 15 (Apr. 10, 1866): 235.

35. Lipscomb, "Churches across the Mountains," 4. It is clearer that Lipscomb's view does affirm both the "common" person's greater "epistemological" and "obediential" capacities when one bears in mind that, at least in part, the phrase "obeying the gospel" functions idiomatically in Lipscomb's religious community to refer especially to submitting to baptism by immersion upon confession of faith in Jesus Christ. See, for example, David Lipscomb, "What Constitutes Acceptable Obedience," in *Salvation from Sin,* J. W. Shepherd, ed. (Nashville: Gospel Advocate Co., 1950), 208–30.

36. Eagleson and Scharper, *Puebla and Beyond,* 265.

37. Lipscomb, "The Destitute South," 172.

38. D. L. [David Lipscomb], "The Spirit of the Church," *Gospel Advocate* 8, no. 7 (Feb. 13, 1866): 107–8.

39. Lipscomb, "The Destitute South," 171.

40. Second General Conference of Latin American Bishops, *Conclusions,* 190.

41. Eagleson and Scharper, *Puebla and Beyond,* 140, 267.

42. D. L.[David Lipscomb], "Fine Houses for Worship," *Gospel Advocate* 39, no. 4 (Jan. 28, 1892): 52. Compare the following statement by the bishops at Medellín: "Many

causes have contributed to create [an] . . . impression of a rich hierarchical Church. The great buildings, the rectories and religious houses that are better than those of the neighbor . . . have been some of those causes" (Second General Conference of Latin American Bishops, *Conclusions*, 188).

43. D. L. [David Lipscomb], "Human Societies Lead from God," *Gospel Advocate* 50, no. 49 (Dec. 3, 1908): 776.

44. Lipscomb, "Societies and the Gospel Advocate," 392.

45. Lipscomb, "Churches across the Mountains," 4.

46. Lipscomb, "Educational Prospects and Difficulties," 233–34.

47. David Lipscomb, *Civil Government: Its Origin, Mission, and Destiny, and the Christian's Relation to It* (Nashville: McQuiddy Printing Co., 1913), 132–33.

48. Lipscomb also commends the Christian religion for making people happy, "not by changing their lot" but by "making them content in their position." (Lipscomb, "Who Are to Blame?" 425).

49. Gustavo Gutiérrez, "Liberation Praxis and Christian Faith," 23–24.

50. Gutiérrez, *Power of the Poor in History*, 7.

51. D. L. [David Lipscomb], "Christians in Politics," *Gospel Advocate* 50, no. 23 (June 4, 1908): 361; Lipscomb's approving quotation of Neander is significant: "Neander's conception of the history of the church was that of a divine life gaining increasing control over the lives of men. That life is manifested in individuals . . . [This conception's] weaknesses were its overemphasis on the influence of individuals and its scanty appreciation of the institutional or corporate life of the church." (Williston Walker et al., *A History of the Christian Church*, 4th ed. [New York: Charles Scribner's Sons, 1985], 634–35).

52. D. L. [David Lipscomb], "Objects to Be Accomplished by a Church," *Gospel Advocate* 10, no. 47 (Nov. 19, 1868): 2007, 2009. It is noteworthy that the ministry to the poor is *not* confined to the poor *of the Church*. See also D. L. [David Lipscomb], "Shall Christians Administer to the Alien?" *Gospel Advocate* 10, no. 44 (Oct. 29, 1868): 1049. Lipscomb's attitudes were reflected both in his pacifism during the Civil War and in his recommendations relative to the freed slaves after the Civil War. That is, it was to be through the church and not through politics that the Black former slaves were to be helped (Hooper, *Call to Remember*, 60–62). Consistent with his overall theology was Lipscomb's view that racial discrimination within the church was far less tolerable than social and political discrimination (62–66).

53. D. L. [David Lipscomb], "Some Thoughts Suggested by the Political Contest," *Gospel Advocate* 38, no. 45 (Nov. 12, 1896): 724.

54. Ibid.

55. Hooper, *Crying in the Wilderness*, 230–32.

56. Harrell, *Social History of the Disciples*, 2:132.

57. D. L. [David Lipscomb], "Mob Law," *Gospel Advocate* 34, no. 22 (June 2, 1892): 340.

58. *Integral liberation* has been a controversial term. The understanding of it embraced by Gutiérrez would be that it refers to "the totality and complexity of the liberation

process." This includes "economic liberation, social liberation, political liberation, liberation of the human being from all manner of servitude, liberation from sin and communion with God as the ultimate basis of a human community of brothers and sisters." Gutiérrez sees this understanding of "integral liberation" as underlying the Puebla documents (*Power of the Poor in History,* 144–48).

59. Lipscomb, "Who Are to Blame?" 422. In spite of this statement, Lipscomb sometimes seemed to have agreed with the position of the bishops at Puebla that "the poor merit preferential attention, whatever may be the moral or personal situation in which they find themselves" (Eagleson and Scharper, *Puebla and Beyond,* 265). See, for example, D. L. [David Lipscomb], "Preaching to the Poor," *Gospel Advocate* 15, no. 17 (Apr. 24, 1873): 390–91.

60. This phrase is from Elsa Tamez. Of course, she was not referring to David Lipscomb but to the general danger of such a spiritualization. For Lipscomb, *both* material poverty (understood not as "destitution" but as a "modest competency") *and* the privilege of the poor in God's sight are idealized ("Good News for the Poor," in *Third World Liberation Theologies: A Reader,* ed. Deane William Ferm [Maryknoll, N.Y.: Orbis Books, 1986], 195; Lipscomb, "Who Are to Blame?" 422–24). Gutiérrez's approach to synthesizing material and spiritual understandings of poverty through "solidarity and protest" is most clearly distinguishable from Lipscomb's in the area of "protest" (*Theology of Liberation,* 299–302).

61. Lipscomb, "Christians in Politics," 361.

62. Harrell, *Social History of the Disciples,* 2:134.

63. The writer gratefully acknowledges the assistance of William R. Barr (professor of theology), Michael Kinnamon (dean), and Sharyn Dowd (associate professor of the New Testament) of Lexington Theological Seminary in the preparation of this article. This research was presented, in abbreviated form, to both the faculty of Lexington Theological Seminary and the Evangelical Theology group of the American Academy of Religion. The helpful responses of both of these groups are appreciated. Portions of this essay appeared as "David Lipscomb on the Church and the Poor," in *Restoration Quarterly* 33 (second quarter 1991): 75–85, and are reprinted here with the permission of the publisher.

Disciples of Christ Pacifism in Nineteenth-Century Tennessee

David Edwin Harrell Jr.

One of the new religious groups spawned by the religious ferment in the early-nineteenth-century American West was the Disciples of Christ. Biblical literalists with a gigantic faith, the early Disciples reformers' aim was "the restoration of the Ancient Gospel," and their central plea was "to speak where the Bible speaks and be silent where the Bible is silent." They fervently believed that they had found the long-sought platform for Christian unity. By the early 1830s the Disciples of Christ had emerged as an independent denomination, and under the capable and energetic leadership of the Bethany, Virginia, preacher, debater, and editor Alexander Campbell, they made startling numerical gains from 1830 to 1860. On the eve of the Civil War the church had a membership of well over 200,000.[1]

After the war the movement continued its rapid growth. By 1880 the number of Disciples exceeded half a million, and by the first decade of the twentieth century the church had well over a million members.[2] Hundreds of religious periodicals and scores of large and small educational institutions promoted the cause. Although the Disciples were never strongly centralized in the nineteenth century (there was a persistent minority within the church that opposed any organization above the congregational level), a national missionary society was formed in 1849. In the years after the Civil War, strengthening the organizational union of the church became one of the major aims of many of the group's leaders.

The Disciples early made significant progress in Tennessee. Alexander Campbell made several preaching tours of the state; a number of prominent Tennessee Baptist clergymen were early converts to the cause; and by 1860 the Disciples had more than one hundred congregations and an estimated membership of around fifteen thousand in the state.[3] A group of Middle Tennessee preachers that included Philip Fall and Tolbert Fanning were nationally important leaders in antebellum Disciples history.

In 1880 there were about three hundred Disciples churches in Tennessee with nearly forty thousand members; by 1916 the movement claimed well over eighty thousand members in the state.[4] During the postbellum period the most powerful church leader in the state was unquestionably the protégé of Tolbert Fanning, David Lipscomb. Lipscomb, as editor of the influential Nashville paper the *Gospel Advocate,* had an enormous impact on the history of the Disciples in the South during the half century after the end of the war.

The growth of the Disciples of Christ from 1830 to 1900 was not accomplished without the development of serious internal tensions. The loose-knit movement was repeatedly shaken by divisive problems—the slavery question, diverging sectional economic patterns, the Civil War, and diverse and incompatible theological emphases. During the fervent early years of the movement these schismatic tendencies were blurred by enthusiasm and the primary concern of church leaders with the sins of others, but by 1850 it was obvious that a crisis was developing within the church. The Disciples had no authoritative organization to pronounce the church divided, and nominally they remained united until the religious census of 1906 separately listed the Disciples of Christ and the Church of Christ; but in actual fact the lines of the division had been hardening for decades. The doctrinal basis of the division was the objection of Church of Christ leaders to organized missionary societies, the use of instrumental music in worship, and a number of similar "innovations."[5]

The causes of the Disciples schism are complex: theological motivations were intricately interwoven with sociological factors. However involved the causes of the division may be, it is obvious from a cursory investigation of census returns that the rupture was decidedly sectional in character. According to the religious census of 1916, the Disciples of Christ had a membership of 1,226,028, while the Church of Christ had only 317,937. In the former slave states, however, Disciples membership totaled only 485,740, over half of which was in the two border states of Kentucky and Missouri. On the other hand, 246,553 of the Church of Christ members were in the former slave states. In Tennessee, the Disciples listed 21,672 members, while the Church of Christ claimed 63,521.[6] While there is no simple explanation for these statistics, the influence of such Middle Tennessee preachers as Fall, Fanning, and Lipscomb, and their doctrine of Christian pacifism, is unquestionably an important and long unappreciated factor.

The first practical test of Disciples' reactions to the war question came with the outbreak of the Mexican War in May 1846. Although scattered Disciples throughout the nation had given some notice to the budding peace movement during the early years of the century, church leaders demonstrated little sustained interest in the subject until the beginning of hostilities with Mexico.[7]

In general, the reaction of American churches to the Mexican War reflected the geographic distribution of their membership.[8] The most vigorous protests against the war came from the Northeast. On the other hand: "No church with its members concentrated in the Southwest or with a strong stake there opposed the war."[9] The Disciples of Christ generally followed this pattern. While most church leaders in the North denounced the war in uncompromising terms, a number of southern preachers defended it as a struggle to free the oppressed people of Mexico from Catholic despotism and to fulfill the providential destiny of the United States.[10]

The most significant exception to this sectional pattern was the uncompromising antiwar stand taken by the influential Tennessean Tolbert Fanning. Fanning militantly condemned the struggle as a violation of Christian ethics. Although he was cautioned repeatedly by other Tennessee church leaders of the unpopularity of his views, the outspoken preacher firmly stood his ground to the end of the war.[11]

While the Mexican War initiated considerable discussion of the whole war question, agitation of the issue soon subsided. Unquestionably the most significant development during the brotherhood debate had been the prophetic stand of Fanning. In the crucial decade that followed the Mexican War, Tolbert Fanning, more than any other man, trained the corps of Disciples preachers who dominated the church in Tennessee, and much of the lower South, for the next half century. The Tennessee editor's pacifist pronouncements during the popular Mexican War were a solid foundation for the later militant pacifism of church leaders in the state.

As the national crisis of 1861 approached, the Disciples of Christ, with large interests in both North and South, was by no means united. The same potent complex of forces that divided every major intersectional Protestant denomination was at work within the Disciples. As the cries of prophets of peace were slowly overwhelmed by the crescendo of galloping hoofs, clattering caissons, and bellowing demagogues—the sounds of a nation converging on Bull Run—most young Disciples packed their Bibles into saddlebags and rode off to do homage before the altar of Mars. For the next four years Disciples North and Disciples South prayed and preached as they fought and died.

There were two significant groups within the church, however, that persistently worked for peace. One group of antiwar Disciples was composed of practical neutralists—men who were not opposed to war in general but to the Civil War in particular. The border states of Kentucky and Missouri were Disciples strongholds on the eve of the Civil War, and many of the church leaders in these areas, along with some in both the North and South, repeatedly denounced the fratricidal war and encouraged church members in both sections to remain neutral.[12]

There was also a significant number of doctrinaire pacifists within the church. While Disciples pacifists were not confined to any one section, the most solid core of conscientious objectors was in Middle Tennessee. In the vanguard of the peace movement in Tennessee in 1861 was Tolbert Fanning. In spite of his strong stand, Fanning's school, Franklin College, was soon almost deserted as his students poured into the mushrooming volunteer regiments of the Confederate army. The aging teacher's college soon closed, but Fanning continued to preach his views in the churches of Middle Tennessee.[13]

Equally as important as Fanning's stand was that of his brother-in-law, Philip Fall, minister of the leading Christian church in Nashville. Soon after the beginning of hostilities, Fall announced that he would not "think of taking up arms against his brethren in Christ who live on Either side" and urged the members of his congregation to "stand aloof from this controversy."[14] On June 13, 1861, a day set aside for prayer and religious services by Confederate president Jefferson Davis, Fall refused to open the church building, much to the chagrin of the more ardent secessionists within the congregation.[15] The widely respected minister was never partisan in his actions, however, and in April 1863, when the Federal commander of Nashville issued orders that all white persons over eighteen must take an oath to be "quiet and peaceable citizens of the United States," Fall petitioned for exemption from the oath. He wrote the officer: "An Apostle has said when repeating the words of the Messiah: 'But above all things my brethren, swear not: neither Heaven, nor by earth, *nor by any other oath*' . . . With this authority before me I do not feel at liberty to take the oath of allegiance *now* required."[16] Fall staunchly maintained his position of nonintervention in civil affairs throughout the war, and his enormous influence unquestionably affected the course of the church in Middle Tennessee.

While the stand of such venerated patriarchs as Fanning and Fall was important, the Civil War pacifist attack in Tennessee was led by a group of fervent and vocal young preachers. The troop included O. T. Craig, Robert B. Trimble, and Elisha G. Sewell, but the impassioned leader was David Lipscomb.[17] In 1860 Lipscomb began preaching "all through Middle Tennessee that it was wrong for Christians to go to war, or to encourage the war spirit in others."[18] According to Sewell, who later coedited the *Gospel Advocate* with Lipscomb for nearly half a century, Lipscomb was the first preacher in Tennessee publicly to take this position.[19] Lipscomb was warned repeatedly by his friends that it was dangerous to preach such views. On one occasion, after Lipscomb had preached a pacifist sermon, a distraught listener proposed that if twelve men would join him, they would hang the preacher. Lipscomb was certainly not one to be intimidated, however, and, in spite of a number of harrowing experiences, he preached his pacifist doctrine throughout the war and never was harmed physically.[20]

Sewell reports that Lipscomb's work had considerable effect on the church in Middle Tennessee: "Other preachers fell in line, and many of the members saw at once the scripturalness of the position, adopted it, talked it, preached it publicly in the congregations, advocated it everywhere, and firmly stood by it to the end of the conflict."[21] Early in the war a number of Middle Tennessee church leaders petitioned the Confederate officer who was "head and superintendent of the conscript business in Middle Tennessee" for exemption from service because of their religious convictions. Their plea was courteously received and several Disciples conscientious objectors who had been drafted were released from service.[22] Later, when the state came under Federal control, Lipscomb, Sewell, and Trimble personally presented a similar petition to Gov. Andrew Johnson. The document was signed by evangelists from "ten or fifteen" Middle Tennessee congregations in the "counties of Davidson, Williamson, Maury, Hickman, and many scattered through other counties of Middle Tennessee."[23] Sewell writes that after Governor Johnson read the report, he said: "Gentlemen, I think you need not be uneasy. I do not think anybody will be hurt."[24] Lipscomb also reports that the petition was effective: "This document . . . was the means of saving all those members of the church who would take this position . . . and stand firmly to it, from service in the war."[25]

It is difficult to assess the impact of the Tennessee pacifist leaders' work on the churches of the state. Although there were many Disciples in the section who joined in the fight, there are indications that a considerable number of church members shared the pacifist views of their leaders. Sewell summarized: "The churches were much weakened by many of their members going into the conflict, leaving vacant seats in their weekly assemblies . . . But while these things abounded and many fell away, it is refreshing to know that in almost every congregation, even in the very hottest of the varied conflicts, there were some brethren and sisters of such strong faith and so earnestly devoted to the will of God that they stood firm to the truth."[26] Lipscomb's estimate of pacifist strength in Tennessee was even more optimistic: "Among the disciples, the churches, and especially the preachers in Tennessee, had kept more out of the war than other religious people."[27]

The motivation for Disciples pacifism during the Civil War was at least twofold. Some church leaders were doctrinal pacifists in the full stream of the left-wing Protestant tradition of noninvolvement in civil affairs. David Lipscomb fully elaborated his left-wing philosophy in the years after the Civil War; his book *Civil Government* is the best doctrinal statement of the southern Disciples pacifist position.

The influential editor carefully and concisely summed up his views in his brief book:

1. God created man as his own servant, to govern and control him; and in pursuance of this design has at all times kept in existence a government of his own . . .

2. That institution gave room for no human legislation . . .
3. Man, in the spirit of rebellion against God . . . instituted governments of his own, and those governments in their changing forms have existed from the days of Nimrod to the present time.
4. God, from its beginning, recognized this human government as rebellion against him . . .
5. Regarding them thus, God always forbade that his subjects should join affinity or affiliate with the subjects of human government, or that they should make any alliance with, enter into, support, maintain and defend, or appeal to, or depend upon, these human governments for aid or help.
6. That alliances with these human governments . . . were sins against God, and without exception were punished. That these alliances were sources of corruption to the children of God, weaned them from God . . . and from fidelity to his appointments . . .
8. That God ordained the human government to punish those who rebelled against his government . . .
9. The builders, rulers, and supporters of these governments were wicked, rebellious men . . .
10. God's government was his medium for receiving the service of loyal children, and was his instrumentality through which he bestowed blessings upon them . . .
12. The government of God and those of man were antagonistic and rivals of each other, each contending for the rule and dominion of the world. Between them there was an irrepressible conflict."[28]

Lipscomb's pointed conclusion: "They [early Christians] paid taxes and treated human rulers with respect, when they did not interfere with their duty to God . . . They showed in this that they were subjects of the kingdom of God and only in a secondary sense of a human ruler."[29]

Not long after the close of the war the Tennessee pacifists were saddled with an entirely different motive by the Disciples of the North who had supported the Union war effort. Southern Disciples deeply resented the wartime actions of their northern brethren; especially obnoxious to them was the action taken by the church's only national organization, the American Christian Missionary Society. In the 1863 meeting of the society in Cincinnati, a group of militant northern preachers engineered the passage of a resolution affirming the convention's support of the Union cause. In 1866 a disgruntled Georgia preacher wrote a prophetic protest in which conservative theology, pacifist conviction, and sectional prejudice were inseparably intermingled: "We hear that the brotherhood formed societies, and organizations, unscriptural in name, and without precedent in the word of the Lord.—And in this zeal for God (which I fear is not according to knowledge,) they have passed sundry resolutions of a political character and import, maintaining that men may fight and kill each other, that Christian men may go to war."[30]

In January 1866, the Nashville *Gospel Advocate,* which had been published as a monthly before the war, was revived as a weekly under the editorship of Tolbert Fanning and David Lipscomb. The rejuvenated paper quickly became the center of southern pacifist protest against the wartime actions of the church in the North. Within a few months Lipscomb was engaged in an editorial battle with the leading northern Disciples editor, Isaac Errett, whose Cincinnati paper, the *Christian Standard,* was founded in 1866 by a group of prowar churchmen that included among its members the Ohio congressman and former general James A. Garfield.[31] After some spirited sparring, the northern editor bluntly charged that most southern pacifists were not motivated by the Scriptures: "With many, this [pacifism] is a new-born faith, unknown before the recent civil war, and chiefly prevailing among those who were in sympathy with a lost cause."[32] Errett bitterly denounced Lipscomb's apparent attempts to use sectional prejudice to line up support for his conservative theology: "We have no doubt that our good brother of the *Advocate* imagines himself entirely free from political bias in this matter. We question not his motives. But we are frank to say that the course of the *Advocate* has not carried conviction to us of its freedom from political bias. It commenced its new issue with an appeal to men of southern blood, and proposed cooperation among them only. It has constantly denounced the brethren of the North who shared in the military defense of the government . . . We seriously do not think that these facts furnish evidence of freedom from political bias, or superlative devotion to religious interests."[33] The *Advocate-Standard* debate continued with increasing bitterness and misunderstanding until finally in 1868 it was broken off by Errett, with each editor convinced that the other was trying to establish a sectional party within the church. In the years that followed the charge that Lipscomb and other Tennessee preachers were attempting "to run a Mason and Dixon line through the Bible and the Church of Christ" became commonplace.[34]

The Disciples of Christ–Church of Christ division of the late nineteenth century was deeply affected by this acrid controversy. Lipscomb's militant pacifism was attractive in the post–Civil War South, and the wily editor refused to let his southern readers forget that northern church leaders had "supported the government in its war."[35] Whether pacifists or not, most Tennessee Disciples approved of Lipscomb's attacks on northern preachers. While many other factors were involved, it is safe to say that the pacifism-sectionalism emphasis of the *Gospel Advocate* contributed potently to the growth of the Church of Christ in Tennessee.

It is not so obvious that the continued emphasis of the *Gospel Advocate* on doctrinaire pacifism in the postbellum period was of major importance.

Lipscomb continued to write on the subject frequently. He believed that "these questions ought to be discussed at any and all times"; he reminded his readers that during the Civil War the government had been unreceptive to the appeals of many conscientious objectors because they had not earlier "let their faith be known."[36]

Lipscomb had little use for the organized peace movements that flowered after 1866. When a North Carolina Disciples minister, John T. Walsh, notified the *Advocate* office that he had been appointed an agent for the American Peace Society and solicited the Tennessee editor's aid, Lipscomb curtly replied that he had "no faith in any peace organization." "Some of the bitterest war men in the land," wrote Lipscomb, "are leaders of this peace association."[37] The embittered southerner was not interested in accepting pacifist leadership from men who a few years before had been ardent advocates of war. Lipscomb also had theological reasons for not supporting the organized peace movement. He was opposed to all "moral societies"; he insisted that the "church of the living God" was the only organization that could promote peace and warned that "a Christian is wasting time in seeking peace for the world in other institutions."[38]

But if the *Advocate* ignored the organized peace movement, the paper was never very long without a pacifist article. Throughout the decades of the seventies and eighties such prominent Tennessee preachers as Lipscomb, Sewell, John T. Poe, Justus M. Barnes, and Fletcher D. Srygley kept up a steady stream of antiwar articles. They twitted the northern Disciples, who in these decades became rabid supporters of the organized peace movement, for their recent conversion,[39] wrote long biblical apologies,[40] condemned veterans' rallies in both the North and South,[41] and in general defended the traditional left-wing position of the paper.

During the bellicose decade of the 1890s, when the United States moved from one international crisis to another until the somewhat contrived war with Spain in 1898, Lipscomb and other leading Tennessee preachers kept busy in the *Gospel Advocate* denouncing each successive war scare. During the Anglo-American crisis of 1896 over the Venezuelan boundary dispute, Lipscomb, co-editor Fletcher D. Srygley, and the influential Middle Tennessee preacher John D. Floyd all wrote articles in the *Advocate* advising calm.[42] Lipscomb sneered at what some prowar preachers were calling "Christian patriotism" and caustically asked whether or not the Christians in England were supposed to be "patriots."[43]

The war with Spain in 1898 was a severe test for southern Disciples pacifism. By and large American ministers, including northern Disciples, threw their support behind the struggle against Catholic Spain. The *Advocate*, however, stood firm. Lipscomb republished the pacifist petition that had been circulated during the Civil War and advised that it "should be adhered to by Christians at all times."[44] The colorful J. D. Tant summed up the *Advocate* position on the Spanish War: "I would as soon risk my chance of heaven to die drunk in a bawdy house as to die on the battlefield, with murder in my heart, trying to kill my fellow man."[45]

As in the case of the Civil War, it is difficult to evaluate the influence that the Tennessee pacifist preachers had on the church members of the state in the 1890s. Obviously the church was not solidly behind its leaders. John Floyd of Flat Creek reported that the *Advocate*'s policy "aroused quite a feeling" both in and out of the church. According to Floyd, the pacifist articles in the paper prompted "a few articles in a secular paper and condemnatory resolutions by soldier organizations."[46] In summary, while the church in Tennessee was by no means solidly pacifist in 1900, the radical left-wing Protestant doctrine of non-involvement in civil affairs was still supported by the most articulate church leaders in the state and received wide circulation through the columns of the *Gospel Advocate*.

NOTES

1. Winfred Ernest Garrison and Alfred T. DeGroot, *The Disciples of Christ* (St. Louis, 1948), 327–29. In addition to this book, the most useful general accounts of Disciples history are Winfred Ernest Garrison, *Religion Follows the Frontier* (New York, 1931) and Earl Irvin West, *The Search for the Ancient Order*, 2 vols. (Nashville, 1953). The first two of these works are by liberal Disciples historians, while the last is by a Church of Christ minister. Although each of the works is a valuable contribution to Disciples historiography, none of them is without symptoms of bias.

2. West, *The Search for the Ancient Order*, 2:167–68. For statistics in 1916, see Dept. of Commerce, Bureau of Census, *Religious Bodies, Part II* (Washington, 1919), 209, 249.

3. Garrison and DeGroot, *Disciples of Christ*, 329.

4. West, *The Search for the Ancient Order*, 2:167; *Religious Bodies*, 209, 249.

5. Standard treatments of the division may be found in any of the general histories of the movement. The influence of sociological factors is one of the themes of David Edwin Harrell Jr., *Quest for Christian America: The Disciples of Christ and American Society to 1866* (Nashville: Disciples of Christ Historical Society, 1966). The question of names is rather confusing in Disciples history. During the early years of the movement three names were rather widely used: "Disciples of Christ," "Christian Church," and "Church of Christ." Throughout most of the nineteenth century all of the divergent elements within the group accepted all three of the names as permissible. As the conservative-liberal rift became clear in the decades following the Civil War, however, the conservatives more and more adopted the name "Church of Christ," while "Disciples of Christ" and "Christian Church" were generally associated with the liberal wing. In the course of time these distinctive names have become quasi-official for each group, although they are still not exclusive. The title "Disciples of Christ" is used in this article to describe the movement as a whole, as it

is probably the most widely accepted all-inclusive name at the present time. A good discussion of the early differences between Campbell and Stone on this question may be found in William Garrett West, *Barton Warren Stone* (Nashville, 1954), 153–57. See also Garrison and DeGroot, *Disciples of Christ,* 14–16. Several other early-nineteenth-century religious reform movements used the name "Christian." Two of these groups, one initiated by Abner Jones and Elias Smith in New England and the other started by James O'Kelly in North Carolina, formed the "Christian Connection" church shortly after the turn of the century.

6. *Religious Bodies,* 209, 249.

7. See Harrell, *Quest for Christian America,* 139–41.

8. For general accounts of the churches' reactions to the Mexican War, see Clayton Sumner Ellsworth, "The American Churches and the Mexican War," *American Historical Review* 45 (1940): 301–26; Anson Phelps Stokes, *Church and State in the United States,* 3 vols. (New York, 1959), 2:75–83; John R. Bodo, *The Protestant Clergy and Public Issues, 1812–1848* (Princeton, 1954), 216–23.

9. Ellsworth, "Churches and the Mexican War," 326.

10. See Harrell, *Quest for Christian America,* 142–44.

11. See T[olbert] F[anning], "War Remarks," *Christian Review* 4 (1847): 213–14; James E. Scobey, ed., *Franklin College and Its Influence* (reprint, Nashville, 1954), 36. In quotations from nineteenth-century publications the spelling and punctuation of the original has been retained.

12. For a general account of the Disciples and the Civil War, see Harrell, *Quest for Christian America,* 144–74.

13. See J. R. H[oward] and D. T. W[right], "A Vindication of Ourselves and the Christian Pioneer," *Christian Pioneer* 1 (1861): 170; S. T. Meng, "The Church and World Powers," *Gospel Advocate* 11 (Jan. 28, 1869): 76–78; Scobey, *Franklin College,* 321–22.

14. D. P. Henderson to Fall, July 8, 1861, Philip Fall Papers, Disciples of Christ Historical Society, Nashville, microfilm copy.

15. W. P. Payne to Fall, June 17, 1861, Fall Papers.

16. Fall to Brig. Gen. R. B. Mitchell, Apr. 30, 1863, Fall Papers.

17. For a description of the trials of another member of the Tennessee group, see Edward Alexander Elam, *Twenty-five Years of Trust* (Nashville, 1893), 50–51.

18. D[avid] L[ipscomb], "Correction," *Gospel Advocate* 34 (July 21, 1892): 453.

19. "Reminiscences of the Civil War Again," *Gospel Advocate* 49 (July 18, 1907): 456.

20. "Correction," *Gospel Advocate* 34 (July 21, 1892): 453.

21. "Reminiscences of the Civil War Again," 456.

22. E. G. Sewell, "Reminiscences of Civil War Times—No. 3," *Gospel Advocate* 49 (July 25, 1907): 473.

23. David Lipscomb, *Civil Government* (reprint, Nashville, 1957), 128–32.

24. Sewell, "Reminiscences of Civil War Times—No. 3," 473.

25. Lipscomb, *Civil Government,* 130.

26. Sewell, "Reminiscences of Civil War Times—No. 3," 473.
27. D[avid] L[ipscomb], "Thirty Years' Work," *Gospel Advocate* 38 (Jan. 2, 1896): 4.
28. Lipscomb, *Civil Government*, 40–43.
29. Ibid., 68.
30. Nathan W. Smith, "A Letter from Georgia," *Christian Standard* 1 (June 9, 1866): 76.
31. There is much material of a sectional nature in the *Gospel Advocate* and *Christian Standard* from 1866 to 1868. For a short statement of the sectional motives behind the founding of the *Christian Standard*, see Harrell, *Quest for Christian America*, 166–68.
32. "Religion and Politics," *Christian Standard* 1 (Oct. 20, 1866): 228.
33. "The Gospel Advocate," *Christian Standard* 2 (Feb. 16, 1867): 52.
34. "No North or South in Christ," *Missionary Weekly* 12 (Feb. 26, 1891): 4. See also "From the Papers," *Gospel Advocate* 33 (Mar. 25, 1891): 177; "Curtain Lecture for the Georgia Brethren," *Gospel Advocate* 13 (Dec. 9, 1871): 388; F. D. Srygley, "Concerning the Width and Sweetness of Things," *Gospel Advocate* 34 (June 16, 1892): 370; William D. Dorris to I. T. Reneau, Dec. 26, 1866, Isaac Tipton Reneau Papers, College of the Bible, Lexington, Ky.
35. "The Truth of History," *Gospel Advocate* 34 (July 14, 1892): 436.
36. "Education in War," *Gospel Advocate* 38 (Feb. 20, 1896): 196.
37. "'Put Up Thy Sword,'" *Gospel Advocate* 12 (Jan. 27, 1870): 73–74.
38. Ibid. See also John T. Walsh, "Peace and War," *Gospel Advocate* 12 (Mar. 31, 1870): 307–8.
39. See B. U. Watkins, "President Benton on War," *Gospel Advocate* 10 (Jan. 1869): 9–10; D[avid] L[ipscomb], "What Is War," *Gospel Advocate* 12 (Sept. 29, 1870): 892–95.
40. See, for example, E. G. S[ewell], "Flesh and Blood Warfare No More," *Gospel Advocate* 31 (Mar. 27, 1889): 199; D[avid] L[ipscomb], "Passing Events," *Gospel Advocate* 23 (May 30, 1883): 338; James B. Parker, "Christianity and War," *Gospel Advocate* 34 (Oct. 6, 1892): 630–31.
41. See, for example, "From the Papers," *Gospel Advocate* 37 (Aug. 22, 1895): 529; (Aug. 29, 1895): 545.
42. Ibid., 38 (Jan. 9, 1896), 17; D[avid] L[ipscomb], "The Monroe Doctrine," *Gospel Advocate* 38 (Jan. 16, 1896): 37; J. D. Floyd, "A Few Thoughts on War," *Gospel Advocate* 38 (Feb. 20, 1896): 118.
43. "The Monroe Doctrine," 37.
44. "War and Christianity," *Gospel Advocate* 40 (May 10, 1898): 317.
45. "War—Its Effect Upon the Church," *Gospel Advocate* 40 (July 14, 1898): 443.
46. "A Few Thoughts on War," *Gospel Advocate* 38 (Feb. 20, 1896): 118.

From Pacifism to Patriotism

The Emergence of Civil Religion in the Churches of Christ during World War I

Michael W. Casey

Peter Brock, in his outstanding history of American pacifism, identifies the Churches of Christ as one of America's leading pacifist sects from the Civil War to World War I. However, by the time of the Vietnam War the Churches of Christ were overwhelmingly in favor of the war effort. This essay explores the key era that began the transformation of the Churches of Christ into a politically conservative prowar group.[1]

With an estimated membership of 1.3 million concentrated in Kentucky, Tennessee, Texas, Arkansas, and Oklahoma, the Churches of Christ are the third largest southern church tradition (after the Baptists and Methodists).[2] "The spirited offspring of the religious rednecks of the postbellum South," the Churches of Christ divided from the larger Disciples of Christ late in the last century to better pursue the "restoration of the New Testament church."[3] The tradition believed that a "pattern" for church polity and practice could be found in the New Testament and should be restored in the present age. Because they were perceived as part of the original primitive church, some of the distinctive practices of the Churches of Christ include believer's baptism, weekly communion, a cappella music in worship, and radical congregationalism. After the Civil War and especially in the 1890s, the northern urban and wealthy Disciple churches moved to less exclusivist positions and forced the rural, southern, and poor Churches of Christ into a separate tradition when organs and pianos were introduced into the worship assemblies of local congregations.

The sectional rift of the Disciples, inflamed by the Civil War and the terrible conditions of the defeated South, prompted most leaders of the Churches of Christ to hold radical pacifist views. The war, with its "bloodshed, destruction and desolation" and the spectacle of "disciples of the Prince of Peace with murderous weapons seeking the lives of their fellowman," moved David

Lipscomb, a key early leader of the Churches of Christ and editor of the *Gospel Advocate* of Nashville, Tennessee, to speak out. He wrote *Civil Government,* the key treatise setting out the tradition's theology on the relationship between church and state. He believed that human government or civil government was not needed at creation. God ruled humans directly in a harmonious relationship. When sin entered the world through Adam and Eve, humans rebelled by organizing their own government "to oppose, counteract, and displace the government of God on earth." War was one of the clearest examples of the evil of civil government. Lipscomb said, "All the wars . . . from the beginning until now, have been the result of man's effort to govern himself and the world, rather than submit to the government of God." Lipscomb argued that, instead of human wealth and power, the humble members of the Churches of Christ should focus on another world, heaven: "The kingdoms of the world are recognized by Christ as the kingdoms of the devil. Christ's subjects are in the world but not of it. His kingdom is not of this world; his subjects cannot fight with carnal weapons. Their citizenship is in heaven, the weapons of their warfare are not carnal, but mighty through God to the pulling down of strongholds. His children are pilgrims and strangers in the earthly kingdoms. They seek a city which hath foundations, whose maker and builder is God. They are not to seek for earthly honors."[4] Because all civil governments are evil, Lipscomb frowned on any political activity, even voting, on the part of Christians. Instead of politics and fighting in war, Christians were to follow "the living and essential principles" of the Sermon on the Mount. For Lipscomb and others in the Churches of Christ, following the New Testament included the pacifist ethic of Christ as well as the pattern or structure of the New Testament church.[5]

Lipscomb articulated the views on politics and war that most people in the Churches of Christ held through the nineteenth and twentieth centuries until World War I. In his social history of the Disciples of Christ, David Edwin Harrell Jr. documented the consistent pacifist position of the Churches of Christ. The *Gospel Advocate* chided the unionist Disciples, who supported the Civil War, which aggravated the growing tensions between the liberal Disciples and conservative Churches of Christ. Austin McGary, editor of the *Firm Foundation,* a journal established to combat the liberals in Texas, announced his agreement with Lipscomb's position on civil government and war in 1884.[6] While the liberal Disciples, who were assimilated into mainstream America, praised the Spanish-American War, the Churches of Christ opposed it. J. D. Tant, a prominent Texas preacher, caustically attacked the Disciples of Christ: they had "introduced the organ" and "divided the Church of Christ." They also would "go fight Spain; for many of them are political men who vote and hold office." Tant even declared, "I would as soon risk my chance of heaven to die drunk in a bawdy house as to die on the battlefield, with murder in my heart, trying to kill my fellow man."[7]

Periodical articles praising war and America or encouraging Christians to involve themselves in the political process were rare until America's entry into World War I. The otherworldly pacifist position of the Churches of Christ was sorely tested during the superpatriotism of World War I, and it began to crumble under the severe societal pressures of the prowar forces.[8]

When the war began, the Churches of Christ continued to state their opposition to war and to Christians participating in killing. Fred Rowe, editor of the *Christian Leader,* based in Cincinnati, Ohio, thought the war in Europe was "something terrible to think of." J. C. McQuiddy, who succeeded David Lipscomb as the editor of the *Gospel Advocate,* hoped that the United States could keep out of the war. McQuiddy, G. H. P. Showalter, editor of *Firm Foundation,* and others reaffirmed that it was wrong for Christians to "engage in carnal warfare" even if the government tried to force Christians to participate. McQuiddy suggested that while Christians were to be subject to the government, it did not mean that they "were to give of their means to buy machine guns in order to destroy or kill."[9]

Slowly America moved from neutrality to involvement in the conflict. As patriotic and anti-German feelings rose, church leaders held to their positions. Showalter argued that the war showed there were no "Christian nations." Another writer called patriotism a "devilish sentiment." When the Germans sank the *Lusitania* and inflamed anti-German feelings in America, McQuiddy asked Christians to avoid giving inflammatory speeches and stirring up talk of war. When President Wilson began the "preparedness" issue, church leaders reacted negatively. McQuiddy thought patriotic activities that encouraged a "war spirit" were wrong. He believed Christians, for example, should not sing the national anthem in Sunday assemblies on July 4. One writer said that preparedness "whoopers" or advocates "shame and outrage Christianity by trying to drape their devilish work in the mantle of Christianity."[10]

Even on the eve of America's entry into the war, the journals of the Churches of Christ maintained their pacifist stance. A. B. Lipscomb, nephew of David Lipscomb and a contributing editor of the *Gospel Advocate,* in March 1917 wrote that a man with a "sneer in his voice" asked Lipscomb if he were a pacifist and Lipscomb replied, "Yes," since "Jesus was a pacifist." Just days before America entered the war, McQuiddy naively hoped: "It is hardly probable that the United States government will force people to go to war who have conscientiously and consistently opposed it."[11]

When the United States entered the war there was significant opposition to America's participation. But over time the propaganda of the Creel Committee on Public Information generally converted public opinion. Under the severe pressures of government propaganda and the change in societal opinion, American Christianity and most southern churches supported America's involvement in the war, endorsing it as a holy war to defend democracy and Christianity.[12]

As with broader American Christianity, the initial reaction of the Churches of Christ to the American entrance into the war was mixed. The *Gospel Advocate* maintained the pacifist position, arguing that the only weapon of Christians must be the "sword of the spirit" or the Bible. A. B. Lipscomb advised conscientious objectors to seek humanitarian service in the military. He encouraged pacifists "to stand up for this principle *now*" and "to bear contemptuous little gibes" and "adverse criticism." Both McQuiddy and Lipscomb said, "When a Christian lays aside the sword of the Spirit and engages in carnal warfare, he cannot conscientiously claim to be following the meek and lowly Christ." In contrast to the *Advocate* and to what he had said earlier, G. H. P. Showalter, editor of *Firm Foundation,* believed that the unprecedented "crisis" of the war and the "broad philanthropy" and "utter unselfishness" of the United States in entering the war justified Christian support of the war.[13]

The *Christian Leader* published prowar and pacifist articles. One writer argued that war was "the only rod of chastening" for God and for just nations in disciplining evil nations. If a war was for freedom and justice, then Christians could fight in it. If any country "would threaten the future peace and liberty of the peoples" of the world, then Christians "must fight against such men and nations." Pacifists used a "sickly sentimentality" when they quoted the Golden Rule in opposition to war, and their position would "throw away all guarantee of social order and justice."[14] However, another writer said he was a "dove" and that he felt sad for those who were "blindly led by the jingo press."[15]

However, the balance between pacifist and prowar articles abruptly shifted. The *Gospel Advocate* suddenly reversed its editorial stance on August 16, 1917. It refused to publish any more pacifist articles and announced it "vigorously opposes the policy that is for encouragement of the slacker, coward and the selfish egotist." Editor McQuiddy said the "journal proposes to be helpful in every possible way to the government."[16] Brute force was the reason for the change. On June 15, 1917, the Espionage Act of 1917 became law, intended to silence any remaining antiwar sentiment. Under the Espionage Act U.S. district attorneys had broad powers to shut down pacifist publications. In addition, numerous semiofficial and private organizations were created to suppress pacifism. Some of them included the American Defense Society, the Liberty League, the Anti-Yellow Dog League, the Boys Spies of America, and the Sedition Slammers. Patriots were turning in their neighbors and fellow church members they suspected were pacifists.[17] A reader of the *Advocate* complained to Lee Douglas, the U.S. attorney general of the Middle District of Tennessee, about the *Advocate*'s pacifist position. One article was perceived as "seditious" and had "the effect of discouraging registration of young men under the Selective Service or Draft Act." Douglas summoned McQuiddy to his office and warned him "that the government did not approve of such articles" and that he would arrest McQuiddy "if such publications did not cease." McQuiddy agreed to stop the articles, and Douglas was satisfied during the rest of the war that McQuiddy was "a patriotic citizen."[18] The overall efforts to suppress pacifist sentiments were so successful that the attorney general declared in 1918, "It is safe to say that never in its history has this country been so thoroughly policed."[19]

While an occasional pacifist article appeared in the other journals of the Churches of Christ, the prowar patriotic view dominated and reached levels heretofore reserved for religious fervor. The lines between politics and religion became so blurred that the Churches of Christ began to equate the political prowar position with Christianity itself. Brute force, however, cannot explain this wholesale change adequately, because the majority of the Churches of Christ embraced the nonpacifist beliefs willingly. The civil religion of the war as a righteous cause and America as a Christian nation was persuasive and seductive to most of the Churches of Christ. This civil religion was aptly summarized by one writer who reflected years later: "The gospel of service and of unselfish devotion to the ideals of Christian democracy was the heart of the appeal as felt by all."[20] This suggests one persuasive aspect of the civil religion: it appeared to be consonant with the Christian ideal of unselfish love and service.

This civil religion was structured around three intertwining concepts: God had chosen and blessed America and made her an instrument of his purposes; patriotism was now a "true and pure religion";[21] and American civilization was a Christian civilization, meaning that American soldiers were dying for both God and country.

E. A. Elam, a Tennessee preacher and regular staff writer for the *Gospel Advocate*, thought that the United States followed God's principles of justice and righteousness and "always will be the most generous, most enlightened, most advanced . . . and the most powerful and invincible nation on earth."[22] God would give the United States victory in the war. Another writer believed that God had made America great and that, like Israel of old, America did not go into battle without the God of hosts." This part of the ideology developed into an optimistic postmillennial position: America would usher in God's reign on earth. Thereby the prowar position co-opted traditional Christian eschatology. Now, in addition to doing Christian service, a Christian who supported the war was also carrying out God's will for his kingdom. At the end of the war Fred

Rowe believed that the war would be used by God to establish his kingdom on earth. America would take pride in the role that God gave her as the leader of all nations, "and by possessing and manifesting the Spirit of the Master, will lead them to the great Lord of all when his truth shall be heard and his kingdom established in every corner of the earth." M. C. Kurfees, who preached most of his life in Louisville, Kentucky, and was a staff writer for the *Gospel Advocate*, also reiterated this millennial theme when he urged Christians to support the Versailles Treaty and the League of Nations because "it would be a long step in the direction of establishing the claims of the Prince of Peace."[23]

Patriotism was equated with Christianity and true piety. One writer thought the churches were "fortresses of the loftiest and holiest patriotism." America needed to be united by a "high and holy enthusiasm, in the ways of outspoken patriotism, true and pure religion, and a noble and earnest living."[24] The equation of patriotism and Christian piety manifested itself in various ways. Several preachers and colleges of the Churches of Christ urged Christians to buy liberty bonds in support of the war effort.[25] Even McQuiddy, as editor of the *Gospel Advocate*, said that to refuse to buy a liberty bond "would be rebellion against God." Also, E. A. Elam, a committed pacifist, said, "Patriotism is the purest and greatest thing on earth, except Christianity."[26]

Probably the most persuasive aspect of the civil religion of the war was the way people could rhetorically cope with the death of their sons in war. Church members' sons who fought and died in the war were sanctified by sacrificing their lives for the war effort. Their deaths were for God's cause as well as America's. The church in Lebanon, Tennessee, wrote to the American soldiers in France: "If for the sake of the orphan, the widow, the oppressed, and the downtrodden, your life is sacrificed, you may fall as a Christian soldier in the triumph of your faith." J. W. Chism, who preached for churches in Texas and Oklahoma, eulogized his son who was killed in "freedom's cause." He was "a faithful citizen [who] gave his life on the altar, a sacrifice to the cause of righteousness against brutal might."[27]

M. C. Kurfees, a regular staff writer for the *Gospel Advocate*, complained soon after the war that many Christians and preachers thought that soldiers who died "for righteous causes" would be saved "regardless of their former lives." This, according to Kurfees, "set aside" the "wisdom of God" and "the plan of salvation."[28] His complaint shows the difficulty that the sectarian pacifism encountered. If the pacifists were right, then many of the fallen soldiers were "damned to hell," a thought that few church members would find palatable.

The more comfortable theology of the fallen "Christian" soldier spread to such an extent that in many congregations service flags honoring their young men slain in battle were placed in church buildings. Elam protested when a service flag was hung at the South College Street Church building in Nashville, and later J. M. McCaleb, a missionary to Japan, was shocked when he returned to the United States at the large number of service flags in congregations "all over the land."[29]

Apparently in many churches political songs and ceremonies honoring their war dead began to creep into the worship ceremonies of some Churches of Christ. As late as 1920 J. W. Shepherd, a preacher in Detroit and a longtime associate of David Lipscomb, complained: "The church must free herself of *politics* and *policies* . . . It must hear other songs than *The Star Spangled Banner* and *My Country 'Tis of Thee* in her assemblies, and see other sights than the '*consecration*, with *imposing religious ceremonies*' of 'service flags' and of the 'banners' of warriors on her altars!"[30]

For the first time in the Churches of Christ the fate of America was intertwined with the fate of Christianity. The barrier between politics and religion that the sectarian theology of David Lipscomb had erected was now breached. U. G. Wilkinson, who preached in Comanche, Oklahoma, mocked the sectarian pacifists:

> Where are the servants of the God of Moses, David fled?
> Is the spirit of martyrs and the heroes lost and dead?
> Have we no more like Lincoln's boys who died to make men free?
> Where are the sons of veterans who followed Grant and Lee?
> If we would sacred rights preserve we MUST meet might with might,
> There's no other alternative, no refuge but in fight;
> The conqueror's minions must be stayed, the WORLD must now be free,
> Our sword, our father's sword must win, for God and Liberty![31]

This intertwining created additional new attitudes and changes in the Churches of Christ. Thorp Springs Christian College and Abilene Christian College formed Student Army Training Corps to recruit students. The students had their tuition paid for by the government and delayed their draft into the military by receiving military training while in school. Several young men, including those who wanted to preach, took advantage of this government program. There was widespread involvement in government programs by preachers. Several preachers joined the YMCA and began to work and preach at the various military training camps. These ministers encouraged the soldiers "to get as many 'Huns'" as possible and tried to get conscientious objectors to change their minds and fight the enemy.[32]

In this civil religion, pacifists and conscientious objectors were now seen as heretics, and any idea that could be labeled German, along with Germany, was considered fallen and evil. Christians who opposed pacifism continued to turn in to the government members of the Churches of Christ who remained pacifists, because the pacifists committed "treason" against the United States. In Kentucky several preachers were "brought before" government authorities for "criticizing the government"—or preaching "the gospel of peace," depending upon one's perspective.[33]

The churches also promoted attacks against the "heresy" of conscientious objectors, or "slackers" as they were derisively called in their own journals and books. Wilkinson's attack shows the depth of the hatred toward the conscientious objector:

> Must we still suffer those who cry, "Peace when there is no peace."
> And war and all its horrors over all our lands and seas? . . .
> Have we not held the subject up in all its shades and lights.
> Entreated, supplicated, prayed and all that so delights
> The slacker and the talker? Shall we cast our pearls to hogs,
> Or longer give (what Christ forbids), "things holy to the dogs?"[34]

G. H. P. Showalter doubted the sincerity of any of the imprisoned objectors to war, since they were really aiding the enemy. Showalter believed press reports that German agents were transformed into "ministers of righteousness" to influence young men to become conscientious objectors. He also thought the government had carefully investigated the cases and found that no one's "religious protection guaranteed by the constitution of the American government" had been disregarded. Christians, instead of supporting the objectors to war, "should support the government."[35] W. H. Carter, a Tennessee preacher, agreed with Showalter: "We should remember, too, that a seditionist is condemned in the Bible, as well as by the government . . . Every Christian should be patriotic."[36] Many in Nashville still held to pacifist views, especially at David Lipscomb College, where Lipscomb's influence was still felt.[37] Austin McGary, former editor of the *Firm Foundation,* sarcastically attacked the Nashville pacifists: "Nashville, Tennessee is the headquarters of that character of slackery. These sanctimonious fanatics claim that their 'citizenship is in heaven' in such an exclusive sense as will not admit of their being citizens of any nation."[38]

The "treason" or "heresy" against the United States became the grounds for the government in crushing the First Amendment rights of the pacifist minority of the Churches of Christ. A government officer searched the home of a preacher "in the South" for pacifist articles "printed or written" by the minister and "made it plain" that 'anti-war articles would not be tolerated" by the government.[39] Lee Douglas, of the U.S. attorney's office in Nashville, after the war admitted that several publications and preachers of the Churches of Christ were under investigation for antiwar activities. McQuiddy on one occasion was able to convince Douglas not to arrest one preacher. Fred Rowe, editor of the *Christian Leader,* tried to "explain" that since the government was arresting ministers, his paper and others should defend "the integrity of the government." He did not think it was the appropriate time to "raise any objection to our Government's participation in the war."[40] Rowe did allow the giving of publicity to efforts to gain conscientious objector status for any Christian who desired it. J. W. Shepherd, who led the efforts for the COs of the Churches of Christ in Washington, D.C., was threatened by prowar activists. One Sunday morning he was visited by government officials at the congregation for which he preached. Another preacher was also harassed by a government official for preaching against Christians "bearing arms." The preacher confronted the officer: "I made it manifest to him that I had not transcended my rights under the Constitution of the United States." The officer replied, "That thing is going to be changed. It has been an alibi for many a conscientious objector."[41]

Several draft-age men and some students at Cordell Christian College had their First Amendment rights suspended by local draft boards. The draft board of Cordell, Oklahoma, refused to acknowledge the objections of some of Cordell's students to doing any military service. These students were sent to prison at Ft. Leavenworth. Fourteen COs from the Churches of Christ were imprisoned there for refusing to do any military service. The local draft board and some of the prowar members of the Churches of Christ were so angered by the pacifist stance of Cordell that the local defense council intervened and ordered the school to be shut down and then reorganized under a new prowar management.[42]

While American ideals and government were righteous and Christian, Germany and anything German were demonic and corrupt. "Never, from the day when the unprincipled Attila led his demonic and merciless hordes of Huns in the Fifth Century," according to M. C. Kurfees, "was there ever such a foe to civilization." Germany might destroy "every principle fought and died for by the fathers" of America "in the War of Revolution."[43] The kaiser of Germany became the incarnation of evil. One writer of the Churches of Christ said, "Kaiserism is a fact, a great, black, menacing, Satanic fact . . . and the greatest menace to humanity's upward march the world has ever seen."[44] Because the Germans believed that they were a "chosen" or superior nation, they had "set aside" God and God's revelation with "German higher criticism." The Germans planned to "destroy the religion of Jesus Christ from the face of the earth."[45] McQuiddy, in the *Gospel Advocate,* concluded: "We cannot hope for the millennium" until the "pharisaic, self-righteous spirit" of German higher criticism and superiority "is driven from the whole world."[46]

The fear of anything German suggests that the civil religion was persuasive, because, in the opinion of these leaders of the Churches of Christ, German higher criticism was undermining the authority of the Bible. Since the goal of the tradition was "restoring the New Testament church," this meant that the basis of the theology of the Churches of Christ—the authority of the New Testament—would be undermined. In their opinion, Germany was also threatening the freedom of America. These Christians were alarmed at the thought of losing both their homes and their religion. The overthrow of this evil force justified the actions of the war. The pacifism of the tradition became impotent in the face of this evil.

These themes of politics and religion were not merely an intellectual ideology for some in the tradition; several saw this as a grand drama in which American patriotism and Christianity were fused together. A cosmic struggle between the forces of good and evil was being waged on the battlefields of Europe. The fate of all civilization and of Christianity hung in the balance. However, it was the eschatological destiny of America to bring God's liberty to all the earth. Wilkinson stated the drama best:

> And since our immortal Washington first drew his country's sword,
> To drive back the foreign despot with his mercenary hoard,
> The principles of Liberty marched on from day to day,
> And must still march till EARTH shall yield to its benignant sway.[47]

No longer would pacifist arguments capture the imagination of the majority of the Churches of Christ. In the new theology the fallen government of this world had been transformed into the guarantor of Christianity itself. As American ideals were upheld by the war, so Christianity was also being defended. The mythic heroes of America were also the heroes of Christianity. The separation of religion and politics had disappeared in the heat of the zealous patriotism of the war. The hope of the millennium and the end of the world was bound up in the hope that American democracy would spread to all nations and that World War I would end all wars.

While the grandiose promise of the patriotism of the war effort quickly changed to disillusionment, and some backlash occurred against the prowar preachers, the Churches of Christ did not and could not turn back the clock and revert to their sectarian isolationist ways. Congregations were flourishing in southern cities, and many church members were beginning to achieve lower-middle-class status in their communities. The emergent civil religion gave them respectability in their neighbors' eyes. Hence, although the millennial dreams of the prowar preachers died, as did postmillennialism in general, the majority of Churches of Christ still thought that America was a Christian civilization. As the 1920s progressed, the tradition began to blame evolutionists and theological liberals who had accepted "German" higher criticism for the failure of the war to bring its promised rewards. In order to combat the evil of teaching evolution in public schools, many of the Churches of Christ joined the fundamentalists and actively entered the political process that they had disdained before the war. The otherworldly pacifism still remained in places. However, on the whole, the Churches of Christ had started down the road to a full-blown prowar position.[48] For the Churches of Christ the idea of restoring the structures of a New Testament church remained, but the New Testament pacifist ethic from the Sermon on the Mount began to disappear.[49] The spirited sons of southern rednecks had clearly begun to turn their backs on their pacifist religious fathers during World War I.

NOTES

1. Peter Brock, *Pacifism in the United States: From the Colonial Era to the First World War* (Princeton, N.J.: Princeton Univ. Press, 1968), 911–15.

2. Mac Lynn, *Churches of Christ in the United States* (Nashville: Gospel Advocate Co., 1990), xviii.

3. David Edwin Harrell Jr., "The Sectional Origins of the Churches of Christ," *Journal of Southern History* (1964): 277. The names for the overall tradition are at times confusing. "Disciples of Christ," "Christian Church," and "Churches of Christ" were used interchangeably in the beginning of the Campbell-Stone or restoration movement. As time progressed "Disciples of Christ" and "Christian Church" were used by the "liberals," while "Churches of Christ' was preferred by the "conservatives." The 1906 U.S. Census of Religious Bodies is the first time the Churches of Christ were recognized as a distinct tradition separate from the Disciples of Christ.

4. David Lipscomb, *Civil Government: Its Origins, Mission, and Destiny* (Nashville: Gospel Advocate Co., 1889), iii, iv, 9, 10, 89–90.

5. Ibid., 133.

6. Austin McGary, no title, *Firm Foundation* (hereafter cited as *FF*) (Dec. 1884): 22.

7. As cited by David Edwin Harrell Jr., *The Social Sources of Division in the Disciples of Christ, 1865–1900: A Social History of the Disciples of Christ* (Atlanta, Ga.: Publishing Systems, 1973), 243–52, and Harrell, "Disciples of Christ Pacifism in Nineteenth Century Tennessee," *Tennessee Historical Society Quarterly* 21 (Sept. 1962): 263–74.

8. Undoubtedly there may have been some prowar members of the Churches of Christ, for the radically congregational tradition never has had a central organizational headquarters or bureaucracy enforcing theological control. Each individual congregation is autonomous, and individual members are free to some extent to decide theological matters for themselves. However, while the tradition has no "popes," it does have editors. Periodicals have filled the usual role of a denominational bureaucracy. Prominent preachers and church members publish articles that set out the beliefs of the Churches of Christ, hence the periodicals provide an excellent window to what members of the tradition thought. Unfortunately, sometimes writers well known to the editors are difficult to identify today.

9. Fred Rowe, "European War," *Christian Leader* (hereafter cited as *CL*) (Aug. 4, 1914): 9; J. C. McQuiddy, "Spirit of the Press" *Gospel Advocate* (hereafter cited as *GA*) (Aug. 13,

1914): 869; G. H. P. Showalter, "False Glory," *FF* (June 1914): 2; E. A. Elam, "Questions, Letters and Answers," *GA* (Mar. 11, 1915): 231–32; J. C. McQuiddy, "Query Department," *GA* (Feb. 3, 1916): 114.

10. G. H. P. Showalter, "Peace on Earth," *FF* (Dec. 22, 1914): 2; O. E. Enfield, "Sermonettes," *FF* (May 30, 1916): 7; J. C. McQuiddy, "Our President," *GA* (May 20, 1915): 490; McQuiddy, "Spirit of the Press," *GA* (July 15, 1915): 701; A. M. George, "The Preparedness Craze," *FF* (Oct. 17, 1916): 3.

11. A. B. Lipscomb, "Why I Am a Pacifist," *GA* (Mar. 8, 1917): 225; J. C. McQuiddy, "Query Department," *GA* (Mar. 22, 1917): 312.

12. Harold L. Nelson, ed., *Freedom of the Press from Hamilton to the Warren Court* (Indianapolis: Bobbs-Merrill Co., 1967), 247–48; Ray Abrams, *Preachers Present Arms* (New York: Round Table Press, 1933), 49–75; E. Clinton Gardner, "Ethics, Christian," in *Encyclopedia of Religion in the South*, ed. Samuel S. Hill (Macon, Ga.: Mercer Univ. Press, 1984), 235–36; Kenneth K. Bailey, *Southern White Protestantism* (New York: Harper and Row, 1964), 42; and James J. Thompson, *Tried as by Fire: Southern Baptists and the Religious Controversies of the 1920s* (Macon, Ga.: Mercer Univ. Press, 1982), 3–5, 68, 70.

13. A. B. Lipscomb, "Edifying As the Need May Be," *GA* (Apr. 26, 1917): 400–401, and *GA* (May 3, 1917): 425; J. C. McQuiddy and A. B. Lipscomb, "What Action Should Christians Take?" *GA* (May 17, 1917): 473–74; and G. H. P. Showalter, "Present Responsibilities," *FF* (May 22, 1917): 2.

14. Fred Sommer, "Should Christians Go to War?" *CL* (Apr. 3, 1917): 2–3.

15. Flavil Hall, "Field Notes and Helpful Thoughts," *CL* (Mar. 20, 1917): 6; (May 8, 1917): 6.

16. J. C. McQuiddy, "Conscience and Conscription," *GA* (Aug. 16, 1917): 790–91.

17. H. C. Peterson and Gilbert Fite, *Opponents of War, 1917–1918* (Madison, Wis.: Univ. of Wisconsin Press, 1957), 12–20.

18. Lee Douglas to J. C. McQuiddy, Aug. 20, 1920, in F. W. Smith, "As a Matter of Simple Justice," *GA* (Sept. 23, 1920): 931.

19. Peterson and Fite, *Opponents of War*, 20.

20. William Webb Freeman, "A History of the Campbell Movement and Its Educational System" (master's thesis, Abilene Christian Univ., 1933), 693. Civil Religion is defined as religious nationalism, whereby the nation is the object of glorification and adoration. Further, the "national life is apotheosized, national values are religionized, national heroes are divinized," and "national history is experienced as a Heilsgeschichte, as a redemptive history." Christianity and love of one's country are frequently equated. See Russell E. Richey and Donald G. Jones, *American Civil Religion* (New York: Harper and Row, 1974), 14–18.

21. "Cultivation of Patriotism," *CL* (June 5, 1917): 3.

22. E. A. Elam, "When Will God Stop the War?" *GA* (Aug. 15, 1918): 777.

23. R. W. L., "Will Our Nation Forget God?" *CL* (June 5, 1917): 2; Fred L. Rowe, "God Reigns," *CL* (Nov. 26, 1918): 3; and M. C. Kurfees, "The League of Nations and the Prince of Peace," *GA* (Jan. 8, 1920): 30–31.

24. "Cultivation of Patriotism," *CL* (June 5, 1917): 3.

25. George Klingman, "A Happy Golden Year," *FF* (June 25, 1918): 1; and Boyd Morgan, *Arkansas Angels* (Paragould, Ark.: College Press and Bookstore, 1967), 97.

26. J. C. McQuiddy, "Buy a Liberty Bond," *GA* (May 2, 1918): 420; and E. A. Elam, "But Can God Really Stop the War?" *GA* (Sept. 26, 1918): 922.

27. John A Klingman, "A Pressing Duty for Every Congregation," *GA* (Apr. 25, 1918): 398; and J. W. Chism, "He Fell in Freedom's Cause," *FF* (Dec. 24, 1918): 7.

28. M. C. Kurfees, "Does Fighting and Dying for Religious Principles Save?" *FF* (Jan. 23, 1919): 78.

29. J. M. McCaleb, "And Why Beholdest Thou the Mote?" *GA* (May 13, 1920): 468. Also see J. M. McCaleb, "The Service Flag," *FF* (Oct. 28, 1919): 6, where he said he saw a service flag at the Gallatin, Tennessee, church building when he spoke there on October 8, 1919.

30. J. W. Shepherd, "Should Christians Engage in War?" *CL* (July 20, 1920): 5. Italics his.

31. U. G. Wilkinson, *The Great Conflict* (Comanche, Okla.: U. G. Wilkinson, 1919), 83.

32. J. P. Sewell, "Students in Training to Get Thirty Dollars a Month," *FF* (Sept. 3, 1918): 3; W. W. Freeman, "Abilene Christian College," *CL* (Oct. 1, 1918): 5; W. F. Ledlow, "Student Army Training Corps," *FF* (Sept. 3, 1918): 6, Roy Lanier, oral history interview by Lawrence Smith in Abilene Christian College Archives; Earl West, *The Search for the Ancient Order: A History of the Restoration Movement, 1900–1918* (Indianapolis: Religious Book Service, 1979), 3:379–83, chronicles the involvement of the preachers of the Churches of Christ in government agencies; Flavil Hall, "Field Notes and Helpful Thoughts," *CL* (Nov. 11, 1919): 6. See Ray Abrams, *Preachers Present Arms*, 139, 171–76, on how the YMCA encouraged the war spirit and anti-German feelings and pressured COs to give up their beliefs.

33. G. C. Brewer, "Christians and War," *GA* (July 4, 1940): 626, and E. A. Elam, "What Have Christians to Do with Judging Them That Are Without?" *GA* (Oct. 16, 1919): 1018; M. C. Kurfees, "The League of Nations and the Peace of the World," *GA* (Sept. 4, 1919): 866, and C. E. W. Dorris, "The League of Nations and the Peace of the World," *Tidings of Joy* (Dec. 1919): 91. Kurfees was prowar and Dorris was pacifist.

34. Wilkinson, *The Great Conflict*, 83.

35. G. H. P. Showalter, "So-Called Conscientious Objectors," *FF* (June 18, 1918): 2.

36. W. H. Carter, "Our Country's Greatest Need—No. 2," *CL* (May 14, 1918): 9.

37. J. C. McQuiddy, "Spirit of the Press," *GA* (Apr. 25, 1918): 396, and H. Leo Boles, "Our Friends," *Babbler* (Apr. 10, 1925): 2.

38. Austin McGary as cited by Flavil Hall, "Field Notes and Helpful Thoughts," *CL* (Nov. 6, 1917): 6.

39. F. W. Smith, "As a Matter of Simple Justice," *GA* (Sept. 23, 1920): 931. This article published an entire letter of Douglas to J. C. McQuiddy about the events of the pacifist controversy.

40. Fred Rowe, "An Official Warning," *CL* (June 11, 1918): 5. Also see J. C. McQuiddy, "An Official Warning," *GA* (June 20, 1918): 581.

41. Mary Shepherd French, "I Remember My Dad—J. W. Shepherd," *GA* (Mar. 1, 1979): 138; E. A. Elam, "Some Questions about Christians Going to War," *GA* (Apr. 16, 1919): 343; and Flavil Hall, "Field Notes and Helpful Thoughts," *CL* (Sept. 23 1919): 6.

42. Michael W. Casey, "The Closing of Cordell Christian College: A Microcosm of American Intolerance during World War I," *Chronicles of Oklahoma* 76 (Spring 1996): 20–37.

43. M. C. Kurfees, "Some Queries on Brother Dunn's Work," *GA* (Feb. 7, 1918): 326.

44. J. Y. E., "Why Does God Permit the Kaiser?" *CL* (Sept. 3, 1918): 2; (Sept. 10, 1918): 6. See Abrams, *Preachers Present Arms*, 103–9, on how American Christianity portrayed Germany as evil and the kaiser as the devil.

45. J. C. McQuiddy, "The German View of War," *GA* (Jan. 31, 1917): 104.

46. J. C. McQuiddy, "Are the Germans Chosen People?" *GA* (July 12, 1917): 671–72.

47. Wilkinson, *The Great Conflict*, 81.

48. On the backlash against the prowar people, see H. Leo Boles, *The New Testament Teaching on War* (Nashville: Gospel Advocate Co., 1923); and A. N. Trice, *Correspondence between the Author and F. B. Srygley, M. C. Kurfees, F. W. Smith and a Brief Review of the Gospel Advocate on War: With Quotations from David Lipscomb* (Nashville: Organ Printing Co., 1922). On the political participation of the Churches of Christ in fundamentalism, see Michael Casey, "From Sectarianism to Participation: The Involvement of the Churches of Christ in the Fundamentalist Movement of the 1920s" (paper presented at the American Academy of Religion Meeting, Anaheim, Calif., Nov. 21, 1989). David Lipscomb College in Nashville, Harding College in Searcy, Arkansas, and Pepperdine University in Los Angeles, California, had several faculty members who took the pacifist position through World War II. Two minor divisions within the Churches of Christ—those who opposed Sunday school classes and those who opposed multiple cups in communion—maintained a pacifist majority in their congregations. The Great Depression encouraged many Americans, including many in the Churches of Christ, to be isolationists and favor keeping America out of World War II. Pearl Harbor quickly transformed the attitudes of most Americans, including those in the Churches of Christ. There was enough pacifist sentiment in the three colleges and the minor divisions for approximately two hundred men from the Churches of Christ to serve in the Civilian Public Service during World War II. On the minority status of pacifists in the Churches of Christ during World War II, see J. L. Hines, "Christians Made Slaves," *Gospel Broadcast* (Jan. 16, 1947): 2. Also see Johnnie Andrew Collins, "Pacifism in the Churches of Christ: 1866–1945," (D.A. diss., Middle Tennessee State Univ., 1984), 167–98. Royce Lynn Money, "Church-State Relations in the Churches of Christ since 1945: A Study in Religion and Politics" (Ph.D. diss., Baylor Univ., 1975); and Melvin Earl Hailey, "The Political and Social Attitudes of Churches of Christ Ministers" (Ph.D. diss., Texas Tech Univ., 1988) traces the politically conservative views of the present-day Churches of Christ.

49. A similar shift for pacifism occurred in other restorationist groups, especially Holiness and Pentecostal traditions. See Jay Beaman, *Pentecostal Pacifism: The Origin, Development, and*

Rejection of Pacific Belief among the Pentecostals (Hillsboro, Kans.: Center for Mennonite Brethren Studies, 1989); Mitchell K. Hall, "A Withdrawal of Peace: The Historical Response to War of the Church of God (Anderson, Indiana)," *Journal of Church and State* (Spring 1985): 301–14; Merle D. Strege, "The Demise[?] of a Peace Church: The Church of God (Anderson), Pacifism and Civil Religion," *MQR* 65 (1991): 128–40; Mickey Crews, *The Church of God: A Social History* (Knoxville, Tenn.: Univ. of Tennessee Press, 1990); Edith L. Blumhofer, *The Assemblies of God: A Chapter in the Story of Pentecostalism, Volume I–To 1941* (Springfield, Mo.: Gospel Publishing House, 1989).

Who Speaks for the Christians?

The Great War and Conscientious Objection Movement in the Churches of Christ: A View from the Wigan Coalfield

Peter Ackers

Conscientious objection to conscription into the armed forces, from January 1916 onward, was a highly complex phenomenon.[1] Quakers and Socialists are the best-known conscientious objectors, but the lesser-known religious sects made up a higher proportion of the total, and their contribution has been neglected. The motives for objection were varied—as Ceadel's classification suggests.[2] Some, like many Quakers, were "absolute pacifists" guided by a universal moral imperative usually grounded in Protestant Christianity. Others, including some Socialists, were "selective objectors" to this particular war or to imperialist wars in general. Then there were the "quasi-pacifists"; the "elitists" who believed they should be exempted because of their special gifts; and the "esoterics," such as the Christadelphians, Jehovah's Witnesses, Seventh-day Adventists, and the Peculiar People of Essex, whose objection was based not on some straightforward pacifism but on "unorthodox religious tenets."

Individual objectors often combined a mixture of motives, and even within the same grouping their degree of objection varied, from objecting to combat service and any military command to objecting even to alternative war work. Overall, the religious motive was strongest, and while this included individuals from almost every conceivable group, most came from Nonconformist bodies. However, only a few groups contributed to conscientious objection as a *movement* to the extent that it could be regarded as a fundamental expression of their corporate beliefs. Of these, the Quakers were the best known and the Christadelphians the most heavily represented. In both cases, although individuals went their own way according to their conscience, the sect as a whole was committed to conscientious objection.

The situation in the Churches of Christ was rather different.[3] Their group of conscientious objectors was sufficiently large and concerted to constitute a movement linked to certain first principles. But, by 1916 the Churches' leadership, and perhaps the majority of members, had come round to supporting the war and even conscription. Thus "the First World War had a polarising effect on the British churches."[4] The portion of the Churches' objection movement described here is that centered on the Wigan coalfield. This was distinctive in that many of the objectors and their spokesmen came from the poorer, working-class chapels of this northern mining town. Such origins mark it off from the rather genteel Nonconformist pacifism that dominates much of the literature. Of course these are generalisations, and individuals of all backgrounds chose different attitudes toward the war. After all, Lloyd George had grown up in the Welsh Churches of Christ,[5] and William Robinson, the Churches' leading interwar theologian and author of *Christianity Is Pacifism* (1933), enlisted in January 1915 and was subsequently wounded.

The Churches of Christ had begun in the mid-nineteenth century as a loose-knit movement calling for a restoration of primitive New Testament Christianity. A particular blend of beliefs and practices—believer's baptism, weekly celebration of the Lord's Supper, lay congregational leadership, and a general anticlericalism—gave it a distinctive "new sectarian" identity.[6] But, by the onset of the Great War, the Churches were already on the path from sect to denomination, and their beliefs and identify were in a state of flux. Behind them, for the most part, lay the otherworldly isolationism, biblical literalism, and working-class primitivism of the early days. Ahead lay full-time ministers, a theological training college, and growing integration into the largely middle-class Nonconformist mainstream. This was, however, a complicated and uneven development, proceeding fastest at the large "West End chapels,"[7] such as Rodney Street, Wigan, discussed here,[8] and slowest at the back street Bethels, such as Albert Street and Platt Bridge.

There are dangers in writing the history of a group like the Churches of Christ with the hindsight of a modern denominational perspective. A too selective reading tends to iron out those primitive and working-class, even sectarian and biblical-literalist, elements that sparked the sect's formation. For the Churches of Christ, which in places came as close to a "labour sect" as any group,[9] these currently unfashionable elements are central to understanding its impact on the outside world as a source of labor leaders and conscientious objectors. Arguably, as the sect became more hierarchical and theologically liberal, more middle class, and like other Nonconformist denominations, it lost this cutting edge and ceased to make a distinctive contribution to local working-class communities. From this perspective, conscientious objection among Wigan's Churches of Christ during the Great War is best understood as the last stand of a humble primitivism behind the "old attitude" and against these new compromises.[10]

This article arises from a wider doctoral study of the Churches in the Wigan coalfield, as perceived through the life of W.T. Miller (1880–1963). Miller became president (1926–39), then national secretary (1939–43), of the Pit Deputies trade union.[11] Apart from national material, my sources are those closest to his life: the Miller family itself and the coalfield chapels of Victoria Road, Platt Bridge and Albert Street, Newtown. Miller's brothers and friends were drawn into conscientious objection, and these small chapels became a national focus for the movement, each with its own large constituency of objectors. What follows aims to bring to light the experience of a little-known group of conscientious objectors, within a relatively obscure religious denomination, as one contribution toward telling "the full story of those who remained loyal to their pacifist convictions during the war."[12]

Like other English Nonconformists, the Churches of Christ had traditionally opposed war and militarism. This was their mood at the 1900 Annual Meeting, which regretted "the military spirit now so prevalent in British society generally."[13] Henry Tickle's 1901 conference paper called, in the spirit of "the early days of the church," for members to refuse all military service, "whether voluntary or compulsory," even if this should involve "penalties in person or property." This paper was reprinted in 1914, but the rhetoric was soon forgotten once war was declared. As elsewhere in English Dissent, the outbreak of hostilities prompted an abrupt about-turn of attitudes.[14] Whereas only a minority in the Churches of Christ had supported the Boer war, the struggle to save Belgium won much wider assent. However, while most leading national figures had already shifted their ground in favor of the war, pacifists within the Churches hoped that they would remain firm against conscription. Radical Protestantism has a strong voluntarist tendency, suspicious of the "world," and, in the past, the Churches of Christ had opposed compulsory vaccination schemes and education rates.

When war came, it pitched the patriotic leadership in many chapels against pacifist sections of their congregations: "Leaders urged our young men to enlist and fight for King and Country, and scant sympathy was given to those who stood for the old attitude. With the coming of conscription, we saw our young men turned down by tribunals of which leaders of their own Churches were chairmen. Brethren, some of whom were elders in the Churches, sat on magisterial benches and handed over their own Brethren to their persecutors."[15] In Wigan, this split partly took the form of a division between the more respectable and middle-class Rodney Street and the smaller, outlying mining chapels.

The debate raged through the pages of the *Bible Advocate*, particularly during 1916 as the conscription bill loomed ever larger. An editorial hoped its "conditions and exemptions" would meet most objections.[16] It also noted that a petition against the war in the name of the Churches of Christ was "in circulation." While this only represented the views of "some members," it probably expressed "what many of the young men desire." The following week's editorial, "Sympathy," weighed the case for pacifism against the "just war" argument and found in favor of the latter.[17] But it asked chapels to show "sympathy . . . in prayer" for objectors. Yet, by now, the many brethren already in the armed forces were suffering horrific casualties, and the atmosphere had become much more emotionally charged. The same edition saw the launch of W. Marshall's regular epistle from the front, "Letter to Soldiers."

The antiwar brethren had begun both to campaign against the war and to form self-help groups to prepare themselves for the threat of conscription. One letter offered constructive "Suggestions to Non-conscriptionists" facing prosecution and attempting to establish their genuine religious reasons and referred, tellingly, to "young brethren who are taking this stand."[18] But in the same edition, under the heading "Our Soldiers and Sailors," Julian Elwes informed readers that the list of "Our Boys" had now passed six hundred. They wanted "sympathy not scorn" and to be spared the "amputations of careless consciences." The editor promised to continue publishing any advice for conscientious objectors who opposed "all war,"[19] but he insisted: "We as a people do not take that view." Another "Letter to Soldiers" evoked the "Just War" and claimed the armed forces contained "the finest manhood of our nation and Empire."[20]

For the rest of the war, the words, actions, and experiences of Robert Price, from Albert Street chapel in Wigan, encapsulated the pacifist predicament. His opening communication reported a meeting at another Wigan coalfield chapel, Platt Bridge, of "conscientious objectors of the Churches of Christ" to discuss "future policy under the Military Service (No. 2) Act."[21] He outlined the three-stage procedure for claiming exemption on conscientious grounds: the Local Tribunal, the Appeal Tribunal, and, finally, the Central Tribunal. The meeting had recommended that brethren "ask for complete or absolute exemption and accept nothing less." They should use all three tribunals, and if exemption were ultimately refused, "patiently await the next move by the authorities." They were then "liable to be called up," and each who refused would "become a deserter"—subject to imprisonment, though the death penalty had been amended from the act. Thomas Miller of Platt Bridge issued what appears to be an ironic rejoinder to the "King and Country" mood of the times, thanking God for continuing "voluntary enlistment into the army of Jesus" and praying they "'fight the good fight' that at the end we may receive at the hands of our King that glorious reward for faithful service—the victor's crown."[22] Robert Price next produced a remarkable "manifesto," agreed at a meeting on February 26, 1916, entitled "Brethren and an Anti-War Attitude," and "Issued by members of the Churches of Christ who object, on conscientious grounds, to rendering military service of any kind, or to taking the military oath."[23] This stressed the sanctity of individual conscience and struck a pacifist position based on fundamental Christian values and biblical authority:

> The case for compulsion is being urged by many who, because they have no conscientious scruples, fail to realise the position of the conscientious objector. Therefore we deem it imperative to voice our protest against the Military Service (No. 2) Act. Our voice is the voice of a number of men who are bound by deep conscientious convictions to refuse to render military service of any kind, whatever the consequences for refusal. Our objection to taking any part in military service is not merely negative, but rests fundamentally upon a recognition of a positive obligation to Christ, whose whole life was a protest against force and militarism. We firmly believe in the sanctity of human life. And to us "Thou shalt not kill" means what it says. We believe it to be a definitive and absolute command, admitting of no exception. To us the human race is one grand brotherhood. We admit the rights of a community to impose duties upon its members for the common good, but we absolutely deny the right of Government to make the slaughter of our fellows a bounden duty. We are uncompromisingly opposed to any Act of Compulsion, because it strikes at the foundation of the Christian Church, national well-being, and, what is more, will tend to fan into religious persecution. It will also mean the serious violation of the consciences of thousands of the most loyal subjects in the land. We are prepared to sacrifice as much in the case of world's peace as our fellows are sacrificing in the cause of the nation's war. Our motto is that of the old Christian martyrs, who died fighting a similar warfare to this—"We are Christians, and therefore cannot fight."

Conscription came into force on March 2, 1916, and the prosecution of conscientious objectors began. In Nottingham "several young brethren" had appeared before the local tribunal.[24] Moreover, Robert Price warned that exemptions were being refused and described the objectors' predicament:

> Some of these brethren have already left their occupations, they being "deemed to be deserters" and are now awaiting their arrest by the authorities; how long or how soon it will be they do not know. Brethren taking this course require no less courage than is required by a soldier. To combat public opinion, to be still while everybody is active, to stand by a principle, and yet be branded a coward, and last of all, to face what may be the death of a deserter, though misunderstood, none but a man can do. Let it, therefore, not be forgotten that peace has its martyrs as well as war, that peace also can boast her "rolls of honour" none the less.[25]

Meanwhile, the debates in Wigan resounded through the pages of the *Bible Advocate*. An official-sounding "Day Open Conference on the War,"[26] representing the views of the Churches' leadership, was held at Rodney Street chapel on Good Friday. Present were James Marsden, J.P. (1841–1927), Coop's religious and business successor and a leading national figure in the Churches of Christ, the mayor of Wigan, and two church evangelists. The two main sessions concerned "(1) The outlook of the churches as affected by the war; (2) The Fulfilment of Old Testament Prophecy and its relations to the present war."

The anticonscription movement came to a head on Saturday, April 22, with a Platt Bridge conference of those who had "signed the protest form," drawing brethren from Ashton-under-Lyne, Blackburn, Manchester, and Swindon, as well as the Wigan District.[27] Its aim was to provide a moral and financial support system for arrested brethren, "who may have to testify their deep Christian conviction against military service." Two resolutions were passed to this end, a manifesto agreed, and a committee established to organize a future national conference. A further meeting in Birmingham was suggested.[28] The Platt Bridge conference was well supported and another was held in Leicester during the 1917 Annual Meeting.[29] Robert Price convened a further national objectors conference to be held at the Total Abstinence Hall, Greenough Street, Wigan, on Saturday, June 10.[30] By then there were 125 conscientious objectors in all, 35 requiring assistance, 17 currently in military hands, 5 released—altogether including 166 Church and Sunday school workers.[31]

The issue had already arisen of what the Churches' position was and who spoke for it. Their whole tradition resisted the idea of a centralized "authority" pronouncing on issues of "the world" without a direct biblical reference, and brethren were reminded of this.[32] Nevertheless, by the late spring of 1916, the absence of an "official" church position was leading to a dispute over "who spoke for the Church." The publication of a pamphlet by W. Nelms of Glasgow, *Peace: A Principle of the Churches of Christ*, brought this problem to a head.[33] Walter Crosthwaite, who supported the "Peace" pamphlet, pleaded for more clarity on the war issue.[34] George Talbot from Glasgow likewise expressed concern over the confusion but blamed the pacifist pamphlet for "masquerading under false colours," claimed the Churches were close to "schism" over the war, and argued that the issue was the Christian attitude toward the "present war" and not "war" in general, "as discussed in the various peace propaganda." The editor regretted attempts "to represent the Churches of Christ by brethren on both sides of this question" and begged them to "forbear and respect each others' convictions." Then, for a short time the debate over principles was sidetracked into a plea for chapel elders (in the absence of an official paid ministry) to share the "total exemption . . . granted to clergymen and ministers of all denominations."[35]

By the summer of 1916, brethren conscientious objectors were being "ill treated by military men."[36] Robert Price gave a vivid report of one such case:

> At Richmond Castle, on June 10th, he was ordered to open out his kit for inspection. This he refused to do. He was at once thrown on the floor, being thumped and kicked while there. He was then taken to the guard-room, and again thrown-down, receiving a kick in the back. This was followed by one kneeling on him. His foot was then twisted, and so was one of his arms. This process caused him so much pain that he was compelled to open his kit. His kit having been examined, it was strapped on him, and later he was taken before the Commanding Officer, who sentenced him to fourteen days detention. This expired on the 24th. Although he persists in breaking all orders, he says they will not permit him in the guardroom, and is now waiting to be sent out to France with other NCCs.[37]

Another was sentenced to death in France—although this was commuted afterward to ten years penal servitude—an indication that the military could still impose the death penalty by forcing the recalcitrant onto the battlefield and then charging him with desertion.[38] Robert Price pleaded again for those suffering hardship and detailed the circumstances of twenty-two brethren "in the hands of the authorities,"[39] including "Wm Miller," the son of Platt Bridge chapel labor councilor W.T. Miller, "at Walton" gaol for "two years without hard labour, not yet commuted."[40] He returned to the case for peace and Christian internationalism:

> The great brotherhood of man has gone to ruin . . . The Church of Christ has not found itself proof against this storm, and now we think of our fellow-members in Germany, Austria or Bulgaria as being in the enemy's camp. It is impossible that all the brethren should be born in England. It is necessary that the Kingdom of God be world-wide, and take into its number those of all nations. So let us return to our charitable feelings which we once held towards those brethren who live (or die) in Germany. I would submit that the Christian should recognise no enemy other than Satan, and that he should repudiate the rights of Governments to decide who are his enemies.[41]

By the end of 1916 the objectors' position, including that of "Wm Miller" of Platt Bridge chapel was "considerably improved."[42] In Wigan, J. B. Kendrick of Albert Street reported an October 27 meeting[43] and later "a social of brethren objectors . . . held at Baren's Cafe, on the night of November 16th."[44] This involved brethren from Earlestown, Platt Bridge, Albert Street, and Rodney Street chapels, "Bro William Miller . . . paid us a visit from HM Prison at Wakefield," where he had been "under arrest for six or seven months."

From December 1916, the two Price brothers of Albert Street themselves faced prosecution. Edward was called up "after being rejected eight months ago."[45] On refusing to attend parade, he was "placed in the guard-room at Grimsby" to await a "district court-marshall." Soon after, Robert Price was also recalled to the army.[46] Meanwhile, the "Central Committee of the anti-war brethren" had met again in Blackburn, and J. B. Kendrick communicated Robert Price's complaint of "illegal treatment." And by the summer of 1917 the news was worse: "Bro. Robert Price, after serving one sentence in Wormwood Scrubs for conscience's sake, and being returned to camp at Cleethorpes, where for fourteen days he was kept on bread and water, besides other cruel treatment, was on Friday, June 8th, forcibly taken across to France from Folkestone."[47] Rumors circulated that he had been "accidentally killed" in France. In fact, "he had been returned to this country" and was now serving "another twelve months hard labour" in Wandsworth prison.[48] As Price had insisted, determined conscientious objection was no soft option. The official report of a Wigan District of the Churches of Christ meeting at Platt Bridge a couple of weeks before barely reflected all this—even though Thomas Miller of Platt Bridge was chairman—except to report another "official" war conference at Chorley.[49] The chapel minutes, however, indicate how solidly it was behind the conscientious objectors, how serious was the rift with the district leadership, and how close the chapel came to leaving the co-operation.

From the beginning, Platt Bridge agreed to rent a room to "conscientious objectors to Military Service,"[50] and the secretary was instructed to announce their Friday night meetings in chapel.[51] When brethren began to be prosecuted, a "Special Officers Meeting" agreed unanimously to send a letter "to the President of the Central Tribunal concerning Bro. Wm Miller's release."[52] The Albert Street chapel conscientious objectors, Robert Price and J. B. Kendrick, were among five preachers the chapel asked "for dates on the next plan."[53] When the former was arrested a few weeks later, this precipitated open conflict with the Rodney Street–based district Churches leadership.

The chapel officers were "very willing to give testimony" to Robert Price's character" and sent a resolution to the District "disapproving of their action in erasing Bro Robert Price's name from the plan."[54] A "Special Church Meeting" agreed that unless his name was restored they would "leave the committee." Over the next three months, a series of chapel meetings maintained the call for Price's reinstatement, and by now the threat was to "withdraw from the association."[55] A delegation from the district was received cordially,[56] but a conciliatory move to drop the issue (since Price could not fulfill his "plan" obligations while under arrest) moved by W.T. Miller and his father, Simon, was defeated in favor of standing by the threat to withdraw—only to be reversed at the next meeting.[57] It was perhaps with a view to healing the wounds that the district annual conference was held at Platt Bridge in July 1917.[58]

If there were differences over tactics toward the district, there seems to have been virtual unanimity over principles. The dispute was reverberating round the Wigan churches, and when the district wrote to other chapels about "brethren setting up another table" (that is, breaking away) and circulated "statements alleged to have been made" by two leading Platt Bridge pacifists, Thomas Bennett and William Speakman, the secretary wrote "explaining errors" in their report and asked them to withdraw it.[59] A little later, he wrote to the War Office "protesting very strongly against the treatment served out to conscientious objectors." He and any two officers were "Empowered to write to the War Office at any other future time that they think it desirable in the interests of men being punished for their convictions against militarism." A resolution to "send parcels" to brethren "serving in the army" was also defeated.[60]

The issue revived after February 1918, when the cabinet introduced "clean cut," which ended the exempt status of occupations like coal mining and took all men below a certain age.[61] During 1918, both the *Bible Advocate* (Bro. J. Luck remained a contact for conscientious objectors "in prison, detention camps, or work centres"), and the Platt Bridge chapel minutes are largely silent on the subject. Nonetheless, many of the younger brethren at Platt Bridge and Albert Street were coal miners, including the trade union leader W.T. Miller and three of his brothers, John, James, and George. It seems that at least two of them became conscientious objectors at this time. W.T.'s daughter, Betty, remembers her father visiting them at Ditton Priors army camp in Shropshire. James eventually went to war and George gained a reprieve for ill health, but John joined those at Dartmoor. Others from Platt Bridge included Bill and Jim Speakman and Isaac Miller, who refused active service but worked in the medical corps. The chapel asked the district to "petition the Government for the immediate release of the conscientious objectors" and wrote to their local mining MP, Stephen Walsh, on their behalf.[62] After the war, they also suggested the topic "Can a Christian Be a Soldier, Compulsory or Voluntary?" for the Annual Conference paper.[63]

Overall, sixty-one Churches of Christ objectors were arrested and twelve spent more than a year in prison. One died of influenza in Strangeways prison, Manchester. Another, as we have seen, was sentenced to death in France but had the sentence commuted. Groups of Christian Brethren objectors in Wakefield and Dartmoor prisons held regular services for the "breaking of the bread." Thompson argues that "the strongly committed pacifist group was very small."[64] His estimate, including the 125 from the Platt Bridge meeting, totals no more than 300—half the number of brethren enlisted by 1916 and just under 2 percent of the 15,191 national membership. Yet it was still a fairly high proportion of so small a religious body compared to the total complement of objectors, who amounted to only 0.33 percent of those who were conscripted or volunteered to fight.[65]

The sympathy was probably much wider, especially among the young brethren, who were notable by their prominence in the antiwar campaign. We have already seen the situation at Platt Bridge chapel. According to his daughter,

Betty, the trade union leader, W.T. Miller, "would have been with them if he hadn't had an essential job," and almost everyone was "against war." Harry Ackers, then a teenager at Albert Street chapel, remembers the Price brothers and others, who came together in the young men's classes, where they trained as lay preachers. He recalls that "practically all the young men" were conscientious objectors and that he too would not have fought at the time had he been of age, because war was against their basic principles. There seems no doubt that the mining chapels of Platt Bridge and Albert Street were at the center of a sizable movement for conscientious objection, strongly supported by the young brethren. Thompson's national history, inevitably centered on the large, middle-class chapels such as Rodney Street, may understate this strength of feeling.

The Churches' leadership tried to accommodate both sides in a highly charged atmosphere of great suffering all around. The 1916, 1917, and 1918 Annual Meetings passed resolutions that referred both to those resisting and fighting.[66] The mood was never bellicose, and the *Bible Advocate* spoke of the "horrors of war and evils of militarism" in "this the hour of darkness and sorrow."[67] The end was greeted with: "Thank God the dawn of a better day has come."[68] Nevertheless, relations were not easy in those chapels with sizable concentrations of objectors, such as Platt Bridge and Albert Street. The Price brothers and J. B. Kendrick attended the latter, but so did families with sons like Peter Yates, who was on active service:[69] "He enlisted in the Army in March, 1915, and went to France in December, 1915. He received wounds in the legs and head on July 22nd, 1917, which necessitated an operation to have the leg amputated. On the following day he passed away, at the age of 34 years." Harry Ackers recalled at least one bereaved father who left the chapel for good because of its pacifist atmosphere.

What kind of conscientious objectors were the Churches of Christ? How did their motives and experiences compare with those of other objectors? Rae describes both those motivated by the corporate position of their church or sect, and individual Christians, exercising, in characteristic Protestant fashion, their individual consciences. With the Churches of Christ's objectors we find a combination of the two, reflecting the reluctance of their tradition to take positions on the "world." Individuals drew inspiration from a personal understanding of their primitive Christian plea, which was at variance with that of their Churches' establishment. This was apparent in the varying degrees of resistance: some were absolutists, taking the full path to prison; others accepted alternative work; some finally relented and went to war. As absolute pacifists formed only 10 percent of all objectors, the Churches seemed to have produced a fairly high proportion.[70]

Given that support for the objectors went well beyond the number who faced the conscription test, what was the general basis for their objection?

Here again Ceadel's classification is instructive. It would be easy to lump the Churches' group with "esoteric quasi-pacifists,"[71] such as the Christadelphians, Seventh-day Adventists, or Jehovah's Witnesses, for whom objection reflected not an earthly pacifism inspired by Christ's teaching but an "interim ethic" awaiting the Second Coming and the creation of God's kingdom on earth. Rae refers to the Churches' "biblical literalism" and places them with unusual groups such as the Dowie Church, Dependent Cocklers, and Peculiar People.[72] Ceadel takes a broader swipe at "unsophisticated religious beliefs" and those who "expressed an objection primarily in terms of a literal reading of selected biblical texts"—virtually making religious sophistication a condition of conscience.[73]

Biblical authority was certainly an important anchor for the Churches of Christ's objectors' case. Moreover, the Churches' earlier nineteenth-century congregations had strong millenarian elements, which indeed had fed Christadelphianism. But, by the Great War the Churches had long abandoned this aspect and were already moving in a quite different direction. A more important influence was the Churches' original plea for a restoration of primitive, New Testament Christianity. This "otherworldly" perspective linked naturally to the more widespread Christian pacifist interest in the pacifist traditions of the church before Constantine.[74] Hence, while attention to scriptural support was important to the Churches, as to other bible Christians, the letters and manifestos quoted above appeal to a more general early Christian ethic of absolute nonviolence.

Critics of the objectors voiced suspicions of a "selective pacifism." Was their objection to just this war, rather than to all war, and did the labor atmosphere and strong collier representation in these chapels exercise an influence? The question is hypothetical, since people had to confront the war they were faced with, not some abstract problem. However, there is circumstantial evidence to suggest that political objections may have exercised a greater influence than is immediately apparent. Religious and political considerations were inseparable for many objectors, and the sources used here would tend to encourage religious rationalizations, as would the primacy of the religious test at tribunals. At Platt Bridge chapel the "two W.T.s," a coal-mining trade union official and a labor councilor, were related to many objectors and in close contact with others. There were similar figures at Albert Street, and it would be surprising if the coalfield antipathy to conscription, especially after the "clean cut" of 1918, was not a factor.[75]

Finally, it seems likely that the experience of these Churches of Christ objectors was harsher than that of most others. They were mainly young working men from backstreet chapels in a northern mining town. They were not high-profile pacifist intellectuals, nor could they look to Bloomsbury for character witnesses.[76] To compound this, they were members of a relatively little-known sect with a deliberately weak sectarian identity who often described themselves simply as "Christians." They lacked the corporate identity of the Quaker or even the Christadelphian,[77] whose ideas were more likely to be understood by the tribunal, and this must have encouraged suspicion about their true religious commitments. In addition, their own Churches' hierarchy, which in Wigan was very well connected, tended to support the war. Furthermore, they seem to have been isolated from the two main middle-class national objector movements, the political No-Conscription Fellowship and the Christian Fellowship of Reconciliation. After the war, while others rose to political and religious prominence, they simply faded away, and there is a suggestion that some, such as Robert Price, may have suffered in consequence.

This question of the links between the Churches of Christ objectors and the wider religious and socialist conscientious objection movement is an intriguing one. Even though it was well organized and concentrated in working-class chapels attended by labor and trade union activists, the antiwar movement appears insular and characterized by a withdrawal from the "world." The language of fundamental pacifist values and universal brotherhood has a wider Christian and socialist resonance, but I have little evidence that, as a group, they forged wider links. It seems to have been the stubborn, primitive Christian attitudes of these "backstreet bethels" that fueled their subculture of resistance to the war.

NOTES

1. This account of conscientious objection draws on M. Ceadel, *Pacifism in Britain, 1914–1945* (Oxford, 1980), and J. Rae, *The Politics of Conscience: The British Government and the Objector to Military Service, 1916–19* (Oxford, 1970).

2. Ceadel, *Pacifism in Britain*, 8–10.

3. I draw heavily here on D. M. Thompson, *Let Sects and Parties Fall: A Short History of the Association of Churches of Christ in Britain and Ireland* (Birmingham, 1980).

4. Thompson, *Let Sects and Parties Fall*, 121.

5. T. Witton Davies, "The McLeanist (Scotch) and Campbellite Baptists of Wales," in vol. 7 of *Transactions of the Baptist Historical Society*.

6. A. D. Gilbert, *Religion and Society in Industrial England: Church, Chapel, and Social Change, 1740–1914* (London, 1976).

7. H. McLeod, *Religion and the Working-Class in Nineteenth-Century Britain* (London, 1984). Rodney Street had engaged an "evangelist," or de facto full-time minister from the outset. The smaller chapels had depended more on lay resources and were most resistant to these changes. What was new were moves toward the recognition and training of a formal ministry.

8. Wigan became one of the main centers for the Churches of Christ. The church reached the town in 1841 through the efforts of Timothy Coop, a clothing store manager and former Wesleyan who became a major industrialist. The first permanent meetinghouse was the town-center Rodney Street (1858), with 398 members in 1916. This meetinghouse joined the URC in 1980 and closed in 1989. The manufacturing dynasty dominated the chapel's history, and it played an important part in the Churches nationally. The movement spread into the outlying coalfields from the 1870s, through chapels such as Platt Bridge (1883) and Albert Street (1878), with more working-class, mainly mining, congregations. In 1916 they had 111 and 136 members respectively. The latter left the association in 1947 and has now closed. The former remained with the Churches until 1980 and continues outside the URC. See W. T. Moore, *The Life of Timothy Coop* (London, 1889) and my "Churches of Christ in the Wigan area," *Chapels Society Newsletter*, no. 4 (June 1991): 44–5.

9. E. J. Hobsbawm, *Primitive Rebels* (Manchester, 1971); B. Lancaster, *Radicalism, Cooperation, and Socialism: Leicester Working-Class Politics, 1860–1906* (Leicester, 1987), see the Churches in these terms. In reality, their social composition was more complex, even in the Wigan coalfield chapels, where local tradesmen were well represented at officer level. See also M. and D. Clague, "Churches of Christ in Furness, Cumbria, 1842–1981," *Journal URCHS* 4 (1991): 504–8, which discusses the Churches' history in terms of its contribution to the URC and the ecumenical movement.

10. Thompson, *Let Sects and Parties Fall*, 123.

11. See my "W.T. Miller" in *Dictionary of Labour Biography* (Hull, 1992). See also entries for Robert Fleming of Belfast and Amos Mann of Leicestershire.

12. K. W. Clements, "Baptists and the Outbreak of the First World War," *Baptist Quarterly* 26, no. 2 (1975): 76.

13. Thompson, *Let Sects and Parties Fall*, 121.

14. For Baptists, see Clements, "Baptists and the Outbreak of the First World War."

15. Walter Crosthwaite, quoted Thompson, *Let Sects and Parties Fall*, 123.

16. *Bible Advocate*, Jan. 14, 1916. (the Churches' main national publication).

17. Ibid., Jan. 21, 1916.

18. Ibid., Jan. 28, 1916.

19. Ibid., Feb. 4, 1916.

20. Ibid., Feb. 11, 1916.

21. Ibid., Feb. 18, 1916.

22. Ibid., March 3, 1916.

23. Ibid.

24. Ibid., Apr. 7, 1916.

25. Ibid.

26. Ibid., Apr. 14, 1916.

27. Ibid., Apr. 28, 1916.

28. Ibid., May 12, 1916.

29. Thompson, *Let Sects and Parties Fall,* 123.
30. *Bible Advocate,* June 2, 1916.
31. Ibid., June 16, 1916.
32. Ibid., June 2, 1916.
33. Ibid., May 17, 1916.
34. Ibid., May 26, 1916.
35. Ibid., June 2, 1916.
36. Ibid., June 23, 1916.
37. Ibid., June 30, 1916.
38. Ibid., July 7, 1916.
39. Ibid., July 14, 1916.
40. Ibid., July 28, 1916. This is a second W.T. Miller, labor councilor and cousin to the Pit Deputies leader, and also at Platt Bridge.
41. *Bible Advocate,* Aug 8, 1916.
42. Ibid., Sept. 15, 1916.
43. Ibid., Nov. 17, 1916.
44. Ibid., Dec. 1, 1916.
45. Ibid., Dec. 8, 1916. The Price brothers attended Albert Street but lived out in the country. Harry Ackers (1902–), soon to be an engineering apprentice, remembers them bringing sandwiches for the daylong chapel Sabbath. Edward managed Platt Bridge Co-op (near the other chapel), and Robert was probably a teacher. I believe Robert died in 1926.
46. *Bible Advocate,* Jan. 1, 1917.
47. Ibid., June 22, 1917.
48. Ibid., July 20, 1917.
49. Ibid., Aug. 10, 1917.
50. Platt Bridge Chapel Minutes, Feb. 6, 1916.
51. Ibid., Feb 27, 1916.
52. Ibid., Sept. 3, 1916.
53. Ibid., Oct. 11, 1916.
54. Ibid., Jan. 7, 1917.
55. Ibid., Jan. 24, 1917, Feb. 18, 1917, Mar. 18 1917.
56. Ibid., Mar. 25, 1917.
57. Ibid., Aug. 8, 1917.
58. Ibid., July 8, 1917.
59. Ibid., June 3, 1917; June 17, 1917.
60. Ibid., Oct. 28, 1917.
61. Rae, *The Politics of Conscience,* 68.
62. Platt Bridge Chapel Minutes, Nov. 25, 1918. The M.P. for Ince, which included Platt Bridge. Wigan politics were at a point of transition from Tory to labor. Harry Twist a Nonconformist mining leader, first won the Wigan seat, briefly, in 1910, anticipating

the dominance of mining labor from 1918. See D. Brown, "The Labour Movement in Wigan" (master's thesis, Liverpool Univ., 1969). Another mining leader and Churches of Christ member, Joseph Parkinson, J.P. (1854–1929), was elected to the council in 1906 and became an early labor mayor.

63. Platt Bridge Chapel Minutes, Sept. 21, 1919.
64. Thompson, *Let Sects and Parties Fall*, 123–24.
65. Rae, *The Politics of Conscience*, 71.
66. Thompson, *Let Sects and Parties Fall*, 124.
67. *Bible Advocate*, Apr. 5, 1918.
68. *Bible Advocate*, Nov. 15, 1918.
69. Ibid., July 27, 1917.
70. Ceadel, *Pacifism in Britain*, 32.
71. Ibid., 20.
72. Rae, *The Politics of Conscience*, 77.
73. Ceadel, *Pacifism in Britain*, 44.
74. Ibid., 19.
75. Rae, *The Politics of Conscience*, 69.
76. Ibid., 82.
77. Ibid., 72–73.

Part V

Traditions Related to the Stone-Campbell Movement

A Different Kind of Loyalist

The Sandemanians of New England during the Revolutionary War

Jean F. Hankins

Members of New England's Sandemanian sect were not run-of-the-mill Loyalists during the Revolution.[1] Like other supporters of Great Britain, the followers of Robert Sandeman were geographically concentrated in coastal and urban areas as well as in southwestern Connecticut. Like the Anglicans and other Loyalists, they swam outside the main religious current. They, too, were feared, vilified, shot at, jailed, and exiled. What does separate the Sandemanians from other New England Loyalists is their determined passivity: they supplied no soldiers to Loyalist regiments, piloted no ships, counterfeited no money, engaged in no spying missions, published no pro-British propaganda, and contributed no food, materiel, or information to the English.

This unusual sect has received scant attention from historians of New England since Williston Walker issued his comprehensive study in 1902.[2] Perhaps the American Sandemanians have been neglected because they seem never to have numbered more than one hundred persons. If we overlook them, however, we risk committing the same error as did many of their contemporaries, that of failing to distinguish among varieties of loyalism. By examining the religious motivation that compelled the Sandemanians to bear allegiance to the British Crown even as many sought to live peaceably among their patriot neighbors, we will better understand the nuances of a term like "Loyalist."

I

Robert Sandeman, the Scottish founder of the Sandemanian churches in Great Britain and America, arrived in America in 1764. He was the chief disciple of his father-in-law, John Glas, a Scottish clergyman deposed in 1728 by his Presbyterian synod for his dissenting theological views. Both Glas and Sandeman urged the separation of church and state and called for a return to the religious practices of the primitive Christians. Sandeman's *Letters on Theron and Aspasio* (1757), written in response to James Hervey's *Dialogues between Theron and Aspasio* (1755), was widely read in both Britain and America.[3] The cornerstone of Sandeman's theology, as expressed in this and other works, was his conception of faith, which he defined as simple assent to scriptural testimony about Christ. Like the antinomian Calvinists, Sandeman taught that faith alone, not deeds, is the way to salvation. Faith is bare intellectual belief, he stated, and nothing that man does will help him find God or even assure him that he is on the right track.[4] Bypassing the Arminian Calvinists' argument that such a definition of faith destroys any incentive to lead a moral life, Sandeman also rejected Jonathan Edwards's theory of evangelical repentance as well as Edwards's belief that the heart or will is the seat of holiness. The conversion experience through which one gained membership in New England's Congregationalist churches played no role in the Glasite or Sandemanian service.[5]

Despite their emphasis on separation of church and state, Glas and Sandeman also insisted that the Bible enjoined people to be loyal to their rulers. As Samuel Pike, a prominent Sandemanian spokesman, wrote in 1766, "We think every Christian must be a *loyal Subject,* submitting himself in civil Concerns to every ordinance of Man for the Lord's sake, punctually regarding the Rules laid down [in] Rom. xiii.1–7, 1 Peter ii.13–17. This was required of the Disciples and Churches, when they were under a tyrannical and persecuting Government; and it cannot be less a Duty, under the present mild and peaceable one."[6] Sandeman's publications, coming at a time when New England Congregationalism was in a somewhat depressed state, struck a responsive chord in the souls of several New England Congregational clergymen, notably Connecticut's David Judson of Newtown and Ebenezer White of Danbury and his two sons, Joseph Moss White and Ebenezer Russell White. Encouraged by the Americans' letters expressing their acceptance of his definition of faith, Sandeman in the fall of 1764 brought his mission to America.

He found it tough going. Preaching in towns up and down the Atlantic coast from Maine to Philadelphia, he attracted large audiences at first but few converts. He sometimes spoke in taverns and public houses but also from the pulpits of separated congregations. His reception was not always kind. On December 14, 1764, a Portsmouth mob broke the windows of the meetinghouse in which he was preaching, and Sandeman was given four days to leave town.[7] Just six months later, however, the first Sandemanian church was established there.[8] Composed "in no small part of persons of intelligence," the Portsmouth church included two prominent merchants, the brothers

Colburn and Nathaniel Barrell, the latter a member of New Hampshire's Governor's Council.[9]

Sandeman's theological beliefs were hardly a radical brand of Calvinism, and the worship service, with its emphasis on mutual exhortation and scriptural readings, was probably less alarming to many Congregationalists than the emotional excesses wrought by the Great Awakening. Still, the Sandemanians were considered peculiar. Included in their liturgy were such oddities as foot washing, a love feast, and the kiss of peace, for which the group earned the derisive nickname of "Kissites."[10] The Sandemanians insisted that all congregational decisions be unanimous, a rule that led to excommunications, schisms, and perhaps the eventual decline of the sect. They also practiced a modified form of communism unusual both in Scotland and New England; renouncing any form of "covetousness," church members were required to share their surplus goods and money with their less fortunate brethren.

If Sandeman had come to America twenty years later, his followers might have been better able to withstand the public's censure. Unlike the early American Quakers and Shakers, the first American Sandemanian converts did not actively proselytize and thereby avoided public confrontations with members of other churches. Once Sandeman's own missionary work was over, the sect never placed any emphasis on evangelism; some, in fact, carried the Sandemanian doctrine of exclusivism to an extreme, even avoiding social contacts with nonmembers.[11] Despite this exclusivism, the Sandemanians were unable to shut out the rest of the world. For the Portsmouth congregation, in particular, the timing was bad: the church had been established there on May 4, 1765, and a small meetinghouse erected in July. On March 22 of that year the British Parliament finally had passed the Stamp Act. Even before that news reached America, sides were taken. Some Sandemanians, unwisely speaking out, proclaimed it their duty to be obedient to the divinely established secular powers and "not to meddle with those who are given to change."[12] At the same time, following Sandeman's example, the new Portsmouth converts made themselves both conspicuous and unpopular by criticizing the teachings of other clergymen in the city. Nathaniel Barrell boldly pronounced, "Christ will come in flaming fire to take Vengeance on all who know not God and Obey not the Gospel."[13] Sandeman himself, never characterized as a man of tact and forbearance, admonished Barrell at different times that he really should not label the opposition clergy "base, dirty, infamous & villanous."[14]

The Stamp Act went into effect on November 1. On that same day a Portsmouth mob attacked the small Sandemanian church on Divinity Street and caused considerable damage. In their petition to New Hampshire's governor, the Sandemanians, seeking redress, spelled out the mob's motive: "the 1st of November last a number of People were assembled together in a Riotuous [*sic*] manner in the Town of Portsmouth in profess'd design to oppose the Stamp Act taking place, & in a riotous manner did damage, break & spoil a house built at our expense for the purpose of Worshipping God."[15] It is worth noting that the crowd's hostility toward the Stamp Act was vented not against the Anglican church (now St. John's), established in 1732, but against the fledgling society of Sandemanians, its "persons of intelligence" included. The Sandemanian meetinghouse may simply have been an easier target and the Sandemanians a less risky adversary; however, one suspects that because of Barrell's outspokenness, the Sandemanians in their six months' existence had become far more notorious than the Anglicans.

Between 1765 and 1770, a period of rapidly increasing tension between America and England, several American Sandemanian churches were established. Within a few months in 1765, Sandemanians founded churches in Boston and Danbury, Connecticut. The churches in Providence and several southwestern Connecticut towns were established between 1770 and the outbreak of the Revolution.[16]

The most important and enduring of the Sandemanian churches founded in this period was that in Danbury. Ebenezer White, who had encouraged Sandeman to come to America, had been ousted from his pulpit in 1764 for "heresy and Sandemanianism."[17] White had formed his own church, known as the New Danbury Church, but, despite his prior influence, Sandeman "could not persuade Mr. White and his adherents to adopt their [Sandeman's] peculiar Plan of Worship and Discipline."[18] However, about July 1765, probably induced by Sandeman himself, then living in Danbury, Ebenezer White's son, Joseph Moss White, led "a small party of pure Sandemanians from his father's church" to form a separate society fully Sandemanian in practice as well as doctrine.[19]

The existence of a Sandemanian church in Danbury as well as the presence of Sandeman, who had settled permanently in Danbury by 1766, drew a number of young converts to the town. Among them were Theophilus Chamberlain and Titus Smith, both Yale graduates, who in 1765 had been ordained by the commissioners of the Scottish Society for the Propagation of Christian Knowledge as Indian missionaries to the Oneidas in New York. Returning to Connecticut, they became converted to Sandemanianism and were reordained as Sandemanian elders in 1768 in Boston. Both men, with their families, moved to Danbury in 1768 or 1769.[20] Sandeman himself had no family or visible means of income and continued to make occasional missionary forays outside the town. As late as 1770 Danbury townspeople regarded Sandeman, as well as his recently arrived adherents, as strangers in their midst, much as they had regarded the itinerant preachers spawned by the religious revivals of the 1730s and 1740s.

Even those Sandemanians who were native born and otherwise respectable, however, were viewed as strange. Take the case of Thomas Gold, son of Stratford's longtime Congregational minister and brother of another Congregational minister. Married in 1755 in the Redding Congregational Church, Thomas Gold at the age of thirty-two inexplicably joined the Sandemanian church. What was more, he took his new religion seriously. Evidently a prosperous farmer in Redding, a town bordering Danbury to the south, Gold tried very hard to follow Sandemanian principles, including the difficult injunction against laying up treasure on earth. About 1769 or 1770 Gold started getting rid of his earthly treasure. He sent thirty-six bushels of wheat and a barrel of pork to Boston "as present to his friends." He gave Sandeman twenty-five pounds of sugar and a large quantity of building nails. In the fall of 1771 Titus Smith received a barrel of pork, thirty bushels of wheat, £10, a two-hundred-pound hog, three cows, some sheep, fifty pounds of flax, seven pounds of wool, cloth for a coat, leather for his breeches, and six yards of "flaxxen shirting." Gold also gave a "Sattin waistcoat to Bob Sandeman and Cloath to Thos. Cozicar for a loose coat."[21]

The Redding selectmen were naturally alarmed by this unusual behavior. In September 1771 they appointed an overseer for Gold and impounded his goods in order to prevent him from bankrupting himself and becoming a public charge through "mismanagement and bad Husbandry." In January Gold appealed the selectmen's action to the Fairfield County court.[22] The overseer, Gold complained, "was appointed in order to tie up his hand & prevent him from feeding the hungry and cloathing the naked, especially his despised & afflicted Brethren." In deciding the case, the court had opportunity to examine depositions given by Gold's friends and neighbors, among them Theophilus Chamberlain and Asa Church, good Sandemanians both, who concurred that Thomas Gold had indeed given away substantial amounts of his livestock, produce, and cash.[23] There is no record that the Fairfield court ever made a decision on the case; however, on the outside cover of the original documents relating to the case are a few lines, probably written by one of the county judges: "Law severe. Not designed to take in such Case. It appears he acts conscientiously. Charity recommended. A tender Pain. Court will rather Err on the other side." In October 1772, the case was finally decided when the General Assembly annulled the action of the Redding selectmen.[24]

The clemency shown by Connecticut's legislature only emphasizes the worries and fears of the Redding selectmen. It was easy enough for officials convening in distant Hartford or New Haven to condone the Sandemanians' behavior; it was quite another matter for the local residents to put up with it.

In 1770, about the same time Gold was displaying his Christian charity in Redding, Sandeman was urging his followers to restrain themselves in expressing their political beliefs. Throughout New England, in the aftermath of the Stamp Act, Townshend Acts, and the Boston Massacre, anti-British feelings were running at fever pitch, especially in Boston. "In such times," Sandeman wrote

Colburn Barrell in Boston, "it is not our part to rebuke our neighbours for their disloyalty, but as quietly as possible to preserve our own loyalty till God either strengthen the hands of those in authority or give us new masters."[25] He urged the brethren to say as little as possible about "contentious matters" during their church services. The danger was not only that they would be misunderstood, but also that they would lose sight of their true goal; it would become all too easy, he wrote, for the loyal brethren to "preach up the British king and constitution, with more zeal than Jesus Christ."[26]

Barrell did not take Sandeman's advice. By the fall of 1770 he had moved to Boston, which was still inflamed by the events of the recent massacre and where his public pronouncements did little to dampen hostilities. In November, for example, at a Sandemanian service, he announced that the people of Boston "were disaffected to the Laws of the Land" and that they were in fact "in open Rebellion, Disobedience, & Disloyalty." Furthermore, he charged, the Congregationalist clergy were taking the lead in "oppugning the Authority of the Laws of the Land."[27]

About the same time that Colburn Barrell was getting into trouble in Boston, Sandeman became caught up in a situation not wholly of his own making. The Danbury selectmen, probably disliking Sandeman's politics as much as his religion, decided to force him to leave town. On February 28, 1770, Asa Church, at whose home Sandeman and his nephew Bob had been staying, was fined £40 by the town of Danbury for lodging the undesirable strangers for more than two weeks.[28]

About three weeks later, Sandeman and his adherent Theophilus Chamberlain were brought before Danbury Justice of the Peace Thomas Benedict and charged by the town selectmen with being strangers and transient persons who had remained in town four weeks after being warned to leave. For this the two men could be fined £40 each. Sandeman reported in a letter to his brother William (March 27, 1770) that he made a long and vigorous defense, arguing that the law against transients "was intended not against harmless strangers but against persons of ungoverned and dishonest conversations." After some hesitation the justice, by all accounts an honorable man, found Sandeman and Chamberlain guilty but did not attempt to execute the judgment.[29] Both Sandeman and Chamberlain remained in Danbury until Sandeman's death, at the age of fifty-three, in Chamberlain's house, on April 2, 1771.

Sandeman's death did not bring an immediate end to the selectmen's problems. A group of citizens immediately protested plans to bury Sandeman's remains in the town cemetery. In due course more reasonable sentiments did prevail, and he was properly interred in the Old Wooster Street graveyard.

"There could be no loyalists until there were rebels," Mary Beth Norton has pointed out, and there were no rebels until after 1773, when independence became "the chief point of contention."[30] The Sandemanians were passive rather than active Loyalists. As New England became caught up in the anti-British fervor of the Revolutionary period, the Sandemanians, like all other Loyalists, became targets of the patriots' hostility. Because they would not renounce their allegiance to the British king, the Sandemanians were associated in the patriots' minds with the Tories, who from pulpit and in newspapers opposed the Revolution, as well as those who gave military aid to the English. Though most Sandemanians carefully refrained from making political pronouncements, this restraint made little difference in the treatment they received.

II

When fighting broke out, the Sandemanians had two possible courses of action: they could stay or they could leave. The choices made by different groups and individuals reveal an interesting variety of responses to a common threat.

Unlike their brethren in New Haven, the Boston Sandemanian Loyalists ever distinguished themselves from other Loyalists. Given the small size of the Boston congregation (twenty-five to thirty families is a good guess), the Sandemanians nevertheless made up a significant percentage of those in Boston or Massachusetts who are identified as Loyalists by virtue of having signed certain documents. Eight of the 124 signing the address to Governor Hutchinson on his departure from Boston were Sandemanians.[31] The June 8, 1774, address to Governor Gage, in content very similar to the address to Hutchinson, was signed by nine Sandemanians. Later in June, nine Sandemanians were among the 128 persons who signed a protest against the Solemn League and Covenant, a nonimportation pledge never popular in Boston.[32] Immediately after the outbreak of fighting at Concord and Lexington, twelve known Sandemanians joined other Boston Loyalists in forming an association to keep peace in the city.[33] Although the intentions expressed in all of these documents may now appear moderate and peaceful, anyone brave enough to sign any of them set himself up as a target "for radical opprobrium,"[34] which in some cases turned destructive and violent. One Boston Sandemanian, Isaac Winslow Jr., further defied the wrath of the Sons of Liberty when he took the oath of mandamus councilor, a position he resigned a few days later under pressure or, as he put it, "more owing to the perswasion of others than to his own inclination."[35] A contemporary observer, Ezra Stiles, chillingly characterized the mood of the day: "They hunt the new Councillors in Mass."[36] Two weeks after Winslow moved his family into Boston, his Roxbury home was razed.[37] When the British evacuated Boston in March 1776, thirteen Sandemanian families, including all of those who had signed the addresses, went with them. Most of the Bostonians continued on to Halifax or Shelburne, Nova Scotia.[38]

Although Connecticut did not absolve its residents of allegiance to the British Crown until October 1776, the revolutionaries controlled Connecticut town affairs at a much earlier date.[39] In New Haven, the Friends of Constitutional Liberty were organized in the fall of 1774.[40] A year later, on November 6, 1775, the New Haven town meeting voted that anyone siding with George III should be asked to leave town, and New Haven's selectmen became its Committee of Inspection to enforce that decision.[41] All this spelled trouble for the Sandemanians.

In New Haven the group of nine or ten Sandemanian families included several who had moved there from the Danbury area after Sandeman's death in 1771. Among these were the families headed by Titus Smith, Theophilus Chamberlain, Thomas Gold, and Daniel Humphreys. The elders of the New Haven church, formally established about 1774, were Chamberlain and Richard Woodhull.[42] Woodhull, an attorney and merchant, was the only one of the New Haven group with roots in that city.[43]

Unlike the Boston Sandemanians, the New Haven group had refrained from making any public declaration concerning their loyalty to either America or Great Britain. Still, they became known as Tories. The Reverend Samuel Andrew Peters recounted an episode witnessed around the time the Friends of Constitutional Liberty was being formed. He had been

> at Newhaven in the Colony of Connecticut in Septembr 1774 and saw Joseph Pynchon Esqr. and many other Gentlemen called Sandemanians barbarously insulted by three Mobs (headed by Arnold, Wooster & Mansfield) composed of the Sect called (in their Law Book) sober Dissenters, for refusing to sign the League & Covenant the mobs cried along the streets, *that the Sandemanians had proved themselves to be guilty of the Damnable Sin of Loyalty to the King of England by not signing the Covenant.*[44]

In early December 1775 John Sparhawk, a leading Sandemanian from Portsmouth, was visiting members of the Sandemanian church in New Haven. He reported in a letter to Isaac Winslow Jr., of Boston, that the church at New Haven was "scattered, the body of inhabitants having insisted upon all our [leaving] the town—in consequence of which T.& B. Smith have gone to Newtown—Mr. Pynchon to Guilford—Mr. Humphreys to Derby." Sparhawk said he was "called upon by the Select Men to give them my principal [view] of government etc. etc."[45]

Despite such periodic inquisitions, no civil charges were made against any of the Sandemanians until the fall of 1777, following the British attack on military stores in Danbury. Fearing a similar invasion across Long Island Sound, citizens of coastal communities like New Haven grew worried for their own safety and anxious about possible enemies in their midst. On September 12, 1777, complaints were lodged against Theophilus Chamberlain as being "Inimical and Dangerous to the United American States." The New Haven Committee of Inspection quickly found him guilty and sought a statement from the Sandemanians concerning their beliefs and loyalties. On September 14 the Sandemanians submitted the following document:

> [We consider it our duty] to be faithful & loyal Subjects to our Sovereign King George the Third . . . to whose Government we are heartily attached . . . That as according to the Scriptures the Kingdoms of this World are to be defended by the Sword, a Command from the Sovereign to his faithful Subjects to assist in the Defence of his Government at the peril of their Lives, when they are in a Situation that admits of it, is a lawful Command. And even in the Situation in which we now are, we are bound to a dutiful, loyal, obedient Conduct such as our Situation will admit of. And although we earnestly wish to live in peace, & have no inclination to bear arms or become Soldiers in a lawful Warr, yet the Exhortation of John the Baptist and the case of Cornelius oblige us to conclude that the Soldiers calling is a lawful one for Christians as well as other men . . .
>
> We hold ourselves equally obliged . . . to live peacefully with all men; to do good to all men as we have Opportunity; to be inoffensive among our Neighbours, to love & pray for our Enemies; never to avenge ourselves, nor to bear ill-will to any men; to be no busy-bodies in other men's matters . . . If we are to be deprived of that Liberty, which we have in no wise forfeited, happy shall we be if it be given to us from above to suffer with patience. We are able to get a subsistence in this place in our lawful Callings without being a burden to our Neighbours. If we are removed or confined, this is taken from us. We would be glad therefore to be permitted to continue here if we may live in quiet & unmolested. We wish not to be sent into the Country, or to be separated to prevent our assembling on the first day of the Week to continue stedfastly in the Apostle's doctrine & fellowship and the breaking of bread & the Prayers . . . But if we are not to be permitted the free exercise of the Christian Profession in this place . . . Our wish is, that we may be suffered peaceably to retire with our families to some convenient place more immediately under the King's Protection . . . and that this may be allowed in such a way that we may not be molested by the people in departing.

The document concludes by requesting that their brother, Oliver Burr, be released from prison so that he might join them. It is signed by Daniel Humphreys, Titus Smith, Richard Woodhull, Thomas Gold, Joseph Pynchon, Theophilus Chamberlain, Benjamin Smith, and William Richmond.[46]

The following day, September 15, the Committee of Inspection forwarded the Sandemanians' declaration to Governor Trumbull with the comment that the Sandemanians' view was "Diametrically opposite to the Resent System of Politicks adopted by the American States for Their Preservation and Safety . . .

& by the Late Conduct of some of their Number we believe them to be Enimies to our Common Cause." They requested that the governor "adopt some method regarding them whereby the Publick . . . may be rid of Their Fears." What perhaps made the Sandemanians even more repugnant was their determination, according to the committee, "not to advance a Shilling . . . in Support of the Resent Dispute as They say their [Consciences] will not allow them to support this Warr."[47]

The New Haven Committee apparently pressed the Sandemanians for a more direct statement concerning their loyalty. This request elicited a second, more equivocating statement: "I do not feel myself bound either from Conscience or Choice to give Intelligence to his Majesty's Officers or troops nor do I feel my self bound either from Conscience or Choice to take an active part, or to take up arms against this town or the united Colonies . . . I also feel my self bound in Conscience to seek the Peace of this town."[48] The five signers were Woodhull, Burr, Gold, Humphreys, and Chamberlain. Although this statement appears designed to keep the Sandemanians out of trouble with the authorities and their neighbors, the signers had second thoughts about what they had professed and quickly issued a repudiation, dated simply October 1777:

> On reflection, we have great reason to fear & tremble before our Maker & judge, on Account of the above Answer . . . For it appears to us that it is a Shamefull, evasive & wicked Answer, exposing us to everlasting shame & Confusion of faith. We were not in giving the above Answer acting in the Fear of God . . . but of Man . . . The answer which ought to have been given, is plain & simple, viz; *that we hold our Selves bound in Conscience to yield Obedience to the Commands of his Majesty King George 3d as far as to take up Arms against this town, or the united Colonies.*[49]

Strong, brave words—and the New Haven authorities promptly threw all the Sandemanian brothers in jail. On October 22 the selectmen, evidently bewildered by the Sandemanians' position, sent a copy of their last declaration to their General Assembly delegate, commenting that it contained "[s]entiments so very extraordinary that the minds of the People were raised to so high a Pitch as induced the . . . Committee immediately to take up the matter . . . and [decide] that their madness was so great that they aught to be Confin'd, they are now in gaol, to quiet the Inhabitants. You will therefore immediately lay their Declaration . . . before the General Assembly and Strenuously urge on the House the necessity of their being removed out of this Town[.] [If] they are not possibly the Consequence may be attended with very disagreeable Curcumstances."[50]

If the Sandemanians' declaration indicated their willingness to fight, their intentions, like their actions, were clearly peaceful. They did not fight for the British (or Americans), and as far as can be determined, none ever did anything detrimental to his patriotic American kinsmen and neighbors. Even if the General Assembly could not consider the Sandemanians to be neutral or pacifists, it nevertheless gave them the benefit of the doubt. In October 1777 the assembly resolved that they could "continue in this state upon giving their Parole . . . that they will not do any thing injurious to this state or the united States of America, or give any intelligence, or Assistance to the British offices or forces at war with this and the other united States."[51] Obviously the Sandemanians would not compromise again, and on November 10 Ezra Stiles recorded in his diary: "I saw some of the Sandemanian Brethren who were lately imprisoned in N. Haven for their Declara. in Favor of the King & agt. America. They are embarkg. for L. Isld."[52]

The exodus of so many Sandemanian families from Boston and New Haven meant the end, at least temporarily, of the Sandemanian churches in those cities.[53] But not all Sandemanians left Boston and New Haven, and most of the Danbury church members remained in their homes throughout the Revolution. They may have come to regret their decision.

The case of Hopestill Capen of Boston is noteworthy. Capen, a Boston merchant, stayed behind with his wife and children when the British evacuated the city in March 1776. Because he had signed the addresses to Hutchinson and Gage and joined the Boston Association of Loyalists, his political position was well known. On August 6 he was "impeached as an Enemy to [his] Country, and cast into Prison." On August 29 he petitioned the court of enquiry for release, arguing that he had been misunderstood. He maintained that he was simply following God's commandments as revealed in the Scriptures. "But as to the charge of my being an enemy to my country, no accusation can be more unjust." Capen maintained that "had I not been check'd by the command of God . . . to be subject to the Higher Powers . . . I should have been one of the foremost in opposing the measure of the British Parliament . . . neither do I think myself in any ways bound in conscience to become an informer against my country . . . but to be subject to all the laws that are made that are not contrary to the laws of my Maker." Then Capen added a variation on this familiar theme: "But . . . whenever it shall appear to my conscience that a change in government has taken place, and is so established that the power is of God, I shall know myself to be as tenaciously bound to adhere to God's law respecting being subject to that power, and to what I am from its support with cheerfulness."[54] In other words, Capen was saying that he would switch his loyalty if the Americans proved victorious. He was also implying that he would welcome that outcome. But the court was not impressed with Capen's attempt to be the good American while still clinging to his Sandemanian principles. Despite another petition by Capen's wife (March 1778), he remained in jail until at least October 1778.[55]

Although Boston had dealt more harshly with one of the town's remaining Sandemanians than had New Haven with its own, patriotic fervor was still causing problems for Connecticut's Sandemanians. Late in September 1775, the rumor spread through western Connecticut, noted for its large share of British sympathizers, that the resident Loyalists were planning to join forces with invading royal troops to wreak havoc on Fairfield by "coming down in the night, and setting fire to the houses and barns and destroying all before them."[56] Whatever the truth of the rumor, it became an excuse for several hundred Whig militia from eastern Connecticut to march to the western part of the state, rounding up whatever Tories could be found. Two months later, about November 20, the scene was repeated over a wider area. This time Connecticut's restless, disbanded army regiments, recently returned from Boston, were engaged in the Tory hunt. They started at Newtown but continued on to Redding, Danbury, Ridgefield, and later Woodbury, forcibly disarming Loyalists as they went.[57] Some of Danbury's Sandemanians were caught in their net, including Ebenezer Russell White and John Sparhawk, who had recently moved to Danbury with his family. Returning to town late one night, Sparhawk recounted in a letter dated December 5:

> to my surprize [I] found there were several hundreds of armed men [near?] the Town on the Sea Coast, who had taken prisoners about 30 Tories (as they are called) & among them 8 or 9 of our Brethren . . . I did not think it expedient to fly—the next morning Mr. White & I were taken from our homes by [adjective illegible] men, & were conducted to the place where the other prisoners were, [some] of our Brethren had been already two days prisoner—we continued in [this] situation [until] about twelve where all of us who were distinguished by the name of "Glasites" were carried before a kind of Court Martial, composed of many of the Militia Officers of the County & some of the Committee of this Town, here we were examined in an [inquisitorial?] way for they had nothing to charge us with, we were first ask'd whether we would take up arms against the Country, to this we answd we were bound to be subject to any ordinance of man etc. . . . We were then asked if we would discover all plots & conspiracies against the Country—I answered that they were equivocal times & a direct answer could not be given without they were explained—I added, however, we might be class'd with Tories—It was with us a point of Conscience, a religious test—that we could in no sense join with them without giving up a Commandment of the Lords—than which it would be far better for us not only to suffer imprisonment but Death itself.—This contrary to my expectations exasperated them beyond measure—I was called a Scoundrell not fit to live in this world.[58]

The court-martial continued until three the next morning, by which time, Sparhawk admitted, "I can assure you that however a persecution may look at a distance, at a closer view the heart shrinks—at least my heart did." Sparhawk's release was brought about through the help of a former member of the sect, a "Lieut. St[even]s, whose conscience was somewhat touch'd." Sparhawk was released on bond of £200, the other brethren collectively on a bond of £1,000.[59]

Nor was this the last time Sparhawk and White were arrested. The British attack on Danbury took place April 26–28, 1777, and Sparhawk and White, along with Munson Gregory, were jailed immediately after the British withdrew (at which time several other Sandemanians fled to Long Island). Daniel Humphreys wrote an account of Sparhawk and Gregory's experiences in a letter dated June 6: "[Sparhawk] had been a Prisoner above 30 days, sometimes out for a day and sometimes for a night on some person's word. He has been greatly threatened & to appearance in eminent hazard of life—Men loading their Pieces in his Sight, before or when he was taken, and swearing by their Maker that he should die, threatened to be shot when carried along the street by the Guard . . . The most that was alledged against him was that he was in the Streets while the Troops were there." Humphreys's next comment is worth special note: "it appeared that his being a Leader among the Brethren there, was what made him so obnoxious." This statement adds weight to the suspicion that much of the religious hostility to the Sandemanians was given political expression. As for Munson Gregory, Humphreys continued,

> his case is this—Sabbath Morng. just as the King's Troops were leaving the Town—a certain Capt. belonging to the town came to him & gave him to understand that there would be the utmost hazard to any man's tarrying who was a friend of government, that such were shot at by ye people, that he had been shot at, & his son shot dead by his side (it appeared afterward that this was not so, he was only wounded). This alarmed bror. Gregory to such a degree, that he packed up a few things, and went down to Mr. Sparhawk to ask his advice respecting going off. He advised him to return home & not to go. He was accordingly returning to his own house with a view to tarry; but taken up, carried over to ye Province of New York, treated with great severity, finally brot back, & released on bond.[60]

The man whose son was shot may have been Hezekiah Benedict, a Sandemanian.[61] In 1787 Samuel Hoyt, also a Sandemanian, petitioned the General Assembly for restoration of his estate, confiscated following the Danbury raid after Hoyt escaped to Long Island. Hoyt fled, he reported, because "he was informed and really believed that the justly incensed multitude of the people threatened to put to death all those people who had remained at their homes while the enemy was there, and that they had so far carried their threats into execution as to fire upon one Hezh. Benedict & his sons of sd Danbury and had shot one of sd Benedicts sons thro' the thigh."[62]

The motives of those doing the firing were doubtless mixed, and it would be going too far to say that Danbury's patriot defenders singled out the Sandemanians for attack. Clearly, during the intense hours of the British occupation of Danbury, what really counted was not a man's religion, or who his relatives and friends were, but which side he was taking.[63]

Shortly after the British raid on Danbury, the Sandemanians were subjected to another kind of pressure, the military draft. Evidently most of them had been able to avoid earlier drafts by one means or another.[64] In March 1778 nineteen Danbury men petitioned Governor Trumbull for exemption from military service. The signers, nearly all of whom have been identified through other sources as Sandemanians, complained that even though "they have at all times behaved peaceably among their Neighbours & Countrymen, and most of them have payed fines without murmuring for not going into the war which they look upon as unjust—they are now drafted & understand no fine can excuse them—and as they declare it to be utterly against their Concience to take up Arms against the King; and as . . . [they] have been frequently told that if they would remain quietly at home & diligently follow their respective occupations They might be Suffered to remain in peace." Their aim, they declared, was to be allowed that "liberty of Conscience" that they had hitherto enjoyed and "which is enjoyed in all protestant Countries."[65]

One of the signers of this petition was Comfort Benedict, already in jail. Benedict was drafted in the summer of 1777 but escaped to Long Island. When he subsequently returned to Danbury, he was thrown in jail, where he languished for three years. Benedict's plea to the General Assembly poignantly argued "that from his infancy he has been educated in the principles commonly called Sandemanian . . . & tis well known that, that Sect of Christians have ever professed . . . that in their Opinion Inhabitants of America was contrary to the Law of God to take up arms against the King of Great Britain. [They] have strictly adhered to their profession aforesaid." After being drafted, Benedict said, he "remonstrated" to the Danbury officer in charge, "supposing himself exempt by a resolution of Congress purporting that persons who supposed themselves bound by the Law of God not to take arms should be excused from Draughts—yet notwithstanding all his remonstrances he was carried to Camp and delivered to Genl. Putnam, to whom he made the same objections & urged that he could not fight even were it to save his Life." Benedict was held in the Fairfield jail until early 1778, when he was sent to Hartford and put "under the care of Sheriff Williams, with whom he has found so much favor that he has suffered him to work out for a considerable Time, but the people with whom he has labored have tho't generally that twas [wrong for] . . . such a Malefactor to be allowed his Victuals for his Labor . . . & the Sheriff has no publick provisions to feed your memorialist with & he has no Cloaths wherewith to cover himself." Insisting that he never intended to take up arms against his country, Benedict asked permission to go home to his mother. The General Assembly, again acting compassionately, ruled that Benedict should be discharged and could return to Danbury if the selectmen there so permitted.[66]

The American Revolution did not extinguish the Sandemanians. Like other religious groups through history, the sect may have gained strength from physical and verbal abuse. During the early nineteenth century, their numbers grew somewhat, especially in Danbury. Everywhere the Sandemanians were noted as people of substance and good character. Doubtless by the mid-nineteenth century the Sandemanians were regarded in most communities much as they were in Halifax, where, one historian has commented, "a Sandemanian's word in business stood just a little bit higher and his charity was carried just a little bit further."[67] Ironically, as their respectability and social conformity increased, the Sandemanians became enfeebled through internal dissension and schism. Excommunications were frequent, and disharmony grew to the point where the churches in Danbury and Portsmouth would no longer communicate with those in Boston and London. By about 1850, even in Danbury few if any new members were joining the church, and well before 1900 the last regular Sandemanian services in America ended.[68]

The Sandemanians thought of themselves not as revolutionaries but as true disciples of Christ. Some of their eighteenth-century contemporaries, however, considered their doctrines a threat to pure religion; others thought them a threat to social stability. As things turned out, the Sandemanians, as Loyalists, were never a political danger. Their neighbors, misunderstanding the Sandemanians' political stand, treated them like all the other Tories—in some cases, perhaps, just a bit worse. The patriots' dislike for the Sandemanians' odd religious life probably merged with a dislike for their politics at a time when direct attacks on a religious institution or group were neither legal nor socially acceptable. So the mob wrecking the Portsmouth church, the fearful New Haven citizens seeking the exile of the nine or ten Sandemanian families there, the militiamen interrogating the Danbury elders—these all may have been displays of religious hostility masked behind an acceptable political motive, the protection of society from real or supposed enemies in its midst.

The Sandemanians of the Revolutionary period earn our respect for their unflinching fidelity to their religious principles. Even Hopestill Capen of Boston and Comfort Benedict of Danbury, while insisting that they were good Americans, put their religion first. The Sandemanians themselves may have been confused over the issue of political loyalty, but they acted in remarkably consistent fashion. Sounding like activists but acting like pacifists, New England's Sandemanians emerge as a different kind of Loyalist.

NOTES

1. My definition of *Loyalist* is a composite of those of Robert Brown, *The Good Americans: The Loyalists in the American Revolution* (New York: William Morrow, 1969), 229–30, and *The King's Friends* (Providence: Brown Univ. Press, 1965), 20–33, 62, 250–52; Robert M. Calhoon, *The Loyalists in Revolutionary America, 1760–1781* (New York: Harcourt, 1973), xi, 281–83; Franklin B. Dexter, "Notes on Some of the New Haven Loyalists," *Papers of the New Haven Historical Society* (New Haven: Society, 1902), 9:33, 36; William H. Nelson, *The*

American Tory (Oxford: Oxford Univ. Press, 1961), 86–92; and Mary Beth Norton, *The British-Americans: The Loyalist Exiles in England, 1774–1789* (Boston: Little, Brown, 1972), 6–7. Also useful were Bruce E. Steiner, *Connecticut Anglicans in the Revolutionary Era: A Study in Communal Tensions* (n.p.: American Revolution Bicentennial Commission of Connecticut, 1978); and David Henry Villers, "Loyalism in Connecticut, 1763–1783" (Ph.D. diss., Univ. of Connecticut, 1975).

2. Williston Walker, *The Sandemanians of New England* (Annual Report, 1901, American Historical Association; published, Washington, D.C., 1902), is the major secondary source for this paper. Ezra Stiles was one of Walker's primary sources. See also H. H. Edes, "The Places of Worship of the Sandemanians in Boston," *Publications of the Colonial Society of Massachusetts*, vol. 6 (Boston: CSM, 1904); and George W. Hallock, "The Sandemanians," *New England Magazine* 13 (Apr. 1896): 239–44. For British theological background, see John Thomas Hornsby, "John Glas: A Study of the Origins, Development, and Influence of the Glasite Movement" (Ph.D. diss., Univ. of Edinburgh, 1936); and Lynn McMillon, "The Quest for the Apostolic Church: A Study of Scottish Origins of American Restorationism" (Ph.D. diss., Baylor Univ., 1972).

3. That New England's Congregational clergy were worried about Sandeman's possible impact is demonstrated in the Stiles Collection at Yale, which contains more than twenty letters about Sandeman. The authors of the letters, written between 1764 and 1769, were twelve clergymen throughout New England. Several letters contain accounts of meeting Sandeman or hearing him preach. All express considerable uncertainty about how to react to him.

4. Walker, *Sandemanians*, 138, 139.

5. Members of the sect are called Sandemanians in America and England but Glasites in Scotland. The American Sandemanians often referred to themselves simply as Disciples of Christ. Indeed, the present church known as Disciples of Christ has its origin in the 1817 schism within the Danbury Sandemanian church when Levi Osborn and others seceded over the issue of infant baptism.

6. Samuel Pike, *A Plain and Full Account of the Christian Practices of the Church in St. Martin's-le-Grand* (Boston, 1766), 13. Italics are Pike's.

7. Edes, "Places of Worship," 4.

8. Walker, *Sandemanians*, 152–53.

9. Charles H. Bell, *The Bench and Bar of New Hampshire* (Boston: Houghton, Mifflin, 1894), 450.

10. William G. McLoughlin, *New England Dissent, 1630–1833: The Baptists and the Separation of Church and State*, 2 vols. (Cambridge: Harvard Univ. Press, 1971), 2:240.

11. Nathaniel Barrell of Portsmouth, for example, distressed his wealthy father-in-law by refusing to let his children visit their grandfather, lest they be tainted by Congregationalist errors. George Ernst, *New England Miniature: A History of York, Maine* (Freeport, Maine: Bond Wheelwright Co., 1961), 71–73.

12. *Connecticut Courant*, Sept. 2, 1765; *Connecticut Gazette*, Sept. 6, 1765; *New London Gazette*, Aug. 23, 1765; all quoted in Oscar Zeichner, *Connecticut's Years of Controversy*,

1750–1776 (published for the Institute of Early American History and Culture, Williamsburg, Va., by the Univ. of North Carolina Press, 1949), 230.

13. Nathaniel Barrell to [?], June 19, 1766, Sandeman-Barrell Papers, Massachusetts Historical Society, Boston. The Sandeman-Barrell Papers are all bound in one volume, in a kind of scrapbook arrangement. The Massachusetts Historical Society has given permission for material to be quoted from this collection.

14. Robert Sandeman to Nathaniel Barrell, Jan. 8, 1767, Sandeman-Barrell Papers.

15. Petition of June 9, 1766, signed by Nathaniel Barrell, Benjamin Hart, Moses Noble, Colburn Barrell, Nathaniel Rogers, and William Fullerton. The text of this petition is given in *Provincial Papers,* vol. 7, *Province of New Hampshire, 1764 to 1776,* ed. Nathaniel Bouton (Nashua: Orren C. Moore, 1873), 112, but the names of only three of the signers (the Barrells and Hart) are included. The Sandeman-Barrell Papers at the Massachusetts Historical Society includes a paper that appears to be the original petition; all six signatures are on it.

16. Providence's Sandemanian church was established by 1771 (Ezra Stiles, *The Literary Diary,* ed. Franklin B. Dexter, 3 vols. [New York: Scribner's, 1901], 1:184). The church in Bethel, Conn., was established in 1774 (Walker, *Sandemanians,* 156); in Fairfield about 1774 (Steiner, *Connecticut Anglicans,* 50); in Newtown in 1774 (Ebenezer Russell White, *The Biography of Ebenezer Russell White,* 1818; photocopy of modern handwritten copy, Scott-Fanton Museum and Historical Society, Danbury, Conn., p. 50; location of original manuscript is unknown). The date when the Sandemanian church in North Stratford (now Trumbull) was founded is not known, but its existence is indicated by a letter from Ebenezer Russell White to Sturges Burr, Sept. 7, 1791 (Baldwin Family Papers, Yale Univ. Library). Following the outbreak of the Revolution, more churches were established in Deerfield and Taunton, Mass.; Newark, N.J.; and Halifax, Nova Scotia. The churches in Deerfield and Newark were small and probably of short duration. Sandemanian loyalist émigrés from Boston and New Haven were responsible for forming the church in Halifax. See Charles St. C. Stayner, "The Sandemanian Loyalists," *Collections of the Royal Nova Scotia Historical Society* 29 (1951): 62–123.

17. Walker, *Sandemanians,* 150. The Fairfield East Association of Congregational clergy met at Bethel, Conn., on May 29, 1763, to investigate complaints against White, the Reverend James Taylor of New Fairfield, and the Reverend Noah Wetmore of Bethel. Wetmore was cleared, but White and Taylor eventually were dismissed from their pastorates. See Congregational Churches, Connecticut, General Association, *Contributions to the Ecclesiastical History of Connecticut* (New Haven: William L. Kingsley, 1861), 298.

18. Chauncey Whittelsey to Ezra Stiles, Mar. 9, 1765, Stiles Collection, Beinecke Library, Yale Univ. Library, New Haven, Conn. The Yale University Library has granted permission to quote from this letter.

19. Franklin B. Dexter, *Biographical Sketches of the Graduates of Yale College* (New York: Holt, 1903), 2:681; Walker, *Sandemanians,* 153. Joseph Moss White is a mysterious figure. After this instance, his name does not occur again in reference to the Sandemanians. Apparently he lived his entire life in Danbury; he died there in 1822. Several contemporary

letters mention his brother, Ebenezer Russell White, as a church elder, and one wonders if Dexter's sources confused the two.

20. Dexter, *Biographical Sketches* (New York: Holt, 1903), 3:105–8, 168; M. Chamberlain to F. B. Dexter, Sept. 28, 1900, Dexter Papers, Yale Univ. Library, New Haven, Conn.

21. Connecticut Archives, Ecclesiastical Records, 15:196–99, 201, Connecticut State Library, Hartford.

22. Conn. Archives, Ecclesiastical Records, 15:193.

23. Ibid., 196–203.

24. Ibid., 196b.

25. Robert Sandeman et al., *Letters in Correspondence* . . . (Dundee, Scotland: Hill & Alexander, 1851), 108.

26. Ibid., 114.

27. Massachusetts Supreme Court of Judicature, "Indictment of Colburn Barrell for Preaching about Rebellion," Boston, Nov. 21, 1770. Boston Public Library, Chamberlain Collection. Quoted by courtesy of the Trustees of the Boston Public Library.

28. Walker, *Sandemanians,* 154; and Sandeman, *Letters in Correspondence,* 102–4.

29. Sandeman, *Letters in Correspondence,* 104.

30. Norton, *British-Americans,* 7.

31. Peter Force, ed., *American Archives,* 4th ser., vol. 1 (Washington, D.C., 1837), 364; Massachusetts Historical Society, *Proceedings,* 1st ser., vol. 11 (Boston: MHS, 1869–70), 392–94.

32. Massachusetts Historical Society, *Proceedings,* 1st ser., vol. 11 (Boston: MHS, 1869–70), 394–95.

33. L. Kinvin Wroth, ed., *Province in Rebellion: A Documentary History of the Founding of the Commonwealth of Massachusetts, 1774–1775* (microfiche and book) (Cambridge, Mass.: Harvard Univ. Press, 1975), doc. 2079–81.

34. Norton, *British-Americans,* 13.

35. *Province in Rebellion,* doc. 531; declaration of Aug. 29, 1774. The unpopular Massachusetts Government Act of 1774 created the mandamus councilors. The governor's councilors had heretofore been elected; henceforth the Crown would appoint them. The legal term *mandamus* implies the royal prerogative. See *English Historical Documents,* vol. 9, *American Colonial Documents to 1776,* ed. Merrill Jensen (New York: Oxford Univ. Press, 1962), 781–82.

36. Stiles, *Literary Diary,* 1:455.

37. Unlike most of the other Boston Sandemanians, the two Isaac Winslows (uncle and nephew), both Harvard educated, prosperous merchants, were Loyalists not only by religious scruple but also "by family ties, and by financial investment" (*Sibley's Harvard Graduates,* ed. Clifford K. Shipton [Boston: Massachusetts Historical Society, 1951], 8:337).

38. See Stayner, "Sandemanian Loyalists."

39. Zeichner, *Connecticut's Years,* 216.

40. Thomas C. Barrow, *Connecticut Joins the Revolution* (Chester, Conn.: Pequot Press, 1973), 41–42.

41. Edward E. Atwater, *History of the City of New Haven* (New York: Munsell, 1887), 140; Royal R. Hinman, *Historical Collection* (Hartford: Gleason, 1842), 588–89.

42. Both Chamberlain and Woodhull, like several other Sandemanians, were graduates of Yale. For Chamberlain see Dexter, *Biographical Sketches*, 3:105–8; for Woodhull, *Biographical Sketches*, 2:301–2.

43. Atwater, *History of the City of New Haven*, 139. See also Kenneth Scott and Rosanna Conway, comps., *Genealogical Data from Colonial New Haven Newspapers* (Baltimore: Genealogical Publishing Co., 1979), 215.

44. Samuel Andrew Peters, Declaration on Joseph Pynchon, Jan. 8, 1784, in Betts Autograph Collection, Yale Univ. Library, New Haven, Conn. Yale University Library has granted permission to quote from this manuscript.

45. John Sparhawk to Isaac Winslow Jr., Dec. 12, 1775, Winslow Papers, Massachusetts Historical Society, Boston.

46. Conn. Archives, Revolutionary War Records, 8:239a–239c. Daniel Humphreys (1740–1827), son of the Reverend Daniel Humphreys of Derby, Connecticut, and brother of Col. David Humphreys, one of Washington's aides, graduated from Yale in 1757 and eventually became a Portsmouth attorney (Dexter, *Biographical Sketches*, 2:471; Bell, *Bench and Bar*, 450). Thomas Gold (1732/3–?) was the son of the Reverend Hezekiah Gold of Stratford (Conn. Vital Records). Joseph Pynchon, who graduated from Yale in 1757, was the son of Col. William Pynchon of Springfield, Mass. (Dexter, *Biographical Sketches*, 2:488–89). Benjamin Smith (1732–?) was the brother of Titus Smith (1734–1807); both were born in Hadley, Massachusetts (Sylvester Judd, *History of Hadley* [Springfield, Mass.: H. R. Huntting & Co., 1905], 2:129). William Richmond, originally of Providence (Sandeman to Barrell, Mar. 25, 1767, Sandeman-Barrell Papers), was probably the William Richmond (1744–1828) who later became a judge in Providence (Joshua B. Richmond, *The Richmond Family* [Boston, 1897], 172). Oliver Burr (1745–1797) was the youngest son of Col. Andrew Burr of Fairfield, Conn. (Charles T. Burr, *A Genealogical History of the Burr Family*, 2d ed. (New York: Knickerbocker, 1891], 140). The other signers of this petition have been identified elsewhere.

47. Conn. Archives, Revolutionary War Records, 8:238b.

48. Ibid., 240a.

49. Ibid., 240a–240b. Italics occur in the original document.

50. Ibid., 241.

51. Ibid., 242.

52. Stiles, *Literary Diary*, 2:228. Richard Woodhull was the only declaration signer who did not leave New Haven. There is no record that he gave his parole. The General Assembly expressly stated that Woodhull's daughter would not be required (or allowed?) to leave because she was "Heiress to a considerable Real Estate in sd. New Haven Descended to her from her mother" (Conn. Archives, Revolutionary War Records, 8:242). All the Sandemanians except Woodhull and Oliver Burr eventually settled at least temporarily in Nova Scotia, many joining the Boston Sandemanians at Halifax. For an illuminating article on the Sandemanians' subsequent lives in Nova Scotia, see Stayner, "Sandemanian Loyalists."

53. The church in New Haven was never reestablished. The church in Boston was re-formed in March 1787 and continued until about 1823. See Isaac Winslow Jr. to Benjamin Davis Sr., Mar. 26, 1787, Winslow Papers; Edes, "Places of Worship," 10.

54. Petition to Court of Enquiry, Aug. 29, 1775, broadside, Massachusetts Historical Society, Boston. The society has granted permission to quote from this document.

55. Calhoon, *Loyalists*, 319; Massachusetts Historical Society, *Catalog of Manuscripts* (Boston: G. K. Hall, 1969), 1:109.

56. Force, *American Archives*, 4th ser., 3:851; Nelson, *American Tory*, 97–98.

57. Steiner, *Connecticut Anglicans*, 50.

58. John Sparhawk to Isaac Winslow, Dec. 5, 1775, Winslow Papers. The right margin of the manuscript is damaged; hence my interpolations, some conjectural, in the quotation.

59. John Sparhawk to Isaac Winslow, Dec. 5, 1775, Winslow Papers.

60. Daniel Humphreys to Joseph Hastings, June 6, 1777, Sandeman-Barrell Papers.

61. The three Benedicts mentioned in this essay—Thomas, Hezekiah, and Comfort—were not closely related. Benedict was a common Danbury name.

62. Conn. Archives, Revolutionary War Records, 37:136–44.

63. Ebenezer White presents an interesting historical problem here. He was never a full-fledged Sandemanian himself, but his two sons were. We can conjecture that he was a Loyalist from two pieces of evidence: (1) in 1775 Samuel Andrew Peters, the Anglican priest, included White and his two sons in his list of five Danbury Loyalists (Villers, "Loyalism in Connecticut," 487); (2) a number of British officers made their headquarters in White's house (Robert McDevitt, *Connecticut Attacked: A British Viewpoint, Tryon's Raid on Danbury* [Chester, Conn.: Pequot Press, 1974], 37–38). Generally officers chose the homes of Loyalists to lodge in, and the Loyalist scouts who aided Tryon's entry into the town were Danbury natives and would have known who was safe. About twenty houses in Danbury were burned during the British raid (McDevitt, *Connecticut Attacked*, 43). James Bailey, Danbury's historian, states that White's house was one of them (*History of Danbury, Conn., 1684–1896* [New York: Burr, 1896], 73). Bailey probably made this statement because White was one of the eighteen individuals who submitted "fire claims" to the General Assembly after the raid. However, the amount of his claim, £1,637.60, was markedly smaller than most claims for destroyed houses. That it was not his house that was burned can also be argued because when White died two years later, he left considerable household furnishings, including an extensive library (Danbury Probate Records). If White's house had burned, this library almost certainly would have been destroyed. It seems much more likely that it was not his house for which he was seeking recompense but either a small outbuilding or the meetinghouse for the New Danbury Church, built by his congregation in 1768 but unused for several years. Bailey (73) says that the meetinghouse was burned, and no further mention of the building appears in Danbury records. Assuming, then, that it was White's church and not house that burned, we are left with three possibilities: the British burned it; it burned accidentally; or the American patriots burned it in retaliation for losses inflicted by the British.

64. For a list of the Danbury men drafted May 2, 1777, to serve in the 16th Regiment, Continental Army, see Conn. Archives, Revolutionary War Records, 6:104. The names of several Sandemanian men, including Joseph Moss White and Comfort Benedict, appear also in the list of men drafted May 1, 1778, but again there is no evidence that any of them actually served (Connecticut Historical Society, *Collections* [Hartford: Society, 1909], 12:119).

65. Conn. Archives, Revolutionary War Records, 13:285.

66. Ibid., 20:96.

67. Stayner, "Sandemanian Loyalists," 113.

68. There are still (1987) two small congregations left, in London and in Edinburgh. Gerard Sandeman, the great-great-grandson of Robert Sandeman's brother David, is one of the Edinburgh elders. The London congregation, which sold its meetinghouse in 1985, is not a formal church because it has only one elder. I am indebted to Kenneth Weller of London for this information. [Editor's note: Gerard Lionel Sandeman died Nov. 11, 1999. See Lynn McMillon, "End of an Era in Edinburgh: Gerard Lionel Sandeman, the Last of Glasite Restoration Leaders, Dies," *Christian Chronicle* 57 (Feb. 2000): 1.]

Unity and Separation

Contrasting Elements in the Thought and Practice of Robert and James Alexander Haldane

Deryck W. Lovegrove

In June 1799 the General Assembly of the Church of Scotland issued a pastoral admonition to its congregations denouncing the missionaries of the newly formed Society for Propagating the Gospel at Home (SPGH). They were, it alleged, "a set of men whose proceedings threatened no small disorder to the country."[1] In issuing this warning the assembly brought to public attention for the first time the work of two of the most prominent Scottish leaders of the Evangelical Revival, Robert and James Alexander Haldane. The Haldane brothers, two of the moving spirits behind the offending organization, were wealthy Presbyterian converts to an undenominational activism already much in evidence south of the border. For a decade spanning the turn of the century their religious enterprise challenged Scottish ecclesiastical conventions, provoking strong contemporary reactions and leading to a marked divergence in subsequent historical assessment. From "the Wesley and Whitefield of Scotland,"[2] at one extreme, they have been described less fulsomely as the source of a movement that, though it alarmed all the Presbyterian churches, proved to be short-lived, dying away "among its own domestic quarrels," "marred by bitterness of speech, obscurantism and fanaticism."[3]

Contemporaries seem to have found it little easier to agree on the leaders' personal qualities. In 1796 Thomas Jones, the minister of Lady Glenorchy's Chapel in Edinburgh, commended Robert Haldane to William Wilberforce as "a man of strickt honour integrity religion prudence and virtue," who being "possessed of a fortune from £50,000 to £60,000 . . . thinks it is his duty . . . to employ a considerable portion of it in promoting the cause of God."[4] By 1809 Haldane's former friend and colleague, Greville Ewing, had become so disenchanted with his methods that, having referred to him scornfully as "the POPE of independents," he accused him bitterly of "the greatest effort [he had ever seen] from any motive whatsoever, to ruin the comfort, and the usefulness, of a minister of the gospel."[5] Though his brother, James, appears to have inspired a more universal affection, the forcefulness of both personalities ensured that mere neutrality would never be easy.

From the fleeting comments offered by historians the most positive evaluation of the Haldanes centers upon their "undenominationalism" or "catholicity."[6] Their obvious dislike of denominational division and their willingness to make common cause in Evangelical ventures with all people of similar sentiments has prompted the most recent work on Scottish Congregationalism to speak of their advocacy of "ecumenical Christianity."[7] While this is to some extent misleading, a more widespread view is that the diminished emphasis on ecclesiastical distinctions was accompanied by a beneficial release from the tyranny of conventional and external forms of worship.[8] In its best moments the Haldane movement focused upon the more fundamental issues at the heart of religious life.

Negatively, most commentators have noted the link within the new movement between the propensity for innovation and the appearance of a critical spirit leading to division, disenchantment, and ultimately to failure;[9] a tendency to ignore the wider principles of religion in favor of tithing mint, dill, and cumin. In one or two summaries, however, there is an interesting variation on the latter theme, for while the work of the Haldanes is not seen as accomplishing anything significant in its own right, it is regarded as a necessary goad, having the most salutary effect upon a neglectful and complacent religious establishment.[10] In January 1798, following a lengthy but encouraging exploratory tour to the north of Scotland by James Haldane, John Aikman, and Joseph Rate, an itinerancy which discovered a ready response to evangelism in many places, and especially in the remote county of Caithness, a group of laymen met in Edinburgh to draw up the constitution of the SPGH.[11] At the heart of the new society was the conviction that many parts of the country were deprived of adequate means of religious instruction.

The founding address set out in unequivocal terms the undenominational character of the new body, declaring: "it is not our design to form or to extend the influence of any sect. Our sole intention is to make known the everlasting gospel of our Lord Jesus Christ." It was envisaged that the society would "be composed of persons of every denomination, holding unity of faith in the leading doctrines of Christianity." Its agents, both itinerant preachers and catechists, were required "to endeavour to strengthen the hands of all faithful ministers of Jesus Christ of whatever denomination, and as far as they [could] discourage all bitter party spirit, wherever they discover[ed] it among Christians."[12]

In adopting these aims the new society stood firmly in the Evangelical tradition of the 1790s, a decade which saw the formation of many similar co-operative schemes from the village itinerancy and the Religious Tract Society to the [London] Missionary Society. Against a background of population movement, social and political upheaval, and growing dissatisfaction with the established forms of religion, the new co-operative Christian spirit suited the needs of the age.

Nor was co-operation merely a matter of expedience. Throughout their careers as church leaders the Haldanes were prepared to work with anyone whose aims were compatible with their own. In their early, Presbyterian phase both brothers gave their support to the Society in Scotland for Propagating Christian Knowledge (SSPCK). James served a regular three-year term on the committee of directors from March 1796 until December 1798, the eve of his ordination as an independent pastor.[13] From his 1796 tour with Charles Simeon to the welcome he extended at his own pulpit in Edinburgh to ministers of various persuasions, including Anglicans, Independents, and Baptists, the former ship's captain displayed an evangelist's disregard for the niceties of denominational distinction.[14] On his preaching tours, while he tended at first to criticize laxity, error, and narrowness wherever he found them, he readily identified with those of similar views, such as the parish minister at Tain in Easter Ross and George Cowie, the Antiburgher minister at Huntly, who shared the same interest in evangelism.[15]

Although the Haldane movement evoked little response in Scottish Episcopalian circles, apart from the brief itinerancy of William Ward based on the Chapel of Old Deer in Aberdeenshire, friendly contacts with English Evangelical clergymen were more substantial.[16] In addition to the dubious help of Rowland Hill, a considerable influence came through the correspondence of John Campbell with leading figures in the English revival.[17] Campbell, the "philanthropic ironmonger" of Edinburgh's Grassmarket, was both an intimate friend of the Haldanes and other Scottish Evangelicals and of the venerable Anglican clergyman John Newton, Rector of Saint Mary Woolnoth in the City of London.[18] These personal contacts were supplemented by the monthly appearance of the *Missionary Magazine*,[19] an Edinburgh-based periodical that copied the format and content of the English *Evangelical Magazine*.[20] The Scottish publication gave those associated with the SPGH a detailed awareness of the wider scale of Christian expansion, including ventures that received Anglican support.

As the Scottish movement achieved a degree of stability and success, plans were set in motion for the creation in the largest and most strategically sited burghs of tabernacles or preaching centers on the Whitefieldite model, meeting places the poor could attend freely in order to hear a succession of Evangelical preachers.[21] Though the new buildings soon acquired a quasi-denominational character, serving as homes for congregations of "tabernacle people,"[22] their existence, especially in the early stages of the movement, represented a genuine expression of the undenominational spirit. The substance of the message preached from their pulpits, as in the open air, was biblical and conversionary, and as such devoted little thought to the weightier matters of church order. While in the longer term the experiment proved unstable,[23] the immediate effect of the tabernacles was to provide a visible focus of unity and achievement.

Despite its essential concern for the common elements of Reformed Protestantism, the initial success of the Haldane movement provoked a strong reaction from the Scottish churches. Unconvinced by its protestations that it had no intention of creating another sect, the opponents of the new Evangelicalism were alarmed precisely by its indifference toward existing forms of Presbyterianism. Within the established church the hostility of the dominant moderate party, with its distaste for any form of enthusiasm, was both predictable and obvious. As the 1799 Pastoral Admonition, Declaratory Act, and associated correspondence reveal, leaders such as George Hill of Saint Mary's College, Saint Andrews, objected strongly to what they regarded as an attempt by the missionary preachers to alienate the affections of the people from their parish ministers.[24] The smaller Presbyterian bodies, the Antiburgher and Relief synods, reacted against the Haldane preachers with similar proscriptive measures.[25] The very existence and operations of a new and aggressively expansionist body such as the SPGH seemed to imply a measure of criticism and to threaten the future viability of local congregations.

For the established church there was the additional fear that this new unitive movement concealed more sinister republican and democratic ideals. As early as January 1797 William Porteous, a Glasgow minister, had voiced this concern in connection with Robert Haldane's contemporary application to the East India Company to go as a missionary to Benares. Writing to Robert Dundas, the Lord Advocate, Porteous stated his belief "that the whole of this missionary business grows from a democratical root."[26] In this, as in the other areas of concern, the substance and force behind the complaint stemmed from the recognition that a new and unprecedented combination of interests had appeared that paid scant regard to conventional norms.

If the confrontation that developed during the late 1790s represented a clash between the opposing interests of religious revival and traditional churchmanship, the Haldanes appeared two decades later in more surprising circumstances: at the heart of a bitter dispute involving one of the primary instruments of Evangelicalism. The new controversy erupted in 1821, when Robert Haldane began investigating the practices of the British and Foreign Bible Society.

In the Apocrypha Controversy, as it came to be known, there were no factors of ecclesiastical polity or ministry to cloud the issue. The debate centered upon the practical expression of Christian unity made possible by the fundamental rule of the Bible Society, the circulation of the Scriptures without note or comment. In August that year it had come to Haldane's notice that Continental versions of the Bible circulated by the society included the Apocrypha.[27] Not only in his eyes was scriptural purity at stake, but also the clarity and effectiveness of evangelism, for the Bible Society had been created in 1804 as a primary instrument of the Evangelical Revival. Out of the many societies formed in that period, it alone, by virtue of its simple and unexceptionable aim, had been able genuinely to transcend denominational barriers and thereby attract the widest measure of support.[28]

Over the ensuing twelve years Robert Haldane fought a tireless campaign in conjunction with the leading Church of Scotland evangelical, Andrew Thomson, and the Edinburgh auxiliary of the Bible Society, against what he believed to be the compromising policies of the Earl Street committee of the parent body. In a succession of lengthy tracts Haldane sought to expose the naiveté, expediency, and duplicity of the London directors, the heterodoxy of many of their Continental agents, the hostile attitude of the latter toward evangelical activity, the deficiency of certain translations employed by the society, and the theological harm caused by circulating the Apocrypha with its mixture of "absurdities" and "pernicious doctrines."[29]

As an opponent of Bible Society policy Haldane did not stand alone, yet there cannot have been many more forthright attacks upon the directors than those that flowed from his pen. If they persisted in their errors, he believed, their clear duty was to adopt a more appropriate name, one which emphasized the inclusion of the Apocrypha. The society's supporters would then be under no illusion as to the object to which their donations were applied. The published reports, he suggested with unconcealed scorn, should state that "[t]his is a Society which does *not* confine itself with rigorous exactness to the dissemination of the Holy Scriptures, as they are received by Christians of different denominations in this country, who have all resolved to merge their peculiarities so as to agree in publishing, as the Bible, whatever shall be considered to be the Bible, whether in Christian, Mahometan, or Pagan countries: to all of which it has pledged itself to extend its influence."[30]

Despite the catholicity of his intentions and the interdenominational unity of the Edinburgh committee, a body which included both Churchmen and Dissenters, it is all too easy, given Haldane's developing reputation for controversy, to see his Calvinist and biblical susceptibilities as shibboleths standing in the way of a wider cooperation between Christians of different persuasions. The Scottish controversialist would, of course, have regarded any such collaboration as entirely spurious.

I

Like many exponents of Evangelicalism operating in a climate of disdain for ideas associated with enthusiastic manifestations of religious revival, the author of *The Evidence and Authority of Divine Revelation* and the *Exposition of the Epistle to the Romans* was fond of emphasizing his wholehearted commitment to the classical doctrines of the Christian faith.[31] In his *Letter to the Editor of the Edinburgh Christian Instructor* (1820) he set his own concern for orthodoxy against various erroneous notions culled from the writings of eminent Churchmen, including William Warburton and William Paley. Four years later, in his reply to strictures made by Professor Chenevière of Geneva in the pages of the *Monthly Repository*, he drew an even more powerful contrast between his own affinity with the teachings of Calvin and his fellow Reformers, and the deviation from those doctrines displayed by the Venerable Company of Pastors.[32]

Yet the impressive list of writings published by the Haldanes in their very titles denoted a strong controversial tendency. Repeatedly the authors emphasized their differences with contemporary church leaders on many of the central issues of Christian theology. Moderate parish ministers in Scotland, encountered by James Haldane during his 1797 tour, were castigated for their resort to a pulpit doctrine enshrining the merit of good works, rather than justification by faith alone.[33] The Genevan pastors, led by Chenevière, were rebuked by his brother for their denial of the divinity of Christ and their rejection of a range of biblical ideas contemptuously dismissed as "the mysterious points of the Christian religion."[34] Professor Tholuck of Halle University, quoted elsewhere sympathetically for his negative assessment of the vitality of Continental religion in the mid 1820s,[35] was censured a decade later for his own Neology.[36] Even fellow Evangelicals and Dissenters were taken to task for errors ranging from an overemphasis on the human response to God and a rejection of limited atonement[37] to Edward Irving's insistence on the corruptibility of the human nature of Christ.[38] Ironically, this eagerness to criticize the doctrinal shortcomings of others conveys an impression not of mainstream sympathies but of an outlook essentially sectarian.

The opposition mounted by both writers to the theological errors they detected around them was well argued and logical. Robert Haldane in particular emphasized the destructive effect of false belief on the complex of doctrines that constituted the gospel. In his reply to Chenevière he recounted his own systematic use of the Epistle to the Romans to demonstrate to the Genevan theological students who had gathered in his house in 1817 the principal Pauline teachings concerning the person and work of Christ. He attempted also to show the steps by which he believed the city's pastors had undermined the doctrinal integrity of the faith. In this work, as in the tracts concerning the Bible Society, he displayed a low regard for the theological condition of Continental Protestantism. Many Continental theologians, in his eyes, were beyond the pale of Christian cooperation. Their heterodoxy merely lent weight to a deliberate campaign to subvert, neutralize, and even persecute orthodox Christianity. As can be seen from both the Geneva and Apocrypha controversies, a constant polemical barrage was maintained against the insidious effects of Arminianism. Yet in the end no one error or set of mistakes was regarded as all-important. Both writers saw themselves confronted by a shifting network of ideas, not always consistent but possessing the same debilitating and destructive potential in their effect on vital belief and, therefore, claiming their best attention as defenders of the faith.

In his "Summary of the Theological Controversies Which of Late Years Have Agitated the City of Geneva," published in 1824, Chenevière had defined his adversary's views as intolerant and partisan. The baneful influence upon the Genevan students he described as "A Scotchman, Mr Haldane, a rigid Calvinist, whose theological principles are to be found in print, especially in his Commentary on the Epistle to the Romans, in which those who have the courage to undertake the task may judge of his doctrines."[39] Assuming a substantial measure of truth in Haldane's own portrayal of Chenevière, the Genevan professors' description was entirely predictable. Yet even the more sympathetic Ami Bost, himself a participant in the Swiss *Réveil*, had reservations concerning the Scotsman's views: "On peut admettre qu'il fallait au commencement de l'oeuvre, et en présence d'une incrédulité presque absolue, des principes rigoureux: et tous ceux qui ont connu M. Haldane s'accordent, sans exception, à en parler avec un amour, une reconnaissance et un respect également profonds. Quant à moi . . . je ne l'ai pas connu personnellement. Il est probable que, même après avoir subi son influence, je l'eusse secouée plus tard dans ce qu'elle avait de trop étroit."[40]

Given the use made of reasoned argument by Robert Haldane in pursuit of his apologetic aims, especially in his approach to the early-nineteenth-century quest for convincing evidences with which to supplement, or supplant, revelation, it might be possible to ignore the Swiss evidence and to regard his theological views as a synthesis between traditional Calvinism and more optimistic beliefs stemming from the Enlightenment. Such an interpretation might appear to gain credibility from his unwavering interest in evangelism. Yet his approach to the pursuit of Christian evidences was not characteristic of the genre. In *The*

Evidence and Authority of Divine Revelation he declared that he had long been deeply convinced that it was necessary "to attend not merely to the arguments which can be adduced to prove the Bible to be true, but to the Salvation which it reveals." He aimed to treat the evidences of Christianity not in the abstract, but in close association with doctrine and as a means of vindicating "the full inspiration and unspeakable value of the Holy Scriptures." Obliquely he criticized many of his eighteenth-century predecessors for portraying natural religion based on evidences as an adequate substitute for a faith dependent upon divine revelation.[41]

At a comparatively late point in his life, Robert Haldane reiterated his firm adherence to Calvinist doctrine. Writing against certain views expressed in Tholuck's *Exposition of St Paul's Epistle to the Romans* he described the "moderate Calvinism" professed by some of his contemporaries as "refined Arminianism." It was, he argued, "impossible to modify the former without sliding into the latter." Election, though a doctrine unpalatable to many Christians because of their faulty conception of divine truth, was explicitly taught in Scripture and was essential to the biblical concept of salvation.[42] In each of the brothers' writings, reliance upon reason was ultimately limited by deference to biblical authority. Repeated appeals were made to the obvious meaning of Scripture, and if their Calvinism has to be qualified it can only be so by the addition of a prefix such as "biblical" or "evangelical." Haldaneism was not a resurgence of early-eighteenth-century Calvinism, with its gloomy emphasis upon the doctrine of reprobation. Of the two men, Robert evinced the greater concern for the philosophical aspect of theology, yet even he made little mention of hell or reprobation. In his reply to Chenevière, as in his later exposition of Romans, he treated election as a positive concept, one which was a source of joy to the Christian believer.[43] Ultimate respect was accorded to the idea of divine sovereignty, since every other doctrine was seen to be contingent upon it. In consequence he displayed a marked reluctance to probe the adverse significance of limited atonement, despite his willingness to affirm his belief in the doctrine only days before his death.[44]

Though James Haldane restated his own adherence to the doctrines of the Westminster Confession as late as 1846,[45] his writings display a less formal commitment to Calvinism than that expressed by his brother. While their differences in matters of belief were minimal, James made little if any reference to any inherited system of doctrine, appealing only to scriptural authority and apostolic practice. It was that biblicism that led him, rather exceptionally given the confessional nature of Scottish churchmanship, to reject explicitly as early as 1806 the authority of the Confession.[46] In practice, that rejection is not so surprising, for there was in this period a widespread movement away from belief in the covenanted community.[47] His anticonfessional stance was, moreover, far from complete, for although he had withdrawn his formal assent to the Confession, he had not rejected its theology. His objections were concerned with its social and political implications, and with the idea of so much significance being attached to historical and, therefore, ultimately fallible human constructs, in preference to the authority of the divinely inspired text.

II

If the first signs of the Haldanes's sensitivity toward civil religion began to emerge, as the testimony of Greville Ewing and James Somerville suggests, in private discussions following their adoption of Evangelicalism,[48] the period prior to the Pastoral Admonition remained one of close connections with the established church. However strongly they felt about the lethargy and theological shortcomings of the Scottish clergy, their new active faith led them to regard themselves as agents of the wider church, whose duty was to engage with others of similar philanthropic intentions. It was in this spirit that Robert Haldane conceived the plan of selling his estate at Airthrey, near Stirling, and with the proceeds establishing a privately sponsored mission in Bengal. Of his three projected companions, two were active ministers of the established church, while the other, though a Dissenter in England because of his nonepiscopal ordination, had received his training at the Edinburgh Divinity Hall.[49]

In the stream of importunate letters and the printed *Memorial* directed in turn between September 1796 and the following summer at the lord advocate, the secretary of state for war and the colonies, and the directors of the East India Company, the Airthrey landowner emphasized his broad Christian concern for the people of India. In an early letter to Henry Dundas he argued that plans in hand to create an extensive religious establishment in India would not be affected by his own proposal: "My plan does not supersede theirs. The field is by much too ample for us all; & I am sure the Gentlemen will rejoice at any assistance which can be given them."[50] Writing to the secretary of state's nephew, Robert Dundas, in a markedly more insistent and less deferential vein, Haldane took care to align his project with the Scottish establishment: "Indeed we can scarcely suppose that you will not grant our request, when we are assured that you countenanced the Scotch Society for propagating the Gospel, & expressed your affection for the Christian Religion, your predeliction [*sic*] for the Church of Scotland, & approbation of the general views & objects of the Society—Our views are entirely the same as theirs & therefore they ought also to meet with your Countenance & approbation. At the same time we think it proper to observe that we are no bigots to any sect. What we wish to propagate is the great Doctrines & principles of Christianity—Modes & Forms of Worship are with us things of far inferiour consideration."[51]

When the plans for the Bengal mission were rejected in January 1797 by the East India Company directorate, Robert Haldane turned his attention to another possible means of realizing his aim with semiofficial church blessing. At the beginning of February he wrote to the committee of directors of the SSPCK requesting a commission from the society "and authority to such as are Ministers among us to preach the Gospel abroad, and to those of us who are not Ministers to assist them as Catechists." In March a general meeting of the society, having carefully considered a report from a subcommittee appointed to investigate the matter, approved the request and the text of the commission. The latter stipulated that Ewing, Innes, and Bogue, the ministers involved, should demit their charges in a regular manner, that the expenses of the work should be borne entirely by those commissioned, that a regular report of the work should be submitted to the society, and that the commission should not in any way be deemed to interfere with the legal rights of any other corporate body or chartered company.[52] Although the plan never came to fruition, Robert Haldane's acceptance by the society in the relatively humble role of catechist marked the closest the Haldane movement came to a formal expression of its catholic aspirations.

Although, as William Innes later recalled, the source of inspiration for the India project was the first account of William Carey's mission to Bengal,[53] too much significance should not be attached to the Dissenting aspect of that English precedent. The Scottish plan owed more to the zeal of a new convert, and to the undenominational character of the Christianity embraced, than to any consideration of the relationship between religion and the state. When, therefore, the dream of an overseas venture proved impossible and the Haldanes turned to domestic evangelism, there is little reason for doubting the sincerity of the nonsectarianism they expressed in 1799 through the SPGH. Nor is it surprising that two years earlier Robert Haldane rounded indignantly on John Robison for a serious calumny against him. The Edinburgh professor in a purported exposé of a sinister international conspiracy had attributed to the would-be missionary, with thinly veiled anonymity, the statement that "he would willingly wade to the knees in blood to overturn the establishment of the Kirk of Scotland."[54]

Yet, as the discussions within the Haldane-Ewing circle indicate, doubts existed from a very early stage concerning the validity of religious establishments, a debate which in the form of an untimely leak almost certainly provided the basis for Robison's lurid attribution. After 1797 the force of questioning intensified as relationships between the evangelists and the established church began to deteriorate. With the publication of the General Assembly's 1799 Declaratory Act against unqualified ministers and preachers, and a further report investigating the most effective method of regulating "vagrant teachers and Sunday schools,"[55] leading churchmen openly appealed to the civil power for assistance in controlling the new expansionist religious movement.[56] William Robertson, the procurator of the Church of Scotland, obligingly provided the Lord Advocate with a long and detailed list of relevant legislation already to be found on the statute book.[57] Nor was recourse to the law only contemplated in Edinburgh. Both the records of the Presbytery of Caithness and private correspondence reveal that prosecutions were brought against the SPGH preachers John Cleghorn and William Ballantine at Inverness justiciary court in September 1799 on the grounds of their unauthorized celebration of marriages. Those who supported the accused feared a sentence of transportation, though in the event no penalty was imposed.[58]

Even before the established church had begun to apply formal methods of control the Haldanes's attitude had hardened. On February 3, 1799, James was ordained as pastor of the Congregational church newly constituted in the Edinburgh Circus. What had commenced the previous summer as a means of providing indoor accommodation for evangelistic preaching to the city's poorer inhabitants had begun to evolve into a gathered church. Under the twin influences of practical necessity and scriptural exposition the rationale of the new type of ecclesiastical organization gradually developed, with the pastor providing an impetus for the process through his numerous publications setting out the apostolic ideal and the appropriate forms of order and discipline. By 1808 his mature view of the local church, as "a body of persons collected together by the influence of the truth, and appearing to walk according to it,"[59] not only embraced the principle of separation from the world, including the state, but had begun in its quest for purity to discover certain tensions between that goal and the original task of evangelism.[60]

In the gradual emergence of the new form of church community three important elements can be detected. The confluence of Enlightenment thinking and Whitefieldite Evangelicalism had produced an attitude that defined religious life in individual terms. Such an approach allowed the recognition of the essentially secular character of contemporary society. Within the Haldane movement there was from the outset a marked preference for a literal and commonsense treatment of the biblical text. Under the influence of this tendency the earlier Calvinist focus upon Old Testament covenant theology gave way to a simple, pragmatic quest for apostolicity. As the concept of apostolic order developed, so, in turn, the initial practical aims began to yield to more theoretical considerations. In 1807, at Kingsland Chapel on the northern outskirts of London, the pastor, John Campbell, found himself facing solemn warnings and even sarcasm from Robert Haldane regarding the danger of preferring "usefulness" to "duty." Campbell was only able to resist the pressure exerted by his Scottish friend with the help of letters he had received over many years from his nonseparatist confidant, John Newton.[61]

By 1808 the transition from national church to radical Independency had been completed. The former willingness to subordinate matters of organization and government to the all-consuming task of evangelism had been replaced by the conviction that any formal link between church and state was indefensible, being intrinsically harmful to true religion. The earlier insistence upon common action had given way to an equally striking preoccupation with order and discipline. Yet James Haldane, whose writings most clearly illustrate the new focus of attention, steadily refused to advocate any form of resistance to the established church other than that of scriptural argument. Instead, he portrayed the later refusal of the voluntaries to pay the annuity tax, levied for the support of the established clergy, as a rejection of the biblical injunction to be subject to civil government.[62] Though he could not himself support the principle of establishment, he warned in 1832 that the growing enthusiasm for the forcible separation of church and state marked not a coming triumph for Christianity, but rather the entrance upon an apocalyptic struggle with the forces of infidelity.[63]

III

Prominent among James Haldane's reasons for disapproving of establishment was his belief that the civil connection exerted a deleterious influence upon the church's ministry. In a reply to Thomas Chalmers he suggested that worldliness and professionalism were the hallmarks of an established clergy.[64] Although he was able to maintain a lasting friendship with parish ministers who shared his Evangelical convictions, his relationship with others was less satisfactory. Haldane's early strictures against the clergy emerged in the context of his own itinerant preaching. They were concerned not primarily with moral weakness or practical shortcomings, but with the doctrinal and spiritual contribution made by the individual to public worship. Gone was the old respect for clerical learning: in its place a more subjective assessment based upon what was regarded as the only appropriate qualification, a knowledge of "the doctrine of Christ" necessarily denied to those who had not experienced regeneration.[65] At Kirriemuir in 1797, having attended communion in the parish church, the evangelist told a large crowd assembled in the market place "that what they had heard was not the gospel."[66] This aggressive practice directed against individuals aroused widespread ill feeling. It was one of the factors which, in spite of its rapid abandonment, persuaded moderate Evangelical ministers not to denounce the Pastoral Admonition and Declaratory Act.[67]

Yet this early polemical tone, and the encouragement given to alternative forms of ministry, did not indicate a complete disregard for existing conventions. Contrary to the impression created by the Pastoral Admonition, with its denunciation of those who assumed "the character of missionaries" without the "advantages of regular education," the new movement did not reject the Reformed concern for adequate theological preparation.[68] Instead, it transferred the balance of emphasis from the moral and intellectual sphere to that of spirituality. There was a recognition that even the new type of itinerant preacher needed not only to be literate, but also to receive appropriate instruction in doctrine, biblical exposition, and homiletics. The English model of evangelical expansion, from which much of the Scottish impetus derived, had already created a prominent role for a revised version of the traditional Dissenting academy.[69] It was this that influenced Robert Haldane in the establishment of a series of seminary classes at Glasgow, Dundee, and Edinburgh between 1799 and 1808.[70]

Those accepted for training were left under no illusion concerning their sponsor's intentions, nor of the strict limitations they were expected to place on personal ambition. As a former journeyman-printer and member of the 1799 class later recalled: "Mr Haldane, most distinctly gave us, his students, to understand that by that means we were not to rise above the level on which he found us. He was mistaken, for by the very fact that we had become educated persons, and ministers of religion, without indulging any self conceit, we were raised considerably in the social scale."[71] Though many of the three hundred men trained in the seminary classes spent some while as itinerant preachers, the majority eventually became settled pastors. Several attained prominence within the wider church, while a few achieved some measure of academic distinction. The intellectual content of the courses may have improved when Haldane extended the training period from twelve months to two years, but disagreements connected with the syllabus revealed the sponsor's somewhat limited aims. In 1800 he acceded grudgingly to Greville Ewing's concern to instruct the students in Greek, but he refused to consider Latin and Hebrew on the grounds of time and relative usefulness.[72] The possession of a two-year seminary education was sufficient to expose the weakness of most contemporary allegations of ignorance, but the academic training afforded to Haldane students did not compare with the traditional standards set for Presbyterian ordinands.

The practical estrangement from the parish ministry created by these differences in educational attainment and social status was of comparatively little consequence, however, compared to that which stemmed from the apparently amorphous character of the Haldaneite ministry. With their unregulated band of itinerant preachers, catechists, Sabbath school teachers, and peregrinating ministers, the operations of the SPGH outraged the Presbyterian sense of propriety. The blurring of the traditional distinction between lay status and that of the ordained preaching ministry offended many within the established church, including the widely respected Evangelical leader John Erskine, who believed that laymen at most should confine their activities to private exhortation.[73] Despite a spirited defense of lay preaching,[74] there is no sign that the passage of time lessened this alienation, and the appearance in 1800 of the first products of the Haldane seminary classes, with their dedication to an itinerant ministry, merely served to emphasize the division.

The ordination of James Haldane as pastor of the Circus church might be interpreted as the first sign of a return to a more conventional view of ministry, but this was not the case. Guided by biblical and apostolic practice and influenced by his reading of the eighteenth-century separatists Glas and Sandeman, he moved steadily to a more radical position. By 1806 he was advocating a form of leadership based on a plurality of elders. These men would not be a reiteration of the Presbyterian concept of the ruling elder, for Haldane had already come to reject the lay-clerical distinction as unscriptural. They were instead a group of members set apart and ordained by the congregation for the task of ministry. Quoting a Presbyterian author, he argued that ordination conferred no special status or honor, conveyed no supernatural character, and signified only an appointment to a task within the church. Nor was it correct to associate the practice primarily with the administration of the ordinances, for baptism and the Lord's Supper had wrongly usurped the place of preaching.[75]

In 1808 the quest for an apostolic ministry reached its final stage at the Edinburgh Tabernacle, with mutual exhortation being accorded a prominent place in public worship. The significance of this development lay less in its extension of the ministerial function to all church members than in its implications for conventional attitudes toward selection and preparation for the pastoral office. In a pamphlet commending mutual exhortation as a divine ordinance James Haldane argued that existing methods of selecting pastors depended upon human judgment and learning. The process leading to ordination, even among the new Independent congregations, presupposed at least a formal trial of gifts. More commonly, he suggested, "Young men are obtained from academies; and if they appear to possess a little learning, and a tolerable facility in speaking, every other pastoral qualification is overlooked." By contrast, the new practice, when incorporated in congregational worship, provided a natural means for the divine choice of pastoral leadership to become apparent.[76] The implications of his views were obvious. Not only did mutual exhortation have the effect of eliminating the element of rational selection, it also removed the need for theological institutions with their manifest reliance upon human learning.[77] Not surprisingly the new elements of worship at the tabernacle aroused strong opposition. John Aikman described them as "destructive, both of the pastoral office and of all order in the house of God."[78] More generally the Haldanes became identified, even in the thinking of many of their former associates, with a restless desire for innovation.

IV

Accusations of that character were by no means new. Almost a decade earlier opponents of the SPGH had criticized the society's agents for believing that they possessed "some secret and novel method of bringing men to heaven." The ecclesiastical legislation of 1799 had sought to combat contempt for "the rules . . . for the orderly dispensation of the word and sacraments."[79] Yet the Haldanes and their disciples, at the outset at least, had shown few signs of renouncing accepted patterns of worship and discipline. Practical itinerancy provided little scope for experiment in either sphere.

During the early preaching tours attendance at parish worship was not uncommon, and while the less congenial sermons were often subjected to public scrutiny, there is no suggestion that the itinerant's presence at the service betrayed any kind of ulterior motive. Where sympathetic clergy were involved the situation was more straightforward. In May 1798 Joseph Rate, an itinerant with the SPGH, attended the Kirk at East Wemyss, where he "heard an evangelical lecture from Mr Gib, the minister there." A few days earlier another of the society's agents had preached by invitation in the parish church at Croy, near Inverness.[80] The following summer, before the ban on unauthorized preaching had been imposed by the General Assembly, the English itinerant Rowland Hill not only gained access to pulpits at Paisley and Greenock, but with equal significance chose to remain silent in the town of Dumbarton in deference to the Evangelical parish minister, who had not been warned of his coming.[81]

Though the general state of the church did not impress the early itinerants, little was said concerning the subject of discipline. While presbytery minutes recorded routine cases of Sabbath-breaking and sexual impropriety, evangelists' journals passed over such matters in silence. Only James Haldane dealt with the wider issue during his first visit to Caithness. Commenting on the low state of religion in that area he drew a firm parallel between the lack of "faithful," or Evangelical, preaching in the ten parishes of Caithness and the sharp deterioration in ecclesiastical discipline within the county. In particular, he lamented the contemporary practice of commuting for a fine the public profession of repentance for the sins of adultery and fornication. Still worse in his opinion was the general and unhesitating admission of offenders to the communion table once they had paid their fine.[82]

While his remarks indicated a latent concern, they gave no direct hint of his future doubts concerning the possibility of effective discipline within a national church.[83] In 1797 Haldane still appeared to adhere to the traditional concept of the godly commonwealth and to accept the need for the effective operation of the ecclesiastical courts as the primary agents of Christian discipline.

There was, therefore, prior to the formation of the Circus church in 1799, a largely uncritical acceptance of the existing forms of order and discipline. Preaching occupied a preeminent position in worship. Observance of the Lord's Supper and baptism remained the province of the parochial clergy. The proper exercise of ecclesiastical discipline was expected. And until February that year neither brother formally renounced Presbyterianism. The early use of the Circus building was merely an extension of the semidetached attitude to established religion exemplified by Lady Glenorchy's Chapel and other similar proprietary places of worship. Even after the new church had been constituted, in January 1799, an element of ambiguity remained, for of the 310 persons who united in communion 30 maintained their membership of the established church, seeking admission to the Lord's table only on an occasional basis.[84] More significantly for future developments, James Haldane at his ordination to the pastorate, while indicating his approval of the simple and scriptural plan of the church, "disavowed any confidence in it as a perfect model of a church of Christ, to the exclusion of all others."[85]

While the pattern of congregational autonomy adopted by the Circus church permitted a more consistent emphasis on discipline, it did not involve a revolution in church order. The professionalism of the educated ministry had given way to a simpler concept, yet the pastoral function continued to be the responsibility of a single leader. Mutual exhortation appeared but only at informal weeknight gatherings confined to church members.[86] The Lord's Supper, no longer regarded as a sacrament, was limited to monthly observance,[87] while in similar fashion the ordinance of baptism retained its traditional character as a rite of inclusion in the Christian community associated primarily with infants.[88] Although the scriptural ideal had begun to exert its influence, reason and custom continued to be powerful factors. In 1802 the innate conservatism of early Independency was openly acknowledged by James Haldane in a pamphlet that argued for a weekly observance of the Lord's Supper. Reviewing the progress of his own thinking, he confessed to his fellow church members: "From the time of the formation of the church, I should have esteemed it a privilege to have shewed forth [our Lord's] death as often as I commemorated his resurrection. I thought, however, this would have been inexpedient."[89] In the transitional period between 1799 and 1808 the ordering of church life and worship had more in common with inherited forms than the new principle of congregational government might appear to suggest.

With a suddenness reminiscent of its origins the Haldane movement in 1808 suffered a serious and permanent setback. A damaging schism, which dislocated the Tabernacle congregations, was precipitated by the adoption of antipaedobaptist views by James Haldane. While the example of English Evangelicalism warns that the divisive potential of baptism should not be underestimated, and personal animosities served to intensify the disagreement, other factors were also involved.[90] Those who clung to the original form of Independency attributed most of the blame to the reckless pursuit of change.

By 1805 the practice of weekly communion had spread beyond the Edinburgh Tabernacle. During a visit to Breadalbane, John Campbell noted its regular observance in that area.[91] Yet frequency of communion did not lie at the heart of the 1808 division, in spite of its place among a list of "ecclesiastical novelties," to which Campbell and others subsequently showed resistance. Far more damaging to unity were changes involving less familiar or popular elements of church order, most notably the elevation to public prominence of exhortation and ecclesiastical discipline. Both prompted objections based on the mixed character of Sunday gatherings. With little prospect of success James Haldane sought to appease his critics by arguing that unbelievers who happened to be present could not fail to be impressed and attracted by the seriousness and integrity of the new proceedings.[92]

The opposition generated by these changes in public worship was merely strengthened by the parallel adoption of a plural eldership. Not only did this further innovation appear to threaten the pastoral office, it also showed little evidence of positive success. According to one observer when either of Haldane's colleagues was scheduled to preach, congregational numbers declined dramatically.[93] More significantly, a permanent difficulty was encountered in finding suitable persons who were willing to assume the pastoral role on a shared basis.

The introduction of the new practices was indicative of a sea change in attitudes. In their quest for purity of order the innovators showed that they were prepared to jettison any realistic chance of harmony for the sake of adherence to the letter of Scripture. Still more destructive was the missionary zeal with which they pursued that goal. In spite of their awareness of the dangers of Glasite intolerance, the Haldanes failed to apply to their own context the historical lesson it offered concerning obsession with detail, and the resulting sequence of strife, debility, and ultimate irrelevance.

Nevertheless, even James Haldane was prepared to set limits on experimentation. He recognized the impossibility of re-creating with absolute faithfulness an apostolic model of Christianity. While certain practices were linked to specific circumstances, the meaning and character of other features of apostolic life were no longer evident.[94] In one marginal example, that of salutation, he overturned his own earlier suggestion of cultural relativity only to find that its introduction provoked a further minor schism within the Tabernacle congregation and a harsh lampoon in an anonymous poem entitled *Hypocrisy Detected* (1812), a work which showed an intimate knowledge of the Haldane movement.[95]

Viewed overall, the attitudes of the Tabernacle pastor embodied a curious mixture of idealism and reality; elements that were capable of acting in concert as much as in opposition, and with not entirely predictable consequences. Far from welcoming the later Irvingite movement, Haldane's view of the extraordinary nature of New Testament glossolalia led him to join the majority in criticizing the 1830s outburst of tongues, especially the involvement of women.[96] In similar fashion his own determination at the Tabernacle to revive the principal features of apostolic worship experienced a measure of restraint from a combination of concern to avoid unnecessary confrontation and belief in the Christian principle of forbearance.[97]

V

With the coming of schism the evolution perceptible in the thought and activity of the Haldanes had reached its final stage. The original lack of interest in forms and organization had given way to a self-conscious insistence on apostolic propriety. At the same time unity had to all outward appearances been ousted by the persuasive logic of separation. Yet subsequent events reveal the existence of a continuing tension between these opposing elements. The new and uncompromising biblicism that lay at the roots of the emphasis on separation was itself a unitive phenomenon; a transdenominational development whose origins owed much to Robert Haldane.[98]

In their relationships with Scottish churchmen the Haldanes continued to display considerable ambiguity. While the younger brother showed no hesitation in publicly challenging the pro-establishment views of Thomas Chalmers,[99] private correspondence between Robert Haldane and the Evangelical leader expressed a close affinity of interests. In comments accompanying an exchange of publications concerning the Epistle to the Romans the Scottish Dissenter manifested a warm regard for Chalmers as a Christian of kindred sympathies to whom the utmost respect and charity was due.[100] As late as 1842 only a few months before his death, he showed himself willing, moreover, to identify publicly with representatives of the national church when he condemned the Edinburgh and Glasgow Railway Company for introducing a Sunday train service. In his attack on the company directors, his call for the exercise of disciplinary powers by the Presbytery of Edinburgh contained a wistful if somewhat inconsistent reminder of the outmoded concept of the Christian commonwealth.[101]

This sustained evidence of unity in the face of separation goes some way toward accounting for the sharply diverging historical assessments of the two Scottish Dissenters. Their essential paradox was that of a curious and antipathetic combination of broad Evangelical aims and overzealous interest in detail and the apportionment of blame. At one and the same time the Haldanes were both catholic and sectarian, irenic yet controversial. The sentiments engendered by these apparent contradictions, even among those potentially sympathetic, were expressed in contemporary polemic in the form of an open charge of hypocrisy.[102] In the light of this and other complicating factors arising from political tensions and personality, some loss of unanimity in historical judgment is not altogether surprising.

NOTES

1. *Acts of the General Assembly of the Church of Scotland, 1638–1842* (Edinburgh, 1843), 871.

2. G. Yuille, ed., *History of the Baptists in Scotland from Pre-Reformation Times* (Glasgow, 1927), 55.

3. A. J. Campbell, *Two Centuries of the Church of Scotland, 1707–1929* (Paisley, 1930), 160.

4. Thomas Snell Jones to William Wilberforce, Sept. 14, 1796, Edinburgh Univ. Library, Laing MSS La.II.500; Lady Glenorchy's Chapel was a proprietary building linked to the Church of Scotland.

5. G. Ewing, *Facts and Documents respecting the Connections which have subsisted between Robert Haldane, Esq. and Greville Ewing, laid before the public, in consequence of Letters which the Former has addressed to the Latter, respecting the Tabernacle at Glasgow* (Glasgow, 1809), 249–50.

6. J. MacInnes, *The Evangelical Movement in the Highlands of Scotland, 1688 to 1800* (Aberdeen, 1951), 128; C. G. Brown, *The Social History of Religion in Scotland since 1730* (London, 1987), 121–22.

7. H. Escort, *A History of Scottish Congregationalism* (Glasgow, 1960), 80.

8. W. L. Mathieson, *Church and Reform in Scotland: A History from 1797 to 1843* (Glasgow, 1916), 69; Campbell, *Two Centuries*, 161.

9. G. Struthers, *The History of the Rise, Progress, and Principles of the Relief Church, Embracing Notices of the Other Religious Denominations in Scotland* (Glasgow, 1843), 391, 405–7; J. Ross, *A History of Congregational Independency in Scotland* (Glasgow, 1900), 82–84.

10. J. Cunningham, *Church History of Scotland* (Edinburgh, 1859), 2:577; MacInnes, *Evangelical Movement*, 150–51.

11. The wholly lay character of the SPGH was unusual. The long-established society in Scotland for Propagating Christian Knowledge had always exhibited strong clerical direction, but even in newer bodies such as the Edinburgh and Glasgow Missionary Societies the ministerial element remained prominent.

12. *An Account of the Proceedings of the Society for Propagating the Gospel at Home, from their commencement, December 28, 1797, to May 16, 1799* (Edinburgh, 1799), 8, 11, 14.

13. Edinburgh, Scottish Record Office, MS GD 95/2/11.

14. A. Haldane, *The Lives of Robert Haldane of Airthrey and of His Brother James Alexander Haldane*, 3d ed. (London, 1853), 136–44, 219, 232, 298; D. Reeves, "The Interaction of Scottish and English Evangelicals, 1790–1810" (master's thesis, Glasgow, 1973), 119–21.

15. J. A. Haldane, *Journal of a Tour through the Northern Counties of Scotland and the Orkney Isles, in Autumn 1797* (Edinburgh, 1798), 79, 90–91.

16. John Craigie to William Robertson, Apr. 6, 1799, SRO, MS GD 214/659; Dundee Univ. Library, Br. MS 3/DC/7; *Missionary Magazine* 4 (1799): 110–11.

17. Hill's practical assistance was reinforced by the journals of his two Scottish preaching tours, which were published in 1799 and 1800, and by his *Series of Letters, Occasioned by the Late Pastoral Admonition of the Church of Scotland* (Edinburgh, 1799).

18. R. Philip, *The Life, Times, and Missionary Enterprises, of the Rev. John Campbell* (London, 1841), 79–100.

19. *The Missionary Magazine, a Periodical Monthly Publication, Intended as a Repository of Discussion, and Intelligence Respecting the Progress of the Gospel throughout the World* (Edinburgh, 1796–1813).

20. The *Evangelical Magazine* had commenced publication in 1793.

21. A. Haldane, *Robert and James Alexander Haldane*, 230, 233; D. E. Wallace, "The Life and Work of James Alexander Haldane"(Ph.D. diss., Edinburgh, 1955), 111–12, 121–22.

22. Struthers, *Relief Church*, 387.

23. Ewing, *Facts and Documents*, Appendix, 257–62; Catherine McNeil to Alexander Haldane, May 27, 1851, Gleneagles, Haldane MSS.

24. *Acts of the General Assembly*, 868–73; George Hill to Henry Dundas, May 30, 1799, SRO, MSS GD 51/5/427/6–7.

25. Struthers, *Relief Church*, 404–5; Haldane, *Robert and James Alexander Haldane*, 260–61.

26. William Porteous to Robert Dundas, Jan. 24, 1797, EUL, Laing MSS La.II.500.

27. A. Haldane, *Robert and James Alexander Haldane*, 517–18.

28. R. H. Martin, *Evangelicals United: Ecumenical Stirrings in Pre-Victorian Britain, 1795–1830* (Metuchen, N.J., 1983), 84–87, 92–93.

29. R. Haldane, *Review of the Conduct of the Directors of the British and Foreign Bible Society, Relative to the Apocrypha and to Their Administration on the Continent* (Edinburgh, 1825), 50–51, 72–73; *Review of the Conduct of the Rev. Daniel Wilson, on the Continent, as a Member of the Society for Promoting Christian Knowledge, and of the British and Foreign Bible Society* . . . (Edinburgh, 1829), cap. 3.

30. R. Haldane, *Review of the Conduct of the Directors of the British and Foreign Bible Society*, 35–36.

31. The first editions of these works were published in 1816 and 1835 respectively.

32. R. Haldane, *Letter to M. J. J. Chenevière, Pastor and Professor of Divinity at Geneva: Occasioned by His "Summary of the Theological Controversies Which of Late Years Have Agitated the City of Geneva," Published in the Monthly Repository of Theology and General Literature* (Edinburgh, 1824), 2–8, 24–25.

33. J. A. Haldane, *Journal of a Tour*, 58, 71.

34. R. Haldane, Letter to M. J. J. Chenevière, 22.

35. R. Haldane, *A Second Review of the Conduct of the Directors of the British and Foreign Bible Society, Containing an Account of the Religious State of the Continent* (Edinburgh, 1826), 52.

36. R. Haldane, *For the Consideration of the Ministers of the Church of Scotland. Remarks on Dr Tholuck's Exposition of St Paul's Epistle to the Romans, Translated by One of Themselves* (Edinburgh, 1837), 4–5.

37. J. A. Haldane, *Man's Responsibility; the Nature and Extent of the Atonement; and the Work of the Holy Spirit; in Reply to Mr Howard Hinton and the Baptist Midland Association* (Edinburgh, 1842), pt. 2, caps. 1–2.

38. J. A. Haldane, *Refutation of the Heretical Doctrine Promulgated by the Rev. Edward Irving, Respecting the Person and Atonement of the Lord Jesus Christ* (Edinburgh, 1829), 9.

39. *Monthly Repository* 19 (1824): 4.

40. A. Bost, *Memoires pouvant servir à l'Histoire du Réveil Religieux des Églises Protestantes de La Suisse et de La France, etc.*, 3 vols. (Paris, 1854–55), 1:81.

41. Ibid., 2d ed., 2 vols. (London, 1834), 1:i–ii, xvi–xviii.

42. R. Haldane, *Tholuck's Exposition*, 18.

43. R. Haldane, *Letter to M. J. J. Chenevière*, 36–37, 38, 93–95; *Exposition of the Epistle to the Romans: With Remarks on the Commentaries of Dr Macknight, Professor Moses Stuart, and Professor Tholuck*, 8th ed., 3 vols. (Edinburgh, 1859), 2:302–27, Commentary on Romans 8.29–30.

44. A. Haldane, *Robert and James Alexander Haldane*, 633.

45. Ibid., 652.

46. J. A. Haldane, *A View of the Social Worship and Ordinances Observed by the First Christians, Drawn from the Sacred Scriptures Alone: Being an attempt to Enforce their Divine Obligation; and to represent the guilt and evil consequences of neglecting them*, 2d ed. (Edinburgh, 1806), 108; *Observations on Mr Brown's Vindication of the Presbyterian Form of Church Government, As Professed in the Standards of the Church of Scotland* (Edinburgh, 1806), 33, 40–41.

47. Mathieson, *Church and Reform*, 32–33, 45–46, 57–62.

48. Ewing, *Facts and Documents*, 7–8; R. Haldane, *Address to the Public Concerning Political Opinions, and Plans Lately Adopted to Promote Religion in Scotland*, 2d ed. (Edinburgh, 1800), 32. Somerville was the senior parish minister at Stirling from 1793 until 1817.

49. Greville Ewing was an assistant to Thomas Jones at Lady Glenorchy's Chapel, Edinburgh, until December 1798, when he left the established church in order to become a Congregational minister at the Haldane Tabernacle in Glasgow. William Innes held the second parish charge at Stirling until he resigned in 1799 to become the resident minister at the Dundee Tabernacle. David Bogue was pastor of an Independent church at Gosport, Hampshire, a position he held from 1777 until 1825.

50. Robert Haldane to Henry Dundas, Sept. 30, 1796, Edinburgh, National Library of Scotland, MS 2257 fol. 53ʳ

51. Robert Haldane to Robert Dundas, Sept. 28, 1796, EUL, Laing MSS La.II.500.

52. SRO, MSS GD 95/2/11 and GD 95/1/6. I am indebted to David Currie for bringing these references to my attention.

53. William Innes to Alexander Haldane, undated, Gleneagles, Haldane MSS.

54. J. Robison, *Proofs of a Conspiracy against all the Religions and Governments of Europe, Carried on in the Secret Meetings of Free Masons, Illuminati and Reading Societies* (Edinburgh, 1797), 485; A. Haldane, *Robert and James Alexander Haldane*, 212–17.

55. *Acts of the General Assembly*, 868–69, 873–75.

56. George Hill to Henry Dundas, May 30, 1799, SRO, MS GD 51/5/427/6, fol. 2.$^{v.}$

57. William Robertson to Robert Dundas, to May 1799, SRO, MS GD 214/659.

58. Presbytery of Caithness, minutes Jan. 8, 1799, to Jan. 12, 1802, passim, SRO, MS CH 2/47/6; William Sutherland to William Robertson, undated, SRO, MS GD 214/659; Catherine McNeil to Miss Haldane, Apr. 28, 1851, Gleneagles, Haldane MSS.

59. J. A. Haldane, *Presbyterian Form of Church Government*, 10.

60. J. A. Haldane, *Observations on the Association of Believers; Mutual Exhortation; the Apostolic Mode of Teaching, Qualifications and Support of Elders, Spiritual Gifts, &c.* (Edinburgh, 1808), 65, 86–88.

61. Philip, *John Campbell*, 359–61.

62. J. A. Haldane, *The Voluntary Question Political, Not Religious: A Letter to the Rev. Dr John Brown, Occasioned by the Allusion in His Recent Work to the Author's Sentiments upon National Churches* (Edinburgh, 1839), 4–5.

63. J. A. Haldane, *The Signs of the Times Considered, with the Duty of Preparation for the Approaching Crisis; Being the Substance of Five Discourses* (Edinburgh, 1832), 57–58.

64. J. A. Haldane, *Two Letters to the Rev. Dr Chalmers, on His Proposal for Increasing the Number of Churches in Glasgow*, 2d ed. (Edinburgh, 1820), 16–17.

65. J. A. Haldane, *Two Letters to the Rev. Dr Chalmers*, 17.

66. J. A. Haldane, *Journal of a Tour*, 40.

67. Evangelical parish ministers in Edinburgh had, with the opening of the Circus, a more local cause of resentment. Not only did its preference for Independency accentuate the schismatic tendency within Evangelicalism, but the succession of visiting preachers ensured a constant leaching of support from their own congregations.

68. *Acts of the General Assembly*, 872. Contrary also to Mathieson, *Church and Reform*, 84.

69. Reeves, "Scottish and English Evangelicals," 1; D. W. Lovegrove, *Established Church, Sectarian People: Itinerancy and the Transformation of English Dissent, 1780–1830* (Cambridge, 1988), cap. 4.

70. R. F. Calder, "Robert Haldane's Theological Seminary," *TCHS* 13 (1937–39): 53, 59–63.

71. David Sutherland to Alexander Haldane, Nov. 7, 1853, Gleneagles, Haldane MSS.

72. Ewing, *Facts and Documents*, 68–70. Haldane argued that more time should be devoted to reading church history and divinity and to "searching and explaining the Scriptures."

73. Philip, *John Campbell*, 139, 223–24.

74. G. Ewing, *A Defence of Itinerant and Field Preaching* (Edinburgh, 1799); R. Hill, *Journal of a Tour through the North of England and Parts of Scotland: With Remarks on the Present State of the Established Church of Scotland, and the different Secessions therefrom. Together with . . . Some Remarks on the Propriety of What Is Called Lay and Itinerant Preaching* (London, 1799).

75. J. A. Haldane, *Social Worship*, 211–17, 255–62.

76. J. A. Haldane, *Observations on . . . Mutual Exhortation*, 41–46.

77. Although his seminary classes ended in 1808, Robert Haldane continued to show an interest in theological education. Apart from well-publicized activities at Geneva and Montauban between 1817 and 1819, he provided financial support during the 1820s for the training of Baptist home missionaries at Grantown-on-Spey and for a small institution in Paris. A. Haldane, *Robert and James Alexander Haldane*, 331; Robert Haldane to Sergeant Lefroy, Sept. 4, 1822, Gleneagles, Haldane MSS.

78. A. Haldane, *Robert and James Alexander Haldane*, 361.

79. *Acts of the General Assembly*, 869, 871.

80. *Proceedings of the SPGH*, 45, 27, 35.

81. R. Hill, *Journal of a Tour*, 31–34.

82. J. A. Haldane, *Journal of a Tour*, 76.

83. J. A. Haldane, *The Obligation of Christian Churches to Observe the Lord's Supper Every Lord's Day, Stated in a Letter to the Church of Christ Assembling in the Tabernacle, Edinburgh. To Which Are Added, Miscellaneous Observations* (Edinburgh, 1802), 48–49.

84. A. Haldane, *Robert and James Alexander Haldane*, 237.

85. *Missionary Magazine* 4 (1799): 78.

86. J. A. Haldane, *Observations on . . . Mutual Exhortation*, 42–43.

87. J. A. Haldane, *Lord's Supper*, 4.

88. J. A. Haldane, *Reasons of a Change of Sentiment & Practice on the Subject of Baptism; Containing a Plain View of the Signification of the Word, and of the Persons for Whom the Ordinance Is Appointed; Together with a Full Consideration of the Covenant Made with Abraham, and Its Supposed Connexion with Baptism* (Edinburgh, 1808), 1–9.

89. J. A. Haldane, *Lord's Supper*, 4–5.

90. Lovegrove, *Established Church, Sectarian People*, 36–37.

91. J. Campbell, "Journal of a Tour to the North in ye Year 1805," June 9, 1805, Gleneagles, Haldane MSS.

92. J. A. Haldane, *Observations on . . . Mutual Exhortation*, 64–65, 88–90.

93. Robert Kinniburgh to Alexander Haldane, Mar. 15, 1851, Gleneagles, Haldane MSS.

94. J. A. Haldane, *Lord's Supper*, 20–30.

95. Kinniburgh to A. Haldane, Mar. 15, 1851.

96. J. A. Haldane, *Signs of the Times*, 31.

97. J. A. Haldane, *Observations on Forbearance* (Edinburgh, 1811), [iii].

98. D. W. Bebbington, *Evangelicalism in Modern Britain: A History from the 1730s to the 1980s* (London, 1989), 87–88.

99. J. A. Haldane, *Two Letters to the Rev. Dr Chalmers,* esp. letter I.

100. Robert Haldane to Thomas Chalmers, Dec. 29, 1837, Edinburgh, New College Library, Chalmers MS CHA 4.264–46.

101. R. Haldane, *On the Purposed Desecration of the Sabbath, by the Directors of the Edinburgh and Glasgow Railway* (Edinburgh, 1842), 29–30.

102. Anon., *Hypocrisy Detected; in a Letter to the Late Firm of Haldane, Ewing, and Co. With a Preface Containing the Narrative of Mr James Reid, a Missionary Sent by These Gentlemen to Upper Canada* (Aberdeen, 1812), 72.

"To Hear a Free Gospel"

The Christian Connexion in Canada

Philip G. A. Griffin-Allwood

The awakenings and newlight stirs of the late eighteenth and early nineteenth century produced a number of new denominations that embodied the principles of revivalism.[1] The religious identity of these new denominations was expressed in a number of ways; as preaching or hearing "a free gospel,"[2] as "[propagation of] free principles and [development of] the free spirit,"[3] as giving people "free course to the Bible,"[4] or as professing a "spirit of liberty."[5] They described themselves as "free brethren"[6] or "free Christeans."[7]

The major "radical sects" of revolutionary New England, the Freewill Baptists, the United Society of Believers (Shakers), the Universalists, and the Allinites, have been the study of Stephen Marini and George Rawlyk.[8] They were the first generation of the "free gospel" denominations. One group that belongs to the second generation of the movement is the Christian Connexion, who expressed their identity as rejection of "all names, appellation, and badges of distinctive party among the followers of Christ."[9]

In the early 1830s there were two Christian Connexion conferences in British North America, in Upper Canada and New Brunswick, both with about twenty churches. The Upper Canadian conference had about twelve hundred members in 1833, while by 1847 the New Brunswick conference had about two thousand members. The subsequent histories of the two conferences are a study in contrast. By the beginning of the twentieth century, the Ontario conference had declined to about one thousand members, while that in New Brunswick had increased to more than twelve thousand members. Growth or decline was in direct relation to the degree of indigenousness.

CHRISTIAN CONNEXION

The Christian Connexion, which by the late nineteenth century had formed the American Christian Convention as its major transcongregational organization, was a union of three separate "free gospel" movements: the James O'Kelly–led Republican Methodists of Virginia and North Carolina, the Barton Stone–led Christians of Kentucky and Tennessee, and the New England Christians associated with Elias Smith and Abner Jones.[10] The latter branch entered present-day Canada.

Near the end of the eighteenth century Abner Jones, a Regular Baptist, rejected "sectarian names and human creeds." The bond of Christian fellowship and communion was defined as "true piety alone" with the Bible as the only source of doctrine.[11] Jones was ordained by Freewill Baptist ministers, although he never claimed to be a Freewill Baptist.[12] He gathered his first "free Christian Church" in September 1800 in Lyndon, Vermont. Similar churches were gathered in Vermont in 1802 and in New Hampshire in 1803.[13]

About the same time Elias Smith, a Regular Baptist minister, revolted against the institutional practices of that denomination. He provided leadership for disenchanted Regular and Freewill Baptists, organizing churches throughout New England.

The churches of the Christian Connexion were considered to be independent with full authority to enact their own polities. On the transcongregational level, conferences were organized. A conference assumed authority for ordination of ministers and for annual examination of ministers' character and of their maintenance of "purity in ministry."[14] Smith summed up the Christian Connexion position in the following manner: "We mean to be New Testament Christians, without any sectarian name connected to it, without any sectarian creeds, articles, or confessions, or discipline to illumine the Scriptures . . . It is our design to remain free from all human laws, confederations and unscriptural combinations; and to stand fast in the liberty wherewith Christ has made us free."[15]

When the Christian Connexion developed a transcongregational identity is a matter for debate. During the first decade of the nineteenth century Christians and Freewill Baptists moved freely among one another.[16] Smith's advocacy of a "loose notion of church order" distinguished congregations under his influence from Freewill Baptist churches. The latter group used church covenants and adhered to an organizational order that had to be adopted before a congregation could be recognized as a church.[17]

Smith applied for membership at the New Durham Quarterly Meeting of the Freewill Baptists in August 1805 and expected to formally join them the following November at the Gorham Yearly Meeting. His disavowal of written creeds and denominational names, except Christian, the one mentioned in the Bible, led to rejection of his application by the Freewill Baptists.[18]

Specifically, Smith, and many of those who followed him, rejected metaphysical Trinitarianism. This frequently led to the charge that the Christian

Connexion were Unitarian. Yet they did affirm Christ's divinity.[19] Milo Morrill, in his early-twentieth-century history of the Christian denomination, described their position as belief "in the Biblical Trinity but not in the theological."[20] This theological vagueness led to reference to them as "Evangelical Unitarians" or "Unitarian Baptists."[21]

Smith continued to enjoy support among the Freewill Baptists after the decision by the Yearly Meeting not to accept him. Tension existed over, one, the ecclesial authority of the Freewill Baptist Monthly, Quarterly, and Yearly Meetings and, two, the use of the name "Freewill Baptist." Smith's supporters among the Freewill Baptists sought to "keep no records, more than a list of names of persons baptized, as Elias Smith did."[22] The issue was resolved at the Yearly Meeting in June 1810, when after consultation with local churches, the decision was made to cease calling local Freewill Baptist congregations by the designation Monthly Meeting and to have any business referred to the Quarterly Meeting by a church "done in sequestered conference."[23]

This marked the moment of creation of a separate transcongregational identity for the Christian Connexion among proponents of the "free gospel." While, as noted above, the Freewill Baptists had an denominational order or structure into which congregations were organized,[24] Christian churches were "acknowledged [as being] in New Testament order"[25] or "united . . . in a church, on the New Testament plan."[26]

This led to the inclusion in the Christian Connexion of a revivalist movement in Maine that called its congregations by the designation "Christian Band." In the first decade of the nineteenth century, the "Christian Band" appeared to be independent of, but drawn to, both the Christians and the Freewill Baptists. By 1821, though, "Christian Band" was synonymous with the Christian Connexion.[27]

In addition to the 1810 decision of the Freewill Baptists, two other things contributed to the creation of a distinct transcongregational identity for the churches of the New England Christian Connexion by the third decade of the nineteenth century. One, Elias Smith began publication of a periodical, *The Herald of Gospel Liberty*, in September 1808.[28] Second, after 1809 "elders' conferences" were convened in conjunction with the informal "general meetings" and in 1820 the U.S. Christian Conference was organized. With respect to the conferences the denominational principle of liberty meant that there was no continuing organization from meeting to meeting and that minimal records were kept.[29]

THE CANADAS

Adherents of the Christian Connexion migrated from New England to western New York State, where the Great Revival of 1800–1825 bolstered the denomination.

Sixty New York preachers met in 1825 to protest the "evils of the Methodist episcopacy" and to make overtures to the Christian Connexion.[30] The migration of people and revival extended beyond the Niagara into Upper Canada.

There was a Christian Connexion presence in Lower Canada beginning in 1812. Two churches were formed, both in Hatley, with John Orcutt as the resident elder. They joined the Vermont Conference of the Christian Connexion.[31] The story of the Christian Connexion in Lower Canada parallels that of the other immersionist denominations in the border region of Lower Canada, the Freewill Baptists and the Regular Baptists. There was a surge of activity early in the nineteenth century but declined to almost oblivion as the century progressed.[32]

In Upper Canada at the beginning of the third decade of the nineteenth century, a revival occurred among American migrants who had previously been affiliated with "free gospel" denominations. This extension of the Great Revival in western New York State was strengthened by preachers from the migrants' former places of residence. The preachers came, not on their own initiative, but in response to requests for assistance.[33]

In 1821, Mary Stodgill moved to Newmarket. She had been immersed in Greenville, New York, in 1817 by Elder David Millard. She wrote Elder Thomas Brown of Porter, New York, requesting that he send a Christian Connexion preacher to her community. Elder Doubleday and a brother McIntire apparently were supposed to go but did not. In May 1821 she again wrote to Brown requesting that he send a preacher. Brown passed her request on to Millard, who in turn was unable to go, but forwarded the letter to the *Christian Herald*.[34]

Allen Huntley, a lay preacher, responded to the invitation. He labored in Upper Canada for a number of months, in Newmarket and other communities. Huntley reported to the General Meeting in Pomsret, Chateaugay County, New York, in October 1821, bringing with him a letter from North Gwillimbury (Keswick) requesting his ordination.[35] Joseph Bailey described the meeting: "The Conference took into consideration the said request and after much consultation and prayer to the Lord for wisdom, it seemed good unto us to send chosen men with brother Huntly that they might be set in order the things that were wanting. And the Spirit bade Elder Simeon Bishop and myself [Joseph Bailey] to go with him, nothing doubting. Moreover the Conference gave us letters of commendation to the said brethren in Canada, who had believed through grace."[36]

Bishop, Bailey, and Huntley went to Upper Canada in November 1821. First they went to Newmarket, then to Lake Simcoe (North Gwillimbury), where the revival was still in process. Bailey stated, "The meetings we held with them were truly refreshing. The groans of the wounded were mingled with songs of the saints, while the spiritual exhortation from the lips of the heavenborn converts, seemed sufficient to move the heardest [sic] heart."[37]

Huntley was ordained on the following Sunday and ten converts were immersed in Lake Simcoe. "A church was acknowledged in New Testament order" of forty-three members.[38] A second church was founded in East Gwillimbury (Newmarket) in November 1822 through the labors of Nathan Harding and Asa C. Morrison, who were also sent to Upper Canada by the New York Christians.[39] Churches were gathered throughout the province and the Christian Conference of Upper Canada was organized in 1825.[40] By 1834 the conference contained about twenty churches, twenty preachers, and had a membership of about twelve hundred.[41]

A crisis occurred in that year at the annual conference meeting at Whitby, when Joseph Ash, clerk of the conference, proposed union between the Christians and the Disciples of Christ. This would have meant a reduction of the conference's oversight of the churches within it. There was a keen debate, resulting in a tied vote, which was broken when the chairman voted in the negative. Although no churches left the Christian Conference, Ash and other ministers and members joined the Disciples.[42]

Interest in the Disciples had been prompted by Ash's reading of Barton Stone's *Christian Messenger*. Stone's Christians had united with Alexander Campbell's Reformers, the Disciples of Christ, in 1832. The Disciples, who formed a distinct identity between 1825 and 1830, emphasized a rationalistic adherence to the "ancient gospel" in contrast to revivalistic emotionalism of the "free gospel" denominations.[43]

Ash had hoped to promote a similar union in Upper Canada but encountered a response similar to that of some of Stone's followers who refused to accept the 1832 merger.[44] The issues of disagreement were, one, the Disciples accent on baptism and, two, the extreme Independency of their congregations. Although the Upper Canadian Christians tended to emphasize immersion, it was not a prerequisite. The charge that the Christians were Unitarians was not an issue because the Ontario Christians were "'progressive conservative' in theology."[45]

With competition for the antisectarian "market" in Canadian religious life, Christian Connexion growth was slowed. Nevertheless, before 1838 an Eastern Conference of Upper Canada was organized. But by 1850 the denomination's growth had ended.[46] The story of the "2nd Division Quarterly Conference" illustrates the declension of the post-1850 period.

The conference was organized in April 1852 by the King, Georgiana, North Gwillimbury, East Gwillimbury, West Gwillimbury, and Newmarket churches. The purpose of the conference was to provide coordination of ministerial service in the area served by the churches. Despite the good intentions, regular meetings had ended by 1853.[47]

By 1862 the Ontario conferences of the Christian Connexion had been reorganized as the Christian Church in Canada. A fourth district was formed to cover part of the area previously served by the Second Division conference. The number of churches was reduced to three, King, Newmarket, and West Gwillimbury. In 1863, the three churches formed a union, known as the Newmarket District, to coordinate the Christian ministry in the area.[48]

Decline continued for the Christian Church throughout the nineteenth century.[49] Unsuccessful union negotiations again took place with the Disciples in 1896.[50] Affiliation with the American Christian Connexion was maintained, with the Ontario conference hosting the American Christian Convention in Oshawa in 1870 and in Newmarket in 1898. A limited fresh vitality was experienced as the denomination entered the twentieth century due to the establishment of a periodical, the *Christian Vanguard*, an educational effort, and new home mission churches in Toronto (1899), Stouffville (1905), and in Saskatchewan.[51]

The Ontario Christians were forced to consider their future by plans, begun in 1923 and consummated in 1931, for the union of the American Christians with the Congregationalists.[52] The Canadian Christian Church, consisting of nine active churches with about one thousand members, opened negotiations with the United Church of Canada in 1926.[53] When the information concerning union was submitted to the Christian's annual conference in June 1928, action was deferred. A decision was made to permit individual churches to join the United Church of Canada. The Oshawa church did so, becoming the Centre Street United Church. The Bathurst Street Christian Church in Toronto voted to disband and transferred members to the United Church.[54]

The other Canadian churches remained part of the Congregational Christian Churches until the latter united with the Evangelical and Reformed Church in 1957 to form the United Church of Christ.[55] In 1949, though, the Newmarket Church joined the Baptist Convention of Ontario and Quebec.[56] At least one church is now part of the Fellowship of Evangelical Baptist Churches in Canada.[57] Six churches with 275 members continue as the Conference of Congregational Christian Churches in Ontario, part of the international Conservative Congregationalist Christian Conference.[58]

THE MARITIMES

Governor Lawrence's second proclamation of invitation to New Englanders in January 1759 included guarantees of "full liberty of conscience" with respect to religion. This "charter of religious freedom" attracted revivalistic Separate Baptists and Separate Congregationalists to Nova Scotia.[59] As a result, one of the last "fires" of the First New England Great Awakening occurred in Nova Scotia among the Separate Baptist settlements from 1765 to 1767.[60]

The revival in Nova Scotia history was the Nova Scotia Great Awakening of 1776 to 1784. Led by the Separate Congregationalist preacher Henry Alline, it was part of the newlight stirs that occurred in the period surrounding the American Revolution.[61] The awakening transformed Maritime religious life, creating an indigenous denomination, similar to the other "free gospel" movements in New England, with its own Articles of Faith and Practice, clergy, and sense of mission.[62] Pressure to have a "name," a reaction to the existence of an established church in Nova Scotia, caused most of the leadership of the Allinite churches to become Regular Baptist. Division resulted.[63]

The adoption of Regular Baptist polity was not immediately nor universally accepted by Allinites. Advocates of Free Christianity continued to be a force in the Maritimes. The tendency in Maritime Baptist historiography has been to interpret the development of the Free Christian Baptists and Freewill Baptists as a phenomenon of the 1820s.[64] Thanks to the labors of contemporary researchers, the continuity of these denominations with the Allinite tradition has been discovered.[65]

After Alline's death in 1784, Allinite congregations continued to exist and be gathered in both New Brunswick and Nova Scotia, with the greatest strength in the former province. Distance from the leadership of the Nova Scotia Baptist Association was perhaps a significant contributing factor to greater vitality in New Brunswick. A number of preachers provided leadership among the congregations; for example, Thomas Crowell and Clark Alline in Nova Scotia and Daniel Shaw, Matthew Fenwick, Nathaniel Churchill, and Robert Colpitts in New Brunswick.[66]

In New Brunswick the Christian Connexion position of "acknowledging New Testament order" would be crucial for their successful entry into the province. The Allinite congregations considered themselves to be churches and resisted Regular and Freewill Baptist efforts to put them into their perceived proper order. But, they readily accepted Christian Connexion recognition of their spiritual propriety.[67]

In June 1817 Samuel Nutt, an ordained Christian Connexion minister, commenced preaching at St. Andrews, New Brunswick. About the same time, Elder William O. Grant was preaching on Deer Island. Nutt settled briefly in St. David, where he formed a Christian church in 1826. In 1828 Elder George Kilton gathered a Christian church on Deer Island. In 1831 the Maine Christian Conference included churches at St. Andrews, Deer Island, and Bocabec.[68]

Early in 1830 Nutt visited Wakefield. He was invited by his innkeeper, Charles McMullin, to preach in the Wakefield Allinite Meetinghouse. A revival resulted, both in Wakefield and in the communities above there on the river. Nutt described it in a letter to the *Christian Herald:* "I found the Lord had a work for me to do in that land, the power of God attended the work and fell on the people in marvellous manner in as much that scarcely a dry eye was found in all the congregation; and as there was quite a number of old pilgrims present, that was in a low state of mind they took encouragement and came forward and witnessed to the gospel they had heard and encouraged the trembling sinner to seek salvation of their souls."[69]

After six months, Nutt returned to Maine, but by autumn he was back on the St. John River. At Bear Island a revival was followed by the "uniting" of a church. He journeyed to Sussex, where he found a revival in process, led in all likelihood by Samuel Hartt. The latter, an Allinite preacher from Wakefield, was ordained in 1831.[70]

The Maine Conference recognized Hartt's ordination and in 1832 added William Pennington of Queensbury to its list of licensed preachers. During Nutt's second visit to New Brunswick in 1832, he brought a letter from the Maine Conference.[71] This was recognition by the Maine Christian Connexion churches of the New Brunswick churches as sister churches. In September of that year, Nutt "mentioned to the rest of the preachers that it would be in furtherance of the cause to have a [New Brunswick] General Conference . . . organized for the better regulation of the churches."[72]

On October 13, 1832, representatives of six churches met at Wakefield to establish the New Brunswick Christian Conference. Two elders, Nutt and McMullin, and six churches joined the conference. The Charlotte County churches remained within the orbit of the Maine Conference. Hartt and Churchill did not join the conference.[73] The organization of this Christian Conference marked the transcongregational institutionalization of the Allinites in New Brunswick. The Allinites did not perceive themselves as changing their order, they simply were being recognized by similar proponents of the "free gospel."

A similar pattern occurred in Nova Scotia, although a recognized Christian Connexion conference was not organized. Jacob Norton, who had been ordained by a "Church of Christ" in Swansville, Maine, in 1814, moved to Shag Harbour, Shelburne County, in 1817. In 1818, no doubt drawing on former Allinite congregations, he was responsible for the organization of churches in Barrington Passage, Bear Point, and Lower Argyle. Similarly, in 1819, a Christian church was organized in Lower Horton. In the early 1820s, Norton settled in Cornwallis, Kings County, where he would be a bane to the Regular Baptist ministers, Edward Manning and T. S. Harding. While there he gathered churches consisting of Allinites in Habitant, Hall's Harbour, Black Rock, Scot's Bay, and Mount Denison. He returned to the south shore by 1825.[74]

Doubt exists about whether Norton was a member of the Christian Connexion. The earliest material identifies him as a member of the "Christian Band" in Maine.[75] In 1868, he was identified as a "strict trinitarian" from the Christian Connexion.[76] His name does not appear on any list of Christian Connexion ministers. That may be because he chose to cooperate with other "free gospel" movements in Nova Scotia rather than seeking recognition from the American denomination. The nature of the churches Norton founded and his linkage to the "Christian Band" would suggest that he may have been the Christian Connexion link in Nova Scotia to which Elias Smith referred.[77]

The Christian Connexion influence in Nova Scotia was thus limited to the influence of preaching. In 1837 a union conference of churches led by Norton, Crowell, and Asa McGray, a Freewill Baptist, was formed using the name "Free Christian Baptist." The Freewill Baptists withdrew in 1840 but reunited in 1866 to form the Nova Scotia Conference of Free Baptists.[78] The history of the Free Christian Baptists in Nova Scotia was one of maintaining independence from American affiliations.

Pressures would result in a similar indigenization in New Brunswick. For three years after the founding of the New Brunswick Christian Conference, only one meeting was held. After 1835 two conferences were held, one in the spring and one in the fall, until 1849. The standard interpretation is that the division was a peaceful break with Fredericton as the geographical boundary.[79] This description reflects a late harmonization of the facts, for both upper and lower conferences met in Nashwalk.[80] There were tensions among the New Brunswick Christians.

Three things created the tension among the Christians. At the 1834 annual conference the New Brunswick Christians debated the issue "should persons be recognized as members of our churches without baptism?" One participant was an unimmersed deacon.[81] The churches were experiencing conflict over the Allinite definition of baptism as a nonessential.

Another source of the pressure came from the presence of two competing "Christian" denominations. The Disciples of Christ drew on the Christian Conference for members and leadership. A Christian Connection schism, the "Hamiltonites" had a great influence in New Brunswick beginning in 1835. Jonathan Hamilton and his followers stressed an antiformalism that was compatible with the Allinite heritage.[82] The presence of advocates from both these American denominations, one stressing a reasonable faith, the other an emotional, would not have been conducive to harmony among the former Allinites.

Perhaps the greatest pressure experienced by the former Allinites was the same one that had led the earlier leadership to become Regular Baptist; the need for recognition in a province with an established church. Ministers of the Christian Conference had been denied the privilege of officiating in marriages. Thus in 1847 a petition campaign was organized to obtain recognition.[83]

Although the conference had been known as Trinitarian,[84] the need for recognition required that confessional orthodoxy be established. The conference responded to criticism of their fellowship with the Christian Connexion by adopting a negative creed. It stated that they did "not believe in infant purity—

in the destruction of the wicked, or annihilation—in Unitarianism—Universalism."[85] To further ease tensions, the name Free Christian Baptist was adopted in 1847. Two reasons were given for the decision: " (1) to relieve the minds of many of our brethren who were never fully reconciled to the name 'Christian' only, and thereby cultivate a greater union among ourselves; and (2) to open a door for union with our brethren in Nova Scotia bearing that name."[86]

Thus the surviving Allinite tradition in New Brunswick declared its independence from American influences and affirmed its indigenous nature and heritage. Communication with the American Christian Connexion ended by 1840.[87] The sign of departure from the Christian Connexion was the adoption by both the Nova Scotia and New Brunswick Free Baptists of a condensed version of the 1834 Freewill Baptist *Treatise* in 1841 and 1848 respectively.[88] Despite this use of the American theological document and repeated overtures from the Freewill Baptists, the New Brunswick Free Christian Baptists never formally joined them.[89]

As noted at the beginning of this article, in 1833 the Upper Canadian Christian Conference contained about 20 ordained elders, 20 churches, and 1,200 members. In 1882 there were 16 ordained ministers and by in 1898, when the Ontario Conference played host to the American Christian Convention, it included 25 churches. But in 1926, when they began negotiations with the United Church of Canada, they had decreased to 9 active churches and 1,000 members.[90] The New Brunswick Christian Conference contained 8 ministers and 20 churches in 1835; 14 elders, 40 churches, and 2,000 members in 1847; 49 ministers, 156 churches with a membership of 12,428 in 1901, just before their union in 1905 with the Regular Baptists to create the United Baptist denomination.[91]

The major difference between the two conferences was the indigenousness of the Maritime Christians, in contrast to the Ontario Conference's continued affiliation with the American denomination. The divergence was derived from the revivals that gave the conferences their genesis. The Ontario conference was a product of a revival that was an extension of Great Revival in New York State's "Burned-over district." Unlike other revivalistic denominations, particularly the Methodists, who formed an indigenous identity through resolution of tensions derived from British and American expressions of their movements,[92] the Ontario Christians maintained an identity as American. This affiliation was reflected in the founding declaration of the Newmarket Christian Church, which described the congregation as "a church of Christ in connection with the people called Christians in the United States of America."[93]

The Maritime churches drew their indigenous identity from the Allinite Awakening. They eventually became part of a growing Canadian transcongregational unity among immersing denominations, which focused on mission to the Canadian West, French Canada, and overseas.[94] This transcongregational unity was part of a larger movement, the institutionalization of revivalism as Evangelicalism. In the Canadian context this was expressed as "National Protestantism." While Canadian Evangelicalism would divide between proponents of organic and federated union, nevertheless, the evangelical premise that Canada was "God's last best country" was the dominant influence in Canadian Protestant religious life as the nineteenth century progressed; a premise shared by Maritime immersing denominations.[95]

Evangelicalism advocated Christian unity on the basis of a number of principles. First was an affirmation of "no creed but the Bible." The initial prospectus for the founding of the international Evangelical Alliance in 1846 had described the doctrinal "Consensus" as a "Profession of Faith." But, at the founding assembly itself, the "Consensus" was explicitly denied status as a "creed or confession."[96] Second, Evangelicalism advocated a personal piety, expressed in terms of "religious liberty," the "priesthood of believers," "united prayer," and missionary activity.[97] Third, Evangelicalism sought visible unity among churches, viewing the "visible catholic church as constructed of denominations of Christians."[98]

With the ascendancy of Canadian Evangelicalism, the Ontario Christian Connexion found itself without a raison d'être. The Christian Connexion found its denominational genesis in advocacy of anticreedalism, Christian unity, and personal piety. By the mid-nineteenth century those principles were the standard for Canadian evangelical Protestantism as a whole.

Lacking an indigenous psyche the Ontario denomination simply had nothing to offer. Why join a Christian Church if your own denomination was offering the same things? To join the Ontario Christian Church was to join an American denomination. To join a New Brunswick Free Christian Baptist church, on the other hand, was, in Henry Alline's words, to join God's "chosen people."[99] This psyche was expressed by 1865 as "Jerusalem" responding to the province's "Macedonian Cry."[100]

The story of the Christian Connexion in Canada illustrates a phenomena of Canadian religious life. To thrive in the Canadian context a denomination had to indigenize and participate in the Canadian religious vision of "His Dominion."[101]

NOTES

1. Whitney Cross has described the "ultraism" of western New York State. Whitney R. Cross, *The Burned-Over District: The Social and Intellectual History of Enthusiastic Religion in Western New York, 1800–1850* (Ithaca and London: Cornell Univ. Press, 1950). Cf. Leonard I. Sweet, *The Evangelical Tradition in America* (Macon, Ga.: Mercer Univ. Press, 1984). T. Scott

Miyakawa examined individualism and conformity on the American frontier. T. Scott Miyakawa, *Protestants and Pioneers: Individualism and Conformity on the American Frontier* (Chicago and London: Univ. of Chicago Press, 1964). William McLoughlin explored religious dissent in New England. William G. McLoughlin, *New England Dissent 1630–1833*, 2 vols. (Cambridge, Mass.: Harvard Univ. Press, 1971). The religion of the Old South has been examined by Donald Mathews. Donald G. Mathews, *Religion in the Old South* (Chicago: Univ. of Chicago Press, 1977). Significant attention was paid to Canadian revivalism by S. D. Clark. S. D. Clark, *Church and Sect in Canada* (Toronto: Univ. of Toronto Press, 1948). Clark, though, concentrated on the five denominations that would form Canadian National Protestantism: Anglicans, Methodists, Presbyterians, Congregationalists, and Baptists.

2. I. D. Stewart, *The History of the Freewill Baptists for Half a Century* (Dover: Freewill Baptist Printing Establishment, 1862), 170. The quotation in the title comes from a report that precedes that of David Millard in the *Christian Herald* 4, no. 2 (1821): 42.

3. "The Last Will and Testament of the Springfield Presbytery," quoted in Winfred Ernest Garrison and Alfred T. DeGroot, *The Disciples of Christ: A History*, rev. ed. (St. Louis: Bethany, 1958), 109.

4. *Minutes of the Annual Conference of the Free Baptists of Nova Scotia*, 1887, 32.

5. David Millard, "History of the Christians, or Christian Connexion," in *History of the Religious Denominations in the United States*, ed. John Winebrenner (Harrisburg, Pa.: John Winebrenner, 1848), 164.

6. Letter of Elder David Millard, July 10, 1821, *Christian Herald* 4, no. 2 (1821): 42–43.

7. Brian C. Cuthbertson, ed., *The Journal of the Reverend John Payzant (1749–1834)* (Hantsport, N.S.: Lancelot, 1981), 59.

8. Stephen A. Marini, *Radical Sects of Revolutionary New England* (Cambridge, Mass., and London: Harvard Univ. Press, 1982) and George A. Rawlyk, *Ravished by the Spirit: Religious Revivals, Baptists, and Henry Alline* (Kingston and Montreal: McGill-Queen's Univ. Press, 1984). The Freewill Baptists are the most studied of the new denominations, although studies tend to see them as a homogeneous movement. See Marini and Norman Allen Baxter, *History of the Freewill Baptists: A Study in New England Separatism* (Rochester, N.Y.: American Baptist Historical Society, 1957). The Freewill Baptists by mid-nineteenth century, although dominated by the New England Freewill Baptists, were a amalgam of Freewill Baptists, Free Communion Baptists, and a southern free will Baptist movement.

9. Millard, "History of the Christians," 164. I have chosen to use the early-nineteenth-century spelling "Connexion" rather than the late-nineteenth-century "Connection."

10. Millard, "History of the Christians," 164–65. Cf. Milo True Morrill, *A History of the Christian Denomination in America* (Dayton, Ohio: Christian Publishing Association, 1912), 15–119. Elias Smith used the appellation Christ-ian (Christ-yan) to describe those associated with him, but it did not gain universal acceptance.

11. Ibid., 165.

12. Stewart, *The History of the Freewill Baptists*, 252, and Garrison and DeGroot, *The Disciples of Christ*, 89.

13. Millard, "History of the Christians," 165, and Louis H. Gunnemann, *The Shaping of the United Church of Christ: An Essay in the History of American Christianity* (New York: United Church Press, 1977), 162.

14. Millard, "History of the Christians," 165, 169.

15. Quoted in Garrison and DeGroot, *The Disciples of Christ*, 90.

16. David Benedict, *A General History of the Baptist Denomination in America and Other Parts of the World* (1848; reprint, Lafayette, Tenn.: Church History Research & Archives, 1977), 915–16.

17. Stewart, *The History of the Freewill Baptists*, 193.

18. Ibid., 270–71.

19. Millard, "History of the Christians," 166–69.

20. Morrill, *A History*, 184.

21. Garrison and DeGroot, *The Disciples of Christ*, 91 and Barry M. Moody, "From Itinerant to Pastor: The Case of Edward Manning (1767–1851)," *Papers of the Canadian Society of Church History 1981* (Montreal: Canadian Society of Church History, 1982), 19.

22. John Buzzell in the *Repository*, vol. 8, no. 23, quoted in Stewart, *The History of the Freewill Baptists*, 273.

23. Stewart, *The History of the Freewill Baptists*, 275.

24. See Stewart, *The History of the Freewill Baptists*, for descriptions of organization of churches.

25. Letter of Joseph Bailey, Oct. 31, 1821, in *Christian Herald* 4, no. 5 (1821): 106.

26. Letter of Samuel Nutt to the *Christian Herald* 14, no. 4 (1831), quoted in F. C. Burnett, "Notes on the Christian Connection Preachers on the River St. John" (Griffin-Allwood library), 3.

27. Stewart, *The History of the Freewill Baptists*, 90, 114, 217, 349, and *Christian Herald* 4, no. 3 (1821): 63. Cf. G. A. Burgess and J. T. Ward, *Free Baptist Cyclopaedia* (N.p.: Free Baptist Cyclopaedia Co., 1889), 353–68.

28. Garrison and DeGroot, *The Disciples of Christ*, 89.

29. Morrill, *A History*, 108, 139–41, 378.

30. Cross, *The Burned-Over District*, 15–17, 38.

31. *Christian Herald* 4, no. 3 (1821): 64. During the War of 1812 Elder Joseph Badger went into Lower Canada to visit his parents. He preached along the way and, due to suspicions caused by the war, he was arrested. The same thing happened when he returned at a later date with two other young ministers, J. L. Peavy and Joseph Boody. As a result of his perseverance a reformation took place in Ringsey. Morrill, *A History*, 113. The revival spread throughout Wickham, Kingsey, Melbourn, Shiftan, Brompton, Oxford, Ascott, Hatley, Barnston, Stanstead, and Campion. Badger returned to Lower Canada in 1821, visiting the former site of his revivalistic efforts. He was able to report that "many of the converts still stand in the liberty wherewith Christ has made them free." "Journal of Joseph Badger," *Christian Herald* 4, no. 7 (1821): 157–58. Orcutt had left the Freewill Baptists and induced the Hatley Freewill Baptist church to change denominations in

1823. Stewart, *The History of the Freewill Baptists*, 382, and Burgess and Ward, *Free Baptist Cyclopaedia*, 501, 669. Revivalistic anglophone churches on the American border in Lower Canada tended to join American transcongregational organizations.

32. Morrill, *A History*, 113 and Philip G. A. Griffin-Allwood, "The Canadianization of Baptists: From Denominations to Denomination, 1760–1912" (Ph.D. diss., Southern Baptist Theological Seminary, 1986), 158, 178.

33. Thus the Free Communion and Freewill Baptist denominations began in Upper Canada. Griffin-Allwood, "The Canadianization of Baptists," 177–78.

34. Letter of David Millard and letter of Mary Stogdell, *Christian Herald* 4, no. 2 (1821): 42–43.

35. Letter of Joseph Bailey, *Christian Herald* 4, no. 5 (1821): 105.

36. Ibid., 105–6. The latter was a requirement for recognition by Upper Canadian legal authorities. See John S. Moir, ed., *Church and State in Canada, 1627–1867: Basic Documents*, Carleton Library No. 33 (Toronto: McClelland and Stewart, 1967), 147–48.

37. Letter of Joseph Bailey, 106.

38. Ibid.

39. Letter from Nathan Harding to Thomas Henry, Sept. 2, 1853, quoted in Mrs. P. A. Henry, *Memoir of Rev. Thomas Henry: Christian Minister, York Pioneer, and Soldier of 1812* (Toronto: Mrs. P. A. Henry, 1880). Cf. Harold Hilton, *Christian Baptist: 160 Years of Ministry* (Newmarket, Ont.: Newmarket Christian Baptist Church, 1982), 1.

40. Morrill, *A History*, 125.

41. Joseph Ash, "Reminiscences No. 1 or History of the Rise and Progress of Our Cause in Canada," *Christian Worker* 2, no. 1 (1882): 3. Cf. Reuben Butchart, *The Disciples of Christ in Canada Since 1830* (Toronto: Canadian Headquarters' Publications, Church of Christ [Disciples], 1949), 62.

42. Joseph Ash, "Reminiscences No. 3 or History of the Rise and Progress of Our Cause in Canada," *Christian Worker* 2, no. 5 (1883): 1; "Reminiscences No. 4 or History of the Rise and Progress of Our Cause in Canada," *Christian Worker* 2, no. 6 (1883): 1; and "Reminiscences No. 8 or History of the Rise and Progress of Our Cause in Canada," *Christian Worker* 2, no. 10 (1883): 1. Cf. Butchart, *The Disciples of Christ*, 9, 143, 412.

43. Garrison and DeGroot, *The Disciples of Christ*, 201–13. For Canadian illustrations of the differences between the Disciples and other immersionist denominations, see the *Christian Worker* 1–5 (1883–88), published in Meadford, Ontario, and *The Christian* 1–4 (1839–41, 1847–48), published in Saint John, New Brunswick.

44. Durward T. Stokes and William T. Scott, *A History of the Christian Church in the South* (Elon, N.C.: Elon College, 1975), 46–47.

45. Joseph Ash, "Reminiscences No. 17 or History of the Rise and Progress of Our Cause in Canada," *Christian Worker* 3, no. 7 (1884): 4. Morrill, *A History*, 183, 342; and *The United Church of Canada Year Book*, 1928, 429.

46. Morrill, *A History*, 126, 384.

47. "Minutes of the 2nd Division Quarterly Conference" (Canadian Baptist Archives, McMaster Divinity College, Hamilton, Ontario).

48. "Minutes of District No. 4 of the Christian Church in Canada" (Canadian Baptist Archives, McMaster Divinity College, Hamilton, Ontario). The Georgiana and North Gwillimbury (Keswick) churches were farther north on Lake Simcoe.

49. Morrill, *A History*, 342–43.

50. Butchart, *The Disciples of Christ*, 496.

51. Morrill, *A History*, 343, 348, 379. The educational effort was an affiliation. Cf. "The Story of the Christian Church in Ontario," *Christian Vanguard*, June 11, 1921, 1–7.

52. Gunnemann, *The Shaping of the United Church of Christ*, 162.

53. *The United Church of Canada Year Book*, 1926, 354. Three other churches were inactive.

54. *The United Church of Canada Year Book*, 1928, 479–80.

55. See the Yearbooks of the Congregationalist Christians and the United Church of Christ.

56. Hilton, *Christian Baptist*, 8.

57. *The Evangelical Baptist*, June 1986, 12. The Little Britain church had been reopened in 1936.

58. Constant H. Jacquet Jr., ed., *Year Book of the American and Canadian Churches 1987* (Nashville: Abingdon, 1987), 131. Active churches are Keswick; Stoufville Memorial; Ringwood; Crawford Street, Toronto; Emmanuel, Toronto; and Kingston Mission. Letter from Harold G. Hilton to P. G. A. Griffin-Allwood, May 13, 1988, and letter from Cathy Horlick to P. G. A. Griffin-Allwood, July 22, 1988.

59. Separate Baptists and Separate or Strict Congregationalists were the two denominations birthed by the First Great Awakening. Although some Separate Baptist churches were formed through withdrawal from Regular Baptist churches, the majority were created by the adoption of immersion by Separate Congregationalist churches that had withdrawn from Standing Order Congregationalist churches. See C. C. Goen, *Revivalism and Separatism in New England, 1740–1800: Strict Congregationalists and Separate Baptists in the Great Awakening* (New Haven and London: Yale Univ. Press, 1962).

60. This revival is discussed in Griffin-Allwood, "The Canadianization of Baptists," 65–69. Further research needs to be done on the religious affiliation of the pre-Loyalist migrants.

61. See Marini, *Radical Sects*, and Rawlyk, *Ravished by the Spirit*.

62. See Gordon Stewart and George Rawlyk, *A People Highly Favoured of God: Yankees and the American Revolution* (Toronto: Macmillan, 1972), George Rawlyk and Gordon Stewart, "Nova Scotia's Sense of Mission," *Histoire Sociale* 2 (1968): 5–17; and Frederick C. Burnett, "Henry Alline's 'Articles & Covenant of a Gospel Church,'" *Nova Scotia Historical Review* 4 (1984): 13–24. The classic description of the revival is found in Maurice W. Armstrong, *The Great Awakening in Nova Scotia, 1776–1809* (Hartford: American Society of Church History, 1948).

63. See Griffin-Allwood, "The Canadianization of Baptists," 82–98, and David G. Bell, ed., *Newlight Baptist Journals of James Manning and James Innis* (Hantsport, N.S.: Lancelot, 1985), 2–53.

64. Cf. George E. Levy, *The Baptists of the Maritime Provinces, 1753–1946* (Saint John, N.B.: Barnes-Hopkins, 1946), 235–39.

65. In particular, David Bell, a barrister and sometime law and history professor, and Elder Frederick Burnett, of the Upper Brighton (New Brunswick) Free Baptist Church, for New Brunswick; and the Reverend Roland McCormick, a retired minister and teacher, for Nova Scotia.

66. See Roland K. McCormick, *The Free Baptists of Nova Scotia: An Anthology*, Baptist Collection, Vaughan Memorial Library, Wolfville, N.S., 3–45; F. C. Burnett, "Early Baptists from New Brunswick Who Went to Upper Canada," Griffin-Allwood library, 1–2; Bell, *Newlight Baptist Journals*; David G. Bell, "From Newlight to Arminian Baptist in New Brunswick 1776–1832" (Paper, Harvard Univ., May 1981); and Griffin-Allwood, "The Canadianization of Baptists," 98–104.

67. For example, one prominent member of the Waterborough Allinite congregation was surprised when the Regular Baptists would not recognize their congregation as a proper church. J. M. Bumsted, ed., "The Autobiography of Joseph Crandall," *Acadiensis* 3, no. 1 (1973): 88. Cf. Griffin-Allwood, "The Canadianization of Baptists," 98–147.

68. Bell, *Newlight Baptist Journals*, 73–75.

69. Nutt quoted in Burnett, "Notes."

70. Bell, *Newlight Baptist Journals*, 53–55, and Burnett, "Notes."

71. Bell, *Newlight Baptist Journals*, 55.

72. George Garraty, *Rise and Progress of the "New-Brunswick Christian Conference"* (Saint John: n.p., 1840), 4.

73. Bell, *Newlight Baptist Journals*, 54–55. George Garraty gives as the reason that the latter two did not join as "jealousy" between them. They could not join the conference because they "could in no wise agree." Garraty, *Rise and Progress*, 5. Underlying it may have been concern about the authority that the conference exercised over preachers. Memories of the Baptist Association may have prohibited acceptance of even this limited delegation of the authority of the local church. Daniel Shaw, who was alive at the time of the founding of the conference, appears not to have been involved in the organizational events of the 1830s.

74. Edwin Crowell, "A Sketch of the Free Baptists of Nova Scotia" in E. M. Saunders, *History of the Baptists of the Maritime Provinces* (Halifax: Press of John Burgoyne, 1902), 399, and McCormick, *Free Baptists of Nova Scotia*, 57–60, 175–77. Positive identification of the Barrington church is a matter for further inquiry. McCormick has done more research since the preparation of *Free Baptists of Nova Scotia*. Letter from R. K. McCormick to P. G. A. Griffin-Allwood, Apr. 24, 1988. Cf. Moody, "From Itinerant to Pastor," 12–13; Charles Tupper, "History of the Baptist Churches in Nova-Scotia," *Baptist Missionary Magazine of Nova-Scotia and New Brunswick* 1 (1829): 315–16; and Roland K. McCormick,

"Jacob Norton: The Forgotten Christian of Atlantic Baptist History," *Nova Scotia Historical Review* 7, no. 1 (1987): 100–105.

75. See Clark, *Church and Sect in Canada,* 280–82.

76. Article in *Religious Intelligencer* quoted in McCormick, *Free Baptists of Nova Scotia,* 175.

77. Morrill, *A History,* 112. Another "Christian Band" preacher in Nova Scotia was W. W. Ashley, but his significance is diminished by his constant shifting of denominational allegiance. McCormick, *Free Baptists of Nova Scotia,* 82, 88, 204, 208, and Butchart, *The Disciples of Christ,* 353.

78. McGray, a minister from Maine, had his ministry revitalized by Norton, but in 1831 he organized a Freewill Baptist conference. Crowell joined the conference but may have at least temporarily withdrawn when he refused to participate in the ordination of Asa Bent in 1832. This conference was the organizational framework used for the creation of the union conference in 1837. "Cape Sable Island Church Book" (Baptist Collection, Vaughan Memorial Library, Acadia Univ., Wolfville, N.S.), entry for Apr. 5, 1832, and notes in the back of the book. Conflict between Norton and McGray resulted in the affiliation of the Cape Sable Island church with the Freewill Baptists' Farmington Quarterly meeting in 1840. See Griffin-Allwood, "The Canadianization of Baptists," 107–14. McCormick, *The Free Baptists of Nova Scotia,* 30, 46–54, 87, 126, 173, 176–78. Cf. Cape Sable Island Free Baptist Church Book, entries for May 5 and May 28, 1840 (Baptist Collection, Vaughan Memorial Library, Acadia Univ., Wolfville, N.S.). After the schism, the first Freewill Baptist messenger attended the Free Christian Baptist Conference in 1860. After the 1866 union, the Freewill Baptist connection with the Maine Central Yearly Meeting was ended and the new conference was considered to be a yearly meeting. The name Free Baptist is the same designation used in the United States for the union of the Freewill and Free Communion Baptists. *Free Baptist Faith,* 143. Crowell, "A Sketch of the Free Baptists of Nova Scotia," 402–3. In 1901, the Nova Scotia conference joined the Freewill Baptist General Conference in response to the socio-ecclesial pressures brought to bear by the union of the New Brunswick Free Baptists with the Maritime Regular Baptists. Crowell, "A Sketch of the Free Baptists of Nova Scotia," 409.

79. Joseph McLeod, "A Sketch of the History of the Free Baptists of New Brunswick," in Saunders, *History of the Baptists of the Maritime Provinces,* 423.

80. Frederick C. Burnett, "The New Brunswick Christian Conference," Griffin-Allwood library, 2.

81. W. W. Eaton, "History of the Christian Connexion," *Christian* 2 (Dec. 1840): 161, and Garraty, *Rise and Progress,* 7. Cf. Philip G. A. Griffin-Allwood, "Maritime Baptists and Unimmersed Christians: The Influence of Societies on Church Membership Practice," *Papers of the Canadian Society of Church History 1984* (Ottawa: Canadian Society of Church History, 1985), 66–88.

82. See Eaton, "History of the Christian Connexion"; Garraty, *Rise and Progress*; Butchart, *The Disciples of Christ,* 97–100, 129–33; Bell, *Newlight Baptist Journals,* 76–77; and Stewart, *The History of the Freewill Baptists,* 355–56.

83. "Petition to His Excellency Sir Edmund Walker Head," 1847. Cf. D. G. Bell, "Religious Liberty and Protestant Dissent in Loyalist New Brunswick," *UNB Law Journal* 36 (1987): 146–62.

84. Frederick C. Burnett, "Hamiltonians," Griffin-Allwood library.

85. Eaton, "History of the Christian Connexion," 161–62. Jonathan Hamilton's orthodox Trinitarian theological position may have helped prompt this response. Cf. Stewart, *The History of the Freewill Baptists*, 356.

86. *A Treatise on the Faith of the Free Christian Baptists of Nova-Scotia and New-Brunswick* (Saint John, N. B.: Bailey & Day, 1848), 2–3 and McLeod, "A Sketch of the History of the Free Baptists of New Brunswick," 424.

87. Bell, *Newlight Baptist Journals*, 75. Fred Burnett suggests that the identification of the New Brunswick churches with the Christian Connexion may have ceased as early as the mid-1830s. On October 17, 1839, the Maine Eastern Christian Conference responded to "unfavorable reports ... against some of our preachers ... with regard to the churches [in New Brunswick] being gathered by our preachers" by affirming that "more than thirty churches were gathered in [New Brunswick] by our preachers." Quoted in a letter from F. C. Burnett to P. G. A. Griffin-Allwood, Apr. 20, 1988. Individual Christian Connexion ministers and churches continued to join the New Brunswick Free Christian Baptists until 1864. "Free Baptist Church Record Book Deer Island, N.B." (Public Archives of New Brunswick, Fredericton, N.B.); *Minutes of the General Conference of Free Christian Baptists of New Brunswick*, 1863, 10, and 1864, 10; and letter from F. C. Burnett to P. G. A. Griffin-Allwood, Mar. 28, 1988. Burnett is preparing a catalog of Free Christian Baptist churches and elders in Nova Scotia and New Brunswick.

88. *A Treatise on the Faith of the Free Christian Baptists of Nova-Scotia and New-Brunswick* (Yarmouth: Free Christian Baptist Connexion, 1841) and *Treatise*, 1848.

89. Griffin-Allwood, "Canadianization of Baptists," 132. Cf. *Free Baptist Banner*, Oct. 1902, 226. The New Brunswick Free Baptists were approached as late as 1902 and the proposal was greeted with "no favour, and apparently with scant courtesy."

90. Ash, "Reminiscences No. 4," 1; Butchart, *The Disciples of Christ*, 103; *United Church Year Book, 1928*, 479; and *The Christian Church in Ontario*, 2.

91. *Treatise*, 1848, 2, and McLeod, "A Sketch of the History," 434.

92. Cf. John S. Moir, "The Canadianization of the Protestant Churches," *Canadian Historical Association Papers* (1966), 56–59.

93. Hilton, *Christian Baptist*, 2.

94. See Griffin-Allwood, "The Canadianization of Baptists," for the story.

95. C. J. Cameron, *Foreigners or Canadians?* (Toronto: Baptist Home Mission Board of Ontario and Quebec, 1913), 5. For a description of Canadian Evangelicalism see Philip G. A. Griffin-Allwood, "Contemporary Evangelicalism: A Question of Continuity," *Atlantic Baptist*, Feb. 1988, 57–61. Cf. *Free Baptist Banner*, May 1902, 102–3; Oct. 1904, 219–20; Nov. 1904, 254–55; Jan. 1905, 9–11; Oct. 1905, 226–27.

96. Philip Schaff and Ireneus Prime, eds., *History, Essays, Orations, and Other Documents of the Sixth General Conference of the Evangelical Alliance* (London: Sampson Low, Marston, Low, & Searle, 1874), 760; Philip Schaff, "The Doctrinal Consensus of Evangelical Christendom," *Evangelical Alliance Extra: Montreal Daily Witness* (Oct. 1874): 9–11; Professor MacKnight, "On Confessions of Faith—On Their Use and Abuse," *Evangelical Alliance Extra,* 28–29; "Christian Union," *Montreal Register,* Jan. 29, 1846, 2; and J. E. Pinnington, "Denominational Loyalty and Loyalty to Christ: The Problem a Century Ago and Today," *Canadian Journal of Theology* 14 (1968): 125–30.

97. A. J. Arnold, "The Work of the British Evangelical Alliance," *Christianity Practically Applied* (New York: Baker & Taylor, 1894), 234–48, and W. Noel, "The Evangelical Alliance: Its Objects and Influence in Promoting the Universal Priesthood of Believers to the Communion of Saints," in Schaff and Prime, *History, Essays, Orations,* 197–200.

98. R. L. Dabney, "The Scriptural Idea of the Visible Church as Constituted of Denominations of Christians," *Evangelical Alliance Extra,* 13–18; G. M. Grant, "The Church of Canada—Can Such a Thing Be?" *Evangelical Alliance Extra,* 40–45; "Christian Union," in Schaff and Prime, *History, Essays, Orations,* 139–200; and "Christian Union and Cooperation," in *Christianity Practically Applied,* 221–340.

99. Henry Alline, *Two Mites . . . Points of Divinity* (1781) quoted in Rawlyk and Stewart, "Nova Scotia's Sense of Mission," 12.

100. *Minutes of the New Brunswick Free Christian Baptist General Conference,* 1865, 32–33.

101. William T. Gunn, *His Dominion* (Toronto: The Canadian Council of the Missionary Education Movement, 1918). Cf. H. C. Priest, *Canada's Share in World Tasks* (Toronto: Canadian Council of the Missionary Education Movement, 1920). In recent years affiliation with the Conservative Congregational Christian Conference, which occurred between 1965 and 1968, has given the Canadian churches a fresh vitality. Significant, in light of the above analysis, is the adoption of a modified form of the World Evangelical Fellowship's "Statement of Faith" as the "Statement of Faith" of the Congregational Christians. *The Congregational Christian Church* (Keswick, Ont.: Conference of the Congregational Christian Churches in Ontario, n.d.). Cf. *1984 Yearbook of the Conservative Congregational Christian Conference,* 43–44, 87–88.

The Boston Church of Christ

Russell Paden

In the past decade few religious groups have gained as much attention from the media and the anticult forces as the Boston Church of Christ. Controversial recruiting practices, high commitment expectations of members, use of discipleship partners, and teachings on church authority have brought a barrage of criticism from outsiders and ex-members alike.

Boston Church of Christ is the name given to a religious movement that began with a single congregation in Boston, Massachusetts. This movement has been known by a variety of names (the Crossroads movement,[1] Multiplying Ministries, the Discipling movement, and the International Churches of Christ, among others), but for the purposes of this study, the term *Boston movement* will be used for two reasons. One, for the sake of clarity, it is useful to distinguish between the founding church in Boston and the churches worldwide that affiliate themselves with the Boston Church of Christ. Two, the name is not chosen arbitrarily, for those in the Boston movement both think of and refer to themselves as a movement and, indeed, the term *Boston movement* appears in much of their literature.

EARLY HISTORY

Although the Boston Church of Christ officially came into existence in 1979, its roots run much deeper. The Boston movement is born of the traditions of the nineteenth-century Restoration movement in America. Leaders of the Restoration movement such as Thomas Campbell, his son Alexander, and Barton Stone sought a return to first-century Christianity. Their two main objectives were to do away with denominational divisions and to return to the Bible as the sole authority for the faith and practice of the church.

The Restoration movement pledged itself to the axiom "Where the scriptures speak, we speak; and where the scriptures are silent, we are silent,"[2] but applying this interpretive rule was problematic. When some restorationists began using musical instruments in the worship service and instituting missionary societies, a small conservative faction felt that neither had biblical precedence or authority. This faction, which became the traditional or mainline Churches of Christ, separated itself from the remainder of the Restoration movement. Major doctrinal differences developed among restorationist leaders as early as the 1860s,[3] and the Churches of Christ officially went their own way in 1906, growing from 160,000 members[4] to 1.2 million in the United States by the 1990s.[5]

In 1967, the Fourteenth Street Church of Christ in Gainesville, Florida (later renamed the Crossroads Church of Christ), borrowing and adapting some techniques learned from Campus Crusade,[6] began a "pilot project [at the University of Florida] for a campus ministry program with a strong evangelistic thrust."[7] Under the direction of the minister, Chuck Lucas, the campus ministry, called Campus Advance, grew rapidly. Campus Advance was not without critics. Two practices in particular, "soul talks" and "prayer partners," led to accusations of cultism. Soul talks, evangelistic Bible studies with prayer and sharing, were held in student residences.[8] Each soul talk had a leader who was given delegated authority over the members of his group.[9] *Prayer partners* was the term used for the practice of pairing up a new Christian with a more mature Christian so that the new Christian could be given one-on-one direction.[10] Both practices emphasized "in-depth involvement of each member in one another's lives,"[11] and critics thought the practices led to manipulation and abuse of members.

In 1972 a freshman at the University of Florida, the future leader of the Boston movement, Kip McKean, was converted through Campus Advance. The impact of the campus ministry of the Crossroads Church of Christ on him was significant: "The innovations of 'one another Christianity,' evangelistic small group Bible studies, and the vision of dynamic campus ministries were put on my heart through the powerful preaching of Chuck Lucas and his associate, Sam Laing. The seeds of discipling were placed in my life as I saw personally how one man could affect another's daily lifestyle and eternal destiny for God."[12] McKean trained at Crossroads while finishing his education at the University of Florida. He left Crossroads and served as campus minister at other mainline Churches of Christ until, in 1979, he was invited to take over as the pulpit and campus minister of a struggling, thirty-member church in a Boston suburb, the Lexington Church of Christ.

GROWTH

The Lexington Church of Christ was renamed the Boston Church of Christ and saw tremendous growth under McKean's tutelage. By 1981, the thirty-member church had grown to a membership of three hundred. In 1981–82 Kip McKean felt the Lord had placed on his heart a "vision for the world." His vision was to establish "pillar churches" in key metropolitan centers of the world that could in turn evangelize the cities around them.[13]

In 1982 the Boston Church of Christ planted churches in Chicago and London and in 1983 in New York City. This heavy emphasis on evangelism and the trend of church plantings continued, until by 1993 the movement had grown to 42,855 members in 130 congregations worldwide, with 27,055 members and 48 congregations in the United States. The largest congregations, New York and Boston, both currently have a Sunday morning attendance over 5,000, while the Los Angeles congregation has attendance over 4,000.[14]

Much of the movement's vision has been fueled by the perceived lethargy of denominational churches, particularly the mainline Churches of Christ from which it originated. Church growth has become the litmus test of a true church. While members would probably concede that there are false religions that experience growth, they would contend that a true church of God *must* be experiencing growth.

Lack of growth among the mainline Churches of Christ provided much of the impetus for the Boston movement. Between 1945 and 1965 the mainline Churches of Christ was one of the fastest growing religious movements in America. By the 1970s, however, the Churches of Christ saw a decrease in conversions and a decline in growth until the net annual growth rate was less than 1 percent.[15] Kip McKean stated that he visited numerous mainline Churches of Christ between 1976 and 1979 and found their spiritual condition "ranged from lukewarm to disgusting."[16] It was this attitude, plus the decline in growth of the Churches of Christ, that spurred him on in his belief that Christ's church had to be revitalized and restored.

BELIEFS AND PRACTICES

Many of the beliefs and practices of the Boston movement would fit easily within the evangelical tradition in America. A typical Sunday morning service consists of singing, praying, preaching, and the taking of the Lord's Supper. Members of the movement accept the inspiration of the Bible, the virgin birth, the subsitutionary atonement, the bodily resurrection of Jesus, the Trinity, and the Second Coming.

However, the movement is very exclusivistic, believing that it alone has "rediscovered" numerous first-century Bible doctrines and that it is virtually impossible to be among the elect outside the ranks of the Boston movement. Movement leaders have a vision for converting the whole world by training individual members to be highly evangelistic and very submissive to the leadership of the church.

Part of their commitment to evangelism is seen in their financial practices. Very rarely will a congregation affiliated with the movement own a church building. A congregation will typically rent a facility to meet in on Sunday morning (the Boston Church of Christ meets in the Boston Garden); the money that would have gone toward a church mortgage is funneled into paid staff, the majority of whom are involved directly or indirectly in evangelistic efforts.

DISCIPLESHIP

Key to understanding the Boston movement is the concept of discipleship. The movement sees a sharp distinction between "the world's" view of a Christian and a true disciple of Christ. Marty Wooten, missionary and leader in the Boston movement, has written, "In the Boston movement, 'disciple' was soon to gain momentum and come to represent those who are faithfully following Christ in contrast to someone in another congregation who had been immersed [baptized] for the forgiveness of sins but never repented and took on the lifestyle and purpose of the early disciples, that is, making disciples of all nations."[17] Boston movement missionary Andrew Giambarba echoed those sentiments: "Every single member of every congregation must be committed to making disciples. If any are not, then they are not disciples themselves. And if they are not disciples themselves, then they will not be going to heaven."[18] As these quotations show, the most important characteristic of a disciple, according to the Boston movement, is making other disciples. Part of the process of making disciples includes the use of discipleship partners. McKean felt that the practice of prayer partners that was employed at the Crossroads Church of Christ was not "directive enough," since Crossroads members chose their own partners. At Boston, McKean decided it was better for the leaders of the congregation to arrange for "older, stronger Christians to give direction to each of the younger, weaker ones."[19] Discipleship partners were always of the same sex and were to have daily contact and meet weekly.[20]

Discipleship partners are not considered optional: "Similarly we expect every member to be discipled by a more spiritually mature Christian who is given the authority to teach him to obey everything that Jesus commanded."[21] Kip McKean writes: " We need to make it abundantly clear . . . that every brother in the congregation needs to have a discipleship partner. To not have a discipleship partner is to be rebellious to God and to the leadership of this congregation."[22] The soul talks concept from Crossroads was also continued in Boston, renamed "Bible talks." Bible talks are held once a week at regular times and places and attended consistently by an average of six to ten members.[23] Some Bible talks are for men or women only, while others are mixed.

Each Bible talk has a Bible talk leader and assistants who are given authority over the members of the group by the elders and evangelists of the congregation to see that the leadership's "expectations" are implemented by the members of the group.[24] The Bible talk is the main outreach instrument of the local congregations, and members are expected to bring visitors with them. In many ways, the Bible talk is the foundation of the movement, for if the Bible talks do not grow, the local churches do not grow.[25]

It should be noted that this concept of discipling is not new. Other religious movements have made use of this system of training and close personal supervision. Two parachurch organizations, Campus Crusade for Christ and the Navigators, use variants of this system. Similar "shepherding" movements arose within charismatic circles during the 1970s under the names Christian Growth Ministries and Maranatha Christian Churches.

BAPTISM

There is probably no biblical passage that is more important or more pivotal to the teachings of the Boston movement than Matthew 28:19–20: "Therefore go and make disciples of all nations, baptizing them in the name of the Father and of the Son and of the Holy Spirit, and teaching them to obey everything I have commanded you. And surely I am with you always, to the very end of the age."[26] This passage (often called the Great Commission) reiterates the movement's commitment to evangelism; it also is used as a source outlining the proper form of baptism. There are two important things to know about the movement's teachings on baptism: (1) The only acceptable form of baptism is immersion; and (2) although adherents deny that they teach baptismal regeneration, they do in fact believe that one is saved at the time of baptism.[27] Using Matthew 28:19–20 as their proof text, they further contend that one must be a disciple *first*, before baptism, for the baptism to be valid. Their reasoning is that since "make disciples" comes before "baptizing" in the text, the one must precede the other.[28]

Since salvation is dependent upon a correct and valid baptism, a person who was baptized in any other religious group (including the mainline Churches of Christ) is almost always rebaptized upon joining the Boston movement. Often, a member who was initially baptized within the Boston movement will decide he or she did not have a proper understanding of baptism or was not a true disciple at the time of the first baptism and will be baptized a second time.[29] This was particularly true in the fall of 1986 and spring of 1987. It was during this time that the current understanding of Matthew 28:19–20 began to be taught: that a person had to be a disciple first, before baptism, for the baptism to be valid.[30] Kip McKean stated that he and other leaders in the church "rediscovered" this first-century Bible doctrine.[31] With its discovery came a rash of rebaptisms throughout the movement, including rebaptisms of many of the top leaders of the church.

ORGANIZATION

Based on its interpretation of the second and third chapters of the book of Revelation, the movement adheres to a "one church, one city" concept. They believe it is unscriptural to have more than one congregation per city. Typically, but not always, a church affiliated with the Boston movement will simply take the name of the city as its name, such as the Los Angeles Church of Christ or the Chicago Church of Christ.

There is a very clear hierarchy in the Boston movement. In 1988 Kip McKean established nine world sector leaders who would each be responsible for the churches in a portion of the world. World Sector Administrators were also appointed to oversee the administration and finances of each world sector. Elders and evangelists make up the leadership core of individual congregations. Although the terminology differs from congregation to congregation, each church is usually divided geographically into sectors or quadrants with a sector or quadrant leader. The sectors are further subdivided (again, geographically) into zones, and the sector leader oversees the zone leaders. The zone leader then oversees the individual Bible talks and the Bible talk leaders. Typically, anyone in the position of zone leader or higher is a paid employee of the church.[32]

Kip McKean founded the Boston Church of Christ and continues as its undisputed leader today. In 1988 McKean removed himself from the position of lead evangelist of the Boston Church of Christ so that he could focus his attention on the newly appointed world sector leaders. In 1990 he moved to Los Angeles to oversee the Los Angeles Church of Christ and continue to serve as missions evangelist for the movement worldwide.

Those within the movement enthusiastically follow McKean as leader and have nothing but the highest praise for him. Andrew Giambarba says, "In spanning twenty centuries of history it is my belief that there has never been a disciple since the apostle Paul who has given spiritual sight to so many."[33] Steve Johnson, world sector leader and evangelist for the New York City Church of Christ, writes: "With eyes wide open I'm following Kip McKean; Consciously, Intentionally; Thankfully. I guess I'm just not as strong as some folks and I need help in following Jesus. And so far, I've found no better help, no better leader, no more righteous a man—no better friend than Kip."[34]

CONTROVERSY

While the Boston movement is untainted by sexual scandal or financial impropriety, it has been the focus of intense controversy. The mainline Churches of Christ disavowed the Boston movement in the mid-1980s and are now ardent opponents of it; numerous universities around the country either restrict or bar Boston movement activities on their campuses; anticult forces charge the movement with mind control and abusive practices; and many ex-members have taken up personal crusades against the movement.

The majority of the controversy surrounding the Boston movement centers on the commitment level that is expected of church members and the authority the church exercises in members' lives. It is clear from *Making Disciples* (a manual to train potential converts) that members are expected to put the church above all else, including job, friends, and family.[35] Each week the average member attends at least four or five meetings for worship and/or Bible study. Those in any position of leadership (assistant Bible talk leader and up) might also attend a leadership meeting on a weekly basis. Every member is involved with a discipleship partner, and many, if not most, are involved with multiple discipleship partners.[36] Partners usually meet once a week and keep in daily contact. In many congregations Saturday night has been set aside as a time when singles are expected to date other singles in the church.[37] Members are expected, on a daily basis, to contact people with the intention of recruiting; some leaders set guidelines as to how many contacts a member is to have each day. As Nick Young said in a sermon in Tulsa, Oklahoma, "You are going to go out with the gospel of Jesus, and you're not going to have a problem with inviting thirty a day . . . I have heard that some of you have actually had an attitude about having to share with thirty people a day. That makes me sick! And you know, it makes God sicker! Where is your heart? You've lost your faith. You've lost your heart. You can't even take a simple challenge like sharing with thirty people a day and not get all bent out of shape about it."[38] Many congregations make use of accountability sheets that each member is to fill out and turn in on a weekly basis. For each day of the week members are to indicate whether they spent time praying (alone and with spouse), studying the Bible, and sharing their faith. Accountability sheets from some congregations have also included checklists for such things as whether they had sex with their spouses, whether they went to bed and arose on time, and how much sleep and exercise they were getting.[39]

It is these intrusions into private areas of people's lives that are cited by critics and ex-members alike. Ex-members charge that church leaders dictated to them regarding the use of their money, how they spent their free time, whom they dated and for how long, and with whom they associated. Critics believe that the church attempts to isolate members from anyone who might cause them to question the teachings of the Boston movement. As support for this contention, critics claim that members are encouraged to live together and to limit their contact with nonmember family and friends. They also note that college students are often urged not to go home for the summer if there are no Boston movement churches near their homes.[40]

It is clear that the movement does maintain rigid teachings on authority: part of being a disciple is submitting to the leadership of the church. It is assumed that someone in a leadership position knows what is best for an individual even more than the individual does. As Kip McKean has said,

> Let me tell you this, the people that are easiest to disciple are those individuals who are the ones who most want to imitate you. Because the moment you start saying, "Well, there are some parts about this brother I am a little bit unsure of," what that person begins to do, is they begin to filter through the direction and advice that's given to them. And when they start filtering through, they begin to filter out. And when they start filtering out, they're going to filter out what seems best to them, and the whole point of being a disciple is that they don't know what is best for them. But their discipler knows what is best for them. And so I believe a challenge for us is to say, "Listen, I really love and appreciate my Zone leader. But more than that, I want to be like him."[41]

He further states: "The only time [the evangelist] is not to be obeyed is when he calls you to disobey Scripture or disobey your conscience and even if he calls you [to] do something that disobeys your conscience, you still have an obligation to study it out and prayerfully change your opinion so you can be totally unified."[42] Critics of the Boston movement believe the church's teachings on authority, its influence in members' daily lives, and the discipling relationships have all led to emotional abuse of members. It should be noted that the leadership of the Boston movement recognizes that abuses of authority have occurred, and it has retracted some of its earlier teachings on authority and submission.[43] However, while the movement claims it has attempted to "readjust what was previously taught,"[44] those who have recently left the movement claim that the old teachings and practices regarding authority in the church persist.[45]

Along with the tremendous growth there has been a tremendous dropout rate as well. Although more people come into the Boston movement than leave it, large numbers leave the movement every year. Although 22,135 people joined the movement in 1991, the total growth for the year was only 8,880, indicating that 13,255 people left the movement.[46] Kip McKean states that the dropout rate for the movement is 50 percent,[47] while ex-Boston Elder Jerry Jones has put the figure at 59 percent.[48]

Many ex-members have proved quite nettlesome to the movement. Those who leave are often "marked" as people that members are to have no contact with. Ex-members routinely recount their stories (which usually portray the movement in a negative light) to the media, and others such as Jerry Jones and

Rick Bauer have produced books denouncing the movement.[49] Kip McKean has pronounced any publications critical of the Boston movement as "spiritual pornography,"[50] and in a recent article stated, "Listening to men like Jerry Jones is ultimately in violation of Scripture."[51]

The challenge facing the Boston movement in its second decade is sustaining its tremendous growth. While the movement continues to increase its numbers each year, its percentage of growth declines.[52] Many of the larger congregations are experiencing a leveling off of their membership growth. For a movement that is theologically centered on expansive evangelism and that often justifies its existence and its practices based on its numerical growth, a substantial decline in growth could raise serious questions among members as to the righteousness of the movement.

It is unlikely that critics will become fewer in number as the Boston movement expands. The movement has already experienced a few cases of forcible deprogramming and will continue to have to deal with the ranks of ex-members, critics, and anticult forces. But the strong opposition encountered by the movement has done little to diminish its zeal and in fact often strengthens the conviction that this is truly a movement of God.

NOTES

1. This term has been used due to the key role of the Crossroads Church of Christ in the history of the Boston movement. The term is a misnomer since the Crossroads and Boston Church of Christ have severed all ties and the Boston movement has become its own distinct movement.

2. First spoken by Thomas Campbell in 1809. Robert Richardson, *Memoirs of Alexander Campbell*, vol. 1 (Philadelphia: L. B. Lippincott, 1868; reprint, Indianapolis: Religious Book Service, n.d.), 236.

3. David Edwin Harrell Jr., *Emergence of the "Church of Christ" Denomination* (Athens Ala.: Christian Enterprises International, 1972), 9.

4. U.S. Dept. of Commerce and Labor, Bureau of the Census, *Religious Bodies, 1906* (U.S. Printing Office, 1910), 236.

5. Mac Lynn, comp., *Churches of Christ in the United States* (Nashville: Gospel Advocate Co., 1991), xiii.

6. Flavil R. Yeakley, ed., *The Discipling Dilemma: A Study of the Discipling Movement Among Churches of Christ* (Nashville: Gospel Advocate Co., 1988), 137. Campus Crusade for Christ International is an evangelistic organization committed to spreading the gospel throughout the world, particularly among college students. Daniel G. Reid, ed., *Dictionary of Christianity in America* (Downers Grove, Ill.: InterVarsity Press, 1990), s.v. "Campus Crusade for Christ International," by K. L. Staggers, 215.

7. Rick Rowland, "The History of Campus Ministry," *Campus Journal* 32 (Summer 1990): 8.

8. Ibid., 9.

9. Unless all the participants of the soul talk were female, then a male always led the meeting.

10. Rowland, "History of Campus Ministry," 9.

11. Martin Edward Wooten, "The Boston Movement as a 'Revitalization Movement'" (D.Min. thesis, Harding Graduate School of Religion, 1990), 86–87.

12. Kip McKean, "Revolution through Restoration," *UpsideDown* 1 (Apr. 1992): 6.

13. Ibid., 8–9.

14. Attendance figures are as of February 1993. Roger Lamb, managing editor *UpsideDown* magazine, private correspondence to Russell R. Paden, Mar. 24, 1993.

15. Flavil R. Yeakley Jr., *Why Churches Grow* (Broken Arrow, Okla.: Christian Communications, 1979), 1.

16. K. McKean, "Revolution through Restoration, " 6.

17. Wooten, "The Boston Movement as a 'Revitalization Movement,'" 70.

18. Andrew Giambarba, *Bent on Conquest* (Boston: Boston Church of Christ Printing, 1988), 7.

19. K. McKean, "Revolution through Restoration," 8.

20. Ibid., 8–9.

21. Al Baird, *Boston Bulletin*, "Authority and Submission," pt. 5, Oct. 4, 1987.

22. Kip McKean, 1988 Leadership Conference (Boston), "Discipleship Partners," audiocassette.

23. Lamb, private correspondence.

24. Wooten, "The Boston Movement as a 'Revitalization Movement,'" 86.

25. Sarah Bauer, *A Time to Speak: A Personal Journal of My Years in the Boston Movement* (Upper Marlboro, Md.: Freedom House, 1992), 24.

26. I have used the New International Version due to its popularity within the Boston movement.

27. Randy McKean, ed., *Making Disciples* (Woburn, Mass.: Kingdom Media Resources, 1991), 22.

28. Biblical scholars have noted that the Boston movement's rendering of this passage is problematic in an English translation, but is particularly dubious in the original Greek. See J. Paul Pollard, "An Analysis of Matthew 28:19–20" in *The Boston Movement: Analysis, Commentary, and Media Reports* (Upper Marlboro, Md.: Freedom House, 1992), no page number.

29. "Letter to Boston Leaders from Scott and Robyn Deal," in Jerry Jones, *What Does the Boston Movement Teach?* (Bridgeton, Mo.: By the author, 1993), 3:73.

30. Jones, *What Does the Boston Movement Teach?* 3:7.

31. K. McKean, "Revolution through Restoration," 8.

32. Susan McGunnigle Condon, *A Diary: Why I Left the Boston Movement* (Atlanta: By the author, 1991), 9.

33. Giambarba, *Bent on Conquest,* from the dedication, no page number.

34. Steve Johnson, "A Tribute to the Boston Church of Christ," *Discipleship Magazine* 1 (Spring 1989): 26.

35. R. McKean, *Making Disciples,* 45.

36. Giambarba, *Bent on Conquest,* 9.

37. Both the Boston and Chicago congregations have printed "Dating Guidelines" for singles to use. Jones, *What Does the Boston Movement Teach?* (reprint, 1991), 1:9, 88.

38. "Tulsa Reconstruction," (Tulsa, Okla.), Aug. 1992, audiocassette.

39. Photocopies of accountability sheets appear in Jones, *What Does the Boston Movement Teach?* 1: 16–17, 128, 163; 2: 117.

40. Carlene B. Hill, "Church Grows Amidst Controversy," *New England Church Life* (Dec. 1987): 10.

41. Kip McKean, 1988 Leadership Retreat (Boston), audio cassette in Jones, *What Does the Boston Movement Teach?* 1: 13.

42. Kip McKean, 1987 World Mission Seminar (Boston), "Why Do You Resist the Spirit?' audio cassette.

43. K. McKean, "Revolution through Restoration,' 15; Wooten, "The Boston Movement as a 'Revitalization Movement,'" 157; Al Baird, "A New Look at Authority," *Upside-Down* 1 (Apr. 1992): 18–19, 49.

44. Baird, "A New Look at Authority," 18.

45. "Open Letter from Daniel Eng," in Jones, *What Does the Boston Movement Teach?* 3:75.

46. Ibid., 34. Using statistics from the *Boston Bulletin,* Jerry Jones has provided growth figures in tabular form.

47. K. McKean, "Revolution through Restoration," 8.

48. Jones, *What Does the Boston Movement Teach?* 3:34.

49. They have also set up ministries to aid those leaving the Boston movement.

50. Roger Lamb, Tom Jones, and Dedan Joyce, "Who's Brainwashing Who?" *Upside-Down* 2 (Jan. 1993): 24.

51. Ibid., 30.

52. Wooten, "The Boston Movement as a 'Revitalization Movement,'" 194. See also growth statistics in Jones, *What Does the Boston Movement Teach?* 3:34.

Contributors

PETER ACKERS is a reader in employment relations, Loughborough University Business School, Loughborough, Leicestershire.

LOUIS BILLINGTON is a retired professor of American studies, University of Hull, United Kingdom.

MONROE BILLINGTON is a professor of history at New Mexico State University, Las Cruces.

PAUL BLOWERS is a professor of church history at Emmanuel School of Religion, Johnson City, Tennessee.

MICHAEL W. CASEY is Carl P. Miller Chair of Communication, Pepperdine University, Malibu, California.

ANTHONY DUNNAVANT was dean and professor of church history at Lexington Theological Seminary, Lexington, Kentucky.

DAVID B. ELLER is director of the Young Center for Anabaptist and Pietist Groups, Elizabethtown College, Elizabethtown, Pennsylvania.

DOUGLAS A. FOSTER is an associate professor of church history and director of the Center for Restoration Studies, Abilene Christian University, Abilene, Texas.

PHILIP G. A. GRIFFIN-ALLWOOD is an associate minister of the First Baptist Church, Halifax, Nova Scotia, Canada.

JEAN F. HANKINS is an independent scholar in Otisfield, Maine.

DAVID EDWIN HARRELL JR. is Breeden Eminent Professor of Humanities, Auburn University, Auburn, Alabama.

NATHAN O. HATCH is provost, University of Notre Dame, South Bend, Indiana.

L. EDWARD HICKS is chair of the social and behavior science department and professor of history, Faulkner University, Montgomery, Alabama.

RICHARD T. HUGHES is a Distinguished Professor of Religion, Pepperdine University, Malibu, California.

Contributors

DERYCK W. LOVEGROVE is a professor of church history at University of St. Andrews School of Divinity, St. Andrews, Fife, Scotland.

JOHN L. MORRISON is a retired professor of education at Milligan College, Tennessee.

RUSS PADEN is director of Academic Affairs, Center for Distance Education, University of Phoenix, Phoenix, Arizona.

PAUL D. PHILLIPS is a retired professor of history, Tennessee State University, Nashville.

WILLIAM C. RINGENBERG is a professor of history at Taylor University, Upland, Indiana.

STEPHEN VAUGHN is a professor of journalism at University of Wisconsin, Madison.

EARL I. WEST is professor emeritus of church history, Harding Graduate School of Religion, Memphis, Tennessee.

MONT WHITSON is professor emeritus of sociology, Morehead State University, Morehead, Kentucky.

GLENN ZUBER is a doctoral student in religious studies, Indiana University, Bloomington.

Acknowledgments

David Edwin Harrell Jr.'s "The Sectional Origins of the Churches of Christ," *Journal of Southern History* 30 (August 1964): 261–77, is reprinted with the permission of the Southern Historical Association. Richard T. Hughes's "Apocalyptic Origins of Churches of Christ and the Triumph of Modernism," *Religion and American Culture: A Journal of Interpretation* 2 (Summer 1992): 181–214, and **David Edwin Harrell Jr.**'s "The Agrarian Myth and the Disciples of Christ in the Nineteenth Century," *Agricultural History* 41 (April 1967): 181–92, are reprinted with the permission of the University of California Press. **Nathan Hatch's** "The Christian Movement and Demand for a Theology of the People," *Journal of American History* 67 (1980): 545–67, is reprinted with the permission of the Organization of American Historians. **John L. Morrison's** "A Rational Voice Crying in an Emotional Wilderness," *West Virginia History* 34 (January 1973): 125–40, and **Mont Whitson**, "Campbell's Post-Protestantism and Civil Religion," *West Virginia History* 37 (October 1975): 109–21, are reprinted with the permission of *West Virginia History*. **Earl Irvin West's** "Early Cincinnati's 'Unprecedented Spectacle,'" *Ohio History* 79 (Winter 1970): 5–17, is reprinted courtesy of the Ohio Historical Society. **L. Edward Hicks's** "Republican Religion and Republican Institutions: Alexander Campbell and the Anti-Catholic Movement," *Fides et Historia* 22 (Fall 1990): 42–52, is reprinted with the permission of the Conference on Faith and History. **William C. Ringenberg's** "The Religious Thought and Practice of James A. Garfield," *Old Northwest* 8 (1982–83): 365–82, is reprinted with the permission of William C. Ringenberg. **Monroe Billington's** "Lyndon B. Johnson: The Religion of a Politician," *Presidential Studies Quarterly* 17, no. 3 (Summer 1987): 519–30, and **Stephen Vaughn's** "The Moral Inheritance of a President: Reagan and the Dixon Disciples of Christ," *Presidential Studies Quarterly* 25, no. 1 (Winter 1995): 109–27, are reprinted with permission granted by the Center for the Study of the Presidency, publisher of *Presidential Studies Quarterly*.

Glenn Michael Zuber's "'Mainline Women Ministers: One Beginning Point'; Women Missionary and Temperance Organizers Become 'Disciples of Christ' Ministers, 1888–1908," *Mid-America: An Historical Review* 78 (Summer 1996): 109–37, is reprinted with the permission of *Mid-America*. **Paul M. Blowers's** "'Living in a Land of Prophets': James T. Barclay and an Early Disciples of Christ Mission to Jews in the Holy Land," *Church History* 62 (December 1993): 494–513, is reprinted with the permission of the American Society of Church History. **Paul D. Phillips's** "The Interracial Impact of Marshall Keeble Black Evangelist, 1878–1968," *Tennessee Historical Quarterly* 36 (Spring 1977): 62–74, and **David Edwin Harrell Jr.'s** "Disciples of Christ Pacifism in Nineteenth Century Tennessee," *Tennessee Historical Quarterly* 21 (September 1962): 263–74, are reprinted with the permission of the

Tennessee Historical Society. **David B. Eller's** "Hoosier Brethren and the Origins of the Restoration Movement," *Indiana Magazine of History* 76 (1980): 1–20, is reprinted with the permission of the *Indiana Magazine of History*. **Richard T. Hughes's** "Two Restoration Traditions: Mormons and Churches of Christ in the Nineteenth Century,"*Journal of Mormon History* 19 (Spring 1993): 34–51, is reprinted with the permission of Richard T. Hughes.

Louis Billington's "The Churches of Christ in Britain: A Study of Nineteenth-Century Sectarianism," *Journal of Religious History* 8 (1974–75): 21–48, is reprinted with the permission of the *Journal of Religious History*. **Peter Ackers's** "West End Chapel, Back Street Bethel: Labour and Capital in the Wigan Churches of Christ, c. 1845–1945," *Journal of Ecclesiastical History* 47 (April 1996): 298–329, is reprinted with the permission of Cambridge University Press. **Anthony Dunnavant's** "David Lipscomb and the 'Preferential Option for the Poor' among Post-Bellum Churches of Christ," in *Poverty and Ecclesiology: Nineteenth-Century Evangelicals in the Light of Liberation Theology*, ed. Anthony Dunnavant, 27–50 (Collegeville, Minn.: Liturgical Press, 1992), is reprinted with the permission of Anthony Dunnavant. **Michael W. Casey's** "From Pacifism to Patriotism: The Emergence of Civil Religion in the Churches of Christ," *The Mennonite Quarterly Review* 66 (July 1992): 376–90, is reprinted with the permission of the *Mennonite Quarterly Review*. **Peter Ackers's** "Who Speaks for the Christians? The Great War Conscientious Objection Movement in the Churches of Christ: A View from the Wigan Coalfield," *Journal of the United Reformed Church History Society* 5 (1993): 153–66, is reprinted with the permission of the *Journal of the United Reformed Church History Society*. **Jean F. Hankins,** "A Different Kind of Loyalist: The Sandemanians of New England during the Revolutionary War, *The New England Quarterly* 60 (June 1987), copyright held by *The New England Quarterly*. Reprinted by permission of the publisher and author. **Deryck W. Lovegrove's** "Unity and Separation: Contrasting Elements in the Thought and Practice of Robert and James Alexander Haldane,"in *Protestant Evangelicalism: Britain, Ireland, Germany and America, c.1750–c.1950,* ed. Keith Robbins, 153–77 (Oxford: Basil Blackwell, 1990), is reprinted with the permission of the Ecclesiastical History Society. **Philip G. A. Griffin-Allwood's** "'To Hear a Free Gospel': The Christian Connexion in Canada," in *Historical Papers*, ed. Michael Owen, 73–86 (Windsor: Canadian Society of Church History, 1988), is reprinted with the permission of the Canadian Society of Church History. **Russell Paden's** "The Boston Church of Christ," in *America's Alternative Religions*, ed. Timothy Miller, 133–40 (Albany: State University of New York Press, 1995), is reprinted with the permission of the State University of New York Press.

Index

A Kempis, Thomas, *Imitation of Christ*, 221
Abilene Christian College, 472
Abilene Christian University, 3, 17, 23, 32, 39; Center for Restoration Studies, 26
Abolitionists, 279
Abrahamic League for the Restoration of Israel, 279
Ackers, Harry, 490
Ackers, Peter, 21, 40, 42, 51, 62, 65
Adams, Charles Francis, 139
Adams, Harry, 57
Adams, John, 121
Adams, Joseph, 404
Adams, John Quincy, 192
Adventists, 282, 370, 372, 384, 386, 388
Aesthetics, 27–28, 45
African-Americans, 37
Agrarian myth, 35–36, 147–55; threats to, 153; west as safety valve, 150
Ahlstrom, Sydney S., 108, 142, 186
Ahorey church (Ireland), 206
Aikman, John, 521, 533
Alabama, 88
Albert Street, 482–84, 487–91
Albert Street, Newtown chapel, 403, 406–7, 409, 411, 415, 417
Alberta, Canada, 45
Alcott, Bronson, 109
Alexander, Charles C., 61
Allen, C. Leonard, 2, 3, 13, 23, 32, 46, 48, 49, 53, 61, 108, 110, 112
Allen, Victor, 44
Alline, Clark, 550

Alline, Henry, 549
Allinite churches, 550–51, 553
Allinites, 544
Alsup, Mike, 43
Amburn, Ellis, 64
America, 281
America in prophecy, 281
American Board of Commissioners for Foreign Missions, 272
American Christian Bible Society, 94
American Christian Convention, 544, 553
American Christian Missionary Society (ACMS), 11, 19, 76, 94, 273, 279, 281–82, 460–61; Pro-union Civil War resolutions, 12, 72–74
American Christian Review, 20, 73, 78, 79
American Peace Society, 462
American Revolution, 121–22, 124, 130, 134, 136, 181. *See* Revolutionary War
Americans as Chosen people, 18
Ames, Edward Scribner, 25
Amundsen, Darrel W., 58
Anabaptists, 30, 53
ancient gospel, 548
Anderson, James, 391n. 25, 396n. 108
Andros, Thomas, 133
Anglicanism, 17
Anglo-Prussian bishopric, 274
Anglo-Saxons, superiority of, 151–52
annihilationism, 553
Annual Meeting (Dunker), 332–37, 341
Anthony, Susan B., 230
Antiburgher Synod, 523
anticlericalism, 387
Antifederalists, 135

antipaedobaptist, 536
apocalyptic revivalism, 354
Apocalyptic worldview, 3, 4, 6, 7, 13, 18, 85–86, 91–101, 109, 111–12; loss of, 102–7
Apocrypha Controversy, 524
Apostolic Times, 370
apostolicity, 530
Arendt, Hannah, 187
Arminianism, 32, 526–27
Asbury, Francis, 34, 124, 125, 129, 130
Ash, Joseph, 548
Association of Churches of Christ, 40. *See* British Churches of Christ
Atlanta, Ga., 77
Atlanta Symphony Orchestra, 43
Atonement, 54; Moral government theory, 17, 25; Moral influence theory, 6, 17, 25, Penal substitution, 6, 17, 25
Auger, Arlene, 43
Austin, Benjamin, Jr., 123, 136
Australia, 21, 42, 373
autonomy, congregational, 535, 548

Babcock, Clara C., 300–301, 307
Back-street bethels, 40, 398–432
Backus, Isaac, 125, 128, 130
Bacon, Francis, 90
Baconian hermeneutic, 275, 282, 355
Baconianism, 7, 89, 206, 275–76. *See* Scottish Common Sense philosophy
Badger, Joseph, 556n. 31
Bailey, Garry, 54
Bailey, Joseph, 547
Bailyn, Bernard, 139
Baines, George Washington, Jr., 235
Baines, George Washington, Sr., 235
Bales, James D., 37
Ballentine, William, 530
Ballou, Hosea, 219
Banner, Lois, 140

Banowsky, William, 55
baptism, 7, 9, 54, 323, 332, 335–37, 340–41, 368, 375, 385, 401, 404, 406, 442, 533, 535–36, 548, 552, 566–67
Baptist Convention of Ontario and Quebec, 549
Baptists, 5, 169, 335, 337, 339, 352, 368, 372, 381–82, 384–85, 400; in Virginia, 128; in Texas 234
Baptists, English, 42
Baptists, Freewill, 122, 129, 544–47, 550, 552–53, 555n. 8
Baptists, Northern, 23
Baptists, Scotch, 40, 41
Baptists, Scottish, 63
Baptists, Southern, 23
Barber, James David, 247
Barclay, James Turner, 19, 50, 73, 273–84; first mission to Jerusalem, 277–79; millennialism, 274; primitivism, 274, 278; and return of Jews to Palestine, 279–82; second mission to Jerusalem, 279
Barclay, Robert, 273
Barlow, Philip, 359
Barnes, Justus M., 462
Barnes, Robert E., 80
Barnes, Timothy, 60
Barnhart, Elbert B., 55
Barr, William R. 24, 53
Barrell, Colburn, 501, 504
Barrell, Nathaniel, 501
Basen, Neil, 65
Bathurst Street Christian Church (Toronto), 549
Bauer, Rick, 571
Baylor University, 235
Beck, Ella, 302
Becker, Edwin L., 61
Beech Hill chapel, 418
Beecher, Henry Ward, 226

Index

Beecher, Lyman, 205
Belcastro, Joseph, 6, 47
Belfast, Northern Ireland, 45
Bell, Jack, 242
Bellah, Robert, 181, 183, 187
Bellamy, Joyce M., 63
Belmont Church of Christ, 43
Ben-Arieh, Yehoshua, 284, 288, 289
Benedict, Comfort, 512–13
Benedict, Hezekiah, 511
Benedict, Thomas, 504
Bengal mission (Haldane), 528–29
Bennett, Thomas, 489
Benson, George, 15, 36, 49
Bentham, Jeremy, 191
Bentley Miners Fund, 410
Bentley, William, 122–23
Bercovitch, Sacvan, 47, 290
Berry, Stephen Pressley, 53
Berryhill, Carisse, 26, 55
Best, Thomas F., 52
Bestor, Arthur Eugene, Jr., 201, 203
Bethany, Va., 206
Bethany College, W.V., 19, 92, 149, 163, 211, 222, 281
Bethel, Dunker, Ind., 333
Bever, Ronald, 55
Bible Advocate, 382, 483, 485, 489–90
Bible Christians, 373
Bible colleges, 443
Bible talks (Boston Church of Christ), 566–67, 569
Bible, 359, 401
biblical authority, 527
biblical criticism, 15
biblical literalism, 417
biblicism, 537
Bicha, Karel D., 60
Billington, Louis, 40, 63
Billington, Monroe, 36, 61, 246
Billington, Ray Allen, 212, 213, 215

Bing, H. F., 65
Bird, Janet, 64
Birmingham District Association, England, 378
Bishop, Simeon, 547
Blackstone, W. E., 102, 103
Blakemore, W. B., 57
Blanco County, Tex., 233
Bloom, Harold, 356
Blowers, Paul, 19, 32, 47, 50, 59
Blue River (Ind.) Baptist Church, 339
Board of Church Extension, 77
Boden, Brian, 41–42, 63
Bodo, John, 81
Boer war, the, 483
Boggs, John, 72
Bogue, David, 529, 540n. 49
Boles, H. Leo, 55
Boles, John B., 59, 140, 142
Boll, Robert H., 4, 5, 17, 20, 102–3, 105–7; pacifism, 102, *Word and Work*, 103
Book of Mormon, 349, 353, 359
Boone, Debbie, 43
Boone, Pat, 43, 53
Boorstin, Daniel J., 145
Bordin, Ruth, 298
Bost, Ami, 526
Boston, Mass., 279
Boston Association of Loyalists, 509
Boston Church of Christ, 15, 35, 563. *See* International Churches of Christ
Boston Independent Chronicle, 123, 136
Boston Massacre, 503
Boston Movement, 34. *See* International Churches of Christ
Boston Sandemanians, 505
Bouchard, Larry D., 57
Bower, Adam, 334
Bower, William C., 155
Bozeman, Theodore Dwight, 213

Brandon, George, 28, 57
Brents, J. W., 321
Brethren. *See* Plymouth Brethren
Brethren, German, and 1827 Union with Campbell movement, 13
Brightwell, W. E., 105, 324
Britain, 21, 150
Brite Divinity School, 8
British and Foreign Bible Society, 524
British Churches of Christ, 21, 39–42, 63, 367–97; Annual Meeting, 40; Old Paths Churches of Christ, 41, 63. *See* Campbellites, British Churches of Christ
British Evolution Protest Movement, 37
British Millennial Harbinger, 376, 400
British working-class religion, 40
Brock, Peter, 466
Bronowski, J., 201
Brooks, James, 100
Brooks, Pat, 23, 53
Brown, Harry J., 231–33
Brown, Ira, 157
Brown, Rev. Antonette L., 230
Brown, Richard D., 139
Brown, Robert McAfee, 435
Brown, Sterling, 155
Brown, Thomas, 547
Brumberg, Joan Jacobs, 146
Brumley, Al, 43
Brumley, Albert E., 43
Brush Run Church, 178, 194, 206
Bucer, Martin, 351
Buchanan, Darrell, 62
Buchanan, James, 44
Buckley, William, 36, 61
Bullinger, Heinrich, 351
Burned-over District, New York, 553
Burnet, David S., 152
Burnet, Isaac G., 189
Burnet, Judge Jacob, 199

Burnett, Thomas R., 75, 78
Burns, Edward McNall, 158
Burr, Oliver, 507
Burton, A. M., 318–19
Business in Christianity, 77
Butchard, Reuben, 41, 63
Butler, Jonathan, 12, 49
Butler, T. D., 380
Byars, Ronald, 50

Cage, John, 44
Caldwell, Robert G., 231–33
Caldwell, William, 93
Calhoon, Robert M., 60
Califano, Joseph A., Jr., 246
Callen, Barry, 23, 52
Calvin, John, 90, 130
Calvinism, 4, 32, 33, 87, 90, 109, 129–30, 200, 354, 369, 525–27, 530
Calvinists, Calvinism, 500–501
Cambridge University, 40
Campbell, Alexander, 1, 3, 7, 11, 12, 14, 28, 29, 40, 49, 54, 56, 58, 69, 72, 89–91, 92, 94, 101, 122, 124, 128, 131, 132, 163–74, 177–86, 194–96, 222, 249, 274–79, 282–83, 331, 336–37, 352, 354–59, 361, 367–70, 383, 400, 455, 548, 563; and agrarian myth, 147–50; anti-Calvinism, 171–72; anti-Catholicism, 29, 94, 205–12; anti-clericalism, 126, 164–67; attacks on revivalism, 169–70; Campbell-Owen debate, 27, 168, 177, 189–200, 254, 276; Campbell-Purcell debate, 27, 56, 205, 208, 211; civil religion, 184–86; *Christian Baptist*, 11, 14, 85, 86, 108, 126, 165–66, 178, 181, 189, 196; as a debater, 165; and destiny of America, 152, 182, 185, 207, 276; dispensationalism, 179–80; ecclesiology, 54, 129; ecumenicism,

Index

30–31; and education, 163–64, 210–11; free will, 171; and gospel, 30–31; interpretation of the Bible, 172–73, 210; *Millennial Harbinger,* 11, 14, 91, 147, 165–66, 178, 181, 207; opposition to moral societies, 183–84; postmillennialism, 19, 86, 88, 90–91, 110, 150–51, 181–82; post-Protestantism, 183; preaching, 26, 55, 165–67, 194–96, 226, 254; racism, 151; rationalism, 168–74, 180–81, 206; restorationism, 30–31, 90, 125, 174, 180, 181, 207; rhetoric, 55; return of Jews to Palestine, 276–77; sectarianism, 31, 85, 96; Sermon on the Law, 179–80, 195, 214; slavery, 71, 80–81; view of the Bible, 167–68, 207; view of the Holy Spirit, 23–24, 53, 168
Campbell, Archibald, 206
Campbell, George, 26
Campbell, Glen, 43, 64
Campbell, John, 522, 530, 536
Campbell, Selina, 32–33, 100, 165
Campbell, Thomas, 33, 125, 194, 199, 206, 249, 352, 563; Christian Association of Washington, 178, 206, 214; *Declaration and Address,* 131, 178, 214, 261; millennial views, 131, 163, 177, 178
Campbell Movement, 10, 11, 14, 41, 71, 340; 1832 Union with Stone movement, 11, 13, 88, 89, 125, 147
Campbell-Stone Movement, 436
Campbellites, British Churches of Christ, 367–97, 398–432
Campus Advance, 564
Campus Crusade for Christ, 564, 567
Canada, 21, 41–42, 63; British expatriates, 42; Doctor, first licensed female, 38; Maritime provinces, 34; Nova Scotia, 34; Ontario, 34, 41, 63

Canada, Christian Connexion, 544–62
Cane Ridge Revival, 14, 32, 92, 93, 124
Cannon, Lou, 260
Cantor, Gregory, 64
Cape Girardeau, Mo., 249, 253
Capen, Hopestill, 509, 513
Carey, William, 529
Carnegie-Mellen University, 43
Caro, Robert A., 243
Carpenter, Joel, 48
Carter, W. H., 473
Cartwright, Peter, 11
Carver, Fran, 65
Case, Shirley Jackson, 107
Casey, Michael, 21, 26, 41, 51, 55, 63, 65
Caskey, T. W. (on women's rights), 306
Catholicism, 8, 30, 47–48, 204–5, 274, 400; in America, 211–12; Provincial Council of Catholicity, 205, 213
Catholics, 7, 277–78
Cawood, Marion, 43
Census, 1906 religious, 69, 70, 80, 86, 95, 154
Census, 1936 religious, 75–76, 80, 83
Chalmers, David M., 61
Chalmers, Thomas, 531, 537
Chamberlain, Theophilus, 502–4, 506–7
Chaney, Charles L., 285
Channing, William Ellery, 170
Chapman, Graeme, 42, 63
Charismatic movement, 24, 29
Chenevière, 525–57
Cherry, Conrad, 290
Chesnut, Roderick, 60
Chicago Church of Christ, 565, 568
Chiliasm, chiliasts, 271
Chism, J. W., 471
Christ, divinity of, 525, 546
Christ, humanity, 525
Christ, person and work, 526

Christadelphians, 33, 370, 372, 375, 377, 384–85, 388, 421, 426n. 74
Christian, Chris, 43
Christian, Persis L., 311n. 22
Christian, The, 29
Christian Advocate, 413, 417, 421
Christian Association (British), 381–82, 411–12
Christian Band, 546, 551
Christian Baptist, 336–37, 368–69, 379
Christian calendar, 405
Christian Church in Canada, 548–49
Christian Churches/Churches of Christ, 1, 9, 16; unity meetings with Church of God (Anderson, Ind.), 23; unity meetings with Churches of Christ, 23; Stone-Campbell dialogue, 23. *See* independent Christian Churches
Christian Commonwealth, 381
Christian Conference of Upper Canada, 548
Christian Connection, 338
Christian Connexion, 33, 42, 63
Christian Connexion, Canada, 544–62
Christian Echo, 318
Christian evidences, 526–27
Christian Growth Ministries, 567
Christian Herald, 547, 550
Christian History, 126
Christian Humanists, 351
Christian Leader, 20, 468–69, 474
Christian Messenger, 338, 548
Christian Messenger and Reformer (British), 369, 371
Christian Missionary Society, 72–73, 279
Christian Movement, 14, 123–24, 129, 131; legacy of, 137–38, millennialism, 132
Christian Observer, 192
Christian Oracle, 100
Christian Standard, 10, 20, 70, 73–74, 75, 78, 79, 229, 298, 303, 305, 307, 461

Christian Theological Seminary, 5
Christian unity, 554
Christian Vanguard, 549
Christian Woman's Board of Missions, 38, 293 ff
Christian-Evangelist, 7, 20, 29, 78, 298, 305
Christianity is Pacifism, 482
Christmas, 405
Christology, 24
Church, Asa, 503–4
church, separation from world, 445
church, socioeconomic responsibility, 446–47
church, tasks in the world, 445–46
church and state, 445, 500, 529–31
church discipline, 382
church government, 405–6, 410
Church Missionary Society (Anglican), 273
Church of Christ, listed separately from Disciples, 456; division with Disciples, 461
Church of England, Anglican Church, 367, 375, 400
Church of God (Anderson, Ind.), 23
Church of Scotland, 367–68, 520, 530
Churches of Christ, 1, 3, 6, 7, 9, 12, 13, 15–16, 18, 22–24, 27, 34, 70, 71, 85, 86, 94, 179, 183; anti-evolution, 37; anti-institutional or noninstitutional Churches of Christ, 3, 7; charismatic movement, 24; church edifices, value of, 75–76; Cuba, 39; cultural alienation, 7; division with Disciples, 85–88, 103; economic pattern of division with Disciples, 76–77; and Equal Rights Amendment, 37; mainstream Churches of Christ, 7, 102, 107; membership, urban and rural, 75; music styles, 28–29;

Index

noninstitutional controversy, 7; pacifism, 21, 95, 102, 103–5, 113; preaching, 26; Premillennial Churches of Christ, 7, 17–18, 106, 283; premillennial controversy, 17–18, 102–7, 113; racism, 16; rural-urban pattern of division with Disciples, 76–77, 154–55; sectarianism, 96; Sectional origins, 2, 3, 69–84, 87–88, 108, 109, 294, 340, 348–63, 367, 380, 398, 436, 443; sex education, 37; Spain, 39; unity meetings with other groups, 23

Churchill, Nathaniel, 550–51

Cincinnati, Ohio, 72, 76, 77, 189–90, 198–99, 205

Cincinnati Bible Seminary, 9

Cincinnati Chronicle and Literary Gazette, 197, 200

City of the Great King, 278

Civil Government (David Lipscomb), 459–60, 467

Civil War, American, 2, 3, 11, 13, 20, 69, 71, 72, 76, 87, 281, 292, 349, 437, 447, 457, 466–67

Clapper-Dickey, Roberta, 250

Clarke, James Freeman, 227

Clay, Henry, 163–64

Clayson, Alan, 64

Cleaver, Ben, 248–55, 257, 259–60

Cleaver, Helen, 248, 259

Cleaver, Margaret, 248, 250–51, 253, 256, 257, 258, 259

Cleaver, Thomas, 249

Cleghorn, John, 530

Cleland, Thomas, 165

Cleveland Orchestra and Chorus, 43

Clevenger, Dale, 43

closed communion, 379, 385, 416–17

Cobb, Richard, 52

Cole, G. D. H., 201, 202

collections, 382, 402

Collins, Johnnie Andrews, 113

Colpitts, Robert, 550

Communication Studies, 25–27

Communion, Open, 41

communion, weekly, 536

Communist Party, 44

Confederacy, 70

Conference of Congregational Christian Churches in Ontario, 549

congregational autonomy, 369, 375, 377, 379, 406

Congregational Christian Churches, 549

Congregational Church, 293, 305, 309, 381, 400, 403, 530, 549

Congregationalism, 500–501, 503–4, 530

Congregationalists, 123, 133

Conkin, Paul, 1, 46, 59

Conrad, David E., 243

conscientious objectors, 459, 462

Conservative Congregationalist Christian Convention, 549

Constitution of the United States, 135

Contemporary Christian Music, 24, 43

conversion, 404

Conway, John, 285

Coop, Lois, 411

Coop, Timothy, 41, 374, 380–81, 383, 399–401, 404, 410–11, 414

Cope, Brian, 22, 52

Cordell Christian College, 474

Corf, John, 401

Cormier, Frank, 244, 245

Council of Trent, 208

Cowie, George, 522

Cox, Claude, 41–42, 63

Craddock, Emmie, 243

Craddock, Fran, 39, 62

Craddock, Fred, 26, 57

Craden, Maren Lockwood, 109

Craig, Laura Gerould, 302

Craig, O. T., 458
Crain, James, 265
Creath, Jacob, Jr., 150
Creation Research Society, 37
Creationism, 36–37
creeds, 400–401
Crihfield, Arthur, 19, 85, 103, 108
Crook, John, 412
Crook, Robert Burton, 413
Crook, Robert Kay, 413
Cross, Robert A., 139
Crossroads Church of Christ (Gainesville, Fla.), 35, 564
Crossroads Movement, 563
Crosthwaite, Walter, 486
Crowell, Thomas, 550, 552
Cuba, 39
Cunningham, Merce, 44

Dains, Mary K., 58
Dale, David, 190
Danbury, Conn., 502, 506, 509, 511–13
Danner, Dan, 50
Darwinism, 15
David Lipscomb University, 15. *See* Nashville Bible School
Davidson, James West, 144
Davies, T. Witton, 62
Davis, David Brion, 139
Davis, Dr. George R., 238, 239
Davis, Jefferson, 458
Davis, Moshe, 273, 284, 285, 288
Day, Heather, 42, 64, 65
Dayton, Donald W., 16–18, 50, 290; Methodist Paradigm of evangelicalism, 16–18; Presbyterian paradigm of evangelicalism, 16
De Pillis, Mark, 146
de Tocqueville, Alexis, 137, 204, 211–12, 236
deacons, 368, 375–76, 401

Dean, Camille K., 60
Dean, Doug, 37
debates, religious, 11, 25–27, 56
debating style, 7
Declaratory Act (1799), 523, 529, 531
DeGroot, Alfred T., 49, 79, 84, 108, 155, 186
Delmore Brothers, 43
Dembski, Peter E. Paul, 62
Democratization of Christianity, 123–25, 138–39. *See* egalitarian protest
Denton, William, 222
Dewey, Donald, 65
Dewey, Orville, 170
Dewhitt, Samuel, 348, 355, 357
Dialogues between Theron and Aspasia (James Hervey), 500
Dickinson, Hoke S., 110–11
Disciple Year Book, 300, 304, 309
The Disciple, 29
Disciples of Christ, 1, 6, 9, 15–16, 19, 27, 35, 44, 69, 70, 89, 100, 178–79, 220, 249, 367–68, 380, 548–49, 552; abolitionism, 71–72, 279; agrarian myth, 147–55, 250; anti-Catholicism, 153, 253, 265; Christology, 24, 54; church edifices, value of, 75; Council on Christian Unity, 22; division with Churches of Christ, 85–88, 154–55; division with Independents, 10, 83; Disciples Renewal, 15; evangelism, 26; Hispanics/Latinos, 39; membership, rural and urban, 75; millennial views, 20, 70, 150–52, 282; ministry, 26, 55; missions, 58, 273–82; pacifism, 21; primitivism, 148, 151, 206–7; Puerto Rican Disciples, 39; racism, 253; Restructure, 22; return of Jews to Palestine, 275, 283; social views, 250; in Tennessee, 455–65; in Texas, 235; unity meetings, 23; and women,

38–39; women preachers, 38; worship, 57
Disciples of Christ Historical Society, 29, 31
discipleship (Boston Church of Christ), 566
discipleship partners (Boston Church of Christ), 566, 569
Discipliana, 39
discipline (church), 402, 406, 419, 534–35, 537
Discipling Movement, 563
Dissenters, 524
Divine, Robert A., 243
Dixon, Ill., 36, 248, 253, 256
Douglas, Lee, 470, 473–74
Doyle, Don Harrison, 146
Dozier, Dan, 57
Drinkhouse, Edward J., 141
Dugger, Robert, 243
Dull, C. J., 48
Dundas, Henry, 528
Dundas, Robert, 523, 528
Dunker, Dunkard. See German Baptist Brethren
Dunlavy, John, 93
Dunn, Holly, 43
Dunnavant, Anthony, 21–22, 32, 47, 51–52, 54, 59
Dutch Reformed Church, 221

Eames, Samuel Morris, 110
Earl Street committee (British and Foreign Bible Society), 524
Earle, H. S., 381
East India Company, 523, 528–29
Easter, 405
Eastern Conference of Upper Canada (Christian Connexion), 548
Eastman Kodak, 38
Ecclesiastical Observer, 380, 386

ecclesiology, 7, 23, 129
Eckman, George, 107
ecumenical Christianity, 521
Ecumenical movement, 22, 23
ecumenism, 7, 9, 22–23, 384, 417
Eden Theological Seminary, 22
Edict of Nantes, 206
Edinburgh, Ind., Conference, Baptists and Dunkers, 338
Edinburgh, Scotland, 368, 520–22, 524, 530, 532
Edinburgh Divinity Hall, 528
Edinburgh Tabernacle, 533, 536
editor-bishops, 25–26, 104
Edwards, Anne, 260, 261
Edwards, Jonathan, 130, 133, 500
egalitarian protest, 127–28, 134–35; in interpretation of the Bible, 128, 132–34, 138; in law, 136; in politics, 134–36
Elam, E. A., 470–71
elders, 304, 306, 314n. 47, 333, 338, 355, 368, 375–78, 401, 412, 533, 536, 546
elders (Boston Church of Christ), 568
election, doctrine of, 527
Eller, David B., 13, 49
Ellis, Bartley, 375
Ellis, Carroll, 27, 55, 56
Ellis, Geoffrey H., 63
Ellis, Richard E., 136, 139, 145
Elwes, Julian, 484
Emerson, Ralph Waldo, 87
Emmanuel School of Religion, 19
English labor movement, 40
Enlightenment, 2, 8, 17, 90, 206, 354, 356, 358, 360
Episcopalians, 170
Equal Rights Amendment, 37
Erie (Ill.) Christian Church, 301
Errett, Isaac, 22, 73, 78, 293, 305, 461
Erskine, John, 533

Espionage Act of 1917, 469
Essex County, Mass., 122
Established churches, U.K., 40
Estevez, E. R., 39, 62
Eubanks, Wayne C., 55
Eureka, Ill., 249, 260
Evangelical Alliance, 554
Evangelical and Reformed Church, 549
Evangelical historians, new, 3–4, 16–17. See also Noll, Mark; Hatch, Nathan; Marsden, George; Wacker, Grant
Evangelical Magazine, 522
Evangelical Revival, 520, 522
Evangelical Unionists, 382
Evangelical Unitarians, 546
Evangelicalism, 3, 10, 16–18, 525, 554
Evangelist Committee (of General Meeting of the British Churches of Christ), 379–80, 412
evangelists, 376–79, 387, 405; Boston Church of Christ, 568; the poor as, 438
Evans, Rowland, 242
Evidence and Authority of Divine Revelation, Robert Haldane, 525, 527
Ewing, Greville, 194, 520–21, 528–29, 532, 540n. 49
excommunication, 382
Exposition of St. Paul's Epistle to the Romans, Tholuck, 527
Exposition of the Epistle to the Romans, Robert Haldane, 525

Faber, George Stanley, 275
faith, 500, 525
Fall, Philip, 99, 455, 458
Family Policy Advisory Board, 37
Fanning, Tolbert, 20, 23, 51, 53, 74, 85, 95–96, 97, 98, 99, 103, 104, 156, 455–58, 461
Faraday, Michael, 44

Farrar, Francis "Birdie," 299
Faulkner, Joseph E., 55
Faulkner University, Ala., 30
Faw, Martha, 39, 62
Federalists, 123, 135
Fellowship of Evangelical Baptist Churches in Canada, 549
Fenwick, Matthew, 550
Field, Nathaniel, 71
Fife, Robert O., 80
Finn, James, 278
Finto, Don, 24, 53
Firm Foundation, 20, 317, 467–69
First Christian Church (Dixon, Ill.), 248, 249, 251–53, 255, 257–59
First Christian Church (Johnson City, Tex.), 235, 238
First Great Awakening, 14, 122, 125, 132
Fischer, David Hackett, 139
Fisk University, 320
Fisk, Pliny, 272–74
Fitch, Alger, 59
Fleming, Robert, 45, 409
Flint, Timothy, 189, 190, 193, 198, 199, 200
Florence, Franklin, 38
Florida, 39
Floyd, John D., 462–63
foot washing, 13, 340–41, 368, 375
Foreign Christian Missionary Society, 381
Forrest H. Kirkpatrick Seminar, 39
Foster, Douglas A., 17, 22, 50, 52, 61
Fourteenth Street Church of Christ (Gainesville, Fla.), 564
Franklin College, 458
Franklin, Benjamin, 20, 72, 85
Free Christian Baptists, 550, 552–54
free gospel, 544 ff
Friedman, Milton, 44
Friends of Constitutional Liberty, 506
Friskney, Thomas, 55

Frontier religion, 134
Ft. Worth, Tex., 8
Fuller, Edmund, 232
Fundamentalism, 9, 107. See fundamentalist movement
fundamentalist movement, 3, 10, 16, 103
fundamentalists, 271

Gabriel, Ralph, 157
Gaebelain, Arno, 102, 103
Gainesville, Tex., 78
Galbreath, Leslie, 42, 64, 65
Gandhi, Mahatma, 255
Garfield, Abram, 219
Garfield, Eliza Ballou, 219
Garfield, James A., 36, 61, 74, 219–33, 461; conversion, 220; criticism of denominations, 221; criticism and praise of sermons, 225–28; debate on science and Christianity, 222; and Disciples of Christ, 219–26, 229; as preacher, 219, 223–24; and public role for women, 230
Garrett, Leroy, 31, 32, 53, 58, 59
Garrison, J. H., 22
Garrison, Winfred E., 79, 80, 81, 84, 108, 145, 155, 169, 176, 178, 186, 187, 261, 262
Gary, James, 102
Gates, Isaac, 142
Gaustad, Edwin S., 108, 109
Geertz, Clifford, 21, 52, 65
General Annual Meeting (British Churches of Christ), 403, 405, 417
General Christian Missionary Convention, 294
General Evangelical Committee (British Churches of Christ), 411
General Federation of Firemen, Examiners and Deputies Association of Great Britain, 45
General Meeting of the Churches of Christ (British), 368–69, 371, 373–75, 377–78, 403, 405
Geneva, 526
Genovese, Eugene 121, 139
George, King of England 33
George, Lloyd, 412, 482
Georgetown University, 32
Georgia, 75, 83
Gerlach, Luther P., 140
German Baptist Brethren, 331–47
Gerrard, William A., III, 50
Geyelin, Philip, 243
Giambarba, Andrew, 566, 568
Gilbert, Bentley Brinkerhoff, 65
Gillmore, William, 25
Gilpin, W. Clark, 49, 55
Givens, Randall J., 58
Glas, John, 194, 368, 499–500, 533
Glasgow University, 27, 177, 194, 206
Glasgow, Scotland, 523, 532
Glasites, 40, 367–68, 510, 536. See Sandemanians
glossolalia, 537
Goen, C. C., 143
Golbourne chapel, 403
Gold, Thomas, 502–3, 506–7
Goldman, Eric F., 242, 245
Gonzalez, Samuel, 39, 62
Goodacre, Isabelle, 300
Goode, Richard C., 60
Gooding, David, 65
Goodwin, Doris Kearns, 246, 247
Goodwin, E[lijah], 293–94
Gospel Advocate, 7, 20, 38, 70, 74, 77, 95, 99, 101, 104, 148, 149, 294, 298, 324, 326, 436, 456, 458, 461–63, 467–71, 474
Gospel Banner, 370–71
Grace, Fran, 65. *See* Fran Carver
Graham, Billy, 238

Grant, Amy, 43, 64
Grant, David, 51
Grant, William O., 550
Gray, Fred, 38, 61
Great Awakening, 354, 501, 549, 558n. 59
Great Depression, 13, 21
Great Revival (1800–1825), 546–47
Great Songs of the Church, 28
Great War. *See* World War I
Green, David E., 232
Greene, Michael, 47
Gregory, Munson, 511
Gresham, Perry E., 58, 64
Grey, Norman Q., 285
Gribben, William, 212
Griffin, Russell A., 203
Griffin-Allwood, Philip, 34, 60
Gutiérrez, Gustavo, 444–45

Haggard, Merle, 43, 64
Haldane, James Alexander, 33, 60, 194, 520–43
Haldane, Robert, 33, 60, 194, 520–43
Haldane movement, 33, 59
Haldanes, 367–68
Haldeman, Isaac M., 102
Haley, J. Evetts, 243
Halle University, 525
Hallmark, James, 54
Ham, John, 334
Hamilton, Jonathan, 552
Hamiltonites, 552
Handy, Robert T., 285
Hankins, Jean, 33, 60
Hannibal, Mo., 6
Hansen, Klaus, 360
Hardeman, N. B., 55, 103
Harding University, 36, 37
Harding, B. B., 62
Harding, James A., 19, 99, 102, 104
Harding, Nathan, 548

Harding, T. S., 551
Hargis, Billy James, 15, 37, 49–50, 61
Harper, E. R., 106
Harrell, David Edwin, Jr., 2, 3, 7, 8, 10, 17, 35, 37, 46, 47, 51, 58, 60, 80, 82, 84, 87–88, 108, 109, 111–12, 113, 114, 142, 157, 158, 186, 212, 213, 214, 261–62, 265, 266, 349, 390n. 4, 467
Harrison, J. F. C., 146
Harrison, Richard, 54, 59
Hartt, Samuel, 551
Harvard University, 37, 121
Hatch, Nathan O., 3, 10, 32, 35, 46, 54, 59, 60, 144, 261, 349, 352
Hatchitt, Joseph, 338
Haymes, Don, 56
Hazelrigg, Clara H., 300, 303
Healey, Robert, 285
Hedges, Virginia, 303, 309
Heimer, Nancy, 39, 62
Henretta, James A., 139
Hensley, Carl Wayne, 18–19, 50–51, 55, 110
Herald of Gospel Liberty (Elias Smith), 546
Herberg, Will, 184
Heren, Louis, 242, 247
Hervey, James, 500
Hicks, John Mark, 25, 47, 54
Hicks, L. Edward, 30, 36, 49, 58, 61
Higham, John, 10–12, 48–49
Higher criticism, 41
Hill, Christopher, 146
Hill, George, 523
Hill, Rowland, 522, 534
Hill, Samuel S., Jr., 56
Hindley chapel, 403–4, 417
Hine, Virginia H., 140
Hines, Joshua, 374
Hinsdale, Burke, 225, 229
Hinsdale, Mary, 233
Hiram, Ohio, 223

Index

Hiram College, 220, 222, 223, 225, 229
Hobbs, Lottie Beth, 37
Hofstadter, Richard, 108
Holifield, E. Brooks, 56
Holiness Movement, 16–17, 24, 388–89
Holland, Harold, 28, 57
Holloway, Gary, 54
Hollywood Beverley Christian Church, 251
Holm, James N., Jr., 27, 56
Holman, Selina Moore, 38, 61
Holy Land, 19, 271–91
Holy Spirit, 358, 360
Holy Trinity Episcopal Church, 99
homiletics, 26
Hon, Peter, 334, 337, 339–40
Hooper, Robert, 15, 50, 113, 447
Hopkins, Mark, 222, 226
Horner, Arthur Lewis, 44
Hostetler, Adam, 333–35, 337
Hostetler, Christian, 334, 340
Hostetler, Joseph, 335–40
Houston, Ross 95
Houston, Tex., 37
Howard, Goldena Roland, 262, 263
Howard, John R., 85, 103, 108, 154
Hoyt, Samuel, 511
Hudson, Winthrop S., 108
Huffman, Ella M., 295
Hughes, John Archbishop, 210
Hughes, Richard T., 2–8, 10, 13, 16, 17, 20, 23, 30, 31, 32, 45–51, 53, 54, 65, 108, 110, 112, 114, 287, 436
Hughs, Jesse, 338, 340
Hull, Debra, 38–39, 62, 64
Humberstone Cooperative (U.K.), 45
Humble, Bill, 56, 108
Humphrey, Dr. Herman, 167
Humphries, Daniel, 506–7, 511
Huntley, Allen, 547–48
hymnody, 28–29

Hypocrisy Detected (anti-Haldane), 537

Iglesias de Christo, 39, 62
Illinois Christian Missionary Society, 305
immersion, 6
Independency, 531, 548
independent Christian Churches, 6, 9, 15, 26, 179, 183; division with Disciples of Christ, 10, 83n. 37; millennial views, 20. *See* Christian Churches/Churches of Christ
Independent Methodists, 373, 385–86, 389, 400
Indiana, 6, 70, 75, 80, 85, 331–47
Indians, Flathead, 228
individualism, 8
inerrancy, 17
Ingersoll, Robert, 228
Innes, William, 529, 540n. 49
instrumental music in worship, 380, 382, 416, 418, 456, 564; opposition to, 27–28, 78, 80, 86, 95, 101, 154; use of, 69, 70, 71, 76
Intellectual history, 2–8, 37
interchurch cooperation, 377
International Churches of Christ, 33–35, 563. *See* Boston Movement and Boston Church of Christ
Ireland, Ballymena, 194
Irving, Edward, 525
Irvingite Movement, 537
Isaac, Rhys, 143, 349
Israel, 19
itinerancy, 534

Jackson, Andrew, 121
Jackson, Kenneth T., 61
Jackson Street Church of Christ (Nashville, Tenn.), 317–18, 320
Jacksonian America, 204–5
James, Frank A. J. L., 65

James, Sonny, 43
Jameson, J. Franklin, *The American Revolution Considered as a Social Movement*, 129, 144
Jameson, Marie, 295
Jardine, George, 27
Jarratt, Deveraux, 139
Jefferson, Thomas, 127
Jeffersonians, 134
Jeffersonville, Ind., 71
Jehovah's Witnesses, 385, 388–89
Jerusalem, 19, 273, 274, 276 ff
Jeter, Joseph, Jr., 26, 55
Jews, 271–84
Jews, conversion of, 272–74, 277, 280–81; repatriation of, 272–73, 275–77, 279–81, 283–84
Jimenez, J. R., 39, 62
Johnson, Andrew, 459
Johnson, Lady Bird, 238
Johnson, Lyndon B., 36, 234–42; Baptist background of mother's family, 235; and civil rights, 240–41; and Disciples of Christ, 235–40; Great Society program, 239–40; religious beliefs, 236–42; and Vietnam War, 241–42
Johnson, Rebekah Baines, 235–36, 241
Johnson, Sam Ealy, Jr., 236
Johnson, Steve, 568
Johnston, Robert L., Jr., 62
Jones, Abner, 141, 545
Jones, Charles T., 64
Jones, Dean, 44
Jones, Donald, 187
Jones, Isaac, 91
Jones, Jerry, 570
Jones, Thomas, 520
Jones, William, 369
Jordanaires, 43
Jorgenson, Dale 27, 56–57, 64
Jorgenson, E. L., 28

Journal of Communication and Religion, 25, 54
Journalism, religious, 25–26, 54, 126
Jovellanos Church of Christ (Cuba), 39
Joyce, William L., 54
Judson, David, 500

Kanawha county, W.V., 37
Kansas City, Mo., 44
Kark, Ruth, 288, 290
Kearns, Doris, 243, 247
Keck, Leander, 26
Keeble, Horace P., 319
Keeble, Marshall, 37–38, 317–28
Keeble, Minnie, 320
Keeble, Robert, 319
Kelly, Louise, 302
Kendal, Ohio, 196
Kendrick, J. B., 487–88, 490
kenosis, 21, 437–38
Kentucky, 6, 13, 38, 70, 75, 80, 85, 88, 89, 91
Kentucky Revival, 338, 354
Kerber, Linda K., 212
Kern, Abraham, 335, 340–41
Kershner, Frederick, 25, 29, 44
Ketelas, William, 135
Kettner, James H., 145
Kilgore, Charles Franklin, 141
Kilton, George, 550
King, David, 370, 374, 376–80, 382–38, 385, 388
King, Keith Lynn, 60
King, Martin Luther, Jr., 38
Kingsland Chapel, London, 530
Kinnamon, Michael, 22, 52
Kirriemuir, Scotland, 531
Kissites (Sandemanians), 501
Klatzker, David, 290
Knight, Frank, 44
Knox, John, 351

Index

Kragenbrink, Kevin, 48
Ku Klux Klan, 37, 61, 265, 321
Kurfees, M. C., 104, 471, 474

labor movement, 405, 410, 419, 421
Labour Party, 40, 45
Lady Glenorchy's Chapel, Edinburgh, 520, 535
Laing, Sam, 564
Lamar, James S., 81, 84
Lambert, O. C., 105
Lancashire, U.K., 40
Lancashire and Cheshire District Conference, 405–6, 419
Lancaster, Bill, 62
Landis, Benson Y., 79
Lane College, 322
Lard, Moses, 19, 77, 149, 165, 166, 283; and return of Jews to Palestine, 283–84
Larimore, T. B., 22
Last Will and Testament of the Springfield Presbytery, 19, 124, 128
Latter Day Saints. *See* Mormons
Lawrence, Kenneth, 43
Lea Avenue Christian Church (Nashville, Tenn.), 319
League of Nations, 104, 409
Lears, T. J. Jackson, 267
Leathers, Dale, 49
Lee, John D., 348, 350, 357–58
Leech, Margaret, 231, 233
Leicester, U.K., 45
Leicester Church of Christ, 399
Lessner, Richard E., 265
Letter to the Editor of the Edinburgh Christian Instructor, Robert Haldane, 525
Letters on Theron and Aspasia, Robert Sandeman, 500
Levi, David, 275
Lewis, Jack, 50, 288

Lewis, R. W. B., 108, 187
Lewis, Tim, 43
Lexington, Ky., 73, 89
Lexington (Mass.) Church of Christ, 35, 564
Lexington Theological Seminary, 21, 22
liberalism, 9, 25
Liberation Theology, Latin American, 21, 435, 437–38, 441, 443–34
liberty, 10, 121; religious, 128–30
Lilly Endowment, 22
Lincoln, Evelyn, 243
Lindley, D. Ray, 58, 215
Lindsay, Vachel, 43
Lindsey, David L., 44
Lipman, Vivian, 284, 285, 288
Lippy, Charles, 34, 50, 60
Lipscomb, A. B., 104, 320–21, 468–69
Lipscomb, David, 4, 5, 15, 17, 20, 22, 38, 74, 77, 78, 94–101, 102, 104, 105–6, 294, 436–48, 456, 458–62, 466–68, 472; apocalypticism, 96–101; attacks on, 105–6; *Civil Government*, 97, 98, 459–60; millennial views, 98–100, 113; myth of yeoman farmer, 149; pacifism, 100, 113; politics, rejection of, 97, 100–101, 113; return of the Jews to Palestine, 291
Lloyd, Richard, 377
Lloyd-George, David, 44, 65
Locke, John, 28, 90, 165, 177, 180, 186–87
Lockean empiricism, 355
Lockean epistemology, 8, 53
Log Cabin Myth, 36
London Church of Christ, 565
London Jew's Society, 273, 277
London Missionary Society, 522
London Society for the Propagation of Christianity Among the Jews, 273. *See also* London Jew's Society

London Times, 197
Long, Kathryn Teresa, 49
Long, Loretta, 32
Lord's Supper, 368, 375, 382, 385, 401, 404, 406, 418–19, 533, 535–36
Los Angeles Church of Christ, 565, 568
Lost River, Dunker, Ind., 333, 335, 340
Loughborough University, 21
Louisville, Ky., 28, 106
Love, Bill, 56
love feast, 332, 334
Lovegrove, Deryck, 33, 60
Lowe, James, 403
Lower Canada, 547
Loyalists, 499, 505, 510, 513
Lucas, Chuck, 35, 564
Luce, Elder Matthias, 194
Lunger, Harold, 58, 180, 182, 186
Luther, Martin, 90
Lyda, Hap C. S., 38, 61
Lyndon, Vt., 545
Lyons, Mary, 296–97

Machado, Daisy, 39, 62
Madison, James, 163, 166
Madison Church of Christ (Tenn.), 318
Mahoning Baptist Association, 213
Main, Jackson Turner, 139
Maine Conference (Christian Connexion), 551
Mains, George Preston, 107
Major, James Brooks, 25, 54
Making Disciples (Boston Church of Christ), 569
Malcolm X, 38
Manchester, England, 190
Mankin, Jim, 28, 57
Mann, Amos, 45, 384, 393n. 44, 396n. 105, 409
Manning, Edward, 551
Mansfield, E. D., 195

Maranatha Christian Churches, 567
Marini, Stephen, 544
Markham, Edwin, 43
Marsden, George, 3, 48
Marsden, Harry, 413
Marsden, James, 404, 411, 413–14, 486
Marsden, Sidney James, 413
Marshall, John, 163
Marshall, W., 484
Martin, William C., 36, 50, 61
Marty, Martin, 109, 215, 262, 265
Mason, Bertha C., 302
Mason, Dr. John, 167
Mason, Millie W., 303, 307
Massa, Mark, 39, 62
Mathews, Donald G., 140
Mathews, Shailer, 107
Matthews, James E., 95
Mauro, Philip, 102, 103
May, Henry, 140
Mazlish, Bruce, 201
McAllister, Lester G., 108, 142, 265
McBride, Jim, 43
McCaleb, J. M., 472
McCalla, William L., 89, 195
McCann, Forrest, 28, 57
McCloud, Barry, 64
McCorkle, Samuel, 90–91
McCoy, Sadie, 301
McDormand, Francis, 44
McDougale, William, 400–401
McGarvey, J. W., 73, 82, 284, 380
McGary, Austin, 467
McGray, Asa, 552
McKean, Kip, 35, 564–68, 570
McLean, Archibald, 368
McLoughlin, William G., 14–15, 49, 141, 143, 145
McMillon, Lynn, 59, 213
McMullen, Ernan, 37
McMullin, Charles, 550–51

Index

McNemar, Richard, 10, 19, 48, 138
McQuiddy, J. C., 103–4, 468–71, 474
Mead, Sidney, 177, 184, 186, 202
Meadows, Swithin, 409
Meat Loaf, 43
Medellín, Colombia, Conference of the Latin American Episcopal Council, Second General, 435, 439, 442
Meithe, Terry, 58
Mell, Glen W., 81
Mendelsson Choir of Pittsburgh, 43
Meredith, Don, 55
Merrick, Daniel B., 57
Methodist Protestant Church, 310n. 4
Methodists, Methodism, 11, 16–17, 34, 40, 123–24, 129, 165, 221; in Texas, 235, 352, 372–73, 375, 378, 381–83, 386, 398, 415, 547, 553
Mexican War, 456–57
Mexico, 39, 198
Meyers, Marvin, 212
Mid-Stream, 22
Miles, Johnny, 56
Millard, Bob, 64
Millard, David, 547
Millenarianism. See Premillennial
Millennial Harbinger and Voluntary Church Advocate (British), 369
Millennial Harbinger, 369
Millennialism. *See* Premillennial
Miller, Betty, 489–90
Miller, George, 406, 409, 418, 489
Miller, Isaac, 489
Miller, James, 407, 409, 489
Miller, John, 489
Miller, Merle, 242
Miller, Perry, 140, 170, 176, 202
Miller, Sally M., 65
Miller, Simon, 407, 488
Miller, Thomas, 408–9, 484, 488
Miller, W. T., 45, 182, 409, 483, 487–90

Miller, William, 109, 138, 370, 487–88. *See* Millerite movement
Millerite movement, 12. *See* William Miller
Millerites. *See* Adventists
Milligan, Robert, 19, 24–25, 277
Milligan College, 9, 44
Mills, Dean, 110
Milner, Thomas, 374
miners, 40
ministry, 401; educated, 439–40; preaching, 439
miracles, 358
Missionary Magazine, 522
missionary society, 69, 70, 71, 76, 78, 80, 82, 86, 95, 101, 154, 455–56, 460, 564
missionary society controversy, 439, 443
Missionary Tidings (CWBM), 301
Missouri, 6, 70, 80
Miyakawa, T. Scott, 169, 176
modernity, 17, 89, 107
Monroe, James, 163
Monroy, Juan Antonio, 39
Monthly Repository, 525
Monticello, 273
Moody, Dwight, 102, 227
Mooney, Booth, 243, 244, 245
Moore, Alice, 37
Moore, Arthur, 157, 158
Moore, Ephraim, 95
Moore, R. Laurence, 1, 15–16, 46, 50, 56
Moore, William T., 25, 54, 77, 80, 381
Morgan, Edmund S., 121, 139, 145
Morgan, Peter, 28, 57
Mormons, 24, 230, 282, 322, 348–63, 374, 384, 386
Morrill, Milo True, 59, 141, 546
Morris, Don H., 62
Morris, Edmund, 267
Morrison, Asa C., 548
Morrison, John, 29, 58

Morrow, Ralph, 142
Morse, F. B., 205
Moser, K. C., 54
Muir, John, 44
multiculturalism, 37–39
multiplying ministries, 563
Mungazi, Dickson, 65
Muñiz, Manuel, 39, 62
Murch-Witty unity meetings, 23
Murdock, John, 24, 358
Murfreesboro, Tenn., 319
Murrah, Roger, 43
Muslims, 277
Mussulman, Joseph, 64
mutual exhortation, 533, 535
myth of the garden, 148, 181; and primitivism, 152. *See* agrarian myth
myth of yeoman farmer, 148–49, 153

Nashville, Tenn., 95, 99, 102, 317, 319, 458
Nashville Bible School, 99, 102, 104. *See* David Lipscomb University
Nashville Christian Institute, 318, 321, 324–25
Nation, Carry, 44
Nation, David, 44
National Association for the Advancement for Colored People, 253
National Benevolent Association, 306
National City Christian Church (Washington, D.C.), 238, 239
National Pro-Family Rally, 37
National Women's Conference, 37
Native Americans, 37
Navigators, 567
Neander, Johann August Wilhelm, 445
Nelms, W., 486
Nevin, John W., 138
New Brunswick Conference (Christian Connexion), 544, 550–53

New Harmony Gazette, 193, 196, 198
New Harmony, Ind., 189, 192–94, 196, 197
New Haven Committee of Inspection, 507–8
New Haven, Conn., 506–7
New Lanark, Scotland, 190–91
New Lights, 338–40
New London, Mo., 254
New Orleans, 106, 196–7
New Testament (as constitution), 355
New Testament Christians, 545
New Testament Church, 10, 18
New York Church of Christ, 565, 568
New York City, 39, 99, 135
New York Observer, 167
New York Tribune, 99
New Zealand, 21, 42, 373
New Zealand Churches of Christ, 44
Newcastle Daily Chronicle, 375
Newmarket District, Canada (Christian Connexion), 549
Newton, 90
Newton, John, 522, 531
Newton, Wales, 190
Niebuhr, H. Richard, 148, 156
Nigeria, 317
Noah, Mordecai, 275
Noll, Mark, 3, 48
Nonconformists, Nonconformity, 40–41, 383, 386, 389, 398, 404–5, 412, 414
North Carolina, 70, 80, 83
North Western Christian Magazine, 72
North Western Christian University, 72
North, James B., 9, 23, 47–48
North, S. N. D., 95
North-South tensions in Disciples, 460–61
Northern Baptist Convention, 293, 305
Norton, Jacob, 551–52
Norton, Mary Beth, 139, 504
Norwood, Frederick, 34, 60

Nottingham, 399
Nova Scotia, 505, 549–52
Nova Scotia Baptist Association, 550
Nova Scotia Conference of Free Baptists, 552
Nova Scotia Great Awakening, 34
Novack, Robert, 242
Noyes, John Humphreys, 109, 138
Numbers, Ronald, 36, 58, 61
Nutt, Samuel, 550–51

O'Hare, Kate Richards, 44
O'Kelly, James, 34, 60, 122–23, 125, 129, 131, 545, Republican Methodists, 123
Octographic Review, 77
Ohio, 6, 85, 89
Ohio River, 6, 70
Oklahoma, 70, 80
Olbricht, Thomas, 23, 33, 53, 58, 59, 141
Old Christians, Christian Connection, 338
old paths, 415, 417, 426n. 74
Old Princeton Theology, 16
Olive Branch (Dunker, Ind.), 332, 334, 339–41
Oliver, Bobbie, 51
Ontario Conference (Christian Connexion), 544, 553–54
open communion, 379–80, 412
open membership, 6
Orban, Donald K., 50
Orbison, Roy, 43, 64
Orcutt, John, 547
ordination, 380
organizers (CWBM, WCTU), 295–97, 299–300, 302, 305, 308, 311n. 17
Osborn, Carroll D., 62
Osborn, Ronald, 22, 49, 52, 57
Otis, Harrison Gray, 121, 139
Ottoman Empire, 276
Overdale Theological College, 413, 418

Owen, Robert, 27, 166, 168, 171, 183, 189–94, 196–200, 254; debate with Alexander Campbell, 276
Owen, Robert Dale, 190, 198

pacifism, 5, 13, 17, 21, 40, 63, 81, 100, 102, 332, 414, 455–65, 466–80, 507
Paden, Russ, 34, 60
Page, Patti, 43
Page, Robert, 43
paid pastorate, 373, 375, 378–80, 386–87, 416, 418
Palestine, 271–74. *See* Holy Land
Paley, William, 525
Paris, Andrew, 56
Parkinson, Joseph, 45, 409
Parks, Rosa, 38
Parsons, Levi, 272–74
Particular Baptists, 368
pastor system, 69, 76, 78, 154
Pastoral Admonition (1799), 523, 528, 531–32
pastors, 401
Paulsell, William O., 29, 57
peace movement, 462
Peace: A Principle of the Churches of Christ, 486
Pearl Harbor, attack on, 105
Peel, Sir Robert, 192
Pelagianism, 16
Pennington, William, 551
Pentecostal Movement, 16, 24
Pentecostal, Pentecostalism, 388
Pepperdine University, 3, 21, 23, 37
Perry, Lewis, 144
Peskin, Allan, 231–33
Peters, Samuel Andrew, Rev., 506
pew rents, 402
Philippines, 58
Phillips, Paul, 37, 61
Phillips, Thomas W., 74

Pierard, Richard W., 245
Pike, Samuel, 500
pillar churches, 565
Pinkerton, Lewis L., 76
Pittsburgh Symphony Orchestra, 43
Platt Bridge, 482–85, 487–91
Platt Bridge chapel, 403–4, 406–9, 411, 415, 417–19, 422
Plymouth Brethren, 367–68, 375–77, 382, 385–86, 397n. 112, 421
pneumatology, 23–25, 53
Pocock, J. G. A., 143
Poe, John T., 462
Poestenkill, N.Y., 223
political involvement, 382–84, 389, 396n. 105; prohibited by David Lipscomb, 444
Political movements, right-wing, 36–37
Politics, rejection of 5, 93, 95
polity, 550; Boston Church of Christ, 568
Pool, William C., 243, 247
Poor Brethren Fund, 410
Pope Clement XIII, 209
Pope Gregory XVI, 209
Popkin, R. H., 286
Populism, 35
populist, religion, 122
Porteous, William, 523
Portsmouth, 500–502
Portsmouth, N.H., 123
Posey Walter B., 11, 49, 56, 165, 175
Postliberal theology, 15
postmillennial, postmillennialism, 6, 18, 19, 87, 181, 276, 280, 282, 355, 379
postmodernism, 15, 18
Potter, David, 212
poverty, 447
Powell, Monty, 43
practical theology, 25–29
Pratt, Parley P., 24, 357
prayer partners, 564, 566

preaching, 25–26
preferential option for the poor, 435–54; in evangelism, 440
premillennial, premillennialism, 5–7, 17–20, 86, 93, 99–100, 271–76, 279–80, 282–83, 354, 359, 370–71, 375, 384, 391n. 20; Bible and Prophecy Conference, First American, 99; dispensational, 17–18, 100, 102, 103, 107
Presbyterian church, 92, 129; Antiburger, 177; Old Light Seceder, 194
Presbyterians, Presbyterianism, 125, 133, 165, 221, 351; Old School, 189, 195; Scotch-Irish, 30, 124; in Texas 235
Presbytery of Edinburgh, 537
Price, Robert, 484–88
priesthood of all believers, 401, 417
Prill, Paul, 55
Primitive Baptist Church, 321
primitive Christianity, 367, 385–87, 416
Primitive Methodists, 372, 383, 386, 389, 396n. 100
primitivism, 3, 8, 13, 30, 33, 40, 46, 49, 87, 89–90, 94, 107, 108–9, 174, antimodern, 87–88, 94, 107. *See* restorationism
print media, 25–26
Prohibition, 383
Protestant Reformation, 351
Protestantism, 24
Protestantism, liberal, 15
Puebla, Mexico, Conference of Catholic Bishops, 435, 438, 441–42
Puerto Rico, 39
Pulley, Kathy J., 62
Purcell, John B., 27, 205, 210
Puritans, Puritanism, 4, 14, 27–28, 128, 350–51, 400, 421
Purviance, Levi, 93
Pynchon, Joseph, 507

Index

Quakers, 339, 373, 501
Quill, J. Michael, 243, 247
Qunicy, Josiah, 140

Raines, Aylette, 73
Ralls County, Mo., 249, 253
Ramos, Marcos, 39, 62
Rate, John, 521
Rate, Joseph, 534
rationalism, 8, 27, 29–30, 32, 45, 95
Rausch, David, 291
Rauschenburg, Robert, 44
Rawlyk, George, 60, 544
Reagan, Jack, 255–56
Reagan, Michael, 251
Reagan, Neil, 251, 256
Reagan, Nelle Wilson, 36, 248, 251–53, 255–58, 260
Reagan, Ronald, 36, 44, 61; and alcohol, 255–56; anticommunism, 254; and Disciples of Christ, 248–49, 251–52, 254–60; racial attitudes, 252
reason, 527
rebaptism, 567
Redstone Baptist Association, 178–80, 195, 206, 213, 214
Reformed Theology, 2, 16
Reformed tradition, 4
Regular Baptists, 545, 547, 550–53
Reigel, Robert, 201
Relief Synod (Church of Scotland), 523
Religious communication, 25
Religious Communication Association, 25
religious insiders, 15–16
religious outsiders, 15–16
Religious right, 37
Religious Tract Society, 522
Renaissance, 351
Reno, Milo, 60
Republican Methodists, 545
Republican religion, 204

Restoration, restorationism, 9, 18, 30, 35, 40, 49, 69, 70, 90–91, 278, 348–53, 356, 359, 367–68, 380, 389n. 1, 410. *See* primitivism
Restoration lectures, 39
Restoration Movement, 8, 563–64. *See* Stone-Campbell movement; Stone-Campbell tradition
Revitalization movement, 13
Revivalism, nineteenth-century, 16
Revivals, revivalism, 386, 395n. 91, 544, 546, 554
Revolutionary War (American), 14, 33, 35, 131, 499–519
Rhetoric, classical, 26
Rhetoric, enlightenment, 26
Rice, David, 138, 144
Richardson, Robert, 23, 29, 31, 53, 59, 80, 164, 165, 167
Richesin, L. Dale, 57
Richey, Russell E., 187
Richmond, William, 507
Ridge Meetinghouse Debate (Church of Christ v. Mormons), 348, 350, 355, 357
Rigdon, Sidney, 24, 353
Ringenberg, William C., 36, 61
Roberts, R. L., 46, 51, 88, 109
Robertson, Eck, 43
Robertson, William, 530
Robinson, Edward, 278
Robinson, William, 418, 482
Robison, John, 529
Rodney Street, 482–83, 485, 487–88, 490
Rodney Street Church, 400, 402–4, 406–7, 411–15, 417–18
Roe, Marty, 43
Rogers, John, 91
Rollins, Richard M., 144
Rollman, Hans, 33, 59
Rolph, William Kirby, 65

Romanticism, 356, 359, 360–61
Roper, David, 42, 63
Ross, Dorothy, 212
Roth, Herbert, 51
Rotherham, Joseph, 391n. 15
Rowe, David L., 146
Rowe, Fred, 468, 470–71, 474
ruling elder, 533
Russell, Charles Taze, 105
Russell, W. S., 24, 53
Russellism. *See* Jehovah's Witnesses
Russia, 409
Rutherford County, Tenn., 319
Rutledge, John, 135

Sagan, Carl, 37
Salem, Mass., 123
Sallee, Abraham, 348, 355, 357
Salvation Army, 382, 388
San Diego Orchestra, 43
Sandeen, Ernest R., 285, 287
Sandeman, Robert, 194, 499–500, 503–4, 533
Sandeman, William, 504
Sandemanians, 33, 44, 59, 60, 367–68, 375, 499–519
Sanderson, L. O., 28, 57
Sanford, Charles L., 155, 158
Sargent, Able M., 127, 131, 143
Saville, John, 63
Schlesinger, Arthur, Jr., 180, 186
Scholes chapel, 403, 415, 417
Schug, Howard L., 62
Schultz, Daisy, 302
Scofield, Cyrus, 102
Scotch Baptists, 367–69, 375, 384
Scott, Walter, 19, 24, 32, 178, 277, 353; millennial views, 152, 276; plan of salvation, 178–79; return of Jews to Palestine, 275–76, 282, *The Evangelist*, 275

Scott, William T., 59
Scottish Common Sense philosophy, 177, 206. *See* Baconianism
Scottish Congregationalism, 521
Scottish Episcopalians, 522
Scottish Society for the Propagation of Christian Knowledge, 502, 528
Scottsville, Va., 273
Sears, Clara E., 109
Sears, Jack Wood, 37
2nd Division Quarterly Conference (Christian Connexion), 548–59
Second Great Awakening, 14, 138
sect to denomination development, 5, 7, 10, 18, 399, 414–15, 426n.74
sectarianism, 525
secularism, 374, 383, 388
seminaries, Haldane, 532
Separate Baptists, 349, 549, 558n. 59
Separate Congregationalists, 549, 558n. 59
Separatists of New England, 128
Seventh-Day Adventists, 12
Sewell, Elisha G., 20, 51, 99, 458–59
Seyter, Rev. David Franklin, 251
Shakers, 501
Shalhope, Robert E., 212
Shaw, Daniel, 550
Shaw, Nelle, 43
Shaw, Robert, 43
Shaw, Shirley R., 43
Shepherd, J. W., 472, 474
Shepherd, Naomi, 271, 284, 288, 290
shepherding movements, 567
Sherrill, Robert, 243
Shi, David, 12–13, 49
Shipps, Jan, 359
Short, Foy, 62
Short, Howard, 61
Showalter, G. H. P., 468–69, 473
Sikes, Walter, 57
Silberman, Neil Asher, 285

Simeon, Charles, 522
simplicity, 12–13, 27–28
Singletary, Amos, 135
slavery, 5, 71, 72, 74, 383
Smith, B. K., 282
Smith, Benjamin Lyon, 156, 507
Smith, David E., 157
Smith, Elias, 25, 54, 122–23, 125, 130, 131, 132–33, 136, 143, 545–46, 552; anticlericalism, 126; *Herald of Gospel Liberty*, 123, 124, 127, 128, 130, 132
Smith, F. W., 51
Smith, George T., 300
Smith, Henry Nash, 147, 155, 156, 158
Smith, James, 406, 408
Smith, Joseph, 138, 348, 350–52, 356, 359–61
Smith, Lucy, 350
Smith, Mrs. S. H., 193
Smith, Theodore Clarke, 231–32
Smith, Titus, 502–3, 506–7
Smylie, James H., 244
Snow, Lorenzo, 360
Snowden, James, 107
Sobrino, John, 438
social activism, 409, 414
Social Gospel, 15
social history, 2–3, 37. *See* Churches of Christ, sectional origins and cultural alienation
Society for Propagating the Gospel at Home (SPGH), 520–21, 529, 532, 534
Society in Scotland for Propagating Christian Knowledge (SSPCK), 522, 529
Socknat, Thomas P., 51
Sokolow, Nahum, 275, 286
Solemn League and Covenant (1774), 505–6
Somerville, James, 528
Sommer, Daniel, 19, 78, 85

Sons of Liberty, 505
soul talks, 564, 566
South, The 71, 74, 75, 79, 87–88
South Carolina, 83
Southern Baptist Home Mission Board, 23
Southern District, Christian, 338
Southwest State Teachers College, 241
Spain, 39
Spanish American War, 151, 462, 467
Sparhawk, John, 506, 510–11
Speakman, James, 410, 489
Speakman, Peter, 408
Speakman, William, 489
Spencer, Claude, 55
spirituality, 29, 57
Spurgeon, Charles H., 226–27
Srygley, Fletcher D., 77, 462
St. Andrews University, 33, 523
St John's Episcopal Church (Washington, D.C.), 238
St. Mark's Episcopal Church (San Antonio, Tex.), 238
St. Mark's Episcopal Church (Washington, D.C.), 238
Stainton, Elmer S., 63
Stamp Act, 501–3
Stamps-Baxter Gospel Music, 43
Stanton, Elizabeth Cady, 230
Star Bible Publications, 32
Steinberg, Alfred, 242, 243
Stevens, John, 49
Stiles, Ezra, 505, 509
Stodgill, Mary, 547
Stokes, Durwood T., 59
Stone, Barton W., 1, 3, 6, 12, 19, 24, 26, 29, 32, 46, 47, 53, 59, 85, 86, 87, 88, 91–94, 96, 97, 104, 107, 122, 124, 125, 131, 178, 275, 331, 338, 342, 352, 354, 356, 359, 545, 548, 563; anti-Calvinism, 129–30, 134; *Christian Messenger*, 19, 32, 91, 92, 93; view of the Holy Spirit, 23

Stone, Sam E., 55
Stone-Campbell movement, 2, 7–9, 13–14, 16, 18–19, 21, 24, 26, 33, 35–36; African-Americans in, 37–38; Canada, 41–42; debates, 26–27; unity efforts in, 9; women in, 38–39; worship, 27–29, 57. *See* Stone-Campbell tradition
Stone-Campbell studies, 1, 2
Stone-Campbell tradition, 8, 13, 17, 24–25, 35–36; Australia, 42, 63; cultural significance 42–45; New Zealand, 42. *See* Stone-Campbell movement
Stone movement, 10, 11, 14, deprivation and poverty, 91–92; ecclesiastical societies, rejection of, 94; 1832 union with Campbell movement, 11, 13, 88, 89, 125, 147; eschatology, 92–93, 131; politics, rejection of, 92–93; separation from world, 92–93
Stout, Harry S., 143
Stowe, Charles Hambrick, 59–60
Strait, Jimmy Odell, 53
Strict Baptists, 372
Student Army Training Corps, 472
Student Christian Movement, 419
Stutzman, Jacob, 332
subordination of women, 305
Summit, Ga., 321
Sunday school, 384, 404, 415–16
Swanson, Guy E., 144
Sweet, Leonard I., 4, 25, 46–47, 54
Sweet, William Warren, 145
Swick, Danny, 23, 53
Synan, Vinson, 53, 64

Tabbernee, William, 63
tabernacles, 522–23
Talbot, George, 486
Tampico, Ill., 248
Tampico Church of Christ, 251
Tant, J. D., 462–63, 467
Taylor, J. T., 45, 409
Taylor University, 36
temperance movement, 380, 383, 409
Tennessee, 38, 75, 85, 88, 89
Terrell, A. P., 298
Texas, 20, 74, 75, 89, 234
Texas Baptist, 235
Texas Missionary Society, 78
Theisen, Lee Scott, 64
Third Great Awakening, 15
Tholuck, 525, 527
Thomas, Cecil K., 58
Thomas, John, 19, 370–71
Thompson, David, 40, 63
Thompson, Doris, 51
Thompson, William, 135
Thomson, Andrew, 524
Thornton, J. Mills, 212
Thorp Springs Christian College, 472
Thrasher, Thomas, 56
Three Dog Night, 43
Tickle, George, 374
Todd, Sir Garfield, 44, 65
Tolles, Frederick B., 140
Torrey, Reuben, 102, 103
Toulouse, Mark, 8, 9, 48; *Walter Scott: A Nineteenth Century Evangelical*, 32, 59
Townshend Acts, 503
Travis, Randy, 43
Treat, J. W., 62
Treatise (1834, Freewill Baptist), 553
Tribe, Ivan, 64
Trimble, Robert B., 458–59
Trinitarianism, 545, 552
Trinity, doctrine of, 130
Tristano, Richard, 7, 47–48
Troeltsch, 41
Trollope, Francis, 189, 190, 199

Index

Trout, Jennie, 38, 61
Tucker, William E., 108, 142, 265
Tully, J. C., 100
Tuvenson, Ernest L., 181, 183, 184, 187
Twain, Mark, 183

Ulster, 206
Underwood, Grant, 351
Unitarian Baptists, 546
Unitarianism, Unitarians, 129, 170, 546, 553
United Baptist Church, 553
United Christian Missionary Society, 37
United Church of Canada, 549, 553
United Church of Christ, 22, 549
United Reformed Church (U.K.), 40, 416, 426n. 74
United Society of Believers (Shakers), 544
unity, 69, 70, 554. *See* ecumenicism
Universalism, Universalists, 123, 129, 219, 334, 544, 553
University of Chicago, 44, 250
University of Florida, 564
University of Notre Dame, 37
Upper Canada, 544, 547–48
Upper Canadian Conference (Christian Connexion), 544, 553
Urquhart, Henry Ritchie, 21, 52
U.S. Christian Conference (Christian Connexion), 546

Valenti, Jack, 245
Van Deusen, Kenneth, 51
Vandergrift, Eileen Gordon, 80, 81, 289
VanRheenen, Dwayne, 55, 56
Vargas, Joaquin, 62
Vaughn, Stephen, 36, 61
Vawter, Beverley, 338
Vercoe, Millie, 297
Vietnam War, 466
Virginia, 70, 80, 83

Virginia Constitutional Convention of 1829, 163, 166, 187
Vogel, Dan, 350

Wacker, Grant, 3
Walker, Granville T., 58
Walker, Ray, 43
Wallace, Anthony F. C., 13, 49
Wallace, Foy E., Jr., 17, 105–6; *Bible Banner*, 105, 106; *Gospel Guardian*, 105
Wallace, Gen. Lewis, 43
Wallace, Zerelda, 43
Waller, John, 195
Wallis, James, 369–70, 374, 377
Walsh, James Patrick, 143
Walsh, John T., 462
Walsh, Stephen, 489
Walters, Ronald G., 47
War of 1812, 14
Warburton, William, 525
Ward, Rita Rhodes, 37
Ward, William, 522
Warner, Wayne E., 53
Warren Baptist Association, 125
Washington, Booker T., 317–18, 320
Washington, Pa., 178, 194
Washington College, Pa., 170
Washington National Intelligencer, 190
Washington Reporter (Pa.), 183
Wasson, W. W., 231–32
Watch Tower Bible and Tract Society, 105
Waters, Chris, 43
Waters, Ken, 53
Watkins, Benjamin U., 76
Watkins, Keith, 54, 57
Webb, Henry, 9, 10, 48, 58
Weber, Max, 41
Weber, Timothy, 112, 114, 115
Weed, Michael, 2, 46
Weedman, Mark, 27, 56
Weiss, Ruth, 65

Index

Weld, Timothy, 205
Wells, Kitty, 43
Wells, R. C., 318
Welsh Campbellites, 373
Wesleyan Methodists, 381, 399
West, Earl I., 27, 56, 62, 79, 80, 108, 113, 155
West, Robert Frederick, 58, 110, 142, 163–65, 174, 175
West, William G., 32, 59, 142
West End Chapel, 40–41
West Virginia, 70, 80
Western Reserve (Ohio), 219, 223
Westminster Confession, 194, 527–28
White, Ebenezer, 500, 502, 510, 518n. 63
White, Jackie, 43
White, James, 27, 56
White, Joseph Moss, 500, 502
White, William S., 244, 245
White River (Dunker, Ind.), 333, 335
Whitefield model of evangelism, 522–23, 530
Whitefield, George, 123
Whitley, Oliver Read, 79
Whitney, Elizabeth Ann, 24, 358
Whitney, Newel K., 358
Whitney, Orson F., 360
Whitson, Mont, 50, 157
Wicker, Tom, 243
Wigan, 482, 484–85, 487
Wigan and District Association, 405, 413
Wigan Churches of Christ, 398–432
Wigan Lane Church, 400, 402
Wigan Miner's Association, 45
Wigan miners' strike (1853), 402
Wilberforce, William, 520
Wilburn, James R., 53, 112
Wilburn, Ralph G., 49
Wilkes, Lanceford B., 74
Wilkinson, U. G., 472–73

Williams, D. Newell, 5, 6, 10, 23, 30–32, 47–48, 51–53, 55, 58–59, 110
Williams, Dennis, 65
Williams, Don, 43
Williams, Frederick D., 232–33
Williams College, 222, 223
Williamson, Clarke, 54
Wills, Garry, 260, 261, 263, 268
Wilson, Bryan, 388
Wilson, Joshua, 189
Wilson, Major L., 87, 108, 212
Wilson, Martha, 92
Wilson, Virgil, 92
Winslow, Isaac, Jr., 505–6
Witherspoon, John, 130
Woburn, Mass., 123, 125
Wolfe, Charles K., 64
Wolfgang, James Stephen, 61
Womack, S. W., 317
Women's Christian Temperance Union (WCTU), 38, 62, 293 ff
women's role, 95, 407, 416, 537; preaching, 297 ff; ordination, 292–316
Wood, Gordon S., 122, 140, 145, 349
Wood, Henry Wise, 45, 60
Woodhull, Richard, 506–7
Woods, L. Shelton, 58
Woodworth-Etter, Maria, 24, 53
Wooten, Martin Edward, 49
Wooten, Mary, 566
World Sector Administrators (Boston Church of Christ), 568
World War I, 21, 63, 102, 103–4, 105, 409, 414, 416, 466–68, 482 ff
World War II, 21, 105, 415–16
worldliness, 383
Worldly Church: A Call for Biblical Renewal, The, 2
Worship, 27–29
Worship styles, Evangelical/Charismatic, 15

Worship traditions, frontier, 27,
  Reformed, 27–28
Wrather, Eva Jean, 31, 56, 213
Wright, Amos, 339
Wright, Harold Bell, 43–44
Wright, John, 335, 337–40
Wright, Peter, 337–39
Wylie, Irvin G., 61
Wylie, Wayne E., 58

Yadkinville, N.C., 92
Yankovich, "Weird" Al, 43
Yearbook of American Churches, 70, 155
YMCA, 472

Yoakam, Dwight, 43
Young, Alfonso, 348, 357
Young, Brigham, 227, 360
Young, C. A., 214
Young, Marguerite, 201–2
Young, Nick, 569
Young People's Department (of CWBM), 302

Zelinsky, Wilbur, 79
Zimbabwe, 44
Zuber, Glenn, 38, 62
Zwingli, 90

The Stone-Campbell Movement was designed and typeset on a Macintosh computer system using QuarkXPress software. The text is set in Stone Serif and the chapter openings are set in Stone Sans. This book was designed by Bill Adams, typeset by Kimberly Scarbrough, and manufactured by Thomson-Shore, Inc. The paper used in this book is designed for an effective life of at least three hundred years.